This is No. 543 of Everyman's Library. A list of authors and their works in this series will be found at the end of this volume. The publishers will be pleased to send freely to all applicants a separate, annotated list of the Library.

J. M. DENT & SONS LIMITED
10–13 BEDFORD STREET LONDON W.C.2

E. P. DUTTON & CO. INC.
286–302 FOURTH AVENUE
NEW YORK

EVERYMAN'S LIBRARY
EDITED BY ERNEST RHYS

HISTORY

THE HISTORY OF ROME
BY THEODOR MOMMSEN · INTRO-
DUCTION BY E. A. FREEMAN, LL.D.
TRANSLATED BY W. P. DICKSON
IN 4 VOLS.   VOL. 2

THEODOR MOMMSEN, born in 1817 in Schleswig-Holstein. From 1848 was professor of Roman Law and Ancient History at Berlin and other universities. From 1873 to 1895 was secretary to the Berlin Academy of Sciences. From 1873 to 1888 was a member of the Prussian House of Representatives. Died in 1903.

THE HISTORY OF ROME

VOLUME TWO

THEODOR MOMMSEN

LONDON: J. M. DENT & SONS LTD.
NEW YORK: E. P. DUTTON & CO. INC.

All rights reserved
Made in Great Britain
at The Temple Press Letchworth
and decorated by Eric Ravilious
for
J. M. Dent & Sons Ltd.
Aldine House Bedford St. London
First Published in this Edition 1911
Reprinted 1921, 1929

CONTENTS

BOOK THIRD

FROM THE UNION OF ITALY TO THE SUBJUGATION OF CARTHAGE AND THE GREEK STATES

CONTENTS

BOOK THIRD

FROM THE UNION OF ITALY
TO THE
SUBJUGATION OF CARTHAGE AND THE GREEK STATES

Arduum res gestas scribere.—Sallust.

THE HISTORY OF ROME

BOOK THIRD

CHAPTER I

CARTHAGE

THE Semitic stock occupied a place amidst, and yet aloof from, the nations of the ancient classical world. The true centre of the former lay in the East, that of the latter in the region of the Mediterranean; and, however wars and migrations may have altered the line of demarcation and thrown the races across each other, a deep sense of diversity has always severed, and still severs, the Indo-Germanic peoples from the Syrian, Israelite, and Arabic nations. This diversity was no less marked in the case of that Semitic people, which spread more than any other in the direction of the west—the Phoenicians. Their native seat was the narrow border of coast bounded by Asia Minor, the highlands of Syria, and Egypt, and called Canaan, that is, the " plain." This was the only name which the nation itself made use of ; even in Christian times the African farmer called himself a Canaanite. But Canaan received from the Hellenes the name of Phoenike, the " land of purple," or " land of the red men," and the Italians also were accustomed to call the Canaanites Punians, as we are accustomed still to speak of them as the Phoenician or Punic race.

The land was well adapted for agriculture; but its excellent harbours and the abundant supply of timber and of metals eminently favoured the growth of commerce, and it was there perhaps, where the opulent eastern continent abuts on the wide-spreading Mediterranean so rich in harbours and islands, that commerce first dawned in all its greatness upon man. The Phoenicians directed all the resources of courage, acuteness, and enthusiasm to the full development of commerce and its attendant arts of navigation, manufacturing, and colonisation, and thus connected the East and the West. At an incredibly

3

early period we find them in Cyprus and Egypt, in Greece and
Sicily, in Africa and Spain, and even on the Atlantic Ocean and
the North Sea. The field of their commerce reached from
Sierra Leone and Cornwall in the west, eastward to the coast of
Malabar. Through their hands passed the gold and pearls of
the East, the purple of Tyre, slaves, ivory, lions' and panthers'
skins from the interior of Africa, frankincense from Arabia, the
linen of Egypt, the pottery and fine wines of Greece, the copper
of Cyprus, the silver of Spain, tin from England, and iron from
Elba. The Phoenician mariners supplied every nation with
whatever it needed or was likely to purchase; and they roamed
everywhere, yet always returned to the narrow home to which
their affections clung.

The Phoenicians are entitled to be commemorated in history
by the side of the Hellenic and Latin nations; but their case
affords a fresh proof, and perhaps the strongest proof of all, that
the development of national energies in antiquity was of a one-
sided character. Those noble and enduring creations in the
field of intellect, which owe their origin to the Aramaean race,
did not emanate from the Phoenicians. While faith and knowledge in a certain sense were the especial property of the
Aramaean nations and reached the Indo-Germans only from the
East, neither the Phoenician religion nor Phoenician science
and art ever, so far as we can see, held an independent rank
among those of the Aramaean family. The religious conceptions of the Phoenicians were rude and uncouth, and it seemed
as if their worship was meant to foster rather than to restrain
lust and cruelty. No trace is discernible, at least in times of
clear historical light, of any special influence exercised by their
religion over other nations. As little do we find any Phoenician
architecture or plastic art at all comparable even to those of
Italy, to say nothing of the lands where art was native. The
most ancient seat of scientific observation and of its application
to practical purposes was Babylon, or at any rate the region of
the Euphrates. It was there probably that men first followed
the course of the stars; it was there that they first distinguished
and expressed in writing the sounds of language; it was there
that they began to reflect on time and space and on the powers
at work in nature: the earliest traces of astronomy and chronology, of the alphabet, and of weights and measures, point to
that region. The Phoenicians doubtless availed themselves of
the artistic and highly developed manufactures of Babylon for
their industry, of the observation of the stars for their naviga-

tion, of the writing of sounds and the adjustment of measures
for their commerce, and distributed many an important germ
of civilisation along with their wares; but it cannot be demonstrated that the alphabet or any other ingenious product of the
human mind belonged peculiarly to them, and such religious
and scientific ideas as they were the means of conveying to the
Hellenes were scattered by them more after the fashion of a
bird dropping grains than of the husbandman sowing his seed.
The power which the Hellenes and even the Italians possessed,
of civilising and assimilating to themselves the nations susceptible of culture with whom they came into contact, was
wholly wanting in the Phoenicians. In the field of Roman
conquest the Iberian and the Celtic languages have disappeared
before the Romanic tongue; the Berbers of Africa speak at the
present day the same language as they spoke in the times of the
Hannos and the Barcides.

Above all, the Phoenicians, like the rest of the Aramaean
nations as compared with the Indo-Germans, lacked the instinct
of political life — the noble idea of self-governed freedom.
During the most flourishing times of Sidon and Tyre the land
of the Phoenicians was a perpetual apple of contention between
the powers that ruled on the Euphrates and on the Nile, and
was subject sometimes to the Assyrians, sometimes to the
Egyptians. With half its power Hellenic cities had achieved
their independence; but the prudent Sidonians calculated that
the closing of the caravan-routes to the East or of the ports of
Egypt would cost them more than the heaviest tribute, and so
they punctually paid their taxes, as it might happen, to Nineveh
or to Memphis, and even gave their ships, when they could not
avoid it, to help to fight the battles of the kings. And, as at
home the Phoenicians patiently submitted to the oppression of
their masters, so also abroad they were by no means inclined to
exchange the peaceful career of commerce for a policy of conquest. Their colonies were factories. It was of more moment
in their view to deal in buying and selling with the natives than
to acquire extensive territories in distant lands, and to carry
out there the slow and difficult work of colonisation. They
avoided war even with their rivals; they allowed themselves to
be supplanted in Egypt, Greece, Italy, and the east of Sicily
almost without resistance; and in the great naval battles, which
were fought in early times for the supremacy of the western
Mediterranean, at Alalia ($\frac{217}{537}$) and at Cumae ($\frac{280}{474}$), it was the
Etruscans, and not the Phoenicians, that bore the brunt of the

struggle with the Greeks. If rivalry could not be avoided, they
compromised the matter as best they could; no attempt was
ever made by the Phoenicians to conquer Caere or Massilia.
Still less, of course, were the Phoenicians disposed to enter on
aggressive war. On the only occasion in earlier times when
they took the field on the offensive—in the great Sicilian expedition of the African Phoenicians which terminated in their
defeat at Himera by Gelo of Syracuse ($\frac{274}{480}$)—it was simply as
dutiful subjects of the great king and in order to avoid taking
part in the campaign against the Hellenes of the east, that they
entered the lists against the Hellenes of the west; just as their
Syrian kinsmen were in fact obliged in that same year to share
the defeat of the Persians at Salamis (i. 323).

This was not the result of cowardice; navigation in unknown
waters and with armed vessels requires brave hearts, and that
such were to be found among the Phoenicians, they often showed.
Still less was it the result of any lack of tenacity and idiosyncracy
of national feeling; on the contrary the Aramaeans defended
their nationality with spiritual weapons as well as with their
blood against all the allurements of Greek civilisation and all
the coercive measures of eastern and western despots, and that
with an obstinacy which no Indo-Germanic people has ever
equalled, and which to us who belong to the West seems to be
sometimes more sometimes less than human. It was the result
of that want of political instinct, which amidst all their lively
sense of the ties of race, and amidst all their faithful attachment
to the city of their fathers, formed the most essential feature in
the character of the Phoenicians. Liberty had no charms for
them, and they aspired not after dominion; "quietly they
lived," says the Book of Judges, "after the manner of the
Sidonians, careless and secure, and in possession of riches."

Of all the Phoenician settlements none attained a more rapid
and secure prosperity than those which were established by the
Tyrians and Sidonians on the south coast of Spain and the north
coast of Africa—regions that lay beyond the reach of the arm of
the great king and the dangerous rivalry of the mariners of
Greece, and in which the natives held the same relation to the
strangers as the Indians in America held to the Europeans.
Among the numerous and flourishing Phoenician cities along
these shores, the most prominent by far was the "new town,"
Karthada or, as the Occidentals called it, Karchedon or Carthago.
Although not the earliest settlement of the Phoenicians in this
region, and originally perhaps a dependency of the adjoining

Utica the oldest of the Phoenician towns in Libya, it soon out-stripped its neighbours and even the motherland through the incomparable advantages of its situation and the energetic activity of its inhabitants. It was situated not far from the (former) mouth of the Bagradas (Mejerda), which flows through the richest corn district of Northern Africa, and was placed on a fertile rising ground, still occupied with country houses and covered with groves of olive and orange trees, falling off in a gentle slope towards the plain, and terminating towards the sea in a sea-girt promontory. Lying in the heart of the great North-African roadstead, the Gulf of Tunis, at the very spot where that beautiful basin affords the best anchorage for vessels of larger size, and where drinkable spring water is got close by the shore, the place proved singularly favourable for agriculture and commerce and for the exchange of their respective com-modities—so favourable, that not only was the Tyrian settle-ment in that quarter the first of Phoenician mercantile cities, but even in the Roman period Carthage was no sooner restored than it became the third city in the empire, and still, under circumstances far from favourable and on a site far less judi-ciously chosen, there exists and flourishes in that quarter a city of a hundred thousand inhabitants. The prosperity, agricul-tural, mercantile, and industrial, of a city so situated and so peopled, needs no explanation; but the question requires an answer—In what way did this settlement come to attain such a development of political power as no other Phoenician city possessed?

That the Phoenician stock did not even in Carthage renounce its passive policy, there is no lack of evidence to prove. Carthage paid, even down to the times of its prosperity, a ground-rent for the space occupied by the city to the native Berbers, the tribe of Maxitani or Maxyes; and although the sea and the desert sufficiently protected the city from any assault of the eastern powers, Carthage appears to have recognised—although but nominally—the supremacy of the great king, and to have paid tribute to him occasionally, in order to secure its commercial communications with Tyre and the East.

But with all their disposition to be submissive and cringing, circumstances occurred which compelled the Phoenicians to adopt a more energetic policy. The stream of Hellenic migra-tion was pouring ceaselessly towards the west: it had already dislodged the Phoenicians from Greece proper and Italy, and it was preparing to supplant them also in Sicily, in Spain, and even in Libya itself. The Phoenicians had to make a stand somewhere, if they were not willing to be totally crushed. In this case, where they had to deal with Grecian traders and not with the great king, submission did not suffice to secure the continuance of their commerce and industry on its former footing, liable merely to tax and tribute. Massilia and Cyrene were already founded; the whole east of Sicily was already in the hands of the Greeks; it was full time for the Phoenicians to think of serious resistance. The Carthaginians undertook the task; after long and obstinate wars they set a limit to the advance of the Cyrenaeans, and Hellenism was unable to establish itself to the west of the desert of Tripolis. With Carthaginian aid, moreover, the Phoenician settlers on the western point of Sicily defended themselves against the Greeks, and readily and gladly submitted to the protection of the powerful cognate city (i. 146). These important successes, which occurred in the second century of Rome, and which saved for the Phoenicians the south-western portion of the Mediterranean, served of themselves to give to the city which had achieved them the hegemony of the nation, and to alter at the same time its political position. Carthage was no longer a mere mercantile city; it aimed at the dominion of Libya and of a part of the Mediterranean, because it could not avoid doing so. It is probable that the custom of employing mercenaries contributed materially to these successes. That custom came into vogue in Greece somewhere about the middle of the fourth century of Rome, but among the Orientals and the Carians more especially it was far older, and it was perhaps the Phoenicians themselves that began it. By the system of foreign recruiting war was converted into a general pecuniary speculation, which was quite in keeping with the character and habits of the Phoenicians.

It was probably the reflex influence of these successes abroad, that first led the Carthaginians to change the character of their occupation in Africa from a tenure of hire and sufferance to one of proprietorship and conquest. It appears to have been about the year $\frac{300}{450}$ that the Carthaginian merchants got rid of the rent for the soil, which they had hitherto been obliged to pay to the natives. This change enabled them to prosecute husbandry on a great scale. The Phoenicians were at all times anxious to employ their capital as landlords as well as traders, and to practise agriculture on a large scale by means of slaves or hired labourers; a large portion of the Jews in this way served

the merchant-princes of Tyre for daily wages. The Carthaginians could now without restriction extract the produce of the
rich Libyan soil by a system akin to that of the modern planters;
slaves in chains cultivated the land—we find single citizens
possessing as many as twenty thousand of them. Nor was this
all. The agricultural villages of the surrounding region—
agriculture appears to have been introduced among the Libyans
at a very early period, probably anterior to the Phoenician
settlement, and in all likelihood from Egypt—were subdued by
force of arms, and the free Libyan farmers were transformed
into fellahs, who paid to their lords a fourth part of the produce
of the soil as tribute, and were subjected to a regular system of
recruiting for the formation of a home Carthaginian army.
Hostilities were constantly occurring with the roving pastoral
tribes (νόμαδες) on the borders; but a chain of fortified posts
secured the territory enclosed by them, and the Nomades were
slowly driven back into the deserts and mountains, or were
compelled to recognise Carthaginian supremacy, to pay tribute,
and to furnish contingents. About the period of the first Punic
war their great town Theveste (Tebessa, at the sources of the
Mejerda) was conquered by the Carthaginians. These formed
the " towns and tribes (ἔθνη) of subjects," which appear in the
Carthaginian state-treaties; the former being the non-free
Libyan villages, the latter the subject Nomades.

To this fell to be added the sovereignty of Carthage over the
other Phoenicians in Africa, or the so-called Libyphoenicians.
These included, on the one hand, the smaller settlements sent
forth from Carthage along the whole north and part of the north-
west coast of Africa—which must have been not unimportant,
for on the Atlantic alone there were settled at one time 30,000
such colonists—and, on the other hand, the old Phoenician
settlements especially numerous along the coast of the present
province of Constantine and Beylik of Tunis, such as Hippo
afterwards called Regius (Bona), Hadrumetum (Susa), Little
Leptis (to the south of Susa)—the second city of the Phoenicians
in Africa—Thapsus (in the same quarter), and Great Leptis
(near Tripoli). In what way all these cities came to be subject
to Carthage—whether voluntarily, for their protection perhaps
from the attacks of the Cyrenaeans and Numidians, or by constraint—cannot be now ascertained; but it is certain that they
are designated as subjects of the Carthaginians even in official
documents, that they had to pull down their walls, and that
they had to pay tribute and furnish contingents to Carthage.

They were not liable however to the recruiting system or to the
land-tax, but contributed a definite amount of men and money,
Little Leptis for instance paying the enormous sum annually of
365 talents (£90,000); moreover there was equality of law
between them and the Carthaginians, and they could contract
marriage on equal terms.[1] Utica alone escaped a similar fate and
had its walls and independence preserved to it, less perhaps from
its own power than from the pious feeling of the Carthaginians
towards their ancient protectors; in fact the Phoenicians
cherished a remarkable feeling of reverence for such relations,
presenting a thorough contrast to the indifference of the Greeks.
Even in intercourse with foreigners " Carthage and Utica "
always stipulate and promise in conjunction; which, of course,
did not preclude the far more important " new town " from
practically asserting its hegemony over Utica. Thus the Tyrian
factory was converted into the capital of a mighty North-
African empire, which extended from the desert of Tripoli to
the Atlantic Ocean, contenting itself in its western portion
(Morocco and Algiers) with the occupation, and that to some
extent superficial, of a belt along the coast, but in the richer
portion to the east (the present districts of Constantine and
Tunis) stretching its sway over the interior also and constantly
pushing its frontier farther to the south. The Carthaginians
were, as an ancient author significantly expresses it, converted
from Tyrians into Libyans. Phoenician civilisation prevailed
in Libya just as Greek civilisation prevailed in Asia Minor and
Syria after the campaigns of Alexander, although not with the

---

[1] The clearest description of this important class occurs in the Carthaginian treaty (Polyb. vii. 9), where in contrast to the Uticenses on the one
hand, and to the Libyan subjects on the other, they are called οἱ Καρχη-
δονίων ὕπαρχοι ὅσοι τοῖς αὐτοῖς νόμοις χρῶνται. Elsewhere they are spoken
of as cities allied (συμμαχίδες πόλεις, Diod. xx. 10) or tributary (Liv.
xxxiv. 62; Justin, xxii. 7, 3). Their *conubium* with the Carthaginians is
mentioned by Diodorus, xx. 55; the *commercium* is implied in the " equal
laws." That the old Phoenician colonies were included among the Libyphoenicians, is shown by the designation of Hippo as a Libyphoenician city
(Liv. xxv. 40); on the other hand as to the settlements derived from
Carthage it is said in the Periplus of Hanno: " the Carthaginians resolved
that Hanno should sail beyond the Pillars of Hercules and found cities of
Libyphoenicians." In substance the word " Libyphoenicians " was used
by the Carthaginians not as a national designation, but as a term denoting
a class in constitutional law. This view is quite consistent with the fact
that grammatically the name denotes Phoenicians mingled with Libyans
(Liv. xxi. 22, an addition to the text of Polybius); in reality, at least in
the institution of very exposed colonies, Libyans were frequently associated
with Phoenicians (Diod. xiii. 79; Cic. *pro Scauro*, 42). The analogy in
name and constitutional relations between the Latins of Rome and the
Libyphoenicians of Carthage is unmistakable.

same intensity. Phoenician was spoken and written at the courts of the Nomad sheiks, and the more civilised native tribes adopted for their language the Phoenician alphabet;[1] to Phoenicise them completely suited neither the genius of the nation nor the policy of Carthage.

The epoch, at which this transformation of Carthage into the capital of Libya took place, admits the less of being determined, because the change doubtless took place gradually. The author just mentioned names Hanno as the reformer of the nation. If the Hanno is meant who lived at the time of the first war with Rome, he can only be regarded as having completed the new system, the carrying out of which probably occupied the fourth and fifth centuries of Rome.

The flourishing of Carthage was accompanied by a parallel decline in the great cities of the Phoenician mother-country, in Sidon and especially in Tyre, the prosperity of which was destroyed partly by internal commotions, partly by the pressure of external calamities, particularly of its sieges by Salmanassar in the first, Nebuchodrossor in the second, and Alexander in the fifth century of Rome. The noble families and the old firms of Tyre emigrated for the most part to the secure and flourishing daughter-city, and carried thither their intelligence, their capital, and their traditions. At the time when the Phoenicians came into contact with Rome, Carthage was as decidedly the first of Canaanite cities as Rome was the first of the communities of Latium.

But the empire of Libya was only half of the power of Carthage; its maritime and colonial dominion had acquired, during the same period, a not less powerful development.

In Spain the chief station of the Phoenicians was the primitive Tyrian settlement at Gades (Cadiz). Besides this they possessed to the west and east of it a chain of factories, and in the interior the region of the silver mines; so that they had

---

[1] The Libyan or Numidian alphabet, by which we mean that which was and is employed by the Berbers in writing their non-Semitic language—one of the innumerable alphabets derived from the primitive Aramaean one—certainly appears to be more closely related in several of its forms to the latter rather than the Phoenician alphabet; but it by no means follows from this, that the Libyans derived their writing not from Phoenicians but from earlier immigrants, any more than the partially older forms of the Italian alphabets prohibit us from deriving these from the Greek. We must rather assume that the Libyan alphabet has been derived from the Phoenician at a period of the latter earlier than the time at which the records of the Phoenician language that have reached us were written.

occupied nearly the modern Andalusia and Granada, or at least the coasts of these provinces. They made no effort to acquire the interior from the warlike native nations; they were content with the possession of the mines and of stations for traffic and for shell and other fisheries; and they had difficulty in maintaining their ground even in these against the adjoining tribes. It is probable that these possessions were not strictly Carthaginian but Tyrian, and Gades was not reckoned among the cities tributary to Carthage; but practically, like all the western Phoenicians, it was under Carthaginian hegemony, as is shown by the aid sent by Carthage to the Gaditani against the natives, and by the institution of Carthaginian trading settlements to the westward of Gades. Ebusus and the Baleares, again, were occupied by the Carthaginians even at an early period, partly for the fisheries, partly as advanced posts against the Massiliots, with whom furious conflicts were waged from these stations.

In like manner the Carthaginians already at the end of the second century of Rome, established themselves in Sardinia, which was turned to account by them precisely in the same way as Libya. While the natives withdrew into the mountainous interior of the island to escape from the bondage of agricultural serfs, just as the Numidians in Africa withdrew to the borders of the desert, Phoenician colonies were conducted to Caralis (Cagliari) and other important points, and the fertile districts along the coast were rendered productive by the introduction of Libyan cultivators.

In Sicily the straits of Messana and the larger eastern half of the island had fallen at an early period into the hands of the Greeks; but the Phoenicians, with the help of the Carthaginians, retained the smaller adjacent islands, the Aegates, Melita, Gaulos, Cossyra—the settlement in Malta especially was rich and flourishing—and they kept the west and north-west coast of Sicily, whence they maintained communication with Africa by means of Motya and afterwards of Lilybaeum and with Sardinia by means of Panormus and Soluntum. The interior of the island remained in the possession of the native Elymi, Sicani, and Siceli. After the further advance of the Greeks was checked, a state of comparative peace had prevailed in the island, which even the campaign undertaken by the Carthaginians at the instigation of the Persians against their Greek neighbours in the island ($\frac{274}{480}$) did not permanently interrupt, and which continued on the whole to subsist till the Attic expedition to Sicily ($\frac{339-341}{415-413}$). The two competing nations made up their minds to tolerate each other, and confined themselves in the main each to its own field.

All these settlements and possessions were important enough in themselves; but they were of still greater moment, inasmuch as they became the pillars of the Carthaginian maritime supremacy. By their possession of the south of Spain, of the Baleares, of Sardinia, of western Sicily and Melita, and by their prevention of Hellenic colonies on the east coast of Spain, in Corsica, and in the region of the Syrtes, the masters of the north coast of Africa rendered their sea a closed one, and monopolised the western straits. In the Tyrrhene and Gallic seas alone the Phoenicians were obliged to admit the rivalry of other nations. This state of things might be endured so long as the Etruscans and the Greeks served to counterbalance each other in these waters; with the former as the less dangerous rivals Carthage even entered into an alliance against the Greeks. But when, on the fall of the Etruscan power—a fall which, as is usually the case in such forced alliances, Carthage had hardly exerted all her power to avert—and after the miscarriage of the great projects of Alcibiades Syracuse stood forth as indisputably the first Greek naval power, not only did the rulers of Syracuse naturally begin to aspire to dominion over Sicily and lower Italy and at the same time over the Tyrrhene and Adriatic seas, but the Carthaginians also were compelled to adopt a more energetic policy. The immediate result of the long and obstinate conflicts between them and their equally powerful and infamous antagonist, Dionysius of Syracuse ($\frac{348-389}{406-365}$), was the annihilation or weakening of the intervening Sicilian states—a result which both parties had an interest in accomplishing—and the division of the island between the Syracusans and Carthaginians. The most flourishing cities in the island—Selinus, Himera, Agrigentum, Gela, and Messana—were thoroughly destroyed by the Carthaginians in the course of these unhappy conflicts: and Dionysius was not displeased to see Hellenism destroyed or suppressed there, so that, leaning for support on foreign mercenaries enlisted from Italy, Gaul, and Spain, he might rule in greater security over provinces which lay desolate or which were occupied by military colonies. The peace, which was concluded after the victory of the Carthaginian general Mago at Kronion ($\frac{371}{383}$), and which subjected to the Carthaginians the Greek cities of Thermae (the ancient Himera), Segesta, Heraclea Minoa, Selinus, and a part of the territory of Agrigentum as far as the Halycus, was regarded by the two powers contending for the possession of the island as only a temporary accommodation; on both sides the rivals were ever renewing their attempts to dispossess each other. Four several times—in $\frac{360}{394}$ in the time of Dionysius the elder; in $\frac{410}{344}$ in that of Timoleon; in $\frac{445}{309}$ in that of Agathocles; in $\frac{476}{278}$ in that of Pyrrhus—the Carthaginians were masters of all Sicily excepting Syracuse, and were baffled by its solid walls; almost as often the Syracusans, under able leaders, such as were the elder Dionysius, Agathocles, and Pyrrhus, seemed equally on the eve of dislodging the Africans from the island. But more and more the balance inclined to the side of the Carthaginians, who were, as a rule, the aggressors, and who, although they did not follow out their object with Roman steadfastness, yet conducted their attack with far greater method and energy than the Greek city, vexed and torn by factions, conducted its defence. The Phoenicians might with reason expect that a pestilence or a foreign *condottiere* would not always snatch the prey from their hands; and for the time being, at least at sea, the struggle was already decided (i. 409): the attempt of Pyrrhus to restore the Syracusan fleet was the last. After the failure of that attempt, the Carthaginian fleet commanded without a rival the whole western Mediterranean; and their endeavours to occupy Syracuse, Rhegium, and Tarentum, showed the extent of their power and the objects at which they aimed. Hand in hand with these attempts went the endeavour to monopolise more and more the maritime commerce of this region, at the expense alike of foreigners and of their own subjects; and it was not the wont of the Carthaginians to recoil from any violence that might help forward their purpose. A contemporary of the Punic wars, Eratosthenes, the father of geography ($\frac{479-560}{275-194}$), affirms that every foreign mariner sailing towards Sardinia or towards the Straits of Gades, who fell into the hands of the Carthaginians, was thrown by them into the sea; and with this statement the fact completely accords, that Carthage by the treaty of $\frac{406}{348}$ (i. 410) declared the Spanish, Sardinian, and Libyan ports open to Roman trading vessels, whereas by that of $\frac{448}{306}$ (i. 412) it totally closed them, with the exception of the port of Carthage itself, against the same.

Aristotle, who died about fifty years before the commencement of the first Punic war, describes the constitution of Carthage as having changed from a monarchy to an aristocracy, or to a democracy inclining towards oligarchy, for he designates it by both names. The conduct of affairs was immediately vested in the hands of the Council of Ancients, which, like the Spartan

Gerusia, consisted of the two kings nominated annually by the citizens, and of twenty-eight gerusiasts, who were also, as it appears, chosen annually by the citizens. It was this council which mainly transacted the business of the state—making, for instance, the preliminary arrangements for war, appointing levies and enlistments, nominating the general, and associating with him a number of gerusiasts from whom the sub-commanders were regularly taken; and to it despatches were addressed. It is doubtful whether along with this small council there existed a larger one; at any rate it was not of much importance. As little does any special influence seem to have belonged to the kings; they acted chiefly as supreme judges, and they were frequently so named (Shofetes, *praetores*). The powers of the general were greater. Isocrates, the senior contemporary of Aristotle, says that the Carthaginians had an oligarchical government at home, but a monarchical government in the field; and thus the office of the Carthaginian general may be correctly described by Roman writers as a dictatorship, although the gerusiasts attached to him must have practically at least restricted his power and, after he had laid down his office, a regular official reckoning unknown among the Romans awaited him. There existed no fixed term of office for the general, and for this very reason he was doubtless different from the annual king, from whom Aristotle also expressly distinguishes him. The combination however of several offices in one person was not unusual among the Carthaginians, and it is not therefore surprising that often the same person appears as at once general and shofete.

But the Gerusia and the magistrates were subordinate to the corporation of the Hundred and Four (in round numbers the Hundred), or the Judges, the main bulwark of the Carthaginian oligarchy. It had no place in the original constitution of Carthage, but, like the Spartan Ephorate, it originated in an aristocratic opposition to the monarchical elements of that constitution. As public offices were purchasable and the number of members forming the supreme board was small, a single Carthaginian family, eminent above all others in wealth and military renown, the clan of Mago (i. 319), threatened to unite in its own hands the management of the state in peace and war and the administration of justice. This led, nearly about the time of the decemvirs, to an alteration of the constitution and to the appointment of this new board. We know that the holding of the quaestorship gave a title to admission into the body of judges, but that the candidate had nevertheless to be elected by certain self-electing Boards of Five (Pentarchies); and that the judges, although probably by law chosen from year to year, practically remained in office for a longer period or indeed for life, for which reason they are usually called "senators" by the Greeks and Romans. Obscure as are the details, we recognise clearly the nature of the body as an oligarchical board constituted by aristocratic cooptation; an isolated but characteristic indication of which is found in the fact that there were in Carthage special baths for the judges over and above the common baths for the citizens. They were primarily intended to act as political jurymen, who summoned the generals in particular, but beyond doubt the shofetes and gerusiasts also when circumstances required, to a reckoning on resigning office, and inflicted even capital punishment at pleasure, often with the most reckless cruelty. Of course in this as in every instance, where administrative functionaries are subjected to the control of another body, the reality of power was transferred from the controlled to the controlling authority; and it is easy to understand on the one hand how the latter came to interfere in all matters of administration—the Gerusia for instance submitted important despatches first to the judges, and then to the people—and on the other hand how fear of the control at home, which regularly meted out its award according to success, hampered the Carthaginian statesman and general in council and action.

The body of citizens in Carthage, though not expressly restricted, as in Sparta, to the attitude of passive bystanders in the business of the state, appears to have had but a very slight amount of practical influence on it. In the elections to the Gerusia a system of open corruption was the rule; in the nomination of a general the people were consulted, but only after the nomination had really been made by proposal on the part of the Gerusia; and other questions only went to the people when the Gerusia thought fit or could not otherwise agree. Assemblies of the people with judicial functions were unknown in Carthage. The powerlessness of the citizens was probably in the main occasioned by their political organisation: the mess-associations, which are mentioned among the Carthaginian institutions and compared with the Spartan Pheiditia, were probably guilds under oligarchical management. Mention is made even of a distinction between "burgesses of the city" and "manual labourers," which leads us to infer that the latter held a very inferior position, perhaps approaching to servitude.

On a comprehensive view of its several elements, the Carthaginian constitution appears to have been a government of capitalists, such as would naturally arise in a civic community which had no opulent middle class but consisted on the one hand of a city rabble without property and living from hand to mouth, and on the other hand of great merchants, planters, and overseers of quality. The system of enriching decayed grandees at the expense of the subjects, by despatching them as tax-assessors and overseers to the dependent communities—that infallible token of a rotten civic oligarchy—was not wanting in Carthage; Aristotle describes it as the main cause of the tried durability of the Carthaginian constitution. Up to his time no revolution worth mentioning had taken place in Carthage either from above or from below. The multitude remained without leaders in consequence of the material advantages which the governing oligarchy was able to offer to all ambitious or necessitous men of rank, and was satisfied with the crumbs which in the form of electoral corruption or otherwise fell to it from the table of the rich. A democratic opposition indeed could not fail with such a government to emerge; but at the time of the first Punic war it was still quite powerless. At a later period, partly under the influence of the defeats which were sustained, its political influence appears on the increase, and that far more rapidly than the influence of the similar party at the same period in Rome; the popular assemblies began to assume the final decision in political questions, and broke down the omnipotence of the Carthaginian oligarchy. After the termination of the second Punic war it even was enacted, on the proposal of Hannibal, that no member of the council of a Hundred could hold office for two consecutive years; and thereby a complete democracy was introduced, which certainly was under existing circumstances the only means of saving Carthage, if there still was time to do so. The opposition was swayed by a strong patriotic and reforming enthusiasm; but the fact cannot withal be overlooked, that it rested on a corrupt and rotten basis. The body of citizens in Carthage, which is compared by well-informed Greeks to the people of Alexandria, was so disorderly that on that account it well deserved to be powerless; and it might well be asked, what good could arise from revolutions, where, as in Carthage, the boys helped to make them.

From a financial point of view, Carthage held in every respect the first place among the states of antiquity. At the time of the Peloponnesian war this Phoenician city was, according to the

testimony of the first of Greek historians, financially superior
to all the Greek states, and its revenues were compared to those
of the great king; Polybius calls it the wealthiest city in the
world. The intelligent character of the Carthaginian husbandry
—which, as was the case subsequently in Rome, generals and
statesmen did not disdain scientifically to practise and to teach
—is attested by the agricultural treatise of the Carthaginian
Mago, which was universally regarded by the later Greek and
Roman rural authors as the fundamental code of rational
husbandry, and was not only translated into Greek, but was
edited also in Latin by command of the Roman senate and
officially recommended to the Italian landholders. A characteristic feature was the close connection between this Phoenician agriculture and capital: it was quoted as a leading maxim
of Phoenician husbandry that one should never acquire more
land than he could thoroughly manage. The rich resources of
the country in horses, oxen, sheep, and goats, in which Libya
by reason of its Nomad husbandry perhaps excelled at that time,
as Polybius testifies, all other lands of the earth, were of great
advantage to the Carthaginians. As these were the instructors
of the Romans in the art of profitably working the soil, they were
so likewise in the art of turning to good account their subjects;
by virtue of which Carthage reaped indirectly the rents of the
" best part of Europe," and of the rich—and in some portions,
such as in Byzacitis and on the lesser Syrtis, surpassingly productive—region of northern Africa. Commerce, which was
always regarded in Carthage as an honourable pursuit, and the
shipping and manufactures which commerce rendered flourishing, brought even in the natural course of things golden harvests
annually to the settlers there; and we have already indicated
how skilfully, by an extensive and ever-growing system of
monopoly, not only all the foreign but also all the inland commerce of the western Mediterranean, and the whole carrying
trade between the west and east, were more and more concentrated in that single harbour.

Science and art in Carthage, as afterwards in Rome, seem to
have been mainly dependent on Hellenic influences, but they
do not appear to have been neglected. There was a respectable
Phoenician literature; and on the conquest of the city there
were found rich treasures of art—not created, it is true, in
Carthage, but carried off from Sicilian temples—and considerable libraries. But even intellect there was in the service of
capital; the prominent features of its literature were chiefly

agricultural and geographical treatises, such as the work of
Mago already mentioned and the account by the admiral Hanno
of his voyage along the west coast of Africa, which was originally
deposited publicly in one of the Carthaginian temples, and
which is still extant in a translation. Even the general diffusion
of certain attainments, and particularly of the knowledge of
foreign languages,[1] as to which the Carthage of this epoch probably stood almost on a level with Rome under the empire,
forms an evidence of the thoroughly practical turn given to
Hellenic culture in Carthage. It is absolutely impossible to
form an idea of the mass of capital accumulated in this London
of antiquity, but some notion at least may be gained of the public
revenues from the fact, that, in spite of the costly system on
which Carthage organised its wars and in spite of the careless
and faithless administration of the state property, the contributions of its subjects and the customs-revenue completely
covered the expenditure, so that no direct taxes were levied from
the citizens; and further, that even after the second Punic war,
when the power of the state was already broken, the current
expenses and the payment to Rome of a yearly instalment of
£48,000 could be met, without levying any tax, merely by a somewhat stricter management of the finances, and fourteen years
after the peace the state proffered immediate payment of the
thirty-six remaining instalments. But it was not merely the
sum total of its revenues that evinced the superiority of the
financial administration at Carthage. The economical principles of a later and more advanced epoch are found by us in
Carthage alone of all the more considerable states of antiquity.
Mention is made of foreign state-loans, and in the monetary
system we find along with gold and silver mention of a token-
money having no intrinsic value—a species of currency not used
elsewhere in antiquity. In fact, if government had resolved
itself into mere mercantile speculation, never would any state
have solved the problem more brilliantly than Carthage.

Let us now compare the respective resources of Carthage
and Rome. Both were agricultural and mercantile cities, and
nothing more; art and science had substantially the same altogether subordinate and altogether practical character in both,

---

[1] The steward on a country estate, although a slave, ought, according
to the precept of the Carthaginian agricultural writer Mago (*ap.* Varro,
R. R. i. 17), to be able to read, and ought to possess some culture. In the
prologue of the "Poenulus" of Plautus, it is said of the hero of the title:—

> *Et is omnes linguas scit ; sed dissimulat sciens*
> *Se scire ; Poenus plane est ; quid verbis opus't ?*

except that in this respect Carthage had made greater progress than Rome. But in Carthage the moneyed interest preponderated over the landed, in Rome at this time the landed still preponderated over the moneyed; and, while the agriculturists of Carthage were universally large landlords and slave-holders, in the Rome of this period the great mass of the burgesses still tilled their fields in person. The majority of the population in Rome held property, and was therefore conservative; the majority in Carthage held no property, and was therefore accessible to the gold of the rich as well as to the cry of the democrats for reform. In Carthage there already prevailed all that opulence which marks powerful commercial cities, while the manners and police of Rome still maintained at least externally the severity and frugality of the olden times. When the ambassadors of Carthage returned from Rome, they told their colleagues that the relations of intimacy among the Roman senators surpassed all conception; that a single set of silver plate sufficed for the whole senate, and had reappeared in every house to which the envoys had been invited. The sneer is a significant token of the difference in their economic condition.

In both the constitution was aristocratic; the Judges governed in Carthage, as did the senate in Rome, and both on the same system of police-control. The strict state of dependence in which the governing board at Carthage held the individual magistrate, and the injunction to the citizens absolutely to refrain from learning the Greek language and to communicate with a Greek only through the medium of a public interpreter, originated in the same spirit as the system of government at Rome; but in comparison with the cruel harshness and the categorical precision, bordering on silliness, of this Carthaginian state-tutelage, the Roman system of fining and censure appears mild and reasonable. The Roman senate, which was open to eminent ability and represented in the best sense the nation, was able also to trust the nation, and had no need to fear the magistrates. The Carthaginian senate, on the other hand, was based on a jealous control of administration by the government, and represented exclusively the leading families; its essence was mistrust of all above and below it, and therefore it could neither be confident that the people would follow whither it led, nor free from the dread of usurpations on the part of the magistrates. Hence the steady course of Roman policy, which never receded a step in times of misfortune, and never threw away the favours of fortune by negligence or indifference; whereas the Carthaginians desisted from the struggle when a last effort might perhaps have saved all, and weary or forgetful of their great duties as a nation allowed the half-completed building to fall to pieces, only to begin it in a few years anew. Hence the able magistrate in Rome was ordinarily on a good understanding with his government; in Carthage he was frequently at decided feud with his masters at home, and was forced to resist them by unconstitutional means and to make common cause with the reform party which constituted the opposition.

Both Carthage and Rome ruled over communities of lineage kindred with their own, and over numerous others of alien race. But Rome had thrown open her citizenship to one district after another, and had rendered it even legally accessible to the Latin communities; Carthage from the first maintained her exclusiveness, and did not permit the dependent districts even to cherish a hope of being some day placed upon an equal footing. Rome granted to the communities of kindred lineage a share in the fruits of victory, especially in the acquired domains; and sought, by conferring material advantages on the rich and noble, to gain over at least a party to her own interest in the other subject states. Carthage not only retained for herself the produce of her victories, but even deprived the most privileged cities of their freedom of trade. Rome did not wholly take away the independence of even the lowest grade of her subject communities, and imposed a fixed tribute on none; Carthage despatched her overseers everywhere, and loaded even the old Phoenician cities with a heavy tribute, while her subject tribes were practically treated as state-slaves. In this way there was not in the compass of the Carthagino-African state a single community, with the exception of Utica, that would not have been politically and materially benefited by the fall of Carthage; in the Romano-Italic there was not one that had not much more to lose than to gain in rebelling against a government, which was careful to avoid injuring material interests, and which never at least by extreme measures challenged political opposition to conflict. If Carthaginian statesmen believed that they had attached to the interests of Carthage her Phoenician subjects by their greater dread of a Libyan revolt and all the landholders by means of token-money, they transferred mercantile calculation to a sphere to which it did not apply. Experience proved that the Roman symmachy, notwithstanding its seemingly looser bond of connection, held out against Pyrrhus like a wall of rock, whereas the Carthaginian fell to pieces like a gossamer web as soon as a hostile army set foot on African soil. It was so on the landing of Agathocles and of Regulus, and likewise in the mercenary war; the spirit that prevailed in Africa is illustrated by the fact, that the Libyan women voluntarily contributed their ornaments to the mercenaries for their war against Carthage. In Sicily alone the Carthaginians appear to have exercised a milder rule, and to have attained on that account better results. They granted to their subjects in that quarter comparative freedom in foreign trade, and allowed them to conduct their internal commerce, probably from the outset and exclusively, with a metallic currency; far greater freedom of movement generally was allowed to them than was permitted to the Sardinians and Libyans. Had Syracuse fallen into Carthaginian hands, their policy would doubtless soon have changed. But that result did not take place; and so, owing to the well-calculated mildness of the Carthaginian government and the unhappy distractions of the Sicilian Greeks, there actually existed in Sicily a party really friendly to the Phoenicians; for example, even after the island had passed to the Romans, Philinus of Agrigentum wrote the history of the great war in a thoroughly Phoenician spirit. Nevertheless on the whole the Sicilians must, both as subjects and as Hellenes, have been at least as averse to their Phoenician masters as the Samnites and Tarentines were to the Romans.

In a financial point of view the state revenues of Carthage doubtless far surpassed those of Rome; but this advantage was partly neutralised by the facts, that the sources of the Carthaginian revenue—tribute and customs—dried up far sooner (and just when they were most needed) than those of Rome, and that the Carthaginian mode of conducting war was far more costly than the Roman.

The military resources of the Romans and Carthaginians were very different, yet in many respects not unequally balanced. The citizens of Carthage still at the conquest of the city amounted to 700,000, including women and children,[1] and were probably

---

[1] Doubts have been expressed as to the correctness of this number, and the highest possible number of inhabitants, taking into account the available space, has been reckoned at 250,000. Apart from the uncertainty of such calculations, especially as to a commercial city with houses of six stories, we must remember that the numbering is doubtless to be understood in a political, not in an urban, sense, just like the numbers in the Roman census, and that thus all Carthaginians would be included in it, whether dwelling in the city or its neighbourhood, or resident in its subject territory or in other lands. There would, of course, be a large number of such absentees in the case of Carthage; indeed it is expressly stated that in Gades, for the same reason, the burgess-roll always showed a far higher number than that of the citizens who had their fixed residence there.

at least as numerous at the close of the fifth century; in that century they were able in case of need to set on foot a burgess army of 40,000 hoplites. At the very beginning of the fifth century, Rome had in similar circumstances sent to the field a burgess army equally strong (i. 420); after the great extension of the Roman domain in the course of that century the number of full burgesses capable of bearing arms must at least have doubled. But far more than in the number of men capable of bearing arms, Rome excelled in the effective condition of the burgess-soldier. Anxious as the Carthaginian government was to induce its citizens to take part in military service, it could neither furnish the artisan and the manufacturer with the bodily vigour of the husbandman, nor overcome the native aversion of the Phoenicians to warfare. In the fifth century there still fought in the Sicilian armies a " sacred band " of 2500 Carthaginians as a guard for the general; in the sixth not a single Carthaginian, officers excepted, was to be met with in the Carthaginian armies such as that of Spain. The Roman farmers, again, took their places not only in the muster-roll, but also in the field of battle. It was the same with the cognate dependencies of both communities; while the Latins rendered to the Romans no less service than their own burgess-troops, the Libyphoenicians were as little adapted for war as the Carthaginians, and, as may easily be supposed, still less desirous of it, and so they too disappeared from the armies; the towns bound to furnish contingents probably redeemed their obligation by a payment of money. In the Spanish army just mentioned, composed of some 15,000 men, only a single troop of cavalry of 450 men consisted, and that but partly, of Libyphoenicians. The flower of the Carthaginian armies was formed by the Libyans, whose recruits were capable of being trained under able officers into good infantry, and whose light cavalry was unsurpassed in its kind. To these were added the forces of the more or less dependent tribes of Libya and Spain and the famous slingers of the Baleares, who seem to have held an intermediate position between allied contingents and mercenary troops; and finally, in case of need, the hired soldiery raised abroad. So far as numbers were concerned, such an army might without difficulty be raised almost to any desired strength; and in the ability of its officers, in acquaintance with arms, and in courage, it might be capable of coping with that of Rome. Not only, however, did a dangerously long interval elapse, in the event of mercenaries being required, ere they could be got ready, while the Roman militia was able at any moment to take the field, but—which was the main matter—there was nothing to keep together the armies of Carthage but military honour and profit, while the Romans were united by all the ties that bound them to their common fatherland. The average Carthaginian officer estimated his mercenaries, and even the Libyan farmers, very much as men in modern warfare estimate cannon-balls; hence such disgraceful proceedings as the betrayal of the Libyan troops by their general Himilco in $\frac{358}{396}$, which was followed by a dangerous insurrection of the Libyans, and hence that proverbial cry of "Punic faith," which did the Carthaginians no small injury. Carthage experienced in full measure all the evils which armies of fellahs and mercenaries could bring upon a state, and more than once she found her paid serfs more dangerous than her foes.

The Carthaginian government could not fail to perceive the defects of this military system, and they certainly sought to remedy them by every available means. They insisted on maintaining full chests and full magazines, that they might at any time be able to equip mercenaries. They bestowed great care on those elements which among the ancients represented the modern artillery—the construction of machines, in which we find the Carthaginians regularly superior to the Siceliots, and the use of elephants, after these had superseded in warfare the earlier war-chariots: in the casemates of Carthage there were stalls for 300 elephants. They could not venture to fortify the dependent cities, and were obliged to submit to the occupation of the towns and villages as well as of the open country by any hostile army that landed in Africa—a thorough contrast to the state of Italy, where most of the subject towns had retained their walls, and a chain of Roman fortresses commanded the whole peninsula. But on the fortification of the capital they expended all the resources of money and of art, and on several occasions nothing but the strength of its walls saved the state; whereas Rome held a political and military position so secure that it never underwent a formal siege. Lastly, the main bulwark of the state was their war-marine, on which they lavished the utmost care. In the building as well as in the management of vessels the Carthaginians excelled the Greeks; it was at Carthage that ships were first built of more than three banks of oars, and the Carthaginian war-vessels, at this period mostly quinqueremes, were ordinarily better sailers than the Greek; the rowers, all of them public slaves, who never stirred from the galleys, were excellently trained, and the captains were expert and fearless. In this respect Carthage was decidedly superior to the Romans, who, with the few ships of their Greek allies and still fewer of their own, were unable even to show themselves in the open sea against the fleet which at that time without a rival ruled the western Mediterranean.

If, in conclusion, we sum up the results of this comparison of the resources of the two great powers, the judgment expressed by a sagacious and impartial Greek is perhaps borne out, that Carthage and Rome were, when the struggle between them began, on the whole equally matched. But we cannot omit to add that, while Carthage had put forth all the efforts of which intellect and wealth were capable to provide herself with artificial means of attack and defence, she was unable in any satisfactory way to make up for the fundamental want of a land army of her own and of a symmachy resting on a self-supporting basis. That Rome could only be seriously attacked in Italy, and Carthage only in Libya, no one could fail to see; as little could any one fail to perceive that Carthage could not in the long run escape from such an attack. Fleets were not yet in those times of the infancy of navigation a permanent heirloom of nations, but could be fitted out wherever there were trees, iron, and water. It was clear, and had been several times tested in Africa itself, that even powerful maritime states were not able to prevent a weaker enemy from landing. When Agathocles had shown the way thither, a Roman general could follow the same course; and while in Italy the entrance of an invading army simply began the war, the same event in Libya put an end to it by converting it into a siege, in which, unless some special accident should intervene, even the most obstinate and heroic courage must finally succumb.

CHAPTER II

THE WAR BETWEEN ROME AND CARTHAGE CONCERNING
SICILY

FOR upwards of a century the feud between the Carthaginians and the rulers of Syracuse had devastated the beautiful island of Sicily. On both sides the contest was carried on with the weapons of political proselytism, for, while Carthage kept up communications with the aristocratic-republican opposition in Syracuse, the Syracusan dynasts maintained relations with the national party in the Greek cities that had become tributary to Carthage. On both sides armies of mercenaries were employed to fight their battles—by Timoleon and Agathocles, as well as by the Phoenician generals. And as like means were employed on both sides, so the conflict had been waged on both with a disregard of honour and a perfidy unexampled in the history of the west. The Syracusans were the weaker party. In the peace of $\frac{440}{314}$ Carthage had still limited her claims to the third of the island to the west of Heraclea Minoa and Himera, and had expressly recognised the hegemony of the Syracusans over all the cities to the eastward. The expulsion of Pyrrhus from Sicily and Italy ($\frac{479}{275}$) left by far the larger half of the island, and especially the important city of Agrigentum, in the hands of Carthage; the Syracusans retained nothing but Tauromenium and the south-east of the island.

In the second great city on the east coast, Messana, a band of foreign soldiers had established themselves and held the city, independent alike of Syracusans and Carthaginians. These new rulers of Messana were Campanian mercenaries. The dissolute habits that had become prevalent among the Sabellians settled in and around Capua (i. 352), had made Campania in the fourth and fifth centuries—what Aetolia, Crete, and Laconia were afterwards—the universal recruiting field for princes and cities in search of mercenaries. The partial civilisation that had been called into existence there by the Campanian Greeks, the barbaric luxury of life in Capua and the other Campanian cities, the political impotence to which the hegemony of Rome condemned them, while yet its rule was not so stern as wholly to withdraw from them the right of self-disposal—all tended to drive the youth of Campania in troops to the standards of the recruiting officers. As a matter of course, this wanton and unscrupulous selling of themselves was here as in all cases attended by estrangement from their native land, habits of military violence and lawlessness, and indifference to the breach of their allegiance. These Campanians could see no reason why a band of mercenaries should not seize on their own behalf any city entrusted to their guardianship, provided only they were in a position to hold it—the Samnites had established their dominion in Capua itself, and the Lucanians in a succession of Greek cities, after a fashion not much more honourable. Nowhere was the state of political relations more inviting for such enterprises than in Sicily. Already the Campanian captains who came to Sicily during the Peloponnesian war had insinuated themselves in this way into Entella and Aetna. Somewhere about the year $\frac{470}{284}$ a Campanian band, which had previously served under Agathocles and after his death ($\frac{465}{289}$) took up the trade of free-booters on their own account, established themselves in Messana, the second city of Grecian Sicily, and the chief seat of the anti-Syracusan party in that portion of the island which was still in the power of the Greeks. The citizens were slain or expelled, their wives and children and houses were distributed among the soldiers, and the new masters of the city, the Mamertines or "men of Mars," as they called themselves, soon became the third power in the island, the north-eastern portion of which they reduced to subjection in the times of confusion that succeeded the death of Agathocles. The Carthaginians were no unwilling spectators of these events, which established in the immediate vicinity of the Syracusans a new and powerful adversary instead of a cognate and ordinarily allied or dependent city. With Carthaginian aid the Mamertines maintained themselves against Pyrrhus, and the untimely departure of the king restored to them all their power.

It is not proper in the historian either to excuse the perfidious crime by which the Mamertines seized their power, or to forget that the God of history does not necessarily punish the sins of the fathers to the fourth generation. He who feels it his vocation to judge the sins of others may condemn the human agents; for Sicily it might be a blessing, that a warlike power, and one belonging to the island, thus began to be formed in it—a power which was already able to bring eight thousand men into the field, and which was gradually putting itself in a position to take up at the proper time and on its own resources that struggle against the foreigners, to the maintenance of which the Hellenes, becoming more and more unaccustomed to arms notwithstanding their perpetual wars, were no longer equal.

In the first instance, however, things took another turn. A young Syracusan officer, who by his descent from the family of Gelo and his intimate relations of kindred with king Pyrrhus as well as by the distinction with which he had fought in the campaigns of the latter, had attracted the notice of his fellow-citizens as well as of the Syracusan soldiery—Hiero, son of Hierocles—was called by military election to command the army, which was at variance with the citizens ($\frac{479}{275}-\frac{480}{274}$). By his prudent administration, the nobility of his character, and the moderation of his views, he rapidly gained the hearts of the citizens of Syracuse—who had been accustomed to the most scandalous lawlessness in their despots—and of the Sicilian Greeks in general. He rid himself—in a perfidious manner, it is true—of the insubordinate army of mercenaries, revived the citizen-militia, and endeavoured, at first with the title of general, afterwards with that of king, to re-establish the deeply sunken Hellenic power by means of his civic troops and of fresh and more manageable recruits. With the Carthaginians, who in concert with the Greeks had driven king Pyrrhus from the island, there was at that time peace. The immediate foes of the Syracusans were the Mamertines. They were the kinsmen of those hated mercenaries whom the Syracusans had recently extirpated; they had murdered their own Greek hosts; they had curtailed the Syracusan territory; they had oppressed and plundered a number of smaller Greek towns. In league with the Romans who just about this time were sending their legions against the Campanians in Rhegium, the allies, kinsmen, and confederates in crime of the Mamertines (i. 408), Hiero turned his arms against Messana. By a great victory, after which Hiero was proclaimed king of the Siceliots ($\frac{484}{270}$), he succeeded in shutting up the Mamertines within their city, and after the siege had lasted some years, they found themselves reduced to extremity and unable to hold the city longer against Hiero on their own resources. It was evident that a surrender on favourable terms was impossible, and that the axe of the executioner, which had fallen upon the Campanians of Rhegium at Rome, as certainly awaited those of Messana at Syracuse. Their only means of safety lay in delivering up the city either to the Carthaginians or to the Romans, both of whom could not but be so strongly set upon acquiring that important place as to overlook all other scruples. Whether it would be more advantageous to surrender it into the hands of the Phoenicians or into those of the masters of Italy, was doubtful; after long hesitation the majority of the Campanian burgesses at length resolved to offer the possession of their sea-commanding fortress to the Romans.

It was a moment of the deepest significance in the history of the world, when the envoys of the Mamertines appeared in the Roman senate. No one indeed could then anticipate all that was to depend on the crossing of that narrow arm of the sea; but that the decision, however it should go, would involve consequences far other and more important than had attached to any decree hitherto passed by the senate, must have been manifest to every one of the fathers of the city assembled in council. Strictly upright men might indeed ask how it was possible to hesitate at all, and how any one could even think of suggesting that the Romans should not only break their alliance with Hiero, but should, just after the Campanians of Rhegium had been punished by them with righteous severity, admit their no less guilty Sicilian accomplices to the alliance and friendship of the state, and thereby rescue them from the punishment which they deserved. Such an outrage on propriety would not only afford their adversaries matter for declamation, but must seriously offend all men of moral feeling. But even the statesman, with whom political morality was no mere phrase, might ask in reply, how Roman burgesses, who had broken their military oath and treacherously murdered the allies of Rome, could be placed on a level with foreigners who had committed an outrage on foreigners, where no one had constituted the Romans judges of the one or avengers of the other? Had the question been only whether the Syracusans or Mamertines should rule in Messana, Rome might certainly have acquiesced in the rule of either. Rome was striving for the possession of Italy, Carthage for that of Sicily; the designs of the two powers scarcely then went further. But that very circumstance formed a reason why each desired to have and retain on its frontier an intermediate power—the Carthaginians for instance reckoning in this way on Tarentum, the Romans on Syracuse and Messana —and why, if that course was impossible, each preferred to see these adjacent places given over to itself rather than to its great rival. As Carthage had made an attempt in Italy, when Rhegium and Tarentum were about to be occupied by the Romans, to acquire these cities for itself, and had only been

prevented from doing so by accident, so in Sicily an opportunity
now offered itself to Rome to bring the city of Messana into its
symmachy; should the Romans reject it, it was not to be supposed that the city would remain independent or would become
Syracusan; they would themselves throw it into the arms of
the Phoenicians. Were they justified in allowing an opportunity to escape, such as certainly would never recur, of making
themselves masters of the natural *tête de pont* between Italy and
Sicily, and of securing it by means of a brave garrison on which
they could, for good reasons, depend? Were they justified in
abandoning Messana, and thereby surrendering the command of
the last free passage between the eastern and western seas, and
sacrificing the commercial liberty of Italy? It is true that
other objections might be urged to the occupation of Messana
besides mere scruples of feeling and of honourable policy. That
it could not but lead to a war with Carthage, was the least of
these; serious as was such a war, Rome might not fear it. But
there was the more important objection that by crossing the
sea the Romans would depart from the purely Italian and purely
continental policy which they had hitherto pursued; they
would abandon the system by which their ancesters had founded
the greatness of Rome, to enter upon another system the results
of which no one could foretell. It was one of those moments
when calculation fails, and when faith in men's own and in their
country's destiny alone gives them courage to grasp the hand
which beckons to them out of the darkness of the future, and
to follow it they know not whither. Long and seriously the
senate deliberated on the proposal of the consuls to lead the
legions to the help of the Mamertines; it came to no decisive
resolution. But the burgesses, to whom the matter was referred,
were animated by a lively sense of the greatness of the power
which their own energy had established. The conquest of
Italy encouraged the Romans as that of Greece encouraged
the Macedonians and that of Silesia the Prussians, to enter
upon a new political career. A formal pretext for supporting
the Mamertines was found in the protectorate which Rome
claimed the right to exercise over all Italians. The transmarine
Italians were received into the Italian confederacy; [1] and on the
proposal of the consuls the citizens resolved to send them
aid ($\frac{489}{265}$).

[1] The Mamertines were admitted into precisely the same position towards
Rome as the Italian communities, bound themselves to furnish ships
(Cic. *Verr.* v. 19, 50), and, as the coins show, did not possess the privilege
of coining silver.

Much depended on the way in which the two Sicilian powers, immediately affected by this intervention of the Romans in the affairs of the island, and both hitherto nominally in alliance with Rome, would regard her interference. Hiero had sufficient reason to treat the summons, by which the Romans required him to desist from hostilities against their new confederates in Messana, precisely in the same way as the Samnites and Lucanians in similar circumstances had treated the occupation of Capua and Thurii, and to answer the Romans by a declaration of war. If, however, he remained unsupported, such a war would be folly; and it might be expected from his prudent and moderate policy that he would acquiesce in what was inevitable, if Carthage should be disposed for peace. This seemed not impossible. A Roman embassy was now ($\frac{489}{265}$) sent to Carthage, seven years after the attempt of the Phoenician fleet to gain possession of Tarentum, to demand explanations as to that transaction (i. 407). Grievances not unfounded, but half forgotten, once more emerged—it seemed not superfluous amidst other warlike preparations to replenish the diplomatic armoury with reasons for war, and to be able to claim in the coming manifesto, as was the custom of the Romans, the character of the party aggrieved. This much at least might with entire justice be affirmed, that the respective enterprises on Tarentum and Messana stood upon exactly the same footing in point of design and of pretext, and that it was simply the accident of success that made the difference. Carthage avoided an open rupture. The ambassadors carried back to Rome a disavowal on the part of the Carthaginian admiral who had made the attempt on Tarentum, along with the requisite false oaths: the counter-complaints, which of course were not wanting on the part of Carthage, were studiously moderate, and abstained from characterising the meditated invasion of Sicily as a ground for war. Such, however, it was; for Carthage regarded the affairs of Sicily—just as Rome regarded those of Italy—as internal matters in which an independent power could suffer no interference, and was determined to act accordingly. But Phoenician policy followed a gentler course than that of threatening open war. When the preparations of Rome for sending help to the Mamertines were at length so far advanced that the fleet formed of the war-vessels of Naples, Tarentum, Velia, and Locri, and the vanguard of the Roman land army under the military tribune Gaius Claudius, had appeared at Rhegium (in the spring of $\frac{490}{264}$), unexpected news arrived from Messana that

the Carthaginians, having come to an understanding with the
anti-Roman party there, had as a neutral power arranged a
peace between Hiero and the Mamertines; that the siege had in
consequence been raised; and that a Carthaginian fleet lay in
the harbour of Messana, and a Carthaginian garrison in the
citadel, both under the command of admiral Hanno. The
Mamertine citizens, now under Carthaginian influence, informed
the Roman commanders, with due thanks for the federal help
so speedily accorded to them, that they were glad that they no
longer needed it. The adroit and daring officer who commanded
the Roman vanguard nevertheless set sail with his troops. But
the Carthaginians warned the Roman vessels to retire, and even
made some of them prizes; these, however, the Carthaginian
admiral, remembering his strict orders to give no pretext for
the outbreak of hostilities, sent back to his good friends on the
other side of the straits. It almost seemed as if the Romans
had compromised themselves as uselessly before Messana, as
the Carthaginians before Tarentum. But Claudius did not
allow himself to be deterred, and on a second attempt he succeeded in crossing. Scarcely had he landed when he called a
meeting of the citizens; and, at his wish, the admiral also
appeared at the meeting, still imagining that he should be able
to avoid an open breach. But the Romans seized his person in
the assembly itself; and Hanno and the Phoenician garrison in
the citadel, weak and destitute of a leader, were pusillanimous
enough, the former to give to his troops the command to withdraw, the latter to comply with the orders of their captive
general and to evacuate the city along with him. Thus the
tête de pont of the island fell into the hands of the Romans. The
Carthaginian authorities, justly indignant at the folly and weakness of their general, caused him to be executed, and declared
war against the Romans. It was of especial importance to
recover the lost place. A strong Carthaginian fleet, led by
Hanno, son of Hannibal, appeared off Messana; while the fleet
blockaded the straits, the Carthaginian army landing from it
began the siege on the north side. Hiero, who had only waited
for the Carthaginian attack to begin the war with Rome, again
brought up his army, which he had hardly withdrawn, against
Messana, and undertook the attack on the south side of the city.
But meanwhile the Roman consul Appius Claudius Caudex
had appeared at Rhegium with the main body of his army, and
succeeded in crossing on a dark night in spite of the Carthaginian
fleet. Audacity and fortune were on the side of the Romans;

the allies, not prepared for an attack by the whole Roman army and consequently not united, were beaten in detail by the Roman legions issuing from the city; and thus the siege was raised. The Roman army kept the field during the summer, and even made an attempt on Syracuse; but, when that had failed and the siege of Echetla (on the confines of the territories of Syracuse and Carthage) had to be abandoned with loss, the Roman army returned to Messana, and thence, leaving a strong garrison behind them, to Italy. The results obtained in this first campaign of the Romans out of Italy probably did not quite correspond to the expectations formed at home, for the consul had no triumph; nevertheless, the energy which the Romans displayed in Sicily could not fail to make a great impression on the Sicilian Greeks. In the following year both consuls and an army twice as large entered the island unopposed. One of them, Marcus Valerius Maximus, afterwards called from this campaign the " hero of Messana " (*Messalla*), achieved a brilliant victory over the allied Carthaginians and Syracusans. After this battle the Phoenician army no longer ventured to keep the field against the Romans; Alaesa, Centuripa, and the smaller Greek towns generally joined the victors, and Hiero himself abandoned the Carthaginian side and made peace and alliance with Rome ($\frac{491}{263}$). He pursued a judicious policy in joining the Romans as soon as it appeared that their interference in Sicily was in earnest, and while there was still time to purchase peace without cessions and sacrifices. The intermediate states in Sicily, Syracuse and Messana, which were unable to follow out a policy of their own and had only the choice between Roman and Carthaginian hegemony, necessarily preferred the former; because the Romans had not probably as yet formed the design of conquering the island for themselves, but sought merely to prevent its being acquired by Carthage, and at all events Rome might be expected to substitute a juster treatment and due protection of commercial freedom for the tyrannising and monopolising system that Carthage pursued. Henceforth Hiero continued to be the most important, the steadiest, and the most esteemed ally of the Romans in the island.

The Romans had thus gained their immediate object. By their double alliance with Messana and Syracuse, and the firm hold which they had on the whole east coast, they secured the means of landing on the island and of maintaining—which hitherto had been a very difficult matter—their armies there; and the war, which had previously been doubtful and hazardous,

lost in a great measure its character of risk. Accordingly, no
greater exertions were made for it than for the wars in Samnium
and Etruria; the two legions which were despatched to the
island for the next year $\left(\frac{499}{262}\right)$ sufficed, in concert with the
Sicilian Greeks, to drive the Carthaginians everywhere into
their fortresses. The commander-in-chief of the Carthaginians,
Hannibal son of Gisgo, threw himself with the flower of his
troops into Agrigentum, to defend to the last that most important of the Carthaginian inland cities. Unable to storm a city
so strong, the Romans blockaded it with entrenched lines and a
double camp; the besieged, who numbered 50,000, soon suffered
from want of provisions. To raise the siege the Carthaginian
admiral Hanno landed at Heraclea, and cut off in turn the
supplies from the Roman besieging force. On both sides the
distress was great. At length a battle was resolved on, to put
an end to the state of embarrassment and uncertainty. In
this battle the Numidian cavalry showed itself just as superior
to the Roman horse as the Roman infantry was superior to the
Phoenician foot; the infantry decided the victory, but the
losses even of the Romans were very considerable. The result
of the successful struggle was somewhat marred by the circumstance that, after the battle, during the confusion and fatigue
of the conquerors, the beleaguered army succeeded in escaping
from the city and in reaching the fleet. The victory was nevertheless of importance; Agrigentum fell into the hands of the
Romans, and thus the whole island was in their power, with the
exception of the maritime fortresses, in which the Carthaginian
general Hamilcar, Hanno's successor in command, entrenched
himself to the teeth, and was not to be driven out either by force
or by famine. The war was thenceforth continued only by
sallies of the Carthaginians from the Sicilian fortresses and their
descents on the Italian coasts.

In fact, the Romans now for the first time felt the real difficulties of the war. If, as we are told, the Carthaginian
diplomatists before the outbreak of hostilities warned the
Romans not to push the matter to a breach, because against
their will no Roman could even wash his hands in the sea, the
threat was well founded. The Carthaginian fleet ruled the sea
without a rival, and not only kept the coast towns of Sicily in
due obedience and provided them with all necessaries, but also
threatened a descent upon Italy, for which reason it was necessary in $\frac{492}{262}$ to retain a consular army there. No invasion on a
large scale occurred; but smaller Carthaginian detachments

landed on the Italian coasts and levied contributions on the allies of Rome, and, what was worst of all, completely paralysed the commerce of Rome and her allies. The continuance of such a course for even a short time would suffice entirely to ruin Caere, Ostia, Neapolis, Tarentum, and Syracuse, while the Carthaginians easily consoled themselves for the loss of the tribute of Sicily with the contributions which they levied and the rich prizes of their privateering. The Romans now learned, what Dionysius, Agathocles, and Pyrrhus had learned before, that it was as difficult to conquer the Carthaginians as it was easy to beat them in the field. They saw that everything depended on procuring a fleet, and resolved to form one of twenty triremes and a hundred quinqueremes. The execution, however, of this energetic resolution was not easy. The representation originating in the schools of the rhetoricians, which would have us believe that the Romans then for the first time dipped their oars in water, is no doubt a childish tale; the mercantile marine of Italy must at this time have been very extensive, and there was no want even of Italian vessels of war. But these were war-barks and triremes, such as had been in use in earlier times; quinqueremes, which under the more modern system of naval warfare that had originated chiefly in Carthage were almost exclusively employed in the line, had not yet been built in Italy. The measure adopted by the Romans was therefore much as if a maritime state of the present day were to pass at once from the building of frigates and cutters to the building of ships of the line; and, just as in such a case now a foreign ship of the line would, if possible, be adopted as a pattern, the Romans referred their master shipbuilders to a stranded Carthaginian *penteres* as a model. No doubt the Romans, had they wished, might have sooner attained their object with the aid of the Syracusans and Massiliots; but their statesmen had too much sagacity to desire to defend Italy by means of a fleet not Italian. The Italian allies, however, were largely drawn upon both for the naval officers, who must have been for the most part taken from the Italian mercantile marine, and for the sailors, whose name (*socii navales*) shows that for a time they were exclusively furnished by the allies; along with these, slaves provided by the state and the wealthier families were afterwards employed, and ere long also the poorer class of burgesses. Under such circumstances, and when we take into account, as is but fair, on the one hand the comparatively low state of shipbuilding at that time, and on the other hand the

energy of the Romans, there is nothing incredible in the statement that the Romans solved within a year the problem—which
baffled Napoleon—of converting a continental into a maritime
power, and actually launched their fleet of 120 sail in the spring
of $\frac{494}{260}$. It is true, that it was by no means a match for the
Carthaginian fleet in numbers and efficiency at sea; and these
were points of the greater importance, as the naval tactics of
the period consisted mainly in manœuvring. In the maritime
warfare of that period hoplites and archers no doubt fought
from the deck, and projectile machines were also plied from it;
but the ordinary and really decisive mode of action consisted in
running foul of the enemy's vessels, for which purpose the prows
were furnished with heavy iron beaks: the vessels engaged were
in the habit of sailing round each other till one or the other
succeeded in giving the thrust, which usually proved decisive.
Accordingly the crew of an ordinary Greek trireme, consisting
of about 200 men, contained only about 10 soldiers, but on the
other hand 170 rowers, from 50 to 60 on each deck; that of
a quinquereme numbered about 300 rowers, and soldiers in
proportion.

The happy idea occurred to the Romans that they might
make up for what their vessels, with their unpractised officers
and crews, necessarily lacked in ability of manœuvring, by
again assigning a more considerable part in naval warfare to
the soldiers. They stationed at the prow of each vessel a flying
bridge, which could be lowered in front or on either side; it
was furnished on both sides with parapets, and had space for
two men in front. When the enemy's vessel was sailing up to
strike the Roman one, or was lying alongside of it after the
thrust had been evaded, the bridge on deck was suddenly lowered
and fastened to its opponent by means of a grappling-iron:
this not only prevented the running down, but enabled the Roman
marines to pass along the bridge to the enemy's deck and to
carry it by assault as in a conflict on land. No distinct body
of marines was formed, but land troops were employed, when
required, for this maritime service. In one instance as many
as 120 legionaries fought in each ship on occasion of a great naval
battle; in that case however the Roman fleet had at the same
time a landing-army on board.

In this way the Romans created a fleet which was a match
for the Carthaginians. Those err who represent this building
of a Roman fleet as a fairy tale, and besides they miss their aim;
the feat must be understood in order to be admired. The con-

struction of a fleet by the Romans was in very truth a noble
national work—a work through which, by their clear perception
of what was needful and possible, by ingenuity in invention,
and by energy in resolution and in execution, they rescued their
country from a position which was worse than at first it seemed.

The outset, nevertheless, was not favourable to the Romans.
The Roman admiral, the consul Gnaeus Cornelius Scipio, who had
sailed for Messana with the first seventeen vessels ready for sea
($\frac{494}{260}$), fancied, when on the voyage, that he should be able to capture Lipara by a *coup de main*. But a division of the Carthaginian fleet stationed at Panormus blockaded the harbour of the
island where the Roman vessels rode at anchor, and captured
the whole squadron along with the consul without a struggle.
This, however, did not deter the main fleet from likewise sailing,
as soon as its preparations were completed, for Messana. On
its voyage along the Italian coast it fell in with a Carthaginian
reconnoitring squadron of less strength, on which it had the good
fortune to inflict a loss more than counterbalancing the first
loss of the Romans; and thus successful and victorious it entered
the port of Messana, where the second consul Gaius Duilius took
the command in room of his captured colleague. At the promontory of Mylae, to the north-west of Messana, the Carthaginian fleet, that advanced from Panormus under the command
of Hannibal, encountered the Roman, which here underwent
its first trial on a great scale. The Carthaginians, seeing in the
ill-sailing and awkward vessels of the Romans an easy prey,
fell upon them in irregular order; but the newly invented boarding-bridges proved their thorough efficiency. The Roman
vessels hooked and stormed those of the enemy as they came
up one by one; they could not be approached either in front
or on the sides without the dangerous bridge descending on the
enemy's deck. When the battle was over, about fifty Carthaginian vessels, almost the half of the fleet, were sunk or captured
by the Romans; among the latter was the ship of the admiral
Hannibal, formerly belonging to king Pyrrhus. The gain was
great; still greater the moral effect of the victory. Rome had
suddenly become a naval power, and held in her hand the means
of energetically terminating a war which threatened to be end-
lessly prolonged and to involve the commerce of Italy in ruin.

Two plans were open to the Romans. They might attack
Carthage on the Italian islands and deprive her of the coast
fortresses of Sicily and Sardinia one after another—a scheme
which was perhaps practicable through well-combined operations

by land and sea; and, in the event of its being accomplished, peace might either be concluded with Carthage on the basis of the cession of these islands, or, should such terms not be accepted or prove unsatisfactory, the second stage of the war might be transferred to Africa. Or they might neglect the islands and throw themselves at once with all their strength on Africa, not, in the adventurous style of Agathocles, burning their vessels behind them and staking all on the victory of a desperate band, but covering with a strong fleet the communications between the African invading army and Italy; and in that case a peace on moderate terms might be expected from the consternation of the enemy after the first successes, or, if the Romans chose, they might by pushing matters to an extremity compel the enemy to entire surrender.

They chose, in the first instance, the former plan of operations. In the year after the battle of Mylae ($\frac{495}{259}$) the consul Lucius Scipio captured the port of Aleria in Corsica—we still possess the tombstone of the general, which makes mention of this deed—and made Corsica a naval station against Sardinia. An attempt to establish a footing in Olbia on the northern coast of that island failed, because the fleet wanted troops for landing. In the succeeding year ($\frac{496}{258}$), it was repeated with better success, and the open villages along the coast were plundered; but no permanent establishment of the Romans took place. Nor was greater progress made in Sicily. Hamilcar conducted the war with energy and adroitness, not only by force of arms on sea and land, but also by political proselytism. Of the numerous small country towns some every year fell away from the Romans, and had to be laboriously reclaimed from the Phoenician grasp; while in the coast fortresses the Carthaginians maintained themselves without challenge, particularly in their head-quarters of Panormus and in their new stronghold of Drepana, to which, on account of its easier defence by sea, Hamilcar had transferred the inhabitants of Eryx. A second great naval engagement off the promontory of Tyndaris ($\frac{497}{257}$), in which both parties claimed the victory, made no change in the position of affairs. In this way no progress was made, whether in consequence of the divided command and the rapid changes in the commanders of the Roman troops, which rendered the concentrated management of a series of operations on a small scale exceedingly difficult, or from the general strategical relations of the case, which certainly, as the science of war then stood, were unfavourable to the attacking party in general (i. 407), and particularly so to the Romans, who were still on the mere threshold of scientific warfare. Meanwhile, although the pillaging of the Italian coasts had ceased, the commerce of Italy suffered not much less than it had done before the fleet was built.

Weary of a course of operations without results, and impatient to put an end to the war, the senate resolved to change its system, and to assail Carthage in Africa. In the spring of $\frac{498}{256}$ a fleet of 330 ships of the line set sail for the coast of Libya: at the mouth of the river Himera on the south coast of Sicily it embarked the army for landing, consisting of four legions, under the charge of the two consuls Marcus Atilius Regulus and Lucius Manlius Volso, both experienced generals. The Carthaginian admiral suffered the embarkation of the enemy's troops to take place; but on continuing their voyage towards Africa the Romans found the Punic fleet drawn up in order of battle off Ecnomus to protect its native land from invasion. Seldom have greater numbers fought at sea than were engaged in the battle that now ensued. The Roman fleet of 330 sail contained at least 100,000 men in its crews, besides the landing army of about 40,000; the Carthaginian of 350 vessels was manned by at least an equal number; so that wellnigh three hundred thousand men were brought into action on this day to decide the contest between the two mighty peoples. The Phoenicians were placed in a single widely-extended line, with their left wing resting on the Sicilian coast. The Romans arranged themselves in a triangle, with the ships of the two consuls as admirals at the apex, the first and second squadrons drawn out in oblique line to the right and left, and a third squadron, having the vessels built for the transport of the cavalry in tow, forming the line which closed the triangle. They thus bore down in close order on the enemy. A fourth squadron placed in reserve followed more slowly. The wedge-shaped attack broke without difficulty the Carthaginian line, for its centre, which was first assailed, intentionally gave way, and the battle resolved itself into three separate engagements. While the admirals with the two squadrons drawn up on the wings pursued the Carthaginian centre and were closely engaged with it, the left wing of the Carthaginians drawn up along the coast wheeled round upon the third Roman squadron, which was prevented by the vessels which it had in tow from following the two others, and by a vehement onset in superior force drove it against the shore; at the same time the Roman reserve was turned on the open sea, and assailed from behind, by the right wing of the Carthaginians. The first of these three engagements was soon at an end; the ships of the Carthaginian centre, manifestly much weaker than the two Roman squadrons with which they were engaged, took to flight. Meanwhile the two other divisions of the Romans had a severe encounter with the superior enemy; but in close fighting the dreaded boarding-bridges stood them in good stead, and by this means they succeeded in maintaining their ground till the two admirals with their vessels could come up. By their arrival the Roman reserve was relieved, and the Carthaginian vessels of the right wing retired before the superior force. And now, when this conflict had been decided in favour of the Romans, all the Roman vessels that still could keep the sea fell on the rear of the Carthaginian left wing, which was obstinately following up its advantage, so that it was surrounded and almost all the vessels composing it were taken. The losses otherwise were nearly equal. Of the Roman fleet 24 sail were sunk; of the Carthaginian 30 were sunk, and 64 were taken.

Notwithstanding its considerable loss, the Carthaginian fleet did not give up the protection of Africa, and with that view returned to the gulf of Carthage, where it expected the descent to take place and purposed to give battle a second time. But the Romans landed, not on the western side of the peninsula which helps to form the gulf, but on the eastern side, where the bay of Clupea presented a spacious harbour affording protection from almost all winds, and the town, situated close by the sea on a shield-shaped eminence rising out of the plain, supplied an excellent defence for the harbour. They disembarked the troops without hindrance from the enemy, and established themselves on the hill; in a short time an entrenched naval camp was constructed, and the land army was at liberty to commence operations. The Roman troops ranged over the country and levied contributions: they were able to send as many as 20,000 slaves to Rome. Through the rarest good fortune the bold scheme had succeeded at the first stroke, and with but slight sacrifices: the end seemed attained. The feeling of confidence that in this respect animated the Romans is evinced by the resolution of the senate to recall to Italy the greater portion of the fleet and half of the army; Marcus Regulus alone remained in Africa with 40 ships, 15,000 infantry, and 500 cavalry. Their confidence, however, was seemingly not over-strained. The Carthaginian army, which was disheartened, did not venture forth into the plain, but waited to sustain discomfiture in the wooded defiles, in which it could make no use of its two best arms, the cavalry and the elephants. The towns surrendered *en masse;* the Numidians rose in insurrection, and overran the open country far and wide. Regulus might hope to begin the next campaign with the siege of the capital, and with that view he pitched his camp for the winter in its immediate vicinity at Tunes.

The spirit of the Carthaginians was broken: they sued for peace. But the conditions which the consul proposed—not merely the cession of Sicily and Sardinia, but the conclusion of an alliance on unequal terms with Rome, which would have bound the Carthaginians to renounce their own war-marine and to furnish vessels for the Roman wars—conditions which would have placed Carthage on a level with Neapolis and Tarentum, could not be accepted, so long as a Carthaginian army kept the field and a Carthaginian fleet kept the sea, and the capital stood unshaken.

The mighty enthusiasm, which kindles into a noble flame among Oriental nations, even the most abased, on the approach of extreme peril—the energy of dire necessity—impelled the Carthaginians to exertions, such as were by no means expected from a nation of shopkeepers. Hamilcar, who had carried on the guerilla war against the Romans in Sicily with so much success, appeared in Libya with the flower of the Sicilian troops, who furnished an admirable nucleus for the newly levied force. The connections and gold of the Carthaginians, moreover, brought to them troop after troop of excellent Numidian horse, and also numerous Greeks mercenaries; amongst whom was the celebrated captain Xanthippus of Sparta, whose talent for organisation and strategical skill were of great service to his new masters.[1] While the Carthaginians were thus making their preparations in the course of the winter, the Roman general remained inactive at Tunes. Whether it was that he did not anticipate the storm which was gathering over his head, or that a sense of military honour prohibited him from doing what his position demanded—instead of renouncing a siege which he was not in a condition even to attempt, and shutting himself up in the stronghold of Culpea, he remained with a handful of men

[1] The statement, that the military talent of Xanthippus was the primary means of saving Carthage, is probably coloured; the officers of Carthage can hardly have waited for foreigners to teach them that the light African cavalry could be more appropriately employed on the plain than among hills and forests. From such stories, the echo of the talk of Greek guard-rooms, even Polybius is not free. The statement that Xanthippus was put to death by the Carthaginians after the victory is a fiction; he departed voluntarily, perhaps to enter the Egyptian service.

before the walls of the hostile capital, neglecting even to secure his line of retreat to the naval camp; and neglecting to provide himself with—what above all he wanted, and what might have been so easily obtained through negotiation with the revolted Numidian tribes—a good light cavalry. He thus wantonly brought himself and his army into a plight similar to that which formerly befell Agathocles in his desperate adventure.

When spring came ($\frac{499}{255}$), the state of affairs had so changed, that now the Carthaginians were the first to take the field and to offer battle to the Romans. It was natural that they should do so, for everything depended on their getting quit of the army of Regulus, before reinforcements could arrive from Italy. The same reason should have led the Romans to desire delay; but, relying on their invincibleness in the open field, they at once accepted battle notwithstanding their inferiority of strength— for, although the numbers of the infantry on both sides were nearly the same, their 4000 cavalry and 100 elephants gave to the Carthaginians a decided superiority—and notwithstanding the unfavourable nature of the ground where the Carthaginians were drawn up, a broad plain probably not far from Tunes. Xanthippus, who on this day commanded the Carthaginians, first threw his cavalry on that of the enemy, which was stationed, as usual, on the two flanks of the line of battle; the few squadrons of the Romans were scattered like dust in a moment before the masses of the enemy's horse, and the Roman infantry found itself outflanked by them and surrounded. The legions, un-shaken by their apparent danger, advanced to attack the enemy's line; and, although the row of elephants placed as a protection in front of it checked the right wing and centre of the Romans, the left wing at any rate, marching past the elephants, engaged the mercenary infantry on the right of the enemy, and overthrew them completely. But this very success broke up the Roman ranks. The main body indeed, assailed by the elephants in front and by the cavalry on the flanks and in the rear, formed square, and defended itself with heroic courage, but the close masses were at length broken and swept away. The victorious left wing encountered the still fresh Carthaginian centre, where the Libyan infantry prepared a similar fate for it. From the nature of the ground and the superior number of the enemy's cavalry, all the combatants in these masses were cut down or taken prisoners; only two thousand men, chiefly, in all probability, the light troops and horsemen who were dispersed at the commencement, gained—while the Roman legions stood to be slaughtered—a start sufficient to enable them with difficulty to reach Clupea. Among the few prisoners was the consul himself who afterwards died in Carthage; his family, under the idea that he had not been treated by the Carthaginians according to the usages of war, wreaked a most revolting vengeance on two noble Carthaginian captives till even the slaves were moved to pity, and on their information the tribunes put a stop to the shameful outrage.[1]

When the terrible news reached Rome, the first care of the Romans was naturally directed to the saving of the force shut up in Clupea. A Roman fleet of 350 sail immediately started, and after a noble victory at the Hermaean promontory, in which the Carthaginians lost 114 ships, it reached Clupea just in time to deliver from their hard-pressed position the remains of the defeated army which were there entrenched. Had it been despatched before the catastrophe occurred, it might have converted the defeat into a victory that would probably have put an end to the Punic wars. But so completely had the Romans now lost their judgment, that after a successful conflict before Clupea they embarked all their troops and sailed home, voluntarily evacuating that important and easily defended position which secured to them facilities for landing in Africa, and abandoning their numerous African allies without protection to the vengeance of the Carthaginians. The Carthaginians did not neglect the opportunity of filling their empty treasury, and of making their subjects clearly understand the consequences of rebellion. An extraordinary contribution of 1000 talents of silver (£244,000) and 20,000 oxen was levied, and the sheiks in all the communities that had revolted were crucified; it is said that there were three thousand of them, and that this revolting atrocity on the part of the Carthaginian authorities really laid the foundation of the revolution which broke forth in Africa some years later. Lastly, as if to fill up the measure of misfortune to the Romans even as their measure of success had been filled before, on the homeward voyage of the fleet three-fourths of the Roman vessels perished with their crews in a violent storm; only eighty reached their

[1] Nothing further is known with certainty as to the end of Regulus; even his mission to Rome—which is sometimes placed in $\frac{503}{251}$, sometimes in $\frac{513}{241}$—is very imperfectly attested. The later Romans, who sought in the fortunes and misfortunes of their forefathers mere materials for school themes, made Regulus the type of heroic misfortune as they made Fabricius the type of heroic poverty, and circulated a number of anecdotes in his name—incongruous embellishments, contrasting ill with serious and sober history.

port (July $\frac{4 \, 9 \, 9}{2 \, 5 \, 5}$). The captains had foretold the impending mischief, but the extemporised Roman admirals had nevertheless given orders to sail.

After successes so immense the Carthaginians were able to resume their offensive operations, which had long been in abeyance. Hasdrubal, son of Hanno, landed at Lilybaeum with a strong force, which was enabled, particularly by its enormous number of elephants—amounting to 140—to keep the field against the Romans: the last battle had shown that it was possible to make up for the want of good infantry to some extent by elephants and cavalry. The Romans also resumed the war in Sicily; the annihilation of their invading army had, as the voluntary evacuation of Clupea shows, at once restored ascendancy in the senate to the party which was opposed to the war in Africa and was content with the gradual subjugation of the islands. But for this purpose too there was need of a fleet; and, since that which had conquered at Mylae, at Ecnomus, and at the Hermaean promontory was destroyed, they built a new one. Keels were at once laid down for 220 new vessels of war—they had never hitherto undertaken the building of so many simultaneously--and in the incredibly short space of three months they were all ready for sea. In the spring of $\frac{5 \, 0 \, 0}{2 \, 5 \, 4}$ the Roman fleet, numbering 300 vessels mostly new, appeared on the north coast of Sicily; Panormus, the most important town in Carthaginian Sicily, was acquired through a successful attack from the seaboard, and the smaller places there, Soluntum, Cephaloedium, and Tyndaris, likewise fell into the hands of the Romans, so that along the whole north coast of the island Thermae alone was retained by the Carthaginians. Panormus became thenceforth one of the chief stations of the Romans in Sicily. The war by land, nevertheless, made no progress; the two armies stood face to face before Lilybaeum, but the Roman commanders, who knew not how to encounter the mass of elephants, made no attempt to compel a pitched battle.

In the ensuing year ($\frac{5 \, 0 \, 1}{2 \, 5 \, 3}$) the consuls, instead of pursuing sure advantages in Sicily, preferred to make an expedition to Africa, for the purpose not of landing but of plundering the coast towns. They accomplished their object without opposition; but, after having first run aground in the troublesome, and to their pilots unknown, waters of the Lesser Syrtis, whence they with difficulty got clear again, the fleet encountered a storm between Sicily and Italy, which cost more than 150 ships. On this occasion also the pilots, notwithstanding their representations and entreaties to be allowed to take the course along the coast, were obliged by command of the consuls to steer straight from Panormus across the open sea to Ostia.

Despondency now seized the fathers of the city; they resolved to reduce their war-fleet to sixty sail, and to confine the war by sea to the defence of the coasts, and to the convoy of transports. Fortunately, just at this time, the languishing war in Sicily took a more favourable turn. In the year $\frac{502}{252}$, Thermae, the last point which the Carthaginians held on the north coast, and the important island of Lipara, had fallen into the hands of the Romans, and in the following year (summer of $\frac{503}{251}$) the consul Gaius Caecilius Metellus achieved a brilliant victory over the army of elephants under the walls of Panormus. These animals, which had been imprudently brought forward, were wounded by the light troops of the Romans stationed in the moat of the town; some of them fell into the moat, and others fell back on their own troops, who crowded in wild disorder along with the elephants towards the beach, that they might be picked up by the Phoenician ships. One hundred and twenty elephants were captured, and the Carthaginian army, whose strength depended on these animals, was obliged once more to shut itself up in its fortresses. Eryx soon fell into the hands of the Romans ($\frac{505}{249}$), and the Carthaginians retained nothing in the island but Drepana and Lilybaeum. Carthage a second time offered peace; but the victory of Metellus and the exhaustion of the enemy gave to the more energetic party ascendancy in the senate.

Peace was declined, and it was resolved to prosecute in earnest the siege of the two Sicilian cities, and for this purpose to send to sea once more a fleet of 200 sail. The siege of Lilybaeum, the first great and regular siege undertaken by Rome, and one of the most obstinate known in history, was opened by the Romans with an important success: they succeeded in introducing their fleet into the harbour of the city, and in blockading it on the side facing the sea. The besiegers, however, were not able to close the sea completely. In spite of their sunken vessels and their palisades, and in spite of the most careful vigilance, dexterous mariners, accurately acquainted with the shallows and channels, maintained with swift-sailing vessels a regular communication between the besieged in the city and the Carthaginian fleet in the harbour of Drepana. In fact, after a time, a Carthaginian squadron of 50 sail succeeded in running into the harbour, in throwing a large quantity of provisions and a reinforcement of 10,000 men into the city, and in returning unmolested. The besieging land army was not much more fortunate. They began with a regular attack; machines were erected, and in a short time the batteries had demolished six of the towers flanking the walls, so that the breach soon appeared to be practicable. But the able Carthaginian commander Himilco parried this assault by giving orders for the erection of a second wall behind the breach. An attempt of the Romans to enter into an understanding with the garrison was likewise frustrated in proper time. And, after a first sally made for the purpose of burning the Roman set of machines had been repulsed, the Carthaginians succeeded during a stormy night in effecting their object. Upon this the Romans abandoned their preparations for an assault, and contented themselves with blockading the city by land and water. The prospect of success in this way was indeed very remote, so long as they were unable wholly to preclude the entrance of the enemy's vessels; and the army of the besiegers was in a condition not much better than that of the besieged in the city, because their supplies were frequently cut off by the numerous and bold light cavalry of the Carthaginians, and their ranks began to be thinned by the diseases indigenous to that unwholesome region. The capture of Lilybaeum, however, was of sufficient importance to induce a patient perseverance in the laborious task, which promised to be crowned in time with the desired success.

But the new consul Publius Claudius considered the task of maintaining the investment of Lilybaeum too trifling: he preferred to change once more the plan of operations, and with his numerous newly manned vessels suddenly to surprise the Carthaginian fleet which was waiting in the neighbouring harbour of Drepana. With the whole blockading squadron, which had taken on board volunteers from the legions, he started about midnight, and sailing in good order with his right wing by the shore, and his left in the open sea, he safely reached the harbour of Drepana at sunrise. The Phoenician admiral Atarbas commanded there. Although surprised, he did not lose his presence of mind or allow himself to be shut up in the harbour, but as the Roman ships entered the harbour, which opens to the south in the form of a sickle, on the one side, he withdrew his vessels from it by the opposite side which was still free, and stationed them in line on the outside. No other course remained to the Roman admiral but to recall as speedily as possible the foremost vessels from the harbour, and to make his arrangements for battle in like manner in front of it; but in consequence of this retrograde movement he lost the free choice of his position, and was obliged to accept battle in a line, which on the one hand was outflanked by that of the enemy to the extent of five ships—for there was not time fully to deploy the vessels as they issued from the harbour—and on the other hand was crowded so close on the shore that his vessels could neither retreat, nor sail behind the line so as to come to each other's aid. Not only was the battle lost before it began, but the Roman fleet was so completely ensnared that it fell almost wholly into the hands of the enemy. The consul indeed escaped, for he was the first who fled; but 93 Roman vessels, more than three-fourths of the blockading fleet, with the flower of the Roman legions on board, fell into the hands of the Phoenicians. It was the first and only great naval victory which the Carthaginians gained over the Romans. Lilybaeum was practically relieved on the side towards the sea, for though the remains of the Roman fleet returned to their former position, they were much too weak seriously to blockade a harbour which had never been wholly closed, and they could only protect themselves from the attack of the Carthaginian ships with the assistance of the land army. That single imprudent act of an inexperienced and criminally thoughtless officer had thrown away all that had been with so much difficulty attained by the long and galling warfare around the fortress; and those war-vessels of the Romans which his presumption had not forfeited were shortly afterwards destroyed by the folly of his colleague. The second consul, Lucius Junius Pullus, who had received the charge of lading at Syracuse the supplies destined for the army at Lilybaeum, and of convoying the transports along the south coast of the island with a second Roman fleet of 120 war-vessels, instead of keeping his ships together, committed the error of allowing the first set of transports to depart unattended and of only following with the second. When the Carthaginian vice-admiral, Carthalo, who with a hundred select ships blockaded the Roman fleet in the port of Lilybaeum, received the intelligence, he proceeded to the south coast of the island, cut off the two Roman squadrons from each other by interposing between them, and compelled them to take shelter in two harbours of refuge on the inhospitable shores of Gela and Camarina. The attacks of the Carthaginians were indeed bravely repulsed by the Romans with the help of the shore batteries, which had for some time been erected there as everywhere along the coast; but, as the Romans could not hope to effect a junction and continue their voyage, Carthalo could leave the elements to finish his work. The next great storm, accordingly, completely annihilated the two Roman fleets in their wretched roadsteads, while the Phoenician admiral easily weathered it on the open sea with his light and well-managed ships. The Romans, however, succeeded in saving the greater part of the crews and cargoes $\left(\frac{505}{249}\right)$.

The Roman senate was in perplexity. The war had now reached its sixteenth year; and they seemed to be farther from their object in the sixteenth than in the first. In this war four large fleets had perished, three of them with Roman armies on board; a fourth select land army had been destroyed by the enemy in Libya; to say nothing of the numerous losses which had been occasioned by the minor naval engagements, and by the battles, and still more by the guerilla warfare and the diseases, of Sicily. What a multitude of human lives the war swept away may be seen from the fact that the burgess-roll from $\frac{502}{252}$ to $\frac{507}{247}$ alone decreased by about 40,000, a sixth part of the whole; and this does not include the losses of the allies, who bore the whole brunt of the war by sea, and, in addition, at least an equal proportion with the Romans of the warfare by land. Of the financial loss it is not possible to form any conception; but both the direct damage sustained in ships and *matériel*, and the indirect injury through the paralysing of trade, must have been immense. An evil still greater than this was the exhaustion of all the methods by which they had sought to terminate the war. They had tried a landing in Africa with their forces fresh and in full career of victory, and had totally failed. They had undertaken to storm Sicily town by town; the lesser places had fallen, but the two mighty naval strongholds of Lilybaeum and Drepana stood more invincible than ever. What were they to do? In fact, there was to some extent reason for despondency. The fathers of the city became faint-hearted; they allowed matters simply to take their course, knowing well that a war protracted without object or end was more pernicious for Italy than the straining of the last man and the last penny, but without that courage and confidence in the nation and in fortune, which could stimulate new sacrifices in addition to those that had already been lavished in vain. They discarded the fleet; at the most they encouraged privateering, and with that view placed the war-vessels of the state at the disposal of captains who were ready to undertake a piratical warfare on their own account. The war by land was continued nominally, because they could not do otherwise; but they were content with observing the

Sicilian fortresses and barely maintaining what they possessed,
—measures which, in the absence of a fleet, required a very
numerous army and extremely costly preparations.

Now, if ever, the time had come when Carthage was in a position to humble her mighty antagonist. She, too, of course must
have felt some exhaustion of resources; but, in the circumstances, the Phoenician finances could not possibly be so disorganised as to prevent the Carthaginians from continuing the
war, which cost them little beyond money, offensively and
with energy. The Carthaginian government, however, was not
energetic, but on the contrary weak and indolent, unless impelled to action by an easy and sure gain or by extreme necessity.
Glad to be rid of the Roman fleet, they foolishly allowed their
own also to fall into decay, and began after the example of the
enemy to confine their operations by land and sea to the petty
warfare in and around Sicily.

Thus there ensued six years of uneventful warfare $\left(\frac{506-511}{248-243}\right)$,
the most inglorious in the history of this century for Rome, and
inglorious also for the Carthaginian people. One man, however,
among the latter thought and acted differently from his nation.
Hamilcar, named Barak or Barca (*i.e.* lightning), a young
officer of great promise, was entrusted with the supreme command in Sicily in the year $\frac{507}{247}$. His army, like every Carthaginian one, was defective in a trustworthy and experienced
infantry; and the government, although it was perhaps in a
position to create such an infantry and at any rate was bound
to make the attempt, contented itself with passively looking on
at its defeats or at most with nailing the defeated generals to the
cross. Hamilcar resolved to take the matter into his own hands.
He knew well that his mercenaries were as indifferent to Carthage
as to Rome, and that he had to expect from his government
not Phoenician or Libyan conscripts, but at the best a permission
to save his country with his troops in his own way, provided it
cost nothing. But he knew himself also, and he knew men. His
mercenaries cared nothing for Carthage; but a true general is
able to substitute his own person for his country in the affection
of his soldiers; and such an one was this young commander.
After he had habituated his men to face the legionaries in the
warfare of outposts before Drepana and Lilybaeum, he established himself with his force on Mount Ercte (Monte Pellegrino
near Palermo), which commands like a fortress the neighbouring
country; and making them settle there with their wives and
children, levied contributions from the plains, while Phoenician

privateers plundered the Italian coast as far as Cumae. He thus provided his people with copious supplies without asking money from the Carthaginians, and, keeping up the communication with Drepana by sea, he threatened to surprise the important town of Panormus in his immediate vicinity. Not only were the Romans unable to expel him from his stronghold, but after the struggle had lasted awhile at Ercte, Hamilcar formed for himself another similar position at Eryx. This mountain, which bore half way up the city of the same name and on its summit a temple of Aphrodite, had been hitherto in the hands of the Romans, who made it a basis for annoying Drepana. Hamilcar deprived them of the town and besieged the temple, while the Romans in turn blockaded him from the plain. The Celtic deserters from the Carthaginian army who were stationed by the Romans at the forlorn post of the temple—a reckless pack of marauders, who in the course of this siege plundered the temple and perpetrated every sort of outrage—defended the summit of the rock with desperate courage; but Hamilcar did not allow himself to be again dislodged from the town, and kept his communications constantly open by sea with the fleet and the garrison of Drepana. The war in Sicily seemed to be assuming a turn more and more unfavourable to the Romans. The Roman state was losing in that warfare its money and its men, and the Roman generals their honour; it was already clear that no Roman general was a match for Hamilcar, and the time might be calculated when even the Carthaginian mercenary would be able boldly to measure himself against the legionary. The privateers of Hamilcar appeared with ever-increasing audacity on the Italian coast: already a praetor had been obliged to take the field against a band of Carthaginian rovers which had landed there. A few years more, and Hamilcar might with his fleet have accomplished from Sicily what his son subsequently undertook by the land route from Spain.

The Roman senate, however, persevered in its inaction; the desponding party for once had the majority there. At length a number of sagacious and high-spirited men determined to save the state even without the interposition of the government, and to put an end to the ruinous Sicilian war. Successful corsair expeditions, if they had not raised the courage of the nation, had aroused energy and hope in a portion of the people; they had already joined together to form a squadron, burnt down Hippo on the African coast, and sustained a successful naval conflict with the Carthaginians off Panormus. By a private subscription—such as had been resorted to in Athens also, but not on so magnificent a scale—the wealthy and patriotic Romans equipped a war fleet, the nucleus of which was supplied by the ships built for privateering and the practised crews which they contained, and which altogether was far more carefully fitted out than had hitherto been the case in the shipbuilding of the state.

This fact—that a number of citizens in the twenty-third year of a severe war voluntarily presented to the state two hundred ships of the line, manned by 60,000 sailors—stands perhaps unparalleled in the annals of history. The consul Gaius Lutatius Catulus, to whom fell the honour of conducting this fleet to the Sicilian seas, met with almost no opposition: the two or three Carthaginian vessels, with which Hamilcar had made his corsair expeditions, disappeared before the superior force, and almost without resistance the Romans occupied the harbours of Lilybaeum and Drepana, the siege of which was now undertaken with energy by water and by land. Carthage was completely taken by surprise; even the two fortresses, weakly provisioned, were in great danger. A fleet was equipped at home; but with all the haste which they displayed, the year came to an end without any appearance of Carthaginian sails in the Sicilian waters; and when at length, in the spring of $\frac{513}{241}$, the hurriedly prepared vessels appeared in the offing of Drepana, they deserved the name of a fleet of transports rather than that of a war fleet ready for action. The Phoenicians had hoped to land undisturbed, to disembark their stores, and to be able to take on board the troops requisite for a naval battle; but the Roman vessels intercepted them, and forced them, when about to sail from the island of Hiera (now Maritima) for Drepana, to accept battle near the little island of Aegusa (Favignano) (10 March, $\frac{513}{241}$). The issue was not for a moment doubtful; the Roman fleet, well built and manned, and admirably handled by the able praetor Publius Valerius Falto (for a wound received before Drepana still confined the consul Catulus to his bed), defeated at the first blow the heavily laden and poorly and inadequately manned vessels of the enemy; fifty were sunk, and with seventy prizes the victors sailed into the port of Lilybaeum. The last great effort of the Roman patriots had borne fruit; it brought victory, and with victory peace.

The Carthaginians first crucified the unfortunate admiral—a step which did not mend the matter—and then despatched to the Sicilian general unlimited authority to conclude a peace.

Hamilcar, who saw his heroic labours of seven years undone
by the fault of others, magnanimously submitted to what was
inevitable without on that account sacrificing either his military
honour, or his nation, or his own designs. Sicily indeed could
not be retained, seeing that the Romans had now command of
the sea; and it was not to be expected that the Carthaginian
government, which had vainly endeavoured to fill its empty
treasury by a state-loan in Egypt, would make even any further
attempt to vanquish the Roman fleet. He therefore surrendered
Sicily. The independence and integrity of the Carthaginian
state and territory, on the other hand, were expressly recognised in the usual form. Rome bound herself not to enter into
a separate alliance with the Carthaginian, and Carthage engaged
not to enter into separate alliance with the Roman, symmachy
—that is, with their respective subject or dependent communities; neither was to make war, or exercise rights of sovereignty,
or undertake recruiting within the other's dominions.[1] The
secondary stipulations included, of course, the gratuitous return
of the Roman prisoners of war and the payment of a war-contribution; but the demand of Catulus that Hamilcar should
deliver up his arms and the Roman deserters was resolutely
refused by Hamilcar, and with success. Catulus desisted from
his second request, and allowed the Phoenicians a free departure
from Sicily for the moderate ransom of 18 *denarii* (11s. 6d.) per
man.

If the continuance of the war appeared to the Carthaginians
undesirable, they had reason to be satisfied with these terms.
It may be that the natural wish to bring to Rome peace as well
as triumph, the recollection of Regulus and of the many vicissitudes of the war, the consideration that such a patriotic effort
as had at last decided the victory could neither be enjoined nor
repeated, perhaps even the personal character of Hamilcar,
concurred in influencing the Roman general to yield so much as
he did. It is certain that there was dissatisfaction with the proposals of peace at Rome, and the assembly of the people, doubtless under the influence of the patriots who had effected the
equipment of the last fleet, at first refused to ratify it. We do
not know with what view this was done, and therefore we are
unable to decide whether the opponents of the proposed peace

---

[1] The statement (Zon. viii. 17) that the Carthaginians had to promise
that they would not send vessels of war into the territories of the Roman
symmachy—and therefore not to Syracuse, perhaps even not to Massilia
—sounds credible enough; but the text of the treaty says nothing of it
(Polyp. iii. 27).

in reality rejected it merely for the purpose of exacting some
further concessions from the enemy, or whether, remembering
that Regulus had summoned Carthage to surrender her political
independence, they were resolved to continue the war till they
had gained that end—so that it was no longer a question of peace,
but a question of conquest. If the refusal took place with the
former view, it was probably mistaken; compared with the gain
of Sicily every other concession was of little moment, and looking to the determination and the inventive genius of Hamilcar,
it was very rash to stake the securing of the principal gain on the
attainment of secondary objects. If on the other hand the
party opposed to the peace regarded the complete political
annihilation of Carthage as the only end of the struggle that
would satisfy the Roman community, it showed political tact
and anticipation of coming events; but whether the resources
of Rome would have sufficed to renew the expedition of Regulus
and to follow it up as far as might be required not merely to
break the courage but to breach the walls of the mighty Phoenician city, is another question, to which no one now can venture
to give either an affirmative or a negative answer.

At last the settlement of the momentous question was entrusted to a commission which was to decide it upon the spot
in Sicily. It confirmed the proposal in substance; only, the
sum to be paid by Carthage for the costs of the war was raised
to 3200 talents (£790,000), a third of which was to be paid down
at once, and the remainder in ten annual instalments. The
definitive treaty included, in addition to the surrender of Sicily,
the cession also of the islands between Sicily and Italy, but this
can only be regarded as an alteration of detail made on revision;
for it is self-evident that Carthage, when surrendering Sicily,
could hardly desire to retain the island of Lipara which had long
been occupied by the Roman fleet, and the suspicion, that an
ambiguous stipulation was intentionally introduced into the
treaty with reference to Sardinia and Corsica, is unworthy and
improbable.

Thus at length they came to terms. The unconquered
general of a vanquished nation descended from the mountains
which he had defended so long, and delivered to the new masters
of the island the fortresses which the Phoenicians had held in
their uninterrupted possession for at least four hundred years,
and from whose walls all assaults of the Hellenes had recoiled
unsuccessful. The west had peace ($\frac{513}{241}$).

Let us pause for a moment over the conflict, which extended

the dominion of Rome beyond the circling sea that encloses the peninsula. It was one of the longest and most severe which the Romans ever waged; many of the soldiers who fought in the decisive battle were unborn when the contest began. Nevertheless, despite the incomparably noble incidents which it now and again presented, we can scarcely name any war which the Romans managed so wretchedly and with such vacillation, both in a military and in a political point of view. It could hardly be otherwise. The contest occurred amidst a transition in their political system—the transition from an Italian policy, which no longer sufficed, to the policy of a great state, which was not yet matured. The Roman senate and the Roman military system were excellently organised for a purely Italian policy. The wars which such a policy provoked were purely continental wars, and always rested on the capital situated in the middle of the peninsula as the primary basis of operations, and on the chain of Roman fortresses as a secondary basis. The problems to be solved were mainly tactical, not strategical; marches and operations occupied but a subordinate, battles held the first, place; siege warfare was in its infancy; the sea and naval war hardly for a moment crossed men's thoughts. We can easily understand—especially if we bear in mind that in the battles of that period, where the naked weapon predominated, it was really the hand-to-hand encounter that proved decisive—how a deliberative assembly might direct such operations, and how any one who was mayor of the city might command the troops. All this was changed in a moment. The field of battle stretched away to an incalculable distance, to the unknown regions of another continent, and beyond a broad expanse of sea; every wave was a highway for the enemy, every harbour might send forth an invading fleet. The siege of strong places, particularly maritime fortresses, in which the first tacticians of Greece had failed, had now for the first time to be attempted by the Romans. A land army and the system of a civic militia no longer sufficed. It was necessary to create a fleet, and, what was more difficult, to employ it; it was necessary to find out the true points of attack and defence, to combine and to direct masses, to calculate expeditions extending over long periods and great distances, and to adjust their co-operation; if these things were not attended to, even an enemy far weaker in the tactics of the field might easily vanquish a stronger opponent. Is there any wonder that the reins of government in such an exigency slipped from the hands of a deliberative assembly and of commanding burgomasters?

It was plain, that at the beginning of the war the Romans did not know what they were undertaking; it was only during the course of the struggle that the inadequacies of their system, one after another, forced themselves on their notice—the want of a naval power, the lack of fixed military leadership, the incapacity of their generals, the total uselessness of their admirals. In part these evils were remedied by energy and good fortune; as was the case with the want of a fleet. That mighty creation, however, was but a grand make-shift, and always remained so. A Roman fleet was formed, but it was rendered national only in name, and was always treated with the affection of a stepmother; the naval service continued to be little esteemed in comparison with the high honour of serving in the legions; the naval officers were in great part Italian Greeks; the crews were composed of subjects or even of slaves and outcasts. The Italian farmer was at all times distrustful of the sea; one of the three things in his life which Cato regretted was, that he had travelled by sea when he might have gone by land. This result arose partly out of the nature of the case, for the vessels were oared galleys and the service of the oar can scarcely be ennobled; but the Romans might at least have formed separate legions of marines and taken steps towards the rearing of a class of Roman naval officers. Taking advantage of the impulse of the nation, they should have made it their aim gradually to establish a naval force important not only in numbers but in sailing powers and practice, and for such a purpose they had a valuable nucleus in the privateering that was developed during the long war; but nothing of the sort was done by the government. Nevertheless the Roman fleet with its unwieldy grandeur was the noblest creation of genius in this war, and, as at its beginning, so at its close it was the fleet that turned the scale in favour of Rome.

Far more difficult to be overcome were those deficiencies, which could not be remedied without an alteration of the constitution. That the senate, according to the strength of the contending parties within it, should leap from one system of conducting the war to another, and perpetrate errors so incredible as the evacuation of Clupea and the repeated discontinuance of the fleet; that the general of one year should lay siege to Sicilian towns, and his successor, instead of urging their surrender, should pillage the African coast or think proper to risk a naval battle; and that at any rate the supreme command should by law change hands every year—all these anomalies could not be reformed without stirring constitutional questions the solution of which was more difficult than the building of a fleet, but as little could their retention be reconciled with the requirements of such a war. Above all, moreover, neither the senate nor the generals could at once adapt themselves to the new mode of conducting war. The campaign of Regulus is an instance how singularly they adhered to the idea that superiority in tactics decides everything. There are few generals·who have had such successes thrown as it were into their lap by fortune: in the year $\frac{498}{256}$ he stood precisely where Scipio stood fifty years later, with this difference, that he had no Hannibal and no experienced army arrayed against him. But the senate withdrew half the army, as soon as they had satisfied themselves of the tactical superiority of the Romans; in blind reliance on that superiority the general remained where he was, to be beaten in strategy, and accepted battle when it was offered to him, to be beaten also in tactics. This was the more remarkable, as Regulus was an able and experienced general of his kind. The rustic method of warfare, by which Etruria and Samnium had been won, was the very cause of the defeat in the plain of Tunes. The principle, quite right in its own province, that every citizen is fit for a general, was no longer applicable; the new system of war demanded the employment of generals who had a military training and a military eye, and every burgomaster had not those qualities. The arrangement was however still worse, by which the chief command of the fleet was treated as an appanage to the chief command of the land army, and any one who chanced to be president of the city thought himself able to act the part not of general only, but of admiral too. The worst disasters which Rome suffered in this war were due not to the storms and still less to the Carthaginians, but to the presumptuous folly of its own citizen-admirals.

Rome was victorious at last. But her acquiescence in a gain far less than had at first been demanded and indeed offered, as well as the energetic opposition which the peace encountered in Rome, very clearly indicate the indecisive and superficial character of the victory and of the peace; and if Rome was the victor, she was indebted for her victory in part no doubt to the favour of the gods and to the energy of her citizens, but still more to the errors of her enemies in the conduct of the war—errors far surpassing even her own.

CHAPTER III

THE EXTENSION OF ITALY TO ITS NATURAL BOUNDARIES

The Italian confederacy as it emerged from the crises of the fifth century—or, in other words, the State of Italy—united the various civic and cantonal communities from the Apennines to the Ionian Sea under the hegemony of Rome. But before the close of the fifth century these limits were already overpassed in both directions, and Italian communities belonging to the confederacy had sprung up beyond the Apennines and beyond the sea. In the north the republic, in revenge for ancient and recent wrongs, had already in $\frac{471}{283}$ annihilated the Celtic Senones; in the south, through the great war from $\frac{490}{264}$ to $\frac{513}{241}$, it had dislodged the Phoenicians from the island of Sicily. In the north there belonged to the combination headed by Rome the Latin town of Ariminum (besides the burgess-settlement of Sena), in the south the community of the Mamertines in Messana, and as both were nationally of Italian origin, so both shared in the common rights and obligations of the Italian confederacy. It was probably the pressure of events at the moment rather than any comprehensive political calculation, that gave rise to these extensions of the confederacy; but it was natural that now at least, after the great successes achieved against Carthage, new and wider views of policy should dawn upon the Roman government—views which even otherwise were obviously enough suggested by the physical features of the peninsula. Alike in a political and in a military point of view Rome was justified in shifting its northern boundary from the low and easily crossed Apennines to the mighty mountain-wall that separates northern from southern Europe, the Alps, and in combining with the sovereignty of Italy the sovereignty of the seas and islands on the west and east of the peninsula; and now, when by the expulsion of the Phoenicians from Sicily the most difficult portion of the task had been already achieved, various circumstances united to facilitate its completion by the Roman government.

In the western sea which was of far more account for Italy than the Adriatic, the most important position, the large and fertile island of Sicily copiously furnished with harbours, had been by the peace with Carthage transferred for the most part into the possession of the Romans. King Hiero of Syracuse indeed, who during the last twenty-two years of the war had adhered with unshaken steadfastness to the Roman alliance, had a fair claim to an extension of territory; but, if Roman policy had begun the war with the resolution of tolerating only secondary states in the island, the views of the Romans at its close decidedly tended towards the seizure of Sicily for themselves. Hiero might be content that his territory—namely, in addition to the immediate district of Syracuse, the domains of Elorus, Neetum, Acrae, Leontini, Megara, and Tauromenium—and his independence in relation to foreign powers, were (for want of any pretext to curtail them) left to him in their former compass; he might well be content that the war between the two great powers had not ended in the complete overthrow of the one or of the other, and that there consequently still remained at least a possibility of continuance for the intermediate power in Sicily. In the remaining and by far the larger portion of Sicily, at Panormus, Lilybaeum, Agrigentum, Messana, the Romans effected a permanent settlement.

They only regretted that the possession of that beautiful island was not enough to convert the western waters into a Roman inland sea, so long as Sardinia still remained Carthaginian. Soon, however, after the conclusion of the peace there appeared an unexpected prospect of wresting from the Carthaginians the second island of the Mediterranean. In Africa, immediately after peace had been concluded with Rome, the mercenaries and the subjects of the Phoenicians joined in a common revolt. The blame of the dangerous insurrection was mainly chargeable on the Carthaginian government. In the last years of the war Hamilcar had not been able to pay his Sicilian mercenaries as formerly from his own resources, and he had vainly requested that money might be sent to him from home; he might, he was told, send his forces to Africa to be paid off. He obeyed; but as he knew the men, he prudently embarked them in small subdivisions, that the authorities might pay them off by troops or might at least separate them, and he then laid down his command. But all his precautions were thwarted not so much by the emptiness of the exchequer, as by the bureaucratic mode of transacting business and the folly of the government. They waited till the whole army was once more united in Libya, and then endeavoured to curtail the pay promised to the men. Of course a mutiny broke out among the troops, and the hesitating and cowardly demeanour of the authorities showed the mutineers what they might dare. Most of them were natives of the districts ruled by, or dependent on, Carthage; they knew the feelings which had been provoked throughout these districts by the slaughter decreed by the government after the expedition of Regulus (p. 43) and by the fearful pressure of taxation, and they knew also the character of their government, which never kept faith and never pardoned; they were well aware of what awaited them, should they disperse to their homes with pay exacted by mutiny. The Carthaginians had for long been digging the mine, and they now themselves filled it with men who could not but explode it. Like wildfire the revolution spread from garrison to garrison, from village to village; the Libyan women contributed their ornaments to pay the wages of the mercenaries; a number of Carthaginian citizens, amongst whom were some of the most distinguished officers of the Sicilian army, became the victims of the infuriated multitude; Carthage was already besieged on two sides, and the Carthaginian army marching out of the city was totally routed in consequence of the blundering of its unskilful leader.

When the Romans thus saw their hated and still dreaded foe involved in a greater danger than any ever occasioned by the Roman wars, they began more and more to regret the conclusion of the peace of $\frac{513}{241}$—which, if it was not in reality precipitate, now at least appeared so to all—and to forget how exhausted at that time their own state had been and how powerful had been their Carthaginian rival. Shame indeed forbade their entering into communication openly with the Carthaginian rebels; in fact, they gave an exceptional permission to the Carthaginians to levy recruits for this war in Italy, and prohibited Italian mariners from dealing with the Libyans. But it may be doubted whether the government of Rome was very earnest in these acts of friendly alliance; for, in spite of them, the dealings between the African insurgents and the Roman mariners continued, and when Hamilcar, whom the extremity of the peril had recalled to the command of the Carthaginian army, seized and imprisoned a number of Italian captains concerned in these dealings, the senate interceded for them with the Carthaginian government and procured their release. The insurgents themselves appeared to recognise in the Romans their natural allies. The garrisons in Sardinia, which like the rest of the army had declared in favour of the insurgents, offered the possession of

the island to the Romans, when they saw that they were unable
to hold it against the attacks of the unconquered mountaineers
of the interior (about $\frac{515}{238}$); and a similar offer came even from
the community of Utica, which had likewise taken part in the
revolt and was now hard pressed by the arms of Hamilcar. The
latter offer was declined by the Romans, chiefly doubtless because its acceptance would have carried them beyond the natural
boundaries of Italy, and therefore farther than the Roman
government was then disposed to go; on the other hand they
entertained the proposals of the Sardinian mutineers, and took
over from them the portion of Sardinia which had been in the
hands of the Carthaginians ($\frac{516}{238}$). In this instance, more than
in the affair of the Mamertines, the Romans were justly liable to
the reproach that a great and victorious nation had not disdained
to fraternise and share the spoil with a venal pack of mercenaries,
and had not sufficient self-denial to prefer the course enjoined
by justice and by honour to the gain of the moment. The
Carthaginians, whose troubles reached their height just about
the period of the occupation of Sardinia, were silent for the time
being as to the unwarrantable violence; but, after their peril
had been, contrary to the expectations and probably contrary
to the hopes of the Romans, averted by the genius of Hamilcar,
and Carthage had been restored to her full sovereignty in Africa
($\frac{517}{237}$), Carthaginian envoys immediately appeared at Rome to
require the restitution of Sardinia. But the Romans, not inclined to restore their booty, replied with frivolous or at any
rate irrelevant complaints as to all sorts of injuries which they
alleged that the Carthaginians had inflicted on the Roman
traders, and hastened to declare war;[1] the principle, that in
politics power is the measure of right, appeared in its naked
effrontery. Just resentment urged the Carthaginians to accept
that offer of war; had Catulus insisted upon the cession of
Sardinia five years before, the war would probably have pursued
its course. But now, when both islands were lost, when Libya
was in a ferment, and when the state was weakened to the
utmost by its twenty-four years' struggle with Rome and the
dreadful civil war that had raged for nearly five years more,
they were obliged to submit. It was only after repeated

---

[1] That the cession of the islands lying between Sicily and Italy, which
the peace of $\frac{513}{241}$ prescribed to the Carthaginians, did not include the
cession of Sardinia, is an ascertained fact (p. 53); but the statement, that
the Romans made that a pretext for their occupation of the island three
years after the peace, is ill attested. Had they done so, they would merely
have added diplomatic folly to political effrontery.

entreaties, and after the Phoenicians had bound themselves to pay to Rome a ransom of 1200 talents (£292,000) for the warlike preparations which had been wantonly begun, that the Romans reluctantly desisted from war. Thus the Romans acquired Sardinia almost without a struggle; to which they added Corsica, the ancient possession of the Etruscans, where perhaps some detached Roman garrisons still remained over from the last war (p. 38). In Sardinia, however, and still more in the rugged Corsica, the Romans restricted themselves, just as the Phoenicians had done, to an occupation of the coasts. With the natives in the interior they were continually engaged in war or, to speak more correctly, in hunting them like wild beasts; they baited them with dogs, and carried what they captured to the slave market; but they undertook no real conquest. They had occupied the islands not on their own account, but for the security of Italy. Now that the confederacy possessed the three large islands, it might call the Tyrrhene Sea its own.

The acquisition of the islands in the western sea of Italy introduced into the state administration of Rome a distinction, which to all appearance originated in mere considerations of convenience and almost accidentally, but nevertheless came to be of the deepest importance in the sequel—the distinction between the continental and transmarine forms of administration, or to use the appellations afterwards current, the distinction between Italy and the provinces. Hitherto the two chief magistrates of the community, the consuls, had no legally defined sphere of action; on the contrary their field of action extended as far as the Roman government itself. Of course, however, in practice they made a division of functions between them, and of course also they were bound in every particular department of their duties by the existing enactments in regard to it; the jurisdiction, for instance, over Roman citizens had in every case to be left to the praetor, and in the Latin or other autonomous communities the existing treaties had to be respected. The four quaestors who had been since $\frac{487}{287}$ distributed throughout Italy did not, formally at least, curtail the consular authority, for in Italy, just as in Rome, they were regarded simply as auxiliary magistrates dependent on the consuls. This mode of administration appears to have been at first extended also to the territories taken from Carthage, and Sicily and Sardinia were governed for some years by quaestors under the superintendence of the consuls; but the Romans must very soon have become practically convinced that it was indispensable to have superior magistrates specially appointed for the transmarine regions. As they had been obliged to abandon the concentration of the Roman jurisdiction in the person of the praetor as the community extended, and to send to the more remote districts deputy judges (i. 430), so now ($\frac{527}{227}$) the concentration of administrative and military power in the person of the consuls had to be abandoned. For each of the new transmarine regions— viz. Sicily, and Sardinia with Corsica annexed to it—there was appointed a special auxiliary consul, who was in rank and title inferior to the consul and equal to the praetor, but otherwise was —like the consul in earlier times before the praetorship was instituted—in his own sphere of action at once commander-in-chief, chief magistrate, and supreme judge. The direct administration of finance alone was withheld from these new chief magistrates, as from the first it had been withheld from the consuls (i. 250); one or more quaestors were assigned to them, who were in all respects dependent on them and were regarded officially as sons, as it were, in the household of their respective praetors, but had specially to manage the finances and to render account of their administration to the senate after having laid down their office.

This difference in the supreme administrative power was the only legal distinction between the continental and transmarine possessions. The principles in other respects, on which Rome had organised her dependencies in Italy, were transferred also to the extra-Italian districts. As a matter of course, these communities without exception forfeited their independence in external relations. As to internal intercourse, no provincial could thenceforth acquire valid property in the province out of the bounds of his own community, or perhaps even conclude a valid marriage. On the other hand the Roman government tolerated, at least in Sicily, the federative organisation of the cities, which was fraught with little danger, and even the general Sicilian diets with their harmless right of petition and complaint.[1] In monetary arrangements it was not practicable at once to declare the Roman currency to be the only valid tender in the islands; but it seems from the first to have obtained legal circulation, and in like manner, at least as a rule, the right of coining

---

[1] That this was the case may be gathered partly from the appearance of the " Siculi " against Marcellus (Liv. xxvi. 26, *seq.*), partly from the " conjoint petitions of all the Sicilian communities " (Cicero, *Verr.* ii. 42, 102; 45, 114; 50, 146; iii. 88, 204), partly from well known analogy (Marquardt, *Handb.* iii. 1, 267). Because there was no *commercium* between the different towns, it by no means follows that there was no *concilium*.

the precious metals seems to have been withdrawn from the cities in Roman Sicily.[1] On the other hand not only was the landed property in all Sicily left untouched—the principle, that the land out of Italy fell by right of war to the Romans as their property, was still unknown in this century—but all the Sicilian and Sardinian communities retained self-administration and some sort of autonomy. The democratic constitutions were no doubt set aside in all the communities, and in every city the power was transferred to the hands of a council representing the civic aristocracy; and the Sicilian communities, at least, were required to institute a general valuation corresponding to the Roman census every fifth year. But both these measures were only the necessary result of subordination to the Roman senate, which in reality could not govern with Greek *ecclesiae*, or without a view of the financial and military resources of each dependent community; in the various districts of Italy also the same course was in both respects pursued.

But, side by side with this essential equality of rights, there was established a distinction between the Italian communities on the one hand, and the transmarine communities on the other —a distinction indeed only *de facto*, but yet very important in its effects. The transmarine communities furnished no fixed contingent to the army or fleet of the Romans;[2] and they lost the right of arms, at least in so far that they could not be employed otherwise than on the summons of the Roman praetor for the defence of their own homes, and that the Roman government was at liberty to send Italian troops at its pleasure into the islands. In lieu of contingents a tenth of the field-produce of Sicily, and a tax of 5 per cent. on the value on all articles of commerce exported from or imported to the Sicilian harbours, were paid to Rome. Neither tax was in itself new. The imposts levied by the Persian great king and the Carthaginian republic were substantially of the same character with that tenth; and in Greece also such a taxation had for long been, after Oriental precedent, associated with the *tyrannis* and often also with an

---

[1] The right of coining gold and silver was not monopolised by Rome in the provinces so strictly as in Italy, evidently because gold and silver money not struck after the Roman standard was of less importance. But in their case too the mints were doubtless, as a rule, restricted to the coinage of copper, or at most silver, small money; even the most favourably treated communities of Roman Sicily, such as the Mamertines, the Centuripans, the Alaesines, the Segestans, and the Panormitans also in the main, coined only copper.

[2] This is implied in Hiero's expression (Liv. xxii. 37): that he knew that the Romans made use of none but Roman or Latin infantry and cavalry, and employed " foreigners " at most only among the light-armed troops.

hegemony. The Sicilians, in particular, had long paid their tenth either to Syracuse or to Carthage, and had long levied customs-dues on account of others. "We received," says Cicero, "the Sicilian communities into our clientship and protection in such a way that they continued under the same law under which they had lived before, and obeyed the Roman community in the same manner in which they had obeyed their own rulers." It is fair that this should not be overlooked; but to continue an injustice is to commit injustice. Viewed in relation not to the subjects, who merely changed masters, but to their new rulers, the abandonment of the equally wise and magnanimous principle of Roman statesmanship—viz., that Rome should accept from her subjects simply military aid, and never pecuniary compensation in lieu of it—was of a fatal importance, in comparison with which all alleviations in the rates and the mode of levying them, as well as all exceptions in detail, were as nothing. Such exceptions were, no doubt, made in various cases. Messana was directly admitted to the confederacy of the *togati*, and, like the Greek cities in Italy, furnished its contingent to the Roman fleet. Various other cities—Segesta and Halicyae, which were the first towns of Carthaginian Sicily that joined the Roman alliance, Centuripa, an inland town in the east of the island, which was destined to keep a watch over the Syracusan territory in its neighbourhood,[1] Alaesa on the northern coast, which was the first of the free Greek towns to join the Romans, and above all Panormus, hitherto the capital of Carthaginian, and now destined to become that of Roman, Sicily—while not admitted to the Italian military confederacy, yet received in addition to other favours immunity from tribute and tenths, so that their position in a financial point of view was even more favourable than that of the Italian communities. The Romans thus applied to Sicily the ancient principle of their policy, that of subdividing the dependent communities into carefully graduated classes with different privileges; but the Sardinian and Sicilian communities on the whole occupied a position not of dependent alliance, but of recognised tributary subjection.

It is true that this thorough distinction between the communities that furnished contingents and those that paid tribute,

[1] This is shown at once by a glance at the map, and also by the remarkable exceptional provision which allowed the Centuripans to settle in any part of Sicily. They required, as Roman spies, the utmost freedom of movement. Besides, Centuripa appears to have been among the first cities that went over to Rome (Diodorus, *l.* xxiii. p. 501).

or at least did not furnish contingents, was not in law necessarily coincident with the distinction between Italy and the provinces. Transmarine communities might belong to the Italian confederacy; the Mamertines for example were substantially on a level with the Italian Sabellians, and there existed no legal obstacle to the establishment even of new communities with Latin rights in Sicily and Sardinia any more than in the country beyond the Apennines. Communities on the mainland might be deprived of the right of bearing arms and become tributary; this arrangement was already the case with certain Celtic districts on the Po, and was introduced to a considerable extent in after times. But, in reality, the communities that furnished contingents as decidedly preponderated on the mainland as the tributary communities in the islands; and while Italian settlements were not contemplated on the part of the Romans either in Sicily with its Hellenic civilisation or in Sardinia, the Roman government had beyond doubt already determined not only to subdue the barbarian land between the Apennines and the Alps, but also, as their conquests advanced, to establish in it new communities of Italic origin and Italic rights. Thus their transmarine possessions were not merely reduced to a state of subjection, but were destined to remain subject in all time to come; whereas the official field recently marked off by law for the consuls, or, which is the same thing, the continental territory of the Romans, was to become a new and more extended Italy, which should reach from the Alps to the Ionian sea. In the first instance, indeed, this essentially geographical conception of Italy was not altogether coincident with the political conception of the Italian confederacy; it was partly wider, partly narrower. But even now the Romans regarded the whole space up to the boundary of the Alps as *Italia*, that is, as the present or future domain of the *togati*, and, just as was and still is the case in North America, the boundary was provisionally marked off in a geographical sense, that the field might be gradually occupied in a political sense also with the advance of colonisation.[1]

---

[1] This distinction between Italy as the Roman mainland or consular sphere on the one hand, and the transmarine territory or praetorial sphere on the other, already appears variously applied in the sixth century. The ritual rule, that certain priests should not leave Rome (Val. Max. i. 1, 2), was explained to mean, that they were not allowed to cross the sea (Liv. *Ep.* 19, xxxvii. 51; Tac. *Ann.* iii. 58, 71; Cic. *Phil.* xi. 8, 18; comp. Liv. xxviii. 38, 44, *Ep.* 59). The distinction is still more definitely brought out in the interpretation which was proposed in $\frac{544}{210}$ to be put upon the old rule, that the consul could nominate the dictator only on " Roman

In the Adriatic sea, at the entrance of which the important and long-contemplated colony of Brundisium had at length been founded before the close of the war with Carthage ($\frac{510}{244}$), the supremacy of Rome was from the very first decided. In the western sea Rome had been obliged to rid herself of rivals; in the eastern, the quarrels of the Hellenes themselves prevented any of the states in the Grecian peninsula from acquiring or retaining power. The most considerable of them, that of Macedonia, had through the influence of Egypt been dislodged from the upper Adriatic by the Aetolians and from the Peloponnesus by the Achaeans, and was scarcely even in a position to defend its northern frontier against the barbarians. How desirous the Romans were to keep down Macedonia and its natural ally, the king of Syria, and how closely they associated themselves with the Egyptian policy directed to that object, is shown by the remarkable offer which after the end of the war with Carthage they made to king Ptolemy III. Euergetes, to support him in the war which he waged with Seleucus II. Callinicus of Syria (who reigned $\frac{507-529}{247-225}$) on account of the murder of Berenice, and in which Macedonia had probably taken part with the latter. Generally, the relations of Rome with the Hellenistic states became closer; the senate already negotiated even with Syria, and interceded with the Seleucus just mentioned on behalf of the Ilians with whom the Romans claimed affinity.

No direct interference of the Romans in the affairs of the eastern powers took place for the present, simply because Rome had no need for her own ends to interfere. The Achaean league, the prosperity of which was arrested by the narrow-minded coterie-policy of Aratus, the Aetolian republic of military adventurers, and the decayed Macedonian empire kept down each other's power without the necessity of Roman intervention for the purpose; and the Romans of that time avoided rather than sought transmarine acquisitions. When the Acarnanians, ap-

ground ": viz. that " Roman ground " comprehended all Italy (Liv. xxvii. 5). The erection of the Celtic land between the Alps and Apennines into a special province, distinct from that of the consuls and subject to a separate chief magistrate, was the work of Sulla. Of course no one will consider it an objection to this view, that already in the sixth century Gallia or Ariminum is very often designated as the " official district " (*provincia*) ordinarily of one of the consuls. *Provincia*, as is well known, denoted in the older language not what we now call *province*, a definite space assigned as a district to a standing chief magistrate, but simply the department of duty prescribed for the particular magistrate by law, decree of the senate, or agreement; and in that sense it was certainly allowable, and was even for a time the rule, that one of the consuls should undertake the government of Northern Italy.

pealing to the ground that they alone of all the Greeks had taken no part in the destruction of Ilion, besought the descendants of Aeneas to help them against the Aetolians, the senate did indeed attempt a diplomatic mediation; but when the Aetolians returned an answer drawn up in their own saucy fashion, the antiquarian interest of the Roman senators by no means provoked them into undertaking a war by which they would have freed the Macedonians from their hereditary foe (about $\frac{51}{239}$).

Even the evil of piracy, which was naturally in such a state of matters the only trade that flourished on the Adriatic coast, and from which the commerce of Italy suffered greatly, was submitted to by the Romans with an undue measure of patience,—a patience intimately connected with their radical aversion to maritime war and their wretched marine. But at length it became too flagrant. Favoured by Macedonia, which no longer found occasion to continue its old function of protecting Hellenic commerce from the corsairs of the Adriatic for the benefit of its foes, the rulers of Scodra had induced the Illyrian tribes— nearly corresponding to the Dalmatians, Montenegrins, and northern Albanians of the present day—to unite for joint piratical expeditions on a great scale. With whole squadrons of their swift-sailing vessels with two banks of oars, the well-known " Liburnian " cutters, the Illyrians waged war by sea and along the coasts against all and sundry. The Greek settlements in these regions, the island-towns of Issa (Lissa) and Pharos (Lesina), the important ports of Epidamnus (Durazzo) and Apollonia (to the north of Avlone on the Aous) of course suffered especially, and were repeatedly beleaguered by the barbarians. Farther to the south, moreover, the corsairs established themselves in Phoenice, the most flourishing town of Epirus; partly voluntarily, partly by constraint, the Epirots and Acarnanians entered into an unnatural symmachy with the foreign freebooters; the coast was insecure even as far as Elis and Messene. In vain the Aetolians and Achaeans collected what ships they had, with a view to check the evil: in a battle on the open sea they were beaten by the pirates and their Greek allies; the corsair fleet was able at length to take possession even of the rich and important island of Corcyra (Corfu). The complaints of Italian mariners, the appeals for aid of their old allies the Apolloniates, and the urgent entreaty of the besieged Issaeans at length compelled the Roman senate to send at least ambassadors to Scodra. The brothers Gaius and Lucius Coruncanius went thither to demand that king Agron should put an end to the nuisance.

The king answered that according to the national law of the Illyrians piracy was a lawful trade, and that the government had no right to put a stop to privateering; whereupon Lucius Coruncanius replied, that in that case Rome would make it her business to introduce better law among the Illyrians. For this certainly not very diplomatic reply one of the envoys was—by the king's orders, as the Romans asserted—murdered on the way home, and the surrender of the murderers was refused. The senate had now no choice left to it. In the spring of $\frac{5\,2\,5}{2\,2\,9}$ a fleet of 200 ships of the line, with a landing-army on board, appeared off Apollonia; the corsair-vessels were scattered before the former, while the latter demolished the piratic strongholds; the queen Teuta, who after the death of her husband Agron conducted the government during the minority of her son Pinnes, besieged in her last retreat, was obliged to accept the conditions dictated by Rome. The rulers of Scodra were again confined both on the north and south to the original limits of their narrow domain, and had to quit their hold not only on all the Greek towns, but also on the Ardiaei in Dalmatia, the Parthini around Epidamnus, and the Atintanes in northern Epirus; no armed Illyrian vessel, and not more than two unarmed in company, were to be allowed in future to sail to the south of Lissus (Alessio, between Scutari and Durazzo). The maritime supremacy of Rome in the Adriatic was asserted, in the most praiseworthy and effective way, by the rapid suppression of the evil of piracy.

But the Romans went further, and established themselves on the east coast. The Illyrians of Scodra were rendered tributary to Rome; Demetrius of Pharos, who had passed over from the service of Teuta to that of the Romans, was installed, as a dependent dynast and ally of Rome, over the islands and coasts of Dalmatia; the Greek cities Corcyra, Epidamnus, Apollonia, and the communities of the Atintanes and Parthini were attached to Rome under mild forms of symmachy. These acquisitions on the east coast of the Adriatic were not sufficiently extensive to require the appointment of a special auxiliary consul; governors of subordinate rank appear to have been sent to Corcyra and perhaps also to other places, and the superintendence of these possessions seems to have been entrusted to the chief magistrates who administered Italy.[1] Thus the most

---

[1] A standing Roman commandant of Corcyra is apparently mentioned in Polyb. xxii. 15, 6 (erroneously translated by Liv. xxxviii. 11, comp. xlii. 37), and a similar one in the case of Issa in Liv. xliii. 9. We have, moreover, the analogy of the *praefectus pro legato insularum Baliarum* (Orelli, 732), and of the governor of Pandataria (*Corp. Inscr. Neapol.* 3528). It

important maritime stations in the Adriatic became subject, like Sicily and Sardinia, to the authority of Rome. What other result was to be expected? Rome was in want of a good naval station in the upper Adriatic—a want which was not supplied by her possessions on the Italian shore; her new allies, especially the Greek commercial towns, saw in the Romans their deliverers, and doubtless did what they could permanently to secure so powerful a protection; in Greece itself no one was in a position to oppose the movement; on the contrary, the praise of the liberators was on every one's lips. It may be a question whether there was greater rejoicing or shame in Hellas, when, in place of the ten ships of the line of the Achaean league, the most warlike power in Greece, two hundred sail belonging to the barbarians now entered her harbours and accomplished at a blow the task, which properly belonged to the Greeks, but in which they had failed so miserably. But if the Greeks were ashamed that the salvation of their oppressed countrymen had to come from abroad, they accepted the deliverance at least with a good grace; they did not fail to receive the Romans solemnly into the fellowship of the Hellenic nation by admitting them to the Isthmian games and the Eleusinian mysteries.

Macedonia was silent; it was not in a condition to protest in arms, and disdained to do so in words. No resistance was encountered. Nevertheless Rome, by seizing the keys to her neighbour's house, had converted that neighbour into an adversary who, should he recover his power, or should a favourable opportunity occur, might be expected emphatically to break the silence. Had the energetic and prudent king Antigonus Doson lived longer, he would have doubtless taken up the gauntlet which the Romans had flung down, for, when some years afterwards the dynast Demetrius of Pharos withdrew from the hegemony of Rome, prosecuted piracy contrary to the treaty in concert with the Istrians, and subdued the Atintanes whom the Romans had declared independent, Antigonus formed an alliance with him, and the troops of Demetrius fought

---

appears, accordingly, to have been a rule in the Roman administration to appoint non-senatorial *praefecti* for the more remote islands. But these "deputies" presuppose in the nature of the case the existence of a superior magistrate who nominates and superintends them; and this superior magistracy can only have been at this period that of the consuls. Subsequently, after the erection of Macedonia and Gallia Cisalpina into provinces, the superior administration was committed to one of these two governors; the very territory now in question, the nucleus of the subsequent Roman province of Illyricum, belonged, as is well known, in part to Caesar's district of administration.

in the army of Antigonus at the battle of Sellasia ($\frac{532}{222}$). But Antigonus died (in the winter $\frac{533-534}{221-220}$); and his successor Philip, still a boy, allowed the consul Lucius Aemilius Paullus to attack the ally of Macedonia, to destroy his capital, and to drive him from his kingdom into exile ($\frac{535}{219}$).

The mainland of Italy proper, south of the Apennines, enjoyed profound peace after the fall of Tarentum: the six days' war with Falerii ($\frac{513}{241}$) was little more than an interlude. But on the north, between the territory of the confederacy and the natural boundary of Italy—the chain of the Alps—there still extended a wide region not absolutely subject to the Romans. Beyond the Apennines they possessed nothing but the narrow space between the Aesis above Ancona and the Rubico below Cesena,[1] nearly the modern provinces of Forli and Urbino. South of the Po the strong Celtic tribe of the Boii still held its ground (from Parma to Bologna); alongside of them, the Lingones on the east and the Anares on the west (in the region of Parma)—two smaller Celtic cantons that were probably clients of the Boii—peopled the plain. At the western end of the plain the Ligurians began, who, mingled with isolated Celtic tribes, and settled on the Apennines westward from Arezzo and Pisa, occupied the region of the sources of the Po. The eastern portion of the plain north of the Po, nearly from Verona to the coast, was possessed by the Veneti, a race different from the Celts and probably of Illyrian extraction. Between these and the western mountains were settled the Cenomani (about Brescia and Cremona) who rarely acted with the Celtic nation and were probably largely intermingled with Veneti, and the Insubres (around Milan). The latter was the most considerable of the Celtic cantons in Italy, and was in constant communication not merely with the minor communities partly of Celtic, partly of non-Celtic extraction, that were scattered in the Alpine valleys, but also with the Celtic cantons beyond the Alps. The gates of the Alps, the mighty stream navigable for 230 miles, and the largest and most fertile plain of the then civilised Europe, still continued in the hands of hereditary foes of the Italian name, who, humbled indeed and weakened, but still scarce even nominally dependent and still troublesome neighbours, persevered in their barbarism, and, thinly scattered over the spacious plains, continued to pasture their herds and

---

[1] According to the most careful recent investigations of the locality, the Rubico is the Fiumicino near Savignano, which however has now changed its channel in the upper part of its course.

to plunder. It was to be anticipated that the Romans would hasten to possess themselves of these regions; the more so as the Celts gradually began to forget their defeats in the campaigns of $\frac{471}{283}$ and $\frac{472}{282}$ and to bestir themselves again, and, what was still more dangerous, the Transalpine Celts began anew to show themselves on the south of the Alps.

In fact the Boii had already renewed the war in $\frac{516}{238}$, and their chiefs Atis and Galatas had—without, it is true, the authority of the general diet—summoned the Transalpine Gauls to make common cause with them. The latter had numerously answered the call, and in $\frac{518}{236}$ a Celtic army, such as Italy had not seen for long, encamped before Ariminum. The Romans, for the moment much too weak to attempt a battle, concluded an armistice, and to gain time allowed envoys from the Celts to proceed to Rome, who ventured in the senate to demand the cession of Ariminum—it seemed as if the times of Brennus had returned. But an unexpected incident put an end to the war before it had well begun. The Boii, dissatisfied with their unbidden allies and afraid probably for their own territory, fell into variance with the Transalpine Gauls. An open battle took place between the two Celtic hosts; and, after the chiefs of the Boii had been put to death by their own men, the Transalpine Gauls returned home. The Boii were thus delivered into the hands of the Romans, and the latter were at liberty to expel them like the Senones, and to advance at least to the Po; but they preferred to grant the Boii peace in return for the cession of some districts of their land ($\frac{518}{236}$). This was probably done, because they were just at that time expecting the renewed outbreak of war with Carthage; but, after that war had been averted by the cession of Sardinia, true policy required the Roman government to take possession as speedily and entirely as possible of the country up to the Alps. Accordingly the constant apprehensions of such a Roman invasion on the part of the Celts were sufficiently justified. The Romans, however, were in no haste; and so the Celts themselves began the war, either because the Roman assignations of land on the east coast ($\frac{522}{232}$), although not a measure immediately directed against them, made them apprehensive of danger; or because they perceived that a war with Rome for the possession of Lombardy was inevitable; or, as is perhaps most probable, because their Celtic impatience was once more weary of inaction and preferred to arm for a new warlike expedition. With the exception of the Ceno-mani, who acted with the Veneti and declared for the Romans, all the Italian Celts concurred in the war, and they were joined by the Celts of the upper valley of the Rhone, or rather by a number of adventurers belonging to them, under the leaders Concolitanus and Aneroestus.[1] With 50,000 warriors on foot, and 20,000 on horseback or in chariots, the leaders of the Celts advanced to the Apennines ($\frac{529}{225}$). The Romans had not anticipated an attack on this side, and had not expected that the Celts, disregarding the Roman fortresses on the east coast and the protection of their own kinsmen, would venture to advance directly against the capital. Not very long before a similar Celtic swarm had in an exactly similar way overrun Greece. The danger was serious, and appeared still more serious than it really was. The belief that Rome's destruction was this time inevitable, and that the Roman soil was fated to become the property of the Gauls, was so generally diffused among the multitude in Rome itself that the government reckoned it not beneath its dignity to allay the absurd superstitious belief of the mob by an act still more absurd, and to bury alive a Gaulish man and a Gaulish woman in the Roman Forum with a view to fulfil the sentence of destiny. At the same time they made more serious preparations. Of the two consular armies, each of which numbered about 25,000 infantry and 1100 cavalry, one was stationed in Sardinia under Gaius Atilius Regulus, the other at Ariminum under Lucius Aemilius Papus. Both received orders to repair as speedily as possible to Etruria, the point of immediate danger. The Celts had already been under the necessity of leaving a garrison at home to face the Cenomani and Veneti, who were allied with Rome; now the levy of the Umbrians was directed to advance from their native mountains down into the plain of the Boii, and to inflict all the injury which they could think of on the enemy upon his own soil. The militia of the Etruscans and Sabines was to occupy the Apennines, and if possible to obstruct the passage till the regular troops could arrive. A reserve was

[1] These, whom Polybius designates as the " Celts in the Alps and on the Rhone, who on account of their character as military adventurers are called Gaesati (free lances)," are in the Capitoline Fasti named *Germani*. It is possible that the contemporary annalists may have here mentioned Celts alone, and that it was the historical speculation of the age of Caesar and Augustus that first induced the editors of these Fasti to treat them as " Germans." If, on the other hand, the mention of the Germans in the Fasti was based on contemporary records—in which case this is the earliest mention of the name—we must regard it as denoting not the Germanic races who were afterwards so called, but a Celtic horde; and this hypothesis may be the more readily adopted, since, according to the view of the best philologists, the name *Germani* is not of Germanic but of Celtic origin, and perhaps signifies " criers."

formed in Rome of 50,000 men. Throughout all Italy, which on this occasion recognised its true champion in Rome, the men capable of service were enrolled, and stores and materials of war were collected.

All this, however, required time. For once the Romans had allowed themselves to be surprised, and it was too late at least to save Etruria. The Celts found the Apennines weakly defended, and plundered unopposed the rich plains of the Tuscan territory, which for long had seen no enemy. They were already at Clusium, three days' march from Rome, when the army of Ariminum, under the consul Papus, appeared on their flank, while the Etruscan militia, which after the passage of the Apennines had assembled in rear of the Gauls, followed the line of the enemy's march. Suddenly one evening, after the two armies had already encamped and the bivouac fires were kindled, the Celtic infantry again broke up and retreated on the road towards Faesulae (Fiesole): the cavalry occupied the advanced posts during the night, and followed the main force next morning. When the Tuscan militia, who had pitched their camp close upon the enemy, became aware of his departure, they imagined that the host had begun to disperse, and marched hastily in pursuit. The Gauls had reckoned on this very result: their infantry, which had rested and was drawn up in order, awaited on a well-chosen battle-field the Roman militia, which came up from its forced march fatigued and disordered. Six thousand men fell after a furious combat, and the rest of the militia, which had been compelled to seek refuge on a hill, would have perished, had not the consular army appeared just in time. This induced the Gauls to return homeward. Their dexterously contrived plan for preventing the union of the two Roman armies and annihilating the weaker in detail, had only partially been successful; now it seemed to them advisable first of all to place in security their considerable booty. For the sake of an easier line of march they proceeded from the district of Chiusi, where they were, to the level coast, and were marching along the shore, when they found an unexpected obstacle in the way. It was the Sardinian legions, which had landed at Pisae; and, when they arrived too late to obstruct the passage of the Apennines, had immediately put themselves in motion and were advancing along the coast in a direction opposite to the march of the Gauls. Near Telamon (at the mouth of the Ombrone) they met with the enemy. While the Roman infantry advanced with close front along the great road, the cavalry, led by the

consul Gaius Atilius Regulus in person, made a side movement
so as to take the Gauls in flank, and to acquaint the other Roman
army under Papus as soon as possible with their arrival. A hot
cavalry engagement took place, in which along with many brave
Romans Regulus fell; but he had not sacrificed his life in vain:
his object was gained. Papus became aware of the conflict, and
guessed how matters stood; he hastily arrayed his legions, and
on both sides the Celtic host was now pressed by the Romans.
Courageously it made its dispositions for the double conflict,
the Transalpine Gauls and Insubres against the troops of Papus,
the Alpine Taurisci and the Boii against the Sardinian legions;
the cavalry combat pursued its course apart on the flank. The
forces were in numbers not unequally matched, and the desperate
position of the Gauls impelled them to the most obstinate resistance. But the Transalpine Gauls, accustomed only to close
fighting, gave way before the missiles of the Roman skirmishers;
in the hand-to-hand combat the better temper of the Roman
weapons placed the Gauls at a disadvantage; and at last an
attack in flank by the victorious Roman cavalry decided the
day. The Celtic horsemen made their escape; the infantry,
wedged in between the sea and the three Roman armies, had no
means of flight. 10,000 Celts, with their king Concolitanus,
were taken prisoners; 40,000 others lay dead on the field of
battle; Aneroestus and his attendants had, after the Celtic
fashion, put themselves to death.

The victory was complete, and the Romans were firmly
resolved to prevent the recurrence of such surprises by the
complete subjugation of the Celts on the south of the Alps. In
the following year ($\frac{530}{224}$) the Boii submitted without resistance
along with the Lingones; and in the year after that ($\frac{531}{223}$) the
Anares; so that the plain as far as the Po was in the hands of the
Romans. The conquest of the northern side of the river cost a
more serious struggle. Gaius Flaminius crossed the river in the
newly-acquired territory of the Anares (somewhere near Piacenza)
in $\frac{531}{223}$; but during the passage, and still more while making
good his footing on the other side, he suffered so heavy losses and
found himself with the river in his rear in so dangerous a position,
that he made a capitulation with the enemy to secure a free
retreat, which the Insubres foolishly conceded. Scarce, however, had he escaped when he appeared in the territory of the
Cenomani, and, united with them, advanced for the second time
from the north into the canton of the Insubres. The Gauls
perceived what was now the object of the Romans, when it was

too late: they took from the temple of their goddess the golden standards called the "immovable," and with their whole levy, 50,000 strong, they offered battle to the Romans. The situation of the latter was critical: they were stationed with their back to a river (perhaps the Oglio), separated from home by the enemy's territory, and left to depend for aid in battle as well as for their line of retreat on the uncertain friendship of the Cenomani. There was, however, no choice. The Gauls fighting in the Roman ranks were placed on the left bank of the stream; on the right, opposite to the Insubres, the legions were drawn up, and the bridges were broken down that they might not be assailed, at least in the rear, by their dubious allies.

In this way undoubtedly the river cut off their retreat, and their homeward route lay through the hostile army. But the superiority of the Roman arms and of Roman discipline achieved the victory, and the army cut its way through: once more the Roman tactics had redeemed the blunders of the general. The victory was due to the soldiers and officers, not to the generals, who gained a triumph only through popular favour in opposition to the just decree of the senate. Gladly would the Insubres have made peace; but Rome required unconditional subjection, and things had not yet come to that pass. They tried to maintain their ground with the help of their northern kinsmen; and, with 30,000 mercenaries whom they had raised amongst these and their own levy, they received the two consular armies advancing once more in the following year ($\frac{532}{222}$) from the territory of the Cenomani to invade their land. Various obstinate combats took place; in a diversion, attempted by the Insubres against the Roman fortress of Clastidium (Casteggio, below Pavia), on the right bank of the Po, the Gallic king Virdumarus fell by the hand of the consul Marcus Marcellus. But, after a battle partially gained by the Celts but ultimately decided in favour of the Romans, the consul Gnaeus Scipio took by assault Mediolanum, the capital of the Insubres, and the capture of that town and of Comum terminated their resistance. Thus the Celts of Italy were completely vanquished, and as, just before, the Romans had shown to the Hellenes in the war with the pirates the difference between a Roman and a Greek sovereignty of the seas, so they had now brilliantly demonstrated that Rome knew how to defend the gates of Italy against freebooters on land very differently from the way in which Macedonia had guarded the gates of Greece, and that in spite of all internal quarrels Italy presented a united front to the common enemy, while Greece exhibited distraction and discord.

The boundary of the Alps was reached, in so far as the whole flat country on the Po was either rendered subject to the Romans or, like the territories of the Cenomani and Veneti, was occupied by dependent allies. It needed time, however, to reap the consequences of this victory and to Romanise the land. In this the Romans did not adopt a uniform mode of procedure. In the mountainous north-west of Italy and in the more remote districts between the Alps and the Po they tolerated, on the whole, the former inhabitants; the numerous wars, as they are called, which were waged with the Ligurians in particular (first in $\frac{516}{238}$) appear to have been slave-hunts rather than wars, and, often as the cantons and valleys submitted to the Romans, Roman sovereignty in that quarter was ordinarily but an empty name. The expedition to Istria also ($\frac{533}{221}$) appears not to have aimed at much more than the destruction of the last lurking-places of the Adriatic pirates, and the establishment of a communication by land along the coast between the Italian conquests of Rome and her acquisitions on the other shore. On the other hand the Celts in the districts south of the Po were doomed irretrievably to destruction; for, owing to the looseness of the ties connecting the Celtic nation, none of the northern Celtic cantons took part with their Italian kinsmen except for money, and the Romans looked on the latter not only as their national foes, but as the usurpers of their natural heritage. The extensive assignations of land in $\frac{522}{232}$ had already filled the whole territory between Picenum and Ariminum with Roman colonists; further measures of the same character were taken, and it was not difficult to dislodge and extirpate a half-barbarous population like the Celtic, but partially devoted to agriculture, and destitute of walled towns. The great northern highway, which had been, probably some eighty years earlier, carried by way of Otricoli to Narni, and had shortly before been prolonged to the newly-founded fortress of Spoletium ($\frac{514}{240}$), was now ($\frac{534}{220}$) carried, under the name of the " Flaminian " road, by way of the newly established market-village Forum Flaminii (near Foligno), through the pass of Furlo to the coast, and thence along the latter from Fanum (Fano) to Ariminum; it was the first artificial road which crossed the Apennines and connected the two Italian seas. Great zeal was manifested in covering the newly-acquired fertile territory with Roman townships. Already on the Po itself the strong fortress of Placentia (Piacenza) had been founded to cover the passage of the river; already had Cremona been laid out on the left bank, and the building of the walls of Mutina (Modena), in the territory acquired from the Boii on the right, had far advanced; already preparations were being made for further assignations of land and for continuing the highway, when a sudden event interrupted the Romans in reaping the fruit of their successes.

CHAPTER IV

HAMILCAR AND HANNIBAL

THE treaty with Rome in $\frac{513}{241}$ gave to the Carthaginians peace, but they paid for it dearly. That the tribute of the largest portion of Sicily now flowed into the enemy's exchequer instead of the Carthaginian treasury, was the least part of their loss. They felt a far keener regret when they found that they had to abandon the hope of monopolising all the lines of traffic between the eastern and the western Mediterranean, just as that hope seemed on the eve of fulfilment. They now beheld their whole system of commercial policy broken up, the south-western basin of the Mediterranean, which they had hitherto exclusively commanded, converted since the loss of Sicily into an open thoroughfare for all nations, and the commerce of Italy rendered completely independent of the Phoenicians. Nevertheless the peaceful Sidonians might perhaps have been induced to acquiesce in this result. They had met with similar blows already; they had been obliged to share with the Massiliots, the Etruscans, and the Sicilian Greeks what they had previously possessed alone; even now the possessions which they retained, Africa, Spain, and the gates of the Atlantic Ocean, were sufficient to confer power and prosperity. But in truth, where was their security that these at least would continue in their hands?

The demands made by Regulus, and his very near approach to the obtaining of what he asked, could only be forgotten by those who were willing to forget; and if Rome should now renew from Lilybaeum the enterprise which she had undertaken with so great success from Italy, Carthage would undoubtedly fall, unless the perversity of the enemy or some special piece of good fortune should intervene to save it. No doubt they had peace for the present; but the ratification of that peace had hung on a thread, and they knew what public opinion in Rome thought of the terms on which it was concluded. It might be that Rome was not yet meditating the conquest of Africa and was content with Italy; but if the existence of the Carthaginian state depended on that contentment, the prospect was but a sorry one; and where was the security that the Romans might not find it even convenient for their Italian policy to extirpate rather than reduce to subjection their African neighbour?

In short, Carthage could only regard the peace of $\frac{513}{241}$ in the light of a truce, and could not but employ it in preparations for the inevitable renewal of the war; not for the purpose of avenging the defeat which she had suffered, nor even with the direct view of recovering what she had lost, but in order to secure for herself an existence that should not be dependent on the good-will of the enemy. But when a war of annihilation is surely, though in point of time indefinitely, impending over a weaker state, the wiser, more resolute, and more devoted men—who would immediately prepare for the unavoidable struggle, accept it at a favourable moment, and thus cover their defensive policy by offensive tactics—always find themselves hampered by the indolent and cowardly mass of the money-worshippers, of the aged and feeble, and of the thoughtless who wish merely to gain time, to live and die in peace, and to postpone at any price the final struggle. So there was in Carthage a party for peace and a party for war, both, as was natural, associating themselves with the political distinction which already existed between the conservatives and the reformers. The former found its support in the governing boards, the council of the Ancients and that of the Hundred, led by Hanno the Great, as he was called; the latter found its support in the leaders of the multitude, particularly the much-respected Hasdrubal, and in the officers of the Sicilian army, whose great successes under the leadership of Hamilcar, although they had been otherwise fruitless, had at least shown to the patriots a method which appeared to promise deliverance from the great danger that beset them. Vehement feud had probably long subsisted between these parties, when the Libyan war intervened to suspend the strife. We have already related how that war arose. After the governing party had instigated the mutiny by their incapable administration which frustrated all the precautionary measures of the Sicilian officers, had converted that mutiny into a revolution by the operation of their inhuman system of government, and had at length brought the country to the verge of ruin by their military incapacity—and particularly that of their leader Hanno, the destroyer of their army—Hamilcar Barca, the hero of Ercte, was in the perilous emergency solicited by the government itself to save it from the effects of its blunders and crimes. He accepted the command, and had the magnanimity not to resign it even when they appointed Hanno as his colleague. Indeed, when the indignant army sent the latter home, Hamilcar had the self-control a second time to concede to him, at the urgent request of the government, a share in the command; and, in spite of his enemies and in spite of such a colleague, he was able by his influence with the insurgents, by his dexterous treatment of the Numidian sheiks, and by his unrivalled genius for organisation and generalship, in a singularly short time to put down the revolt entirely and to recall rebellious Africa to its allegiance (end of $\frac{517}{237}$).

During this war the patriot party had kept silence; now it spoke out the louder. On the one hand this catastrophe had brought to light the utterly corrupt and pernicious character of the ruling oligarchy, their incapacity, their coterie-policy, their leanings towards the Romans. On the other hand the seizure of Sardinia, and the threatening attitude which Rome on that occasion assumed, showed plainly even to the humblest that a declaration of war by Rome was constantly hanging like the sword of Damocles over Carthage, and that, if Carthage in her present circumstances went to war with Rome, the consequence must necessarily be the downfall of the Phoenician dominion in Libya. Probably there were in Carthage not a few who, despairing of the future of their country, counselled emigration to the islands of the Atlantic; who could blame them? But minds of the nobler order disdain to save themselves apart from their nation, and great natures enjoy the privilege of deriving enthusiasm from circumstances in which the multitude of good men despair. They accepted the new conditions just as Rome dictated them; no course was left but to submit and, adding fresh bitterness to their former hatred, carefully to cherish and husband resentment—that last resource of an injured nation. They then took steps towards a political reform.[1] They had become sufficiently convinced of the incorrigibleness of the party in power: the fact that the governing lords had even in the last war neither forgotten their spite nor learned greater wisdom, was shown by the effrontery bordering on simplicity

---

[1] Our accounts as to these events are not only imperfect but one-sided, for of course it was the version of the Carthaginian peace party which was adopted by the Roman annalists. Even, however, in our mutilated and distorted accounts (the most important are those of Fabius, in Polyb. iii. 8; Appian. *Hisp.* 4; and Diodorus, xxv. p. 567) the relations of the parties appear clearly enough. Of the vulgar gossip by which its opponents sought to blacken the "revolutionary combination" (ἑταιρεία τῶν πονηροτάτων ἀνθρώπων) specimens may be had in Nepos (*Ham.* 3), to which it will be difficult perhaps to find a parallel.

with which they now instituted proceedings against Hamilcar as the originator of the mercenary war, because he had without authority from the government promised money to his Sicilian soldiers. Had the club of officers and popular leaders desired to overthrow this rotten and wretched government, it would hardly have encountered much difficulty in Carthage itself; but it would have met with a more formidable obstacle in Rome, with which the chiefs of the government in Carthage already maintained relations that bordered on treason. To all the other difficulties of the position there fell to be added the circumstance, that the means of saving their country had to be created without allowing the Romans, or their own government with its Roman tendencies, to become rightly aware of what was doing.

So they left the constitution untouched, and the chiefs of the government in full enjoyment of their exclusive privileges and of the public property. It was merely proposed and carried, that of the two commanders-in-chief, who at the end of the Libyan war were at the head of the Carthaginian troops, Hanno and Hamilcar, the former should be recalled, and the latter should be nominated commander-in-chief for all Africa during an indefinite period. It was arranged that he should hold a position independent of the governing corporations—his antagonists called it an unconstitutional monarchical power, Cato calls it a dictatorship—and that he could only be recalled and placed upon his trial by the popular assembly.[1] Even the choice of a successor was to be vested not in the authorities of the capital, but in the army, that is, in the Carthaginians serving in the army as Gerusiasts or officers, who were named in treaties also along with the general. Of course the right of confirmation was reserved to the popular assembly. Whether this may or may not have been a usurpation, it clearly indicates that the war party regarded and treated the army as its special domain.

The duties of Hamilcar were modest in form. Wars with the Numidian tribes on the borders never ceased; only a short time previously the "city of a hundred gates," Theveste (Tebessa), in the interior had been occupied by the Carthaginians. The task of continuing this border warfare, which was allotted to

---

[1] The Barcine family conclude the most important state treaties, and the ratification of the governing board is a formality (Pol. iii. 21). Rome enters her protest before them and before the Senate (Pol. iii. 15). The position of that family towards Carthage in many points resembles that of the Princes of Orange towards the States-General.

the new commander-in-chief of Africa, was not in itself of such importance as to prevent the Carthaginian government, which was allowed to do as it liked in its own immediate sphere, from tacitly conniving at the decrees passed in reference to the matter by the popular assembly; and the Romans did not perhaps recognise its significance at all.

Thus there was placed at the head of the army the very man, who had given proof in the Sicilian and in the Libyan wars that fate had destined him, if any one, to be the saviour of his country. Never perhaps was the noble struggle of man with fate waged more nobly than by him. The army was intended to save the state; but what sort of army? The Carthaginian civic militia had fought not badly under Hamilcar's leadership in the Libyan war; but he knew well, that it is one thing to lead out the merchants and manufacturers of a city which is in the extremity of peril for once to battle, and another to form them into soldiers. The patriot party in Carthage furnished him with excellent officers, but it was of course almost exclusively the cultivated class that was represented in it. He had no citizen-militia, at most a few squadrons of Libyphoenician cavalry. The task was to form an army out of Libyan conscripts and mercenaries; a task possible in the hands of a general like Hamilcar, but possible even for him only on condition that he should be able to pay his men punctually and well. But he had learned, by experience in Sicily, that the state revenues of Carthage were expended in Carthage itself on matters much more urgent than the payment of the armies that fought against the enemy. The warfare which he waged, accordingly, had to support itself, and he had to carry out on a great scale what he had already attempted on a smaller scale at Monte Pellegrino. But further, Hamilcar was not only a military chief, he was also a party leader. In opposition to the implacable governing party, which eagerly but patiently waited for an opportunity of overthrowing him, he had to seek support among the citizens; and although their leaders might be ever so pure and noble, the multitude was deeply corrupt and accustomed by the unhappy system of corruption to give nothing without being paid for it. In particular emergencies, indeed, necessity or enthusiasm might for the moment prevail, as everywhere happens even with the most venal corporations; but, if Hamilcar wished to secure the permanent support of the Carthaginian community for his plan, which at the best could only be executed after a series of years, he had to supply his friends at home with regular consignments of money as the means of keeping the mob in good humour. Thus compelled to beg or to buy from the lukewarm and venal multitude permission to save it; compelled to wring from the arrogance of men whom he hated and whom he had constantly conquered, at the price of humiliation and of silence, the respite indispensable for his ends; compelled to conceal from those despised traitors to their country, who called themselves the lords of his native city, his plans and his contempt—the noble hero stood with few friends of congenial sentiments between enemies without and enemies within, building upon the irresolution of the one and of the other, at once deceiving both and defying both, if only he might gain means, money, and men for the contest with a land which, even were the army ready to strike the blow, it seemed difficult to reach and scarce possible to vanquish. He was still a young man, little beyond thirty, but he had apparently, when he was preparing for his expedition, a foreboding that he would not be permitted to attain the end of his labours, or to see otherwise than afar off the promised land. When he left Carthage he enjoined his son Hannibal, nine years of age, to swear at the altar of the supreme God eternal hatred to the Roman name, and reared him and his younger sons Hasdrubal and Mago—the " lion's brood," as he called them—in the camp as the inheritors of his projects, of his genius, and of his hatred.

The new commander-in-chief of Libya departed from Carthage immediately after the termination of the mercenary war (perhaps in the spring of $\frac{518}{236}$). He apparently meditated an expedition against the free Libyans in the west. His army, which was especially strong in elephants, marched along the coast; by its side sailed the fleet, led by his faithful associate Hasdrubal. Suddenly tidings came that he had crossed the sea at the Pillars of Hercules and had landed in Spain, where he was waging war with the natives—with people who had done him no harm, and without orders from his government, as the Carthaginian authorities complained. They could not complain at any rate that he neglected the affairs of Africa: when the Numidians once more rebelled, his lieutenant Hasdrubal so effectually routed them that for a long period there was tranquillity on the frontier, and several tribes hitherto independent submitted to pay tribute. What he personally did in Spain, we are no longer able to trace in detail. His achievements compelled Cato the elder, who, a generation after Hamilcar's death, beheld in Spain the still fresh traces of his working, to exclaim, notwithstanding all his hatred of the Carthaginians, that no king was worthy to be named by the side of Hamilcar Barca. Their results still show to us, at least in a general way, what was accomplished by Hamilcar as a soldier and a statesman in the last nine years of his life ($\frac{518-526}{236-228}$), till in the flower of his age, fighting bravely in the field of battle, he met his death like Scharnhorst just as his plans were beginning to reach maturity. During the next eight years ($\frac{527-534}{227-220}$) the heir of his office and of his plans, his son-in-law Hasdrubal, prosecuted in the spirit of his master the work which Hamilcar had begun. Instead of the small entrepôt for trade, which, along with the protectorate of Gades, was all that Carthage had hitherto possessed on the Spanish coast, and which she had treated as a dependency of Libya, a Carthaginian kingdom was founded in Spain by the generalship of Hamilcar, and confirmed by the adroit statesmanship of Hasdrubal. The fairest regions of Spain, the southern and eastern coasts, became Phoenician provinces. Towns were founded; above all, " Spanish Carthage " (Cartagena) was established by Hasdrubal on the only good harbour along the south coast, containing the splendid " royal castle " of its founder. Agriculture flourished, and still more mining in consequence of the fortunate discovery of the silver-mines of Cartagena, which a century afterwards had a yearly produce of more than £360,000 (36,000,000 sesterces). Most of the communities as far as the Ebro became dependent on Carthage and paid tribute to it. Hasdrubal skilfully by every means, even by intermarriage, attached the chiefs to the interests of Carthage. Thus Carthage acquired in Spain a rich market for its commerce and manufactures; and not only did the revenues of the province sustain the army, but there remained a balance to be remitted to Carthage and reserved for future use. The province at the same time formed and trained the army; regular levies took place in the territory subject to Carthage; the prisoners of war were incorporated with Carthaginian corps. Contingents and mercenaries, as many as were desired, were supplied by the dependent communities. During his long life of warfare the soldier found in the camp a second home, and found a substitute for patriotism in fidelity to his standard and enthusiastic attachment to his great leaders. Constant conflicts with the brave Iberians and Celts created a serviceable infantry, to co-operate with the excellent Numidian cavalry.

So far as Carthage was concerned, the Barcides were allowed to go on. The citizens were not asked for regular contributions, but on the contrary derived benefit from the acquisition; commerce recovered in Spain what it had lost in Sicily and Sardinia; and the Spanish war and the Spanish army with its brilliant victories and important successes soon became so popular that it was even possible in particular emergencies, such as after Hamilcar's fall, to effect the despatch of considerable reinforcements of African troops to Spain, and the governing party, whether well or ill affected, had to maintain silence, or at any rate to content themselves with complaining to each other or to their friends in Rome regarding the demagogic officers and the mob.

On the part of Rome too nothing took place calculated seriously to affect the course of Spanish affairs. The first and chief cause of the inactivity of the Romans was undoubtedly their very want of acquaintance with the circumstances of the remote peninsula—which was certainly also Hamilcar's main reason for selecting Spain and not, as might otherwise have been possible, Africa for the execution of his plan. The explanations with which the Carthaginian generals met the Roman commissioners sent to Spain to procure information on the spot, and their assurances that all this was done only to provide the means of promptly paying the war-contributions to Rome, could not possibly find belief in the senate. But they probably discerned only the immediate object of Hamilcar's plans, viz. to procure compensation in Spain for the tribute and the traffic of the islands which Carthage had lost; and they deemed an aggressive war on the part of the Carthaginians, and in particular an invasion of Italy from Spain—as is evident (both from express statements to that effect and from the whole state of the case—absolute impossibilities. Many, of course, among the peace party in Carthage saw further; but, whatever they might think, they could hardly be much inclined to enlighten their Roman friends as to the impending storm, which the Carthaginian authorities had long been unable to prevent, or that step would accelerate, instead of averting, the crisis; and even if they did so, such denunciations proceeding from partisans would justly be received with great caution at Rome. By degrees, certainly, the inconceivably rapid and mighty extension of the Carthaginian power in Spain could not but excite the observation and awaken the apprehensions of the Romans. In fact, in the course of the later years before the outbreak of war, they did attempt to set bounds to it. About the year $\frac{528}{226}$, mindful of their newborn Hellenism, they concluded an alliance with the two Greek or semi-Greek towns on the east coast of Spain, Zacynthus or Saguntum (Murviedro, not far from Valencia), and Emporiae (Ampurias); and when they acquainted the Carthaginian general Hasdrubal that they had done so, they at the same time warned him not to push his conquests over the Ebro, with which he promised compliance. This was not done to prevent an invasion of Italy by the land route—no treaty would fetter the general who should undertake such an enterprise—but partly to set a limit to the material power of the Spanish Carthaginians which began to be dangerous, partly to secure, in the free communities between the Ebro and the Pyrenees whom Rome thus took under her protection, a basis of operations in case of its being necessary to land and make war in Spain. In reference to the impending war with Carthage, which the senate did not fail to see was inevitable, they hardly apprehended any greater inconvenience from the events that had occurred in Spain than that they might be compelled to send some legions thither, and that the enemy would be somewhat better provided with money and soldiers than, without Spain, he would have been; they were at any rate firmly resolved, as the plan of the campaign of $\frac{536}{218}$ shows and as indeed could not but be the case, to begin and terminate the next war in Africa,—a course which would at the same time decide the fate of Spain. Further grounds for delay were suggested during the first years by the instalments from Carthage, which a declaration of war would have cut off, and then by the death of Hamilcar, which probably induced friends and foes to think that his projects must have died with him. Lastly, during the latter years when the senate certainly began to apprehend that it was not prudent to delay the renewal of the war, there was the very intelligible wish to dispose of the Gauls in the valley of the Po in the first instance, for these, threatened with extirpation, might be expected to avail themselves of any serious war undertaken by Rome to allure the Transalpine tribes once more to Italy, and to renew those Celtic migrations which were still fraught with very great peril. That it was not regard either for the Carthaginian peace party or for existing treaties which withheld the Romans from action, is self-evident; moreover, if they desired war, the Spanish feuds furnished at any moment a ready pretext. The conduct of Rome in this view is by no means unintelligible; but as little can it be denied that the Roman senate in dealing with this matter displayed short-sightedness and slackness—faults which were still more inexcusably manifested in their mode of dealing at the same epoch with Gallic affairs. The policy of the Romans was always more remarkable for tenacity, cunning, and consistency, than for grandeur of conception or power of rapid organisation—qualities in which the enemies of Rome from Pyrrhus down to Mithradates often surpassed her.

Thus the smiles of fortune inaugurated the brilliantly conceived project of Hamilcar. The means of war were acquired —a numerous army accustomed to combat and to conquer, and a constantly replenished exchequer; but in order that the right moment might be discovered for the struggle and that the right direction might be given to it there was wanted a leader. The man, whose head and heart had in a desperate emergency and amidst a despairing people paved the way for their deliverance, was no more, when it became possible to carry out his design. Whether his successor Hasdrubal forbore to make the attack because the proper moment seemed to him to have not yet arrived, or whether, a statesman rather than a general, he believed himself unequal to the conduct of the enterprise, we are unable to determine. When, at the beginning of $\frac{534}{220}$, he fell by the hand of an assassin, the Carthaginian officers of the Spanish army summoned to fill his place Hannibal, the eldest son of Hamilcar. He was still a young man—born in $\frac{505}{249}$, and now, therefore, in his twenty-ninth year; but his life had already been fraught with varied experience. His first recollections pictured to him his father fighting in a distant land and conquering on Ercte; he shared that unconquered father's fortunes, and sympathised with his feelings, on the peace of Catulus, on the bitter return home, and throughout the horrors of the Libyan war. While yet a boy, he had followed his father to the camp; and he soon distinguished himself. His light and firmly built frame made him an excellent runner and fencer, and a fearless rider; the privation of sleep did not affect him, and he knew like a soldier how to enjoy or to want his food. Although his youth had been spent in the camp, he possessed such culture as belonged to the Phoenicians of rank in his day; in Greek, apparently after he had become a general, he made such progress under the guidance of his intimate friend Sosilus of Sparta as to be able to compose state papers in that language. As he grew up, he entered the army of his father, to perform his first feats of arms under the paternal eye and to see him fall in battle by his side. Thereafter he had commanded the cavalry under his sister's husband, Hasdrubal, and distinguished himself by brilliant personal bravery as well as by his talents as a leader. The voice of his comrades now summoned him—the tried, although youthful general—to the chief command, and he could now execute the designs for which his father and his brother-in-law had lived and died. He took possession of the inheritance, and he was worthy of it. His contemporaries tried to cast stains of various sorts on his character; the Romans charged him with cruelty, the Carthaginians with covetousness; and it is true that he hated as only Oriental natures know how to hate, and that a general who never fell short of money and stores can hardly have been other than covetous. But though anger and envy and meanness have written his history, they have not availed to mar the pure and noble image which it presents. Laying aside wretched inventions which furnish their own refutation, and some things which his lieutenants, particularly Hannibal Monomachus and Mago the Samnite, were guilty of doing in his name, nothing occurs in the accounts regarding him which may not be justified in the circumstances, and according to the international law, of the times; and all agree in this, that he combined in rare perfection discretion and enthusiasm, caution and energy. He was peculiarly marked by that inventive craftiness, which forms one of the leading traits of the Phoenician character; he was fond of taking singular and unexpected routes; ambushes and stratagems of all sorts were familiar to him; and he studied the character of his antagonists with unprecedented care. By an unrivalled system of espionage—he had regular spies even in Rome—he kept himself informed of the projects of the enemy; he himself was frequently seen wearing disguises and false hair, in order to procure information on some point or other. Every page of the history of the period attests his genius as a general; and his gifts as a statesman were, after the peace with Rome, no less conspicuously displayed in his reform of the Carthaginian constitution, and in the unparalleled influence which as a foreign exile he exercised in the cabinets of the Eastern powers. The power which he wielded over men is shown by his incomparable control over an army of various nations and many tongues—an army which never in the worst times mutinied against him. He was a great man; wherever he went, he riveted the eyes of all.

Hannibal resolved immediately after his nomination (in the spring of $\frac{534}{220}$) to commence the war. The land of the Celts was still in a ferment, and war seemed imminent between Rome and Macedonia: he had good reason now to throw off the mask without delay and to carry the war whithersoever he pleased, before the Romans began it at their own convenience with a descent on Africa. His army was soon ready to take the field, and his exchequer was tolerably filled by means of some razzias; but the Carthaginian government showed itself far from desirous of issuing a declaration of war against Rome. The place of Hasdrubal, the patriotic national leader, was even more difficult to fill in Carthage than that of Hasdrubal the general in Spain; the peace party had now the ascendancy at home, and persecuted the leaders of the war party with political indictments. The rulers who had already cut down and mutilated the plans of Hamilcar were by no means inclined to allow the unknown young man, who now commanded in Spain, to exercise his youthful patriotism at the expense of the state; and Hannibal hesitated personally to declare war in open opposition to the legitimate authorities. He tried to provoke the Saguntines to break the peace; but they contented themselves with complaining to Rome. When the Romans on receiving their complaint nominated a commission, he tried to drive it to a declaration of war by treating it rudely; but the commissioners saw how matters stood: they kept silence in Spain, with a view to lodge complaints at Carthage, and with a view to send home the news that Hannibal was ready to strike and that war was imminent. Thus the time passed away; accounts had already come of the death of Antigonus Doson, who had suddenly died nearly at the same time with Hasdrubal; in Cisalpine Gaul the establishment of fortresses was carried on by the Romans with redoubled rapidity and energy; preparations were made in Rome for putting a speedy conclusion to the insurrection in Illyria in the course of the next spring. Every day was precious; Hannibal formed his resolution. He sent summary intimation to Carthage that the Saguntines were making aggressions on the Torboletes, subjects of Carthage, and he must therefore attack them; and without waiting for a reply he began in the spring of $\frac{535}{219}$ the siege of a town which was in alliance with Rome, or in other words, war against Rome. We may form some idea of the views and counsels that would prevail in Carthage from the impression produced in certain circles by York's capitulation. All " respectable men," it was said, disapproved an attack made " without orders; " there was talk of disavowal, of surrendering the daring officer. But whether it was that dread of the army and of the multitude nearer home outweighed in the Carthaginian council the fear of Rome; or that they perceived the

impossibility of retracing such a step, now that it was taken;
or that mere inertness prevented any definite action, they determined at length to do nothing, and to suffer the war to go
on, although not prepared to sanction it. Saguntum defended
itself, as only Spanish towns can conduct their defence: had
the Romans showed but a tithe of the energy of their clients, and
not trifled away their time during the eight months' siege of
Saguntum in the paltry warfare with Illyrian brigands, they
might, masters as they were of the sea and of places suitable for
landing, have spared themselves the disgrace of failing to grant
the protection which they had promised, and might perhaps
have given a different turn to the war. But they delayed, and
the town was at length taken by storm. When Hannibal sent
the spoil for distribution to Carthage, patriotism and zeal for
war were roused in the hearts of many who had hitherto felt
nothing of the kind, and the distribution cut off all prospect
of coming to terms with Rome. Accordingly, when after the
destruction of Saguntum a Roman embassy appeared at Carthage
and demanded the surrender of the general and of the Gerusiasts
present in the camp, and when the Roman spokesman, interrupting an attempt at justification, broke off the discussion and,
gathering up his robe, declared that he held in it peace and war
and that the Gerusia might choose between them, the gerusiasts
mustered courage to reply that they left it to the choice of the
Roman; and when he offered war, they accepted it (in the
spring of $\frac{536}{218}$).

Hannibal, who had lost a whole year through the obstinate
resistance of the Saguntines, had as usual retired for the winter
of $\frac{535-536}{219-218}$ to Cartagena, to make all his preparations on the one
hand for the attack of Italy, on the other for the defence of
Spain and Africa; for, as he, like his father and his brother-in-
law, held the supreme command in both countries, it devolved
upon him to take measures also for the protection of his native
land. The whole mass of his forces amounted to about 120,000
infantry and 16,000 cavalry; he had also 58 elephants, 32 quinqueremes manned, and 18 not manned, besides the elephants
and vessels remaining at the capital. Excepting a few Ligurians
among the light troops, there were no mercenaries in this Carthaginian army; the troops, with the exception of some Phoenician
squadrons, consisted mainly of the Carthaginian subjects called
out for service—Libyans and Spaniards. To insure the fidelity
of the latter the general, who knew the men with whom he had
to deal, gave them as a proof of his confidence a general leave of

absence for the whole winter; while, not sharing the narrow-minded exclusiveness of Phoenician patriotism, he promised to the Libyans on his oath the citizenship of Carthage, should they return to Africa victorious. This mass of troops however was only destined in part for the expedition to Italy. Nearly 20,000 men were sent to Africa, the smaller portion of them proceeding to the capital and the Phoenician territory proper, the majority to the western point of Africa. For the protection of Spain 12,000 infantry, 2500 cavalry, and nearly the half of the elephants were left behind, in addition to the fleet stationed there; the chief command and the government of Spain were entrusted to Hannibal's younger brother Hasdrubal. The immediate territory of Carthage was comparatively weakly garrisoned, because the capital afforded in case of need sufficient resources; in like manner a moderate number of infantry sufficed for the present in Spain, where new levies could be procured with ease, whereas a comparatively large proportion of the arms specially African—horses and elephants—was retained there. Great care was taken to secure the communications between Spain and Africa: with that view the fleet remained in Spain, and western Africa was guarded by a very strong body of troops. The fidelity of the troops was secured not only by hostages collected from the Spanish communities and detained in the stronghold of Saguntum, but by the removal of the soldiers from the districts where they were raised to other quarters: the East African militia were moved chiefly to Spain, the Spanish to Western Africa, the West African to Carthage. Adequate provision was thus made for defence. As to offensive measures, a squadron of 20 quinqueremes with 1000 soldiers on board was to sail from Carthage for the west coast of Italy and to pillage it, and a second of 25 sail was, if possible, to re-establish itself at Lilybaeum; Hannibal believed that he might count upon the government making this moderate amount of exertion. With the main army he determined in person to invade Italy; as was beyond doubt part of the original plan of Hamilcar. A decisive attack on Rome was only possible in Italy, as a similar attack on Carthage was only possible in Libya; as certainly as Rome meant to begin her next campaign with the latter, so certainly ought Carthage not to confine herself at the outset to any secondary object of operations, such as Sicily, or to mere defence—defeat would in any case involve equal destruction, but victory would not yield equal fruit.

But how could Italy be attacked? He might succeed in

reaching the peninsula by sea or by land; but if the project was to be no mere desperate adventure, but a military expedition with a strategic aim, a nearer basis for its operations was requisite than Spain or Africa. Hannibal could not rely for support on a fleet and a fortified harbour, for Rome was now mistress of the sea. As little did the territory of the Italian confederacy present any tenable basis. If in very different times, and in spite of Hellenic sympathies, it had withstood the shock of Pyrrhus, it was not to be expected that it would now fall to pieces on the appearance of the Phoenician general; an invading army would without doubt be crushed between the network of Roman fortresses and the firmly consolidated confederacy. The land of the Ligurians and Celts alone could be to Hannibal what Poland was to Napoleon in his very similar Russian campaigns. These tribes still smarting under their scarcely ended struggle for independence, alien in race from the Italians, and feeling their very existence endangered by the chain of Roman fortresses and highways whose first coils were even now being fastened around them, could not but recognise their deliverers in the Phoenician army (which numbered in its ranks numerous Spanish Celts), and would serve as a support for it to fall back upon—a source whence it might draw supplies and recruits. Already formal treaties were concluded with the Boii and the Insubres, by which they bound themselves to send guides to meet the Carthaginian army, to procure for it a good reception from the cognate tribes and supplies along its route, and to rise against the Romans as soon as it should set foot on Italian ground. In fine, the state of Roman relations with the East led the Carthaginians to this same quarter. Macedonia, which by the victory of Sellasia had re-established its sovereignty in the Peloponnesus, was at variance with Rome; Demetrius of Pharos, who had exchanged the Roman alliance for that of Macedon and had been dispossessed by the Romans, lived as an exile at the Macedonian court, and the latter had refused the demand which the Romans made for his surrender. If it was possible to combine the armies from the Guadalquivir and the Karasu anywhere against the common foe, it could only be done on the Po. Thus everything directed Hannibal to northern Italy; and that the eyes of his father had already been turned to that quarter, is shown by the reconnoitring party of Carthaginians, whom the Romans to their great surprise encountered in Liguria in $\frac{524}{230}$.

The reason for Hannibal's preference of the land route to that

by sea is less obvious; for that neither the maritime supremacy
of the Romans nor their league with Massilia could have prevented
a landing at Genoa, is evident, and was shown by the sequel.
Our authorities fail to furnish us with several of the elements,
on which a satisfactory answer to this question would depend,
and which cannot be supplied by conjecture. Hannibal had
to choose between two evils. Instead of exposing himself to
the unknown and unforeseen contingencies of a sea voyage and
of naval war, it must have seemed to him the better course to
accept the assurances, which beyond doubt were seriously meant,
of the Boii and Insubres, and the more so that, even if the army
should land at Genoa, it would still have mountains to cross;
he could hardly know exactly how much smaller are the
difficulties presented by the Apennines at Genoa than by the
main chain of the Alps. At any rate the route which he took
was the primitive Celtic route, by which many much larger
hordes had crossed the Alps: the ally and deliverer of the Celtic
nation might without temerity venture to traverse it.

So Hannibal collected the troops, destined for the grand army,
in Cartagena at the beginning of the favourable season; there
were 90,000 infantry and 12,000 cavalry, of whom about two-
thirds were Africans and a third Spaniards. The 37 elephants
which they took with them were probably destined rather to
make an impression on the Gauls than for serious warfare.
Hannibal's infantry no longer needed, like that led by Xanthippus, to shelter itself behind a screen of elephants, and the general
had too much sagacity to employ otherwise than sparingly and
with caution that two-edged weapon, which had as often
occasioned the defeat of its own as of the enemy's army. With
this force the general set out in the spring of $\frac{536}{218}$ from Cartagena
towards the Ebro. He so far informed his soldiers as to the
measures which he had taken, particularly as to the connections he had entered into with the Celts and the resources
and object of the expedition, that even the common soldier,
whose military instincts lengthened war had developed, felt
the clear perception and the steady hand of his leader, and
followed him with implicit confidence to the unknown and
distant land; and the animated address, in which he laid before
them the position of their country and the demands of the
Romans, the slavery certainly reserved for their dear native
land, and the disgrace of the imputation that they could surrender their beloved general and his staff, kindled a soldierly
and patriotic ardour in the hearts of all.

The Roman state was in a plight, such as easily occurs even in firmly-established and sagacious aristocracies. The Romans knew doubtless what they wished to accomplish, and they took various steps; but nothing was done rightly, or at the right time. They might long ago have been masters of the gates of the Alps and have crushed the Celts; the latter were still formidable, and the former were open. They might either have had friendship with Carthage, had they honourably kept the peace of $\frac{513}{241}$, or, had they not been disposed for peace, they might long ago have conquered Carthage: the peace was practically broken by the seizure of Sardinia, and they allowed the power of Carthage to recover itself undisturbed for twenty years. There was no great difficulty in maintaining peace with Macedonia; but they had forfeited her friendship for a trifling gain. There must have been a lack of some leading statesman to take a comprehensive view of the position of affairs; on all hands either too little was done, or too much. Now the war began at a time and at a place which they had allowed the enemy to determine; and, with all their well-founded conviction of military superiority, they were perplexed as to the object to be aimed at and the course to be followed in their first operations. They had at their disposal more than half a million of serviceable soldiers; the Roman cavalry alone was less good, and relatively less numerous, than the Carthaginian, the former constituting about a tenth, the latter an eighth, of the whole number of troops taking the field. None of the states affected by the war had any fleet corresponding to the Roman fleet of 220 quinqueremes, which had just returned from the Adriatic to the western sea. The natural and proper application of this crushing superiority of force was self-evident. It had been long settled that the war ought to be opened with a landing in Africa. The subsequent turn taken by events had compelled the Romans to embrace in their scheme of the war a simultaneous landing in Spain, chiefly to prevent the Spanish army from appearing before the walls of Carthage. In accordance with this plan they ought above all, when the war had been practically opened by Hannibal's attack on Saguntum in the beginning of $\frac{535}{219}$, to have thrown a Roman army into Spain before the town fell; but they neglected the dictates of interest no less than of honour. For eight months Saguntum held out in vain: when the town passed into other hands, Rome had not even equipped her armament for landing in Spain. The country, however, between the Ebro and the Pyrenees was still free, and its tribes were not only the natural allies of the Romans, but had also, like the Saguntines, received from Roman emissaries promises of speedy assistance. Catalonia may be reached by sea from Italy in not much longer time than from Cartagena by land: had the Romans started, like the Phoenicians, in April, after the formal declaration of war that had taken place in the interval, Hannibal might have encountered the Roman legions on the line of the Ebro.

At length, certainly, the greater part of the army and of the fleet was got ready for the expedition to Africa, and the second consul Publius Cornelius Scipio was ordered to the Ebro; but he proceeded leisurely, and when an insurrection broke out on the Po, he allowed the army that was ready for embarkation to be employed there, and formed new legions for the Spanish expedition. So although Hannibal encountered on the Ebro very vehement resistance, it proceeded only from the natives; and, as under existing circumstances time was still more precious to him than the blood of his men, he surmounted the opposition after some months with the loss of a fourth part of his army, and reached the line of the Pyrenees. That the Spanish allies of Rome would be sacrificed a second time by that delay might have been as certainly foreseen, as the delay itself might have been easily avoided; but probably even the expedition to Italy itself, which in the spring of $\frac{536}{218}$ must not have been anticipated in Rome, would have been averted by the timely appearance of the Romans in Spain. Hannibal had by no means the intention of sacrificing his Spanish " kingdom," and throwing himself like a desperado on Italy. The time which he had spent in the siege of Saguntum and in the reduction of Catalonia, and the considerable corps which he left behind for the occupation of the newly-won territory between the Ebro and the Pyrenees, sufficiently show that, had a Roman army disputed the possession of Spain with him, he would not have been content to withdraw from it; and—which was the main point—had the Romans been able to delay his departure from Spain for but a few weeks, winter would have closed the passes of the Alps before Hannibal reached them, and the African expedition would have departed without hindrance for its destination.

Arrived at the Pyrenees, Hannibal sent home a portion of his troops; a measure which he had resolved on from the first with the view of showing to the soldiers how confident their general was of success, and of counteracting the presentiment that his enterprise was one of those from which there is no return. With an army of 50,000 infantry and 9000 cavalry, entirely veteran soldiers, he crossed the Pyrenees without difficulty, and then took the coast route by Narbonne and Nimes through the Celtic territory, which was opened to the army partly by the connections previously formed, partly by Carthaginian gold, partly by arms. It was not till it arrived in the end of July at the Rhone opposite Avignon, that a serious resistance appeared to await it. The consul Scipio, who on his voyage to Spain had landed at Massilia (about the end of June), had there been informed that he had come too late and that Hannibal had crossed not only the Ebro but the Pyrenees. On receiving these accounts, which appear to have first opened the eyes of the Romans to the course and the object of Hannibal, the consul had temporarily abandoned his expedition to Spain, and had resolved in connection with the Celtic tribes of that region, who were under the influence of the Massiliots and thereby under that of Rome, to receive the Phoenicians on the Rhone, and to obstruct their passage of the river and their march into Italy. Fortunately for Hannibal, opposite to the point at which he meant to cross, there lay at the moment only the general levy of the Celts, while the consul himself with his army of 22,000 infantry and 2000 horse was still in Massilia, four days' march farther down the stream. The messengers of the Gallic levy hastened to inform him. It was the object of Hannibal to convey his army with its numerous cavalry and elephants across the rapid stream under the eyes of the enemy, and before the arrival of Scipio; and he possessed not a single boat. He immediately gave directions that all the boats belonging to the numerous navigators of the Rhone in the neighbourhood should be bought up at any price, and that the deficiency of boats should be supplied by rafts made from felled trees, so that all the numerous army could be conveyed over in one day. While this was done, a strong division under Hanno, son of Bomilcar, proceeded by forced marches up the stream till they reached a suitable point for crossing, which they found undefended, situated two short days' march above Avignon. Here they crossed the river on hastily constructed rafts, with the view of then moving down on the left bank and taking the Gauls, who were impeding the passage of the main army, in the rear. On the morning of the fifth day after they had reached the Rhone, and of the third after Hanno's departure, the preconcerted smoke-signals, which Hannibal was anxiously expecting from the division that had been detached, arose on the opposite bank. Just as the Gauls, seeing that the enemy's fleet of boats began to move, were hastening to occupy the bank, their camp behind them suddenly burst into flames. Surprised and divided, they were unable either to withstand the attack or to resist the passage, and they dispersed in hasty flight.

Scipio meanwhile held councils of war in Massilia as to the proper mode of occupying the ferries of the Rhone, and was not induced to move even by the urgent messages that came from the leaders of the Celts. He distrusted their accounts, and he contented himself with detaching a weak Roman cavalry division to reconnoitre on the left bank of the Rhone. This detachment found the whole enemy's army already transported to that bank, and occupied in bringing over the elephants which alone remained on the right bank of the stream; and, after it had warmly engaged some Carthaginian squadrons in the district of Avignon, merely for the purpose of enabling it to complete its reconnaissance—the first encounter of the Romans and Phoenicians in this war—it hastily returned to report at headquarters. Scipio now started in the utmost haste with all his troops for Avignon; but, when he arrived there, even the Carthaginian cavalry that had been left behind to cover the passage of the elephants had already taken its departure three days ago, and nothing remained for the consul but to return with weary troops and little credit to Massilia, and to revile the " cowardly flight " of the Punic leader. Thus the Romans had for the third time through pure negligence abandoned their allies and an important line of defence; and not only so, but they sacrificed the real means of repairing their error by passing after this first blunder from mistaken slackness to mistaken haste, and by still attempting without any prospect of success to do what might have been done with so much certainty a few days before. When once Hannibal was in the Celtic territory on the Roman side of the Rhone, he could no longer be prevented from reaching the Alps; but if Scipio had at the first accounts proceeded with his whole army to Italy—the Po might have been reached by way of Genoa in seven days—and had united with his corps the weak divisions in the valley of the Po, he might have at least prepared a formidable reception for the enemy. But not only did he lose precious time in the march to Avignon, but, able as otherwise he was, he wanted either the political courage or the military sagacity to change the destination of his corps as the change of circumstances required. He sent the main body under his brother Gnaeus to Spain, and returned himself with a few men to Pisae.

Hannibal, who after the passage of the Rhone had assembled

the army and explained to his troops the object of his expedition, and had brought forward the Celtic chief Magilus himself, who had arrived from the valley of the Po, to address the army through an interpreter, meanwhile continued his march to the passes of the Alps without obstruction. Which of these passes he should choose, could not be at once determined either by the shortness of the route or by the disposition of the inhabitants, although he had no time to lose either in circuitous routes or in combat. He had necessarily to select a route which should be practicable for his baggage, his numerous cavalry, and his elephants, and in which an army could procure sufficient means of subsistence either by friendship or by force; for, although Hannibal had made preparations to convey provisions after him on beasts of burden, these could only meet for a few days the wants of an army which still, notwithstanding its great losses, amounted to nearly 50,000 men. Leaving out of view the coast route, which Hannibal abstained from taking not because the Romans obstructed it, but because it would have led him away from his destination, there were only two well-known routes leading across the Alps from Gaul to Italy in ancient times: [1] the pass of the Cottian Alps (Mont Genèvre) leading into the territory of the Taurini (by Susa or Fenestrelles to Turin), and that of the Graian Alps (the Little St. Bernard) leading into the territory of the Salassi (to Aosta and Ivrea). The former route is the shorter; but, after leaving the valley of the Rhone, it passes by the impracticable and unfruitful valleys of the Drac, the Romanche, and the upper Durance, through a difficult and poor mountain country, and requires at least a seven or eight days' mountain march. A military road was first constructed there by Pompeius, to furnish a shorter communication between the provinces of Cisalpine and Transalpine Gaul.

The route by the Little St. Bernard is somewhat longer; but, after crossing the first Alpine wall that forms the eastern boundary of the Rhone valley, it keeps by the valley of the upper Isère, which stretches from Grenoble by Chambéry up to the very foot of the Little St. Bernard or, in other words, of the chain of the higher Alps, and is the broadest, most fertile, and most populous of all the Alpine valleys. Moreover, the pass of the Little St. Bernard, while not the lowest of all the natural passes of the

[1] It was not till the middle ages that the route by Mont Cenis became a military road. The eastern passes, such as that over the Poenine Alps or the Great St. Bernard—which, moreover, was only converted into a military road by Caesar and Augustus—are, of course, in this case out of the question.

Alps, is by far the easiest; although no artificial road was constructed there, an Austrian corps with artillery crossed the Alps by that route in 1815. And lastly this route, which only leads over two mountain ridges, has been from the earliest times the great military route from the Celtic to the Italian territory. The Carthaginian army had thus in fact no choice. It was a fortunate coincidence, but not a motive influencing the decision of Hannibal, that the Celtic tribes allied with him in Italy inhabited the country up to the Little St. Bernard, while the route by Mont Genèvre would have brought him directly into the territory of the Taurini, who were from ancient times at feud with the Insubres.

So the Carthaginian army marched in the first instance up the Rhone towards the valley of the upper Isère, not, as might be presumed, by the nearest route up the left bank of the lower Isère from Valence to Grenoble, but through the " island " of the Allobroges, the rich, and even then thickly peopled, low ground, which is enclosed on the north and west by the Rhone, on the south by the Isère, and on the east by the Alps. The reason of this movement was, that the nearest route would have led them through an impracticable and poor mountain-country, while the " island " was level and extremely fertile, and was separated by but a single mountain-wall from the valley of the upper Isère. The march along the Rhone into, and across, the " island " to the foot of the Alpine wall was accomplished in sixteen days: it presented little difficulty, and in the " island " itself Hannibal dexterously availed himself of a feud that had broken out between two chiefs of the Allobroges to attach to his interests one of the most important of the chiefs, who not only escorted the Carthaginians through the whole plain, but also supplied them with provisions, and furnished the soldiers with arms, clothing, and shoes. But the expedition narrowly escaped destruction at the crossing of the first Alpine chain, which rises precipitously like a wall, and over which only a single available path leads (over Mont du Chat, near the hamlet Chevelu). The population of the Allobroges had strongly occupied the pass. Hannibal learned the state of matters early enough to avoid a surprise, and encamped at the foot, until after sunset the Celts dispersed to the houses of the nearest town: he then seized the pass in the night. Thus the summit was gained; but on the extremely steep path, which leads down from the summit to the lake of Bourget, the mules and horses slipped and fell. The assaults, which at all available points were made by the Celts upon the army in march, were very annoying, by reason not so much of the direct injury which they inflicted, as of the confusion which they occasioned; and when Hannibal with his light troops threw himself from above on the Allobroges, these were chased indeed without difficulty and with heavy loss down the mountain, but the confusion, in the train especially, was still further increased by the noise of the combat. So, when after much loss he arrived in the plain, Hannibal immediately attacked the nearest town, to chastise and terrify the barbarians, and at the same time to repair as far as possible his loss in sumpter animals and horses. After a day's repose in the pleasant valley of Chambéry the army continued its march up the Isère, without being detained either by want of supplies or by attacks so long as the valley continued broad and fertile. It was only when on the fourth day they entered the territory of the Ceutrones (the modern Tarantaise) where the valley gradually contracts, that they had greater occasion to be on their guard. The Ceutrones received the army at the boundary of their country (somewhere about Conflans) with branches and garlands, furnished cattle for slaughter, guides, and hostages; and the Carthaginians marched through their territory as through a friendly land. When, however, the troops had reached the very foot of the Alps, at the point where the path leaves the Isère, and winds by a narrow and difficult defile along the brook Reclus up to the summit of the St. Bernard, all at once the militia of the Ceutrones appeared partly in the rear of the army, partly on the crests of the rocks enclosing the pass on the right and left, in the hope of cutting off the train and baggage. But Hannibal, whose unerring tact had seen in all the courtesies of the Ceutrones nothing but a scheme to secure at once immunity for their territory and a rich spoil, had in expectation of such an attack sent forward the baggage and cavalry, and covered the march with all his infantry. By this means he frustrated the design of the enemy, although he could not prevent them from moving along the mountain slopes parallel to the march of the infantry, and inflicting very considerable loss by hurling or rolling down stones upon it. At the "white stone" (still called *la roche blanche*), a high isolated chalk cliff standing at the foot of the St. Bernard and commanding the ascent to it, Hannibal encamped with his infantry, to cover the march of the horses and sumpter animals laboriously climbing upward throughout the whole night; and amidst continual and very bloody conflicts he at length on the following day reached the summit of the pass.

There, on the sheltered table-land which spreads to the extent of two and a half miles round a little lake, the source of the Doria, he allowed the army to rest. Despondency had begun to seize the minds of the soldiers. The paths that were becoming ever more difficult, the provisions failing, the marching through defiles exposed to the constant attacks of foes whom they could not reach, the sorely thinned ranks, the hopeless situation of the stragglers and the wounded, the object which appeared chimerical to all save the enthusiastic leader and his immediate staff—all these things began to tell even on the African and Spanish veterans. But the confidence of the general remained ever the same; numerous stragglers rejoined the ranks; the friendly Gauls were near; the watershed was reached, and the view of the descending path, so gladdening to the mountain-pilgrim, opened up: after a brief repose they prepared with renewed courage for the last and most difficult undertaking,—the downward march. In it the army was not materially annoyed by the enemy; but the advanced season—it was already the beginning of September—occasioned troubles in the descent, equal to those which had been occasioned in the ascent by the attacks of the barbarians. On the steep and slippery mountain-slope along the Doria, where the recently fallen snow had concealed and obliterated the paths, men and animals went astray and slipped, and were precipitated into the chasms. In fact, towards the end of the first day's march they reached a portion of the path about two hundred paces in length, on which avalanches are constantly descending from the precipices of the Cramont that overhang it, and where in cold summers snow lies throughout the year. The infantry crossed; but the horses and elephants were unable to pass over the smooth masses of ice, on which there lay but a thin covering of freshly fallen snow, and the general encamped above the difficult spot with the baggage, the cavalry, and the elephants. On the following day the horsemen, by zealous exertion in entrenching, prepared a path for horses and beasts of burden; but it was not until after a further labour of three days with constant reliefs, that the half-famished elephants could at length be conducted over. In this way the whole army was after a delay of four days once more united; and after a further three days' march through the valley of the Doria, which was ever widening and displaying greater fertility, and whose inhabitants the Salassi, clients of the Insurbes, hailed in the Carthaginians their allies and deliverers, the army arrived about the middle of September in the plain of Ivrea, where the exhausted troops were quartered in the villages, that by good nursing and a fortnight's repose they might recruit from their unparalleled hardships. Had the Romans placed a corps, as they might have done, of 30,000 men thoroughly fresh and ready for action somewhere near Turin, and immediately forced on a battle, the prospects of Hannibal's great plan would have been very dubious; fortunately for him, once more, they were not where they should have been, and they did not disturb the troops of the enemy in the repose which was so greatly needed.[1]

The object was attained, but at a heavy cost. Of the 50,000 veteran infantry and the 9000 cavalry, which the army had numbered at the crossing of the Pyrenees, more than half had been sacrificed in the conflicts, the marches, and the passages of the rivers. Hannibal now, according to his own statement, numbered not more than 20,000 infantry—of whom three-fifths were Libyans and two-fifths Spaniards—and 6000 cavalry, part of whom were dismounted: the comparatively small loss

[1] The much discussed questions of topography, connected with this celebrated expedition, may be regarded as cleared up and substantially solved by the masterly investigations of Messrs. Wickham and Cramer. Respecting the chronological questions, which likewise present difficulties, a few remarks may be exceptionally allowed to have a place here.
When Hannibal reached the summit of the St. Bernard, "the peaks were already beginning to be thickly covered with snow" (Pol. iii. 54); snow lay on the route (Pol. iii. 55), perhaps for the most part snow not freshly fallen, but proceeding from the fall of avalanches. At the St. Bernard winter begins about Michaelmas, and the falling of snow in September; when the Englishmen already mentioned crossed the mountain at the end of August, they found almost no snow on their road, but the slopes on both sides were covered with it. Hannibal thus appears to have arrived at the pass in the beginning of September; which is quite compatible with the statement that he arrived there "when the winter was already approaching"—for "συνάπτειν τὴν τῆς πλειάδος δύσιν" (Pol. iii. 54) does not mean anything more than this, least of all the day of the heliacal setting of the Pleiades (about 26th October); comp. Ideler, *Chronol.* i. 241.
If Hannibal reached Italy nine days later, and therefore about the middle of September, there is room for the events that occurred from that time up to the battle of the Trebia towards the end of December (περὶ χειμερινὰς τροπὰς, Pol. iii. 72), and in particular for the transporting of the army destined for Africa from Lilybaeum to Placentia. This hypothesis further suits the statement that the day of departure was announced at an assembly of the army ὑπὸ τὴν ἐαρινὴν ὥραν (Pol. iii. 34), and therefore towards the end of March, and that the march lasted five (or according to App. vii. 4, six) months. If Hannibal was thus at the St. Bernard in the beginning of September, he must have reached the Rhone at the beginning of August—for he spent thirty days in making his way from the Rhone thither—and in that case it is evident that Scipio, who embarked at the beginning of summer (Pol. iii. 41) and so at latest by the commencement of June, must have spent much time on the voyage or remained for a considerable period in singular inaction at Massilia.

of the latter proclaimed the excellence of the Numidian cavalry no less than the consideration of the general in making a sparing use of troops so select. A march of 526 miles or about 33 moderate days' marching—the continuance and termination of which were only rendered possible by unforeseen accidents and still more unforeseen blunders of the enemy, and which, while it was disturbed by no special misfortunes on a great scale that could not be anticipated, not only cost such sacrifices, but so fatigued and demoralised the army, that it needed a long rest in order to be again ready for action—is a military operation of doubtless value, and it may be questioned whether Hannibal himself regarded it as successful. Only in so speaking we may not pronounce an absolute censure on the general: we see well the defects of the plan of operations pursued by him, but we cannot determine whether he was in a position to foresee them— his route lay through an unknown land of barbarians—or whether any other plan, such as that of taking the coast road or of embarking at Cartagena or at Carthage, would have exposed him to fewer dangers. The cautious and masterly execution of the plan in its details at any rate deserves our admiration, and to whatever causes the results may have been due—whether it was due mainly to the favour of fortune, or mainly to the skill of the general—the grand idea of Hamilcar, that of taking up the conflict with Rome in Italy, was now realised. It was his genius that projected this expedition; and as the task of Stein and Scharnhorst was more difficult and nobler than that of York and Blucher, so the unerring tact of historical tradition has always dwelt on the last link in the great chain of preparatory steps, the passage of the Alps, with a greater admiration than on the battles of the Trasimene lake and of the plain of Cannae.

CHAPTER V

THE WAR UNDER HANNIBAL TO THE BATTLE OF CANNAE

THE appearance of the Carthaginian army on the Roman side of the Alps changed all at once the situation of affairs, and disconcerted the Roman plan of war. Of the two principal armies of the Romans, one had landed in Spain and was already engaged with the enemy there: it was no longer possible to recall it. The second, which was destined for Africa under the command of the consul Tiberius Sempronius, was fortunately still in Sicily: in this instance Roman delay for once proved useful. Of the two Carthaginian squadrons destined for Italy and Sicily, the first was dispersed by a storm, and some of its vessels were captured by the Syracusans near Messana; the second had endeavoured in vain to surprise Lilybaeum, and had thereafter been defeated in a naval engagement off that port. But the continuance of the enemy's squadrons in the Italian waters was so inconvenient, that the consul determined, before crossing to Africa, to occupy the small islands around Sicily, and to dislodge the Carthaginian fleet operating against Italy. The summer passed away in the conquest of Melita, in the chase after the enemy's squadron, which he expected to find at the Lipari islands while it had made a descent near Vibo (Monteleone) and pillaged the Bruttian coast, and, lastly, in gaining information as to a suitable spot for landing on the coast of Africa; so that the army and fleet were still at Lilybaeum, when orders arrived from the senate that they should return with all possible speed for the defence of their homes.

In this way, while the two great Roman armies, each in itself equal in numbers to that of Hannibal, remained at a great distance from the valley of the Po, the Romans were quite unprepared for an attack in that quarter. No doubt a Roman army was there, in consequence of an insurrection that had broken out among the Celts even before the arrival of the Carthaginian army. The founding of the two Roman strongholds of Placentia and Cremona, each of which received 6000 colonists, and more especially the preparations for the founding of Mutina in the

territory of the Boii, had already in the spring of $\frac{536}{218}$ driven
the Boii to revolt before the time concerted with Hannibal;
and the Insubres had immediately joined them. The colonists
already settled in the territory of Mutina, suddenly attacked,
took refuge in the town. The praetor Lucius Manlius, who held
the chief command at Ariminum, hastened with his single legion
to relieve the blockaded colonists; but he was surprised in the
woods, and no course was left to him after sustaining great loss
but to establish himself upon a hill and to submit to a siege
there on the part of the Boii, till a second legion sent from Rome
under the praetor Lucius Atilius succeeded in relieving army
and town, and in suppressing for the moment the Gaulish insurrection. This premature rising of the Boii on the one hand, by
delaying the departure of Scipio for Spain, essentially promoted
the plans of Hannibal; on the other hand, but for its occurrence
he would have found the valley of the Po entirely unoccupied,
except the fortresses. But the Roman corps, whose two
severely thinned legions did not number 20,000 soldiers, had
enough to do to keep the Celts in check, and did not think of
occupying the passes of the Alps. The Romans only learned
that the passes were threatened, when in August the consul
Publius Scipio returned without his army from Massilia to Italy,
and perhaps even then they gave little heed to the matter,
because, forsooth, the foolhardy attempt would be frustrated by
the Alps alone. Thus at the decisive hour and on the decisive
spot there was not even a Roman outpost. Hannibal had full
time to rest his army, to capture after a three days' siege the
capital of the Taurini which closed its gates against him, and to
induce or terrify into alliance with him all the Ligurian and
Celtic communities in the upper basin of the Po, before Scipio,
who had taken the command in the Po valley, encountered him.

Scipio, who, with an army considerably smaller and very
weak in cavalry, had the difficult task of preventing the advance
of the superior force of the enemy and of repressing the movements of insurrection which everywhere were spreading among
the Celts, had crossed the Po probably at Placentia, and marched
up the river to meet the enemy, while Hannibal after the capture
of Turin marched downwards to relieve the Insubres and Boii.
In the plain between the Ticino and the Sesia, not far from
Vercelli, the Roman cavalry, which had advanced with the light
infantry to make a reconnaissance in force, encountered the
Punic cavalry sent out for the like purpose, both led by the
generals in person. Scipio accepted battle when offered, not-

withstanding the superiority of the enemy; but his light
infantry, which was placed in front of the cavalry, dispersed
before the charge of the heavy cavalry of the enemy, and while
the latter engaged the masses of the Roman horsemen in front,
the light Numidian cavalry, after having pushed aside the broken
ranks of the enemy's infantry, took the Roman horsemen in flank
and rear. This decided the combat. The loss of the Romans
was very considerable. The consul himself, who made up as a
soldier for his deficiencies as a general, received a dangerous
wound, and owed his safety entirely to the devotion of his son
of seventeen, who, courageously dashing into the ranks of the
enemy, compelled his squadron to follow him and rescued his
father. Scipio, enlightened by this combat as to the strength of
the enemy, saw the error which he had committed in posting
himself, with a weaker army, in the plain with his back to the
river, and resolved to return to the right bank of the Po under
the eyes of his antagonist. As the operations became contracted
into a narrower space and his illusions regarding Roman in-
vincibility departed, he recovered the use of his considerable
military talents, which the adventurous boldness of his youthful
opponent's plans had for a moment paralysed. While Hannibal
was preparing for a pitched battle, Scipio by a rapidly projected
and steadily executed march succeeded in reaching the right
bank of the river which in an evil hour he had abandoned, and
broke down the bridge over the Po behind his army; the Roman
detachment of 600 men charged to cover the process of destruction were, however, intercepted and made prisoners. But as
the upper course of the river was in the hands of Hannibal, he
could not be prevented from marching up the stream, crossing
on a bridge of boats, and in a few days confronting the Roman
army on the right bank. The latter had taken a position in the
plain in front of Placentia; but the mutiny of a Celtic division
in the Roman camp, and the Gallic insurrection breaking out
afresh all around, compelled the consul to evacuate the plain
and to post himself on the hills behind the Trebia. This was
accomplished without much loss, because the Numidian horsemen sent in pursuit lost their time in plundering, and setting
fire to, the abandoned camp. In this strong position, with his
left wing resting on the Apennines, his right on the Po and the
fortress of Placentia, and covered in front by the Trebia—no
inconsiderable stream at that season—Scipio was unable to save
the rich stores of Clastidium (Casteggio), from which in this
position he was cut off by the army of the enemy; nor was he

able to avert the insurrectionary movement on the part of almost all the Gallic cantons, excepting the Cenomani who were friendly to Rome; but he completely checked the progress of Hannibal, and compelled him to pitch his camp opposite to that of the Romans. Moreover, the position taken up by Scipio, and the circumstance of the Cenomani threatening the borders of the Insubres, hindered the main body of the Gallic insurgents from directly joining the enemy, and gave to the second Roman army, which meanwhile had arrived at Ariminum from Lilybaeum, the opportunity of reaching Placentia through the midst of the insurgent country without material hindrance, and of uniting itself with the army of the Po.

Scipio had thus solved his difficult task brilliantly and completely. The Roman army, now close on 40,000 strong, and though not a match for its antagonist in cavalry, at least equal in infantry, had simply to remain in its existing position, in order to compel the enemy either to attempt in the winter season the passage of the river and an attack upon the camp, or to suspend his advance and to test the fickle temper of the Gauls by the burden of winter quarters. Clear, however, as this was, it was no less clear that it was now December, and that under the course proposed the victory might perhaps be gained by Rome, but would not be gained by the consul Tiberius Sempronius, who held the sole command in consequence of Scipio's wound, and whose year of office expired in a few months. Hannibal knew the man, and neglected no means of alluring him to fight. The Celtic villages that had remained faithful to the Romans were cruelly laid waste, and, when this brought on a conflict between the cavalry, Hannibal allowed his opponents to boast of the victory. Soon thereafter on a raw rainy day a general engagement came on, unlooked for by the Romans. From the earliest hour of the morning the Roman light troops had been skirmishing with the light cavalry of the enemy; the latter slowly retreated, and the Romans eagerly pursued it through the deeply swollen Trebia, so as to follow up the advantage which they had gained. Suddenly the cavalry halted; the Roman vanguard found itself face to face with the army of Hannibal drawn up for battle on a field chosen by himself; it was lost, unless the main body should cross the stream with all speed to its support. Hungry, weary, and wet, the Romans came on and hastened to form in order of battle, the cavalry, as usual, on the wings, the infantry in the centre. The light troops, who formed the vanguard on both sides, began the combat: but the Romans had already almost exhausted their missiles against the cavalry, and immediately gave way. In like manner the cavalry gave way on the wings, hard pressed by the elephants in front, and outflanked right and left by the far more numerous Carthaginian horse. But the Roman infantry proved itself worthy of its name: at the beginning of the battle it fought with very decided superiority against the infantry of the enemy, and even when the repulse of the Roman horse allowed the enemy's cavalry and light-armed troops to turn their attacks against the Roman infantry, the latter, although ceasing to advance, obstinately maintained its ground. At this stage a select Carthaginian band of 2000 men, half infantry, half cavalry, under the leadership of Mago, Hannibal's youngest brother, suddenly emerged from an ambush in the rear of the Roman army, and fell upon the densely entangled masses. The wings of the army and the rear ranks of the Roman centre were broken up and scattered by this attack, while the first division, 10,000 men strong, in compact array broke through the Carthaginian line, and made a passage for itself obliquely through the midst of the enemy, inflicting great loss on the opposing infantry and more especially on the Gallic insurgents. This brave body, pursued but feebly, thus reached Placentia. The remaining mass was for the most part slaughtered by the elephants and light troops of the enemy in attempting to cross the river: only part of the cavalry and some divisions of infantry were able, by wading through the river, to gain the camp whither the Carthaginians did not follow them, and thus they too reached Placentia.[1]

---

[1] Polybius's account of the battle on the Trebia is quite clear. If Placentia lay on the right bank of the Trebia where it falls into the Po, and if the battle was fought on the left bank, while the Roman encampment was pitched upon the right—both of which points have been disputed, but are nevertheless indisputable—the Roman soldiers must certainly have passed the Trebia in order to gain Placentia as well as to gain the camp. But those who crossed to the camp must have made their way through the disorganised portions of their own army and through the corps of the enemy that had gone round to their rear, and must then have crossed the river almost in hand to hand combat with the enemy. On the other hand the passage near Placentia was accomplished after the pursuit had slackened; the corps was several miles distant from the field of battle, and had arrived within reach of a Roman fortress; it may even have been the case, although it cannot be proved, that a bridge led over the Trebia at that point, and that the *tête de pont* on the other bank was occupied by the garrison of Placentia. It is evident that the first passage was just as difficult as the second was easy, and therefore with good reason Polybius, military judge as he was, merely says of the corps of 10,000, that in close columns it cut its way to Placentia (iii. 74, 6), without mentioning the passage of the river which in this case was unattended with difficulty.

The erroneousness of the view of Livy, which transfers the Phoenician

Few battles confer more honour on the Roman soldier than this on the Trebia, and few at the same time furnish graver impeachment of the general in command; although the candid judge will not forget that a commandership-in-chief expiring on a definite day was an unmilitary institution, and that figs cannot be reaped from thistles. The victory came to be costly even to the victors. Although the loss in the battle fell chiefly on the Celtic insurgents, yet a multitude of the veteran soldiers of Hannibal died afterwards from diseases engendered by that raw and wet winter day, and all the elephants perished except one.

The effect of this first victory of the invading army was, that the national insurrection now spread and assumed shape without hindrance throughout the Celtic territory. The remains of the Roman army of the Po threw themselves into the fortresses of Placentia and Cremona: completely cut off from home, they were obliged to procure their supplies by way of the river. The consul Tiberius Sempronius only escaped, as if by miracle, from being taken prisoner, when with a weak escort of cavalry he went to Rome on account of the elections. Hannibal, who would not hazard the health of his troops by further marches at that inclement season, bivouacked for the winter where he was; and, as a serious attempt on the larger fortresses would have led to no result, contented himself with annoying the enemy by attacks on the river-port of Placentia and other minor Roman positions. He employed himself mainly in organising the Gallic insurrection: more than 60,000 foot soldiers and 4000 horsemen from the Celts are said to have joined his army.

No extraordinary exertions were made in Rome for the campaign of $\frac{537}{217}$. The senate thought, and not unreasonably, that, despite the lost battle, their position was by no means fraught with serious danger. Besides the coast-garrisons, which were despatched to Sardinia, Sicily, and Tarentum, and the reinforcements which were sent to Spain, the two new consuls Gaius Flaminius and Gnaeus Servilius obtained only as many men as were necessary to restore the four legions to their full complement; additions were made to the strength of the cavalry alone. The consuls had to protect the northern frontier, and stationed themselves accordingly on the two highways which led from Rome to the north, the western of which at that time terminated

---

camp to the right, the Roman to the left bank of the Trebia, has lately been repeatedly pointed out. We may only further mention, that the site of Clastidium, near the modern Casteggio, has now been established by inscriptions (*Orelli—Henzen*, 5117).

at Arretium, and the eastern at Ariminum; Gaius Flaminius
occupied the former, Gnaeus Servilius the latter. There they
ordered the troops from the fortresses on the Po to join them,
probably by water, and awaited the commencement of the
favourable season, when they proposed to occupy in the defensive the passes of the Apennines, and then, resuming offensive
operations, to descend into the valley of the Po and effect a
junction somewhere near Placentia. But Hannibal by no
means intended to defend the valley of the Po. He knew Rome
better perhaps than the Romans knew it themselves, and was
very well aware how decidedly he was the weaker and continued
to be so notwithstanding the brilliant battle on the Trebia; he
knew too that his ultimate object, the humiliation of Rome, was
not to be wrung from the unbending Roman pride either by
terror or by surprise, but could only be gained by the complete
subjugation of the haughty city. It was clearly apparent that
the Italian federation was in political solidity and in military
resources infinitely superior to an adversary, who received only
precarious and irregular support from home, and who was in the
first instance dependent for aid in Italy solely on the vacillating
and capricious nation of the Celts; and that the Phoenician foot
soldier was, notwithstanding all the pains taken by Hannibal,
far inferior in point of tactics to the legionary, had been completely proved by the defensive movements of Scipio and the
brilliant retreat of the defeated infantry on the Trebia. From
this conviction flowed the two fundamental principles which
determined Hannibal's whole method of operations in Italy—
viz., that the war should be carried on, somewhat adventurously,
with constant changes in the plan and in the theatre of operations; and that its favourable issue could only be looked for
as the result of political and not of military successes—of the
gradual loosening and final breaking up of the Italian federation.
This mode of carrying on the war was necessary, because the
single element which Hannibal had to throw into the scale
against so many disadvantages—his military genius—only told
with its full weight, when he constantly foiled his opponents by
unexpected combinations; he was undone, if the war became
stationary. This aim was the aim dictated to him by right policy,
because, mighty conqueror though he was in battle, he saw very
clearly that on each occasion he vanquished the generals but not
the city, and that after each new battle the Romans remained
just as superior to the Carthaginians as he was personally
superior to the Roman commanders. That Hannibal even at

the height of his fortune never deceived himself on this point, is a fact more wonderful than his most wondrous battles.

It was these motives, and not the entreaties of the Gauls that he should spare their country—which would not have influenced him—that induced Hannibal now to forsake, as it were, his newly acquired basis of operations against Italy, and to transfer the scene of war to Italy itself. Before doing so he gave orders that all the prisoners should be brought before him. He ordered the Romans to be separated and loaded with chains as slaves—the statement that Hannibal put to death all the Romans capable of bearing arms, who here and elsewhere fell into his hands, is beyond doubt at least strongly exaggerated. On the other hand, all the Italian allies were released without ransom, and charged to report at home that Hannibal waged war not against Italy, but against Rome; that he promised to every Italian community the restoration of its ancient independence and its ancient boundaries; and that the deliverer was about to follow those whom he had set free, bringing release and revenge. So, when the winter ended, he started from the valley of the Po to search for a route through the difficult defiles of the Apennines. Gaius Flaminius, with the Etruscan army, was still for the moment at Arezzo, intending to move from that point towards Lucca in order to protect the vale of the Arno and the passes of the Apennines, so soon as the season should allow. But Hannibal anticipated him. The passage of the Apennines was accomplished without much difficulty, at a point as far west as possible or, in other words, as distant as possible from the enemy; but the marshy low grounds between the Serchio and the Arno were so flooded by the melting of the snow and the spring rains, that the army had to march four days in water, without finding any other dry spot for resting by night than was supplied by piling the baggage or by the sumpter animals that had fallen. The troops underwent unutterable sufferings, particularly the Gallic infantry, which marched behind the Carthaginians along tracks already rendered impassable: they murmured loudly and would undoubtedly have dispersed to a man, had not the Carthaginian cavalry under Mago, which brought up the rear, rendered flight impossible. The horses, assailed by a distemper in their hoofs, fell in heaps; various diseases decimated the soldiers; Hannibal himself lost an eye in consequence of ophthalmia.

But the object was attained. Hannibal encamped at Fiesole, while Gaius Flaminius was still waiting at Arezzo until the roads should become passable that he might blockade them. After the Roman defensive position had thus been turned, the best course for the consul, who might perhaps have been strong enough to defend the mountain passes but certainly was unable now to face Hannibal in the open field, would have been to wait till the second army, which had now become completely superfluous at Ariminum, should arrive. He himself, however, thought otherwise. He was a political party leader, raised to distinction by his efforts to limit the power of the senate; indignant at the government in consequence of the aristocratic intrigues concocted against him during his consulship; carried away, through a doubtless justifiable opposition to their beaten track of partisanship, into a scornful defiance of tradition and custom; intoxicated by a blind affection for the common people, and by quite as bitter a hatred towards the party of the nobles; and, in addition to all this, possessed with the fixed idea that he was a military genius. His campaign against the Insubres of $\frac{531}{223}$, which to unprejudiced judges only showed that good soldiers often repair the errors of bad generals (p. 75), was regarded by him and by his adherents as an irrefragable proof that the Romans had only to put Gaius Flaminius at the head of the army in order to make a speedy end of Hannibal. Talk of this sort had procured for him his second consulship, and hopes of this sort had now brought to his camp so great a multitude of unarmed followers eager for spoil, that their number, according to the assurance of sober historians, exceeded that of the legionaries. Hannibal based his plan in part on this circumstance. So far from attacking him, he marched past him, and caused the country all around to be pillaged by the Celts who thoroughly understood plundering, and by his numerous cavalry. The complaints and indignation of the multitude which had to submit to be plundered under the eyes of the hero who had promised to enrich them, and the protestation of the enemy that they did not believe him possessed of either the power or the resolution to undertake anything before the arrival of his colleague, could not but induce such a man to display his genius for strategy, and to give a sharp lesson to his inconsiderate and haughty foe.

No plan was ever more successful. In haste, the consul followed the line of march of the enemy, who passed by Arezzo and moved slowly through the rich valley of the Chiana towards Perugia. He overtook him in the district of Cortona, where Hannibal, accurately informed of his antagonist's march, had

had full time to select his field of battle—a narrow defile between two steep mountain walls, closed at its outlet by a high hill, and at its entrance by the Trasimene lake. With the flower of his infantry he barred the outlet; the light troops and the cavalry placed themselves in concealment on either side. The Roman columns advanced without hesitation into the unoccupied pass; the thick morning mist concealed from them the position of the enemy. As the head of the Roman line approached the hill, Hannibal gave the signal for battle; the cavalry, advancing behind the heights, closed the entrance of the pass, and at the same time the mist rolling away revealed the Phoenician arms everywhere along the crests on the right and left. There was no battle; it was a mere rout. Those that remained out of the defile were driven by the cavalry into the lake. The main body was annihilated in the pass itself almost without resistance, and most of them, including the consul himself, were cut down in the order of march. The head of the Roman column, formed of 6000 infantry, cut their way through the infantry of the enemy, and proved once more the irresistible might of the legions; but, cut off from the rest of the army and without knowledge of its fate, they marched on at random, were surrounded on the following day, on a hill which they had occupied, by a corps of Carthaginian cavalry, and—as the capitulation, which promised them a free retreat, was rejected by Hannibal —were all treated as prisoners of war. 15,000 Romans had fallen, and as many were captured; in other words, the army was annihilated. The slight Carthaginian loss—1500 men— again fell mainly upon the Gauls.[1] And, as if this were not enough, immediately after the battle on the Trasimene lake, the cavalry of the army of Ariminum under Gaius Centenius, 4000 strong, which Gnaeus Servilius had sent forward to the support of his colleague while he himself advanced by slow marches, was likewise surrounded by the Phoenician army, and partly slain, partly made prisoners. All Etruria was lost, and Hannibal might without hindrance march on Rome. The Romans prepared themselves for the worst; they broke down the bridges over the Tiber, and nominated Quintus Fabius Maximus dictator to repair the walls and conduct the defence, for which

---

[1] The date of the battle, 23rd June according to the uncorrected calendar, must, according to the rectified calendar, fall somewhere in April, since Quintus Fabius resigned his dictatorship, after six months, in the middle of autumn (Liv. xxii. 31, 7; 32, 1), and must therefore have entered upon it about the beginning of May. The confusion of the calendar (i. 455) in Rome was even at this period very great.

an army of reserve was formed. At the same time two new legions were summoned under arms in the room of those annihilated, and the fleet, which might become of importance in the event of a siege, was put in order.

But Hannibal was more farsighted than king Pyrrhus. He did not march on Rome; nor even against Gnaeus Servilius, an able general, who had with the help of the fortresses on the northern road preserved his army hitherto uninjured, and would perhaps have kept his antagonist at bay. Once more a movement occurred which was quite unexpected. Hannibal marched past the fortress of Spoletium, which he attempted in vain to surprise, through Umbria, fearfully devastated the territory of Picenum which was covered all over with Roman farmhouses, and halted on the shores of the Adriatic. The men and horses of his army had not yet recovered from the painful effects of their spring campaign; here he rested for a considerable time to allow his army to recruit its strength in a pleasant district and at a fine season of the year, and to reorganise his Libyan infantry after the Roman mode, the means for which were furnished to him by the mass of Roman arms among the spoil. From this point, moreover, he resumed his long interrupted communication with his native land, sending his messages of victory by water to Carthage. At length, when his army was sufficiently restored and had been adequately exercised in the use of the new arms, he broke up and marched slowly along the coast into southern Italy.

He had calculated correctly, when he chose this time for remodelling his infantry. The surprise of his antagonists, who were in constant expectation of an attack on the capital, allowed him at least four weeks of undisturbed leisure for the execution of the unprecedentedly bold experiment of changing completely his military system in the heart of a hostile country and with an army still comparatively small, and of attempting to oppose African legions to the invincible legions of Italy. But his hope that the confederacy would now begin to break up was not fulfilled. In this respect the Etruscans, who had carried on their last wars of independence mainly with Gallic mercenaries, were of less moment; the flower of the confederacy, particularly in a military point of view, consisted—next to the Latins—of the Sabellian communities, and with good reason Hannibal had now come into their neighbourhood. But one town after another closed its gates; not a single Italian community entered into alliance with the Phoenicians. This result was a great, in

CHAP. V.   The War under Hannibal   115

fact an all-important, point gained for Rome. Nevertheless it was felt in the capital that it would be imprudent to put the fidelity of their allies to such a test, without a Roman army to keep the field. The dictator Quintus Fabius combined the two supplementary legions formed in Rome with the army of Ariminum, and when Hannibal marched past the Roman fortress of Luceria towards Arpi, the Roman standards appeared on his right flank at Aeca. Their leader, however, pursued a different course from his predecessors. Quintus Fabius was a man advanced in years, of a deliberation and firmness, which to not a few seemed procrastination and obstinacy. Zealous in his reverence for the good old times, for the political omnipotence of the senate, and for the command of the burgomasters, he looked to a methodical prosecution of the war as—next to sacrifices and prayer—the means of saving the state. A political antagonist of Gaius Flaminius, and summoned to the head of affairs in virtue of the reaction against his foolish war-demagogism, Fabius departed for the camp just as firmly resolved to avoid a pitched battle at any price, as his predecessor had been determined at any price to fight one; he was without doubt convinced that the first elements of strategy would forbid Hannibal to advance so long as the Roman army confronted him intact, and that accordingly it would not be difficult to weaken by petty conflicts and gradually to starve out the enemy's army, dependent as it was on foraging for its supplies.

Hannibal, well served by his spies in Rome and in the Roman army, immediately learned how matters stood, and, as usual, adjusted the plan of his campaign in accordance with the individual character of the opposing leader. Passing the Roman army, he marched over the Apennines into the heart of Italy towards Beneventum, took the open town of Telesia on the boundary between Samnium and Campania, and thence turned against Capua, which was the most important of all the Italian cities dependent on Rome, and for that very reason had been oppressed and maltreated in a more vexatious manner than any other community had been by the Roman government. He had formed connections there, which led him to hope that the Campanians might revolt from the Roman alliance; but in this hope he was disappointed. So, retracing his steps, he took the road to Apulia. During all this march of the Carthaginian army the dictator had followed along the heights, and had condemned his soldiers to the melancholy task of looking on with arms in their hands, while the Numidian cavalry plundered the faithful allies far and wide, and the villages over all the plain rose in flames. At length he opened up to the exasperated Roman army the eagerly coveted prospect of attacking the enemy. When Hannibal had begun his retreat, Fabius intercepted his route near Casilinum (the modern Capua), by strongly garrisoning that town on the left bank of the Volturnus and occupying the heights that secured the right bank with his main army, while a division of 4000 men encamped on the road itself that led along by the river. But Hannibal ordered his light-armed troops to climb the heights which rose immediately alongside of the road, and to drive before them a number of oxen with lighted faggots on their horns, so that it seemed as if the Carthaginian army were thus marching off during the night by torchlight. The Roman division, which blocked up the road, imagining that they were evaded and that further covering of the road was superfluous, marched by a side movement to the same height. Along the road thus left free Hannibal then retreated with the bulk of his army, without encountering the enemy; next morning he without difficulty, but with severe loss to the Romans, disengaged and recalled his light troops. Hannibal then continued his march unopposed in a north-easterly direction; and by a widely-circuitous route, after traversing and laying under contribution the lands of the Hirpinians, Campanians, Samnites, Paelignians, and Frentanians without resistance, he arrived with rich booty and a full chest once more in the region of Luceria, just as the harvest there was about to begin. Nowhere in his extensive march had he met with active opposition, but nowhere had he found allies. Clearly perceiving that no course remained for him but to take up winter quarters in the open field, he began the difficult operation of collecting the winter supplies requisite for the army, by means of its own agency, from the fields of the enemy. For this purpose he had selected the broad and mostly flat district of northern Apulia, which furnished grain and grass in abundance, and which could be completely commanded by his excellent cavalry. An entrenched camp was constructed at Gerunium, twenty-five miles to the north of Luceria. Two-thirds of the army were daily despatched from it to bring in the stores, while Hannibal with the remainder took up a position to protect the camp and the detachments sent out.

The master of the horse, Marcus Minucius, who held temporary command in the Roman camp during the absence of the dictator, deemed this a suitable opportunity for approaching the enemy more closely, and formed a camp in the territory of the Larinates; where on the one hand by his mere presence he checked the sending out of detachments and thereby hindered the provisioning of the enemy's army, and on the other hand, in the series of successful conflicts in which his troops encountered isolated Phoenician divisions and even Hannibal himself, drove the enemy from their advanced positions and compelled them to concentrate themselves at Gerunium. On the news of these successes, which of course lost nothing in the telling, reaching the capital, the storm broke forth against Quintus Fabius. It was not altogether unwarranted. Prudent as it was on the part of Rome to abide by the defensive and to expect success mainly from the cutting off of the enemy's means of subsistence, there was yet something strange in a system of defence and of starving out, under which the enemy had laid waste all central Italy without opposition beneath the eyes of a Roman army of equal numbers, and had provisioned themselves sufficiently for the winter by an organised method of foraging on the greatest scale. Publius Scipio, when he commanded on the Po, had not adopted this view of a defensive attitude, and the attempt of his successor to imitate him at Casilinum had failed in such a way as to afford a copious fund of ridicule to the scoffers of the city. It was wonderful that the Italian communities had not wavered, when Hannibal so palpably showed them the superiority of the Phoenicians and the nullity of Roman aid; but how long could they be expected to bear the burden of a double war, and to allow themselves to be plundered under the very eyes of the Roman troops and of their own contingents? Finally, it could not be alleged that the condition of the Roman army compelled the general to adopt this mode of warfare. It was composed, indeed, in part of militia called out for the emergency, but the flower of it consisted of the legions of Ariminum accustomed to service; and, so far from being discouraged by the last defeats, it was indignant at the far from honourable task which its general, "Hannibal's lackey," assigned to it, and it demanded with a loud voice to be led against the enemy. In the assemblies of the people the most violent invectives were directed against the obstinate old man. His political opponents, with the former praetor Marcus Terentius Varro at their head, laid hold of the quarrel—for the understanding of which we must not forget that the dictator was practically nominated by the senate, and the office was regarded as the palladium of the conservative party—and, in concert with the discontented soldiers and the possessors of the plundered estates, they carried an unconstitutional and absurd resolution of the people conferring the dictatorship, which was destined to obviate the evils of a divided command in times of danger, on Marcus Minucius,[1] who had been the lieutenant of Quintus Fabius, in the same way as on Fabius himself. Thus the Roman army, after its hazardous division into two separate corps had just been appropriately remedied, was once more divided; and not only so, but the two sections were placed under leaders who notoriously followed quite opposite plans of war. Quintus Fabius of course adhered more than ever to his methodical inaction; Marcus Minucius, compelled to justify in the field of battle his title of dictator, made a hasty attack with inadequate forces, and would have been annihilated had not his colleague averted greater misfortune by the seasonable interposition of a fresh corps. This last turn of matters justified in some measure the system of passive resistance. But in reality Hannibal had completely attained in this campaign all that arms could attain: not a single material operation had been frustrated either by his impetuous or by his deliberate opponent; and his foraging, though not unattended with difficulty, had yet been in the main so successful that the army passed the winter without complaint in the camp at Gerunium. It was not the *Cunctator* that saved Rome, but the compact structure of its confederacy and, not less perhaps, the national hatred with which the Phoenician hero was regarded by the men of the West.

Despite all its misfortunes, Roman pride stood no less unshaken than the Roman symmachy. The donations which were offered by king Hiero of Syracuse and the Greek cities in Italy for the next campaign—the war affected the latter less severely than the other Italian allies of Rome, for they sent no contingents to the land army—were declined with thanks; the chieftains of Illyria were informed that they could not be allowed to neglect payment of their tribute; and even the king of Macedonia was once more summoned to surrender Demetrius of Pharos. The majority of the senate, notwithstanding the semblance of legitimation which recent events had given to the Fabian system of delay, had firmly resolved to depart from a mode of war that was slowly but certainly ruining the state; if the popular dictator had failed in his more energetic method of

---

[1] The inscription of the gift devoted by the new dictator on account of his victory at Gerunium to Hercules Victor—*Hercolei sacrom M. Minuci(us) C. f. dictator vovit*—was found in the year 1862 at Rome, near S. Lorenzo.

warfare, they laid the blame of the failure, and not without reason, on the fact that they had adopted a half-measure and had given him too few troops. This error they determined to avoid and to equip an army, such as Rome had never sent out before—eight legions, each raised a fifth above the normal strength, and a corresponding number of allies—enough to crush an opponent who was not half so strong. Besides this, a legion under the praetor Lucius Postumius was destined for the valley of the Po, in order, if possible, to draw off the Celts serving in the army of Hannibal to their homes. These resolutions were judicious; everything depended on their coming to an equally judicious decision respecting the supreme command. The stiff carriage of Quintus Fabius, and the attacks of the demagogues which it provoked, had rendered the dictatorship and the senate generally more unpopular than ever: amongst the people, not without the connivance of their leaders, the foolish report circulated that the senate was intentionally prolonging the war. As, therefore, the nomination of a dictator was not to be thought of, the senate attempted to procure the election of suitable consuls; but this only had the effect of thoroughly rousing suspicion and obstinacy. With difficulty the senate carried one of its candidates, Lucius Aemilius Paullus, who had with judgment conducted the Illyrian war in $\frac{535}{219}$ (p. 70); an immense majority of the citizens assigned to him as colleague the candidate of the popular party, Marcus Terentius Varro, an incapable man, who was known only by his bitter opposition to the senate and more especially as the main author of the proposal to elect Marcus Minucius co-dictator, and who was recommended to the multitude solely by his humble birth and his coarse effrontery.

While these preparations for the next campaign were making in Rome, the war had already recommenced in Apulia. As soon as the season allowed him to leave his winter quarters, Hannibal, determining as usual the course of the war and assuming the offensive, set out from Gerunium in a southerly direction, and marching past Luceria crossed the Aufidus and took the citadel of Cannae (between Canosa and Barletta) which commanded the plain of Canusium, and had hitherto served the Romans as one of their principal magazines. The Roman army which, since Fabius had conformably to the constitution resigned his dictatorship in the middle of autumn, was now commanded by Gnaeus Servilius and Marcus Regulus, first as consuls then as proconsuls, had been unable to avert a loss which they could not but feel. On military as well as on political grounds, it became more than ever necessary to arrest the progress of Hannibal by a pitched battle. With definite orders to this effect from the senate, accordingly, the two new commanders-in-chief, Paullus and Varro, arrived in Apulia in the beginning of the summer of $\frac{538}{216}$. With the four new legions and a corresponding contingent of Italians which they brought up, the Roman army was raised to 80,000 infantry, half burgesses, half allies, and 6000 cavalry, of whom one-third were burgesses and two-thirds allies; whereas Hannibal's army numbered 10,000 cavalry, but only about 40,000 infantry. Hannibal wished nothing so much as a battle, not merely for the general reasons which we have explained above, but specially because the wide Apulian plain allowed him to develop the whole superiority of his cavalry, and because the providing supplies for his numerous army would soon, in spite of that excellent cavalry, be rendered very difficult by the proximity of an enemy twice as strong and resting on a chain of fortresses. The leaders of the Roman forces had also, as we have said, made up their minds on the general question of giving battle, and approached the enemy with that view; but the more sagacious of them saw the position of Hannibal, and were disposed accordingly to wait in the first instance and simply to station themselves in the vicinity of the enemy, so as to compel him to retire and accept battle on ground less favourable to him. With this view, confronting the Carthaginian position at Cannae on the right bank of the Aufidus, Paullus constructed two camps farther up the stream, the larger likewise on the right bank, the smaller, at a distance of fully a mile from it and not much more distant from the enemy's camp, on the left, so as to prevent the foraging of the enemy on both banks of the river. But such military pedantry was disapproved by the democratic consul—so much had been said about men taking the field not to set sentinels, but to use their swords—and he gave orders accordingly to attack the enemy, wherever and whenever they found him. According to an old custom foolishly retained, the decisive voice in the council of war alternated between the commanders-in-chief day by day; it was necessary therefore to submit, and to let the hero of the pavement have his way. Only one division of 10,000 men was left in the principal Roman camp, charged to capture the Carthaginian encampment during the conflict and thus to intercept the retreat of the enemy's army across the river. The bulk of the Roman army, at early dawn on the 2nd August according to the uncorrected, probably in June according to the correct, calendar, crossed the river which at this season was shallow and did not materially hamper the movements of the troops, and took up a position in line near the smaller Roman camp—which lay nearest to the enemy, intermediate between the larger Roman camp and that of the Carthaginians, and which had already been the scene of outpost skirmishes—in the wide plain stretching westward from Cannae on the left bank of the river. The Carthaginian army followed and likewise crossed the stream, on which rested the right Roman as well as the left Carthaginian wing. The Roman cavalry was stationed on the wings: the weaker portion consisting of burgesses, led by Paullus, on the right next the river; the stronger consisting of the allies, led by Varro, on the left towards the plain. In the centre was stationed the infantry in unusually deep files, under the command of the proconsul Gnaeus Servilius. Opposite to this centre Hannibal arranged his infantry in the form of a crescent, so that the Celtic and Iberian troops in their national armour formed the advanced centre, and the Libyans, armed after the Roman fashion, formed the retreating wings on either side. On the side next the river the whole heavy cavalry under Hasdrubal was stationed, on the side towards the plain the light Numidian horse. After a short skirmish between the light troops the whole line was soon engaged. Where the light cavalry of the Carthaginians fought against the heavy cavalry of Varro, the conflict was prolonged, amidst constant charges of the Numidians, without decisive result. In the centre, on the other hand, the legions completely overthrew the Spanish and Gallic troops that first encountered them; eagerly the victors pressed on and followed up their advantage. But meanwhile, on the right wing, fortune had turned against the Romans. Hannibal had merely sought to occupy the left cavalry wing of the enemy, that he might bring Hasdrubal with the whole regular cavalry to bear against the weaker right and to overthrow it first. After a brave resistance, the Roman horse gave way, and those that were not cut down were chased across the river and scattered in the plain; Paullus, wounded, rode to the centre to avert or, if not, to share the fate of the legions. These, in order the better to follow up the victory over the advanced infantry of the enemy, had changed their front disposition into a column of attack, which, in the shape of a wedge, penetrated the enemy's centre. In this position they were warmly assailed on both sides by the Libyan infantry wheeling in upon them right and left, and a portion of them were compelled to halt in order to defend themselves against the flank attack; by this means their advance was checked, and the mass of infantry, which was already too closely crowded, now had no longer room to develop itself at all. Meanwhile Hasdrubal, after having completed the defeat of the wing of Paullus, had collected and arranged his cavalry anew and led them behind the enemy's centre against the wing of Varro. His Italian cavalry, already sufficiently occupied with the Numidians, was rapidly scattered before the double attack, and Hasdrubal, leaving the pursuit of the fugitives to the Numidians, rallied his squadrons for the third time, to lead them against the rear of the Roman infantry. This last charge proved decisive. Flight was impossible, and no quarter was given. Never, perhaps, was an army of such size annihilated on the field of battle so completely, and with so little loss to its antagonist, as was the Roman army at Cannae. Hannibal had lost not quite 6000 men, and two-thirds of that loss fell upon the Celts who sustained the first shock of the legions. On the other hand, of the 76,000 Romans who had taken their places in line of battle 70,000 covered the field, amongst whom were the consul Lucius Paullus, the proconsul Gnaeus Servilius, two-thirds of the staff-officers, and eighty men of senatorial rank. The consul Marcus Varro was saved solely by his quick resolution and his good steed, reached Venusia, and was not ashamed to survive the disaster. The garrison also of the Roman camp, 10,000 strong, were for the most part made prisoners of war; only a few thousand men, partly of these troops, partly of the line, escaped to Canusium. Nay, as if in this year Rome was to be altogether ruined, before its close the legion sent to Gaul fell into an ambush, and was, with its general Lucius Posthumius who was nominated as consul for the next year, totally destroyed by the Gauls.

This unexampled success appeared at length to mature the great political combination, for the sake of which Hannibal had come to Italy. He had indeed based his plan primarily upon his army; but with accurate knowledge of the power opposed to him he designed that army to be merely the vanguard, in support of which the powers of the west and east were gradually to unite their forces, so as to prepare destruction for the proud city. That support however, which seemed the most secure, namely the sending of reinforcements from Spain, had been frustrated by the boldness and firmness of the Roman general sent thither, Gnaeus Scipio. After Hannibal's passage of the Rhone Scipio had sailed for Emporiae, and had made himself master first of the coast between the Pyrenees and the Ebro, and then, after conquering Hanno, of the interior also ($\frac{536}{218}$). In the following year ($\frac{537}{217}$) he had completely defeated the Carthaginian fleet at the mouth of the Ebro, and after his brother Publius, the brave defender of the valley of the Po, had joined him with a reinforcement of 8000 men, he had even crossed the Ebro, and advanced as far as Saguntum. Hasdrubal had indeed in the succeeding year ($\frac{538}{216}$), after obtaining reinforcements from Africa, made an attempt in accordance with his brother's orders to conduct an army over the Pyrenees; but the Scipios opposed his passage of the Ebro, and totally defeated him, nearly at the same time that Hannibal conquered at Cannae. The powerful tribe of the Celtiberians and numerous other Spanish tribes had joined the Scipios; they commanded the sea, the passes of the Pyrenees, and, by means of the trusty Massiliots, the Gallic coast also. Now therefore support to Hannibal was less than ever to be looked for from Spain.

On the part of Carthage as much had hitherto been done in support of her general in Italy as could be expected. Phoenician squadrons threatened the coasts of Italy and of the Roman islands and guarded Africa from a Roman landing, and there the matter ended. More substantial assistance was prevented not so much by the uncertainty as to where Hannibal was to be found and the want of a port of disembarkation in Italy, as by the fact that for many years the Spanish army had been accustomed to be self-sustaining, and above all by the murmurs of the peace party. Hannibal severely felt the consequences of this unpardonable inaction; in spite of all his saving of his money and of the soldiers whom he had brought with him, his chests were gradually emptied, the pay fell into arrear, and the ranks of his veterans began to thin. But now the news of the victory of Cannae reduced even the factious opposition at home to silence. The Carthaginian senate resolved to place at the disposal of the general considerable assistance in money and men, partly from Africa, partly from Spain, including 4000 Numidian horse and 40 elephants, and to prosecute the war with energy in Spain as well as in Italy.

The long-discussed offensive alliance between Carthage and Macedonia had been delayed, first by the sudden death of Antigonus, and then by the indecision of his successor Philip and the unseasonable war waged by him and his Hellenic allies against the Aetolians ($\frac{534-537}{220-217}$). It was only now, after the battle of Cannae, that Demetrius of Pharos found Philip disposed to listen to his proposal to cede to Macedonia his Illyrian possessions—which it was necessary, no doubt, to wrest in the first place from the Romans—and it was only now that the court of Pella came to terms with Carthage. Macedonia undertook to land an invading army on the east coast of Italy, in return for which she received an assurance that the Roman possessions in Epirus should be restored to her.

In Sicily king Hiero had during the years of peace maintained a policy of neutrality, so far as he could do so with safety, and he had shown a disposition to accommodate the Carthaginians during the perilous crises after the peace with Rome, particularly by sending supplies of corn. There is no doubt that he saw with the utmost regret a renewed breach between Carthage and Rome; but he had no power to avert it, and when it occurred he adhered with well-considered fidelity to Rome. But soon afterwards (in the autumn of $\frac{538}{216}$) death removed the old man after a reign of fifty-four years. The grandson and successor of the prudent veteran, the young and incapable Hieronymus, entered at once into negotiations with the Carthaginian diplomatists; and, as they made no difficulty in consenting to secure to him by treaty, first, Sicily as far as the old Carthagino-Sicilian frontier, and then, when he rose in the arrogance of his demands, the possession even of the whole island, he entered into alliance with Carthage, and ordered the Syracusan fleet to unite with the Carthaginian which had come to threaten Syracuse. The position of the Roman fleet at Lilybaeum, which already had to deal with a second Carthaginian squadron stationed near the Aegates, became all at once very critical, while at the same time the force that was in readiness at Rome for embarkation to Sicily had, in consequence of the defeat at Cannae, to be diverted to other and more urgent objects.

Above all came the decisive fact, that now at length the fabric of the Roman confederacy began to be unhinged, after it had survived unshaken the shocks of two severe years of war. There passed over to the side of Hannibal Arpi in Apulia, and Uzentum in Messapia, two old towns which had been greatly injured by the Roman colonies of Luceria and Brundisium; all the towns of the Bruttii—who took the lead—with the exception of the Petelini and the Consentini who had to be besieged before yielding; the greater portion of the Lucanians; the Picentes transplanted into the region of Salernum; the Hirpini; the Samnites with the exception of the Pentri; lastly and chiefly, Capua the second city of Italy, which was able to bring into the

field 30,000 infantry and 4000 horse, and whose secession determined that of the neighbouring towns Atella and Calatia. The
aristocratic party, indeed, attached by many ties to the interest
of Rome everywhere, and more especially in Capua, very
earnestly opposed this change of sides, and the obstinate internal
conflicts which arose regarding it diminished not a little the
advantage which Hannibal derived from these accessions. He
found himself obliged, for instance, to have one of the leaders of
the aristocratic party in Capua, Decius Magius, who even after
the entrance of the Phoenicians obstinately contended for the
Roman alliance, seized and conveyed to Carthage; thus furnishing a demonstration, very inconvenient for himself, of the small
value of the liberty and sovereignty which had just been
solemnly guaranteed to the Campanians by the Carthaginian
general. On the other hand, the south Italian Greeks adhered
to the Roman alliance—a result to which the Roman garrisons
no doubt contributed, but which was still more due to the very
decided dislike of the Hellenes towards the Phoenicians and
towards their new Lucanian and Bruttian allies, and their
attachment on the other hand to Rome, which had zealously
embraced every opportunity of displaying its Hellenism, and
had exhibited towards the Greeks in Italy an unwonted gentleness. Thus the Campanian Greeks, particularly Neapolis,
courageously withstood the attack of Hannibal in person: in
Magna Graecia Rhegium, Thurii, Metapontum, and Tarentum
did the same notwithstanding their very perilous position.
Croton and Locri on the other hand were partly carried by
storm, partly forced to capitulate, by the united Phoenicians
and Bruttians; and the citizens of Croton were conducted
to Locri, while Bruttian colonists occupied that important
naval station. The Latin colonies in southern Italy, such as
Brundisium, Venusia, Paestum, Cosa, and Cales, of course
maintained unshaken fidelity to Rome. They were the strongholds by which the conquerors held in check a foreign land,
settled on the soil of the surrounding population, and at feud
with their neighbours; they, too, would be the first to be affected,
if Hannibal should keep his word and restore to every Italian
community its ancient boundaries. This was likewise the case
with all central Italy, the earliest seat of the Roman rule, where
Latin manners and language already everywhere preponderated,
and the people felt themselves to be the comrades rather than
the subjects of their rulers. The opponents of Hannibal in the
Carthaginian senate did not fail to appeal to the fact that not

one Roman citizen or one Latin community had cast itself into the arms of Carthage. This groundwork of the Roman power could only be broken up, like the Cyclopean walls, stone by stone.

Such were the consequences of the day of Cannae, in which the flower of the soldiers and officers of the confederacy, a seventh of the whole number of Italians capable of bearing arms, perished. It was a cruel but righteous punishment for the grave political errors with which not merely some foolish or miserable individuals, but the Roman people themselves, were justly chargeable. A constitution adapted for a small country town was no longer suitable for a great power; it was simply impossible that the question as to the leadership of the armies of the city in such a war should be left year after year to be decided by the Pandora's box of the balloting-urn. As a fundamental revision of the constitution, if practicable at all, could not at any rate be undertaken now, no course was left but at once to commit the practical superintendence of the war, and in particular the bestowal and prolongation of the command, to the only authority which was in a position to undertake such a charge—the senate—and to reserve to the comitia the mere formality of confirmation. The brilliant successes of the Scipios in the difficult arena of Spanish warfare showed what might in this way be achieved. But political demagogism, which was already gnawing at the aristocratic foundations of the constitution, had seized on the management of the Italian war. The absurd accusation, that the nobles were conspiring with the enemy without, had made an impression on the " people." The heroes to whom political superstition looked for deliverance, Gaius Flaminius and Marcus Varro, both " new men " and friends of the people of the purest dye, had accordingly been empowered by the multitude itself to execute the plans of operations which, amidst the approbation of that multitude, they had explained in the Forum; and the results were the battles of the Trasimene lake and of Cannae. Duty required that the senate, which now of course understood its task better than when it recalled half the army of Regulus from Africa, should take into its hands the management of affairs, and should oppose such mischievous proceedings; but when the first of those two defeats had for the moment placed the rudder in its hands, it had hardly acted in a manner unbiassed by the interests of party. Little as Quintus Fabius deserves to be compared with these Roman Cleons, he too conducted the war not as a

mere military leader, but adhered to his obstinate attitude of
defence specially as the political opponent of Gaius Flaminius:
and in the treatment of the quarrel with his subordinate, he did
what he could to exasperate at a time when unity was needed.
The consequence was, first, that the most important instrument
which the wisdom of their ancestors had placed in the hands of
the senate for such uses—the dictatorship—broke down in his
hands; and, secondly—at least indirectly—the battle of Cannae.
But the headlong fall of the Roman power was owing not to the
fault of Quintus Fabius or Marcus Varro, but to the distrust
between the government and the governed—to the variance
between the senate and the burgesses. If the deliverance and
revival of the state were still possible, the work had to begin
with the re-establishment of unity and of confidence at home.
To have perceived this and, what is of more importance, to
have done it, and done it with an abstinence from all recrimina-
tions however justly provoked, constitutes the glorious and
imperishable honour of the Roman senate. When Varro—
alone of all the generals who had command in the battle—
returned to Rome, and the Roman senators met him at the gate
and thanked him that he had not despaired of the salvation of
his country, this was no empty phraseology concealing under
sounding words their real vexation, nor was it bitter mockery
over a poor wretch; it was the conclusion of peace between the
government and the governed. In presence of the gravity of
the time and the gravity of such an appeal, the chattering of
demagogues was silent; henceforth the only thought of the
Romans was how they might be able jointly to avert the common
peril. Quintus Fabius, whose tenacious courage at this decisive
moment was of more service to the state than all his feats of war,
and the other senators of note took the lead in every movement,
and restored to the citizens confidence in themselves and in the
future. The senate preserved its firm and unbending attitude,
while messengers from all sides hastened to Rome to report the
loss of battles, the secession of allies, the capture of posts and
magazines, and to ask reinforcements for the valley of the Po
and for Sicily at a time when Italy was abandoned and Rome
was almost without a garrison. Assemblages of the multitude
at the gates were forbidden; onlookers and women were sent to
their houses; the time of mourning for the fallen was restricted
to thirty days that the service of the gods of joy, from which
those clad in mourning attire were excluded, might not be too
long interrupted—for so great was the number of the fallen.

that there was scarcely a family which had not to lament its
dead. Meanwhile the remnant saved from the field of battle
had been assembled by two able military tribunes, Appius
Claudius and Publius Scipio the younger, at Canusium. The
latter managed, by his spirited bearing and by the brandished
swords of his faithful comrades, to change the views of those
noble young lords who, in indolent despair of the salvation of
their country, were thinking of escape beyond the sea. The
consul Marcus Varro joined them with a handful of men; about
two legions were gradually collected there; the senate gave
orders that they should be reorganised and degraded to serve in
disgrace and without pay. The incapable general was on a
suitable pretext recalled to Rome; the praetor Marcus Claudius
Marcellus, experienced in the Gallic wars, who had been destined
to depart for Sicily with the fleet from Ostia, assumed the chief
command. The utmost exertions were made to organise an
army capable of taking the field. The Latins were summoned
to render aid in the common peril. Rome itself set the example,
and called out all the men above boyhood, armed the debtor-
serfs and criminals, and even incorporated in the army eight
thousand slaves purchased by the state. As there was a want
of arms, they took the old spoils from the temples, and everywhere set the workshops and artisans in action. The senate
was completed, not as timid patriots urged, from the Latins,
but from the Roman burgesses who had the best title. Hannibal
offered a release of captives at the expense of the Roman
treasury; it was declined, and the Carthaginian envoy who had
arrived with the deputation of captives was not admitted into
the city: nothing should look as if the senate thought of peace.
Not only were the allies to be prevented from believing that
Rome was disposed to enter into negotiations, but even the
meanest citizen was to be made to understand that for him as
for all there was no peace, and that safety lay only in victory.

CHAPTER VI

THE WAR UNDER HANNIBAL FROM CANNAE TO ZAMA

THE aim of Hannibal in his expedition to Italy had been to break up the Italian confederacy: after three campaigns that aim had been attained, so far as it was at all attainable. It was clear that the Greek and Latin or Latinised communities of Italy, since they had not been shaken in their allegiance by the day of Cannae, would not yield to terror, but only to force; and the desperate courage with which even in southern Italy isolated little country towns, such as the Bruttian Petelia, maintained their forlorn defence against the Phoenicians, showed very plainly what awaited them among the Marsians and Latins. If Hannibal had expected to accomplish more in this way and to lead even the Latins against Rome, these hopes had proved vain. But it appears as if even in other respects the Italian coalition had by no means produced the results which Hannibal hoped for. Capua had at once stipulated that Hannibal should not have the right to call Campanian citizens compulsorily to arms; the citizens had not forgotten how Pyrrhus had acted in Tarentum, and they foolishly imagined that they should be able to withdraw at once from the Roman and from the Phoenician rule. Samnium and Luceria were no longer what they had been, when king Pyrrhus had thought of marching into Rome at the head of the Sabellian youth. Not only did the chain of Roman fortresses everywhere cut the nerves and sinews of the land, but the Roman rule continued for many years had rendered the inhabitants unused to arms—they furnished only a moderate contingent to the Roman armies—had appeased their ancient hatred, and had gained over a number of individuals everywhere to the interest of the ruling community. They joined the conqueror of the Romans, indeed, after the cause of Rome seemed fairly lost, but they felt that the question was no longer one of liberty; it was simply the exchange of an Italian for a Phoenician master, and it was not enthusiasm, but despair that threw the Sabellian communities into the arms of the victor. Under such circumstances the war in Italy flagged. Hannibal, who commanded the southern part of the peninsula as far up as the Volturnus and Garganus, and who could not simply abandon these lands again as he had abandoned that of the Celts, had now a frontier to protect, which could not be left uncovered with impunity; and for the purpose of defending the districts that he had gained against the fortresses which everywhere defied him and the armies advancing from the north, and at the same time of resuming the difficult offensive against central Italy, his forces—an army of about 40,000 men, without reckoning the Italian contingents—were far from sufficient.

Above all, he found that other antagonists were opposed to him. Taught by fearful experience, the Romans adopted a more judicious system of conducting the war, appointed none but experienced generals to the charge of their armies, and left them, at least where it was necessary, for a longer period in command. These generals were neither mere spectators of the enemy's movements from the mountains, nor did they throw themselves on their adversary wherever they found him; but, keeping the true mean between inaction and precipitation, they took up their positions in entrenched camps under the walls of fortresses, and accepted battle where victory would lead to results and defeat would not be destruction. The soul of this new mode of warfare was Marcus Claudius Marcellus. Instinctively, after the disastrous day of Cannae, the senate and people had turned their eyes to this brave and experienced officer, and entrusted him at once with the actual supreme command. He had received his training in the troublesome warfare against Hamilcar in Sicily, and had given brilliant evidence of his talents as a leader as well as of his personal valour in the last campaigns against the Celts. Although far above fifty, he still glowed with all the ardour of the most youthful soldier, and only a few years before this he had, as general, cut down the mounted general of the enemy (p. 75)—the first and only Roman consul who achieved that feat of arms. His life was consecrated to the two divinities, to whom he erected the splendid double temple at the Capene Gate—to Honour and to Valour; and, while the merit of rescuing Rome from the extremity of danger belonged to no single individual, but pertained to the Roman citizens collectively and pre-eminently to the senate, yet no single man contributed more towards the success of the common enterprise than Marcus Marcellus.

From the field of battle Hannibal had turned his steps to Campania. He knew Rome better than the simpletons, who in ancient and modern times have fancied that he might have terminated the struggle by a march on the enemy's capital. Modern warfare, it is true, decides a war on the field of battle; but in ancient times, when the system of attacking fortresses was far less developed than the system of defence, the most complete success in the field was on numberless occasions neutralised by the resistance of the walls of the capitals. The council and citizens of Carthage were not at all to be compared to the senate and people of Rome; the peril of Carthage after the first campaign of Regulus was infinitely more imminent than that of Rome after the battle of Cannae; yet Carthage had made a stand and been completely victorious. With what colour could it be expected that Rome would now deliver her keys to the victor, or even accept an equitable peace? Instead therefore of sacrificing practicable and important successes for the sake of such empty demonstrations, or losing time in the besieging of the two thousand Roman fugitives enclosed within the walls of Canusium, Hannibal had immediately proceeded to Capua before the Romans could throw in a garrison, and by his advance had induced this second city of Italy after long hesitation to join him. He probably hoped that, in possession of Capua, he would be able to seize one of the Campanian ports, where he might disembark the reinforcements which his great victories had wrung from the opposition at home.

When the Romans learned whither Hannibal had gone, they also left Apulia, where only a weak division was retained, and collected their remaining strength on the right bank of the Volturnus. With the two legions saved from Cannae Marcus Marcellus marched to Teanum Sidicinum, where he was joined by such troops as were at the moment disposable from Rome and Ostia, and advanced—while the dictator Marcus Junius slowly followed with the main army which had been hastily formed—as far as the Volturnus at Casilinum, with a view if possible to save Capua. That city he found already in the power of the enemy; but on the other hand the attempts of the enemy on Neapolis had been thwarted by the courageous resistance of the citizens, and the Romans were still in good time to throw a garrison into that important port. With equal fidelity the two other large coast towns, Cumae and Nuceria, adhered to Rome. In Nola the struggle between the popular and senatorial parties as to whether they should attach themselves to the Carthaginians or to the Romans, was still undecided. Informed that the former were gaining the superiority, Marcellus crossed the river at Caiatia, and marching along the heights of Suessula so as to evade the enemy's army, he reached Nola in sufficient time to hold it against the foes without and within. In a sally he even repulsed Hannibal in person with considerable loss; a success which, as the first defeat sustained by Hannibal, was of far more importance from its moral effect than from its material results. In Campania indeed, Nuceria, Acerrae, and, after an obstinate siege prolonged into the following year ($\frac{539}{215}$), Casilinum also, the key of the Volturnus, were conquered by Hannibal, and the severest punishments were inflicted on the senates of these towns which had adhered to Rome. But terror is a bad weapon of proselytism; the Romans succeeded, with comparatively trifling loss, in surmounting the perilous moment of their first weakness. The war in Campania came to a standstill; then winter came on, and Hannibal took up his quarters in Capua, the luxury of which was by no means fraught with benefit to his troops who for three years had not been under a roof. In the next year ($\frac{539}{215}$) the war acquired another aspect. The tried general Marcus Marcellus, Tiberius Sempronius Gracchus who had distinguished himself in the campaign of the previous year as master of the horse to the dictator, and the veteran Quintus Fabius Maximus, took—Marcellus as pro-consul, the two others as consuls—the command of the three Roman armies which were destined to surround Capua and Hannibal; Marcellus resting on Nola and Suessula, Maximus taking a position on the right bank of the Volturnus near Cales, and Gracchus on the coast near Liternum, covering Neapolis and Cumae. The Campanians, who marched to Hamae three miles from Cumae with a view to surprise the Cumaeans, were thoroughly defeated by Gracchus; Hannibal, who had appeared before Cumae to wipe out the stain, was himself worsted in a combat, and when the pitched battle offered by him was declined, retreated in ill humour to Capua. While the Romans in Campania thus not only maintained what they possessed, but also recovered Compulteria and other minor places, loud complaints were heard from the eastern allies of Hannibal. A Roman army under the praetor Marcus Valerius had taken position at Luceria, partly that it might, in connection with the Roman fleet, watch the east coast and the movements of the Macedonians; partly that it might, in connection with the army of Nola, levy contributions on the revolted Samnites, Lucanians, and Hirpinians. To give relief to these, Hannibal turned first against his most active opponent, Marcus Marcellus;

but the latter achieved under the walls of Nola no inconsiderable victory over the Phoenician army, and it was obliged to depart, without having cleared off the stain, from Campania for Arpi, in order at length to check the progress of the enemy's army in Apulia. Tiberius Gracchus followed it with his corps, while the two other Roman armies in Campania made arrangements to proceed next spring to the attack of Capua.

The clear vision of Hannibal had not been dazzled by his victories. It became every day more evident that he was not by their means gaining his object. Those rapid marches, that adventurous shifting of the war to and fro, to which Hannibal was mainly indebted for his successes, were at an end; the enemy had become wiser; further enterprises were rendered almost impossible by the inevitable necessity of defending what had been gained. The offensive was not to be thought of; the defensive was difficult, and threatened every year to become more so. He could not conceal from himself that the second half of his great task, the subjugation of the Latins and the conquest of Rome, could not be accomplished with his own forces and those of his Italian allies alone. Its accomplishment depended on the council at Carthage, on the head-quarters at Cartagena, on the courts of Pella and of Syracuse. If all the resources of Africa, Spain, Sicily, and Macedonia should now be put forth in earnest against the common enemy; if Lower Italy should become the great rendezvous for the armies and fleets of the west, south, and east; he might hope successfully to finish what the vanguard under his leadership had so brilliantly begun. The most natural and easy course would have been to send to him adequate support from home; and the Carthaginian state, which had remained almost unaffected by the war and had been raised from its deep decline and brought so close to complete victory by a small band of resolute patriots acting of their own accord and at their own risk, could beyond doubt have done this. That it would have been possible for a Phoenician fleet of any desired strength to effect a landing at Locri or Croton, especially as long as the port of Syracuse remained open to the Carthaginians and the fleet at Brundisium was kept in check by Macedonia, is demonstrated by the unopposed disembarkation at Locri of 4000 Africans, whom Bomilcar about this time brought over from Carthage to Hannibal, and still more by Hannibal's undisturbed embarkation, when all had been already lost. But after the first impression of the victory of Cannae had died away, the peace party in Carthage, which was at all times ready to purchase the downfall of its political opponents at the expense of its country, and which found faithful support in the shortsightedness and indolence of the citizens, refused the entreaties of the general for more decided support with the half simple, half malicious reply, that he in fact needed no help inasmuch as he was really victor; and thus contributed not much less than the Roman senate to save Rome. Hannibal, reared in the camp and a stranger to the machinery of civic factions, found no popular leader on whose support he could rely, such as his father had found in Hasdrubal; and he was obliged to seek abroad the means of saving his native country— means which it possessed in rich abundance at home.

For this purpose he might, at least with more prospect of success, reckon on the leaders of the Spanish patriot army, on the connections which he had formed in Syracuse, and on the intervention of Philip. Everything depended on bringing new forces into the field of war against Rome from Spain, Syracuse, or Macedonia; and for the attainment or for the prevention of this object wars were carried on in Spain, Sicily, and Greece. All of these were but means to an end, and historians have often erred in accounting them of greater importance. So far as the Romans were concerned, they were essentially defensive wars, the proper objects of which were to hold the passes of the Pyrenees, to detain the Macedonian army in Greece, to defend Messana and to prevent the communication between Italy and Sicily. Of course this defensive warfare was, wherever it was possible, carried on by offensive means; and, as circumstances favoured its expansion, it led to the expulsion of the Phoenicians from Spain and Sicily, and to the dissolution of Hannibal's alliances with Syracuse and with Philip. The Italian war in itself fell for the time being into the shade, and resolved itself into conflicts about fortresses and razzias, which had no decisive effect on the main issue. Nevertheless, so long as the Phoenicians retained the offensive at all, Italy always remained the central object of operations; and all efforts were directed towards, as all interest centred in, the removal or the continuance of Hannibal's isolation in southern Italy.

Had it been possible, immediately after the battle of Cannae, to bring into play all the resources on which Hannibal thought that he might reckon, he might have been tolerably certain of success. But the position of Hasdrubal at that time in Spain after the battle on the Ebro was so critical, that the supplies of money and men, which the victory of Cannae had roused the Carthaginian citizens to furnish, were for the most part expended on Spain, without producing much improvement in the position of affairs there. The Scipios transferred the theatre of war in the following campaign ($\frac{539}{215}$) from the Ebro to the Guadalquivir; and in Andalusia, in the very centre of the proper Carthaginian territory, they achieved at Illiturgi and Intibili two brilliant victories. In Sardinia communications entered into with the natives led the Carthaginians to hope that they should be able to master the island, which would have been of importance as an intermediate station between Spain and Italy. But Titus Manlius Torquatus, who was sent with a Roman army to Sardinia, completely destroyed the Carthaginian landing force, and reassured to the Romans the undisputed possession of the island ($\frac{539}{215}$). The legions from Cannae sent to Sicily held their ground in the north and east of the island with courage and success against the Carthaginians and Hieronymus; the latter met his death towards the end of $\frac{539}{215}$ by the hand of an assassin. Even in the case of Macedonia the ratification of the alliance was delayed, principally because the Macedonian envoys sent to Hannibal were captured on their homeward journey by the Roman vessels of war. In consequence the dreaded invasion of the east coast was temporarily suspended; and the Romans gained time to secure the very important station of Brundisium first by their fleet and then by the land army which before the arrival of Gracchus was employed for the protection of Apulia, and even to make preparations for an invasion of Macedonia in the event of war being declared. While in Italy the war thus came to a stand, out of Italy nothing was done on the part of Carthage to accelerate the movement of new armies or fleets towards the seat of war. The Romans, again, had everywhere with the greatest energy put themselves in a state of defence, and in that defensive attitude had fought for the most part with good results wherever the genius of Hannibal was absent. Thus the short-lived patriotism, which the victory of Cannae had awakened in Carthage, evaporated; the not inconsiderable forces which had been organised there were, either through factious opposition or through a useless attempt to conciliate the different opinions expressed in the council, so frittered away that they were nowhere of any real service, and but a very small portion arrived at the spot where they would have been most useful. At the close of $\frac{539}{215}$ the reflecting Roman statesman might feel that the urgency of the danger was past, and that the resistance so heroically begun had but to persevere in its exertions at all points in order to achieve its object.

First of all the war in Sicily was brought to an end. It had formed no part of Hannibal's original plan to excite a war on the island; but partly through accident, chiefly through the boyish vanity of the imprudent Hieronymus, a land war had broken out there, which—doubtless because Hannibal had not planned it—the Carthaginian council took up with special zeal. After Hieronymus was killed at the close of $\frac{533}{215}$, it seemed more than doubtful whether the citizens would persevere in the policy which he had pursued. If any city had reason to adhere to Rome, that city was Syracuse; for the victory of the Carthaginians over the Romans could not but give to the former, at any rate, the sovereignty of all Sicily, and no one could seriously believe that the promises made by Carthage to the Syracusans would be actually kept. Partly induced by this consideration, partly terrified by the threatening preparations of the Romans— who made every effort to bring once more under their complete control that important island, the bridge between Italy and Africa, and now for the campaign of $\frac{540}{214}$ sent their best general, Marcus Marcellus, to Sicily—the Syracusan citizens showed a disposition to obtain oblivion of the past by a timely return to the Roman alliance. But, amidst the dreadful confusion in the city—which after the death of Hieronymus was agitated alternately by endeavours to restore the ancient freedom of the people and by the *coups de main* of the numerous pretenders to the vacant throne, while the captains of the foreign mercenary troops were the real masters of the place—Hannibal's dexterous emissaries, Hippocrates and Epicydes, found opportunity to frustrate the projects of peace. They stirred up the multitude in the name of liberty; descriptions, exaggerated beyond measure, of the fearful punishment that the Romans were said to have inflicted on the Leontines who had just been re-conquered, awakened doubts even among the better portion of the citizens whether it was not too late to restore their old relations with Rome; while the numerous Roman deserters among the mercenaries, mostly runaway rowers from the fleet, were easily persuaded that a peace on the part of the citizens with Rome would be their death-warrant. So the chief magistrates were put to death, the armistice was broken, and Hippocrates and Epicydes undertook the government of the city. No course was left to the consul except to undertake a siege; but the skilful conduct of the defence, in which the Syracusan engineer Archimedes, celebrated as a learned mathematician, especially distinguished himself, compelled the Romans after besieging the city for eight months to convert the siege into a blockade by sea and land.

In the meanwhile Carthage, which hitherto had only supported the Syracusans with her fleets, on receiving news of their renewed rising in arms against the Romans had despatched a strong land army under Himilco to Sicily, which landed without interruption at Heraclea Minoa and immediately occupied the important town of Agrigentum. To effect a junction with Himilco, the bold and able Hippocrates marched forth from Syracuse with an army: the position of Marcellus between the garrison of Syracuse and the two hostile armies began to be critical. With the help of some reinforcements, however, which arrived from Italy, he maintained his ground in the island and continued the blockade of Syracuse. On the other hand, the greater portion of the small inland towns were driven into the arms of the Carthaginians not so much by the armies of the enemy, as by the fearful severity of the Roman proceedings in the island, more especially the slaughter of the citizens of Enna, suspected of a design to revolt, by the Roman garrison which was stationed there. In $\frac{542}{212}$ the besiegers of Syracuse during a festival in the city succeeded in scaling a portion of the extensive outer walls that had been deserted by the guard, and in penetrating into the suburbs which stretched from the " island " and the city proper on the shore (Achradina) towards the interior. The fortress of Euryalus, which, situated at the extreme western end of the suburbs, protected these and the principal road leading from the interior to Syracuse, was thus isolated and fell not long afterwards. When the siege of the city thus began to assume a turn favourable to the Romans, the two armies under Himilco and Hippocrates advanced to its relief, and attempted a simultaneous attack on the Roman position, combined with an attempt at landing on the part of the Carthaginian fleet and a sally of the Syracusan garrison; but the attack was repulsed on all sides, and the two relieving armies were obliged to content themselves with encamping before the city, in the low marshy grounds along the Anapus, which in the height of summer and autumn engender pestilences fatal to those that tarry in them. These pestilences had often saved the city, oftener even than the valour of its citizens; in the times of the first Dionysius, two Phoenician armies in the act of besieging the city had been in this way destroyed under its very walls. Now fate turned the special defence of the city into the means of its destruction; while the army of Marcellus quartered in the suburbs suffered but little, fevers desolated the Phoenician and Syracusan bivouacs. Hippocrates died; Himilco and most of the Africans died also; the survivors of the two armies, mostly natives of Sicily, dispersed into the neighbouring cities. The Carthaginians made a further attempt to save the city from the sea side; but the admiral Bomilcar withdrew when the Roman fleet offered him battle. Epicydes himself, who commanded in the city, now abandoned it as lost, and made his escape to Agrigentum. Syracuse would gladly have surrendered to the Romans; negotiations had already begun. But for the second time they were thwarted by the deserters: in another mutiny of the soldiers the chief magistrates and a number of respectable citizens were slain, and the government and the defence of the city were entrusted by the foreign troops to their captains. Marcellus now entered into a negotiation with one of these, which gave into his hands one of the two portions of the city that were still free, the "island;" upon which the citizens voluntarily opened to him the gates of Achradina also (in the autumn of $\frac{542}{213}$). If mercy was to be shown in any case, it might, even according to the far from laudable principles of Roman public law as to the treatment of perfidious communities, have been extended to a city which manifestly had not been at liberty to act for itself, and which had repeatedly made the most earnest attempts to get rid of the tyranny of the foreign soldiers. Nevertheless, not only did Marcellus stain his military honour by permitting a general pillage of the wealthy mercantile city, in the course of which Archimedes and many other citizens were put to death, but the Roman senate lent a deaf ear to the complaints which the Syracusans afterwards presented regarding the celebrated general, and neither returned to individuals their property nor restored to the city its freedom. Syracuse and the towns that had been previously dependent on it were classed among the communities tributary to Rome—Tauromenium and Neetum alone obtained the same privileges as Messana, while the territory of Leontini became Roman domain and its former proprietors Roman lessees—and no Syracusan citizen was henceforth allowed to reside in the "island," the portion of the city that commanded the harbour.

Sicily thus appeared lost to the Carthaginians; but the genius of Hannibal exercised even from a distance its influence there. He despatched to the Carthaginian army, which remained at

Agrigentum in perplexity and inaction under Hanno and Epicydes, a Libyan cavalry officer Mutines, who took the command of the Numidian cavalry, and with his flying squadrons, fanning into an open flame the bitter hatred which the despotic rule of the Romans had excited over all the island, commenced a guerilla warfare on the most extensive scale and with the happiest results; so that he even, when the Carthaginian and Roman armies met on the river Himera, sustained some conflicts with Marcellus himself successfully. The relations, however, which prevailed between Hannibal and the Carthaginian council, were here repeated on a small scale. The general appointed by the council pursued with jealous envy the officer sent by Hannibal, and insisted upon giving battle to the proconsul without Mutines and the Numidians. The wish of Hanno was carried out, and he was completely beaten. Mutines was not induced to deviate from his course; he maintained himself in the interior of the country, occupied several small towns, and was enabled by the not inconsiderable reinforcements which joined him from Carthage gradually to extend his operations. His successes were so brilliant, that at length the commander-in-chief, who could not otherwise prevent the cavalry officer from eclipsing him, deprived him summarily of the command of the light cavalry, and entrusted it to his own son. The Numidian, who had now for two years preserved the island for his Phoenician masters, had the measure of his patience exhausted by this treatment. He and his horsemen who refused to follow the younger Hanno entered into negotiations with the Roman general Marcus Valerius Laevinus, and delivered to him Agrigentum. Hanno escaped in a boat, and went to Carthage to report to his superiors the disgraceful high treason of Hannibal's officer; the Phoenician garrison in the town was put to death by the Romans, and the citizens were sold into slavery ($\frac{5 4 4}{2 1 0}$). To secure the island from such surprises as the landing of $\frac{5 4 0}{2 1 4}$, the city received a Roman colony; the old and glorious Akragas became the Roman fortress Agrigentum. After the whole of Sicily was thus subdued, the Romans exerted themselves to restore some sort of tranquillity and order to the distracted island. The pack of banditti that haunted the interior were driven together *en masse* and conveyed to Italy, that from their head-quarters at Rhegium they might burn and destroy in the territories of Hannibal's allies. The government did its utmost to promote the restoration of agriculture which had been totally neglected in the island. The Carthaginian council more than once talked of sending a fleet to Sicily and renewing the war there; but the project went no further.

Macedonia might have exercised an influence over the course of events more decisive than that of Syracuse. From the Eastern powers neither aid nor resistance was for the moment to be expected. Antiochus the Great, the natural ally of Philip, had, after the decisive victory of the Egyptians at Raphia in $\frac{537}{217}$, to deem himself fortunate in obtaining peace from the indolent Philopator on the basis of the *status quo ante*. The rivalry of the Lagidae and the constant apprehension of a renewed outbreak of the war on the one hand, and insurrections of pretenders in the interior and enterprises of all sorts in Asia Minor, Bactria, and the eastern satrapies on the other, prevented him from joining that great anti-Roman alliance which Hannibal had in view. The Egyptian court was decidedly on the side of Rome, with which it renewed alliance in $\frac{544}{210}$; but it was not to be expected of Ptolemy Philopator, that he would support Rome otherwise than by cargoes of corn. Accordingly there was nothing to prevent Greece and Macedonia from throwing their decisive weight into the great Italian struggle except their own discord; they might save the Hellenic name, if they had the self-control to stand by each other for but a few years against the common foe. Such sentiments doubtless were current in Greece. The prophetic saying of Agelaus of Naupactus, that he was afraid that the prize-fights in which the Hellenes now indulged at home might soon be over; his earnest warning to direct their eyes to the west, and not to allow a stronger power to impose on all the parties now contending a peace of equal servitude—such sayings had essentially contributed to bring about the peace between Philip and the Aetolians ($\frac{537}{217}$), and it was a significant proof of the tendency of that peace, that the Aetolian league immediately nominated Agelaus as its *strategus*.

National patriotism was bestirring itself in Greece as in Carthage: for a moment it seemed possible to kindle a national Hellenic war against Rome. But the general in such a crusade could only be Philip of Macedonia; and he lacked the enthusiasm and the faith in the nation, which alone could carry on such a war. He knew not how to solve the arduous problem of transforming himself from the oppressor into the champion of Greece. His very delay in the conclusion of the alliance with Hannibal damped the first and best zeal of the Greek patriots; and when he did enter into the conflict with Rome, his mode of conducting war was still less fitted to awaken sympathy and confidence.

His first attempt, which was made in the very year of the battle of Cannae ($\frac{538}{216}$), to obtain possession of the city of Apollonia, failed in a way almost ridiculous, for Philip turned back in all haste on receiving the totally groundless report that a Roman fleet was steering for the Adriatic. This took place before there was a formal breach with Rome; when the breach at length ensued, friend and foe expected a Macedonian landing in Lower Italy. Since $\frac{539}{215}$ a Roman fleet and army had been stationed at Brundisium to meet it; Philip, who was without vessels of war, was constructing a flotilla of light Illyrian barks to convey his army across. But when the endeavour had to be made in earnest, his courage failed to encounter the dreaded quinqueremes at sea; he broke the promise which he had given to his ally Hannibal to attempt a landing, and with the view of still doing something he resolved to make an attack on his own share of the spoil, the Roman possessions in Epirus ($\frac{540}{214}$). Nothing would have come of this even at the best; but the Romans, who well knew that offensive was preferable to defensive protection, were by no means content to remain—as Philip probably expected—spectators of the attack from the opposite shore. The Roman fleet conveyed a division of the army from Brundisium to Epirus; Oricum was recaptured from the king, a garrison was thrown into Apollonia, and the Macedonian camp was stormed. Thereupon Philip passed from partial action to total inaction, and notwithstanding all the complaints of Hannibal, who vainly tried to infuse into Philip's halting and shortsighted policy the energy of his own fire and decision, he allowed some years to elapse in armed inactivity.

Nor was Philip the first to renew the hostilities. The fall of Tarentum ($\frac{542}{212}$), by which Hannibal acquired an excellent port on the coast which was the most convenient for the landing of a Macedonian army, induced the Romans to parry the blow at a distance and to give the Macedonians so much employment at home that they could not think of an attempt on Italy. The national enthusiasm in Greece had of course evaporated long ago. With the help of the old antagonism to Macedonia, and of the fresh acts of imprudence and injustice of which Philip had been guilty, the Roman admiral Laevinus found no difficulty in organising against Macedonia a coalition of the intermediate and minor powers under the protectorate of Rome. It was headed by the Aetolians, at whose diet Laevinus had personally appeared and had gained its support by a promise of the Acarnanian territory which the Aetolians had long coveted. They concluded with Rome a modest agreement to rob the other Greeks of men and land on the joint account, so that the land should belong to the Aetolians, the men and movables to the Romans. They were joined by the states of anti-Macedonian, or rather primarily of anti-Achaean, tendencies in Greece proper; in Attica by Athens, in the Peloponnesus by Elis and Messene and especially by Sparta, the antiquated constitution of which had been just about this time overthrown by a daring soldier Machanidas, in order that he might exercise despotic power under the name of king Pelops, a minor, and might establish a government of military adventurers sustained by bands of mercenaries. The coalition was joined moreover by those steadfast antagonists of Macedonia, the chiefs of the half-barbarous Thracian and Illyrian tribes, and lastly by Attalus king of Pergamus, who followed out his own interest with sagacity and energy amidst the ruin of the two great Greek states which surrounded him, and had the acuteness even now to attach himself as a client to Rome when his assistance was still of some value.

It is neither agreeable nor necessary to follow the vicissitudes of this aimless struggle. Philip, although he was superior to each one of his opponents and repelled their attacks on all sides with energy and personal valour, yet consumed his time and strength in that profitless defensive. Now he had to turn against the Aetolians, who in concert with the Roman fleet annihilated the unfortunate Acarnanians and threatened Locris and Thessaly; now an invasion of barbarians summoned him to the northern provinces; now the Achaeans solicited his help against the predatory expeditions of Aetolians and Spartans; now king Attalus of Pergamus and the Roman admiral Publius Sulpicius with their combined fleets threatened the east coast or landed troops in Euboea. The want of a war fleet paralysed Philip in all his movements; he even went so far as to beg vessels of war from his ally Prusias of Bithynia, and even from Hannibal. It was only towards the close of the war that he resolved—as he should have done at first—to order the construction of 100 ships of war; of these however no use was made, if the order was executed at all. All who understood the position of Greece and sympathised with it lamented the unhappy war, in which the last energies of Greece preyed upon itself and the prosperity of the land was destroyed; repeatedly the commercial states, Rhodes, Chios, Mitylene, Byzantium, Athens, and even Egypt had attempted a mediation. In fact both

parties had an interest in coming to terms. The Aetolians, to
whom their Roman allies attached the chief importance, had,
like the Macedonians, suffered greatly by the war; especially
after the petty king of the Athamanes had been gained by Philip,
and the interior of Aetolia had thus been laid open to Macedonian incursions. Many Aetolians too had their eyes gradually opened to the dishonourable and pernicious part which the
Roman alliance condemned them to play; a cry of horror
pervaded the whole Greek nation when the Aetolians in concert
with the Romans sold whole bodies of Hellenic citizens, such as
those of Anticyra, Oreus, Dyme, and Aegina, into slavery. But
the Aetolians were no longer free; they ran a great risk if of
their own accord they concluded peace with Philip, and they
found the Romans by no means disposed, especially after the
favourable turn which matters were taking in Spain and in Italy,
to desist from a war, which on their part was carried on with
merely a few ships, and the burden and injury of which fell
mainly on the Aetolians. At length however the Aetolians
resolved to listen to the mediating cities: and, notwithstanding
the counter efforts of the Romans, a peace was arranged in the
winter of $\frac{548-549}{206-205}$ between the Greek powers. Aetolia had converted an over-powerful ally into a dangerous enemy; but the
Roman senate, which just at that time was summoning all the
resources of the exhausted state for the decisive expedition to
Africa, did not deem it a fitting moment to resent the breach of
the alliance. The war with Philip could not have been carried on
by the Romans without considerable exertions of their own
after the withdrawal of the Aetolians; and it appeared to them
more convenient to terminate it also by a peace, whereby the
state of things before the war was substantially restored and
Rome in particular retained all her possessions on the coast of
Epirus except the worthless territory of the Atintanes. Under
the circumstances Philip might deem himself fortunate in
obtaining such terms; but the fact proclaimed—what could not
indeed be longer concealed—that all the unspeakable misery
which ten years of a warfare waged with revolting inhumanity
had brought upon Greece had been endured in vain, and that
the grand and just combination, which Hannibal had projected
and all Greece had for a moment joined, was shattered irretrievably.

In Spain, where the spirit of Hamilcar and Hannibal was
powerful, the struggle was more severe. Its progress was
marked by the singular vicissitudes incidental to the peculiar

nature of the country and the habits of the people. The farmers and shepherds, who inhabited the beautiful valley of the Ebro and the luxuriantly fertile Andalusia as well as the rough intervening highland region traversed by numerous wooded mountain ranges, could easily be assembled in arms as a general levy; but it was difficult to lead them against the enemy or even to keep them together at all. The inhabitants of the towns could just as little be combined for steady and united action, obstinately as in each case they bade defiance to the oppressor behind their walls. They all appear to have made little distinction between the Romans and the Carthaginians; whether the troublesome guests who had established themselves in the valley of the Ebro, or those who had established themselves on the Guadalquivir, possessed a larger or smaller portion of the peninsula, was probably to the natives very much a matter of indifference; and for that reason the tenacity of partisanship so characteristic of Spain was but little prominent in this war, with isolated exceptions such as Saguntum on the Roman and Astapa on the Carthaginian side. But, as neither the Romans nor the Africans had brought with them sufficient forces of their own, the war necessarily became on both sides a struggle to gain partisans, which was decided rarely by solid attachment, more usually by fear, money, or accident, and which, when it seemed at an end, simply resolved itself into an endless series of fortress-sieges and guerilla conflicts, whence it soon revived with fresh fury. The armies were as shifting as the downs on the sea shore; on the spot where a hill stood yesterday, not a trace of it remains to-day. In general the superiority was on the side of the Romans, partly because they at first appeared in Spain as the deliverers of the land from Phoenician despotism, partly because of the fortunate selection of their leaders and of the stronger nucleus of trustworthy troops which these brought along with them. It is hardly possible, however, with the very imperfect and—in point of chronology especially—very confused accounts which have been handed down to us, to give a satisfactory view of a war so conducted.

The two lieutenant-governors of the Romans in the peninsula, Gnaeus and Publius Scipio—both of them, but especially Gnaeus, good generals and excellent administrators—accomplished their task with the most brilliant success. Not only was the barrier of the Pyrenees steadfastly maintained, and the attempt to re-establish the interrupted communication by land between the commander-in-chief of the enemy and his head-quarters sternly repulsed; not only had a Spanish New Rome been created, after the model of the Spanish New Carthage, by means of the comprehensive fortifications and harbour works of Tarraco, but the Roman armies had already in $\frac{539}{215}$ fought with success in Andalusia (p. 135). Their expedition thither was repeated in the following year ($\frac{540}{214}$) with still greater success. The Romans carried their arms almost to the Pillars of Hercules, extended their protectorate in South Spain, and lastly by regaining and restoring Saguntum secured for themselves an important station on the line from the Ebro to Cartagena, repaying at the same time as far as possible an old debt which the nation owed. While the Scipios thus almost dislodged the Carthaginians from Spain, they knew how to raise up a dangerous enemy to them in western Africa itself in the person of the powerful west African prince Syphax, ruling in the modern provinces of Oran and Algiers, who entered into connections with the Romans (about $\frac{541}{213}$). Had it been possible to supply him with a Roman army, great results might have been expected; but at that time not a man could be spared from Italy, and the Spanish army was too weak to be divided. Nevertheless the troops belonging to Syphax himself, trained and led by Roman officers, excited so serious a ferment among the Libyan subjects of Carthage that the lieutenant-commander of Spain and Africa, Hasdrubal Barca, went in person to Africa with the flower of his Spanish troops. His arrival in all likelihood gave another turn to the matter; king Gala—in what is now the province of Constantine —who had long been the rival of Syphax, declared for Carthage, and his brave son Massinissa defeated Syphax, and compelled him to make peace. Little more is related of this Libyan war than the story of the cruel vengeance which Carthage, according to her wont, inflicted on the rebels after the victory of Massinissa.

This turn of affairs in Africa had an important effect on the war in Spain. Hasdrubal was able once more to proceed to that country ($\frac{543}{211}$), whither he was soon followed by considerable reinforcements and by Massinissa himself. The Scipios, who during the absence of the enemy's general ($\frac{541}{213}$, $\frac{542}{212}$) had continued to plunder and to gain partisans in the Carthaginian territory, found themselves unexpectedly assailed by forces so superior that they were under the necessity of either retreating behind the Ebro or calling out the Spaniards. They chose the latter course, and took into their pay 20,000 Celtiberians; and then, in order the better to encounter the three armies of the enemy under Hasdrubal Barca, Hasdrubal the son of Gisgo, and

Mago, they divided their army and did not even keep their Roman troops together. They thus prepared the way for their own destruction. While Gnaeus with his corps, containing a third of the Roman and all the Spanish troops, lay encamped opposite to Hasdrubal Barca, the latter had no difficulty in inducing the Spaniards in the Roman army by means of a sum of money to withdraw—which perhaps to their free-lance ideas of morals did not even seem a breach of fidelity, seeing that they did not pass over to the enemies of their paymaster. Nothing was left to the Roman general but hastily to begin his retreat, in which the enemy closely followed him. Meanwhile the second Roman corps under Publius found itself vigorously assailed by the two other Phoenician armies under Hasdrubal son of Gisgo and Mago, and the daring squadrons of Massinissa's horse gave to the Carthaginians a decided advantage. The Roman camp was almost surrounded; if the Spanish auxiliaries already on the way should arrive, the Romans would be completely hemmed in. The bold resolve of the proconsul to encounter with his best troops the advancing Spaniards, before their appearance should fill up the gap in the blockade, ended unfortunately. The Romans indeed had at first the advantage; but the Numidian horse, who were rapidly despatched in pursuit, soon overtook them and prevented them both from following up the victory which they had already half gained, and from marching back, until the Phoenician infantry came up and at length the fall of the general converted the lost battle into a defeat. After Publius had thus fallen, Gnaeus, who slowly retreating had with difficulty defended himself against the one Carthaginian army, found himself suddenly assailed at once by three, and all retreat cut off by the Numidian cavalry. Hemmed in upon a bare hill, which did not even afford a possibility of pitching a camp, the whole corps were cut down or taken prisoners. As to the fate of the general himself no certain information was ever obtained. A small division alone was conducted by Gaius Marcius, an excellent officer of the school of Gnaeus, in safety to the other bank of the Ebro; and thither the legate Titus Fonteius also succeeded in bringing safely the portion of the corps of Publius that had been left in the camp; most even of the Roman garrisons scattered in the south of Spain were enabled to flee thither. In all Spain south of the Ebro the Phoenicians ruled without opposition; and the moment seemed not far distant, when the river would be crossed, the Pyrenees would be open, and the communication with Italy would be restored. But the emergency in the Roman camp called the right man to the command. The choice of the soldiers, passing over older and not incapable officers, summoned that Gaius Marcius to become leader of the army; and his dexterous management and, quite as much perhaps, the envy and discord among the three Carthaginian generals, wrested from these the further fruits of their important victory. Such of the Carthaginians as had crossed the river were driven back, and the line of the Ebro was held in the meanwhile, till Rome gained time to send a new army and a new general. Fortunately the turn of the war in Italy, where Capua had just fallen, allowed this to be done. A strong legion—12,000 men—arriving under the propraetor Gaius Claudius Nero, restored the balance of arms. An expedition to Andalusia in the following year ($\frac{544}{210}$) was most successful; Hasdrubal Barca was beset and surrounded, and escaped a capitulation only by ignoble stratagem and open perfidy. But Nero was not the right general for the Spanish war. He was an able officer, but a harsh, irritable, unpopular man, who had little skill in the art of renewing old connections or of forming new ones, or in taking advantage of the injustice and arrogance with which the Carthaginians after the death of the Scipios had treated friend and foe in Further Spain, and had exasperated all against them.

The senate, which formed a correct judgment as to the importance and the peculiar character of the Spanish war, and had learned from the Uticenses brought in as prisoners by the Roman fleet the great exertions which were making in Carthage to send Hasdrubal and Massinissa with a numerous army over the Pyrenees, resolved to despatch to Spain new reinforcements and an extraordinary general of higher rank, the nomination of whom they deemed it expedient to leave to the people. For long—so runs the story—nobody announced himself as a candidate for the perilous and complicated office; but at last a young officer of twenty-seven, Publius Scipio (son of the general of the same name that had fallen in Spain), who had held the offices of military tribune and aedile, came forward to solicit it. It is incredible that the Roman senate should have left to accident an election of such importance in an assembly which it had itself suggested, and equally incredible that ambition and patriotism should have so died out in Rome that no tried officer presented himself for the important post. If on the other hand the eyes of the senate turned to the young, talented, and experienced officer, who had brilliantly distinguished himself in the hotly contested

days on the Trebia and at Cannae, but who still had not the rank
requisite for his coming forward as the successor of men who had
been praetors and consuls, it was very natural to adopt this
course, which compelled the people out of good nature to admit
the only candidate notwithstanding his defective qualification,
and which could not but bring both him and the Spanish expedition, which was doubtless very unpopular, into favour with the
multitude. If the effect of this ostensibly unpremeditated
candidature was thus calculated, it was perfectly successful.
The son, who went to avenge the death of a father whose life he
had saved nine years before at the Trebia; the young man of
manly beauty and long locks, who with modest blushes offered
himself in the absence of a better for the post of danger; the
mere military tribune, whom the votes of the centuries now
raised at once to the roll of the highest magistracies—all this
made a wonderful and indelible impression on the citizens and
farmers of Rome. And in truth Publius Scipio was one, who
was himself enthusiastic, and who inspired enthusiasm. He
was not one of the few who by their energy and iron will con-
strain the world to adopt and to move in new paths for centuries,
or who at any rate grasp the reins of destiny for years till its
wheels roll over them. Publius Scipio gained battles and conquered countries under the instructions of the senate; with the
aid of his military laurels he took also a prominent position in
Rome as a statesman; but a wide interval separates such a man
from an Alexander or a Caesar. As an officer, he rendered at
least no greater service to his country than Marcus Marcellus;
and as a politician, although not perhaps himself fully conscious
of the unpatriotic and personal character of his policy, he
injured his country at least as much as he benefited it by his
military skill. Yet a special charm lingers around the form of
that graceful hero; it is surrounded, as with a dazzling halo, by
the atmosphere of serene and confident inspiration, in which
Scipio with mingled credulity and adroitness always moved.
With quite enough of enthusiasm to warm men's hearts, and
enough of calculation to follow in every case the dictates of intelligence, while not leaving out of account the vulgar; not naïve
enough to share the belief of the multitude in his divine inspira-
tions, nor straightforward enough to set it aside, and yet in
secret thoroughly persuaded that he was a man specially
favoured of the gods—in a word, a genuine prophetic nature;
raised above the people, and not less aloof from them; a man
steadfast to his word and kingly in his bearing, who thought

that he would humble himself by adopting the ordinary title of
a king, but could never understand how the constitution of the
republic should in his case be binding; so confident in his own
greatness that he knew nothing of envy or of hatred, courteously
acknowledged other men's merits, and compassionately forgave
other men's faults; an excellent officer and a refined diplomatist
without presenting offensively the special stamp of either calling,
uniting Hellenic culture with the fullest national feeling of a
Roman, an accomplished speaker and of graceful manners—
Publius Scipio won the hearts of soldiers and of women, of his
countrymen and of the Spaniards, of his rivals in the senate
and of his greater Carthaginian antagonist. His name was soon
on every one's lips, and his was the star which seemed destined to
bring victory and peace to his country.

Publius Scipio went to Spain in $\frac{544}{210}$–$\frac{545}{209}$, accompanied by the
propraetor Marcus Silanus, who was to succeed Nero and to
serve as assistant and counsellor to the young commander-in-
chief, and by his intimate friend Gaius Laelius as admiral, and
furnished with a legion exceeding the usual strength and a well-
filled chest. His appearance on the scene was at once signalised
by one of the boldest and most fortunate *coups de main* that are
known in history. Of the three Carthaginian generals Hasdrubal Barca was stationed at the sources, Hasdrubal son of
Gisgo at the mouth, of the Tagus, and Mago at the Pillars of
Hercules; the nearest of them was ten days' march from the
Phoenician capital New Carthage. Suddenly in the spring of
$\frac{545}{209}$, before the enemy's armies began to move, Scipio set out
with his whole army of nearly 30,000 men and the fleet for this
town, which he could reach by the coast route from the mouth
of the Ebro in a few days, and surprised the Phoenician garrison,
not above 1000 men strong, by a combined attack by sea and
land. The town, situated on a tongue of land projecting into
the harbour, found itself threatened at once on three sides by
the Roman fleet, and on the fourth by the legions; and all help
was far distant. Nevertheless the commandant Mago defended
himself with resolution and armed the citizens, as the soldiers
did not suffice to man the walls. A sortie was attempted; but
the Romans repelled it with ease and, without taking time to
open a regular siege, began the assault on the landward side.
Eagerly the assailants pushed their advance along the narrow
land approach to the town; new columns constantly relieved
those that were fatigued; the weak garrison was utterly exhausted; but the Romans had gained no advantage. Scipio

had not expected any; the assault was merely designed to draw away the garrison from the side next to the harbour, where, having been informed that part of the latter was left dry at ebb-tide, he meditated a second attack. While the assault was raging on the landward side, Scipio sent a division with ladders over the shallow bank "where Neptune himself showed them the way," and they had actually the good fortune to find the walls at that point undefended. Thus the city was won on the first day; whereupon Mago in the citadel capitulated. With the Carthaginian capital there fell into the hands of the Romans 18 dismantled vessels of war and 63 transports, the whole war-stores, considerable supplies of corn, the war-chest of 600 talents (more than £140,000), the hostages of all the Spanish allies of Carthage, and ten thousand captives, among whom were eighteen Carthaginian gerusiasts or judges. Scipio promised the hostages permission to return home so soon as their respective communities should have entered into alliance with Rome, and employed the resources which the city afforded to reinforce and improve the condition of his army. He ordered the artisans of New Carthage, 2000 in number, to work for the Roman army, promising to them liberty at the close of the war, and he selected the able-bodied men among the remaining multitude to serve as rowers in the fleet. But the burgesses of the city were spared, and allowed to retain their liberty and former position. Scipio knew the Phoenicians and was aware that they would obey; and it was important that a city possessing the only excellent harbour on the east coast and rich silver-mines should be secured by something more than a garrison.

Success thus crowned the bold enterprise—bold, because it was not unknown to Scipio that Hasdrubal Barca had received orders from his government to advance towards Gaul and was engaged in fulfilling them, and because the weak division left behind on the Ebro was not in a position seriously to oppose that movement, should the return of Scipio be delayed. But he was again at Tarraco, before Hasdrubal made his appearance on the Ebro. The hazard of the game which the young general played, when he abandoned his primary task in order to execute a dashing stroke, was concealed by the fabulous success which Neptune and Scipio had gained in concert. The marvellous capture of the Phoenician capital so abundantly justified all the expectations which had been formed at home regarding the wondrous youth, that none could venture to utter any adverse opinion. Scipio's command was indefinitely prolonged; he himself resolved no longer to confine his efforts to the mere task of guarding the passes of the Pyrenees. Already, in consequence of the fall of New Carthage, not only had the Spaniards on the north of the Ebro completely submitted, but even beyond the Ebro the most powerful princes had exchanged the Carthaginian for the Roman protectorate.

Scipio employed the winter of $\frac{545-546}{209-208}$ in breaking up his fleet and increasing his land army with the men thus acquired, so that he might at once guard the north and assume the offensive in the south more energetically than before; and he marched in $\frac{546}{208}$ to Andalusia. There he encountered Hasdrubal Barca, who, in the execution of his long cherished plan, was moving northward to the help of his brother. A battle took place at Baecula, in which the Romans claimed the victory and professed to have made 10,000 captives; but Hasdrubal substantially attained his end, although at the sacrifice of a portion of his army. With his chest, his elephants, and the best portion of his troops, he fought his way to the north coast of Spain; marching along the shore, he reached the western passes of the Pyrenees which appear to have been unoccupied, and before the bad season began he was in Gaul, where he took up quarters for the winter. It was evident that the resolve of Scipio to combine offensive operations with the defensive which he had been instructed to maintain was inconsiderate and unwise. The immediate task assigned to the Spanish army, which not only Scipio's father and uncle, but even Gaius Marcius and Gaius Nero had accomplished with much inferior means, was not enough for the arrogance of the victorious general at the head of a numerous army; and he was mainly to blame for the extremely critical position of Rome in the summer of $\frac{547}{207}$, when the plan of Hannibal for a combined attack on the Romans was at length realised. But the gods covered the errors of their favourite with laurels. In Italy the peril fortunately passed over; the Romans were glad to accept the bulletin of the ambiguous victory of Baecula, and, when fresh tidings of victory arrived from Spain, they thought no more of the circumstance that they had had to combat the ablest general and the flower of the Hispano-Phoenician army in Italy.

After the removal of Hasdrubal Barca the two generals who were left in Spain determined for the time being to retire, Hasdrubal son of Gisgo to Lusitania, Mago even to the Baleares; and, until new reinforcements should arrive from Africa, they left the light cavalry of Massinissa alone to wage a desultory

warfare in Spain, as Mutines had done so successfully in Sicily.
The whole east coast thus fell into the power of the Romans.
In the following year ($\frac{547}{207}$) Hanno actually made his appearance
from Africa with a third army, whereupon Mago and Hasdrubal
returned to Andalusia. But Marcus Silanus defeated the united
armies of Mago and Hanno, and captured the latter in person.
Hasdrubal upon this abandoned the idea of keeping the open
field, and distributed his troops among the Andalusian cities,
of which Scipio was during this year able to storm only one,
Oringis. The Phoenicians seemed vanquished; but yet they
were able in the following year ($\frac{548}{206}$) once more to send into the
field a powerful army, 32 elephants, 4000 horse, and 70,000 foot,
far the greater part of whom, it is true, were hastily collected
Spanish militia. Again a battle took place at Baecula. The
Roman army numbered little more than half that of the enemy
and was also to a considerable extent composed of Spaniards.
Scipio, like Wellington in similar circumstances, disposed his
Spaniards so that they should not partake in the fight—the only
possible mode of preventing their dispersion—while on the other
hand he threw his Roman troops in the first instance on the
Spaniards. The day was nevertheless obstinately contested;
but at length the Romans were the victors, and, as a matter of
course, the defeat of such an army was equivalent to its complete dissolution—Hasdrubal and Mago singly made their escape
to Gades. The Romans were now without a rival in the peninsula; the few towns that did not submit with good will were
subdued one by one, and some of them were punished with cruel
severity. Scipio was even able to visit Syphax on the African
coast, and to enter into communications with him and also with
Massinissa with reference to an expedition to Africa—a foolhardy venture, which was not warranted by any corresponding
advantage, however much the report of it might please the
curiosity of the citizens of the capital at home. Gades alone,
where Mago held command, was still Phoenician. For a moment
it seemed as if, after the Romans had entered upon the Carthaginian heritage and had sufficiently undeceived the expectation
cherished here and there among the Spaniards that after the
close of the Phoenician rule they would get rid of their Roman
guests also and regain their ancient freedom, a general insurrection against the Romans would break forth in Spain, in which
the former allies of Rome would take the lead. The sickness
of the Roman general and the mutiny of one of his corps,
occasioned by their pay being in arrear for many years, favoured

the rising. But Scipio recovered sooner than was expected, and dexterously suppressed the tumult among the soldiers; upon which the communities that had taken the lead in the national rising were subdued at once before the insurrection gained ground. Seeing that nothing came of this movement and Gades could not be permanently held, the Carthaginian government ordered Mago to gather together whatever could be got in ships, troops, and money, and with these, if possible, to give another turn to the war in Italy. Scipio could not prevent this—his dismantling of the fleet now avenged itself—and he was a second time obliged to leave in the hands of his gods the defence, with which he had been entrusted, of his country against new invasions. The last of Hamilcar's sons left the peninsula without opposition. After his departure Gades, the earliest and latest possession of the Phoenicians on Spanish soil, submitted on favourable conditions to the new masters. Spain was, after a thirteen years' struggle, converted from a Carthaginian into a Roman province, in which the conflict with the Romans was still continued for centuries by means of insurrections always suppressed and yet never subdued, but in which at the moment no enemy stood opposed to Rome. Scipio embraced the first moment of apparent peace to resign his command (in the end of $\frac{548}{206}$), and to report at Rome in person the victories which he had achieved and the provinces which he had won.

While the war was thus terminated in Sicily by Marcellus, in Greece by Publius Sulpicius, and in Spain by Scipio, the mighty struggle was carried on without interruption in the Italian peninsula. There after the battle of Cannae had been fought and its effects in loss or gain could by degrees be discerned, at the commencement of $\frac{540}{214}$, the fifth year of the war, the dispositions of the opposing Romans and Phoenicians were the following. North Italy had been reoccupied by the Romans after the departure of Hannibal, and was protected by three legions, two of which were stationed in the Celtic territory, the third as a reserve in Picenum. Lower Italy, as far as Mount Garganus and the Volturnus, was, with the exception of the fortresses and most of the ports, in the hands of Hannibal. He lay with his main army at Arpi, while Tiberius Gracchus with four legions confronted him in Apulia, resting upon the fortresses of Luceria and Beneventum. In the land of the Bruttians, where the inhabitants had thrown themselves entirely into the arms of Hannibal, and where even the ports—excepting Rhegium, which the Romans protected from Messana—were occupied by the Phoenicians, there was a second Carthaginian army under Hanno, which in the meanwhile had no enemy to face it. The Roman main army of four legions under the two consuls, Quintus Fabius and Marcus Marcellus, was on the point of attempting to recover Capua. To these there fell to be added on the Roman side the reserve of two legions in the capital, the garrisons placed in all the seaports—Tarentum and Brundisium having been reinforced by a legion on account of the Macedonian landing apprehended there—and lastly the strong fleet which had undisputed command of the sea. If we add to these the Roman armies in Sicily, Sardinia, and Spain, the whole number of the Roman forces, even apart from the garrison service in the fortresses of Lower Italy which was provided for by the colonists occupying them, may be estimated at not less than 200,000 men, of whom one-third were newly enrolled for this year, and about one-half were Roman citizens. It may be assumed that all the men capable of service from the 17th to the 46th year were under arms, and that the fields, where the war permitted them to be tilled at all, were cultivated by the slaves and the old men, women, and children. Of course, under such circumstances the finances were in the most grievous embarrassment; the land-tax, the main source of revenue, came in but very irregularly. Yet notwithstanding these difficulties as to men and money the Romans were able—slowly indeed and by exerting all their energies, but still surely—to recover what they had so rapidly lost; to increase their armies yearly, while those of the Phoenicians were diminishing; to gain ground year by year on the Italian allies of Hannibal, the Campanians, Apulians, Samnites, and Bruttians, who neither sufficed, like the Roman fortresses in Lower Italy, for their own protection nor were adequately protected by the weak army of Hannibal; and finally, by means of the method of warfare instituted by Marcus Marcellus, to develop the talent of their officers and to bring into play the full superiority of the Roman infantry. Hannibal might doubtless still hope for victories, but no longer such victories as those on the Trasimene lake and on the Aufidus; the times of the citizen-generals were gone by. No course was left to him but to wait till either Philip should execute his long promised descent or his own brothers should join him from Spain, and meanwhile to keep himself, his army, and his clients as far as possible free from harm and in good humour. We hardly recognise in the obstinate defensive system which he now began the same general who had carried on the offensive with almost unequalled impetuosity and boldness; it is marvellous in a psychological as well as in a military point of view, that the same man should have accomplished the two tasks prescribed to him—tasks so diametrically opposite in their character—with equal completeness.

At first the war turned chiefly towards Campania. Hannibal appeared in good time to protect its capital, which he prevented from being invested; but he was unable either to wrest any of the Campanian towns held by the Romans from their strong Roman garrisons, or to prevent—in addition to a number of less important country towns—Casilinum, which secured his passage over the Volturnus, from being taken by the two consular armies after an obstinate defence. An attempt of Hannibal to gain Tarentum, with the view especially of acquiring a safe landing-place for the Macedonian army, proved unsuccessful. Meanwhile the Bruttian army of the Carthaginians under Hanno had various encounters in Lucania with the Roman army of Apulia; in the course of which Tiberius Gracchus fought with favourable results, and after a successful combat not far from Beneventum, in which the slave legions pressed into service distinguished themselves, he bestowed liberty and burgess-rights on his slave-soldiers in the name of the people.

In the following year ($\frac{541}{213}$) the Romans recovered the rich and important Arpi, whose citizens, after the Roman soldiers had stolen into the town, made common cause with them against the Carthaginian garrison. In general the bonds of the symmachy formed by Hannibal were relaxing; a number of the leading Capuans and several of the Bruttian towns passed over to Rome; even a Spanish division of the Phoenician army, when informed by Spanish emissaries of the course of events in their native land, passed from the Carthaginian into the Roman service.

The year $\frac{542}{212}$ was more unfavourable for the Romans in consequence of fresh political and military errors, of which Hannibal did not fail to take advantage. The connections which Hannibal maintained with the towns of Magna Graecia had led to no serious result; save that the hostages from Tarentum and Thurii, who were kept at Rome, were induced by his emissaries to make a foolhardy attempt at escape, in which they were speedily recaptured by the Roman posts. But the injudicious spirit of revenge displayed by the Romans was of more service to Hannibal than his intrigues; the execution of all the hostages who had sought to escape deprived them of a valuable pledge, and the exasperated Greeks thenceforth meditated how they might open their gates to Hannibal. Tarentum was actually occupied by the Carthaginians in consequence of an understanding with the citizens and of the negligence of the Roman commandant; with difficulty the Roman garrison maintained itself in the citadel. The example of Tarentum was followed by Heraclea, Thurii, and Metapontum, from which town the garrison had to be withdrawn in order to save the Tarentine Acropolis. These successes so greatly increased the risk of a Macedonian landing, that Rome felt herself compelled to direct renewed attention and apply renewed exertion to the Greek war, which had been almost totally neglected; and fortunately the capture of Syracuse and the favourable state of the Spanish war enabled her to do so.

At the chief seat of war, Campania, the struggle went on with very varying success. The legion posted in the neighbourhood of Capua had not exactly invested the city, but had so greatly impeded the cultivation of the soil and the ingathering of the harvest, that the populous city was in urgent need of supplies from without. Hannibal accordingly collected a considerable supply of grain, and directed the Campanians to receive it at Beneventum; but their tardiness gave the consuls Quintus Flaccus and Appius Claudius time to come up, to inflict a severe defeat on Hanno who protected the grain, and to seize his camp and all his stores. The two consuls then surrounded the town, while Tiberius Gracchus stationed himself on the Appian Way to prevent Hannibal from approaching to relieve it. But that brave officer fell in consequence of the shameful stratagem of a perfidious Lucanian; and his death was equivalent to a complete defeat, for his army, consisting mostly of those slaves whom he had manumitted, dispersed after the fall of their beloved leader. So Hannibal found the road to Capua open, and by his unexpected appearance compelled the two consuls to raise the blockade which they had barely begun. Their cavalry had already, before Hannibal's arrival, been thoroughly defeated by the Phoenician cavalry, which lay as a garrison in Capua under Hanno and Bostar, and by the equally excellent Campanian horse. The total destruction of the regular troops and free bands in Lucania led by Marcus Centenius, a man imprudently promoted from a subaltern to be a general, and the not much less complete defeat of the negligent and arrogant praetor Gnaeus Fulvius Flaccus in Apulia, closed the long series of the misfortunes of this year. But the tough perseverance of the Romans again neutralised the rapid success of Hannibal, at least at the most decisive point. As soon as Hannibal turned his back on Capua to proceed to Apulia, the Roman armies once more gathered around that city, one at Puteoli and Volturnum under Appius Claudius, another at Casilinum under Quintus Fulvius, and a third on the Nolan road under the praetor Gaius Claudius Nero. The three camps, well entrenched and connected by fortified lines, precluded all access to the place, and the large, inadequately provisioned city could not but find itself compelled by the mere investment to surrender at no distant time, should no relief arrive. As the winter of $\frac{542-543}{212-211}$ drew to an end, the provisions were almost exhausted, and urgent messengers, who were barely able to steal through the well-guarded Roman lines, requested speedy help from Hannibal, who was at Tarentum, occupied with the siege of the citadel. With 33 elephants and his best troops he departed by forced marches from Tarentum for Campania, captured the Roman guard at Calatia, and took up his camp on Mount Tifata close by Capua, in the confident expectation that the Roman generals would now raise the siege as they had done the year before. But the Romans, who had had time to entrench their camps and their lines like a fortress, did not stir, and looked on unmoved from the ramparts, while on one side the Campanian horsemen, on the other the Numidian squadrons, dashed against their lines. A serious assault could not be contemplated by Hannibal; he could foresee that his advance would soon draw the other Roman armies after him to Campania, if even before their arrival the scarcity of supplies in a region so systematically foraged did not drive him away. Nothing could be done in that quarter.

Hannibal tried a further expedient, the last which occurred to his inventive genius, to save the important city. After giving the Campanians information of his intention and exhorting them to hold out, he started with the relieving army from Capua and took the road for Rome. With the same dexterous boldness which he had shown in his first Italian campaigns, he threw himself with a weak army between the armies and fortresses of the enemy, and led his troops through Samnium and along the Valerian Way past Tibur to the bridge over the Anio, which he passed and encamped on the opposite bank, five miles from the city. The children's children of the Romans still shuddered, when they were told of "Hannibal at the gate;" real danger there was none. The country houses and fields in the neighbourhood of the city were laid waste by the enemy; the two legions in the city, who went forth against them, prevented the investment of the walls. Besides, Hannibal had never expected to surprise Rome by a *coup de main*, such as Scipio soon afterwards executed against New Carthage, and still less had he meditated a siege in earnest; his only hope was that in the first alarm part of the besieging army of Capua would march to Rome and thus give him an opportunity of breaking up the blockade. Accordingly after a brief stay he departed. The Romans saw in his withdrawal a miraculous intervention of the gods, who by portents and visions had compelled the wicked man to depart, when in truth the Roman legions were unable to compel him; at the spot where Hannibal had approached nearest to the city, at the second milestone on the Appian Way in front of the Capene gate, with grateful credulity the Romans erected an altar to the god " who turned back and protected " (*Rediculus Tutanus*). Hannibal in reality retreated, because this was part of his plan, and directed his march towards Capua. But the Roman generals had not committed the mistake on which their opponent had reckoned; the legions remained unmoved in the lines round Capua, and only a weak corps had been detached on the news of Hannibal's march towards Rome. When Hannibal learned this, he suddenly turned against the consul Publius Galba, who had imprudently followed him from Rome, and with whom he had hitherto avoided an engagement, vanquished him, and took his camp by storm.

But this was a poor compensation for the now inevitable fall of Capua. Long had its citizens, particularly the better classes, anticipated with sorrowful forebodings what was coming; the senate-house and the administration of the city were left almost exclusively to the leaders of the popular party hostile to Rome. Now despair seized high and low, Campanians and Phoenicians alike. Twenty-eight senators chose a voluntary death; the remainder gave over the city to the discretion of an implacably exasperated foe. Of course a bloody retribution had to follow; the only discussion was as to whether the process should be long or short: whether the wiser and more appropriate course was to probe to the bottom the further ramifications of the treason beyond Capua, or to terminate the matter by rapid executions. Appius Claudius and the Roman senate wished to take the former course; the latter view, perhaps the less inhuman, prevailed. Fifty-three of the officers and magistrates of Capua were scourged and beheaded in the market-places of Cales and

Teanum by the orders and before the eyes of the proconsul Quintus Flaccus, the rest of the senators were imprisoned, numbers of the citizens were sold into slavery, and the estates of the more wealthy were confiscated. Similar penalties were inflicted upon Atella and Calatia. These punishments were severe; but, when regard is had to the importance of the revolt of Capua from Rome, and to what was the ordinary if not warrantable usage of war in those times, they were not unnatural. And had not the citizens themselves pronounced their own sentence, when immediately after their defection they put to death all the Roman citizens present in Capua at the time of the revolt? But it was unjustifiable in Rome to embrace this opportunity of gratifying the secret rivalry that had long subsisted between the two largest cities of Italy, and of wholly annihilating, in a political point of view, her hated and envied competitor by abolishing the constitution of the Campanian city.

Immense was the impression produced by the fall of Capua, and all the more that it had not been brought about by surprise, but by a two years' siege carried on in spite of all the exertions of Hannibal. It was quite as much a token that the Romans had recovered their ascendancy in Italy, as its defection some years before to Hannibal had been a token that that ascendancy was lost. In vain Hannibal had tried to counteract the impression of this news on his allies by the capture of Rhegium or of the citadel of Tarentum. His forced march to surprise Rhegium had yielded no result. The citadel of Tarentum suffered greatly from famine, after the Tarentino-Carthaginian squadron closed the harbour; but, as the Romans with their much more powerful fleet were able to cut off the supplies from that squadron itself, and the territory, which Hannibal commanded, scarce sufficed to maintain his army, the besiegers on the side next the sea suffered not much less than did the besieged in the citadel, and at length they left the harbour. No enterprise was now successful; Fortune herself seemed to have deserted the Carthaginians. The consequences of the fall of Capua—the deep shock given to the respect and confidence which Hannibal had hitherto enjoyed among the Italian allies, and the endeavours made by every community that was not too deeply compromised to gain readmission on tolerable terms into the Roman symmachy—affected Hannibal much more sensibly than the immediate loss. He had to choose one of two courses; either to throw garrisons into the wavering towns, in which case he would weaken still more his army already too weak and would expose the troops on whom he could rely to destruction in small divisions or to treachery—500 select Numidian horse were put to death in this way in $\frac{544}{210}$ on the defection of the town of Salapia; or to pull down and burn the towns which could not be depended on, so as to keep them out of the enemy's hands—a course which would not raise the spirits of his Italian clients. On the fall of Capua the Romans felt themselves once more confident as to the final issue of the war in Italy; they despatched considerable reinforcements to Spain, where the existence of the Roman army was placed in jeopardy by the fall of the two Scipios; and for the first time since the beginning of the war they ventured on a diminution in the total number of their troops, which had hitherto been annually augmented notwithstanding the annually increasing difficulty of levying them, and had risen at last to 23 legions. Accordingly in the next year ($\frac{544}{210}$) the Italian war was prosecuted more remissly than hitherto by the Romans, although Marcus Marcellus had after the close of the Sicilian war resumed the command of the main army; he applied himself to the besieging of fortresses in the interior, and had indecisive conflicts with the Carthaginians. The struggle for the Acropolis of Tarentum also continued without decisive result. In Apulia Hannibal succeeded in defeating the proconsul Gnaeus Fulvius Centumalus at Herdoneae. In the following year ($\frac{545}{209}$) the Romans took steps to regain possession of the second large city, which had passed over to Hannibal, the city of Tarentum. While Marcus Marcellus continued the struggle against Hannibal in person with his wonted obstinacy and energy, and in a two days' battle, beaten on the first day, achieved on the second a costly and bloody victory; while the consul Quintus Fulvius induced the already wavering Lucanians and Hirpinians to change sides and to deliver up their Phoenician garrisons; while well-conducted razzias from Rhegium compelled Hannibal to hasten to the aid of the hard-pressed Bruttians; the veteran Quintus Fabius, who had once more—for the fifth time—accepted the consulship and along with it the commission to reconquer Tarentum, established himself firmly in the neighbouring Messapian territory, and the treachery of a Bruttian portion of the garrison surrendered to him the city. Fearful excesses were committed by the exasperated victors. They put to death all of the garrison or of the citizens whom they could find, and pillaged the houses. 30,000 Tarentines are said to have been sold as slaves, and 3000 talents (£730,000) are stated to have been sent to the state treasury. It was the last achievement of the veteran general of eighty; Hannibal arrived to the relief of the city when all was over, and withdrew to Metapontum.

After Hannibal had thus lost his most important acquisitions and found himself hemmed in by degrees to the south-western point of the peninsula, Marcus Marcellus, who had been chosen consul for the next year ($\frac{546}{208}$), hoped that, in connection with his able colleague Titus Quintius Crispinus, he should be able to terminate the war by a decisive attack. The old soldier was not disturbed by the burden of his sixty years; sleeping and waking he was haunted by the one thought of defeating Hannibal and of liberating Italy. But fate reserved that wreath of victory for a younger brow. While engaged in an unimportant reconnaissance in the district of Venusia, both consuls were suddenly attacked by a division of African cavalry. Marcellus maintained the unequal struggle—as he had fought forty years before against Hamilcar and fourteen years before at Clastidium—till he sank dying from his horse; Crispinus escaped, but died of his wounds received in the conflict ($\frac{546}{208}$).

It was now the eleventh year of the war. The danger which some years before had threatened the very existence of the state seemed to have vanished; but all the more the Romans felt the heavy burden—a burden pressing more severely year after year —of the endless war. The finances of the state suffered beyond measure. After the battle of Cannae ($\frac{538}{216}$) a special bank-commission (*tres viri mensarii*) had been appointed, composed of the most eminent men, to form a permanent and circumspect board of superintendence for the public finances in these difficult times. It probably did what it could; but the state of things was such as to baffle all financial sagacity. At the very beginning of the war the Romans had debased the silver and copper coin, raised the legal value of the silver currency more than a third, and issued a gold coinage far above the value of the metal. This very soon proved insufficient; they were obliged to take supplies from the contractors on credit, and connived at their conduct because they needed them, till the scandalous malversation at last induced the aediles to make an example of some of the worst by impeaching them before the people. Appeals were often made, and not in vain, to the patriotism of the wealthy, who in fact were the very persons that suffered comparatively the most. The soldiers of the better classes and the subaltern officers and equites in a body, either voluntarily or constrained by the *esprit de corps*, declined to receive pay. The owners of

the slaves armed by the state and manumitted after the engagement at Beneventum (p. 155) replied to the bank-commission,
which offered them payment, that they would allow it to stand
over to the end of the war ($\frac{540}{214}$). When there was no longer
money in the exchequer for the celebration of the national
festivals and the repairs of the public buildings, the companies
which had hitherto contracted for these matters declared themselves ready to continue their services for a time without remuneration ($\frac{540}{214}$). A fleet was even fitted out and manned,
just as in the first Punic war, by means of a voluntary loan
among the rich ($\frac{544}{210}$). They spent the moneys belonging to
minors; and at length, in the year of the conquest of Tarentum,
they laid hands on the last long-spared reserve fund (£164,000).
The state nevertheless was unable to meet its most necessary
payments; the pay of the soldiers fell dangerously into arrear,
particularly in the more remote districts. But the embarrassment of the state was not the worst part of the material distress.
Everywhere the fields lay fallow: even where the war did not
make havoc, there was a want of hands for the hoe and the
sickle. The price of the *medimnus* (a bushel and a half) had
risen to 15 *denarii* (9s. 7d.), at least three times the average
price in the capital; and many would have died of absolute
want, if supplies had not arrived from Egypt and if, above all,
the revival of agriculture in Sicily (p. 139) had not prevented
the distress from coming to the worst. The effect which such
a state of things must have had in ruining the small farmers, in
eating away the savings which had been so laboriously acquired,
and in converting flourishing villages into nests of beggars and
brigands, is illustrated by similar wars of which more circum-
stantial accounts have been preserved.

Still more ominous than this material distress was the increasing aversion of the allies to the Roman war, which consumed
their substance and their blood. In regard to the non-Latin
communities, indeed, this was of less consequence. The war
itself showed that they could do nothing, so long as the Latin
nation stood by Rome; their greater or less measure of dislike
was therefore of little moment. Now, however, Latium also
began to waver. Most of the Latin communes in Etruria,
Latium, the territory of the Marsians, and northern Campania
—and so in those very districts of Italy which directly had
suffered least from the war—announced to the Roman senate
in $\frac{545}{209}$ that thenceforth they would send neither contingents nor
contributions, and would leave it to the Romans themselves to

defray the costs of a war waged in their interest.   The consternation in Rome was great; but for the moment there were no means of compelling the refractory.   Fortunately all the Latin communities did not act in this way.   The colonies in the land of the Gauls, in Picenum, and in southern Italy, headed by the powerful and patriotic Fregellae, declared on the contrary that they adhered the more closely and faithfully to Rome; in fact, it was very clearly evident to all of these that in the present war their existence was, if possible, still more at stake than that of the capital, and that the war was really waged not for Rome merely, but for the Latin hegemony in Italy, and in truth for the independence of the Italian nation.   That partial defection itself was certainly not high treason, but merely the result of shortsightedness and exhaustion; beyond doubt these same towns would have rejected with horror an alliance with the Phoenicians.   But still there was a variance between Romans and Latins, which did not fail injuriously to react on the subject population of these districts.   A dangerous ferment immediately showed itself in Arretium; a conspiracy organised in the interest of Hannibal among the Etruscans was discovered, and appeared so perilous that Roman troops were ordered to march thither. The military and police suppressed this movement without difficulty; but it was a significant token of what might happen in those districts, if once the Latin strongholds ceased to inspire terror.

Amidst these difficulties and symptoms of variance, news suddenly arrived that Hasdrubal had crossed the Pyrenees in the autumn of $\frac{546}{208}$, and that the Romans must be prepared to carry on the war next year with both the sons of Hamilcar in Italy.   Not in vain had Hannibal persevered at his post throughout the long anxious years; the aid, which the factious opposition at home and the shortsighted Philip had refused him, was at length in the course of being brought to him by his brother, who, like himself, largely inherited the spirit of Hamilcar. Already 8000 Ligurians, enlisted by Phoenician gold, were ready to unite with Hasdrubal; if he gained the first battle, he might hope that like his brother he should be able to bring the Gauls and perhaps the Etruscans into arms against Rome.   Italy, moreover, was no longer what it had been eleven years before; the state and its citizens were exhausted, the Latin league was shaken, their best general had just fallen in the field of battle, and Hannibal was not subdued.   In reality Scipio might bless the star of his genius, if it averted the conse-

quences of his unpardonable blunder from himself and from
his country.

As in the times of the utmost danger, Rome once more called
out twenty-three legions. Volunteers were summoned to arm,
and those legally exempt from military service were included
in the levy. Nevertheless, they were taken by surprise. Far
earlier than either friends or foes expected, Hasdrubal was on
the Italian side of the Alps ($\frac{5\,4\,6}{2\,0\,8}$); the Gauls, now accustomed
to such transits, were readily bribed to open their passes, and
furnished what the army required. If the Romans had any
intention of occupying the outlets of the Alpine passes, they
were again too late; they heard that Hasdrubal was on the Po,
that he was calling the Gauls to arms as successfully as his
brother had formerly done, and that Placentia was invested.
With all haste the consul Marcus Livius proceeded to the
northern army; and it was high time that he should appear.
Etruria and Umbria were in sullen ferment; volunteers from
them reinforced the Phoenician army. His colleague Gaius
Nero summoned the praetor Gaius Hostilius Tubulus from
Venusia to join him, and hastened with an army of 40,000 men
to intercept the march of Hannibal to the north. The latter
collected all his forces in the Bruttian territory, and, advancing along the great road leading from Rhegium to Apulia,
encountered the consul at Grumentum. An obstinate engagement took place in which Nero claimed the victory; but
Hannibal was able at all events, although with some loss, to
evade the enemy by one of his usual adroit flank-marches,
and to reach Apulia without hindrance. There he halted, and
encamped at first at Venusia, then at Canusium: Nero, who
had followed closely in his steps, encamped opposite to him at
both places. That Hannibal voluntarily halted and was not
prevented from advancing by the Roman army, appears to
admit of no doubt; the reason for his taking up his position
exactly at this point and not farther to the north, must have
depended on arrangements concerted between himself and
Hasdrubal, or on conjectures as to the route of the latter's
march, with which we are not acquainted. While the two
armies thus lay inactive, face to face, the despatch from Hasdrubal which was anxiously expected in Hannibal's camp was
intercepted by the outposts of Nero. It stated that Hasdrubal
intended to take the Flaminian road, in other words, to keep in
the first instance along the coast and then at Fanum to turn
across the Apennines towards Narnia, at which place he hoped

to meet Hannibal. Nero immediately ordered the reserve in the capital to proceed to Narnia as the point selected for the junction of the two Phoenician armies, while the division stationed at Capua went to the capital, and a new reserve was formed there. Convinced that Hannibal was not acquainted with the purpose of his brother and would continue to await him in Apulia, Nero resolved on the bold experiment of hastening northward by forced marches with a small but select corps of 7000 men and, in connection with his colleague, compelling Hasdrubal, if possible, to fight. He was able to do so, for the Roman army which he left behind still continued strong enough either to hold its ground against Hannibal if he should attack it, or to accompany him and to arrive simultaneously with him at the decisive scene of action, should he depart.

Nero found his colleague Marcus Livius at Sena Gallica awaiting the enemy; both consuls at once marched against Hasdrubal, whom they found occupied in crossing the Metaurus. Hasdrubal wished to avoid a battle and to escape from the Romans by a flank movement, but his guides abandoned him; he lost his way on the strange ground, and was at length attacked on the march by the Roman cavalry and detained until the Roman infantry arrived and a battle became inevitable. Hasdrubal stationed the Spaniards on the right wing, with his ten elephants in front of it, and the Gauls on the left, which he held back. Long the fortune of battle wavered on the right wing, and the consul Livius who commanded there was hard pressed, till Nero, repeating his strategical operation as a tactical manœuvre, allowed the motionless enemy opposite to him to remain as they stood, and marching round his own army fell upon the flank of the Spaniards. This decided the day. The severely bought and very bloody victory was complete; the army, which had no retreat, was destroyed, and the camp was taken by assault. Hasdrubal, when he saw the admirably conducted battle lost, sought and found like his father an honourable soldier's death. As an officer and a man, he was worthy to be the brother of Hannibal. On the day after the battle Nero started, and after scarcely fourteen days' absence once more confronted Hannibal in Apulia, whom no message had reached, and who had not stirred. The consul brought the message with him; it was the head of Hannibal's brother, which the Roman ordered to be thrown into the enemy's outposts, repaying in this way his great antagonist, who scorned to war with the dead, for the honourable burial which he had given to Paullus, Gracchus, and Marcellus.

Hannibal saw that his hopes had been in vain, and that all was over. He abandoned Apulia and Lucania, even Metapontum, and retired with his troops to the land of the Bruttians, whose ports formed his only means of withdrawal from Italy. By the energy of the Roman generals, and still more by a conjuncture of singular good fortune, a peril was averted from Rome, the greatness of which justified Hannibal's tenacious perseverance in Italy, and which fully bears comparison with the magnitude of the peril of Cannae. The joy in Rome was boundless; business was resumed as in time of peace; every one felt that the danger of the war was surmounted.

Nevertheless the Romans were in no hurry to terminate the war. The state and the citizens were exhausted by the excessive moral and material strain on their energies; men gladly abandoned themselves to carelessness and repose. The army and fleet were reduced; the Roman and Latin farmers were brought back to their desolate homesteads; the exchequer was filled by the sale of a portion of the Campanian domains. The administration of the state was regulated anew and the disorders which had prevailed were remedied; the repayment of the voluntary war-loan was begun, and the Latin communities that remained in arrears were compelled to fulfil their neglected obligations with heavy interest.

The war in Italy made no progress. It forms a brilliant proof of the strategic talent of Hannibal as well as of the incapacity of the Roman generals now opposed to him, that after this he was still able for four years to keep the field in the Bruttian country, and that all the superiority of his opponents could not compel him either to shut himself up in fortresses or to embark. It is true that he was obliged to retire farther and farther, not so much in consequence of the indecisive engagements which took place with the Romans, as because his Bruttian allies were aways becoming more troublesome, and at last he could only reckon on the towns which his army garrisoned. Thus he voluntarily abandoned Thurii; Locri was, on the suggestion of Publius Scipio, recaptured by an expedition from Rhegium ($\frac{549}{205}$). As if at last his projects were to receive a brilliant justification at the hands of the very Carthaginian authorities who had thwarted them, these now, in their apprehension as to the anticipated landing of the Romans, revived of their own accord his plans ($\frac{548}{206}$, $\frac{549}{205}$), and sent reinforcements and subsidies to Hannibal in Italy, and to Mago in Spain, with orders to rekindle the war in Italy so as to achieve some further respite for the trembling possessors of the country houses of Libya and the shops of Carthage. An embassy was likewise sent to Macedonia, to induce Philip to renew the alliance and to land in Italy ($\frac{549}{205}$). But it was too late. Philip had made peace with Rome some months before; the impending political annihilation of Carthage was far from agreeable to him, but he took no step openly at least against Rome. A small Macedonian corps proceeded to Africa, the expenses of which, according to the assertion of the Romans, were defrayed by Philip: this may have been the case, but the Romans had at any rate no proof of it, as the subsequent course of events showed. No Macedonian landing in Italy was thought of.

Mago, the youngest son of Hamilcar, set himself to his task more earnestly. With the remains of the Spanish army, which he had conducted in the first instance to Minorca, he landed in $\frac{549}{205}$ at Genoa, destroyed the city, and summoned the Ligurians and Gauls to arms. Gold and the novelty of the enterprise led them now, as always, to come to him in troops; he had formed connections even throughout Etruria, where political prosecutions never ceased. But the troops which he had brought with him were too few for a serious enterprise against Italy proper; and Hannibal likewise was much too weak, and his influence in Lower Italy had fallen too far, to permit him to advance with any prospect of success. The rulers of Carthage were not willing to save their native country, when its salvation was possible; now, when they were willing, it was possible no longer.

Nobody probably in the Roman senate doubted either that the war on the part of Carthage against Rome was at an end, or that the war on the part of Rome against Carthage must now be begun; but unavoidable as was the expedition to Africa, they were afraid to enter on its preparation. They required for it, above all, an able and beloved leader; and they had none. Their best generals had either fallen in the field of battle, or they were, like Quintus Fabius and Quintus Fulvius, too old for such an entirely new and probably tedious war. The victors of Sena, Gaius Nero and Marcus Livius, would perhaps have been equal to the task, but they were both in the highest degree unpopular aristocrats; it is doubtful whether they would succeed in procuring the command—matters had already reached such a pass that ability, as such, determined the popular choice only in times of grave anxiety—and it was more than doubtful whether these were the men to stimulate the exhausted people to fresh exertions.

At length Publius Scipio returned from Spain, and the favourite of the multitude, who had so brilliantly fulfilled, or at any rate seemed to have fulfilled, the task with which it had entrusted him, was immediately chosen consul for the next year. He entered on office ($\frac{5 4 9}{2 0 5}$) with the firm determination of now realising that African expedition which he had projected in Spain. In the senate, however, not only was the party favourable to a methodical conduct of the war unwilling to entertain the project of an African expedition so long as Hannibal remained in Italy, but the majority was by no means favourably disposed towards the young general himself. His Greek refinement and his modern culture and tone of thought were but little agreeable to the austere and somewhat boorish fathers of the city; and serious doubts existed both as to his conduct of the Spanish war and as to his military discipline. How much ground there was for the objection that he showed too great indulgence towards his officers of division, was very soon demonstrated by the disgraceful proceedings of Gaius Flaminius at Locri, the blame of which certainly was indirectly chargeable to the scandalous negligence which marked Scipio's supervision. In the proceedings in the senate regarding the organisation of the African expedition and the appointment of a general for it, the new consul, wherever usage or the constitution came into conflict with his private views, showed no great reluctance to set such obstacles aside, and very clearly indicated that in case of need he was disposed to rely for support against the governing board on his fame and his popularity with the people. These things could not but annoy the senate and awaken, moreover, serious apprehensions, lest in the impending decisive war and the eventual negotiations for peace with Carthage such a general would not be bound by the instructions which he received— an apprehension which his arbitrary management of the Spanish expedition was by no means fitted to allay. Both sides, however, displayed wisdom enough not to push matters too far. The senate itself could not fail to see that the African expedition was necessary, and that it was injudicious indefinitely to postpone it; it could not fail to see that Scipio was a very able officer and in so far was well adapted for the leader in such a war, and that he, if any one, would be able to induce the people to protract his command as long as was necessary and to put forth their last energies. The majority came to the resolution not to refuse to Scipio the desired commission after he had previously observed, at least in form, the respect due to the supreme governing board and had submitted himself beforehand to the decree of the senate. Scipio was to proceed this year to Sicily to superintend the building of the fleet, the preparation of siege materials, and the formation of the expeditionary army, and then in the following year to land in Africa. For this purpose the army of Sicily—still composed of those two legions that were formed from the remnant of the army of Cannae—was placed at his disposal, because a weak garrison and the fleet were quite sufficient for the protection of the island; and he was permitted moreover to raise volunteers in Italy. It was evident that the senate did not organise the expedition, but merely allowed it: Scipio did not obtain half the resources which had formerly been placed at the command of Regulus, and he got that very corps which for years had been subjected by the senate to intentional degradation. The African army was, in the view of the majority of the senate, a forlorn hope of disrated companies and volunteers, the loss of whom in any event the state had no great occasion to regret.

Any one else than Scipio would perhaps have declared that the African expedition must either be undertaken with other means, or not at all; but Scipio's confidence accepted the terms such as they were solely with the view of attaining the eagerly coveted command. He carefully avoided, as far as possible, the imposition of direct burdens on the people, that he might not injure the popularity of the expedition. Its expenses, particularly those of building the fleet which were considerable, were partly procured by what was termed a voluntary contribution of the Etruscan cities—that is, by a war tribute imposed as a punishment on the Arretines and other communities disposed to favour the Phoenicians—partly laid upon the cities of Sicily. In forty days the fleet was ready for sea. The crews were reinforced by volunteers, of whom seven thousand from all parts of Italy responded to the call of the beloved officer. So Scipio set sail for Africa in the spring of $\frac{550}{204}$ with two strong legions of veterans (about 30,000 men), 40 vessels of war, and 400 transports, and landed successfully, without meeting the slightest resistance, at the Fair Promontory in the neighbourhood of Utica.

The Carthaginians, who had long expected that the plundering expeditions, which the Roman squadrons had frequently made during the last few years to the African coast, would be followed by a more serious invasion, had not only, in order to ward it off, endeavoured to bring about a revival of the Italo-Macedonian

war, but had also made armed preparation at home to receive
the Romans. Of the two rival Berber kings, Massinissa of Cirta
(Constantine), the ruler of the Massylians, and Syphax of Siga
(at the mouth of the Tafna westward from Oran), the ruler of
the Massaesylians, they had succeeded in attaching the latter,
who was far the more powerful and hitherto had been friendly
to the Romans, by treaty and affinity closely to Carthage, while
they cast off the other, the old rival of Syphax and ally of the
Carthaginians. Massinissa had after desperate resistance succumbed to the united power of the Carthaginians and of Syphax,
and had been obliged to leave his territories a prey to the latter;
he himself wandered with a few horsemen in the desert. Besides
the contingent to be expected from Syphax, a Carthaginian
army of 20,000 foot, 6000 cavalry, and 140 elephants—Hanno
had been sent out to hunt elephants for the very purpose—was
ready to fight for the protection of the capital, under the command of Hasdrubal, son of Gisgo, a general who had gained
experience in Spain; in the port there lay a strong fleet. A
Macedonian corps under Sopater, and a consignment of Celtiberian mercenaries, were immediately expected.

On the report of Scipio's landing, Massinissa immediately
arrived in the camp of the general whom not long before he had
confronted as an enemy in Spain; but the landless prince brought
in the first instance nothing beyond his personal ability to the
aid of the Romans, and the Libyans, although heartily weary of
levies and tribute, had acquired too bitter experience in similar
cases to declare at once for the invaders. So Scipio began the
campaign. So long as he was only opposed by the weaker
Carthaginian army, he had the advantage, and was enabled
after some successful cavalry skirmishes to proceed to the siege
of Utica; but when Syphax arrived, according to report with
50,000 infantry and 10,000 cavalry, the siege had to be raised,
and a fortified naval camp had to be constructed for the winter
on a promontory, which easily admitted of entrenchment,
between Utica and Carthage. Here the Roman general passed
the winter of $\frac{550-551}{204-203}$. From the disagreeable situation in which
the spring found him he extricated himself by a fortunate *coup
de main*. The Africans, lulled into security by proposals of
peace suggested by Scipio with more artifice than honour,
allowed themselves to be surprised on one and the same night in
their two camps; the reed huts of the Numidians burst into
flames, and, when the Carthaginians hastened to their help,
their own camp shared the same fate; the fugitives were slain

without resistance by the Roman divisions. This nocturnal surprise was more destructive than many a battle; nevertheless the Carthaginians did not suffer their courage to sink, and they rejected even the advice of the timid, or rather of the judicious, to recall Mago and Hannibal. Just at this time the expected Celtiberian and Macedonian auxiliaries arrived; it was resolved once more to try a pitched battle on the "Great Plains," five days' march from Utica. Scipio hastened to accept it; with little difficulty his veterans and volunteers dispersed the hastily collected host of Carthaginians and Numidians, and the Celtiberians, who could not reckon on any mercy from Scipio, were cut down after obstinate resistance. After this double defeat the Africans could no longer keep the field. An attack on the Roman naval camp attempted by the Carthaginian fleet, while not unsuccessful, was far from decisive, and was greatly outweighed by the capture of Syphax, which Scipio's singular good fortune threw in his way, and by which Massinissa became to the Romans what Syphax had been at first to the Carthaginians.

After such defeats the Carthaginian peace party, which had been reduced to silence for sixteen years, was able once more to raise its head and openly to rebel against the government of the Barcides and the patriots. Hasdrubal son of Gisgo was in his absence condemned by the government to death, and an attempt was made to obtain an armistice and peace from Scipio. He demanded the cession of their Spanish possessions and of the islands of the Mediterranean, the transference of the kingdom of Syphax to Massinissa, the surrender of all their vessels of war except 20, and a war contribution of 4000 talents (nearly £1,000,000)—terms which seem so singularly favourable to Carthage, that the question obtrudes itself whether they were offered by Scipio more in his own interest or in that of Rome. The Carthaginian plenipotentiaries accepted them under reservation of their being ratified by the respective authorities, and accordingly a Carthaginian embassy was despatched to Rome. But the patriot party in Carthage were not disposed to give up the struggle so cheaply; faith in the nobleness of their cause, confidence in their great leader, even the example that had been set to them by Rome herself, stimulated them to persevere, apart from the fact that peace of necessity involved the return of the opposite party to the helm of affairs and their own consequent destruction. The patriotic party had the ascendancy among the citizens; it was resolved to allow the opposition to negotiate for peace, and meanwhile to prepare for a last and decisive effort. Orders were sent to Mago and Hannibal to return with all speed to Africa. Mago, who for three years ($\frac{549}{205}-\frac{551}{203}$) had been labouring to bring about a coalition in Northern Italy against Rome, had just at this time in the territory of the Insubres (about Milan) been defeated by the far superior double army of the Romans. The Roman cavalry had been brought to give way, and the infantry had been thrown into confusion; victory seemed on the point of declaring for the Carthaginians, when a bold attack by a Roman troop on the enemy's elephants, and above all a serious wound received by their beloved and able commander, turned the fortune of the day. The Phoenician army was obliged to retreat to the Ligurian coast, where it received and obeyed the order to embark; but Mago died of his wound on the voyage.

Hannibal would probably have anticipated the order, had not the last negotiations with Philip presented to him a renewed prospect of rendering better service to his country in Italy than in Libya; when he received it at Croton, where he latterly had his head-quarters, he lost no time in complying with it. He caused his horses to be put to death as well as the Italian soldiers who refused to follow him over the sea, and embarked in the transports that had been long in readiness in the roadstead of Croton. The Roman citizens breathed freely, when the mighty Libyan lion, whose departure no one even now ventured to compel, thus voluntarily turned his back on Italian ground. On this occasion the decoration of a grass wreath was bestowed by the senate and burgesses on the only surviving Roman general who had traversed that troubled time with honour, the veteran of nearly ninety years, Quintus Fabius. To receive this wreath —which by the custom of the Romans the army that a general had saved presented to its deliverer—at the hands of the whole community was the highest distinction which had ever been bestowed upon a Roman citizen, and the last honour accorded to the old general, who died in the course of that same year ($\frac{551}{203}$). Hannibal, doubtless not under the protection of the armistice, but solely through his rapidity of movement and good fortune, arrived at Leptis without hindrance, and the last of the "lion's brood" of Hamilcar trode once more, after an absence of thirty-six years, his native soil. He had left it, when still almost a boy, to enter on that noble and yet so thoroughly fruitless career of heroism, in which he had set out towards the west to return homewards from the east, having

described a wide circle of victory around the Carthaginian sea.
Now, when what he had wished to prevent, and what he would
have prevented had he been allowed, was done, he was summoned to help and, if possible, to save; and he obeyed without
complaint or reproach.

On his arrival the patriot party came forward openly; the
disgraceful sentence against Hasdrubal was cancelled; new
connections were formed with the Numidian sheiks through
the dexterity of Hannibal; and not only did the assembly of the
people refuse to ratify the peace practically concluded, but the
armistice was broken by the plundering of a Roman transport
fleet driven ashore on the African coast, and by the seizure even
of a Roman vessel of war carrying Roman envoys. In just
indignation Scipio started from his camp at Tunes ($\frac{552}{202}$) and
traversed the rich valley of the Bagradas (Mejerda), no longer
allowing the townships to capitulate, but causing the inhabitants
of the villages and towns to be seized and sold *en masse*. He
had already penetrated far into the interior, and was at Narag-
gara (to the west of Sicca, now Kaf, near Ras o Dschaber),
when Hannibal, who had marched out from Hadrumetum, fell
in with him. The Carthaginian general attempted to obtain
better conditions from the Roman in a personal conference;
but Scipio, who had already gone to the extreme verge of concession, could not possibly after the breach of the armistice agree
to yield further, and it is improbable that Hannibal had any
other object in this step than to show the multitude that the
patriots were not absolutely opposed to peace. The conference
led to no result.

The two armies accordingly came to a decisive battle at Zama
(probably not far from Sicca).[1] Hannibal arranged his infantry
in three lines; in the first division the Carthaginian hired troops,
in the second the African militia and the Phoenician civic force
along with the Macedonian corps, in the third the veterans
who had followed him from Italy. In front of the line were
placed the 80 elephants; the cavalry were stationed on the
wings. Scipio likewise disposed his legions in three divisions,
as was the wont of the Romans, and so arranged them that the
elephants could pass through and along the line without breaking
it. Not only was this disposition completely successful, but

---

[1] Neither the place nor time of the battle is properly determined. The
former was probably no other than the well-known Zama regia; the time
probably the spring of $\frac{552}{202}$. The fixing of the day as the 19th October,
on account of the solar eclipse, is not to be depended on.

the elephants making their way to the side disordered also the
Carthaginian cavalry on the wings, so that Scipio's cavalry—
which moreover was by the arrival of Massinissa's troops rendered
far superior to the enemy—had little trouble in dispersing them,
and were soon engaged in full pursuit. The struggle of the
infantry was more severe. The conflict lasted long between
the first divisions on both sides; at length in the extremely
bloody hand-to-hand encounter both parties fell into confusion,
and were obliged to seek a support in the second divisions.
The Romans found that support; but the Carthaginian militia
showed itself so unsteady and wavering, that the mercenaries
believed themselves betrayed and a combat arose between them
and the Carthaginian civic force. But Hannibal now hastily
withdrew what remained of the first two lines to the flanks,
and pushed forward his choice Italian troops along the whole
line. Scipio, on the other hand, gathered together in the centre
as many of the first line as still were able to fight, and made
the second and third divisions close up on the right and left of
the first. Once more on the same spot began a still more fearful
conflict; Hannibal's old soldiers never wavered in spite of the
superior numbers of the enemy, till the cavalry of the Romans
and of Massinissa, returning from the pursuit of the beaten
cavalry of the enemy, surrounded them on all sides. This not
only terminated the struggle, but annihilated the Phoenician
army; the same soldiers, who fourteen years before had given
way at Cannae, had retaliated on their conquerors at Zama.
With a handful of men Hannibal arrived, a fugitive, at
Hadrumetum.

After this day folly alone could counsel a continuance of the
war on the part of Carthage. On the other hand it was in the
power of the Roman general immediately to begin the siege
of the capital, which was neither protected nor provisioned,
and, unless unforeseen accidents should intervene, now to subject
Carthage to the fate which Hannibal had wished to bring upon
Rome. Scipio did not do so; he granted peace ($\frac{5}{2}\frac{3}{0}\frac{3}{1}$), but no
longer upon the former terms. Besides the concessions which
had already in the last negotiations been demanded in favour
of Rome and of Massinissa, an annual contribution of 200 talents
(£48,000) was imposed for fifty years on the Carthaginians;
and they had to bind themselves that they would not wage war
against Rome or its allies or indeed beyond the bounds of Africa
at all, and that in Africa they would not wage war beyond their
own territory without having sought the permission of Rome

—the practical effect of which was that Carthage became tribu tary and lost her political independence. It even appears that the Carthaginians were bound in certain cases to furnish ships of war to the Roman fleet.

Scipio has been accused of granting too favourable conditions to the enemy, lest he might be obliged to hand over the glory of terminating the most severe war which Rome had waged, along with his command, to a successor. The charge might have had some foundation, had the first proposals been carried out; it seems to have no warrant in reference to the second. His position in Rome was not such as to make the favourite of the people, after the victory of Zama, seriously apprehensive of recall—already before the victory an attempt to supersede him had been referred by the senate to the burgesses, and by them decidedly rejected. Nor do the conditions themselves warrant such a charge. The Carthaginian city never, after its hands were thus tied and a powerful neighbour was placed by its side, made even an attempt to withdraw from Roman supremacy, still less to enter into rivalry with Rome; besides, every one who cared to know knew that the war just terminated had been undertaken much more by Hannibal than by Carthage, and that it was absolutely impossible to revive the gigantic plans of the patriot party. It might seem little in the eyes of the vengeful Italians, that only the five hundred surrendered ships of war perished in the flames, and not the hated city itself; secret spite and official pedantry might contend for the view, that an opponent is only really vanquished when he is annihilated, and might censure the man who had disdained rigorously to punish the crime of having made Romans tremble. Scipio thought otherwise; and we have no reason and therefore no right to assume that the Roman was in this instance influenced by vulgar motives rather than by the noble and magnanimous impulses which formed part of his character. It was not the consideration of his own possible recall or of the mutability of fortune, nor was it any apprehension of the outbreak of a Mace-donian war at certainly no distant date, that prevented the self-reliant and confident hero, with whom everything had hitherto succeeded beyond belief, from completing the destruction of the unhappy city, which fifty years afterwards his adopted grandson was commissioned to execute, and which might indeed have been equally well accomplished now. It is much more probable that the two great generals, on whom the decision of the political question now devolved, offered and accepted peace on such terms in order to set just and reasonable limits on the one hand to the furious vengeance of the victors, on the other to the obstinacy and imprudence of the vanquished. The noble-mindedness and statesmanlike gifts of the great antagonists are no less apparent in the magnanimous submission of Hannibal to what was inevitable, than in the wise abstinence of Scipio from an extravagant and insulting use of victory. It is to be supposed that one so generous, unprejudiced, and intelligent should not have asked himself of what benefit it could be to his country, now that the political power of the Carthaginian city was annihilated, utterly to destroy that ancient seat of commerce and of agriculture, and wickedly to overthrow one of the main pillars of the then existing civilisation? The time had not yet come when the first men of Rome lent themselves to destroy the civilisation of their neighbours, and frivolously fancied that they could wash away from themselves the eternal infamy of the nation by shedding an idle tear.

Thus ended the second Punic or, as the Romans more correctly called it, the Hannibalic war, after it had devastated the lands and islands from the Hellespont to the Pillars of Hercules for seventeen years. Before this war the policy of the Romans had no higher aim than to acquire command of the mainland of the Italian peninsula within its natural boundaries, and of the Italian islands and seas; it is clearly proved by their treatment of Africa on the conclusion of peace that they also terminated the war with the impression, not that they had laid the foundation of sovereignty over the states of the Mediterranean or of the so-called universal empire, but that they had rendered a dangerous rival innocuous and had given to Italy agreeable neighbours. It is true doubtless that the results of the war, the conquest of Spain in particular, little accorded with such an idea; but their very successes led them beyond their proper design, and it may in fact be affirmed that the Romans came into possession of Spain accidentally. The Romans achieved the sovereignty of Italy, because they strove for it; the hegemony—and the sovereignty which grew out of it—over the territories of the Mediterranean was to a certain extent thrown into the hands of the Romans by the force of circumstances without intention on their part to acquire it.

The immediate results of the war out of Italy were, the conversion of Spain into two Roman provinces—which, however, were in perpetual insurrection; the union of the hitherto dependent kingdom of Syracuse with the Roman province of

Sicily; the establishment of a Roman instead of a Carthaginian protectorate over the most important Numidian chiefs; and lastly the conversion of Carthage from a powerful commercial state into a defenceless mercantile town. In other words, it established the uncontested hegemony of Rome over the western region of the Mediterranean. Moreover, it brought about that decided contact between the state systems of the East and the West which the first Punic war had only foreshadowed; and thereby gave rise to the proximate decisive interference of Rome in the conflicts of the Alexandrine monarchies.

In Italy, first of all the Celts were now doomed to destruction, if indeed their fate had not been decided before; and the execution of the doom was only a question of time. Within the Roman confederacy the effect of the war was to bring into more distinct prominence the ruling Latin nation, whose internal union had been tried and attested by the peril which, notwith-standing isolated instances of wavering, it had surmounted on the whole in faithful fellowship; and to depress still further the non-Latin or Latinised Italians, particularly the Etruscans and the Sabellians of Lower Italy. The heaviest punishment or rather vengeance was inflicted partly on the most powerful, partly on those who were at once the earliest and latest, allies of Hannibal—the community of Capua, and the land of the Bruttians. The Capuan constitution was abolished, and Capua was reduced from the second city into the first village of Italy; it was even proposed to raze the city and level it with the ground. The whole soil, with the exception of a few possessions of foreigners or of Campanians well disposed towards Rome, was declared by the senate to be public domain, and was there-after parcelled out to small occupiers on temporary lease. The Picentes on the Silarus were similarly treated; their capital was razed, and the inhabitants were dispersed among the surround-ing villages. The doom of the Bruttians was still more severe; they were converted *en masse* into a sort of bondsmen to the Romans, and were for ever excluded from the right of bearing arms. The other allies of Hannibal also dearly expiated their offence. The Greek cities suffered severely, with the exception of the few which had steadfastly adhered to Rome, such as the Campanian Greeks and the Rhegines. Punishment not much lighter awaited the Arpanians and a multitude of other Apulian, Lucanian, and Samnite communities, most of which lost portions of their territory. On part of the lands thus acquired new colonies were settled. Thus in the year $\frac{560}{194}$ a succession of burgess-colonies was sent to the best ports of Lower Italy, among which Sipontum (near Manfredonia) and Croton may be named, as also Salernum placed in the former territory of the southern Picentes and destined to hold them in check, and above all Puteoli, which soon became the seat of the fashionable villa-life and of the traffic in Asiatic and Egyptian luxuries. Thurii became a Latin fortress under the new name of Copia ($\frac{560}{194}$), and the rich Bruttian town of Vibo under the name of Valentia ($\frac{562}{192}$). The veterans of the victorious army of Africa were settled singly on various patches of land in Samnium and Apulia; the remainder was retained as public land, and the pasture stations of the grandees of Rome replaced the gardens and arable fields of the farmers. As a matter of course, moreover, in all the communities of the peninsula the persons of note who were not well affected to Rome were got rid of, so far as this could be accomplished by political processes and confiscations of property. Everywhere in Italy the non-Latin allies felt that their name was meaningless, and that they were henceforth subjects of Rome; the conquest of Hannibal was felt as a second subjugation of Italy, and all the exasperation and all the arrogance of the victors vented themselves especially on their Italian allies who were not Latin. Even the colourless Roman comedy of this period, subjected as it was to close censorship, bears traces of this. When the subjugated towns of Capua and Atella were abandoned without restraint to the unbridled wit of the Roman farce, so that the latter town became its very stronghold, and when other writers of comedy jested over the fact that the Campanian serfs had already learned to survive amidst the deadly atmosphere in which even the hardiest race of slaves, the Syrians, pined away; such unfeeling mockeries reflected the scorn of the victors, and re-echoed the cry of distress from the down-trodden nations. The position in which matters stood is shown by the anxious carefulness, which during the ensuing Macedonian war the senate evinced in the watching of Italy, and by the reinforcements which were despatched from Rome to the most important colonies, to Venusia in $\frac{554}{200}$, Narnia in $\frac{555}{199}$, Cosa in $\frac{557}{197}$, and Cales shortly before $\frac{570}{184}$.

What blanks were produced by war and famine in the ranks of the Italian population, is shown by the example of the burgesses of Rome, whose numbers during the war had fallen almost a fourth. The statement, accordingly, that the whole number of Italians who fell in the war under Hannibal was 300,000, seems not at all exaggerated. Of course this loss fell chiefly on the flower of the burgesses, who in fact furnished the core and mass of the combatants. How fearfully the senate in particular was thinned, is shown by the filling up of its complement after the battle of Cannae, when it had been reduced to 123 persons, and was with difficulty restored to its normal state by an extraordinary nomination of 177 senators. That, moreover, the seventeen years' war, which had been carried on simultaneously in all districts of Italy and towards all the four points of the compass abroad, must have shaken to the very heart the national economy, is abundantly evident; but our tradition does not suffice to illustrate this in detail. The state no doubt gained by the confiscations, and the Campanian territory in particular thenceforth remained an inexhaustible source of revenue to the state; but by this extension of the domain system the national prosperity of course lost just about as much as at other times it had gained by the breaking up of the state lands. Numbers of flourishing townships—four hundred, it was reckoned—were destroyed and ruined; the capital laboriously accumulated was consumed; the population were demoralised by camp life; the good old traditional habits of the burgesses and farmers were undermined from the capital down to the smallest village. Slaves and desperadoes associated themselves in robber-bands, of the dangers of which an idea may be formed from the fact that in a single year ($\frac{569}{185}$) 7000 men had to be condemned for robbery in Apulia alone; the extension of the pastures, with their half-savage slave-herdsmen, favoured this mischievous barbarising of the land. Italian agriculture saw its very existence endangered by the proof, first afforded in this war, that the Roman people could be supported by grain from Sicily and from Egypt instead of that which they reaped themselves.

Nevertheless the Roman, whom the gods had allowed to survive the close of that gigantic struggle, might look with pride to the past and with confidence to the future. Many errors had been committed, but much suffering had also been endured; the people, whose whole youth capable of arms had for ten years hardly laid aside shield and sword, might excuse many faults. The living of different nations side by side in peace and amity upon the whole, although maintaining an attitude of mutual antagonism—which appears to be the aim of the peoples of modern times—was a thing foreign to antiquity. In ancient times it was necessary to be either anvil or hammer; and in the final struggle between the victors victory remained with the Romans. Whether they would have the judgment to use it rightly—to attach the Latin nation by still closer bonds to Rome, gradually to Latinise Italy, to rule their dependents in the provinces as subjects and not to abuse them as slaves, to reform the constitution, to reinvigorate and to enlarge the tottering middle class—remained to be seen. If they should have the skill to accomplish these results, Italy might hope to see happy times, in which prosperity based on personal exertion under favourable circumstances, and the most decisive political supremacy over the then civilised world, would impart a just self-reliance to every member of the great whole, furnish a worthy aim for every ambition, and open a career for every talent. It would, no doubt, be otherwise, should they fail to use aright their victory. But for the moment doubtful voices and gloomy apprehensions were silent; from all quarters the warriors and victors returned to their homes; thanksgivings and amusements, and rewards to soldiers and burgesses were the order of the day; the released prisoners of war were sent home from Gaul, Africa, and Greece; and at length the youthful conqueror moved in splendid procession through the decorated streets of the capital, to deposit his laurels in the house of the god by whose direct inspiration, as the pious whispered one to another, he had been guided in counsel and in action.

CHAPTER VII

THE war waged by Hannibal had interrupted Rome in the extension of her dominion to the Alps or to the boundary of Italy, as was even now the Roman phrase, and in her organisation and colonising of the Celtic territories. It was self-evident that the task would now be resumed at the point where it had been broken off, and the Celts were well aware of this. In the very year of the conclusion of peace with Carthage ($\frac{553}{201}$) hostilities had recommenced in the territory of the Boii, who were the most immediately exposed to danger; and a first success obtained by them over the hastily assembled Roman levy, coupled with the persuasions of a Carthaginian officer, Hamilcar, who had been left behind from the expedition of Mago in northern Italy, produced in the following year ($\frac{554}{200}$) a general insurrection spreading beyond the two tribes immediately threatened, the Boii and Insubres. The Ligurians were driven to arms by the nearer approach of the danger, and even the youth of the Cenomani on this occasion listened less to the voice of their cautious chiefs than to the urgent appeal of their kinsmen who were in peril. Of the two fortresses constructed with a view to check the raids of the Gauls, Placentia and Cremona, the former was sacked—not more than 2000 of the inhabitants of Placentia saved their lives—and the second was invested. In haste the legions advanced to save what they could. A great battle took place before Cremona. The dexterous management and the professional skill of the Phoenician leader failed to make up for the deficiencies of his troops; the Gauls were unable to withstand the onset of the legions, and among the numerous dead who covered the field of battle was the Carthaginian officer. The Celts, nevertheless, continued the struggle; the same Roman army which had conquered at Cremona was next year ($\frac{555}{199}$), chiefly through the fault of its careless leader, almost destroyed by the Insubres; and it was not till $\frac{556}{198}$ that Placentia could be partially re-established. But the league of the cantons associated for the desperate struggle suffered from intestine discord; the Boii and Insubres quarrelled, and the Cenomani not only withdrew from the national league, but purchased their pardon from the Romans by a disgraceful betrayal of their countrymen; during a battle in which the Insubres engaged the Romans on the Mincius, the Cenomani attacked in rear, and helped to destroy, their allies and comrades in arms ($\frac{557}{197}$). Thus humbled and deserted, the Insubres, after the fall of Comum, likewise consented to conclude a separate peace ($\frac{558}{196}$). The conditions, which the Romans prescribed to the Cenomani and Insubres, were certainly harder than they had been in the habit of granting to the members of the Italian confederacy; in particular, they were careful to confirm by law the barrier of separation between Italians and Celts, and to enact that no member of these two Celtic tribes should ever be capable of acquiring the citizenship of Rome. But these Transpadane Celtic districts were allowed to retain their existence and their national constitution—so that they formed not townships, but cantons of the several tribes—and no tribute, as it would seem, was imposed on them. They were intended to serve as a bulwark for the Roman settlements south of the Po, and to ward off from Italy the incursions of the migratory northern tribes and the aggressions of the predatory inhabitants of the Alps, who were wont to make regular razzias in these districts. The process of Latinising, moreover, made rapid progress in these regions; the Celtic nationality was evidently far from able to oppose such resistance as the more civilised nations of Sabellians and Etruscans. The celebrated Latin comic poet Statius Caecilius, who died in $\frac{586}{168}$, was a manumitted Insubrian; and Polybius, who visited these districts towards the close of the sixth century, affirms, not perhaps without some exaggeration, that in that quarter only a few villages among the Alps remained Celtic. The Veneti, on the other hand, appear to have retained their nationality longer.

The chief efforts of the Romans in these regions were naturally directed to check the immigration of the Transalpine Celts, and to make the natural wall, which separates the peninsula from the interior of the continent, also its political boundary. That the terror of the Roman name had already penetrated to the adjacent Celtic cantons beyond the Alps, is shown not only by the totally passive attitude which they maintained during the annihilation or subjugation of their Cisalpine countrymen, but still more by the official disapproval and disavowal which the Transalpine cantons—which term we must suppose primarily to apply to the Helvetii (between the lake of Geneva and the Main) and the Carni or Taurisci (in Carinthia and Styria)—expressed to the envoys from Rome, who complained of the attempts made by isolated Celtic bands to settle peacefully on the Roman side of the Alps.   Not less significant was the humble spirit in which these same bands of emigrants first came to the Roman senate entreating an assignment of land, and then without remonstrance obeyed the rigorous order to return over the Alps ($\frac{568-575}{186-179}$), and allowed the town, which they had already founded not far from Aquileia, to be again destroyed.   With wise severity the senate permitted no sort of exception to the principle that the gates of the Alps should be henceforth closed against the Celtic nation, and visited with heavy penalties those Roman subjects in Italy, who had instigated any such schemes of immigration.   An attempt of this kind which was made on a route hitherto little known to the Romans, in the innermost recess of the Adriatic, and still more, as it would seem, the project of Philip of Macedon for invading Italy from the east as Hannibal had done from the west, gave occasion to the founding of a fortress in the extreme north-eastern corner of Italy—Aquileia, the most northerly of the Italian colonies ($\frac{571-573}{183-181}$)—which was intended not only to close that route for ever against foreigners, but also to secure the command of the gulf which was specially convenient for navigation, and to check the piracy which was still not wholly extirpated in those waters.   The establishment of Aquileia led to a war with the Istrians ($\frac{576}{178}$, $\frac{577}{177}$), which was speedily terminated by the storming of some strongholds and the fall of the king, Aepulo, and which was remarkable for nothing except for the panic, which the news of the surprise of the Roman camp by a handful of barbarians occasioned in the fleet and throughout Italy.

A different course was adopted with the region on the south of the Po, which the Roman senate had determined to incorporate with Italy.   The Boii, who were immediately affected by this step, defended themselves with the resolution of despair.   They even crossed the Po and made an attempt to rouse the Insubres once more to arms ($\frac{560}{194}$); they blockaded a consul in his camp, and he was on the point of succumbing; Placentia maintained itself with difficulty against the constant assaults of the exasperated natives.   At length the last battle was fought at Mutina; it was long and bloody, but the Romans conquered ($\frac{561}{193}$); and thenceforth the struggle was no longer a war, but a slave hunt. The Roman camp soon was the only asylum in the Boian territory; thither the better part of the still surviving population began to take refuge; and the victors were able, without much exaggeration, to report to Rome that nothing remained of the nation of the Boii but old men and children. The nation was thus obliged to resign itself to the fate appointed for it. The Romans demanded the cession of half the territory $(\frac{563}{191})$; the demand could not be refused, and even within the diminished district which was left to the Boii, they soon disappeared, amalgamated with their conquerors.[1]

After the Romans had thus cleared the ground for themselves, the fortresses of Placentia and Cremona, whose colonists had been mostly swept away or dispersed by the troubles of the last few years, were reorganised, and new settlers were sent thither. The new foundations were, in or near the former territory of the Senones, Potentia (near Recanati not far from Ancona, in $\frac{570}{184}$) and Pisaurum (Pesaro, in $\frac{570}{184}$), and, in the newly acquired district of the Boii, the fortresses of Bononia $(\frac{565}{189})$, Mutina $(\frac{571}{183})$, and Parma $(\frac{571}{183})$; the colony of Mutina had been instituted before the war under Hannibal, but that war had interrupted the completion of the settlement. The institution of fortresses was associated, as was always the case, with the construction of military roads. The Flaminian way was prolonged from its northern termination at Ariminum, under the name of the Aemilian way, to Placentia $(\frac{567}{187})$. Moreover, the road from Rome to Arretium or the Cassian way, which perhaps had already been long a municipal road, was taken in charge and

---

[1] According to the account of Strabo these Italian Boii were driven by the Romans over the Alps, and from them proceeded that Boian settlement in what is now Hungary between the Neusiedlersee and the Plattensee, which was attacked and annihilated in the time of Augustus by the Getae who crossed the Danube, but which bequeathed to this district the name of the Boian desert. This account is far from agreeing with the well-attested representation of the Roman annals, according to which the Romans were content with the cession of half the territory; and, in order to explain the disappearance of the Italian Boii, we have really no need to assume a violent expulsion—the other Celtic peoples, although visited to a far less extent by war and colonisation, disappeared not much less rapidly and totally from the ranks of the Italian nations. On the other hand, other accounts suggest the derivation of those Boii on the Plattensee from the main stock of the nation, which formerly had its seat in Bavaria and Bohemia before Germanic tribes pushed it towards the south. But it is altogether very doubtful whether the Boii, whom we find near Bordeaux, on the Po, and in Bohemia, were really scattered branches of one stock, or whether this is not an instance of mere similarity of name. The hypothesis of Strabo may have rested on nothing else than an inference from the similarity of name—an inference such as the ancients drew, often without due reason, in the case of the Cimbri, Veneti, and others.

constructed anew by the Roman community probably in $\frac{583}{171}$; while in $\frac{567}{187}$ the track from Arretium over the Apennines to Bononia as far as the new Aemilian road had been put in order, and furnished a shorter communication between Rome and the fortresses on the Po.   By these comprehensive measures the Apennines were practically superseded as the boundary between the Celtic and Italian territories, and were replaced by the Po. South of the Po there henceforth prevailed mainly the civic constitution of the Italians, beyond it mainly the cantonal constitution of the Celts; and, if the district between the Apennines and the Po was still designated *ager Celticus*, it was but an empty name.

In the north-western mountain-land of Italy, whose valleys and hills were occupied chiefly by the much-subdivided Ligurian stock, the Romans pursued a similar course. Those dwelling immediately to the north of the Arno were extirpated. This fate befell chiefly the Apuani, who dwelt on the Apennines between the Arno and the Magra, and incessantly plundered on the one side the territory of Pisae, on the other that of Bononia and Mutina. Those who did not fall victims in that quarter to the sword of the Romans were transported into Lower Italy to the region of Beneventum ($\frac{574}{180}$); and by energetic measures the Ligurian nation, from which the Romans were obliged in $\frac{578}{176}$ to recover the colony of Mutina which it had conquered, was completely crushed in the mountains which separate the valley of the Po from that of the Arno. The fortress of Luna (not far from Spezzia), established in $\frac{577}{177}$ in the former territory of the Apuani, protected the frontier against the Ligurians just as Aquileia did against the Transalpines, and gave the Romans at the same time an excellent port which henceforth became the station for the passage to Massilia or to Spain. The construction of the coast or Aurelian road from Rome to Luna, and of the cross road carried from Luca by way of Florence to Arretium between the Aurelian and Cassian ways, probably belongs to the same period.

With the more western Ligurian tribes, who held the Genoese Apennines and the Maritime Alps, there were incessant conflicts. They were troublesome neighbours, accustomed to pillage by land and by sea: the Pisans and Massiliots suffered no little injury from their incursions and their piracies. But no permanent results were gained amidst these constant hostilities, or perhaps even aimed at; except apparently that, with a view to have a communication by land with Transalpine Gaul and

Spain in addition to the regular route by sea, the Romans endeavoured to clear the great coast road from Luna by way of Massilia to Emporiae, at least as far as the Alps—beyond the Alps it devolved on the Massiliots to keep the coast navigation open for Roman vessels and the road along the shore open for travellers by land. The interior with its impassable valleys and its rocky fastnesses, and with its poor but dexterous and crafty inhabitants, served the Romans mainly as a school of war for the training and hardening of officers and soldiers.

Wars as they are called, of a similar character with those against the Ligurians, were waged with the Corsicans and to a still greater extent with the inhabitants of the interior of Sardinia, who retaliated for the predatory expeditions directed against them by sudden attacks on the districts along the coast. The expedition of Tiberius Gracchus against the Sardinians in $\frac{577}{177}$ was specially held in remembrance, not so much because it gave " peace " to the province, as because he asserted that he had slain or captured as many as 80,000 of the islanders, and dragged slaves thence in such multitudes to Rome that " as cheap as a Sardinian " became a proverb.

In Africa the policy of Rome was substantially summed up in the one idea, as short-sighted as it was narrow-minded, that she ought to prevent the revival of the power of Carthage, and ought accordingly to keep the unhappy city constantly oppressed and apprehensive of a declaration of war suspended over it by Rome like the sword of Damocles. The stipulation in the treaty of peace, that the Carthaginians should retain their territory undiminished, but that their neighbour Massinissa should have all those possessions guaranteed to him which he or his predecessor had possessed within the Carthaginian bounds, looks almost as if it had been inserted not to prevent, but to provoke disputes. The same remark applies to the obligation imposed by the treaty of peace on the Carthaginians not to make war upon the allies of Rome; so that, according to the letter of the treaty, they were not even entitled to expel their Numidian neighbours from their own undisputed territory. With such stipulations and amidst the uncertainty of African frontier questions in general, the situation of Carthage in presence of a neighbour equally powerful and unscrupulous and of a liege lord who was at once umpire and party in the cause, could not but be a painful one; but the reality was worse than the worst expectations. As early as $\frac{561}{193}$ Carthage found herself suddenly assailed under frivolous pretexts, and saw the richest portion of her territory, the province of Emporiae on the lesser Syrtis, partly plundered by the Numidians, partly even seized and retained by them. Encroachments of this kind were multiplied; the level country passed into the hands of the Numidians, and the Carthaginians with difficulty maintained themselves in the larger towns. Within the last two years alone, the Carthaginians declared in $\frac{582}{172}$, seventy villages had been again wrested from them in opposition to the treaty. Embassy after embassy was despatched to Rome; the Carthaginians adjured the Roman senate either to allow them to defend themselves by arms, or to appoint a court of arbitration with power to enforce their award, or to regulate the frontier anew that they might at least learn once for all how much they were to lose; otherwise it were better to make them Roman subjects at once than thus gradually to deliver them over to the Libyans. But the Roman government, which already in $\frac{554}{200}$ had held forth a direct prospect of extension of territory to their client, of course at the expense of Carthage, seemed to have little objection that he should himself take the booty destined for him; they moderated at times the too great impetuosity of the Libyans, who now retaliated fully on their old tormentors for their former sufferings; but it was in reality for the very sake of inflicting this torture that the Romans had assigned Massinissa as a neighbour to Carthage. All the requests and complaints had no result, except that Roman commissions made their appearance in Africa and after a thorough investigation came to no decision, or that in the negotiations at Rome the envoys of Massinissa pretended a want of instructions and the matter was adjourned. Phoenician patience alone was able to submit meekly to such a position, and even to exhibit towards the despotic victors every attention and courtesy, solicited or unsolicited, with unwearied perseverance. The Carthaginians especially courted Roman favour by sending supplies of grain.

This pliability on the part of the vanquished, however, was not mere patience and resignation. There was still in Carthage a patriotic party, and at its head stood the man, who, wherever fate placed him, was still dreaded by the Romans. It had not abandoned the idea of resuming the struggle by taking advantage of those complications that might be easily foreseen between Rome and the eastern powers; and, as the failure of the magnificent scheme of Hamilcar and his sons had been due mainly to the Carthaginian oligarchy, the chief object was internally to reinvigorate the country for this new struggle.

The salutary influence of adversity, and the clear, noble, and commanding mind of Hannibal, effected political and financial reforms. The oligarchy, which had filled up the measure of its guilty follies by raising a criminal process against the great general, charging him with having intentionally abstained from the capture of Rome and with embezzlement of the Italian spoil —that rotten oligarchy was, on the proposition of Hannibal, overthrown, and a democratic government was introduced such as was suited to the circumstances of the citizens (before $\frac{559}{195}$). The finances were so rapidly reorganised by the collection of arrears and of embezzled moneys and by the introduction of better control, that the contribution due to Rome could be paid without burdening the citizens with any extraordinary taxes. The Roman government, just then on the point of beginning its critical war with the great king of Asia, observed the progress of these events, as may easily be conceived, with apprehension; it was no imaginary danger that the Carthaginian fleet might land in Italy and a second war under Hannibal might spring up there, while the Roman legions were fighting in Asia Minor. We can scarcely, therefore, censure the Romans for sending an embassy to Carthage (in $\frac{559}{195}$) which was charged, in all probability, to demand the surrender of Hannibal. The spiteful Carthaginian oligarchs, who sent letter after letter to Rome to denounce to the national foe the hero who had overthrown them as having entered into secret communications with the powers unfriendly to Rome, were contemptible, but their information was probably correct; and, true as it was that that embassy involved a humiliating confession of the dread with which the simple shofete of Carthage inspired so powerful a people, and natural and honourable as it was that the proud conqueror of Zama should take exception in the senate to so humiliating a step, still that confession was nothing but the simple truth, and Hannibal was of a genius so extraordinary, that none but sentimental politicians in Rome could tolerate him longer at the head of the Carthaginian state. The marked recognition thus accorded to him by the Roman government scarcely took himself by surprise. As it was Hannibal and not Carthage that had carried on the last war, so it was he who had to bear the fate of the vanquished. The Carthaginians could do nothing but submit and be thankful that Hannibal, sparing them the greater disgrace of delivering him up by a speedy and prudent flight to the East, left to his ancestral city merely the lesser disgrace of banishing its greatest citizen for ever from his native land, of confiscating his property, and of razing his house. The profound saying that those are the favourites of the gods on whom they lavish infinite joys and infinite sorrows, thus verified itself in full measure in the case of Hannibal.

A graver responsibility than that arising out of their proceedings against Hannibal attaches to the Roman government for their persistence in suspecting and tormenting the city after his removal. Parties indeed fermented there as before; but, after the withdrawal of the extraordinary man who had well-nigh changed the destinies of the world, the patriot party was not of much more importance in Carthage than in Aetolia or Achaia. The most rational of the various ideas which then agitated the unhappy city was beyond doubt that of attaching themselves to Massinissa, and of converting him from the oppressor into the protector of the Phoenicians. But neither the national section of the patriots nor the section with Libyan tendencies attained the helm; on the contrary the government remained in the hands of the oligarchs friendly to Rome, who, so far as they did not altogether renounce thought of the future, clung to the single idea of saving the material prosperity and the communal freedom of Carthage under Roman protection. With this state of matters the Romans might well have been content. But neither the multitude, nor even the senators of the average stamp, could rid themselves of the profound alarm produced by the campaigns of Hannibal; and the Roman merchants with envious eyes beheld the city even now, when its political power was gone, possessed of extensive commerical dependencies and of a firmly established wealth which nothing could shake. Already in $\frac{567}{187}$ the Carthaginian government offered to pay up at once the whole instalments stipulated in the treaty of $\frac{553}{201}$—an offer which the Romans, who attached far more importance to the having Carthage tributary than to the sums of money themselves, naturally declined, and only deduced from it the conviction that, in spite of all the trouble they had taken, the city was not ruined and was not capable of ruin. Fresh reports were ever circulating through Rome as to the intrigues of the faithless Phoenicians. At one time it was alleged that Aristo of Tyre had been seen in Carthage as an emissary of Hannibal, to prepare the citizens for the landing of an Asiatic war-fleet ($\frac{561}{193}$); at another, that the council had, in a secret nocturnal sitting in the temple of the God of Healing, given audience to the envoys of Perseus ($\frac{581}{173}$); at another there was talk of the powerful fleet which was being equipped in Carthage for the Macedonian war ($\frac{583}{171}$). It is probable that these and similar reports were founded on nothing more than, at most, individual indiscretions; but still they were the signal for new diplomatic misrepresentations on the part of Rome, and for new aggressions on the part of Massinissa, and the idea gained ground the more, the less sense and reason there was in it, that the Carthaginian question would not be settled without a third Punic war.

While the power of the Phoenicians was thus declining in the land of their adoption, just as it had long ago sunk in their original home, a new state grew up by their side. The northern coast of Africa has been inhabited from time immemorial, and is inhabited still, by a people who themselves assume the name of Shilah or Tamazigt, whom the Greeks and Romans call Nomades or Numidians, *i.e.* the "pastoral" people, and the Arabs call Berbers, although they also at times designate them as "shepherds" (Shâwie), and to whom we are wont to give the name of Berbers or Kabyles. This people is, so far as its language has been hitherto investigated, related to no other known nation. In the Carthaginian period these tribes, with the exception of those dwelling immediately around Carthage or immediately on the coast, had on the whole maintained their independence, and had also substantially retained their pastoral and equestrian life, such as the inhabitants of the Atlas lead at the present day; although they were not strangers to the Phoenician alphabet and Phoenician civilisation generally (p. 11), and instances occurred in which the Berber sheiks had their sons educated in Carthage and intermarried with the families of the Phoenician nobility. It was not the policy of the Romans to have direct possessions of their own in Africa; they preferred to rear a state there which should not be of sufficient importance to dispense with Roman protection, and yet should be sufficiently strong to keep down the power of Carthage now that it was restricted to Africa, and to render all freedom of movement impossible for the tortured city. They found what they sought among the native princes. About the time of the Hannibalic war the natives of North Africa were subject to three principal kings, each of whom, according to the custom there, had a multitude of princes bound to follow his banner; Bocchar king of the Mauri, who ruled from the Atlantic Ocean to the river Molochath (now Mluia, on the boundary between Morocco and the French territory); Syphax king of the Massaesyli, who ruled from the last-named point to the "Perforated Promontory," as it was called (Seba Rûs, between Djidjeli and Bona), in what

are now the provinces of Oran and Algiers; and Massinissa king
of the Massyli, who ruled from the Tretum Promontorium to the
boundary of Carthage, in what is now the province of Constantine. The most powerful of these, Syphax king of Siga, had
been vanquished in the last war between Rome and Carthage
and carried away captive to Rome, where he died in captivity.
His wide dominions were mainly given to Massinissa; although
Vermina the son of Syphax by humble petition recovered
a small portion of his father's territory from the Romans ($\frac{554}{200}$),
he was unable to deprive the earlier ally of the Romans of his
position as the privileged oppressor of Carthage.

Massinissa became the founder of the Numidian kingdom;
and seldom has choice or accident hit upon a man so thoroughly
fitted for his post. In body sound and supple up to extreme
old age; temperate and sober like an Arab; capable of enduring
any fatigue, of standing on the same spot from morning to
evening, and of sitting four-and-twenty hours on horseback;
tried alike as a soldier and a general amidst the romantic
vicissitudes of his youth as well as on the battle-fields of Spain,
and not less master of the more difficult art of maintaining
discipline in his numerous household and order in his dominions;
with equal unscrupulousness ready to throw himself at the feet
of his powerful protector, or to tread under foot his weaker
neighbour; and, in addition to all this, as accurately acquainted
with the circumstances of Carthage where he was educated and
had been on familiar terms in the noblest houses, as he was
filled with an African bitterness of hatred towards his own and
his people's oppressors,—this remarkable man became the soul
of the revival of his nation, which had seemed on the point of
perishing, and of whose virtues and faults he appeared as it
were a living embodiment. Fortune favoured him, as in everything, so especially in the fact, that it allowed him time for his
work. He died in the ninetieth year of his age ($\frac{516-605}{238-149}$), and
in the sixtieth year of his reign, retaining to the last the full
enjoyment of his bodily and mental powers, leaving behind him
a son one year old, and possessing the reputation of having been
the strongest man and the best and most fortunate king of his
age.

We have already narrated how palpably the Romans in their
management of African affairs displayed their studied leaning
towards Massinissa, and how zealously and constantly the latter
availed himself of the tacit permission to enlarge his territory at
the expense of Carthage. The whole interior to the border of

the desert fell to the native sovereign as it were of its own accord, and even the upper valley of the Bagradas (Mejerda) with the rich town of Vaga became subject to the king; on the coast also to the east of Carthage he occupied the old Sidonian city of Great Leptis and other districts, so that his kingdom stretched from the Mauretanian to the Cyrenaean frontier, enclosed the Carthaginian territory on every side by land, and everywhere pressed, in the closest vicinity, on the Phoenicians. It admits of no doubt, that he looked on Carthage as his future capital; the Libyan party there was significant. But it was not only by the diminution of her territory that Carthage suffered injury. The roving shepherds were converted by their great king into another people. After the example of the king, who brought the fields under cultivation far and wide and bequeathed to each of his sons considerable landed estates, his subjects also began to settle and to practise agriculture. As he converted his shepherds into settled citizens, he converted also his hordes of plunderers into soldiers who were deemed by Rome worthy to fight side by side with her legions; and he bequeathed to his successors a richly-filled treasury, a well-disciplined army, and even a fleet. His residence Cirta (Constantine) became the stirring capital of a powerful state, and a chief seat of Phoenician civilisation, which was zealously fostered at the court of the Berber king—fostered perhaps studiously with a view to the future Carthagino-Numidian kingdom. The hitherto degraded Libyan nationality thus rose in its own estimation, and the native manners and language made their way even into the old Phoenician towns, such as Great Leptis. The Berber began, under the aegis of Rome, to feel himself the equal or even the superior of the Phoenician; Carthaginian envoys at Rome had to submit to be told that they were aliens in Africa, and that the land belonged to the Libyans. The Phoenico-national civilisation of North Africa, which still retained life and vigour even under the levelling times of the empire, was far more the work of Massinissa than of the Carthaginians.

In Spain the Greek and Phoenician towns along the coast, such as Emporiae, Saguntum, New Carthage, Malaca, and Gades, submitted to the Roman rule the more readily, that, left to their own resources, they would hardly have been able to protect themselves from the natives; as for similar reasons Massilia, although far more important and more capable of self-defence than those towns, did not omit to secure a powerful support in case of need by closely attaching itself to the Romans, to whom it was in return very serviceable as an intermediate station between Italy and Spain. The natives, on the other hand, gave to the Romans endless trouble. It is true that there were not wanting the rudiments of a national Iberian civilisation, although of its special character it is scarcely possible for us to acquire any clear idea. We find among the Iberians a widely diffused national writing, which divides itself into two chief kinds, that of the valley of the Ebro, and the Andalusian, and each of these was probably subdivided into various branches: this writing seems to have originated at a very early period, and to be traceable rather to the old Greek than to the Phoenician alphabet. There is a tradition that the Turdetani (round Seville) possessed lays from very ancient times, a metrical book of laws of 6000 verses, and even historical records; at any rate this tribe is described as the most civilised of all the Spanish tribes, and at the same time the least warlike; indeed, it regularly carried on its wars by means of foreign mercenaries. To the same region probably we must refer Polybius' descriptions of the flourishing condition of agriculture and the rearing of cattle in Spain—so that, in the absence of opportunity of export, grain and flesh were to be had at nominal prices—and of the splendid royal palaces with golden and silver jars full of " barley wine." At least a portion of the Spaniards, moreover, zealously embraced the elements of culture which the Romans brought along with them, so that the process of Latinising made more rapid progress in Spain than anywhere else in the transmarine provinces. For example, warm baths after the Italian fashion came into use even at this period among the natives. Roman money, too, was to all appearance not only current in Spain far earlier than elsewhere out of Italy, but was imitated in Spanish coins; a circumstance in some measure explained by the rich silver-mines of the country. The so-called " silver of Osca " (now Huesca in Arragon), *i.e.* Spanish *denarii* with Iberian inscriptions, is mentioned in $\frac{5\,6\,2}{1\,9\,2}$; and the commencement of their coinage cannot be placed much later, because the impression is imitated from that of the oldest Roman *denarii*.

But, while in the southern and eastern provinces the culture of the natives may have so far prepared the way for Roman civilisation and Roman rule that these encountered no serious difficulties, the west and north on the other hand, and the whole of the interior, were occupied by numerous tribes more or less barbarous, who knew little of any kind of civilisation—in Intercatia, for instance, the use of gold and silver was still unknown about $\frac{600}{150}$—and who were on no better terms with each other than with the Romans. A characteristic trait in these free Spaniards was the chivalrous spirit of the men and, at least to an equal extent, of the women. When a mother sent forth her son to battle, she roused his spirit by the recital of the feats of his ancestors; and the fairest maiden unasked offered her hand in marriage to the bravest man. Single combat was common, both with a view to determine the prize of valour, and for the settlement of lawsuits; even disputes among the relatives of princes as to the succession were settled in this way. It not unfrequently happened that a well-known warrior confronted the ranks of the enemy and challenged an antagonist by name; the defeated champion then surrendered his mantle and sword to his opponent, and even entered into relations of friendship and hospitality with him. Twenty years after the close of the second Punic war, the little Celtiberian community of Complega (in the neighbourhood of the sources of the Tagus) sent a message to the Roman general, that unless he sent to them for every man that had fallen a horse, a mantle, and a sword, it would fare ill with him. Proud of their military honour, so that they frequently could not bear to survive the disgrace of being disarmed, the Spaniards were nevertheless disposed to follow any one who should enlist their services, and to stake their lives in any foreign quarrel. The summons was characteristic, which a Roman general well acquainted with the customs of the country sent to a Celtiberian band fighting in the pay of the Turdetani against the Romans—either to return home, or to enter the Roman service with double pay, or to fix time and place for battle. If no recruiting officer made his appearance, they met of their own accord in free bands, with the view of pillaging the more peaceful districts and even of capturing and occupying towns, quite after the manner of the Campanians. The wildness and insecurity of the inland districts are attested by the fact that the being sent into the interior westward of Cartagena was regarded by the Romans as a severe punishment, and that in periods of any excitement the Roman commandants of Further Spain took with them escorts of as many as 6000 men. They are still more clearly shown by the singular relations subsisting between the Greeks and their Spanish neighbours in the Graeco-Spanish double city of Emporiae, at the eastern extremity of the Pyrenees. The Greek settlers, who dwelt on a peninsula separated on the landward side from the Spanish part of the town by a wall, took care that this wall should be guarded every night by a third of their civic force, and that one of the superior magistrates should constantly superintend the watch at the only gate; no Spaniard was allowed to set foot in the Greek city, and the Greeks conveyed their merchandise to the natives only in numerous and well-escorted companies.

These natives, full of restlessness and fond of war—full of the spirit of the Cid and of Don Quixote—were now to be tamed and, if possible, civilised by the Romans. In a military point of view the task was not difficult. It is true that the Spaniards showed themselves, not only when behind the walls of their cities or under the leadership of Hannibal, but even when left to themselves and in the open field of battle, no contemptible opponents; with their short two-edged sword which the Romans subsequently adopted from them, and their formidable assaulting columns, they not unfrequently made even the Roman legions waver. Had they been able to submit to military discipline and to political combination, they might perhaps have shaken off the foreign yoke imposed on them. But their valour was rather that of the guerilla than of the soldier, and they were utterly void of political judgment. Thus in Spain there was no serious war, but as little was there any real peace; the Spaniards, as Cæsar afterwards very justly pointed out to them, never showed themselves quiet in peace or strenuous in war. Easy as it was for a Roman general to scatter a host of insurgents, it was difficult for the Roman statesman to devise any suitable means of really pacifying and civilising Spain. In fact, he could only deal with it by palliative measures; because the only really adequate expedient, a comprehensive Latin colonisation, was not accordant with the general aim of Roman policy at this period.

The territory which the Romans acquired in Spain in the course of the second Punic war was from the beginning divided into two masses—the province formerly Carthaginian, which embraced in the first instance the present districts of Andalusia, Granada, Murcia, and Valencia, and the province of the Ebro, or the modern Arragon and Catalonia, the headquarters of the Roman army during the last war. Out of these territories were formed the two Roman provinces of Further and Hither Spain. The Romans sought gradually to reduce to subjection the interior corresponding nearly to the two Castiles, which they comprehended under the general name of Celtiberia, while they were content with checking the incursions of the inhabitants of the western provinces, more especially those of the Lusitanians in the modern Portugal and the Spanish Estremadura, into the Roman territory; with the tribes on the north coast, the Gallaecians, Asturians, and Cantabrians, they did not as yet come into contact at all. The territories thus won, however, could not be maintained and secured without a standing garrison, for the governor of Hither Spain had no small trouble every year with the chastisement of the Celtiberians, and the governor of the more remote province found similar employment in repelling the Lusitanians. It was needful accordingly to maintain in Spain a Roman army of four strong legions, or about 40,000 men, year after year; besides which the general levy had often to be called out in the districts occupied by Rome, to reinforce the legions. This was of great importance for two reasons: it was in Spain that the military occupation of the land first became continuous, at least on any great scale; and it was there consequently that the military service acquired a permanent character. The old Roman custom of sending troops only where the exigencies of war at the moment required them, and of not keeping the men called to serve, except in very serious and important wars, under arms for more than a year, was found incompatible with the retention of the turbulent and remote Spanish provinces beyond the sea; it was absolutely impossible to withdraw the troops from these, and very dangerous even to relieve them extensively. The Roman burgesses began to perceive that dominion over a foreign people is an annoyance not only to the slave, but to the master, and murmured loudly regarding the odious war-service of Spain. While the new generals with good reason refused to allow the relief of the existing corps as a whole, the men mutinied and threatened that, if they were not allowed their discharge, they would take it of their own accord.

The wars themselves, which the Romans waged in Spain, were but of subordinate importance. They began with the very departure of Scipio (p. 153), and continued as long as the war under Hannibal lasted. After the peace with Carthage (in $\frac{553}{201}$) there was a cessation of arms in the peninsula; but only for a short time. In $\frac{557}{197}$ a general insurrection broke out in both provinces; the commander of the Further province was hard pressed; the commander of Hither Spain was completely defeated, and was himself slain. It was necessary to take up the war in earnest, and although in the meantime the able praetor Quintus Minucius had mastered the first danger, the senate resolved in $\frac{559}{195}$ to send the consul Marcus Cato in person to Spain. On landing at Emporiae he actually found the whole of Hither Spain overrun by the insurgents; with difficulty that seaport and one or two strongholds in the interior were still held for Rome. A pitched battle took place between the insurgents and the consular army, in which, after an obstinate conflict man against man, the Roman military skill at length decided the day with its last reserve. The whole of Hither Spain thereupon sent in its submission: so little, however, was this submission meant in earnest, that on a rumour of the consul having returned to Rome the insurrection immediately recommenced. But the rumour was false; and after Cato had rapidly reduced the communities which had revolted for the second time and sold them *en masse* into slavery, he decreed a general disarming of the Spaniards in the Hither province, and issued orders to all the towns of the natives from the Pyrenees to the Guadalquivir to pull down their walls on one and the same day. No one knew how far the command extended, and there was no time to come to any understanding; most of the communities complied; and of the few that were refractory not many ventured, when the Roman army soon appeared before their walls, to await its assault.

These energetic measures were certainly not without permanent effect. Nevertheless the Romans had almost every year to reduce to subjection some mountain valley or mountain stronghold in the " peaceful province," and the constant incursions of the Lusitanians into the Further province terminated occasionally in the severe defeat of the Romans. In $\frac{563}{191}$, for instance, a Roman army was obliged after heavy loss to abandon its camp, and to return by forced marches into the more tranquil districts. It was not till after a victory gained by the praetor Lucius Aemilius Paullus[1] in $\frac{565}{189}$, and a second still more considerable gained by the brave praetor Gaius Calpurnius beyond the Tagus over the Lusitanians in $\frac{569}{185}$, that quiet for some time

---

[1] The following decree of the praetor Lucius Aemilius Paullus has recently been discovered on a copper tablet found in the neighbourhood of Gibraltar, and now preserved in the Paris Museum: *L. Aimilius L. f. inpeirator decreivit, utei quei Hastensium* [Hasta Regia, not far from Jerez de la Frontera] *servei in turri Lascutana* [known from coins and Plin. iii. 1, 15, but site uncertain] *habitarent, leiberei essent. Agrum oppidumqu[e], quod ea tempestate posedissent, item possidere habereque iousit, dum poplus senatusque Romanus vellet. Act. in castreis, a.d. XII. k. Febr.* [21st Jan. $\frac{564}{190}$ or $\frac{565}{189}$]. This is the oldest Roman document which we possess in the original, drawn up two years earlier than the well-known edict of the consuls of $\frac{568}{186}$ in reference to the affair of the Bacchanalia.

prevailed. In Further Spain the hitherto almost nominal rule of the Romans over the Celtiberian tribes was converted into something more real by Quintus Fulvius Flaccus, who after a great victory over them in $\frac{573}{181}$ compelled at least the adjacent cantons to submission; and especially by his successor Tiberius Gracchus ($\frac{575}{179}$, $\frac{576}{178}$), who achieved results of a permanent character not only by his arms, by which he reduced three hundred Spanish townships, but still more by his adroitness in adapting himself to the views and habits of the simple and haughty nation. He induced Celtiberians of note to take service in the Roman army, and so created a class of dependents; he assigned land to the roving tribes, and collected them in towns—the Spanish town Graccurris preserved the Roman's name—and so imposed a serious check on their freebooter habits; he regulated the relations of the several tribes to the Romans by just and wise treaties, and so stopped, as far as possible, the springs of future rebellion. His name was held in grateful remembrance by the Spaniards, and comparative peace henceforth reigned in the land, although the Celtiberians still from time to time winced under the yoke.

The system of administration in the two Spanish provinces was similar to that of the Sicilo-Sardinian province, but not identical. The superintendence was in both instances vested in two auxiliary consuls, who were first nominated in $\frac{567}{197}$, in which year also the regulation of the boundaries and the definitive organisation of the two provinces took place. The judicious enactment of the Baebian law ($\frac{662}{192}$?), that the Spanish praetors should always be nominated for two years, was not seriously carried out in consequence of the increasing competition for the highest magistracies, and still more in consequence of the jealous supervision exercised over the powers of the magistrates by the senate; and in Spain also, except where deviations occurred in extraordinary circumstances, the Romans adhered to the system of annually changing the governors—a system especially injudicious in the case of provinces so remote and with which it was so difficult to gain an acquaintance. The dependent communities were universally tributary; but, instead of the Sicilian and Sardinian tenths and customs, in Spain fixed payments in money or other contributions were imposed by the Romans, just as formerly by the Carthaginians, on the several towns and tribes: the collection of these by military means was prohibited by a decree of the senate in $\frac{583}{171}$, in consequence of the complaints of the Spanish communities. Grain was not furnished in their case except for compensation, and even then the governor might not levy more than a twentieth; besides, conformably to the just-mentioned ordinance of the supreme authority, he was bound to adjust the compensation in an equitable manner.   On the other hand, the obligation of the Spanish subjects to furnish contingents to the Roman armies had an importance very different from that which belonged to it at least in peaceful Sicily, and it was strictly regulated in the several treaties.   The right, too, of coining silver money of the Roman standard appears to have been very frequently conceded to the Spanish towns, and the monopoly of coining seems to have been by no means asserted by the Roman government with the same strictness as in Sicily.   Rome had too much need of subjects in Spain, not to proceed with all possible caution and tenderness in the introduction and the working of the provincial constitution there.   Among the communities specially favoured by Rome were the great cities along the coast of Greek, Phoenician, or Roman foundation, such as Saguntum, Gades, and Tarraco, which, as the natural pillars of the Roman rule in the peninsula, were admitted to alliance with Rome.   On the whole, Spain was in a military as well as financial point of view a burden rather than a gain to the Roman commonwealth; and the question naturally occurs, Why did the Roman government, whose policy at that time evidently did not contemplate the acquisition of countries beyond the sea, not rid itself of so troublesome a possession?   The not inconsiderable commercial connections of Spain, her important iron-mines, and her still more important silver-mines famous from ancient times even in the far East [1]— the working of which Rome, like Carthage, took into her own hands, and the management of which was specially regulated by Marcus Cato ($\frac{559}{195}$)—must beyond doubt have co-operated to induce its retention; but the chief reason of the Romans for retaining the peninsula in their own immediate possession was, that there were no states in that quarter of similar character to the Massiliot republic in the land of the Celts and the Numidian kingdom in Libya, and that thus they could not abandon Spain without putting it into the power of any adventurer to revive the Spanish empire of the Barcides.

[1] 1 Maccab. viii. 3.   " And Judas heard what the Romans had done in the land of Hispania to become masters of the silver and gold mines there."

CHAPTER VIII

THE EASTERN STATES AND THE SECOND MACEDONIAN WAR

The work, which Alexander king of Macedonia had begun a
century before the Romans acquired their first footing in the
territory which he had called his own, had in the course of time
—while adhering substantially to the great fundamental idea of
Hellenising the East—changed and expanded into the construction of a system of Helleno-Asiatic states. The unconquerable
propensity of the Greeks for migration and colonising, which had
formerly carried their traders to Massilia and Cyrene, to the Nile
and to the Black Sea, now enabled them to retain what the king
had won; and under the protection of the *sarissae*, Greek civilisation peacefully domiciled itself everywhere throughout the
ancient empire of the Achaemenidae. The officers, who divided
the heritage of the great commander, gradually settled their
differences, and a system of equilibrium was established whose
very oscillations manifest some sort of regularity.

Of the three states of the first rank belonging to this system
—Macedonia, Asia, and Egypt—Macedonia under Philip the
Fifth, who had occupied the throne since $\frac{534}{520}$, was externally at
least very much what it had been under Philip the Second, the
father of Alexander—a compact military state with its finances
in good order. On its northern frontier matters had resumed
their former footing, after the waves of the Gallic inundation had
rolled away; the guard of the frontier kept the Illyrian barbarians in check without difficulty, at least in ordinary times.
In the south, not only was Greece in general dependent on
Macedonia, but a large portion of it—including all Thessaly in
its widest sense from Olympus to the Spercheius and the peninsula of Magnesia, the large and important island of Euboea, the
provinces of Locris, Phocis, and Doris, and, lastly, a number of
isolated positions in Attica and in the Peloponnesus, such as
the promontory of Sunium, Corinth, Orchomenus, Heraea, the
Triphylian territory — was directly subject to Macedon and
received Macedonian garrisons; more especially the three important fortresses of Demetrias in Magnesia, Chalcis in Euboea,
and Corinth, "the three fetters of the Hellenes." But the

strength of the state lay above all in its hereditary soil, the province of Macedonia. The population, indeed, of that extensive territory was remarkably scanty; Macedonia, putting forth all her energies, was scarcely able to bring into the field as many men as were contained in an ordinary consular army of two legions; and it was unmistakably evident that the land had not yet recovered from the depopulation occasioned by the campaigns of Alexander and by the Gallic invasion. But while in Greece proper the moral and political energy of the people had decayed, the day of national vigour seemed to have gone by, life appeared scarce worth living for, and even the better spirits there spent their time over the wine-cup, in fencing with their rapiers, or in study by the midnight lamp; while in the East and Alexandria the Greeks were able perhaps to disseminate elements of culture among the dense native population and to diffuse among that population their language and their loquacity, their science and pseudo-science, but were barely sufficient in point of number to supply the nations with officers, statesmen, and schoolmasters, and were far too few to form even in the cities a middle-class of the pure Greek type; there still existed, on the other hand, in northern Greece a goodly portion of the old national vigour, which had produced the warriors of Marathon. Hence arose the confidence with which the Macedonians, Aetolians, and Acarnanians, wherever they made their appearance in the East, claimed and obtained acknowledgment of their superiority; and hence the transcendent position which they occupied at the courts of Alexandria and Antioch. There is a characteristic story, that an Alexandrian who had lived for a considerable time in Macedonia and had adopted the manners and the dress of that country, on returning to his native city, looked upon himself as a man and upon the Alexandrians as little better than slaves. This sturdy vigour and unimpaired national spirit were turned to peculiarly good account by the Macedonians, as the most powerful and best organised of the states of northern Greece. There, no doubt, absolutism had emerged in opposition to the old constitution, which to some extent recognised different estates; but sovereign and subject by no means stood towards each other in Macedonia as they stood in Asia and Egypt, and the people still felt itself independent and free. In steadfast resistance to the public enemy under whatever name, in unshaken fidelity towards their native country and their hereditary government, and in persevering courage amidst the severest trials, no nation in ancient history bears so close a resemblance to the Roman people as the Macedonians; and the almost miraculous regeneration of the state after the Gallic invasion redounds to the imperishable honour of its leaders and of the people whom they led.

The second of the great states, Asia, was nothing but Persia superficially remodelled and Hellenised—the empire of "the king of kings," as its master was wont to call himself in a style characteristic at once of his arrogance and of his weakness—with the same pretensions to rule from the Hellespont to the Punjab, and with the same disjointed organisation; an aggregate of dependent states in various degrees of dependence, of insubordinate satrapies, and of half-free Greek cities. In Asia Minor more especially, which was nominally included in the empire of the Seleucidae, the whole north coast and the greater part of the eastern interior were practically in the hands of native dynasties or of the Celtic hordes that had penetrated thither from Europe; a considerable portion of the west was in the possession of the kings of Pergamus, and the islands and coast towns were some of them Egyptian, some of them free; so that little more was left to the great king than the interior of Cilicia, Phrygia, and Lydia, and a great number of titular claims, not easily made good, against free cities and princes—exactly similar in character to the sovereignty of the German emperor, in his day, beyond his hereditary dominions. The strength of the empire was expended in vain endeavours to expel the Egyptians from the provinces along the coast; in frontier strife with the eastern peoples, the Parthians and Bactrians; in feuds with the Celts, who to the misfortune of Asia Minor had settled within its bounds; in constant efforts to check the attempts of the eastern satraps and of the Greek cities of Asia Minor to achieve their independence; and in family quarrels and insurrections of pretenders. None indeed of the states founded by the successors of Alexander were free from such attempts, or from the other horrors which absolute monarchy in degenerate times brings in its train; but in the kingdom of Asia these evils were more injurious than elsewhere, because, from the lax composition of the empire, they usually led to the severance of particular portions from it for longer or shorter periods.

In marked contrast to Asia, Egypt formed a consolidated and united state, in which the intelligent statecraft of the first Lagidae, skilfully availing itself of ancient national and religious precedent, had established a completely absolute cabinet government, and in which even the worst misrule failed to provoke any attempt either at emancipation or disruption. Very different from the Macedonians, whose national attachment to royalty was based upon their personal dignity and was its political expression, the rural population in Egypt was wholly passive; the capital on the other hand was everything, and that capital was a dependency of the court. The remissness and indolence of its rulers, accordingly, paralysed the state in Egypt still more than in Macedonia and in Asia; while on the other hand when wielded by men, like the first Ptolemy and Ptolemy Euergetes, such a state machine proved itself extremely useful. It was one of the peculiar advantages of Egypt as compared with its two great rivals, that its policy did not grasp at shadows, but pursued definite and attainable objects. Macedonia, the home of Alexander, and Asia, the land where he had established his throne, never ceased to regard themselves as direct continuations of the Alexandrine monarchy and more or less loudly asserted their claim to represent it at least, if not to restore it. The Lagidae never tried to found a universal empire, and never dreamt of conquering India; but, by way of compensation, they drew the whole traffic between India and the Mediterranean from the Phoenician ports to Alexandria, and made Egypt the first commercial and maritime state of this epoch, and the mistress of the eastern Mediterranean and of its coasts and islands. It is a significant fact, that Ptolemy III. Euergetes voluntarily restored all his conquests to Seleucus Callinicus except the seaport of Antioch. Partly by this means, partly by its favourable geographical situation, Egypt attained, with reference to the two continental powers, an excellent military position either for defence or for attack. While an opponent even in the full career of success was hardly in a position seriously to threaten Egypt, which was almost inaccessible on any side to land armies, the Egyptians were able by sea to establish themselves not only in Cyrene, but also in Cyprus and the Cyclades, on the Phoenico-Syrian coast, on the whole south and west coast of Asia Minor, and even in Europe on the Thracian Chersonese. By their unexampled skill in turning to account the fertile valley of the Nile for the direct benefit of the treasury, and by a financial system—equally sagacious and unscrupulous—earnestly and adroitly calculated to foster material interests, the court of Alexandria was constantly superior to its opponents even as a moneyed power. Lastly, the intelligent munificence, with which the Lagidae encouraged the tendency of the age towards earnest inquiry in all departments of enterprise and of knowledge, skilfully confining such inquiries within the bounds of absolute monarchy and entwining them with its interests, was productive of direct advantage to the state, whose ship-building and machine-making showed traces of the beneficial influence of Alexandrian mathematics; and not only so, but also rendered that new development of intellectual power—the most important and the greatest, which the Hellenic nation after its political dismemberment produced—subservient, so far as it would consent to be serviceable at all, to the Alexandrian court. Had the empire of Alexander continued to stand, Greek science and art would have found a state worthy and capable of containing them. Now, when the nation had fallen to pieces, a learned cosmopolitanism grew up in it luxuriantly, and was very soon attracted by the magnet of Alexandria, where scientific appliances and collections were inexhaustible, where kings composed tragedies and ministers wrote commentaries on them, and where pensions and academies flourished.

The mutual relations of the three great states are evident from this description. The maritime power, which ruled the coasts and monopolised the sea, was necessarily led after the first great success—the political separation of the European from the Asiatic continent—to direct its further efforts towards the weakening of the two great states on the mainland, and consequently towards the protection of the several minor states; whereas Macedonia and Asia, while regarding each other as rivals, recognised above all their common adversary in Egypt, and combined, or at any rate should have combined, against it.

Among the states of the second rank, merely an indirect importance, so far as concerned the contact between the East and the West, attached in the first instance to that series of states which, stretching from the southern end of the Caspian Sea to the Hellespont, occupied the interior and the north coast of Asia Minor: Atropatene (in the modern Aderbijan, south-west of the Caspian), next to it Armenia, Cappadocia in the interior of Asia Minor, Pontus on the south-east, and Bithynia on the south-west, shore of the Black Sea. All of these were fragments of the great Persian empire, and were ruled by Oriental, mostly old Persian, dynasties—the remote mountain-land of Atropatene in particular was the true asylum of the ancient Persian system, over which even the expedition of Alexander had swept without leaving a trace—and all were in the same relation of temporary and superficial dependence on the Greek dynasty, which had taken or wished to take the place of the great kings in Asia.

Of greater importance in its general relations was the Celtic state in the interior of Asia Minor. There, intermediate between Bithynia, Paphlagonia, Cappadocia, and Phrygia, three Celtic tribes — the Tolistobogi, the Tectosages, and Trocmi — had settled, without abandoning either their native language and manners or their constitution and their trade as freebooters. The twelve tetrarchs, one of whom was appointed to preside over each of the four cantons in each of the three tribes, formed with their council of 300 men, the supreme authority of the nation, and assembled at the "holy place" (*Drunemetum*), especially for the pronouncing of capital sentences. Singular as this cantonal constitution of the Celts appeared to the Asiatics, equally strange seemed to them the adventurous and marauding habits of the northern intruders, who on the one hand furnished their unwarlike neighbours with mercenaries for every war, and on the other plundered or levied contributions from the surrounding districts. These rude but vigorous barbarians were the general terror of the effeminate surrounding nations, and even of the great kings of Asia themselves, who, after several Asiatic armies had been destroyed by the Celts and king Antiochus I. Soter had even lost his life in conflict with them ($\frac{493}{281}$), agreed at last to pay them tribute.

In consequence of bold and successful measures of opposition to these Gallic hordes, Attalus, a wealthy citizen of Pergamus, received the royal title from his native city and bequeathed it to his posterity. This new court was in miniature what that of Alexandria was on a great scale. Here too the promotion of material interests and the fostering of art and literature formed the order of the day, and the government pursued a cautious and sober cabinet policy, the main object of which was on the one hand to weaken its two dangerous continental neighbours, on the other to establish an independent Greek state in the west of Asia Minor. A well-filled treasury contributed greatly to the importance of these rulers of Pergamus. They advanced considerable sums to the kings of Syria, the repayment of which afterwards formed part of the Roman conditions of peace. They succeeded even in gaining territory in this way; Aegina, for instance, which the allied Romans and Aetolians had wrested in the last war from Philip's allies, the Achaeans, was sold by the Aetolians, to whom it fell in terms of the treaty, to Attalus for 30 talents (£7300). But, notwithstanding the splendour of the court and the royal title, the commonwealth of Pergamus always retained something of an urban character; and in its policy it usually went along with the free cities. Attalus himself, the Lorenzo de' Medici of antiquity, remained throughout life a wealthy burgher; and the family life of the Attalid house, from which harmony and cordiality were not banished by the royal title, formed a striking contrast to the dissolute and scandalous behaviour of more aristocratic dynasties.

In European Greece—exclusive of the Roman possessions on the west coast, in the most important of which, particularly Corcyra, Roman magistrates appear to have resided (p. 68), and the territory directly subject to Macedonia—the powers more or less in a position to pursue a policy of their own were the Epirots, Acarnanians, and Aetolians in northern Greece, the Boeotians and Athenians in central Greece, and the Achaeans, Lacedaemonians, Messenians, and Eleans in the Peloponnesus. Among these, the republics of the Epirots, Acarnanians and Boeotians were in various ways closely knit to Macedonia—the Acarnanians more especially, because it was only Macedonian protection that enabled them to escape the destruction with which they were threatened by the Aetolians; none of them were of any consequence. Their internal condition was very various. The state of things may to some extent be illustrated by the fact, that among the Boeotians—where, it is true, matters reached their worst—it had become customary to make over every property, which did not descend to heirs in the direct line, to the *syssitia ;* and, in the case of candidates for the public magistracies, for a quarter of a century the primary condition of election was that they should bind themselves not to allow any creditor, least of all a foreign one, to sue his debtor.

The Athenians were in the habit of receiving support against Macedonia from Alexandria, and were in close league with the Aetolians. But they too were totally powerless, and hardly anything save the halo of Attic poetry and art distinguished these unworthy representatives of a glorious past from a number of petty towns of the same stamp.

The power of the Aetolian confederacy manifested a greater vigour. The energy of the northern Greek character was still unbroken there, although it had degenerated into a reckless impatience of discipline and control. It was a public law in Aetolia, that an Aetolian might serve as a mercenary against any state, even against a state in alliance with his own country;

and, when the other Greeks urgently besought them to redress
this scandal, the Aetolian diet declared that Aetolia might
sooner be removed from its place than this principle from their
national code. The Aetolians might have been of great service
to the Greek nation, had they not inflicted still greater injury
on it by their system of organised robbery, by their thorough
hostility to the Achaean confederacy, and by their unhappy
antagonism to the great state of Macedonia.

In the Peloponnesus, the Achaean league had united the best
elements of Greece proper in a confederacy based on civilisation,
national spirit, and peaceful preparation for self-defence. But
the vigour and more especially the military efficiency of the
league had, notwithstanding its outward enlargement, been
arrested by the selfish diplomacy of Aratus. The unfortunate
variances with Sparta, and the still more lamentable invocation
of Macedonian interference in the Peloponnesus, had so completely subjected the Achaean league to Macedonian supremacy,
that the chief fortresses of the country thenceforward received
Macedonian garrisons, and the oath of fidelity to Philip was
annually taken there.

The policy of the weaker states in the Peloponnesus, Elis,
Messene, and Sparta, was determined by their ancient enmity
to the Achaean league—an enmity specially fostered by disputes
regarding their frontiers—and their tendencies were Aetolian
and anti-Macedonian, because the Achaeans took part with
Philip. The only one of these states possessing any importance
was the Spartan military monarchy, which after the death of
Machanidas had passed into the hands of one Nabis. With
ever-increasing hardihood Nabis leaned on the support of
vagabonds and itinerant mercenaries, to whom he assigned not
only the houses and lands, but also the wives and children, of
the citizens; and he assiduously maintained connections, and
even entered into an association for the joint prosecution of
piracy, with the great refuge of mercenaries and pirates, the
island of Crete, where he possessed some townships. His
predatory expeditions by land, and the piratical vessels which
he maintained at the promontory of Malea, were dreaded far
and wide; he was personally hated for his baseness and cruelty;
but his rule was extending, and about the time of the battle of
Zama he had even succeeded in gaining possession of Messene.

Lastly, the most independent position among the intermediate
states was held by the free Greek mercantile cities on the
European shore of the Propontis, along the coast of Asia Minor,

and on the islands of the Aegean Sea; they formed, at the same time, the brightest elements in the confused and multifarious picture which was presented by the Hellenic state-system. Three of them, in particular, had after Alexander's death regained their full freedom, and by the activity of their maritime commerce had attained to respectable political power and even to considerable territorial possessions; namely, Byzantium the mistress of the Bosporus, rendered wealthy and powerful by the transit dues which she levied and by the important corn trade carried on with the Black Sea; Cyzicus on the Asiatic side of the Propontis, the daughter and heiress of Miletus, maintaining the closest relations with the court of Pergamus; and lastly and above all, Rhodes. The Rhodians, who immediately after the death of Alexander had expelled the Macedonian garrison, had, by their favourable position for commerce and navigation, secured the carrying trade of all the eastern Mediterranean; and their well-handled fleet, as well as the tried courage of the citizens in the famous siege of $\frac{450}{304}$, enabled them in that age of promiscuous and ceaseless hostilities to become the prudent and energetic representatives and, when occasion required, champions of a neutral commercial policy. They compelled the Byzantines, for instance, by force of arms to concede to the vessels of Rhodes exemption from the transit dues of the Bosporus; and they did not permit the dynast of Pergamus to close the Black Sea. On the other hand they kept themselves, as far as possible, aloof from land warfare, although they had acquired no inconsiderable possessions on the opposite coast of Caria; where war could not be avoided, they carried it on by means of mercenaries. With their neighbours on all sides they were in friendly relations—with Syracuse, Macedonia, Syria, but more especially with Egypt—and they enjoyed high consideration at these courts, so that their mediation was not unfrequently invoked in the wars of the great states. But they interested themselves specially on behalf of the Greek maritime cities, which were so numerously spread along the coasts of the kingdoms of Pontus, Bithynia, and Pergamus, as well as on the coasts and islands of Asia Minor that had been wrested by Egypt from the Seleucidae; such as Sinope, Heracleia Pontica, Cius, Lampsacus, Abydos, Mitylene, Chios, Smyrna, Samos, Halicarnassus and various others. All these were in substance free and had nothing to do with the lords of the soil except to request confirmation of their privileges and, at most, to pay a moderate tribute: such encroachments, as from time to time

were threatened by the dynasts, they skilfully warded off sometimes by cringing, sometimes by strong measures. In this case
the Rhodians were their chief auxiliaries; they emphatically
supported Sinope, for instance, against Mithradates of Pontus.
How firmly amidst the quarrels, and by means of the very
differences, of the monarchs the liberties of these cities of Asia
Minor were established, is shown by the fact, that the dispute
between Antiochus and the Romans some years after this time
related not to the freedom of these cities in itself, but to the
question whether they were to ask confirmation of their charters
from the king or not. This league of the cities was, in its
peculiar attitude towards the lords of the soil as well as in other
respects, a formal Hanseatic association, headed by Rhodes,
which negotiated and stipulated in treaties for itself and its
allies. This league upheld the freedom of the cities against
monarchical interests; and while wars raged around their walls,
public spirit and civic prosperity were sheltered in comparative
peace within, and art and science flourished without the risk of
being crushed by the tyranny of a dissolute soldiery or of being
corrupted by the atmosphere of a court.

Such was the state of things in the East, at the time when the
wall of political separation between the East and the West
was broken down and the Eastern powers, Philip of Macedonia
leading the way, were induced to interfere in the relations of
the West. We have already set forth to some extent the origin
of this interference and the course of the first Macedonian war
($\frac{540-549}{214-205}$); and we have pointed out what Philip might have
accomplished during the second Punic war, and how little of all
that Hannibal was entitled to expect and to count on was really
fulfilled. A fresh illustration had been afforded of the truth,
that of all haphazards none is more hazardous than an absolute
hereditary monarchy. Philip was not the man whom Macedonia
at that time required; yet his gifts were far from insignificant.
He was a genuine king, in the best and worst sense of the term.
A strong desire to rule in person and unaided was the fundamental trait of his character; he was proud of his purple, but
he was no less proud of other gifts, and he had reason to be so.
He not only showed the valour of a soldier and the eye of a
general, but he displayed a high spirit in the conduct of public
affairs, whenever his Macedonian sense of honour was offended.
Full of intelligence and wit, he won the hearts of all whom he
wished to gain, especially of the men who were ablest and most
refined, such as Flamininus and Scipio; he was a pleasant boon

companion, and, not by virtue of his rank alone, a dangerous
wooer. But he was at the same time one of the most arrogant
and flagitious characters which that shameless age produced.
He was in the habit of saying that he feared none save the gods;
but it seemed almost as if his gods were those to whom his
admiral Dicaearchus regularly offered sacrifice—ungodliness
(*Asebeia*) and lawlessness (*Paranomia*). The lives of his advisers
and of the promoters of his schemes possessed no sacredness in
his eyes, nor did he disdain to pacify his indignation against the
Athenians and Attalus by the destruction of venerable monuments and illustrious works of art; it is quoted as one of his
maxims of state, that " whoever puts to death the father must
also kill the sons." Perhaps cruelty was not, strictly, a pleasure
to him; but he was indifferent to the lives and sufferings of
others, and the disposition to relent, which alone renders men
tolerable, found no place in his hard and stubborn heart. So
abruptly and harshly did he proclaim the principle that no
promise and no moral law are binding on an absolute king, that
he thereby interposed the most serious obstacles to the success
of his plans. No one can deny that he possessed sagacity and
resolution, but these were, in a singular manner, combined with
procrastination and supineness; which is perhaps partly to be
explained by the fact, that he was called in his eighteenth year
to the position of an absolute sovereign, and that his ungovernable fury against every one who disturbed his autocratic course
by counter-argument or counter-advice scared away from him
all independent counsellors. What various causes co-operated
to produce the weak and disgraceful management which he
showed in the first Macedonian war, we cannot tell; it may
have been due perhaps to that indolent arrogance which only
puts forth its full energies against danger when it becomes
imminent, or perhaps to his indifference towards a plan which
was not of his own devising and his jealousy of the greatness
of Hannibal which put him to shame. It is certain that his
subsequent conduct betrayed no further trace of the Philip,
through whose negligence the great scheme of Hannibal suffered
shipwreck.

When Philip concluded his treaty with the Aetolians and
Romans in $\frac{548-549}{206-205}$, he seriously intended to make a lasting peace
with Rome, and to devote himself exclusively in future to the
affairs of the East. It admits of no doubt that he saw with
regret the rapid subjugation of Carthage; and it may be, that
Hannibal hoped for a second declaration of war from Macedonia,

and that Philip secretly reinforced the last Carthaginian army
with mercenaries (p. 167). But the tedious affairs in which he
had meanwhile involved himself in the East, as well as the
nature of the alleged support, and especially the total silence
of the Romans as to such a breach of the peace while they were
searching for grounds of war, place it beyond doubt, that Philip
was by no means disposed in $\frac{551}{203}$ to make up for what he ought
to have done ten years before.

He had turned his eyes to an entirely different quarter.
Ptolemy Philopator of Egypt had died in $\frac{547}{207}$. Philip and
Antiochus, the kings of Macedonia and Asia, had combined
against his successor Ptolemy Epiphanes, a child of five years
old, in order completely to gratify the ancient grudge which
the monarchies of the mainland entertained towards the maritime
state. The Egyptian state was to be broken up; Egypt and
Cyprus were to fall to Antiochus; Cyrene, Ionia, and the
Cyclades to Philip. Thoroughly in the spirit of Philip, who
ridiculed such considerations, the kings began the war not
merely without cause, but even without pretext, "just as the
large fishes devour the small." The allies, moreover, had made
their calculations correctly, especially Philip. Egypt had
enough to do in defending herself against the nearer enemy in
Syria, and was obliged to leave her possessions in Asia Minor
and the Cyclades undefended when Philip threw himself upon
these as his share of the spoil. In the year in which Carthage
concluded peace with Rome ($\frac{553}{201}$), Philip ordered a fleet equipped
by the towns subject to him to take on board troops, and to sail
along the coast of Thrace. There Lysimachia was taken from
the Aetolian garrison, and Perinthus, which stood in the relation
of clientship to Byzantium, was likewise occupied. Thus the
peace was broken as respected the Byzantines; and as respected
the Aetolians, who had just made peace with Philip, the good
understanding was at least disturbed. The crossing to Asia was
attended with no difficulties, for Prusias king of Bithynia was
in alliance with Macedonia. By way of recompense, Philip
helped him to subdue the Greek mercantile cities in his territory.
Chalcedon submitted. Cius, which resisted, was taken by storm
and levelled with the ground, and its inhabitants were reduced
to slavery—a meaningless barbarity, which annoyed Prusias
himself who wished to get possession of the town uninjured,
and which excited profound indignation throughout the Hellenic
world. The Aetolians, whose *strategus* had commanded in Cius,
and the Rhodians, whose attempts at mediation had been

summarily and craftily frustrated by the king, were especially offended.

But even had it not been so, the interests of all Greek commercial cities were at stake. They could not possibly allow the mild and almost purely nominal Egyptian rule to be supplanted by the Macedonian despotism, with which civic self-government and freedom of commercial intercourse were not at all compatible; and the fearful treatment of the Cians showed that the matter at stake was not the right of confirming the charters of the towns, but the life or death of one and all. Lampsacus had already fallen, and Thasos had been treated like Cius. No time was to be lost. Theophiliscus, the vigilant *strategus* of Rhodes, exhorted his citizens to avert the common danger by common resistance, and not to suffer the towns and islands to become one by one a prey to the enemy. Rhodes resolved on its course, and declared war against Philip. Byzantium joined it; as did also the aged Attalus king of Pergamus, personally and politically the enemy of Philip. While the fleet of the allies was mustering on the Aeolian coast, Philip directed a portion of his fleet to take Chios and Samos. With the other portion he appeared in person before Pergamus, which however he invested in vain; he had to content himself with traversing the level country and leaving the traces of Macedonian valour on the temples which he destroyed far and wide. Suddenly he departed and re-embarked, to unite with his squadron which was at Samos. But the Rhodo-Pergamene fleet followed him, and forced him to accept battle in the straits of Chios. The number of the Macedonian decked vessels was smaller, but the multitude of their open boats made up for this inequality, and the soldiers of Philip fought with great courage. But he was at length defeated. Almost half of his decked vessels, 24 sail, were sunk or taken; 6000 Macedonian sailors and 3000 soldiers perished, amongst whom was the admiral Democrates; 2000 were taken prisoners. The victory cost the allies no more than 800 men and six vessels. But, of the leaders of the allies, Attalus had been cut off from his fleet and compelled to let his own vessel run aground near Erythrae; and Theophiliscus of Rhodes, whose public spirit had decided the question of war and whose valour had decided the battle, died on the day after it of his wounds. Thus while the fleet of Attalus went home and the Rhodian fleet remained temporarily at Chios, Philip, who falsely claimed the victory, was enabled to continue his voyage and to turn towards Samos, in order to occupy the Carian towns. On the Carian coast the

Rhodians, on this occasion unsupported by Attalus, gave battle for the second time to the Macedonian fleet under Heraclides, near the little island of Lade in front of the port of Miletus. The victory, claimed again by both sides, appears to have been this time gained by the Macedonians; for while the Rhodians retreated to Myndus and thence to Cos, the Macedonians occupied Miletus, and a squadron under Dicaearchus the Aetolian occupied the Cyclades. Philip meanwhile prosecuted the conquest of the Rhodian possessions on the Carian mainland, and of the Greek cities: had he been disposed to attack Ptolemy in person, and had he not preferred to confine himself to the acquisition of his own share in the spoil, he was now in a position to think of an expedition to Egypt. In Caria no army opposed the Macedonians, and Philip traversed without hindrance the country from Magnesia to Mylasa; but every town in that country was a fortress, and the work of besieging was protracted without furnishing, or giving promise of, any material results. Zeuxis the satrap of Lydia supported the ally of his master with the same lukewarmness as Philip had manifested in promoting the interests of the Syrian king, and the Greek cities gave their support only under the pressure of force or fear. The provisioning of the army became daily more difficult; Philip was obliged now to plunder those who but lately had voluntarily supplied his wants, and then he had reluctantly to submit to beg afresh. Thus the good season of the year gradually drew to an end, and in the interval the Rhodians had reinforced their fleet and had also been rejoined by that of Attalus, so that they were decidedly superior at sea. It seemed almost as if they might cut off the retreat of the king and compel him to take up winter quarters in Caria, while the state of affairs at home, particularly the threatened intervention of the Aetolians and Romans, urgently demanded his return. Philip saw the danger; he left garrisons amounting together to 3000 men, partly in Myrina to keep Pergamus in check, partly in the petty towns round Mylasa—Iassus, Bargylia, Euromus, and Pedasa—to secure for him the excellent harbour and a landing place in Caria; and, owing to the negligence with which the allies guarded the sea, he succeeded in safely reaching the Thracian coast with his fleet and arriving at home before the winter of $\frac{553-554}{201-200}$.

In fact a storm was gathering against Philip in the west, which did not permit him to continue the plundering of defenceless Egypt. The Romans, who had at length in this year concluded peace on their own terms with Carthage, began to give serious attention to these complications in the East. It has often been affirmed, that after the conquest of the West they forthwith proceeded to the subjugation of the East; a more thorough consideration will lead to a juster judgment. It is only dull prejudice which fails to see that Rome at this period by no means grasped at the sovereignty of the Mediterranean states, but, on the contrary, simply desired to have neighbours that should not be dangerous in Africa and in Greece; and Macedonia was not really dangerous to Rome. Its power certainly was far from small, and it is evident that the Roman senate only consented with reluctance to the peace of $\frac{548-549}{206-205}$ which left it in all its integrity; but how little any serious apprehensions of Macedonia were or could be entertained in Rome, is best shown by the small number of troops—who yet were never compelled to fight against a superior force—with which Rome carried on the next war. The senate doubtless would have gladly seen Macedonia humbled; but that humiliation would be too dearly purchased at the cost of a land war carried on in Macedonia with Roman troops: and accordingly, after the withdrawal of the Aetolians, the senate voluntarily concluded peace at once on the basis of the *status quo*. It is therefore far from being demonstrated, that the Roman government concluded this peace with any definite design of beginning the war at a more convenient season; and it is very certain that, at the moment, from the thorough exhaustion of the state and the extreme unwillingness of the citizens to enter into a second transmarine struggle, the Macedonian war was in a high degree unwelcome to the Romans. But now it was inevitable. They might have been satisfied with the Macedonian state as a neighbour, such as it stood in $\frac{549}{205}$; but it was impossible that they could permit it to acquire the best part of Asiatic Greece and the important Cyrene, to crush the neutral commercial states, and thereby to double its power. Further, the fall of Egypt and the humiliation, perhaps the subjugation, of Rhodes could not but inflict deep wounds on the trade of Sicily and Italy; and could Rome remain a quiet spectator, while Italian commerce with the East was made dependent on the two great continental powers? Rome had, moreover, an obligation of honour to fulfil towards Attalus her faithful ally since the first Macedonian war, and had to prevent Philip, who had already besieged him in his capital, from expelling him from his dominions. Lastly, the claim of Rome to extend her protecting arm over all the Hellenes was by no means an empty phrase:

the Neapolitans, Rhegines, Massiliots, and Emporienses could testify that that protection was accorded in earnest, and there is no question that at this time the Romans stood in a closer relation to the Greeks than any other nation—one little more remote than that of the Hellenic Macedonians. It is strange that any should dispute the right of the Romans to feel their human, as well as their Hellenic, sympathies revolted at the scandalous treatment of the Cians and Thasians. Thus in reality all political, commercial, and moral motives concurred in inducing Rome to undertake the second war against Philip —one of the most righteous which the city ever waged. It greatly redounds to the honour of the senate, that it immediately resolved on its course and did not allow itself to be deterred from making the necessary preparations either by the exhaustion of the state or by the unpopularity of such a declaration of war. The propraetor Marcus Valerius Laevinus made his appearance as early as $\frac{553}{201}$ with the Sicilian fleet of 38 sail in the eastern waters.

The government, however, were at a loss to discover an ostensible pretext for the war; a pretext which they needed in order to satisfy the people, even although they had not been far too sagacious to undervalue, as was the manner of Philip, the importance of assigning a legitimate ground for hostilities. The support, which Philip was alleged to have granted to the Carthaginians after the peace with Rome, manifestly could not be proved. The Roman subjects, indeed, in the province of Illyria had for a considerable time complained of the Macedonian encroachments. In $\frac{551}{203}$ a Roman envoy at the head of the Illyrian levy had driven Philip's troops from the Illyrian territory; and the senate had accordingly declared to the king's envoys in $\frac{552}{202}$, that if he sought war, he would find it sooner than was agreeable to him. But these encroachments were simply the ordinary outrages which Philip practised towards his neighbours; a negotiation regarding them at the present moment would have led to his humbling himself and offering satisfaction, but not to war. With all the belligerent powers in the East the Roman community was nominally in friendly relations, and might have granted them aid in repelling Philip's attack. But Rhodes and Pergamus, which of course did not fail to request Roman aid, were formally the aggressors; and although Alexandrian ambassadors besought the Roman senate to undertake the guardianship of the boy king, Egypt appears to have been by no means anxious to invoke the direct intervention of the Romans, which would put an end to her difficulties for the moment, but would at the same time open up the eastern seas to the great maritime power of the West. Aid to Egypt, moreover, must have been in the first instance rendered in Syria, and would have entangled Rome simultaneously in a war with Asia and with Macedonia; which the Romans were naturally the more desirous to avoid, as they were firmly resolved not to intermeddle at least in Asiatic affairs. No course was left but to despatch in the meantime an embassy to the East for the purpose, first, of obtaining—what was not in the circumstances difficult—the sanction of Egypt to the interference of Rome in the affairs of Greece; secondly, of pacifying king Antiochus by abandoning Syria to him; and, lastly, of accelerating as much as possible a breach with Philip and promoting a coalition of the minor Graeco-Asiatic states against him (end of $\frac{553}{201}$). At Alexandria they had no difficulty in accomplishing their object; the court had no choice, and was obliged gratefully to receive Marcus Aemilius Lepidus, whom the senate had despatched as " guardian of the king," to uphold his interests, so far as that could be done without an actual intervention. Antiochus did not break off his alliance with Philip, nor did he give to the Romans the definite explanations which they desired; in other respects, however—whether from remissness, or influenced by the declarations of the Romans that they did not wish to interfere in Syria—he pursued his schemes in that direction and left things in Greece and Asia Minor to take their course.

Meanwhile, the spring of $\frac{554}{200}$ had arrived, and the war had recommenced. Philip first threw himself once more upon Thrace, where he occupied all the places on the coast, in particular Maronea, Aenus, Elaeus, and Sestus; he wished to have his European possessions secured against the risk of a Roman landing. He then attacked Abydus on the Asiatic coast, the acquisition of which was an object of great importance to him, for the possession of Sestus and Abydus would bring him into closer connection with his ally Antiochus, and he would no longer need to be apprehensive lest the fleet of the allies might intercept him in crossing to or from Asia Minor. That fleet commanded the Aegean Sea after the withdrawal of the weaker Macedonian squadron: Philip confined his operations by sea to maintaining garrisons on three of the Cyclades, Andros, Cythnos, and Paros, and fitting out privateers. The Rhodians proceeded to Chios, and thence to Tenedos, where Attalus, who had passed the winter at Aegina and had spent his time in listening to the declamations of the Athenians, joined them with his squadron. The allies might probably have arrived in time to help the Abydenes, who heroically defended themselves; but they stirred not, and so at last the city surrendered, after almost all who were capable of bearing arms had fallen in the struggle before the walls; a large portion of the inhabitants fell by their own hand after the capitulation—the mercy of the victor consisted in allowing the Abydenes a term of three days to die voluntarily. Here, in the camp before Abydus, the Roman embassy, which after the termination of its business in Syria and Egypt had visited and dealt with the minor Greek states, met with the king, and submitted the proposals which it had been charged to make by the senate, viz., that the king should wage no aggressive war against any Greek state, should restore the possessions which he had wrested from Ptolemy, and should consent to an arbitration regarding the injury inflicted on the Pergamenes and Rhodians. The object of the senate, which sought to provoke the king to a formal declaration of war, was not gained; the Roman ambassador, Marcus Aemilius Lepidus, obtained from the king nothing but the polite reply, that he would excuse what the envoy had said because he was young, handsome, and a Roman.

Meanwhile, however, the occasion for declaring war, which Rome desired, had been furnished from another quarter. The Athenians in their silly and cruel vanity had put to death two unfortunate Acarnanians, because these had accidentally strayed into their mysteries. When the Acarnanians, who were naturally indignant, asked Philip to procure them satisfaction, he could not refuse the just request of his most faithful allies, and he allowed them to levy men in Macedonia and, with these and their own troops, to invade Attica without a formal declaration of war. This, it is true, was no war in the proper sense of the term; and, besides, the leader of the Macedonian band, Nicanor, immediately gave orders to his troops to retreat, when the Roman envoys, who were at Athens at the time, used threatening language (in the end of $\frac{553}{201}$). But it was too late. An Athenian embassy was sent to Rome to report the attack made by Philip on an ancient ally of the Romans; and, from the way in which the senate received it, Philip saw clearly what awaited him; so that he at once, in the very spring of $\frac{554}{200}$, directed Philocles, his general in Greece, to lay waste the Attic territory and to reduce the city to extremities.

The senate now had what they wanted; and in the summer of $\frac{554}{200}$ they were able to propose to the comitia a declaration of war " on account of an attack on a state in alliance with Rome." It was rejected on the first occasion almost unanimously: foolish or evil-disposed tribunes of the people complained that the senate would allow the citizens no rest; but the war was necessary, and, in strictness, was already begun, so that the senate could not possibly recede. The burgesses were induced to yield by representations and concessions. It is remarkable that these concessions were made mainly at the expense of the allies. The garrisons of Gaul, Lower Italy, Sicily, and Sardinia, amounting in all to 20,000 men, were exclusively taken from the allied contingents that were in active service—quite contrary to the former principles of the Romans. All the burgess troops, on the other hand, that had continued under arms from the Hannibalic war, were discharged; volunteers alone, it was alleged, were to be enrolled for the Macedonian war, but they were, as was afterwards found, for the most part forced volunteers—a fact which in the autumn of $\frac{555}{199}$ gave rise to a dangerous military revolt in the camp of Apollonia. Six legions were formed of the men newly called out; of these two remained in Rome and two in Etruria, and only two embarked at Brundisium for Macedonia, led by the consul Publius Sulpicius Galba.

Thus it was once more clearly demonstrated, that the sovereign burgess assemblies, with their shortsighted resolutions dependent often on mere accident, were no longer at all fitted to deal with the complicated and difficult relations into which Rome was drawn by her victories; and that their mischievous intervention in the working of the state machine led to dangerous modifications of the measures which in a military point of view were necessary, and to the still more dangerous course of treating the Latin allies as inferiors.

The position of Philip was very disadvantageous. The eastern states, which ought to have acted in unison against all interference of Rome and probably under other circumstances would have done so, had been mainly by Philip's fault so incensed at each other, that they were not inclined to hinder, or were inclined even to promote, the Roman invasion. Asia, the natural and most important ally of Philip, had been neglected by him, and was moreover prevented from any immediate active interference by being entangled in the quarrel with Egypt and the Syrian war. Egypt had an urgent interest in keeping the Roman fleet out of the eastern waters; even now an Egyptian embassy intimated at Rome very plainly, that the court of Alexandria was ready to relieve the Romans from the trouble of intervention in Attica. But the treaty for the partition of Egypt concluded between Asia and Macedonia threw that important state thoroughly into the arms of Rome, and compelled the cabinet of Alexandria to declare that it would only intermeddle in the affairs of European Greece with consent of the Romans. The Greek commercial cities, with Rhodes, Pergamus, and Byzantium at their head, were in a position similar, but of still greater perplexity. They would under other circumstances have beyond doubt done what they could to close the eastern seas against the Romans; but the cruel and destructive policy of conquest pursued by Philip had driven them to an unequal struggle, in which for their self-preservation they were obliged to use every effort to obtain the interference of the great Italian power. In Greece proper also the Roman envoys, who were commissioned to organise a second league against Philip there, found the way already substantially paved for them by the enemy. Of the anti-Macedonian party—the Spartans, Eleans, Athenians, and Aetolians—Philip might perhaps have gained the latter, for the peace of $\frac{548}{206}$ had made a deep, and far from healed, breach in their friendly alliance with Rome; but apart from the old differences which subsisted between Aetolia and Macedonia regarding the Thessalian towns withdrawn by Macedonia from the Aetolian confederacy—Echinus, Larissa Cremaste, Pharsalus, and Thebes in Phthiotis—the expulsion of the Aetolian garrisons from Lysimachia and Cius had produced fresh exasperation against Philip in the minds of the Aetolians. If they delayed to join the league against him, the chief reason doubtless was the ill-feeling that continued to prevail between them and the Romans.

It was a circumstance still more ominous, that even among the Greek states firmly attached to the interests of Macedonia —the Epirots, Acarnanians, Boeotians, and Achaeans—the Acarnanians and Boeotians alone stood steadfastly by Philip. With the Epirots the Roman envoys negotiated not without success; Amynander, king of the Athamanes, in particular closely attached himself to Rome. Even among the Achaeans, Philip had offended many by the murder of Aratus; while on the other hand he had thereby paved the way for a more free development of the confederacy. Under the leadership of Philopoemen ($\frac{502-571}{252-183}$, for the first time *strategus* in $\frac{546}{208}$) it had reorganised its military system, recovered confidence in itself by successful conflicts with Sparta, and no longer blindly followed, as in the time of Aratus, the policy of Macedonia. The Achaean league, which had to expect neither profit nor immediate injury from the thirst of Philip for aggrandizement, alone in all Hellas looked at this war from an impartial and national Hellenic point of view. It perceived—what there was no difficulty in perceiving—that the Hellenic nation was thereby surrendering itself to the Romans even before they wished or desired its surrender, and attempted accordingly to mediate between Philip and the Rhodians; but it was too late. The national patriotism, which had formerly terminated the federal war and had mainly contributed to the first war between Macedonia and Rome, was extinguished; the Achaean mediation remained fruitless, and in vain Philip visited the cities and islands to rekindle the zeal of the nation—its apathy was the Nemesis for Cius and Abydus. The Achaeans, as they could effect no change and were not disposed to render help to either party, remained neutral.

In the autumn of $\frac{554}{200}$ the consul, Publius Sulpicius Galba, landed with his two legions and 1000 Numidian cavalry accompanied even by elephants derived from the spoils of Carthage, at Apollonia; on receiving accounts of which the king returned in haste from the Hellespont to Thessaly. But, owing partly to the far advanced season, partly to the sickness of the Roman general, nothing was undertaken by land that year except a reconnaissance in force, in the course of which the places in the vicinity, and in particular the Macedonian colony Antipatreia, were occupied by the Romans. For the next year a joint attack on Macedonia was concerted with the northern barbarians, especially with Pleuratus, the then ruler of Scodra, and Bato, prince of the Dardani, who of course were eager to profit by the favourable opportunity.

More importance attached to the enterprises of the Roman fleet, which numbered 100 decked and 80 light vessels. While the rest of the ships took their station for the winter at Corcyra, a division under Gaius Claudius Cento proceeded to the Piraeeus to render assistance to the hard-pressed Athenians. But, as Cento found the Attic territory already sufficiently protected against the raids of the Corinthian garrison and the Macedonian corsairs, he sailed on and appeared suddenly before Chalcis in Euboea, the chief stronghold of Philip in Greece, where his magazines, stores of arms, and prisoners were kept, and where the commandant Sopater was far from expecting a Roman attack.

The undefended walls were scaled, and the garrison was put to death; the prisoners were liberated and the stores were burnt; unfortunately, there was a want of troops to hold the important position. On receiving news of this invasion, Philip immediately in vehement indignation started from Demetrias in Thessaly for Chalcis, and when he found no trace of the enemy there save the scene of ruin, he went on to Athens to retaliate. But his attempt to surprise the city was a failure, and even the assault was in vain, greatly as the king exposed his life; the approach of Gaius Claudius from the Piraeeus, and of Attalus from Aegina, compelled him to depart. Philip still tarried for some time in Greece; but in a political and in a military point of view his successes were equally insignificant. In vain he tried to induce the Achaeans to take up arms in his behalf; and equally fruitless were his attacks on Eleusis and the Piraeeus, as well as a second attempt on Athens itself. Nothing remained for him but to gratify his natural exasperation in an unworthy manner by laying waste the country and destroying the trees of Academus, and then to return to the north.

Thus the winter passed away. With the spring of $\frac{555}{198}$, the proconsul Publius Sulpicius broke up from his winter camp, determined to conduct his legions from Apollonia by the shortest route into Macedonia proper. This principal attack from the west was to be supported by three subordinate attacks; on the north by an invasion of the Dardani and Illyrians; on the east by an attack on the part of the combined fleet of the Romans and allies, which assembled at Aegina; while lastly the Athamanes, and the Aetolians also, if the attempt to induce them to share in the struggle should prove successful, were to advance from the south. After Galba had crossed the mountains intersected by the Apsus (now the Beratinó), and had marched through the fertile plain of the Dassaretae, he reached the mountain range which separates Illyria from Macedonia, and crossing it, entered the proper Macedonian territory. Philip had marched to meet him; but in the extensive and thinly peopled regions of Macedonia the antagonists for a time sought each other in vain; at length they met in the province of Lyncestis, a fertile but marshy plain not far from the north-western frontier, and encamped not 1000 paces apart. Philip's army, after he had been joined by the corps detached to occupy the northern passes, numbered about 20,000 infantry and 2000 cavalry; the Roman army was nearly as strong. The Macedonians however had the great advantage, that, fighting in their native land and well acquainted with its highways and byways, they had little trouble in procuring supplies of provisions, while they had encamped so close to the Romans that the latter could not venture to disperse for any extensive foraging. The consul repeatedly offered battle, but the king persisted in declining it; and the combats between the light troops, although the Romans gained some advantages in them, produced no material alteration. Galba was obliged to break up his camp and to pitch another eight miles off at Octolophus, where he conceived that he could more easily procure supplies. But here too the divisions sent out were destroyed by the light troops and cavalry of the Macedonians; the legions were obliged to come to their help, whereupon the Macedonian vanguard, which had advanced too far, were driven back to their camp with heavy loss; the king himself lost his horse in the action, and only saved his life through the magnanimous self-devotion of one of his troopers. From this perilous position the Romans were liberated through the better success of the subordinate attacks which Galba had directed the allies to make, or rather through the weakness of the Macedonian forces. Although Philip had instituted levies as large as possible in his own dominions, and had enlisted Roman deserters and other mercenaries, he had not been able to bring into the field (over and above the garrisons in Asia Minor and Thrace) more than the army, with which in person he confronted the consul; and besides, in order to form even this, he had been obliged to leave the northern passes in the Pelagonian territory undefended. For the protection of the east coast he relied partly on the orders which he had given for the laying waste of the islands of Sciathus and Peparethus, which might have furnished a station to the enemy's fleet, partly on the garrisoning of Thasos and the coast and on the fleet organised at Demetrias under Heraclides. For the south frontier he had been obliged to reckon solely upon the more than doubtful neutrality of the Aetolians. These now suddenly joined the league against Macedonia, and immediately in conjunction with the Athamanes penetrated into Thessaly, while simultaneously the Dardani and Illyrians overran the northern provinces, and the Roman fleet under Lucius Apustius, departing from Corcyra, appeared in the eastern waters, where the ships of Attalus, the Rhodians, and the Istrians joined it.

Philip, on learning this, voluntarily abandoned his position and retreated in an easterly direction: whether he did so in order to repel the probably unexpected invasion of the Aetolians, or to draw the Roman army after him with a view to its destruction, or to take either of these courses according to circumstances, cannot well be determined. He managed his retreat so dexterously that Galba, who adopted the rash resolution of following him, lost his track, and Philip was enabled to reach by a flank movement, and to occupy, the narrow pass which separates the provinces of Lyncestis and Eordaea, with the view of awaiting the Romans and giving them a warm reception there. A battle took place on the spot which he had selected; but the long Macedonian spears proved unserviceable on the wooded and uneven ground. The Macedonians were partly turned, partly broken, and lost many men.

But, although Philip's army was after this unfortunate action no longer able to prevent the advance of the Romans, the latter were themselves afraid to encounter further unknown dangers in an impassable and hostile country; and returned to Apollonia after they had laid waste the fertile provinces of Upper Macedonia—Eordaea, Elymaea, and Orestis. Celetrum, the most considerable town of Orestis (now Kastoria, on a peninsula in the lake of the same name), had surrendered to them: it was the only Macedonian town that opened its gates to the Romans. In the Illyrian land Pelium, the city of the Dassaretae, on the upper confluents of the Apsus, was taken by storm and strongly garrisoned to serve as a future basis for a similar expedition.

Philip did not disturb the Roman main army in its retreat, but turned by forced marches against the Aetolians and Athamanians who, in the belief that the legions were occupying the attention of the king, were fearlessly and recklessly plundering the rich vale of the Peneius, defeated them completely, and compelled such as did not fall to make their escape singly through the well - known mountain paths. The effective strength of the confederacy was not a little diminished by this defeat, and not less by the numerous enlistments made in Aetolia on Egyptian account. The Dardani were chased back over the mountains by Athenagoras, the leader of Philip's light troops, without difficulty and with severe loss. The Roman fleet also did not accomplish much; it expelled the Macedonian garrison from Andros, visited Euboea and Sciathus, and then made attempts on the Chalcidian peninsula, which were, however, vigorously repulsed by the Macedonian garrison at Mende. The rest of the summer was spent in the capture of Oreus in Euboea, which was long delayed by the resolute defence of the Macedonian garrison. The weak Macedonian fleet under

Heraclides remained inactive at Heraclea, and did not venture to dispute the possession of the sea with the enemy. The latter went early to winter quarters, the Romans proceeding to the Piraeeus and Corcyra, the Rhodians and Pergamenes going home.

Philip might on the whole congratulate himself upon the results of this campaign. The Roman troops, after an extremely troublesome campaign, stood in autumn precisely on the spot whence they had started in spring; and, but for the well-timed interposition of the Aetolians and the unexpected success of the battle at the pass of Eordaea, perhaps not a man of their entire force would have again seen the Roman territory. The fourfold assault had everywhere failed in its object, and not only did Philip in autumn see his whole dominions cleared of the enemy, but he was able to make an attempt—which, however, miscarried —to wrest from the Aetolians the strong town of Thaumaci, situated on the Aetolo-Thessalian frontier and commanding the plain of the Peneius. If Antiochus, for whose coming Philip vainly supplicated the gods, should unite with him in the next campaign, he might anticipate great successes. For a moment it seemed as if Antiochus was disposed to do so; his army appeared in Asia Minor, and occupied some places belonging to king Attalus, who requested military protection from the Romans. The latter, however, were not anxious to urge the great king at this time to a breach; they sent envoys, who in fact obtained an evacuation of the dominions of Attalus. From that quarter Philip had nothing to hope for.

But the fortunate issue of the last campaign had so raised the courage or the arrogance of Philip, that, after having assured himself afresh of the neutrality of the Achaeans and the fidelity of the Macedonians by the sacrifice of some strong places and of the detested admiral Heraclides, he next spring ($\frac{556}{198}$) assumed the offensive and advanced into the territory of the Atintanes, with a view to form a well-entrenched camp in the narrow pass, where the Aous (Viosa) winds its way between the mountains Aeropus and Asnaus. Opposite to him encamped the Roman army reinforced by new arrivals of troops, and commanded first by the consul of the previous year, Publius Villius, and then from the summer of $\frac{556}{198}$ by that year's consul, Titus Quinctius Flamininus. Flamininus, a talented man just thirty years of age, belonged to the younger generation, who began to lay aside the patriotism as well as the habits of their forefathers and, though not unmindful of their fatherland, were

Titus Quinctius Flamininus

still more mindful of themselves and of Hellenism. A skilful officer and a better diplomatist, he was in many respects admirably adapted for the management of the troubled affairs of Greece. Yet it would perhaps have been better both for Rome and for Greece, if the choice had fallen on one less full of Hellenic sympathies, and if the general despatched thither had been a man who would neither have been bribed by delicate flattery nor stung by pungent sarcasm; who would not amidst literary and artistic reminiscences have overlooked the pitiful condition of the constitutions of the Hellenic states; and who, while treating Hellas according to its deserts, would have spared the Romans the trouble of striving after unattainable ideals.

The new commander-in-chief immediately had a conference with the king, while the two armies lay face to face inactive. Philip made proposals of peace; he offered to restore all his own conquests, and to submit to an equitable arbitration regarding the damage inflicted on the Greek cities; but the negotiations broke down, when he was asked to give up ancient possessions of Macedonia and particularly Thessaly. For forty days the two armies lay in the narrow pass of the Aous; Philip would not retire, and Flamininus could not make up his mind whether he should order an assault, or leave the king alone and reattempt the expedition of the previous year. At length the Roman general was helped out of his perplexity by the treachery of some chiefs among the Epirots, who were otherwise well-disposed to Macedon, and especially of Charops. They conducted a Roman corps of 4000 infantry and 300 cavalry by mountain paths to the heights above the Macedonian camp; and, when the consul attacked the enemy's army in front, the advance of that Roman division, unexpectedly descending from the mountains commanding the position, decided the battle. Philip lost his camp and entrenchments and nearly 2000 men, and hastily retreated to the pass of Tempe, the gate of Macedonia proper. He gave up everything which he had held except the fortresses; the Thessalian towns, which he could not defend, he destroyed; Pherae alone closed its gates against him and thereby escaped destruction. The Epirots, induced partly by these successes of the Roman arms, partly by the judicious moderation of Flamininus, were the first to secede from the Macedonian alliance. On the first accounts of the Roman victory the Athamanes and Aetolians immediately invaded Thessaly, and the Romans soon followed; the open country was easily overrun, but the strong towns, which were friendly to

Macedonia and received support from Philip, fell only after a
brave resistance or withstood even the superior foe—especially
Atrax on the left bank of the Peneius, where the phalanx stood
in the breach as a substitute for the wall. Except these Thessalian fortresses and the territory of the faithful Acarnanians,
all northern Greece was thus in the hands of the coalition.

The south, on the other hand, was still in the main retained
under the power of Macedonia by the fortresses of Chalcis and
Corinth, which maintained communication with each other
through the territory of the Boeotians who were friendly to the
Macedonians, and by the Achaean neutrality; and as it was too
late to advance into Macedonia this year, Flamininus resolved
to direct his land army and fleet in the first place against Corinth
and the Achaeans. The fleet, which had again been joined by
the Rhodian and Pergamene ships, had hitherto been employed
in the capture and pillage of two of the smaller towns in Euboea,
Eretria and Carystus; both however, as well as Oreus, were
thereafter abandoned, and reoccupied by Philocles the Macedonian commandant of Chalcis. The united fleet proceeded
thence to Cenchreae, the eastern port of Corinth, to threaten
that strong fortress. On the other side Flamininus advanced
into Phocis and occupied the country, in which Elatea alone
sustained a somewhat protracted siege: this district and Anticyra in particular on the Corinthian gulf were chosen as winter
quarters. The Achaeans, who thus saw the Roman legions
approaching and the Roman fleet already on their own coast,
abandoned their morally honourable, but politically untenable,
neutrality. After the deputies from the towns most closely
attached to Macedonia—Dyme, Megalopolis, and Argos—had
left the diet, it resolved to join the coalition against Philip.
Cycliades and other leaders of the Macedonian party went into
exile; the troops of the Achaeans immediately united with the
Roman fleet and hastened to invest Corinth by land, which city
—the stronghold of Philip against the Achaeans—had been
guaranteed to them on the part of Rome in return for their joining the coalition. Not only, however, did the Macedonian garrison, which was 1300 strong and consisted chiefly of Italian
deserters, defend with determination the almost impregnable
city, but Philocles also arrived from Chalcis with a division of
1500 men, which after relieving Corinth invaded the territories
of the Achaeans and, in concert with the citizens who were
favourable to Macedonia, wrested from them Argos. But the
recompense of such devotedness was, that the king delivered

over the faithful Argives to the reign of terror of Nabis of Sparta. Philip hoped, after the accession of the Achaeans to the Roman coalition, to gain over Nabis who had hitherto been the ally of the Romans; for his chief reason for joining the Roman alliance was, that he was opposed to the Achaeans and since $\frac{550}{204}$ had been even at open war with them. But the affairs of Philip were in too desperate a condition for any one to feel satisfaction in joining him now. Nabis accepted Argos from Philip, but he betrayed the traitor and remained in alliance with Flamininus, who, in his perplexity at being now allied with two powers that were at war with each other, had in the meantime arranged an armistice of four months between the Spartans and Achaeans.

Thus winter came on; and Philip once more availed himself of it to obtain if possible an equitable peace. At a conference held at Nicaea on the Maliac gulf the king appeared in person, and endeavoured to come to an understanding with Flamininus. With haughty politeness he repelled the forward arrogance of the petty chiefs, and by marked deference to the Romans, as the only antagonists on an equality with him, he sought to obtain from them tolerable terms. Flamininus was sufficiently refined to feel himself flattered by the urbanity of the vanquished prince towards himself and his haughtiness in reference to the allies, whom the Roman as well as the king had learned to despise; but his powers were not ample enough to meet the king's wishes. He granted him a two months' armistice in return for the evacuation of Phocis and Locris, and referred him, as to the main matter, to his government. The Roman senate had long been of opinion that Macedonia must give up all her possessions abroad; accordingly, when the ambassadors of Philip appeared in Rome, they were simply asked whether they had full powers to renounce all Greece and in particular Corinth, Chalcis, and Demetrias, and when they said that they had not, the negotiations were immediately broken off, and it was resolved that the war should be prosecuted with vigour. With the help of the tribunes of the people, the senate succeeded in preventing a change in the chief command—which had often proved so injurious—and in prolonging the command of Flamininus; he obtained considerable reinforcements, and the two former commanders, Publius Galba and Publius Villius, were instructed to place themselves at his disposal. Philip resolved once more to risk a pitched battle. To secure Greece, where all the states except the Acarnanians and Boeotians were now in arms against him, the garrison of Corinth was augmented to

6000 men, while he himself, straining the last energies of exhausted Macedonia and enrolling children and old men in the ranks of the phalanx, brought into the field an army of about 26,000 men, of whom 16,000 were Macedonian *phalangitae*.

Thus the fourth campaign, that of $\frac{557}{197}$, began. Flamininus despatched a part of the fleet against the Acarnanians, who were besieged in Leucas; in Greece proper he became by stratagem master of Thebes, the capital of Boeotia, in consequence of which the Boeotians were compelled to join at least nominally the alliance against Macedonia. Content with having thus interrupted the communication between Corinth and Chalcis, he proceeded to the north, where alone a decisive blow could be struck. The great difficulties of provisioning the army in a hostile and for the most part desolate country, which had often hampered its operations, were now to be obviated by the fleet accompanying the army along the coast and carrying after it supplies sent from Africa, Sicily, and Sardinia. The decisive blow came, however, earlier than Flamininus had expected. Philip, impatient and confident as he was, could not endure to await the enemy on the Macedonian frontier: after assembling his army at Dium, he advanced through the pass of Tempe into Thessaly, and encountered the army of the enemy advancing to meet him in the district of Scotussa.

The Macedonian and Roman armies—the latter of which had been reinforced by the contingents of the Apolloniates and the Athamanes, by the Cretans sent by Nabis, and especially by a strong band of Aetolians—contained nearly equal numbers of combatants, each about 26,000 men; the Romans, however, had the superiority in cavalry. In front of Scotussa, on the plateau of the Karadagh, during a gloomy day of rain, the Roman vanguard unexpectedly encountered that of the enemy, which occupied a high and steep hill named Cynoscephalae, that lay between the two camps. Driven back into the plain, the Romans were reinforced from the camp by the light troops and the excellent corps of Aetolian cavalry, and now in turn forced the Macedonian vanguard back upon and over the height. But here the Macedonians again found support in their whole cavalry and the larger portion of their light infantry; the Romans, who had ventured forward imprudently, were pursued with great loss almost to their camp, and would have wholly taken to flight, had not the Aetolian horsemen prolonged the combat in the plain until Flamininus brought up his rapidly arranged legions. The king yielded to the impetuous cry of his victorious troops demanding the continuance of the conflict, and hastily drew up his heavy-armed soldiers for the battle, which neither general nor soldiers had expected on that day. It was important to occupy the hill, which for the moment was quite denuded of troops. The right wing of the phalanx, led by the king in person, arrived early enough to form without trouble in battle order on the height; the left had not yet come up, when the light troops of the Macedonians, put to flight by the legions, rushed up the hill. Philip quickly pushed the crowd of fugitives past the phalanx into the middle division, and, without waiting till Nicanor had arrived on the left wing with the other half of the phalanx which followed more slowly, he ordered the right phalanx to couch their spears and to charge down the hill on the legions, and the rearranged light infantry simultaneously to turn them and take them in flank. The attack of the phalanx, irresistible on so favourable ground, shattered the Roman infantry, and the left wing of the Romans was completely beaten. Nicanor on the other wing, when he saw the king give the attack, ordered the other half of the phalanx to advance in all haste; by this movement it was thrown into confusion, and while the first ranks were already rapidly following the victorious right wing down the hill, and were still more thrown into disorder by the inequality of the ground, the last files were just gaining the height. The right wing of the Romans under these circumstances soon overcame the enemy's left; the elephants alone, stationed upon this wing, made sad havoc in the broken Macedonian ranks. While a fearful slaughter was taking place at this point, a resolute Roman officer collected twenty companies, and with these threw himself on the victorious Macedonian wing, which had advanced so far in pursuit of the Roman left that the Roman right came to be in its rear. Against an attack from behind the phalanx was defenceless, and this movement ended the battle. From the complete breaking up of the two phalanxes we may well believe that the Macedonian loss amounted to 13,000, partly prisoners, partly fallen—but chiefly the latter, because the Roman soldiers were not acquainted with the Macedonian sign of surrender, the raising of the *sarissae*. The loss of the victors was slight. Philip escaped to Larissa, and, after burning all his papers that nobody might be compromised, evacuated Thessaly and returned home. Simultaneously with this great defeat, the Macedonians suffered other discomfitures at all the points which they still occupied; in Caria the Rhodian mercenaries defeated the

Macedonian corps stationed there and compelled it to shut itself up in Stratonicea; the Corinthian garrison was defeated by Nicostratus and his Achaeans with severe loss, and Leucas in Acarnania was taken by assault after an heroic resistance. Philip was completely vanquished; his last allies, the Acarnanians, yielded on the news of the battle of Cynoscephalae.

It was completely in the power of the Romans to dictate peace; they used their power without abusing it. The empire of Alexander might be annihilated; at a conference of the allies this proposal was actually brought forward by the Aetolians. But what would be the effect of such a course, save to demolish the rampart protecting Hellenic culture from the Thracians and Celts? Already during the war just ended the flourishing Lysimachia on the Thracian Chersonese had been totally destroyed by the Thracians—a serious warning for the future. Flamininus, who had clearly perceived the bitter animosities subsisting among the Greek states, could never consent that the great Roman power should carry into execution the spiteful projects of the Aetolian confederacy, even if his Hellenic sympathies had not been as much won by the polished and chivalrous king as his Roman national feeling was offended by the boastings of the Aetolians, the " victors of Cynoscephalae," as they called themselves. He replied to the Aetolians that it was not the custom of Rome to annihilate the vanquished, and that, besides, they were their own masters and were at liberty to put an end to Macedonia if they could. The king was treated with all possible respect, and, on his declaring himself ready now to entertain the demands formerly made, an armistice for a considerable term was agreed to by Flamininus in return for the payment of a sum of money and the furnishing of hostages, among whom was the king's son Demetrius,—an armistice which Philip greatly needed in order to expel the Dardani out of Macedonia.

The final regulation of the complicated affairs of Greece was entrusted by the senate to a commission of ten persons, the head and soul of which was Flamininus. Philip obtained from it terms similar to those granted to Carthage. He lost all his foreign possessions in Asia Minor, Thrace, Greece, and in the islands of the Aegean Sea; while he retained Macedonia proper undiminished, with the exception of some unimportant tracts on the frontier and the province of Orestis, which was declared free—a stipulation which Philip felt very keenly, but which the Romans could not avoid prescribing, for with his known character it was impossible to leave him free to dispose of subjects who had once revolted from their allegiance. Macedonia was further bound not to conclude any foreign alliances without the previous knowledge of Rome, and not to send garrisons abroad; she was bound, moreover, not to make war out of Macedonia against civilised states or against any allies of Rome at all, and she was to maintain no army exceeding 5000 men, no elephants, and not more than five decked ships; the rest were to be given up to the Romans. Lastly, Philip entered into symmachy with the Romans, which obliged him to send a contingent when requested; indeed, Macedonian troops immediately afterwards fought side by side with the legions. Moreover, he paid a contribution of 1000 talents (£244,000).

After Macedonia had thus been reduced to complete political nullity and was left in possession of only as much power as was needful to guard the frontier of Hellas against the barbarians, the Romans proceeded to dispose of the possessions ceded by the king. The Romans, who just at that time were learning by experience in Spain that transmarine provinces were a very dubious gain, and who had by no means begun the war with a view to the acquisition of territory, took none of the spoil for themselves, and thus compelled their allies also to moderation. They resolved to declare all the states of Greece, which had previously been under Philip, free; and Flamininus was commissioned to read the decree to that effect to the Greeks assembled at the Isthmian games ($\frac{558}{196}$). Thoughtful men doubtless might ask whether freedom was a blessing capable of being thus bestowed, and what was the value of freedom to a nation apart from union and unity; but the rejoicing was great and sincere, as the intention of the senate was sincere in conferring the freedom.[1]

The only exceptions to this general rule were, the Illyrian provinces eastward of Epidamnus, which fell to Pleuratus the ruler of Scodra, and rendered that state of robbers and pirates, which a century before had been humbled by the Romans (p. 68), once more one of the most powerful of the petty principalities in those regions; some districts in western Thessaly, which Amynander had occupied and was allowed to retain; and the three islands of Paros, Scyros, and Imbros, which were presented to Athens in return for the many hardships which she had

---

[1] There are still extant gold staters, with the head of Flamininus and the inscription "*T. Quincti(us)*," struck in Greece under the government of the liberator of the Hellenes. The use of the Latin language is a significant compliment.

suffered, and her still more numerous addresses of thanks and
courtesies of all sorts. The Rhodians, of course, retained their
Carian possessions, and the Pergamenes retained Aegina. The
remaining allies were only indirectly rewarded by the accession
of the newly liberated cities to the several confederacies. The
Achaeans were the best treated, although they were the latest
in joining the coalition against Philip; apparently for the
honourable reason, that this federation was the best organised
and most respectable of all the Greek states. All the possessions
of Philip in the Peloponnesus and on the Isthmus, and consequently Corinth in particular, were incorporated with their
league. With the Aetolians on the other hand the Romans
used little ceremony; they were allowed to receive the towns of
Phocis and Locris into their symmachy, but their attempts to
extend it also to Acarnania and Thessaly were in part decidedly
rejected, in part postponed, and the Thessalian cities were
organised into four small independent confederacies. The
Rhodian city-league reaped the benefit of the liberation of
Thasos, Lemnos, and the towns of Thrace and Asia Minor.

The regulation of the affairs of the Greek states, as respected
both their mutual relations and their internal condition, was
attended with difficulty. The most urgent matter was the war
which had been carried on between the Spartans and Achaeans
since $\frac{550}{204}$, in which the duty of mediating necessarily fell to the
Romans. But after various attempts to induce Nabis to yield,
and particularly to give up the city of Argos belonging to the
Achaean league, which Philip had surrendered to him, no course
at last was left to Flamininus but to have war declared against
the obstinate petty robber-chieftain, who reckoned on the well-
known grudge of the Aetolians against the Romans and on the
advance of Antiochus into Europe, and pertinaciously refused to
restore Argos. This was done, accordingly, by all the Hellenes
at a great diet in Corinth, and Flamininus advanced into the
Peloponnesus accompanied by the fleet and the Romano-allied
army, which included a contingent sent by Philip and a division
of Lacedaemonian emigrants under Agesipolis, the legitimate
king of Sparta ($\frac{559}{195}$). In order to crush his antagonist immediately by an overwhelming superiority of force, no less than
50,000 men were brought into the field, and, the other towns
being disregarded, the capital itself was at once invested; but
the desired result was not attained. Nabis had sent into the
field a considerable army amounting to 15,000 men, of whom
5000 were mercenaries, and he had confirmed his rule afresh

by a complete reign of terror—by the execution *en masse* of the officers and inhabitants of the country whom he suspected. Even when he himself after the first successes of the Roman army and fleet resolved to yield and to accept the comparatively favourable terms of peace proposed by Flamininus, " the people," that is to say the gang of robbers whom Nabis had domiciled in Sparta, not without reason apprehensive of a reckoning after the victory, and deceived by accompanying lies as to the nature of the terms of peace and as to the advance of the Aetolians and Asiatics, rejected the peace offered by the Roman general, so that the struggle began anew. A battle took place in front of the walls and an assault was made upon them; they were already scaled by the Romans, when the setting on fire of the captured streets compelled the assailants to retire.

At last the obstinate resistance came to an end. Sparta retained its independence and was neither compelled to receive back the emigrants nor to join the Achaean league; even the existing monarchical constitution, and Nabis himself, were left intact. On the other hand Nabis had to cede his foreign possessions, Argos, Messene, the Cretan cities, and the whole coast besides; to bind himself neither to conclude foreign alliances, nor to wage war, nor to keep any other vessels than two open boats; and lastly to disgorge all his plunder, to give to the Romans hostages, and to pay to them a war-contribution. The towns on the Laconian coast were given to the Spartan emigrants, and this new community, who named themselves the "free Laconians," in contrast to the monarchically governed Spartans, were directed to enter the Achaean league. The emigrants did not receive back their property, as the district assigned to them was regarded as a compensation for it; it was stipulated on the other hand, that their wives and children should not be detained in Sparta against their will. The Achaeans, although by this arrangement they gained the accession of the free Laconians as well as Argos, were yet far from content; they had expected that the dreaded and hated Nabis would be superseded, that the emigrants would be brought back, and that the Achaean symmachy would be extended to the whole Peloponnesus. Unprejudiced persons, however, will not fail to see that Flamininus managed these difficult affairs as fairly and justly as it was possible to manage them where two political parties, both chargeable with unfairness and injustice, stood opposed to each other. With the old and deep hostility subsisting between the Spartans and Achaeans, the incorporation of Sparta into the Achaean league would have been equivalent to placing Sparta under the Achaean yoke, a course no less contrary to equity than to prudence. The restitution of the emigrants, and the complete restoration of a government that had been set aside for twenty years, would only have substituted one reign of terror for another; the plan adopted by Flamininus was the right one, just because it failed to satisfy either of the extreme parties. At length thorough provision appeared to be made that the Spartan system of robbery by sea and land should cease, and that the government there, such as it was, should prove troublesome only to its own subjects. It is possible that Flamininus, who knew Nabis and could not but be aware how desirable it was that he should personally be superseded, omitted to take such a step from the mere desire to have done with the matter and not to mar the fair impression of his successes by complications that might be prolonged beyond all calculation; it is possible, moreover, that he sought to preserve Sparta as a counterpoise to the power of the Achaean confederacy in the Peloponnesus. But the former objection relates to a point of secondary importance; and as to the latter view, it is far from probable that the Romans condescended to fear the Achaeans.

Peace was thus established, externally at least, among the petty Greek states. But the internal condition of the several communities also furnished employment to the Roman arbiter. The Boeotians openly displayed their Macedonian tendencies, even after the expulsion of the Macedonians from Greece; although Flamininus had at their request allowed the Boeotians who were in the service of Philip to return home, Brachyllas, the most decided partisan of Macedonia, was elected to the presidency of the Boeotian confederacy, and Flamininus was otherwise irritated in every way. He bore it with unparalleled patience; but the Boeotians friendly to Rome, who knew what awaited them after the departure of the Romans, determined to put Brachyllas to death, and Flamininus, whose permission they deemed it necessary to ask, at least did not forbid them. Brachyllas was accordingly killed; upon which the Boeotians were not content with prosecuting the murderers, but lay in wait for the Roman soldiers passing singly or in small parties through their territories, and killed about 500 of them. This was too much to be endured; Flamininus imposed on them a fine of a talent for every soldier; and when they did not pay it, he collected the nearest troops and besieged Coronea ($\frac{558}{196}$). Now they betook themselves to entreaty; Flamininus in reality desisted on the intercession of the Achaeans and Athenians, exacting but a very moderate fine from those who were guilty; and although the Macedonian party remained continuously at the helm in the petty province, the Romans met their puerile opposition simply with the forbearance of superior power. In the rest of Greece Flamininus contented himself with exerting his influence, so far as he could do so without violence, over the internal affairs especially of the newly-freed communities; with placing the councils and courts in the hands of the more wealthy and bringing the anti-Macedonian party to the helm; and with attaching as much as possible the civic commonwealths to the Roman interest, by adding everything, which in each community should have fallen by martial law to the Romans, to the common property of the city concerned. The work was finished in the spring of $\frac{560}{194}$; Flamininus once more assembled the deputies of all the Greek communities at Corinth, exhorted them to a rational and moderate use of the freedom conferred on them, and requested as the only return for the kindness of the Romans, that they would within thirty days send to him the Italian captives who had been sold into Greece during the Hannibalic war. Then he evacuated the last fortresses in which Roman garrisons were stationed, Demetrias, Chalcis along with the smaller forts dependent upon it in Euboea and Acrocorinthus— thus practically giving the lie to the assertion of the Aetolians that Rome had inherited from Philip the " fetters " of Greece —and departed homeward with all the Roman troops and the liberated captives.

It is only contemptible disingenuousness or weakly senti- mentality, which can fail to perceive that the Romans were entirely in earnest in the liberation of Greece; and the reason why the plan so nobly projected resulted in so wretched a struc- ture, is to be sought only in the complete moral and political disorganisation of the Hellenic nation. It was no small matter, that a mighty nation should have suddenly with its powerful arm brought the land, which it had been accustomed to regard as its primitive home and as the shrine of its intellectual and higher interests, into the possession of full freedom, and should have conferred on every community in it deliverance from foreign taxation and foreign garrisons and the unlimited right of self- government; it is mere paltriness that sees in this nothing save political calculation. Political calculation suggested to the Romans the possibility of liberating Greece; it was converted into a reality by the Hellenic sympathies that were at that time indescribably powerful in Rome, and above all in Flamininus himself. If the Romans are liable to any reproach, it is that all of them, and in particular Flamininus who overcame the well-founded scruples of the senate, allowed the magic charm of the Hellenic name to prevent them from perceiving in all its extent the wretched character of the Greek states of that period, and from putting a stop at once to the proceedings of communities who, owing to the impotent antipathies that prevailed alike in their internal and their mutual relations, neither knew how to act nor how to keep quiet. As things stood, it was really necessary at once to put an end to such a freedom, equally pitiful and pernicious, by means of a superior power permanently present on the spot; the feeble policy of sentiment, with all its apparent humanity, was far more cruel than the sternest occupation would have been. In Boeotia for instance Rome had, if not to instigate, at least to permit, a political murder because the Romans had resolved to withdraw their troops from Greece and, consequently, could not prevent the Greeks friendly to Rome from seeking their remedy in the usual manner of the country. But Rome herself also suffered from the effects of this indecision. The war with Antiochus would not have arisen but for the political blunder of liberating Greece, and it would not have been dangerous but for the military blunder of withdrawing the garrisons from the principal fortresses on the European frontier. History has a Nemesis for every sin—for an impotent craving after freedom, as well as for an injudicious generosity.

CHAPTER IX

THE WAR WITH ANTIOCHUS OF ASIA

IN the kingdom of Asia the diadem of the Seleucidae had been worn since $\frac{531}{223}$ by king Antiochus the Third, the great-great-grandson of the founder of the dynasty. He had, like Philip, begun to reign at nineteen years of age, and had displayed sufficient energy and enterprise, especially in his first campaigns in the East, to warrant his being without ludicrous impropriety addressed in courtly style as "the Great." He had succeeded—more, however, through the negligence of his opponents and of the Egyptian Philopator in particular, than through any ability of his own—in restoring in some degree the integrity of the monarchy, and in reuniting with his crown first the eastern satrapies of Media and Parthyene, and then the separate state which Achaeus had founded on this side of the Taurus in Asia Minor. A first attempt to wrest from the Egyptians the coast of Syria, the loss of which he sorely felt, had, in the year of the battle of the Trasimene lake, met with a bloody repulse from Philopator at Raphia; and Antiochus had taken good care not to resume the contest with Egypt, so long as a man—even though he were but an indolent one—occupied the Egyptian throne. But, after Philopator's death ($\frac{549}{205}$), the right moment for crushing Egypt appeared to have arrived; with that view Antiochus entered into concert with Philip, and had thrown himself upon Coele-Syria, while Philip attacked the cities of Asia Minor. When the Romans interposed in that quarter, it seemed for a moment as if Antiochus would make common cause with Philip against them—the course dictated by the position of affairs, as well as by the treaty of alliance. But, not far-seeing enough to repel at once with all his energy any interference whatever by the Romans in the affairs of the East, Antiochus thought that his best course was to take advantage of the subjugation of Philip by the Romans (which might easily be foreseen), in order to secure the kingdom of Egypt, which he had previously been willing to share with Philip, for himself alone. Notwithstanding the intimate relations of Rome with the court of Alexandria and her royal ward, the senate by

no means intended to be in reality, what it was in name, his
" guardian; " firmly resolved to give itself no concern about
Asiatic affairs except in case of extreme necessity, and to limit
the sphere of the Roman power by the Pillars of Hercules and
the Hellespont, it allowed the great king to take his course.　He
himself did not probably contemplate in earnest the conquest
of Egypt proper—which was more easily talked of than achieved
—but he contemplated the subjugation of the foreign possessions
of Egypt one after another, and at once attacked those in Cilicia
as well as in Syria and Palestine.　The great victory, which he
gained in $\frac{556}{198}$ over the Egyptian general Scopas at Mount
Panium near the sources of the Jordan, not only gave him complete possession of that region as far as the frontier of Egypt
proper, but so terrified the Egyptian guardians of the young
king that, to prevent Antiochus from invading Egypt, they submitted to a peace and sealed it by the betrothal of their ward
to Cleopatra the daughter of Antiochus.　When he had thus
achieved his first object, he proceeded in the following year, that
of the battle of Cynoscephalae, with a strong fleet of 100 decked
and 100 open vessels to Asia Minor, to take possession of the
districts that formerly belonged to Egypt on the south and west
coasts of Asia Minor—it is probable that the Egyptian government had ceded these districts, which were actually in the hands
of Philip, to Antiochus under the peace, and had renounced
their foreign possessions generally in Antiochus' favour—and
to recover the Greeks of Asia Minor as a whole to his empire.
At the same time a strong Syrian land-army assembled in
Sardes.

This enterprise had an indirect bearing on the Romans, who
from the first had demanded that Philip should withdraw his
garrisons from Asia Minor and should leave to the Rhodians and
Pergamenes their territory and to the free cities their former
constitution unimpaired, and who had now to witness Antiochus
taking possession of them in Philip's place.　Attalus and the
Rhodians found themselves now directly threatened by Antiochus
with precisely the same danger as had driven them a few years
before into the war with Philip; and they naturally sought to
involve the Romans in this war as well as in that which had just
terminated.　Already in $\frac{555-556}{199-198}$ Attalus had requested from
the Romans military aid against Antiochus, who had occupied
his territory while the troops of Attalus were employed in the
Roman war.　The more energetic Rhodians even declared to
king Antiochus, when in the spring of $\frac{557}{197}$ his fleet appeared off

the coast of Asia Minor, that they would regard its passing beyond the Chelidonian islands (off the Lycian coast) as a declaration of war; and, when Antiochus did not regard the threat, they, emboldened by the accounts that had just arrived of the battle of Cynoscephalae, had immediately begun the war and had actually protected against the king the most important of the Carian cities, Caunus, Halicarnassus, and Myndus, and the island of Samos. Most of the half-free cities had submitted to Antiochus, but some of them, more especially the important cities of Smyrna, Alexandria Troas, and Lampsacus, had, on learning the discomfiture of Philip, likewise taken courage to resist the Syrian; and their urgent entreaties were combined with those of the Rhodians.

It admits of no doubt, that Antiochus, so far as he was at all capable of forming a resolution and adhering to it, had already made up his mind not only to attach to his empire the Egyptian possessions in Asia, but also to make conquests on his own behalf in Europe and, if not to seek, at any rate to risk on that account a war with Rome. The Romans had thus every reason to comply with that request of their allies, and to interfere directly in Asia; but they showed little inclination to do so. They not only delayed as long as the Macedonian war lasted, and gave to Attalus nothing but the protection of diplomacy (which, so far, proved in the first instance effective); but even after their victory, while they doubtless spoke as though the cities which had been in the hands of Ptolemy and Philip ought not to be taken possession of by Antiochus, and while the freedom of the Asiatic cities, Abydus, Cius, and Myrina, figured in Roman documents, they took not the smallest step to give effect to it, and allowed king Antiochus to employ the favourable opportunity presented by the withdrawal of the Macedonian garrisons to introduce his own. In fact, they even went so far as to submit to his landing in Europe in the spring of $\frac{558}{196}$ and invading the Thracian Chersonese, where he occupied Sestus and Madytus and spent a considerable time in the chastisement of the Thracian barbarians and the restoration of the destroyed Lysimachia, which he had selected as his chief stronghold and as the capital of the newly instituted satrapy of Thrace. Flamininus indeed, who was entrusted with the conduct of these affairs, sent to the king at Lysimachia envoys, who talked of the integrity of the Egyptian territory and of the freedom of all the Hellenes; but nothing came of it. The king talked in reply of his undoubted legal title to the ancient kingdom of Lysimachus conquered by his ancestor Seleucus, explained that he was employed not in making territorial acquisitions but only in preserving the integrity of his hereditary dominions, and declined the intervention of the Romans in his disputes with the cities subject to him in Asia Minor. With justice he was enabled to add that peace had already been concluded with Egypt, and that the Romans were thus deprived of any formal pretext for interfering.[1] The sudden return of the king to Asia occasioned by a false report of the death of the young king of Egypt, and the projects which it suggested of a landing in Cyprus or even at Alexandria, led to the breaking off of the conferences without coming to any conclusion, still less producing any result. In the following year, $\frac{559}{195}$, Antiochus returned to Lysimachia with his fleet and army reinforced, and employed himself in organising the new satrapy which he destined for his son Seleucus. Hannibal, who had been obliged to flee from Carthage, came to him at Ephesus; and the singularly honourable reception accorded to the exile was equivalent to a declaration of war against Rome. Nevertheless Flamininus in the spring of $\frac{560}{194}$ withdrew all the Roman garrisons from Greece. This was under the existing circumstances at least a mischievous error, if not a criminal acting in opposition to his own better knowledge; for we cannot dismiss the idea that Flamininus, in order to carry home with him the undiminished glory of having wholly terminated the war and liberated Hellas, contented himself with superficially covering up for the moment the smouldering embers of revolt and war. The Roman statesman might perhaps be right, when he pronounced any attempt to bring Greece directly under the dominion of the Romans, and any intervention of the Romans in Asiatic affairs, to be a political blunder; but the opposition fermenting in Greece, the feeble arrogance of the Asiatic king, the residence, at the Syrian head-quarters, of the bitter enemy of the Romans who had already raised the West in arms against Rome—all these were clear signs of the approach of a fresh appeal to arms on the part of the Hellenic East, which would necessarily seek at least to transfer Greece from the clientship of Rome to that of the states opposed to Rome, and, if this

---

[1] The definite testimony of Hieronymus, who places the betrothal of the Syrian princess Cleopatra with Ptolemy Epiphanes in $\frac{556}{198}$, taken in connection with the hints in Liv. xxxiii. 40 and Appian, *Syr.* 3, and with the actual accomplishment of the marriage in $\frac{561}{193}$, puts it beyond a doubt that the interference of the Romans in the affairs of Egypt was in this case formally uncalled for.

object should be attained, would immediately extend the circle of its operations. It is plain that Rome could not allow this to take place. When Flamininus, ignoring all these sure indications of war, withdrew the garrisons from Greece, and yet at the same time made demands on the king of Asia which he had no intention of employing his army to support, he overdid his part in words as much as he fell short in action, and forgot his duty as a general and as a citizen in the indulgence of his personal vanity—a vanity which wished to enjoy the credit of having conferred peace on Rome and freedom on the Greeks of both continents.

Antiochus employed the unexpected respite in strengthening his position at home and his relations with his neighbours before beginning the war—in which he was the more resolved to engage, the more the enemy appeared to procrastinate. He now ($\frac{561}{193}$) gave his daughter Cleopatra, previously betrothed, in marriage to the young king of Egypt. That he at the same time promised to restore the provinces wrested from his son-in-law, was afterwards affirmed on the part of Egypt, but probably without warrant; at any rate the land remained actually attached to the Syrian kingdom.[1] He offered to restore to Eumenes, who had in $\frac{567}{197}$ succeeded his father Attalus on the throne of Pergamus, the towns taken from him, and to give him also one of his daughters in marriage, if he would abandon the Roman alliance. In like manner he bestowed a daughter on Ariarathes, king of Cappadocia, and gained the Galatians by presents, while he reduced by arms the Pisidians who were constantly in revolt, and other small tribes. Extensive privileges were granted to the Byzantines; respecting the cities in Asia Minor, the king declared that he would concede the independence of the old free cities such as Rhodes and Cyzicus, and would be content in the case of the others with a mere formal recognition of his supremacy; he even gave them to understand that he was ready to submit to the arbitration of the Rhodians. In European Greece he could safely count on the Aetolians, and he hoped to induce Philip again to take up arms. In fact, a plan of Hannibal

---

[1] For this we have the testimony of Polybius (xxviii. 1), which the sequel of the history of Judaea completely confirms; Eusebius (p. 117, *Mai*) is mistaken in making Philometor ruler of Syria. We certainly find that about $\frac{567}{187}$ farmers of the Syrian taxes made their payments at Alexandria (Joseph. xii. 4, 7); but this doubtless took place without detriment to the rights of sovereignty, simply because the dowry of Cleopatra constituted a charge on those revenues; and from this very circumstance probably arose the subsequent dispute.

obtained the royal approval, according to which he was to receive
from Antiochus a fleet of 100 sail and a land army of 10,000
infantry and 1000 cavalry, and was to employ them in kindling
first a third Punic war in Carthage, and then a second Hannibalic
war in Italy; Tyrian emissaries proceeded to Carthage to pave
the way for an appeal to arms there (p. 189). Finally, good
results were anticipated from the Spanish insurrection, which,
at the time when Hannibal left Carthage, was at its height
(p. 197).

While the storm was thus gathering from far and wide against
Rome, it was on this, as on all occasions, the Hellenes implicated
in the enterprise, who, while they were of least moment, took
the most important steps and acted with the utmost impatience.
The exasperated and arrogant Aetolians began by degrees to
persuade themselves that Philip had been vanquished by them
and not by the Romans, and could not even wait till Antiochus
should advance into Greece. Their policy is briefly expressed
in the reply, which their *strategus* gave soon afterwards to
Flamininus, when he requested a copy of the declaration of war
against Rome: that he would deliver it to him in person, when
the Aetolian army should encamp by the Tiber. The Aetolians
acted as the agents of the Syrian king of Greece and deceived
both parties, by representing to the king that all the Hellenes
were waiting with open arms to receive him as their true deliverer, and by telling those in Greece who were disposed to
listen to them that the landing of the king was nearer than it
was in reality. Thus they actually succeeded in inducing the
foolish obstinacy of Nabis to break the peace and to rekindle in
Greece the flame of war two years after Flamininus's departure,
in the spring of $\frac{562}{192}$; but in doing so they missed their aim.
Nabis attacked Gythium, one of the towns of the free Laconians
that by the last treaty had been annexed to the Achaean league,
and took it; but the experienced *strategus* of the Achaeans,
Philopoemen, defeated him at the Barbosthenian mountains,
and the tyrant brought back barely a fourth part of his army to
his capital, in which Philopoemen shut him up. As such a commencement was no sufficient inducement for Antiochus to come
to Europe, the Aetolians resolved to possess themselves of Sparta,
Chalcis, and Demetrias, and by gaining these important towns
to prevail upon the king to embark. In the first place they
thought to become masters of Sparta, by arranging that the
Aetolian Alexamenus should march with 1000 men into the
town under pretext of bringing a contingent in terms of the

alliance, and should embrace the opportunity of making away with Nabis and of occupying the town. This was done, and Nabis was killed at a review of the troops; but, when the Aetolians dispersed to plunder the town, the Lacedaemonians found time to rally and slew them to a man. The city was then induced by Philopoemen to join the Achaean league. This laudable project of the Aetolians had thus not only deservedly failed, but had precisely the opposite effect of uniting almost the whole Peloponnesus in the hands of the other party. It fared little better with them at Chalcis, for the Roman party there called in the citizens of Eretria and Carystus in Euboea, who were favourable to Rome, to render seasonable aid against the Aetolians and the Chalcidian exiles. On the other hand the occupation of Demetrias was successful, for the Magnetes to whom the city had been assigned were, not without reason, apprehensive that it had been promised by the Romans to Philip as a prize in return for his aid against Antiochus; several squadrons of Aetolian horse moreover managed to steal into the town under the pretext of escorting Eurylochus, the recalled head of the opposition to Rome. Thus the Magnetes passed over, partly of their own accord, partly by compulsion, to the side of the Aetolians, and the latter did not fail to make good use of the fact at the court of the Seleucid.

Antiochus took his resolution. A rupture with Rome, in spite of endeavours to postpone it by the diplomatic expedient of embassies, could no longer be avoided. As early as the spring of $\frac{561}{193}$ Flamininus, who continued to have the decisive voice in the senate as to Eastern affairs, had expressed the Roman ultimatum to the envoys of the king, Menippus and Hegesianax; viz., that he should either evacuate Europe and dispose of Asia at his pleasure, or retain Thrace and submit to the Roman protectorate over Smyrna, Lampsacus, and Alexandria Troas. These demands had been again discussed at Ephesus, the chief stronghold and head-quarters of the king in Asia Minor, in the spring of $\frac{562}{192}$, between Antiochus and the envoys of the senate, Publius Sulpicius and Publius Villius; and they had separated with the conviction on both sides that a peaceful settlement was no longer possible. Thenceforth war was resolved on in Rome. In that very summer of $\frac{562}{192}$ a Roman fleet of 30 sail, with 3000 soldiers on board, under Aulus Atilius Serranus appeared off Gythium, where their arrival accelerated the conclusion of the treaty between the Achaeans and Spartans; the eastern coasts of Sicily and Italy were strongly garrisoned, so as to be secure against any attempts at a landing; a land army was expected in Greece in the autumn. In the spring of $\frac{563}{192}$ Flamininus, by direction of the senate, had visited Greece to thwart the intrigues of the opposite party, and to counteract as far as possible the evil effects of the ill-timed evacuation of the country. The Aetolians had already gone so far as formally to declare war in their diet against Rome. But Flamininus succeeded in preserving Chalcis to the Romans by throwing into it a garrison of 500 Achaeans and 500 Pergamenes. He made an attempt also to recover Demetrias; and the Magnetes wavered. Though some towns in Asia Minor, which Antiochus had proposed to subdue before beginning the great war, still held out, he could no longer delay his landing, unless he was willing to let the Romans recover all the advantages which they had surrendered two years before by withdrawing their garrisons from Greece. He collected the vessels and troops which were at hand—he had but 40 decked vessels and 10,000 infantry, along with 500 horse and 6 elephants —and started from the Thracian Chersonese for Greece, where he landed in the autumn of $\frac{563}{192}$ at Pteleum on the Pagasaean gulf, and immediately occupied the adjoining Demetrias. About the same time a Roman army of nearly 25,000 men under the praetor Marcus Baebius landed at Apollonia. The war was thus begun on both sides.

Everything depended on the extent to which that comprehensively planned coalition against Rome, of which Antiochus came forward as the head, might be realised. As to the plan, first of all, of stirring up enemies to the Romans in Carthage and Italy, it was the fate of Hannibal at the court of Ephesus, as through his whole career, to have projected his noble and lofty schemes for the behoof of people narrow-minded and mean. Nothing was done towards their execution, except that some Carthaginian patriots were compromised; no choice was left to the Carthaginians but to show unconditional submission to Rome. The camarilla would have nothing to do with Hannibal —he was too inconveniently great for court cabals; and, after having tried all sorts of absurd expedients—such as accusing the general, with whose name the Romans frightened their children, of concert with the Roman envoys—they succeeded in persuading Antiochus the Great, who like all insignificant monarchs plumed himself greatly on his independence and was influenced by nothing so easily as by the fear of being ruled, into the wise belief that he ought not to allow himself to be thrown into the shade by so illustrious a man. Accordingly

it was in solemn council resolved that the Phoenician should be
employed in future only for subordinate enterprises and for
giving advice—with the reservation, of course, that that advice
should never be followed. Hannibal revenged himself on the
mob of courtiers by accepting every commission and brilliantly
executing all.

In Asia Cappadocia adhered to the great king; Prusias of
Bithynia on the other hand took, as usual, the side of the
stronger. King Eumenes remained faithful to the old policy of
his house, which was now at length to yield to him its true fruit.
He had not only persisted in refusing the offers of Antiochus,
but had constantly urged the Romans to a war, from which he
anticipated the aggrandisement of his kingdom. The Rhodians
and Byzantines likewise joined their old allies. Egypt too took
the side of Rome and offered support in supplies and men;
which, however, the Romans did not accept.

In Europe the result mainly depended on the position
which Philip of Macedonia would take up. True policy ought
perhaps to have induced him, notwithstanding all the injuries
or shortcomings of the past, to unite with Antiochus. But
Philip was ordinarily influenced not by such considerations,
but by his likings and dislikings; and his hatred was naturally
directed much more against the faithless ally, who had left him
to contend alone with the common enemy, had sought merely
to seize his own share in the spoil, and had become a burden-
some neighbour to him in Thrace, than against the conqueror,
who had treated him respectfully and honourably. Antiochus
had, moreover, given deep offence to the hot temper of Philip
by the setting up of absurd pretenders to the Macedonian crown,
and by the ostentatious burial of the Macedonian bones bleach-
ing at Cynoscephalae. Philip therefore placed his whole force
with cordial zeal at the disposal of the Romans.

The second power of Greece, the Achaean league, adhered no
less decidedly than the first to the alliance with Rome. Of the
smaller powers, the Thessalians and the Athenians held by
Rome; among the latter an Achaean garrison introduced by
Flamininus into the citadel brought the patriotic party, which
was somewhat numerous, to reason. The Epirots exerted themselves to keep on good terms, if possible, with both parties.
Thus, in addition to the Aetolians and the Magnetes who were
joined by a portion of the neighbouring Perrhaebians, Antiochus
was supported only by Amynander, the weak king of the Athamanes, who allowed himself to be dazzled by foolish designs on

the Macedonian crown; by the Boeotians, among whom the
party opposed to Rome was still at the helm; and by the Eleans
and Messenians in the Peloponnesus, who were in the habit of
taking part with the Aetolians against the Achaeans. This was
indeed a hopeful beginning; and the title of commander-in-
chief with absolute power, which the Aetolians decreed to the
great king, seemed insult added to injury. There had been,
just as usual, deception on both sides. Instead of the countless
hordes of Asia, the king brought up a force scarcely half as
strong as an ordinary consular army; and instead of the open
arms with which all the Hellenes were to welcome their deliverer
from the Roman yoke, one or two bands of klephts and some
dissolute bodies of citizens fraternised with the king.

For the moment, indeed, Antiochus anticipated the Romans
in Greece proper. Chalcis was garrisoned by the Greek allies of
the Romans, and refused the first summons; but the fortress
surrendered when Antiochus advanced with all his force; and a
Roman division, which arrived too late to occupy it, was annihilated by Antiochus at Delium. Euboea was thus lost to the
Romans. Antiochus also made an attempt in winter, in concert
with the Aetolians and Acarnanians, to gain Thessaly; Thermopylae was occupied, Pherae and other towns were taken,
but Appius Claudius came up with 2000 men from Apollonia,
relieved Larisa, and took up his position there. Antiochus,
tired of the winter campaign, preferred to return to his pleasant
quarters at Chalcis, where the time was spent merrily, and the
king even, in spite of his fifty years and his warlike schemes,
married a fair Chalcidian. So the winter of $\frac{562-563}{192-191}$ passed,
without Antiochus doing much more than sending letters hither
and thither through Greece: he waged war—a Roman officer
remarked—by means of pen and ink.

In the beginning of spring $\frac{563}{191}$ the Roman staff arrived at
Apollonia. The commander-in-chief was Manius Acilius
Glabrio, a man of humble origin, but an able general feared both
by his soldiers and by the enemy; the admiral was Gaius
Livius; and among the military tribunes were Marcus Porcius
Cato, the conqueror of Spain, and Lucius Valerius Flaccus, who
after the old Roman wont did not disdain, although they had
been consuls, to re-enter the army as simple commanders of
legions. They brought with them reinforcements in ships and
men, including Numidian cavalry and Libyan elephants sent by
Massinissa, and the permission of the senate to accept auxiliary
troops to the number of 5000 from the extra-Italian allies, so

that the whole number of the Roman forces were raised to about 40,000 men. The king, who in the beginning of spring had gone to the Aetolians and had thence made an aimless expedition to Acarnania, on learning the arrival of Glabrio, returned to his head-quarters to begin the campaign in earnest. But through his own inconceivable negligence and that of his lieutenants in Asia no reinforcements reached him, so that he had nothing but the weak army—now further decimated by sickness and desertion in its dissolute winter-quarters—with which he had landed at Pteleum in the autumn of the previous year. The Aetolians too, who had professed to send such enormous numbers into the field, now, when their support was of moment, brought to their commander-in-chief no more than 4000 men. The Roman troops had already begun operations in Thessaly, where the vanguard in concert with the Macedonian army drove the garrisons of Antiochus out of the Thessalian towns and occupied the territory of the Athamanes. The consul with the main army followed; the whole force of the Romans assembled at Larisa.

Instead of returning with all speed to Asia and evacuating the field before an enemy in every respect superior, Antiochus resolved to entrench himself at Thermopylae, which he had occupied, and there to await the arrival of the great army from Asia. He himself took up a position in the principal pass, and commanded the Aetolians to occupy the mountain-path, by which Xerxes had formerly succeeded in turning the Spartans. But only half of the Aetolian contingent thought fit to comply with this command of the commander-in-chief; the other 2000 men threw themselves into the neighbouring town of Heraclea, where they took no other part in the battle than that of attempting during its progress to surprise and plunder the Roman camp. Even the Aetolians posted on the heights discharged their duty of watching with remissness and reluctance; their post on the Callidromus allowed itself to be surprised by Cato, and the Asiatic phalanx, which the consul had meanwhile assailed in front, dispersed, when the Romans hastening down the mountain-path fell upon its flank. As Antiochus had made no provision for any case and had not thought of retreat, the army was destroyed partly on the field of battle, partly during its flight; with difficulty a small band reached Demetrias, and the king himself escaped to Chalcis with 500 men. He embarked in haste for Ephesus; Europe was lost to him all but his possessions in Thrace, and even the fortresses could be no longer defended. Chalcis surrendered to the Romans, and Demetrias

to Philip, who received permission—as a compensation for the
conquest of the town of Lamia in Achaia Phthiotis which he
was on the point of accomplishing and then abandoned by
orders of the consul—to make himself master of all the communities that had gone over to Antiochus in Thessaly proper,
and even of the territories bordering on Aetolia, the districts of
Dolopia and Aperantia. All the Greeks that had pronounced in
favour of Antiochus hastened to make their peace; the Epirots
humbly besought pardon for their ambiguous conduct, the
Boeotians surrendered at discretion, the Eleans and Messenians,
the latter after some struggle, submitted to the Achaeans. The
prediction of Hannibal to the king was fulfilled, that no dependence at all could be placed upon the Greeks, who would submit
to any conqueror. Even the Aetolians, when their corps shut
up in Heraclea had been compelled after obstinate resistance to
capitulate, attempted to make their peace with the sorely provoked Romans; but the stringent demands of the Roman
consul, and a consignment of money seasonably arriving from
Antiochus, emboldened them once more to break off the negotiations and to sustain for two whole months a siege in Naupactus.
The town was already reduced to extremities, and its capture or
capitulation could not have been long delayed, when Flamininus,
constantly striving to save every Hellenic community from the
worst consequences of its own folly and from the severity of his
ruder colleagues, interposed and arranged in the first instance
an armistice on tolerable terms. This terminated, at least for
the moment, all resistance in Greece.

A more serious war was impending in Asia—a war which
appeared of a very hazardous character on account not so much
of the enemy as of the great distance and the insecurity of the
communications with home, while yet, owing to the shortsighted obstinacy of Antiochus, the struggle could not well be
terminated otherwise than by an attack on the enemy in his
own country. The first object was to secure the sea. The
Roman fleet, which during the campaign in Greece was charged
with the task of interrupting the communication between Greece
and Asia Minor, and which had been successful about the time
of the battle at Thermopylae in seizing a strong Asiatic transport
fleet near Andros, was thenceforth employed in making preparations for the crossing of the Romans to Asia next year and first
of all in driving the enemy's fleet out of the Aegean Sea. It lay
in the harbour of Cyssus on the southern shore of the tongue of
land that projects from Ionia towards Chios; thither the

Roman fleet proceeded in search of it, consisting of seventy-five Roman, twenty-four Pergamene, and six Carthaginian, decked vessels under the command of Gaius Livius. The Syrian admiral, Polyxenidas, a Rhodian emigrant, had only seventy decked vessels to oppose to it; but, as the Roman fleet still expected the ships of Rhodes, and as Polyxenidas relied on the superior seaworthiness of his vessels, those of Tyre and Sidon in particular, he immediately accepted battle. At the outset the Asiatics succeeded in sinking one of the Carthaginian vessels; but, when they came to grapple, Roman valour prevailed, and it was owing solely to the swiftness of their rowing and sailing that the enemy lost no more than twenty-three ships. During the pursuit the Roman fleet was joined by twenty-five ships from Rhodes, and the superiority of the Romans in those waters was now doubly decisive. The enemy's fleet thenceforth kept the shelter of the harbour of Ephesus, and, as it could not be induced to risk a second battle, the fleet of the Romans and allies broke up for the winter; the Roman ships of war proceeded to the harbour of Cane in the neighbourhood of Pergamus.

Both parties were busy during the winter in preparing for the next campaign. The Romans sought to gain over the Greeks of Asia Minor; Smyrna, which had perseveringly resisted all the attempts of the king to get possession of it, received the Romans with open arms, and the Roman party gained the ascendancy in Samos, Chios, Erythrae, Clazomenae, Phocaea, Cyme, and other places. Antiochus was resolved, if possible, to prevent the Romans from crossing to Asia, and with that view he made zealous naval preparations—employing Polyxenidas to fit out and augment the fleet stationed at Ephesus, and Hannibal to equip a new fleet in Lycia, Syria, and Phoenicia; while he further collected in Asia Minor a powerful land army from all regions of his extensive empire. Early next year ($\frac{564}{190}$) the Roman fleet resumed its operations. Gaius Livius left the Rhodian fleet—which had appeared in good time this year, numbering thirty-six sail—to observe that of the enemy in the offing of Ephesus, and went with the greater portion of the Roman and Pergamene vessels to the Hellespont in accordance with his instructions, to pave the way for the passage of the land army by the capture of the fortresses there. Sestus was already occupied and Abydus reduced to extremities, when the news of the defeat of the Rhodian fleet recalled him. The Rhodian admiral Pausistratus, lulled into security by the representations of his countryman that he wished to desert from

Antiochus, had allowed himself to be surprised in the harbour of Samos; he himself fell, and all his vessels were destroyed except five Rhodian and two Coan ships; Samos, Phocaea, and Cyme on hearing the news went over to Seleucus, who held the chief command by land in those provinces for his father. But when the Roman fleet arrived partly from Cane, partly from the Hellespont, and was after some time joined by twenty new ships of the Rhodians at Samos, Polyxenidas was once more compelled to shut himself up in the harbour of Ephesus. As he declined the offered naval battle, and as, owing to the small numbers of the Roman force, an attack by land was out of the question, nothing remained for the Roman fleet but to take up its position in like manner at Samos. A division meanwhile proceeded to Patara on the Lycian coast, partly to relieve the Rhodians from the very troublesome attacks that were directed against them from that quarter, partly and chiefly to prevent the hostile fleet, which Hannibal was expected to bring up, from entering the Aegean Sea. When the squadron sent against Patara achieved nothing, the new admiral Lucius Aemilius Regillus, who had arrived with twenty war-vessels from Rome and had relieved Gaius Livius at Samos, was so indignant that he proceeded thither with the whole fleet; his officers with difficulty succeeded, while they were on their voyage, in making him understand that the primary object was not the conquest of Patara but the command of the Aegean Sea, and in inducing him to return to Samos. On the mainland of Asia Minor Seleucus had in the meanwhile begun the siege of Pergamus, while Antiochus with his chief army ravaged the Pergamene territory and the possessions of the Mytilenaeans on the mainland; they hoped to crush the hated Attalids, before Roman aid appeared. The Roman fleet went to Elaea and the port of Adramyttium to help their ally; but, as the admiral wanted troops, he accomplished nothing. Pergamus seemed lost; but the laxity and negligence with which the siege was conducted allowed Eumenes to throw into the city Achaean auxiliaries under Diophanes, whose bold and successful sallies compelled the Gallic mercenaries, whom Antiochus had entrusted with the siege, to raise it. In the southern waters too the projects of Antiochus were frustrated. The fleet equipped and led by Hannibal, after having been long detained by the constant westerly winds, attempted at length to reach the Aegean; but at the mouth of the Eurymedon, off Aspendus in Pamphylia, it encountered a Rhodian squadron under Eudamus; and in the battle, which ensued between the two fleets, the excellence of the Rhodian ships and naval officers carried the victory over Hannibal's tactics and his numerical superiority. It was the first naval battle, and the last battle against Rome, fought by the great Carthaginian. The victorious Rhodian fleet then took its station at Patara, and there prevented the intended junction of the two Asiatic fleets. In the Aegean Sea the Romano-Rhodian fleet at Samos, after being weakened by detaching the Pergamene ships to the Hellespont to support the land army which had arrived there, was in its turn attacked by that of Polyxenidas, who now numbered nine sail more than his opponents. On December 23 of the uncorrected calendar, according to the corrected calendar about the end of August, in $\frac{564}{190}$, the battle took place at the promontory of Myonnesus between Teos and Colophon; the Romans broke through the line of the enemy, and totally surrounded the left wing, so that they took or sank forty-two ships. An inscription in Saturnian verse over the temple of the Lares Permarini, which was built in the Campus Martius in memory of this victory, for many centuries thereafter proclaimed to the Romans how the fleet of the Asiatics had been defeated before the eyes of king Antiochus and of all his land army, and how the Romans thus " settled the mighty strife and subdued the kings." Thenceforth the enemy's ships no longer ventured to show themselves on the open sea, and made no further attempt to obstruct the crossing of the Roman land army.

The conqueror of Zama had been selected at Rome to conduct the war on the Asiatic continent; he practically exercised the supreme command for the nominal commander-in-chief, his brother Lucius Scipio, whose intellect was insignificant, and who had no military capacity. The reserve hitherto stationed in Lower Italy was destined for Greece, the army under Glabrio for Asia: when it became known who was to command it, 5000 veterans from the Hannibalic war voluntarily enrolled, to fight once more under their beloved leader. In the Roman July, but according to the true time in March, the Scipios arrived at the army to commence the Asiatic campaign; but they were disagreeably surprised to find themselves involved, in the first instance, in an endless struggle with the desperate Aetolians. The senate, finding that Flamininus pushed his boundless consideration for the Hellenes too far, had left the Aetolians to choose between paying an utterly exorbitant war contribution and unconditional surrender, and thus had driven them anew to arms; none could tell when this warfare among mountains and strongholds would come to an end. Scipio got rid of the inconvenient obstacle by concerting a six-months' armistice, and then entered on his march to Asia. As the one fleet of the enemy was only blockaded in the Aegean Sea, and the other, which was coming up from the south, might daily arrive there in spite of the squadron charged to intercept it, it seemed advisable to take the land route through Macedonia and Thrace and to cross the Hellespont. In that direction no real obstacles were to be anticipated; for Philip of Macedonia might be entirely depended on, Prusias king of Bithynia was in alliance with the Romans, and the Roman fleet could easily establish itself in the straits. The long and weary march along the coast of Macedonia and Thrace was accomplished without material loss; Philip made provision on the one hand for supplying their wants, on the other for their friendly reception by the Thracian barbarians. They had lost so much time however, partly with the Aetolians, partly on the march, that the army only reached the Thracian Chersonese about the time of the battle of Myonnesus. But the marvellous good fortune of Scipio now in Asia, as formerly in Spain and Africa, cleared his path of all difficulties.

On the news of the battle at Myonnesus Antiochus so completely lost his judgment, that in Europe he caused the strongly-garrisoned and well-provisioned fortress of Lysimachia to be evacuated by the garrison and by the inhabitants who were faithfully devoted to the restorer of their city, but forgot even to withdraw in like manner the garrisons or to destroy the rich magazines at Aenus and Maronea; and on the Asiatic coast he opposed not the slightest resistance to the landing of the Romans, but on the contrary, while it was taking place, spent his time at Sardes in upbraiding destiny. It is scarcely doubtful that, had he but provided for the defence of Lysimachia down to the no longer distant close of the summer, and moved forward his great army to the Hellespont, Scipio would have been compelled to take up winter quarters on the European shore, in a position far from being, in a military or political point of view, secure.

While the Romans, after disembarking on the Asiatic shore, paused for some days to refresh themselves and to await their leader who was detained behind by religious duties, ambassadors from the great king arrived in their camp to negotiate for peace. Antiochus offered half the expenses of the war, and the cession of his European possessions as well as of all the Greek cities in

Asia Minor that had gone over to Rome; but Scipio demanded the whole costs of the war and the surrender of all Asia Minor. The former terms, he declared, might have been accepted, had the army still been before Lysimachia, or even on the European side of the Hellespont; but they did not suffice now, when the steed felt the bit and knew its rider. The attempts of the great king to purchase peace from his antagonist after the Oriental manner by sums of money—he offered the half of his year's revenues!—failed as they deserved; the proud burgess, in return for the gratuitous restoration of his son who had fallen a captive, rewarded the great king with the friendly advice to make peace on any terms. This was not in reality necessary: had the king possessed the resolution to prolong the war and to draw the enemy after him by retreating into the interior, a favourable issue was still by no means impossible. But Antiochus, irritated by the probably intentional arrogance of his antagonist, and too indolent for any persevering and consistent warfare, hastened with the utmost eagerness to expose his unwieldy, heterogeneous, and undisciplined mass of an army to the shock of the Roman legions.

In the valley of the Hermus, near Magnesia at the foot of Mount Sipylus not far from Smyrna, the Roman troops fell in with the enemy late in the autumn of $\frac{564}{190}$. The force of Antiochus numbered close on 80,000 men, of whom 12,000 were cavalry; the Romans—who had along with them about 5000 Achaeans, Pergamenes, and Macedonian volunteers—had not nearly half that number, but they were so sure of victory, that they did not wait for the recovery of their general who had remained behind sick at Elaea; Gnaeus Domitius took the command in his stead. Antiochus, in order to be able even to place his immense mass of troops, formed two divisions. In the first were placed the mass of the light troops, the peltasts, bowmen, slingers, the mounted archers of the Mysians, Dahae, and Elymaeans, the Arabs on their dromedaries, and the scythe-chariots. In the second division the heavy cavalry (the Cataphractae, a sort of cuirassiers) were stationed on the flanks; next to these, in the intermediate division, the Gallic and Cappadocian infantry; and in the very centre of the phalanx armed after the Macedonian fashion, 16,000 strong, the flower of the army, which, however, had not room in the narrow space and had to be drawn up in double files 32 deep. In the space between the two divisions were placed 54 elephants, distributed among the companies of the phalanx and of the heavy cavalry. The Romans stationed but a few squadrons on the left wing, where the river gave protection; the mass of the cavalry and all the light armed were placed on the right, which was led by Eumenes; the legions stood in the centre. Eumenes began the battle by despatching his archers and slingers against the scythe-chariots with orders to shoot at the teams; in a short time not only were these thrown into disorder, but the camel-riders stationed next to them were also carried away, and even in the second line the left wing of heavy cavalry placed behind fell into confusion. Eumenes now threw himself with all the Roman cavalry, numbering 3000 horse, on the mercenary infantry, which was placed in the second line between the phalanx and the left wing of heavy cavalry, and, when these gave way, the cuirassiers who had already fallen into disorder also fled. The phalanx, which had just allowed the light troops to pass through and was preparing to advance against the Roman legions, was hampered by the attack of the cavalry in flank, and compelled to stand still and to form front on both sides— a movement which the depth of its disposition favoured. Had the heavy Asiatic cavalry been at hand, the battle might have been restored; but the left wing was shattered, and the right, led by Antiochus in person, had driven before it the little division of Roman cavalry opposed to it, and had reached the Roman camp, which was with great difficulty defended from its attack. In this way the cavalry were at the decisive moment absent from the scene of action. The Romans were careful not to assail the phalanx with their legions, but sent against it the archers and slingers, not one of whose missiles failed to take effect on the densely crowded mass. The phalanx nevertheless retired slowly and in good order, till the elephants stationed in the interstices became frightened and broke the ranks. Then the whole army dispersed in tumultuous flight; an attempt to hold the camp failed, and only increased the number of the dead and the prisoners. The estimate of the loss of Antiochus at 50,000 men is, considering the infinite confusion, not incredible; the legions of the Romans had never been engaged, and the victory, which gave them a third continent, cost them 24 horsemen and 300 foot soldiers. Asia Minor submitted; including even Ephesus, whence the admiral hastily withdrew his fleet, and Sardes the residence of the court.

The king sued for peace and consented to the terms proposed by the Romans, which, as usual, were just the same as those offered before the battle and consequently included the cession of Asia Minor. Till they were ratified, the army remained in

Asia Minor at the expense of the king; which came to cost him not less than 3000 talents (£730,000). Antiochus himself in his careless fashion soon got over the loss of half his kingdom; it was in keeping with his character, that he declared himself grateful to the Romans for saving him the trouble of governing too large an empire. But with the day of Magnesia Asia was erased from the list of great states; and never perhaps did a great power fall so rapidly, so thoroughly, and so ignominiously as the kingdom of the Seleucidae under this Antiochus the Great. He himself was soon afterwards ($\frac{567}{187}$) slain by the indignant inhabitants of Elymais at the head of the Persian gulf, on occasion of the plundering of a temple of Bel, with the treasure of which he had sought to replenish his empty coffers.

After having obtained the victory, the Roman government had to regulate the affairs of Asia Minor and of Greece. In the former Antiochus was conquered, but his allies and satraps in the interior, the Phrygian, Cappadocian, and Paphlagonian dynasts, trusting to their distance, delayed their submission, and the Celts of Asia Minor, who had not strictly been in alliance with Antiochus but had merely after their custom allowed him to raise mercenaries in their land, in like manner saw no reason why they should trouble themselves about the Romans. To the new Roman commander-in-chief, Gnaeus Manlius Volso, who in the spring of $\frac{565}{189}$ relieved Lucius Scipio in Asia Minor, this afforded a welcome pretext for performing in his turn a service to his country and asserting the Roman protectorate over the Hellenes in Asia, just as had been done already in Spain and Gaul; although the more austere men in the senate failed to see either the ground or the object of such a war. The consul started from Ephesus, levied contributions from the cities and princes on the upper Maeander and in Pamphylia without cause and without measure, and then turned northward against the Celts. The most westerly canton of these, the Tolistobogi, had retired with their property to Mount Olympus, and the middle canton, the Tectosages, to Mount Magaba, in the hope that they would be able to defend themselves there, till winter should compel the foreigners to retire. But the missiles of the Roman slingers and archers—which so often turned the scale against the Celts unacquainted with such weapons, somewhat in the same way as in modern times fire-arms have turned the scale against savage tribes—forced the heights, and the Celts succumbed in a battle, such as was often paralleled both before and afterwards on the Po and on the Seine, but which in Asia appears no less singular than the whole phenomenon of this northern race emerging amidst the Greek and Phrygian nations. The number of the slain at both places was very great, and that of the prisoners still greater. The survivors escaped over the Halys to the third Celtic canton of the Trocmi, whom the consul did not disturb, as he did not venture to cross the frontier agreed on in the preliminaries between Scipio and Antiochus.

The affairs of Asia Minor were regulated partly by the peace with Antiochus ($\frac{565}{189}$), partly by the ordinances of a Roman commission presided over by the consul Volso. Antiochus had to furnish hostages, one of whom was his younger son of the same name, and to pay a war-contribution—proportional in amount to the treasures of Asia—of 15,000 Euboic talents (£3,600,000), a fifth of which was to be paid at once and the remainder in twelve annual instalments. He was compelled, moreover, to cede all his possessions in Europe, and all the territory in Asia Minor to the west of the river Halys throughout its course, and of the mountain-chain of the Taurus, which separates Cilicia and Lycaonia, so that he retained nothing in the Anatolian peninsula but Cilicia. His protectorate over the kingdoms and principalities of Asia Minor of course ceased. Even beyond the Roman frontier Cappadocia assumed an independent attitude towards Asia or Syria, as the kingdom of the Seleucidae was now more commonly and appropriately called; and not only so, but the satraps of the two Armenias, Artaxias and Zariadris, became transformed, under the influence of Rome if not exactly in conformity to the Roman treaty of peace, into independent kings and founders of new dynasties. The Syrian king forfeited the right of waging aggressive war against the states of the West, and, in the event of a defensive war, of acquiring territory from them on the conclusion of peace. He was prohibited from navigating the sea to the west of the mouth of the Calycadnus in Cilicia with ships of war, except for the conveyance of envoys, hostages, or tribute; from keeping more than ten decked vessels, except in the event of a defensive war; from taming war-elephants; and finally, from levying mercenaries in the western states, or receiving political refugees and deserters from these states at his court. He gave up the vessels of war which he possessed beyond the prescribed number, the elephants, and the political refugees who had taken shelter with him. The great king received, by way of compensation, the title of a friend of the Roman commonwealth. The state of Syria was thus by land and sea completely and for ever dislodged from the West; it is a significant indication of the feeble and loose organisation of the kingdom of the Seleucidae, that it alone, of all the great states conquered by Rome, never after the first conquest made a second appeal to the decision of arms.

Ariarathes, king of Cappadocia, whose land lay beyond the boundary laid down by the Romans for their protectorate, escaped with a money fine of 600 talents (£146,000); which was afterwards, on the intercession of his son-in-law Eumenes, abated to half that sum.

Prusias, king of Bithynia, retained his territory as it stood, and so did the Celts; but they were obliged to promise that they would no longer send armed bands beyond their bounds—a step which put an end to the disgraceful payments of tribute which many of the towns of Asia Minor made to them. Rome thus conferred on the Asiatic Greeks a real benefit, which they did not fail to repay with golden chaplets and transcendental panegyrics.

In the western portion of Asia Minor the regulation of the territorial arrangements was not without difficulty, especially as the dynastic policy of Eumenes there came into collision with that of the Greek Hansa. At last an understanding was arrived at to the following effect. All the Greek cities, which were free and had joined the Romans on the day of the battle of Magnesia, had their liberties confirmed, and all of them, excepting those previously tributary to Eumenes, were relieved from the payment of tribute to the different dynasts for the future. In this way the towns of Dardanus and Ilium, whose ancient affinity with the Romans was traced to the times of Aeneas, became free, along with Cyme, Smyrna, Clazomenae, Erythrae, Chios, Colophon, Miletus, and other names of old renown. Phocaea also, which in spite of its capitulation had been plundered by the soldiers of the Roman fleet—although it did not fall under the category designated in the treaty—received back by way of compensation its territory and its freedom. Most of the cities of the Graeco-Asiatic Hansa acquired additions of territory and other advantages. Rhodes of course received most consideration; it obtained Lycia exclusive of Telmissus, and the greater part of Caria south of the Maeander; besides, Antiochus guaranteed the property and the claims of the Rhodians within his kingdom, as well as the exemption from customs-dues which they had hitherto enjoyed.

All the rest, forming by far the largest share of the spoil, fell to the Attalids, whose ancient fidelity to Rome, as well as the hardships endured by Eumenes in the war and his personal merit in connection with the issue of the decisive battle, were rewarded by Rome as no king ever rewarded his ally. Eumenes received, in Europe, the Chersonese with Lysimachia; in Asia — in addition to Mysia which he already possessed—the provinces of Phrygia on the Hellespont, Lydia with Ephesus and Sardes, the northern district of Caria to the Maeander with Tralles and Magnesia, Great Phrygia and Lycaonia along with a portion of Cilicia, the district of Milyas between Phrygia and Lycia, and, as a port on the southern sea, the Lycian town Telmissus. There was a dispute afterwards between Eumenes and Antiochus regarding Pamphylia, whether it lay on this side of or beyond the Taurus, and whether accordingly it belonged to the former or to the latter. He further acquired the protectorate over, and the right of receiving tribute from, those Greek cities which did not receive absolute freedom; but it was stipulated in this case that the cities should retain their charters, and that the tribute should not be heightened. Moreover, Antiochus had to bind himself to pay to Eumenes the 350 talents (£85,000) which he owed to his father Attalus, and likewise to pay a compensation of 127 talents (£31,000) for arrears in the supplies of corn. Lastly, Eumenes obtained the royal forests and the elephants delivered up by Antiochus, but not the ships of war, which were burnt: the Romans tolerated no naval power by the side of their own. By these means the kingdom of the Attalids became in the east of Europe and Asia what Numidia was in Africa, a powerful state with an absolute constitution dependent on Rome, destined and able to keep in check both Macedonia and Syria without needing, except in extraordinary cases, Roman support. With this creation dictated by policy the Romans had as far as possible combined the liberation of the Asiatic Greeks, which was dictated by republican and national sympathy and by vanity. About the affairs of the more remote East beyond the Taurus and Halys they were firmly resolved to give themselves no concern. This is clearly shown by the terms of the peace with Antiochus, and still more decidedly by the peremptory refusal of the senate to guarantee to the town of Soli in Cilicia the freedom which the Rhodians requested for it. With equal fidelity they adhered to the fixed principle of acquiring no direct transmarine possessions. After the Roman fleet had made an expedition to Crete and had accomplished the release of the Romans sold thither into slavery, the fleet and land army left Asia towards the end of the summer of $\frac{566}{188}$; on which occasion the land army, which again marched through Thrace, in conse-

quence of the negligence of the general suffered greatly on the
route from the attacks of the barbarians. The Romans brought
nothing home from the East but honour and gold, which were
even at this period usually conjoined in the practical shape
assumed by the address of thanks—the golden chaplet.

European Greece also had been agitated by this Asiatic war,
and needed reorganisation. The Aetolians, who had not yet
learned to reconcile themselves to their insignificance, had, after
the armistice concluded with Scipio in the spring of $\frac{564}{190}$, rendered
intercourse between Greece and Italy difficult and unsafe by
means of their Cephallenian corsairs; and not only so, but even
perhaps while the armistice yet lasted, they, deceived by false
reports as to the state of things in Asia, had the folly to place
Amynander once more on his Athamanian throne, and to carry
on a desultory warfare with Philip in the districts occupied by
him on the borders of Aetolia and Thessaly, in the course of
which Philip suffered several discomfitures. After this, as a
matter of course, Rome replied to their request for peace by the
landing of the consul Marcus Fulvius Nobilior. He arrived
among the legions in the spring of $\frac{565}{189}$, and after fifteen days'
siege gained possession of Ambracia by a capitulation honourable for the garrison; while simultaneously the Macedonians,
Illyrians, Epirots, Acarnanians, and Achaeans fell upon the
Aetolians. There was no such thing as resistance in the strict
sense; after repeated entreaties of the Aetolians for peace the
Romans at length desisted from the war, and granted conditions
which must be reckoned reasonable when viewed with reference
to such pitiful and malicious opponents. The Aetolians lost
all cities and territories which were in the hands of their adversaries, more especially Ambracia which afterwards became free
and independent in consequence of an intrigue concocted in
Rome against Marcus Fulvius, and Oenia[dae] which was given
to the Acarnanians; they likewise ceded Cephallenia. They
lost the right of making peace and war, and were in that respect
dependent on the foreign relations of Rome. Lastly, they paid
a large sum of money. Cephallenia opposed this treaty on its
own account, and only submitted when Marcus Fulvius landed
on the island. In fact, the inhabitants of Same, who feared
that they would be dispossessed from their well-situated town
by a Roman colony, revolted after their first submission and
sustained a four months' siege; the town, however, was finally
taken and the whole inhabitants were sold into slavery.

In this case also Rome adhered to the principle of confining herself to Italy and the Italian islands. She took no portion of the spoil for herself, except the two islands of Cephallenia and Zacynthus, which formed a desirable supplement to the possession of Corcyra and other naval stations in the Adriatic. The rest of the territorial gain went to the allies of Rome. But the two most important of these, Philip and the Achaeans, were by no means content with the share of the spoil granted to them. Philip felt himself aggrieved, and not without reason. He could safely affirm that the chief difficulties in the last war— difficulties which arose not from the character of the enemy, but from the distance and the uncertainty of the communications— had been overcome mainly by his loyal aid. The senate recognised this by remitting his arrears of tribute and sending back his hostages; but he did not receive those additions to his territory which he expected. He got the territory of the Magnetes, with Demetrias which he had taken from the Aetolians; besides, there practically remained in his hands the districts of Dolopia and Athamania and a part of Thessaly, from which also the Aetolians had been expelled by him. In Thrace the interior remained under Macedonian protection, but nothing was fixed as to the coast towns, and the islands of Thasos and Lemnos which were *de facto* in Philip's hands, while the Chersonese was even expressly given to Eumenes; and it was not difficult to see that Eumenes received possessions in Europe, simply that he might in case of need keep not only Asia but Macedonia in check. The exasperation of the proud and in many respects chivalrous king was natural; it was not chicane, however, but an unavoidable political necessity that induced the Romans to take this course. Macedonia suffered for having once been a power of the first rank, and for having waged war on equal terms with Rome; there was much better reason in her case than in that of Carthage for guarding against the revival of her former attitude of power.

It was otherwise with the Achaeans. They had, in the course of the war with Antiochus, gratified their long cherished wish to include the whole Peloponnesus within their confederacy; for first Sparta, and then, after the expulsion of the Asiatics from Greece, Elis and Messene also had more or less reluctantly joined it. The Romans had allowed this to take place, and had even tolerated the intentional disregard of Rome which marked their proceedings. When Messene declared that she wished to submit to the Romans but not to enter the confederacy, and the latter thereupon employed force, Flamininus had not failed to remind the Achaeans that such separate arrangements as to the disposal of a part of the spoil were in themselves unjust, and were, in the relation in which the Achaeans stood to the Romans, more than unseemly; and yet in his very impolitic complaisance towards the Hellenes he had substantially allowed the Achaeans their will. But the matter did not end there. The Achaeans, tormented by their dwarfish thirst for aggrandisement, would not relax their hold on the town of Pleuron in Aetolia which they had occupied during the war, but compelled it to become a member of their league; they bought Zacynthus from Amynander the lieutenant of the last possessor, and would gladly have acquired Aegina also. It was with reluctance that they gave up the former island to Rome, and they heard with great displeasure the good advice of Flamininus that they should content themselves with their Peloponnesus.

The Achaeans believed it their duty to display the independence of their state all the more, the less they really had; they talked of the rights of war, and of the faithful aid of the Achaeans in the wars of the Romans; they asked the Roman envoys at the Achaean diet why Rome should concern herself about Messene when Achaia put no questions as to Capua; and the spirited patriot, who had thus spoken, was applauded and was sure of votes at the elections. All this would have been very right and very dignified, had it not been much more ridiculous. There was a profound justice and a still more profound melancholy in the fact, that Rome, however earnestly she endeavoured to establish the freedom and to earn the thanks of the Hellenes, yet gave them nothing but anarchy and reaped nothing but ingratitude. Undoubtedly very generous sentiments lay at the bottom of the Hellenic antipathy to the protecting power, and the personal bravery of some of the men who took the lead in the movement was unquestionable; but this Achaean patriotism remained not the less a folly and a genuine historical caricature. With all that ambition and all that national susceptibility the whole nation was, from the highest to the lowest, pervaded by the most thorough sense of impotence. Every one was constantly listening to learn the sentiments of Rome, the liberal man no less than the servile; they thanked heaven, when the dreaded decree was not issued; they were sulky, when the senate gave them to understand that they would do well to yield voluntarily in order that they might not need to be compelled; they did what they were obliged to do, if possible, in a way offensive to the Romans, " to save forms; "

they reported, explained, delayed, equivocated, and when all this would no longer avail yielded with a patriotic sigh. Their proceedings might have claimed indulgence at any rate, if not approval, had their leaders been resolved to fight, and had they preferred the destruction of the nation to its bondage; but neither Philopoemen nor Lycortas thought of any such political suicide—they wished, if possible, to be free, but they wished above all to live. Besides all this, the dreaded intervention of Rome in the internal affairs of Greece was not the arbitrary act of the Romans, but was always invoked by the Greeks themselves, who, like boys, brought down on their own heads the rod which they feared. The reproach repeated *ad nauseam* by the mass of the learned in Hellenic and post-Hellenic times—that the Romans strove to stir up internal discord in Greece—is one of the most foolish absurdities which scholars dealing in politics have ever invented. It was not the Romans that carried strife to Greece—which in truth would have been " carrying owls to Athens "—but the Greeks that carried their dissensions to Rome.

The Achaeans in particular, who, in their eagerness to enlarge their territory, totally failed to see how much it would have been for their own good that Flamininus had not incorporated the towns of Aetolian sympathies with their league, acquired in Lacedaemon and Messene a very hydra of intestine strife. Members of these communities were incessantly at Rome, entreating and beseeching to be released from the odious connection; and amongst them, characteristically enough, were even those who were indebted to the Achaeans for their return to their native land. The Achaean league was incessantly occupied in the work of reformation and restoration at Sparta and Messene; the wildest refugees from these quarters dictated the measures of the diet. Four years after the nominal admission of Sparta to the confederacy matters came to an open war and to an insanely thorough restoration, in which all the slaves on whom Nabis had conferred citizenship were once more sold into slavery, and a colonnade was built from the proceeds in the Achaean city of Megalopolis; the old state of property in Sparta was re-established, the laws of Lycurgus were superseded by Achaean laws, and the walls were pulled down ($\frac{566}{188}$). At last the Roman senate was summoned by all parties to arbitrate in reference to the whole matter—an annoying task, which was the righteous punishment of the sentimental policy that the senate had pursued. Far from mixing itself up too much in these affairs, the senate not only bore the sarcasms of Achaean conceit with exemplary composure, but even manifested a culpable indifference while the worst outrages were committed. There was cordial rejoicing in Achaia when, after that restoration, the news arrived from Rome that the senate had found fault with it, but had not annulled it. Nothing was done for the Lacedaemonians by Rome, except that the senate, shocked at the judicial murder of from sixty to eighty Spartans committed by the Achaeans, deprived the diet of criminal jurisdiction over the Spartans—truly a heinous interference with the internal affairs of an independent state! The Roman statesmen gave themselves as little concern as possible about this tempest in a nut-shell, as is best shown by the many complaints regarding the superficial, contradictory, and obscure decisions of the senate; in fact, how could its decisions be expected to be clear, when there were four parties from Sparta simultaneously speaking against each other at its bar? Then the personal impression, which most of these Peloponnesian statesmen produced in Rome, was not favourable; even Flamininus shook his head, when one of them showed him on the one day how to perform some dance, and on the next entertained him with affairs of state. Matters went so far, that the senate at last lost patience and informed the Peloponnesians that it could no longer listen to them, and that they might do what they chose ($\frac{572}{182}$). This was natural enough, but it was not right; situated as the Romans were, they were under a moral and political obligation earnestly and consistently to rectify this melancholy state of things. Callicrates the Achaean, who went to the senate in $\frac{576}{179}$ to enlighten it as to the state of matters in the Peloponnesus and to demand a consistent and sustained intervention, may have had somewhat less worth as a man than his countryman Philopoemen who was the main founder of that patriotic policy; but he was in the right.

Thus the protectorate of the Roman community now embraced all the states from the eastern to the western end of the Mediterranean. There nowhere existed a state that the Romans would have deemed it worth while to fear. But there still lived a man to whom Rome accorded this rare honour—the homeless Carthaginian, who had raised in arms against Rome first all the West and then all the East, and whose schemes had been frustrated solely perhaps by infamous aristocratic policy in the one case, and by stupid court policy in the other. Antiochus had been obliged to bind himself in the treaty of peace to deliver up Hannibal; but the latter had escaped, first to Crete, then to

Bithynia,[1] and now lived at the court of Prusias king of Bithynia, employed in aiding the latter in his wars with Eumenes, and victorious as ever by sea and by land. It is affirmed that he was desirous of stirring up Prusias also to make war on Rome; a folly, which, as it is told, sounds very far from credible. It is more certain that, while the Roman senate deemed it beneath its dignity to have the old man hunted out in his last asylum—for the tradition which inculpates the senate appears to deserve no credit—Flamininus, whose restless vanity sought after new opportunities for great achievements, undertook on his own part to deliver Rome from Hannibal as he had delivered the Greeks from their chains, and, if not to wield—which was not diplomatic—at any rate to whet and to point, the dagger against the greatest man of his time. Prusias, the most pitiful among the pitiful princes of Asia, was delighted to grant the little favour which the Roman envoy in ambiguous terms requested; and, when Hannibal saw his house beset by assassins, he took poison. He had long been prepared to do so, adds a Roman, for he knew the Romans and the faith of kings. The year of his death is uncertain; probably he died in the latter half of the year $\frac{571}{183}$, at the age of sixty-seven. When he was born, Rome was contending with doubtful success for the possession of Sicily; he had lived long enough to see the West wholly subdued, and to fight his own last battle with the Romans against the vessels of his native city which had itself become Roman; and he was constrained at last to remain a mere spectator while Rome overpowered the East as the tempest overpowers the ship that has no one at the helm, and to feel that he alone was the pilot that could have weathered the storm. There was left to him no further hope to be disappointed, when he died; but he had honestly, through fifty years of struggle, kept the oath which he had sworn when a boy.

About the same time, probably in the same year, died also the man whom the Romans were wont to call his conqueror, Publius Scipio. On him fortune had lavished all the successes which she denied to his antagonist—successes which did belong to him, and successes which did not. He had added to the empire Spain, Africa, and Asia; and Rome, which he had found merely the first community of Italy, was at his death

---

[1] The story that he went to Armenia and at the request of king Artaxias built the town of Artaxata on the Araxes (Strabo, xi. p. 528; Plutarch, *Luc.* 31), is certainly a fiction; but it is a striking circumstance that Hannibal should have become mixed up, almost like Alexander, with Oriental fables.

mistress of the civilised world. He himself had so many titles of victory, that some of them were made over to his brother and his cousin.[1] And yet he too spent his last years in bitter vexation, and died when little more than fifty years of age in voluntary banishment, leaving orders to his relatives not to bury his remains in the city for which he had lived and in which his ancestors reposed. It is not exactly known what drove him from the city. The charges of corruption and embezzlement, which were directed against him and still more against his brother Lucius, were beyond doubt empty calumnies, which do not satisfactorily account for such irritation of feeling; although it was characteristic of the man, that instead of simply vindicating himself by means of his account-books, he tore them in pieces in presence of the people and of his accusers, and summoned the Romans to accompany him to the temple of Jupiter and to celebrate the anniversary of his victory at Zama. The people left the accusers on the spot, and followed Scipio to the Capitol; but this was the last glorious day of that illustrious man. His proud spirit, his belief that he was different from, and better than, other men, his very decided family-policy, which in the person of his brother Lucius especially brought forward a clumsy man of straw as a hero, gave offence to many, and not without reason. While genuine pride protects the heart, arrogance lays it open to every blow and every sarcasm, and corrodes even an originally noble-minded spirit. It is throughout, moreover, the distinguishing characteristic of such natures as that of Scipio—strange mixtures of genuine gold and glittering tinsel—that they need the good fortune and the brilliance of youth in order to exercise their charm, and, when this charm begins to fade, it is the charmer himself that is most painfully conscious of the change.

[1] Africanus, Asiagenus, Hispallus.

CHAPTER X

THE THIRD MACEDONIAN WAR

PHILIP OF MACEDONIA was greatly annoyed by the treatment which he met with from the Romans after the peace with Antiochus; and the subsequent course of events was not fitted to appease his wrath. His neighbours in Greece and Thrace, mostly communities that had once trembled at the Macedonian name not less than now they trembled at the Roman, made it their business, as was natural, to retaliate on the fallen great power for all the injuries which since the times of Philip the Second they had received at the hands of Macedonia. The empty arrogance and venal anti-Macedonian patriotism of the Hellenes of this period found vent at the diets of the different confederacies and in ceaseless complaints addressed to the Roman senate. Philip had been allowed by the Romans to retain what he had taken from the Aetolians; but in Thessaly the confederacy of the Magnetes alone had formally joined the Aetolians, while those towns which Philip had wrested from the Aetolians in two of the other Thessalian confederacies—the Thessalian in its narrower sense, and the Perrhaebian—were demanded back by the latter on the ground that Philip had only liberated these towns, not conquered them. The Athamanes conceived that they might request their freedom; and Eumenes demanded the maritime cities which Antiochus had possessed in Thrace proper, especially Aenus and Maronea, although in the peace with Antiochus the Thracian Chersonese alone had been expressly promised to him. All these complaints and numerous minor ones from all the neighbours of Philip as to his supporting king Prusias against Eumenes, as to competition in trade, as to the violation of contracts and the seizing of cattle, were poured forth at Rome. The king of Macedonia had to submit to be accused by the sovereign rabble before the Roman senate, and to accept justice or injustice as the senate chose; he was compelled to witness judgment constantly going against him; he had to submit to withdraw his garrisons from the Thracian coast and from the Thessalian and Perrhaebian towns, and courteously to receive the Roman commissioners, who came to see whether everything required had been properly done. The Romans were not so indignant against Philip as they had been against Carthage; in fact, they were in many respects even favourably disposed to the Macedonian ruler; there was not in his case so reckless a violation of forms as in that of Libya; but the situation of Macedonia was at bottom substantially the same as that of Carthage. Philip, however, was by no means the man to submit to this infliction with Phoenician patience. Passionate as he was, he had after his defeat been more indignant with his faithless ally than with his honourable antagonist; and, long accustomed to pursue a policy not Macedonian but personal, he had regarded the war with Antiochus simply as an excellent opportunity of instantaneously revenging himself on the ally who had disgracefully deserted and betrayed him. This object he had attained; but the Romans, who saw very clearly that the Macedonian was influenced not by friendship for Rome, but by enmity to Antiochus, and who were by no means in the habit of regulating their policy by such feelings of liking and disliking, had carefully abstained from bestowing any material advantages on Philip, and had preferred to confer their favours on the Attalids. From their first elevation the Attalids had been at vehement feud with Macedonia, and were politically and personally the objects of Philip's bitterest hatred; of all the Eastern powers they had contributed most to maim Macedonia and Syria, and to extend the protectorate of Rome in the East; and in the last war, when Philip had voluntarily and loyally embraced the side of Rome, they had been obliged to take part with Rome for the sake of their very existence. The Romans had made use of these Attalids for the purpose of reconstructing in all essential points the kingdom of Lysimachus—the destruction of which had been the most important achievement of the Macedonian rulers after Alexander—and of placing alongside of Macedonia a state, which was its equal in point of power and was at the same time a client of Rome. In the special circumstances a wise sovereign, devoted to the interests of his people, would perhaps have resolved not to resume the unequal struggle with Rome; but Philip, in whose character the sense of honour was the most powerful of all noble, and the thirst for revenge the most potent of all ignoble, motives, was deaf to the voice of timidity or of resignation, and nourished in the depths of his heart a determination once more to try the hazard of the game. When he received the report of fresh invectives, such as were wont to be launched against Macedonia at the Thessalian diets, he replied with the line of Theocritus, that his last sun had not yet set.[1]

Philip displayed in the preparation and the concealment of his designs a calmness, earnestness, and perseverance which, had he shown them in better times, would perhaps have given a different turn to the destinies of the world. In particular the submissiveness towards Rome, by which he purchased the time indispensable for his objects, formed a severe trial for the fierce and haughty man; nevertheless he courageously endured it, although his subjects and the innocent occasions of the quarrel, such as the unfortunate Maronea, paid severely for the suppression of his resentment. It seemed as if war could not but break out as early as $\frac{571\frac{1}{2}}{183}$; but by Philip's instructions, his younger son, Demetrius, effected a reconciliation between his father and Rome, where he had lived some years as a hostage and was a great favourite. The senate, and particularly Flamininus who managed Greek affairs, sought to form a Roman party in Macedonia that would be able to paralyse the exertions of Philip, which of course were not unknown to the Romans; and had selected as its head, and perhaps as the future king of Macedonia, the younger prince who was passionately attached to Rome. With this view they gave it clearly to be understood that the senate forgave the father for the sake of the son; the natural effect of which was, that dissensions arose in the royal household itself, and that the king's elder son, Perseus, who, although the offspring of a marriage of disparagement, was destined by his father for the succession, sought to ruin his brother as his future rival. It does not appear that Demetrius was a party to the Roman intrigues; it was only when he was falsely suspected that he was forced to become guilty, and even then he intended, apparently, nothing more than flight to Rome. But Perseus took care that his father should be duly informed of this design; an intercepted letter from Flamininus to Demetrius did the rest, and induced the father to give orders that his son should be put to death. Philip learned, when it was too late, the intrigues which Perseus had concocted; and death overtook him, as he was meditating the punishment of the fratricide and his exclusion from the throne. He died in $\frac{575}{179}$ at Demetrias, in his fifty-ninth year. He left behind him a shattered kingdom and a distracted household, and with a broken heart confessed to himself that all his toils and all his crimes had been in vain.

His son Perseus then entered on the government, without

---

[1] Ἤδη γὰρ φράσδει πάνθ' ἅλιον ἅμμι δεδύκειν.

encountering opposition either in Macedonia or in the Roman senate. He was a man of stately aspect, expert in all gymnastic exercises, reared in the camp and accustomed to command, imperious like his father and unscrupulous in the choice of his means. Wine and women, which too often led Philip to forget the duties of government, had no charm for Perseus; he was as steady and persevering as his father had been thoughtless and impulsive. Philip, a king while still a boy, and attended by success during the first twenty years of his reign, had been spoiled and ruined by destiny; Perseus ascended the throne in his thirty-first year, and, as he had while yet a boy borne a part in the unhappy war with Rome and had grown up under the pressure of humiliation and under the idea that a revival of the state was at hand, so he inherited along with the kingdom the troubles, resentments, and hopes of his father. In fact he entered with the utmost determination on the continuance of his father's work, and prepared more zealously than ever for war against Rome; he was stimulated, moreover, by the reflection, that he was by no means indebted to the goodwill of the Romans for his wearing the diadem of Macedonia. The proud Macedonian nation looked with pride upon the prince whom they had been accustomed to see marching and fighting at the head of their youth; his countrymen, and many Hellenes of every variety of lineage, conceived that in him they had found the proper general for the impending war of liberation. But he was not what he seemed. He wanted Philip's genius and Philip's elasticity—those truly royal qualities, which success obscured and tarnished, but which under the purifying power of adversity recovered their lustre. Philip was self-indulgent, and allowed things to take their course; but, when there was occasion, he found within himself the vigour necessary for speedy and earnest action. Perseus devised comprehensive and subtle plans, and prosecuted them with unwearied perseverance; but, when the moment arrived for action and his plans and preparations confronted him in stern reality, he was frightened at his own work. As is the wont of narrow minds, the means became to him the end; he heaped up treasures on treasures for war with the Romans, and, when the Romans were in the land, he was unable to part with his golden pieces. It is a significant indication of character that after defeat the father first hastened to destroy the papers in his cabinet that might compromise him, whereas the son took his treasure-chests and embarked. In ordinary times he might have made an average king, as good as or better than many others; but he was not adapted for the conduct of an enterprise, which was from the first a hopeless one unless some extraordinary man should become the soul of the movement.

The power of Macedonia was far from inconsiderable. The devotion of the land to the house of the Antigonids was unimpaired; in this one respect the national feeling was not paralysed by the dissensions of political parties. A monarchical constitution has the great advantage, that every change of sovereign supersedes old resentments and quarrels and introduces a new era of different men and fresh hopes. The king had judiciously availed himself of this, and had begun his reign with a general amnesty, with the recall of fugitive bankrupts, and with the remission of arrears of taxes. The hateful severity of the father thus not only yielded benefit, but conciliated affection, to the son. Twenty-six years of peace had partly of themselves filled up the blanks in the Macedonian population, partly given opportunity to the government to take serious steps towards rectifying this which was really the weak point of the land. Philip urged the Macedonians to marry and raise up children; he occupied the coast towns, whose inhabitants he carried into the interior, with Thracian colonists of reliable valour and fidelity. He formed a barrier on the north to check once for all the desolating incursions of the Dardani, by converting the space intervening between the Macedonian frontier and the barbarian territory into a desert, and by founding new towns in the northern provinces. In short he took step by step the same course in Macedonia, as Augustus afterwards took when he laid afresh the foundations of the Roman empire. The army was numerous—30,000 men without reckoning contingents and hired troops—and the younger men were well exercised in the constant border warfare with the Thracian barbarians. It is strange that Philip did not try, like Hannibal, to organise his army after the Roman fashion; but we can understand it when we recollect the value which the Macedonians set upon their phalanx, often conquered, but still believed to be invincible. Through the new sources of revenue which Philip had created in mines, customs, and tenths, and through the flourishing state of agriculture and commerce, he had succeeded in replenishing his treasury, granaries, and arsenals. When the war began, there was in the Macedonian treasury money to pay the existing army and 10,000 hired troops for ten years, and there were in the public magazines stores of grain for as long a period (18,000,000 *medimni* or 27,000,000 bushels), and arms for an army of three times the strength of the existing one. In fact, Macedonia had become a very different state from what it was when surprised by the outbreak of the second war with Rome. The power of the kingdom was in all respects at least doubled: with a power in every point of view far inferior Hannibal had been able to shake Rome to its foundations.

Its external relations were not in so favourable a position. The nature of the case required that Macedonia should now take up the plans of Hannibal and Antiochus, and should try to place herself at the head of a coalition of all oppressed states against the supremacy of Rome; and certainly threads of intrigue ramified in all directions from the court of Pydna. But their success was slight. It was indeed asserted that the allegiance of the Italians was wavering; but neither friend nor foe could fail to see that an immediate resumption of the Samnite wars was not at all probable. The nocturnal conferences likewise between Macedonian deputies and the Carthaginian senate, which Massinissa denounced at Rome, could occasion no alarm to serious and sagacious men, even if they were not, as is very possible, an utter fiction. The Macedonian court sought to attach the kings of Syria and Bithynia to its interests by intermarriages; but nothing further came of it, except that the immortal simplicity of the diplomacy which seeks to gain political ends by matrimonial means once more exposed itself to derision. Eumenes, whom it would have been ridiculous to attempt to gain, the agents of Perseus would have gladly put out of the way: he was to have been murdered at Delphi on his way homeward from Rome, where he had been active against Macedonia; but the dastardly project miscarried.

Of greater moment were the efforts made to stir up the northern barbarians and the Hellenes to rebellion against Rome. Philip had conceived the project of crushing the old enemies of Macedonia, the Dardani in what is now Servia, by means of another still more barbarous horde of Germanic descent brought from the left bank of the Danube, the Bastarnae, and of then marching in person with these and with the whole avalanche of peoples thus set in motion by the land route to Italy and invading Lombardy, the Alpine passes leading to which he had already sent spies to reconnoitre—a grand project, worthy of Hannibal, and doubtless immediately suggested by Hannibal's passage of the Alps. It is more than probable that this gave occasion to the founding of the Roman fortress of Aquileia (p. 183), which was formed towards the end of the reign of Philip ($\frac{573}{181}$), and did not harmonise with the system followed elsewhere by the Romans in the establishment of fortresses in Italy. The plan, however, was thwarted by the desperate resistance of the Dardani and of the adjoining tribes concerned; the Bastarnae were obliged to retreat, and the whole horde were drowned in returning home by the giving way of the ice on the Danube. The king then sought at least to extend his clientship among the chieftains of the Illyrian land, the modern Dalmatia and northern Albania. One of these who faithfully adhered to Rome, Arthetaurus, perished, not without the cognisance of Perseus, by the hand of an assassin. The most considerable of the whole, Genthius the son and heir of Pleuratus, was, like his father, nominally in alliance with Rome; but the ambassadors of Issa, a Greek town on one of the Dalmatian islands, informed the senate, that Perseus had a secret understanding with the young, weak, and drunken prince, and that the envoys of Genthius served as spies for Perseus in Rome.

In the regions on the east of Macedonia towards the lower Danube the most powerful of the Thracian chieftains, the brave and sagacious Cotys, prince of the Odrysians and ruler of all eastern Thrace from the Macedonian frontier on the Hebrus (Maritza) down to the fringe of coast covered with Greek towns, was in the closest alliance with Perseus. Of the other minor chiefs who in that quarter took part with Rome, one, Abrupolis prince of the Sagaei, was, in consequence of a predatory expedition directed against Amphipolis on the Strymon, defeated by Perseus and driven out of the country. From these regions Philip had drawn numerous colonists, and mercenaries were to be had there at any time and in any number.

Among the unhappy nation of the Hellenes Philip and Perseus had, long before declaring war against Rome, carried on a double system of proselytising, attempting to gain over to the side of Macedonia on the one hand the national, and on the other—if we may be permitted the expression—the communistic party. As a matter of course, the whole national party among the Asiatic as well as the European Greeks was now favourable at heart to Macedonia; not on account of isolated unrighteous acts on the part of the Roman deliverers, but because the restoration of Hellenic nationality by a foreign power involved a contradiction in terms, and now, when it was in truth too late, every one perceived that the most detestable form of Macedonnia rule was less fraught with evil for Greece than a free constitution originating in the noblest intentions of honourable foreigners.

That the most able and upright men throughout Greece should be opposed to Rome was to be expected; the venal aristocracy alone was favourable to the Romans, and here and there an isolated man of worth, who, unlike the great majority, was under no delusion as to the circumstances and the future of the nation. This was most painfully experienced by Eumenes of Pergamus, who was the main supporter of that extraneous liberty among the Greeks. In vain he treated the cities subject to him with every sort of consideration; in vain he sued for the favour of the communities and diets by fair-sounding words and still better-sounding gold; he learned with pain that his presents were declined, and that all the statues that had formerly been erected to him were broken in pieces and the honorary tablets were melted down, in accordance with a decree of the diet, simultaneously throughout the Peloponnesus ($\frac{584}{170}$). The name of Perseus, again, was on every one's lips; even the states that formerly were most decidedly anti-Macedonian, such as the Achaeans, deliberated as to the abolition of the laws directed against Macedonia; Byzantium, although situated within the kingdom of Pergamus, sought and obtained protection and a garrison against the Thracians not from Eumenes, but from Perseus, and in like manner Lampsacus on the Hellespont joined the Macedonian: the powerful and prudent Rhodians escorted the Syrian bride of king Perseus from Antioch with their whole magnificent war-fleet—for the Syrian war-vessels were not allowed to appear in the Aegean—and returned home highly honoured and furnished with rich presents, more especially with wood for ship-building; commissioners from the Asiatic cities, and consequently subjects of Eumenes, held secret conferences with Macedonian deputies in Samothrace. That sending of the Rhodian war-fleet had at least the aspect of a demonstration; and such, certainly, was the object of king Perseus, when he exhibited himself and all his army before the eyes of the Hellenes under pretext of performing a religious ceremony at Delphi. That the king should appeal to the support of this national partisanship in the impending war, was natural and reasonable. But it was wrong in him to take advantage of the fearful economic disorganisation of Greece for the purpose of attaching to Macedonia all those who desired a revolution in matters of property and of debt. It is difficult to form any adequate idea of the unparalleled extent to which the commonwealths as well as individuals in European Greece—excepting the Peloponnesus, which was in a somewhat better position in this respect—were involved in debt. Instances occurred of one city attacking and pillaging another merely to get money—the Athenians, for example, thus attacked Oropus —and among the Aetolians, Perrhaebians, and Thessalians formal battles took place between those that had property and those that had none. Under such circumstances the worst outrages were perpetrated as a matter of course; among the Aetolians, for instance, a general amnesty was proclaimed and a new public peace was made up solely for the purpose of entrapping and putting to death a number of emigrants. The Romans attempted to mediate; but their envoys returned without success, and announced that both parties were equally bad and that their animosities were not to be restrained. In this case there was, in fact, no other remedy than that of the officer and the executioner; sentimental Hellenism began to be as repulsive as from the first it had been ridiculous. Yet king Perseus sought to gain the support of this party, if it deserve to be called such—of people who had nothing, and least of all an honourable name, to lose—and not only issued edicts in favour of Macedonian bankrupts, but also caused placards to be put up at Larisa, Delphi, and Delos, which summoned all Greeks that were exiled on account of political or other offences or on account of their debts to come to Macedonia and to expect full restitution of their former honours and estates. As may easily be supposed, they came; the social revolution smouldering throughout northern Greece now broke out into open flame, and the national-social party there sent to Perseus for help. If Hellenic nationality was to be saved only by such means, the question might well be asked, with all respect for Sophocles and Phidias, whether the object was worth the cost.

The senate saw that it had delayed too long already, and that it was time to put an end to such proceedings. The expulsion of the Thracian chieftain Abrupolis who was in alliance with the Romans, and the alliances of Macedonia with the Byzantines, Aetolians, and part of the Boeotian cities, were equally violations of the peace of $\frac{557}{197}$, and sufficed for the official war-manifesto: the real ground of war was that Macedonia was seeking to convert her formal sovereignty into a real one, and to supplant Rome in the protectorate of the Hellenes. As early as $\frac{581}{173}$ the Roman envoys at the Achaean diet stated pretty plainly, that an alliance with Perseus was equivalent to casting off the alliance of Rome. In $\frac{582}{172}$ king Eumenes came in person to Rome with a long list of grievances and laid open to the senate the whole situation of affairs; upon which the senate unexpectedly in a secret sitting resolved on an immediate declaration of war, and furnished the ports of Epirus with garrisons. . For the sake of form an embassy was sent to Macedonia, but its message was of such a nature that Perseus, perceiving that he could not recede, replied that he was ready to conclude with Rome a new alliance on really equal terms, but that he looked upon the treaty of $\frac{557}{197}$ as cancelled; and he bade the envoys leave the kingdom within three days. Thus war was practically declared. This was in the autumn of $\frac{582}{172}$. Perseus, had he wished, might have occupied all Greece and brought the Macedonian party everywhere to the helm, and he might perhaps have crushed the Roman division of 5000 men stationed under Gnaeus Sicinius at Apollonia and opposed the landing of the Romans. But the king, who already began to tremble at the serious aspect of affairs, engaged in discussions with the consular Quintus Marcius Philippus, with whom he stood in relations of hospitality, as to the frivolousness of the Roman declaration of war, and allowed himself to be induced in this way to postpone the attack and once more to make an effort for peace with Rome: to which the senate, as might have been expected, only replied by the dismissal of all Macedonians from Italy and the embarkation of the legions. Senators of the older school no doubt censured the "new wisdom" of their colleague, and his un-Roman artifice; but the object was gained and the winter passed away without any movement on the part of Perseus. The Roman diplomatists made all the more zealous use of the interval to deprive Perseus of any support in Greece. They were sure of the Achaeans. Even the patriotic party among them—who had neither agreed with those social movements, nor had manifested aught more than a longing after a prudent neutrality— had no idea of throwing themselves into the arms of Perseus; and, besides, the opposition party there had now been brought by Roman influence into power, and attached itself absolutely to Rome. The Aetolian league had doubtless asked aid from Perseus in its internal troubles; but the new *strategus*, Lyciscus, chosen under the eyes of the Roman ambassadors, was more of a Roman partisan than the Romans themselves. Among the Thessalians also the Roman party retained the ascendancy. Even the Boeotians, old partisans as they were of Macedonia, and sunk in the utmost financial disorder, had not in their collective capacity declared openly for Perseus; nevertheless at least two of their cities, Haliartus and Coronea, had of their own accord entered into engagements with him. When on the complaint of the Roman envoy the government of the Boeotian confederacy communicated to him the position of things, he declared that it would best appear which cities adhered to Rome, and which did not, if they would severally pronounce their decision in his presence; and thereupon the Boeotian confederacy fell at once to pieces. It is not true that the great structure of Epaminondas was destroyed by the Romans; it actually collapsed before they touched it, and thus indeed became the prelude to the dissolution of the other still more firmly consolidated leagues of Greek cities.[1] With the forces of the Boeotian towns friendly to Rome the Roman envoy Publius Lentulus laid siege to Haliartus, even before the Roman fleet appeared in the Aegean.

Chalcis was occupied with Achaean, and the province of Orestis with Epirot, forces: the fortresses of the Dassaretae and Illyrians on the west frontier of Macedonia were occupied by the troops of Gnaeus Sicinius; and as soon as the navigation was resumed, Larisa received a garrison of 2000 men. Perseus during all this remained inactive and had not a foot's breadth of land beyond his own territory, when in the spring, or according to the official calendar in June, of $\frac{583}{171}$, the Roman legions landed on the west coast. It is doubtful whether Perseus would have found allies of any mark, even had he shown as much energy as he displayed remissness; but, as circumstances stood, he remained of course completely isolated, and those prolonged attempts at proselytism led, for the time at least, to no result. Carthage, Genthius of Illyria, Rhodes and the free cities of Asia Minor, and even Byzantium hitherto so very friendly with Perseus, offered to the Romans vessels of war; which they, however, declined. Eumenes put his land army and his ships on a war footing. Ariarathes king of Cappadocia sent hostages, unsolicited, to Rome. The brother-in-law of Perseus, Prusias II. king of Bithynia, remained neutral. No one stirred in all Greece. Antiochus IV. king of Syria, designated in court style " the God, the brilliant bringer of victory," to distinguish him from his father the " Great," bestirred himself, but only to wrest the Syrian coast during this war from the entirely impotent Egypt.

But, though Perseus stood almost alone, he was no contemptible antagonist. His army numbered 43,000 men; of

---

[1] The legal dissolution of the Boeotian confederacy, however, took place not at this time, but only after the destruction of Corinth (Pausan. vii. 14, 4; xvi. 6).

these 21,000 were phalangites, and 4000 Macedonian and Thracian cavalry; the rest were chiefly mercenaries. The whole force of the Romans in Greece amounted to between 30,000 and 40,000 Italian troops, besides more than 10,000 men belonging to Numidian, Ligurian, Greek, Cretan, and especially Pergamene contingents. To these was added the fleet, which numbered only 40 decked vessels, as there was no fleet of the enemy to oppose it—Perseus, who had been prohibited from building ships of war by the treaty with Rome, was just erecting docks at Thessalonica—but it had on board 10,000 troops, as it was destined chiefly to co-operate in sieges. The fleet was commanded by Gaius Lucretius, the land army by the consul Publius Licinius Crassus.

The consul left a strong division in Illyria to harass Macedonia from the west, while with the main force he started, as usual, from Apollonia for Thessaly. Perseus did not think of disturbing their arduous march, but contented himself with advancing into Perrhaebia and occupying the nearest fortresses. He awaited the enemy at Ossa, and not far from Larisa the first conflict took place between the cavalry and light troops on both sides. The Romans were decidedly beaten. Cotys with the Thracian horse had defeated and broken the Italian, and Perseus with his Macedonian horse the Greek, cavalry; the Romans had 2000 foot and 200 horsemen killed, and 600 horsemen made prisoners, and might deem themselves fortunate in being allowed to cross the Peneius without hindrance. Perseus employed the victory to ask peace on the same terms which Philip had obtained: he was ready even to pay the same sum. The Romans refused his request: they never concluded peace after a defeat, and in this case the conclusion of peace would certainly have been followed by the loss of Greece.

The wretched Roman commander, however, knew not how or where to attack; the army marched to and fro in Thessaly, without accomplishing anything of importance. Perseus might have assumed the offensive; he saw that the Romans were badly led and dilatory; the news had passed like wildfire through Greece, that the Greek army had been brilliantly victorious in the first engagement; a second victory might lead to a general rising of the patriot party, and, by commencing a guerilla warfare, might produce incalculable results. But Perseus, while a good soldier, was not a general like his father; he had made his preparations for a defensive war, and, when things took a different turn, he felt himself as it were paralysed. He made an unimportant success, which the Romans obtained in a second cavalry combat near Phalanna, a pretext for reverting, as is the habit of narrow and obstinate minds, to his first plan and evacuating Thessaly. This was of course equivalent to renouncing all idea of a Hellenic insurrection: what might have been attained by a different course was shown by the fact that, notwithstanding what had occurred, the Epirots changed sides. Thenceforth nothing serious was accomplished on either side. Perseus subdued king Genthius, chastised the Dardani, and, by means of Cotys, expelled from Thrace the Thracians friendly to Rome and the Pergamene troops. On the other hand the western Roman army took some Illyrian towns, and the consul busied himself in clearing Thessaly of the Macedonian garrisons and making sure of the turbulent Aetolians and Acarnanians by occupying Ambracia. But the heroic courage of the Romans was most severely felt by the two unhappy Boeotian towns which took part with Perseus; Haliartus was captured by the Roman admiral Gaius Lucretius, and the inhabitants were sold into slavery; Coronea was treated in the same manner by the consul Crassus in spite of its capitulation. Never had a Roman army exhibited such wretched discipline as the force under these commanders. They had so disorganised the army that, even in the next campaign of $\frac{584}{170}$, the new consul Aulus Hostilius could not think of undertaking anything serious, especially as the new admiral Lucius Hortensius showed himself to be as incapable and unprincipled as his predecessor. The fleet visited the towns on the Thracian coast without result. The western army under Appius Claudius, whose head-quarters were at Lychnidus in the territory of the Dassaretae, sustained one defeat after another: after an expedition to Macedonia had been utterly unsuccessful, the king in turn towards the beginning of winter assumed the aggressive with the troops which were no longer needed on the south frontier in consequence of the deep snow blocking up all the passes, took from Appius numerous places and a multitude of prisoners, and entered into connections with king Genthius; he was able in fact to attempt an invasion of Aetolia, while Appius allowed himself to be once more defeated in Epirus by the garrison of a fortress which he had vainly besieged. The Roman main army made two attempts to penetrate into Macedonia: first, over the Cambunian mountains, and then through the Thessalian passes; but they were negligently planned, and both were repulsed by Perseus.

The consul employed himself chiefly in the reorganisation of the army—a work which was above all things needful, but which required a sterner man and an officer of greater mark. Discharges and furloughs might be bought, and therefore the divisions were never up to their full numbers; the men were put into quarters in summer, and, as the officers plundered on a great, the common soldiers plundered on a small, scale. Friendly peoples were subjected to the most shameful suspicions: for instance, the blame of the disgraceful defeat at Larisa was imputed to the pretended treachery of the Aetolian cavalry, and, what was hitherto unprecedented, its officers were sent to be criminally tried at Rome; and the Molossians in Epirus were forced by false suspicions into actual revolt. The allied states had war-contributions imposed upon them as if they had been conquered, and if they appealed to the Roman senate, their citizens were executed or sold into slavery: this was done, for instance, at Abdera, and similar outrages were committed at Chalcis. The senate interfered in earnest: it enjoined the liberation of the unfortunate Coroneans and Abderites, and forbade the Roman magistrates to ask contributions from the allies without leave of the senate. Gaius Lucretius was unanimously condemned by the burgesses. But such steps could not alter the fact, that the military result of these first two campaigns had been null, while the political result had been a foul stain on the Romans, whose extraordinary successes in the East were based in no small degree on their reputation for moral purity and soundness as compared with the scandals of Hellenic administration. Had Philip commanded instead of Perseus, the war would probably have begun with the destruction of the Roman army and the defection of most of the Hellenes; but Rome was fortunate enough to be constantly outstripped in her blunders by her antagonists. Perseus was content with entrenching himself in Macedonia—which towards the south and west is a true mountain-fortress—as in a beleaguered town.

The third commander-in-chief also, whom Rome sent to Macedonia in $\frac{585}{169}$, Quintus Marcius Philippus, already mentioned as having honourable relations of hospitality with the king, was not at all equal to his far from easy task. He was ambitious and enterprising, but a bad officer. His hazardous scheme of crossing Olympus by the pass of Lapathus westward of Tempe, leaving behind one division to face the garrison of the pass, and making his way with his main force through impracticable defiles to Heracleum, was not justified by the fact of its success. Not only might a handful of resolute men have blocked

up the route, in which case retreat was out of the question; but
even after the passage, when he stood with the Macedonian
main force in front and the strongly fortified mountain-fortresses
of Tempe and Lapathus behind him, wedged into a narrow plain
on the seashore and without supplies or the possibility of foraging for them, his position was no less desperate than when, in
his first consulate, he had allowed himself to be similarly surrounded in the Ligurian defiles which thenceforth bore his name.
But as an accident saved him then, so the incapacity of Perseus
saved him now. As if he could not comprehend the idea of
defending himself against the Romans otherwise than by the
blockading of the passes, he strangely gave himself over as lost
as soon as he saw the Romans on the Macedonian side of them,
fled in all haste to Pydna, and ordered his ships to be burnt and
his treasures to be sunk. But even this voluntary retreat of
the Macedonian army did not rescue the consul from his painful
position. He advanced indeed without hindrance, but he was
obliged after four days' march to turn back for want of provisions; and, when the king came to his senses and returned in
all haste to resume the position which he had abandoned, the
Roman army would have been in great danger, had not the
impregnable Tempe surrendered at the right moment and
handed over its rich stores to the enemy. The communication
with the south was by this means secured to the Roman army;
but Perseus had strongly barricaded himself in his former well-
chosen position on the bank of the little river Elpius, and there
checked the farther advance of the Romans. So the Roman
army remained, during the rest of the summer and the winter,
hemmed in in the farthest corner of Thessaly; and, while the
crossing of the passes was certainly a success and the first substantial one in the war, it was due not to the ability of the
Roman, but to the blundering of the Macedonian, general. The
Roman fleet in vain attempted the capture of Demetrias, and
performed no exploit whatever. The light ships of Perseus
boldly cruised between the Cyclades, protected the corn-vessels
destined for Macedonia, and attacked the transports of the
enemy. With the western army matters were still worse:
Appius Claudius could do nothing with his reduced division,
and the contingent which he asked from Achaia was prevented
from coming to him by the jealousy of the consul. Moreover,
Genthius had allowed himself to be bribed by Perseus with the
promise of a great sum of money to break with Rome, and to
imprison the Roman envoys; whereupon the frugal king deemed

it superfluous to pay the money which he had promised, since Genthius was now forsooth compelled, independently of it, to substitute an attitude of decided hostility to Rome for the ambiguous position which he had hitherto maintained. Accordingly the Romans had a further petty war by the side of the great one, which had already lasted three years. In fact had Perseus been able to part with his money, he might easily have aroused enemies still more dangerous to the Romans. A Celtic host under Clondicus—10,000 horsemen and as many infantry —offered to take service with him in Macedonia itself; but they could not agree as to the pay. In Hellas too there was such a ferment that a guerilla warfare might easily have been kindled with a little dexterity and a full exchequer; but, as Perseus had no desire to give and the Greeks did nothing gratuitously, the land remained quiet.

At length the Romans resolved to send the right man to Greece. This was Lucius Aemilius Paullus, son of the consul of the same name that fell at Cannae; a man of the old nobility but of humble means, and therefore not so successful in the comitia as on the battle-field, where he had remarkably distinguished himself in Spain and still more so in Liguria. The people elected him for the second time consul in the year $\frac{586}{168}$ on account of his merits—a course which was at that time rare and exceptional. He was in all respects the fitting man: an excellent general of the old school, strict as respected both himself and his troops, and, notwithstanding his sixty years, still hale and vigorous; an incorruptible magistrate—" one of the few Romans of that age to whom one could not offer money," as a contemporary says of him—and a man of Hellenic culture, who, when commander-in-chief, embraced the opportunity of travelling through Greece to inspect its works of art.

As soon as the new general arrived in the camp at Heracleum, he gave orders for the ill-guarded pass at Pythium to be surprised by Publius Nasica, while skirmishes between the outposts occupied the attention of the Macedonians in the channel of the river Elpius; the enemy was thus turned, and was obliged to retreat to Pydna. There, on the Roman 4th of September, $\frac{586}{168}$, or on the 22nd of June of the Julian calendar—an eclipse of the moon, which a scientific Roman officer announced beforehand to the army that it might not be regarded as a bad omen, affords in this case the means of determining the date—the outposts accidentally fell into conflict as they were watering their horses after midday; and both sides determined at once to give

Pydna   168 B.C

the battle, which it was originally intended to postpone till the following day. Passing through the ranks in person, without helmet or shield, the grey-headed Roman general arranged his men. Scarce were they in position, when the formidable phalanx assailed them; the general himself, who had witnessed many a hard fight, afterwards acknowledged that he had trembled. The Roman vanguard dispersed; a Paeliginian cohort was overthrown and almost annihilated; the legions themselves hurriedly retreated till they reached a hill close upon the Roman camp. Here the fortune of the day changed. The uneven ground and the hurried pursuit had disordered the ranks of the phalanx; the Romans in single cohorts entered at every gap, and attacked it on the flanks and in rear; the Macedonian cavalry which alone could have rendered aid looked calmly on, and soon fled in a body, the king among the foremost; and thus the fate of Macedonia was decided in less than an hour. The 3000 select phalangites allowed themselves to be cut down to a man; as if the phalanx, which fought its last great battle at Pydna, had itself wished to perish there. The overthrow was fearful; 20,000 Macedonians lay on the field of battle, 11,000 were prisoners. The war was at an end, on the fifteenth day after Paullus had assumed the command; all Macedonia submitted in two days. The king fled with his gold—he still had more than 6000 talents (£1,460,000) in his chest—to Samothrace, accompanied by a few faithful attendants. But he himself put to death one of these, Evander of Crete, who was to be called to account as instigator of the attempted assassination of Eumenes; and then his pages and remaining comrades also deserted him. For a moment he hoped that the right of asylum would protect him; but he soon perceived that he was clinging to a straw. An attempt to take flight to Cotys failed. So he wrote to the consul; but the letter was not received, because he had designated himself in it as king. He recognised his fate, and surrendered to the Romans at discretion with his children and his treasures, pusillanimous and weeping so as to disgust even his conquerors. With a grave satisfaction, and with thoughts turning rather on the mutability of fortune than on his own present success, the consul received the most illustrious captive whom Roman general had ever brought home. Perseus died a few years after, as a state prisoner, at Alba on the Fucine lake;[1]

---

[1] The story, that the Romans, in order at once to keep the promise which had guaranteed his life and to take vengeance on him, put him to death by depriving him of sleep, is certainly a fable.

his son in after years earned a living in the same Italian country town as a clerk.

Thus perished the empire of Alexander the Great, which had subdued and Hellenised the East, 144 years after his death.

That the tragedy, moreover, might not be without its accompaniment of farce, at the same time the war against "king" Genthius of Illyria was also begun and ended by the praetor Lucius Anicius within thirty days. The piratical fleet was taken, the capital Scodra was captured, and the two kings, the heir of Alexander the Great and the heir of Pleuratus, entered Rome side by side as prisoners.

The senate had resolved that the peril, which the unseasonable gentleness of Flamininus had brought on Rome, should not recur. Macedonia was abolished. In the conference at Amphipolis on the Strymon the Roman commission ordained that the compact, thoroughly monarchical, and united state should be broken up into four republican federative leagues moulded on the system of the Greek confederacies, viz., that of Amphipolis in the eastern provinces, that of Thessalonica with the Chalcidian peninsula, that of Pella on the frontiers of Thessaly, and that of Pelagonia in the interior. Intermarriages between persons belonging to different confederacies were to be invalid, and no one might be a freeholder in more than one of them. All who had held office under the king, as well as their grown-up sons, were obliged to leave the country and proceed to Italy on pain of death; the Romans still dreaded, and with reason, the throbbings of the ancient loyalty. The law of the land and the former constitution otherwise remained in force; the magistrates were of course nominated by election in each community, and the power in the communities as well as in the confederacies was placed in the hands of the upper class. The royal domains and royalties were not granted to the confederacies, and these were specially prohibited from working the gold and silver mines, a chief source of the national wealth; but in $\frac{596}{158}$ they were again permitted to work at least the silver mines.[1] The im-

---

[1] The statement of Cassiodorus, that the Macedonian mines were reopened in $\frac{596}{158}$, receives its more exact interpretation by means of the coins. No gold coins of the four Macedonias are extant; either therefore the goldmines remained closed, or the gold extracted was converted into bars. On the other hand there certainly exist silver coins of Macedonia *prima* (Amphipolis) in which district the silver-mines were situated. For the brief period, during which they must have been struck ($\frac{596-608}{158-146}$), the number of them is remarkably great, and proves either that the mines were very energetically wrought, or that the old royal money was recoined in large quantity.

portation of salt, and the exportation of timber for ship-building, were prohibited. The land-tax hitherto paid to the king ceased, and the confederacies and communities were left to tax themselves; but these had to pay to Rome half of the former land-tax, according to a rate fixed once for all, amounting in all to 100 talents annually (£24,000).[1] The whole land was for ever disarmed, and the fortress of Demetrias was razed; on the northern frontier alone a chain of posts was to be retained to guard against the incursions of the barbarians. Of the arms given up, the copper shields were sent to Rome, and the rest were burnt.

The Romans gained their object. The Macedonian land still on two occasions took up arms at the call of princes of the old reigning house; but otherwise from that time to the present day it has remained without a history.

Illyria was treated in a similar way. The kingdom of Genthius was split up into three small free states. There too the freeholders paid the half of the former land-tax to their new masters, with the exception of the towns, which had adhered to Rome and in return obtained exemption from the tax—an exception which there was no opportunity to make in the case of Macedonia. The Illyrian piratic fleet was confiscated, and presented to the more reputable Greek communities along the coast. The constant annoyances, which the Illyrians inflicted on their neighbours by means of their corsairs, were in this way put an end to, at least for a lengthened period.

Cotys in Thrace, who was difficult to be reached and might conveniently be used against Eumenes, obtained pardon and received back his captive son.

Thus the affairs of the north were settled, and Macedonia also was at last released from the yoke of monarchy. In fact Greece was more free than ever; a king no longer existed anywhere.

But the Romans did not confine themselves to cutting the nerves and sinews of Macedonia. The senate resolved at once to render all the Hellenic states, friend and foe, for ever incapable of harm, and to reduce all of them alike to the same humble state of dependence. The course pursued may itself admit of justification; but the mode in which it was carried out in the

---

[1] The statement that the Macedonian commonwealth was " relieved of seignorial imposts and taxes " by the Romans (Polyb. xxxvii. 4) does not necessarily require us to assume a subsequent remission of these taxes: it is sufficient, for the explanation of Polybius' words, to assume that the hitherto seignorial tax now became a public one. The continuance of the constitution granted to the province of Macedonia by Paullus down to at least the Augustan age (Liv. xlv. 32; Justin xxxiii. 2), would, it is true, be compatible also with the remission of the taxes.

case of the more powerful of the Greek dependent states was unworthy of a great power, and showed that the epoch of the Fabii and the Scipios was at an end.

The state most affected by this change in the position of parties was the kingdom of the Attalids, which had been created and fostered by Rome to keep Macedonia in check, and which now, after the destruction of Macedonia, was forsooth no longer needed. It was not easy to find a tolerable pretext for depriving the prudent and considerate Eumenes of his privileged position, and allowing him to fall into disgrace. All at once, about the time when the Romans were encamped at Heracleum, strange reports were circulated regarding him—that he was in secret intercourse with Perseus; that his fleet had been suddenly, as it were, wafted away; that 500 talents had been offered for his non-participation in the campaign and 1500 for his mediation to procure peace, and that the agreement had only broken down through the avarice of Perseus. As to the Pergamene fleet, the king, after having paid his respects to the consul, went home with it at the same time that the Roman fleet went into winter quarters. The story about corruption was as certainly a fable as any newspaper *canard* of the present day; for that the rich, cunning, and consistent Attalid, who had primarily occasioned the breach between Rome and Macedonia by his journey in $\frac{682}{172}$ and had been on that account well-nigh assassinated by the banditti of Perseus, should—at the moment when the real difficulties of the war were overcome and its final issue, if ever seriously doubted at all, was doubtful no longer—have sold to the instigator of his murder his share in the spoil for a few talents, and should have perilled the work of long years for so pitiful a consideration, may be set down not merely as a fabrication, but as a very silly one. That no proof was found either in the papers of Perseus or elsewhere, is sufficiently certain; for even the Romans did not venture to express those suspicions aloud. But they gained their object. Their intentions were shown in the behaviour of the Roman grandees towards Attalus, the brother of Eumenes, who had commanded the Pergamene auxiliary troops in Greece. Their brave and faithful comrade was received in Rome with open arms and invited to ask not for his brother, but for himself—the senate would be glad to give him a kingdom of his own. Attalus asked nothing but Aenus and Maronea. The senate thought that this was only a preliminary request, and granted it with great politeness. But when he took his departure without having made any further demands, and the senate came to perceive that the reigning family in Pergamus did not live on such terms with each other as were usual in princely houses, Aenus and Maronea were declared free cities. The Pergamenes obtained not a single foot of territory out of the spoil of Macedonia; if after the victory over Antiochus the Romans had still saved forms as respected Philip, they were now disposed to hurt and to humiliate. About this time the senate appears to have declared Pamphylia, for the possession of which Eumenes and Antiochus had hitherto contended, independent. What was of more importance, the Galatians—who had been substantially in the power of Eumenes, ever since he had expelled the king of Pontus by force of arms from Galatia and had on making peace extorted from him the promise that he would maintain no further communication with the Galatian princes—now, reckoning beyond doubt on the variance that had taken place between Eumenes and the Romans, if not directly instigated by the latter, rose against Eumenes, overran his kingdom, and brought him into great danger. Eumenes besought the mediation of the Romans; the Roman envoy declared his readiness to mediate, but thought it better that Attalus, who commanded the Pergamene army, should not accompany him lest the barbarians might be put in ill humour. Singularly enough, he accomplished nothing; in fact, he told on his return that his mediation had only exasperated the barbarians. No long time elapsed before the independence of the Galatians was expressly recognised and guaranteed by the senate. Eumenes determined to proceed to Rome in person, and to plead his cause in the senate. But the latter, as if troubled by an evil conscience, suddenly decreed that in future no kings should be allowed to come to Rome; and despatched a quaestor to meet him at Brundisium, to lay before him this decree of the senate, to ask him what he wanted, and to hint to him that they would be glad to hear of his speedy departure. The king was long silent; at length he said that he desired nothing farther, and re-embarked. He saw how matters stood: the epoch of half-powerful and half-free alliance was at an end; that of impotent subjection began.

Similar treatment befell the Rhodians. They had been singularly favoured: their relation to Rome assumed the form not of symmachy properly so called, but of friendship and equality; they were not prevented from entering into alliances of any kind, and they were not compelled to supply the Romans with a contingent on demand. This very circumstance was probably the real reason why their good understanding with Rome had already for some time been impaired. The first dissensions with Rome had arisen in consequence of the rising of the Lycians, who were handed over to Rhodes after the defeat of Antiochus, against their oppressors who had ($\frac{576}{178}$) cruelly reduced them to slavery as revolted subjects; the Lycians, however, asserted that they were not subjects but allies of the Rhodians, and prevailed with this plea in the Roman senate, which was invited to settle the doubtful meaning of the instrument of peace. But in this result a justifiable sympathy with the victims of grievous oppression had perhaps the chief share; at least nothing further was done on the part of the Romans, who left this as well as other Hellenic quarrels to take their course. When the war with Perseus broke out, the Rhodians, like all other sensible Greeks, viewed it with regret, and blamed Eumenes in particular as the instigator of it, so that his fatal embassy was not even permitted to be present at the festival of Helios in Rhodes. But this did not prevent them from adhering to Rome and keeping the Macedonian party, which existed in Rhodes as well as everywhere else, aloof from the helm of affairs. The permission given to them in $\frac{585}{169}$ to export grain from Sicily shows the continuance of the good understanding with Rome. All of a sudden, shortly before the battle of Pydna, Rhodian envoys appeared at the Roman head-quarters and in the Roman senate, announcing that the Rhodians would no longer tolerate this war which was injurious to their Macedonian traffic and the revenues of their ports, that they were disposed themselves to declare war against the party which should refuse to make peace, and that with this view they had already concluded an alliance with Crete and with the Asiatic cities. Many caprices are possible in a republic governed by popular assemblies; but this insane intervention on the part of a commercial city—which can only have been resolved on after the fall of the pass of Tempe was known at Rhodes—requires special explanation. The key to it is furnished by the well-attested account that the consul Quintus Marcius, that master of the "new-fashioned diplomacy," had in the camp at Heracleum (and therefore after the occupation of the pass of Tempe) loaded the Rhodian envoy Agepolis with civilities and made an underhand request to him to mediate a peace. Republican vanity and folly did the rest; the Rhodians fancied that the Romans had abandoned all hope of success; they were eager to play the part of mediator among four great powers at once; communications were entered into with Perseus;

Rhodian envoys with Macedonian sympathies said more than they should have said; and they were caught. The senate, which doubtless was itself for the most part unaware of such intrigues, heard the strange announcement with natural indignation, and was glad of the favourable opportunity to humble the haughty merchant city. A warlike praetor went even so far as to propose to the people a declaration of war against Rhodes. In vain the Rhodian ambassadors repeatedly on their knees adjured the senate to think of the friendship of a hundred and forty years rather than of the one offence; in vain they sent the heads of the Macedonian party to the scaffold or to Rome; in vain they sent a massive wreath of gold in token of their gratitude for the non-declaration of war. The honourable Cato indeed showed that strictly the Rhodians had committed no offence, and asked whether the Romans were desirous to undertake the punishment of wishes and thoughts, and whether they could blame the nations for being apprehensive that Rome might allow herself all licence if she had no longer any one to fear? His words and warnings were in vain. The senate deprived the Rhodians of their possessions on the mainland, which yielded a yearly produce of 120 talents (£29,000). Still heavier were the blows aimed at the Rhodian commerce. The prohibition of the import of salt to, and of the export of ship-building timber from, Macedonia appears to have been directed against Rhodes. Rhodian commerce was still more directly affected by the erection of the free port at Delos; the Rhodian customs-dues, which hitherto had produced 1,000,000 *drachmae* (£41,000) annually, sank in a very brief period to 150,000 *drachmae* (£6180). Generally, the Rhodians were paralysed in their freedom of action and in their liberal and bold commercial policy, and the state began to languish. Even the alliance asked for was at first refused, and was only renewed in $\frac{589}{164}$ after urgent entreaties. The equally guilty but powerless Cretans escaped with a sharp rebuke.

With Syria and Egypt the Romans could go to work more summarily. War had broken out between them; and Coelesyria and Palaestina formed once more the subject of dispute. According to the assertion of the Egyptians, those provinces had been ceded to Egypt on the marriage of the Syrian Cleopatra; this however the court of Babylon, which was in actual possession, disputed. Apparently the charging of her dowry on the taxes of the Coelesyrian cities gave occasion to the quarrel, and the Syrian side was in the right; the breaking out of the war was occasioned by the death of Cleopatra in $\frac{581}{173}$, with which at latest the payments of revenue terminated. The war appears to have been begun by Egypt; but king Antiochus Epiphanes gladly embraced the opportunity of once more—and for the last time— endeavouring to achieve the traditional aim of the policy of the Seleucidae, the acquisition of Egypt, while the Romans were employed in Macedonia. Fortune seemed favourable to him. The king of Egypt at that time, Ptolemy VI. Philometor, the son of Cleopatra, had hardly passed the age of boyhood and had bad advisers; after a great victory on the Syro-Egyptian frontier Antiochus was able to advance into the territories of his nephew in the same year in which the legions landed in Greece ($\frac{583}{171}$), and soon had the person of the king in his power. Matters began to look as if Antiochus wished to possess himself of all Egypt in Philometor's name; Alexandria accordingly closed its gates against him, deposed Philometor, and nominated as king in his stead his younger brother, Euergetes II., named the Fat. Disturbances in his own kingdom recalled the Syrian king from Egypt; when he returned, he found that the brothers had come to an understanding during his absence; and he then continued the war against both. Just as he lay before Alexandria, not long after the battle of Pydna ($\frac{586}{168}$), the Roman envoy Gaius Popillius, a harsh rude man, arrived, and intimated to him the command of the senate that he should restore all that he had conquered and should evacuate Egypt within a set term. Antiochus asked time for consideration; but the consular drew with his staff a circle round the king, and bade him declare his intentions before he stepped beyond the circle. Antiochus replied that he would comply; and marched off to his capital that he might there, in his character of " the god, the brilliant bringer of victory," celebrate in Roman fashion his conquest of Egypt and parody the triumph of Paullus.

Egypt voluntarily submitted to the Roman protectorate; and thereupon the kings of Babylon also desisted from the last effort to maintain their independence against Rome. Like Macedonia in the war waged by Perseus, the Seleucidae in the war regarding Coelesyria had made a final effort to recover their earlier power; but it is a significant indication of the difference between the two kingdoms, that in the former case the legions, in the latter the abrupt language of a diplomatist, decided the controversy.

In Greece itself, as the two Boeotian cities had already paid more than a sufficient penalty, the Molottians alone remained to be punished as allies of Perseus. Acting on secret orders from the senate, Paullus in one day gave up seventy townships in Epirus to plunder, and sold the inhabitants, 150,000 in number, into slavery. The Aetolians lost Amphipolis, and the Acarnanians Leucas, on account of their equivocal behaviour; whereas the Athenians, who continued to play the part of the begging poet in their own Aristophanes, not only obtained a gift of Delos and Lemnos, but were not ashamed even to petition for the deserted site of Haliartus, which was assigned to them accordingly. Thus something was done for the Muses; but more had to be done for justice. There was a Macedonian party in every city, and therefore trials for high treason began in all parts of Greece. Whoever had served in the army of Perseus was immediately executed; whoever was compromised by the papers of the king or the statements of political opponents who flocked to lodge informations, was despatched to Rome; the Achaean Callicrates and the Aetolian Lyciscus distinguished themselves in the trade of informers. In this way the more conspicuous patriots among the Thessalians, Aetolians, Acarnanians, Lesbians and so forth, were removed from their native land; and, in particular, more than a thousand Achaeans were thus disposed of—a step taken with the view not so much of prosecuting those who were carried off, as of silencing the childish opposition of the Hellenes. To the Achaeans, who, as usual, were not content till they got the answer which they anticipated, the senate, wearied by constant requests for the commencement of the investigation, at length roundly declared that till further orders the persons concerned were to remain in Italy. There they were placed in country towns in the interior, and tolerably well treated; but attempts to escape were punished with death. The position of the former officials removed from Macedonia was, in all probability, similar. This expedient, violent as it was, was still, as things stood, the most lenient, and the enraged Greeks of the Roman party were far from content with the paucity of the executions. Lyciscus had accordingly deemed it proper to have some 500 of the leading men of the Aetolian patriotic party slain at the meeting of the diet; the Roman commission, which had occasion for the man, suffered the deed to pass unpunished, and merely censured the employment of Roman soldiers in the execution of such Hellenic justice. We may presume, however, that the Romans instituted the system of deportation to Italy partly in order to prevent such horrors. As in Greece proper no power existed even of such importance

as Rhodes or Pergamus, there was no need in its case for any
further humiliation; the steps taken were taken only in the
exercise of justice—in the Roman sense, no doubt, of that term
—and for the prevention of the most scandalous and palpable
outbreaks of party discord.

All the Hellenistic states had thus been completely subjected
to the protectorate of Rome, and the whole empire of Alexander
the Great had fallen to the Roman commonwealth just as if
the city had inherited it from his heirs. From all sides kings
and ambassadors flocked to Rome to congratulate her; and they
showed that fawning is never more abject than when kings
are in the antechamber. King Massinissa, who only desisted
from presenting himself in person on being expressly prohibited
from doing so, ordered his son to declare that he regarded himself as merely the usufructuary, and the Romans as the true
proprietors, of his kingdom, and that he would always be content
with what they were willing to leave to him. There was at least
truth in this. But Prusias king of Bithynia, who had to atone
for his neutrality, bore off the palm in this contest of flattery;
he fell on his face when he was conducted into the senate, and
did homage to " the delivering gods." As he was so thoroughly
contemptible, Polybius tells us, they gave him a courteous reply,
and presented him with the fleet of Perseus.

The moment was at least well chosen for such language.
Polybius dates from the battle of Pydna the full establishment
of the universal empire of Rome. It was in fact the last battle
in which a civilised state confronted Rome in the field on a
footing of equality with her as a great power; all subsequent
struggles were rebellions or wars with peoples beyond the pale
of the Romano-Greek civilisation—the barbarians, as they
were called. The whole civilised world thenceforth recognised
in the Roman senate the supreme tribunal, whose commissioners
decided in the last resort between kings and nations; and to
acquire its language and manners foreign princes and youths
of quality resided in Rome. A clear and earnest attempt
to get rid of her dominion was in reality made only once—by
the great Mithradates of Pontus. The battle of Pydna, moreover, marks the last occasion on which the senate still adhered
to the state-maxim that they should, if possible, hold no
possessions and maintain no garrisons beyond the Italian seas,
but should keep the numerous states dependent on them in
order by a mere political supremacy. The aim of their policy
was that these states should neither decline into utter weakness

and anarchy, as had nevertheless happened in Greece, nor emerge out of their half-free position into complete independence, as Macedonia had attempted to do not without success. No state was to be allowed utterly to perish, but no one was to be permitted to stand on its own resources. Accordingly the vanquished foe held at least an equal, often a better, position with the Roman diplomatists than the faithful ally; and, while a defeated opponent was reinstated, those who attempted to reinstate themselves were abased—as the Aetolians, Macedonia after the Asiatic war, Rhodes, and Pergamus learned by experience. But not only did this part of protector soon prove as irksome to the masters as to the servants; the Roman protectorate, with its ungrateful Sisyphian toil that continually needed to be begun afresh, showed itself to be intrinsically untenable. Indications of a change of system, and of an increasing disinclination on the part of Rome to tolerate by its side intermediate states even in such independence as was possible for them, were very clearly given in the destruction of the Macedonian monarchy after the battle of Pydna. The more and more frequent and more and more unavoidable intervention in the internal affairs of the petty Greek states through their misgovernment and their political and social anarchy; the disarming of Macedonia, where the northern frontier at any rate urgently required a defence different from that of mere posts; and, lastly, the introduction of the payment of land-tax to Rome from Macedonia and Illyria, were so many symptoms of the approaching conversion of the client states into subjects of Rome.

If, in conclusion, we glance back at the career of Rome from the union of Italy to the dismemberment of Macedonia, the universal empire of Rome, far from appearing as a gigantic plan contrived and carried out by an insatiable thirst for territorial aggrandisement, appears to have been a result which forced itself on the Roman government without, and even in opposition to, its wish. It is true that the former view naturally suggests itself. Sallust is right when he makes Mithradates say that the wars of Rome with tribes, cities, and kings originated in one and the same prime cause, the insatiable longing after dominion and riches; but it is an error to give forth this judgment—shaped thus by passion and the issue—as an historical fact. It is evident to every one whose observation is not superficial, that the Roman government during this whole period wished and desired nothing but the sovereignty of Italy; that they were simply desirous not to have too powerful neighbours alongside of them; and that—not out of humanity towards the vanquished, but from the very sound view that they ought not to suffer the kernel of their empire to be crushed by the shell—they earnestly opposed the introduction first of Africa, then of Greece, and lastly of Asia into the pale of the Roman protectorate, till circumstances in each case compelled, or at least suggested with irresistible force, the extension of that pale. The Romans always asserted that they did not pursue a policy of conquest, and that they were always the assailed rather than the assailants; and this was something more, at any rate, than a mere phrase. They were in fact driven to all their great wars with the exception of that concerning Sicily—to those with Hannibal and Antiochus, no less than to those with Philip and Perseus—either by a direct aggression or by an unparalleled disturbance of the existing political relations; and hence they were ordinarily taken by surprise on their outbreak. That they did not after victory exhibit the moderation which they ought to have done in the interest more especially of Italy itself; that the retention of Spain, for instance, the undertaking of the guardianship of Africa, and above all the half-fanciful scheme of conferring liberty everywhere on the Greeks, were in the light of Italian policy grave errors, is sufficiently clear. But the causes of these errors were, on the one hand a blind dread of Carthage, on the other a still blinder enthusiasm for Hellenistic liberty; so little did the Romans exhibit during this period the lust of conquest, that they, on the contrary, displayed a very judicious dread of its effects. The policy of Rome throughout was not projected by a single mighty intellect and bequeathed by tradition from generation to generation; it was the policy of a very able but somewhat narrow-minded deliberative assembly, which had far too little power of grand combination, and far too much of an instinctive desire for the preservation of its own commonwealth, to devise projects in the spirit of a Cæsar or a Napoleon. The universal empire of Rome had its ultimate ground in the political development of antiquity in general. The ancient world knew nothing of a balance of power among nations; and therefore every nation which had attained internal unity strove either directly to subdue its neighbours, as did the Hellenic states, or at any rate to render them innocuous, as Rome did,—an effort, it is true, which also issued at last in subjugation. Egypt was perhaps the only great power in antiquity which seriously pursued the system of equilibrium: on the opposite system

Seleucus and Antigonus, Hannibal and Scipio came into collision. And, however melancholy may seem the fact that all the other richly endowed and highly developed nations of antiquity had to perish in order to enrich a single people, as if the ultimate object of their existence had simply been to contribute to the greatness of Italy and to the decay involved in that greatness; yet historical justice must acknowledge that this result was not produced by the military superiority of the legion over the phalanx, but was the necessary consequence of the international relations of antiquity generally—so that the issue was not decided by provoking chance, but was the fulfilment of an unchangeable, and therefore endurable, destiny.

CHAPTER XI

THE GOVERNMENT AND THE GOVERNED

THE fall of the patriciate by no means divested the Roman commonwealth of its aristocratic character. We have already (i. 303) indicated that the plebeian party carried within it that character from the first as well as, and in some sense still more decidedly than, the patriciate; for, while in the old body of burgesses an absolute equality of rights prevailed, the new constitution set out with a distinction between the senatorial houses who were privileged in point of burgess rights and of burgess usufructs, and the mass of the other citizens. Immediately, therefore, on the abolition of the patriciate and the formal establishment of civic equality, a new aristocracy and a corresponding opposition were formed; and we have already shown how the former engrafted itself as it were on the fallen patriciate, and how, accordingly, the first movements of the new party of progress were mixed up with the last movements of the old plebeian opposition (i. 304). The formation of these new parties began in the fifth century, but they assumed their definite shape only in the century which followed. The development of this change is, as it were, drowned amidst the noise of the great wars and victories, and the process of formation is in this case more concealed from our view than in any other in Roman history. Like a crust of ice gathering imperceptibly over the surface of a stream and imperceptibly confining it more and more, this new Roman aristocracy silently arose; and not less imperceptibly, like the concealed current slowly swelling beneath, there arose in opposition to it the new party of progress. It is very difficult to sum up in a general historical view the several, individually insignificant, traces of these two antagonistic movements which do not for the present culminate in any distinct practical catastrophe. But the freedom hitherto enjoyed in the commonwealth was undermined, and the foundation for future revolutions was laid, during this epoch; and the delineation of these as well as of the development of Rome in general would remain imperfect, if we should fail to give some idea of the thickness and strength of that encrusting ice, and of the fearful moaning

and cracking that foretold the mighty breaking up which was
at hand.

The Roman nobility attached itself, in form, to earlier institutions belonging to the times of the patriciate. Persons who
once had filled the highest ordinary magistracies of the state
not only, as a matter of course, practically enjoyed all along a
higher honour, but also had at an early period certain honorary
privileges associated with their position. The most ancient of
these was doubtless the permission given to the descendants of
such magistrates to place the wax images of these illustrious
ancestors after their death in the family hall, along the wall
where the pedigree was painted, and to have these images
carried, on occasion of the death of members of the family, in
the funeral procession (i. 288). To appreciate the importance
of this distinction, we must recollect that the honouring of
images was regarded in the Italo-Hellenic view as unrepublican,
and on that account the Roman state-police did not at all
tolerate the exhibition of effigies of the living, and strictly superintended that of effigies of the dead. With this privilege were
associated various external insignia, reserved by law or custom
for such magistrates and their descendants; the stripe of purple
on the tunic and the golden finger-ring of the men, the silver-
mounted trappings of the youths, the purple border on the *toga*
and the golden amulet-case of the boys [1]—trifling matters, but
still important in a community where civic equality in external
appearance was so strictly adhered to (i. 302), and where, even
during the second Punic war, a burgess was arrested and kept

[1] All these insignia probably belonged at first only to the nobility proper,
i.e. to the agnate descendants of curule magistrates; although, after the
manner of such decorations, all of them in course of time were extended
to a wider circle. This can be distinctly proved in the case of the gold
finger-ring, which in the fifth century was worn only by the nobility (Plin.
H. N. xxxiii. 1, 18), in the sixth by every senator and senator's son (Liv.
xxvi. 36), in the seventh by every one of equestrian rank, under the empire
by every one who was of free birth. So also with the silver trappings,
which still, in the second Punic war, formed a badge of the nobility alone
(Liv. xxvi. 36); and with the purple border of the *toga*, which at first was
granted only to the sons of curule magistrates, then to the sons of equites,
afterwards to those of all free-born persons, lastly—yet as early as the
time of the second Punic war—even to the sons of freedmen (Macrob. *Sat.*
i. 6)   The purple stripe (*clavus*) on the tunic can only be shown to have
been a badge of the senators (i. 86) and equites, the former wearing it broad,
the latter narrow: in like manner the golden amulet-case (*bulla*) is only
mentioned as a badge of the children of senators in the time of the second
Punic war (Macrob. *l.c.*; Liv. xxvi. 36), in that of Cicero as the badge of
the children of the equestrian order (Cic. *Verr.* i. 58, 152), whereas children
of inferior rank wore the leathern amulet (*lorum*). But these seem to be
merely accidental gaps in tradition, and the *clavus* and *bulla* also appear at
first to have been peculiar to the nobility strictly so called alone.

for years in prison because he had appeared in public, in a manner not sanctioned by law, with a garland of roses upon his head.[1]

These distinctions probably already existed in the main in the time of the patrician government, and, so long as families of higher and lower rank were distinguished within the patriciate, served as external insignia for the former. But they only acquired political importance in consequence of the change of constitution in $\frac{387}{367}$, by which the plebeian families that attained the consulate were placed on a footing of equal privilege with the patrician families, all of whom were now probably entitled to carry images of their ancestors. Moreover, it was now settled that the offices of state to which these hereditary privileges were attached should include neither the lower nor the extraordinary magistracies nor the tribunate of the plebs, but merely the consulship, the praetorship which stood on the same level with it (i. 296), and the curule aedileship, which bore a part in the administration of public justice and consequently in the exercise of the sovereign powers of the state.[2] Although this plebeian nobility, in the strict sense of the term, could only be formed after the curule offices were opened to plebeians, yet it exhibited in a short time, if not at the very first, a certain compactness of organisation—doubtless because the germs of such a nobility had long existed in the old senatorial plebeian families. The result of the Licinian laws in reality therefore amounted nearly to what we would now call the creation of a batch of peers. Now that the plebeian families ennobled by their curule ancestors were united into one body with the patrician families and acquired a distinctive position and distinguished power in the commonwealth, the Romans had again arrived at the point whence they had started; there was once more not merely a governing aristocracy and a hereditary

---

[1] Plin. *H. N.* xxi. 3, 6. The right to appear crowned in public was acquired by distinction in war (Polyb. vi. 39, 9; Liv. x. 47); consequently, the wearing a crown without warrant was an offence similar to the assumption, in the present day, of the badge of a military order of merit without due title.

[2] Thus there remained excluded the military tribunate with consular powers (i. 287), the proconsulship, the quaestorship, the tribunate of the people, and several others. As to the censorship, it does not appear, notwithstanding the curule chair of the censors (Liv. xl. 45; comp. xxvii. 8), to have been reckoned a curule office; for the later period, however, when only a man of consular standing could be made censor, the question has no practical importance. The plebeian aedileship certainly was not reckoned originally one of the curule magistracies (Liv. xxiii. 23); it may, however, have been subsequently included amongst them.

nobility—both of which in fact had never disappeared—but there was a governing hereditary nobility, and the feud between the *gentes* in possession of the government and the commons rising in revolt against the *gentes* could not but begin afresh. And matters very soon reached that stage. The nobility was not content with its honorary privileges which were matters of comparative indifference, but strove after exclusive and sole political power, and sought to convert the most important institutions of the state—the senate and the equestrian order—from organs of the commonwealth into organs of the plebeio-patrician aristocracy.

The dependence *de jure* of the Roman senate of the republic, more especially of the larger patricio-plebeian senate, on the magistracy had rapidly become lax, and had in fact been converted into independence. The subordination of the public magistracies to the state-council, introduced by the revolution of $\frac{244}{510}$ (i. 262); the transference of the right of summoning men to the senate from the consul to the censor (i. 290); lastly, and above all, the legal recognition of the right of those who had been curule magistrates to a seat and vote in the senate (i. 314), had converted the senate from a council summoned by the magistrates and in many respects dependent on them into a governing corporation virtually independent, and in a certain sense filling up its own ranks; for the two modes by which its members obtained admission—election to a curule office and summoning by the censor—were both virtually in the power of the governing board itself. The burgesses, no doubt, at this epoch were still too independent to allow the entire exclusion of non-nobles from the senate, and the nobility were perhaps still too prudent even to wish for this; but, owing to the strictly aristocratic gradations in the senate itself—in which those who had been curule magistrates were sharply distinguished, according to their respective classes of *consulares*, *praetorii*, and *aedilicii*, from the senators who had not entered the senate through a curule office and were therefore excluded from debate —the non-nobles, although they probably sat in considerable numbers in the senate, were reduced to an insignificant and comparatively uninfluential position in it, and the senate became substantially a mainstay of the nobility.

The institution of the equites was developed into a second, less important but yet far from unimportant, organ of the nobility. As the new hereditary nobility had not the power to usurp sole possession of the comitia, it necessarily became in the highest degree desirable that it should obtain at least a distinctive position in the representation of the community. In the assembly of the tribes there was no method of managing this; but the equestrian centuries under the Servian organisation seemed as it were created for the very purpose. The 1800 horses which the community furnished [1] were constitutionally

[1] The current hypothesis, according to which the six centuries of the nobility alone amounted to 1200, and the whole equestrian force accordingly to 3600 horse, is not tenable. The method of determining the number of the equites by the number of duplications specified by the annalists is mistaken: in fact, each of these statements has originated and is to be explained by itself. But there is no evidence either for the first number, which is only found in the passage of Cicero, De Rep. ii. 20, acknowledged as erroneous even by the champions of this view, or for the second, which does not appear at all in ancient authors. In favour, on the other hand, of the hypothesis set forth in the text, we have, first of all, the number as indicated not by authorities, but by the institutions themselves; for it is certain that the century numbered 100 men, and there were originally three (i. 72), then six (i. 85), and lastly after the Servian reform eighteen (i. 93), equestrian centuries. The deviations of the authorities from this view are only apparent. The one self-consistent tradition, which Becker has developed (ii. 1, 243), reckons not the eighteen patricio-plebeian, but the six patrician, centuries at 1800 men; and this has been manifestly followed by Livy, i. 36 (according to the reading which alone has manuscript authority, and which ought not to be corrected from Livy's particular estimates), and by Cicero l.c. (according to the only reading grammatically admissible, MDCCC.; see Becker, ii. 1, 244). But Cicero at the same time indicates very plainly, that in that statement he intended to describe the then existing amount of the Roman equites in general. The number of the whole body has therefore been transferred to the most prominent portion of it by a prolepsis, such as is common in the case of annalists not too much given to reflection: just in the same way 300 equites instead of 100 are assigned to the parent-community, including, by anticipation, the contingents of the Tities and the Luceres (Becker, ii. 1, 238). Lastly, the proposition of Cato (p. 66, Jordan), to raise the number of the horses of the equites to 2200, is as distinct a confirmation of the view proposed above, as it is a distinct refutation of the opposite view.

With this view what is known of the equestrian order under the empire very well accords. It was divided into *turmae*, that is, divisions of 30 or 33 men (Marquardt, iii. 2, 258). The slight traces of a division of the cavalry not merely by *turmae*, but at the same time also by tribes (Becker, ii. 1, 261, note 538; and Zonaras, x. 35, p. 421, Bonn: ἵλαρχος τῆς φυλῆς =*sevir eq. R.*), cannot be satisfactorily cleared up; the relation too of the *turma* to the centuries is not quite clear, but cannot well be conceived otherwise than that three *turmae* went to the century. This would accordingly give 54 *turmae*, which number, as all the Roman equites were certainly divided into *turmae*, is doubtless rather too small than too large. Moreover it is self-evident that we have here to do merely with the normal number; by the addition of supernumeraries the number of the equites subsequently far exceeded that normal one. The whole number of the *turmae* is not given by tradition; for, while inscriptions exhibit only the earlier numbers as far as the fifth or sixth, the prominence of these is to be explained simply from the special repute in which the first *turmae* were held—a circumstance which may be compared with the fact that in inscriptions we meet only with the *tribunus a populo* and *laticlavius*, and the *iudex quadringenarius*, never with the *tribunus rufulus* and *angusti-*

disposed of likewise by the censors. It was, no doubt, the duty
of these to make the selection on purely military grounds and
at their musters to insist that all horsemen incapacitated by age
or otherwise, or at all unserviceable, should surrender their
public horse; but the very nature of the institution implied
that the cavalry-horses should be given especially to men of
means, and it was not at all easy to hinder the censors from
looking to superior birth more than to capacity, and from allowing men of standing who were once admitted, senators particularly, to retain their horse beyond the proper time. Accordingly it became practically the rule for the senators to vote in
the eighteen equestrian centuries, and the other places in these
were assigned chiefly to the younger men of the nobility. The
military system, of course, suffered from this not so much through
the unfitness for effective service of no small part of the legionary
cavalry, as through the destruction of military equality to which

---

clavius, or the *iudex ducenarius*. There is no reasonable ground for assuming an aggregate number of six *turmae*, and the fact that it is nevertheless
the usual hypothesis (Becker, ii. 1, 261, 288) is solely due to an inference—
not at all warranted—from the name of the leaders of the *turmae*, the
seviri equitum Romanorum, to the number of *turmae* led by them. The
Roman burgess-cavalry certainly had for a time six centuries under as many
centurions or *tribuni celerum* (i. 72, 85); but, even if we should assume
that this number was retained after the increase of the centuries from six
to eighteen, the *seviri eq. Rom.* could not reasonably be regarded as identical
with these *tribuni celerum*, since on the monuments throughout they appear
in relation not to the cavalry in general, but to the individual *turmae*, as
seviri eq. Rom. turmae primae, and so forth, in Greek Ἵλαρχοι (Zonaras,
x. 35, p. 421 Bonn), and are therefore to be explained not from the arrangement of the centuries, but from that of the *turmae*. In the latter accordingly we find what we are in search of: the six commanders assigned by
the military arrangement to each *turma* (Polyb. vi. 25. 1), the *decuriones*
and *optiones* of Cato (*Fr.* p. 39 Jordan), must just have been these *seviri*,
and there must consequently have been six times as many *seviri* as the
cavalry numbered squadrons. There is no evidence, although it is now
usually assumed, that there was only one *sevir* in each *turma*: this hypothesis would in fact be decidedly opposed to the turmal arrangement. The
objection stated by Henzen (Annali dell' Instituto, 1862, p. 142), that
M. Aurelius gave the Seviral games as *sevir "cum collegis,"* by no means
excludes the large number of *seviri* which we have assumed, for the colleagues mentioned might in fact very well be merely those of the same
turma. It may be even reckoned probable that the *seviri* of the first
turma enjoyed a special distinction, and the *principes iuventutis* were
simply nothing else than the imperial princes acting as *seviri* of the first
turma; the Seviral games, it may be conjectured, devolved exclusively on
this *turma*. It is possible too that in later times the first *turmae* alone were
formally organised and provided with *seviri*, while in the case of the other
equites equo publico this subdivision was discontinued.

Leaving out of view the contingents of the Italian and extra-Italian
subjects, the *equites equo publico* or *equites legionarii* alone composed the
ordinary cavalry of the Roman army; where *equites equo privato* occur,
the expression denotes bands of volunteers or of persons disrated.

the change gave rise; the young men of rank more and more withdrew from serving in the infantry, and the legionary cavalry became a close aristocratic corps. This enables us in some degree to understand why the equites during the Sicilian war refused to obey the order of the consul Gaius Aurelius Cotta that they should work at the trenches with the legionaries ($\frac{502}{252}$), and why Cato, when commander of the army in Spain, found himself under the necessity of addressing a severe reprimand to his cavalry. But this conversion of the burgess-cavalry into a mounted guard of nobles redounded not more decidedly to the injury of the commonwealth than to the advantage of the nobility, which acquired in the eighteen equestrian centuries a suffrage not merely distinct but giving the key-note to the rest.

Of a kindred character was the formal separation of the places assigned to the senatorial order from those occupied by the rest of the multitude as spectators at the national festivals. It was the great Scipio who effected this change in his second consulship in $\frac{560}{194}$. The national festival was as much an assembly of the people as were the centuries convoked for voting; and the circumstance that the former had no decrees to issue made the official announcement of a distinction between the ruling order and the body of subjects—which the separation implied—all the more significant. The innovation accordingly met with much censure even from the ruling class, because it was simply invidious and of no benefit, and because it gave a very obvious contradiction to the efforts of the wiser portion of the aristocracy to conceal their exclusive government under the forms of civil equality.

These circumstances explain why the censorship became the pivot of the later republican constitution; why an office, originally unimportant and on a level with the quaestorship, came to be invested with external insignia which did not at all naturally belong to it and with an altogether unique aristocratico-republican glory, and was viewed as the crown and completion of a well-conducted public career; and why the government looked upon every attempt of the opposition to introduce their men into this office, or even to hold the censor responsible to the people for his administration during or after his term of office, as an attack on their palladium, and presented a united front of resistance to every such attempt. It is sufficient in this respect to mention the storm which the candidature of Cato for the censorship provoked, and the measures, so extraordinarily reckless and in violation of all form, by which the senate prevented the judicial prosecution of the two unpopular censors of the year $\frac{550}{204}$. But with that enhancement of the glory of the censorship the government combined a characteristic distrust of this, their most important and for that very reason most dangerous, instrument. It was thoroughly necessary to leave to the censors absolute control over the personal composition of the senate and the equites; for the right of exclusion could not well be separated from the right of summoning, and it was desirable to retain such a right of exclusion not so much for the purpose of removing from the senate the able men of the opposition—a course which the smooth-going government of that age prudently avoided—as for the purpose of preserving around the aristocracy that moral halo, without which it must have speedily become a prey to the opposition. The right of rejection was retained; but what they chiefly needed was the glitter of the naked blade—the edge of it, which they feared, they took care to blunt. Besides the check involved in the nature of the office—under which the lists of the members of the aristocratic corporations were liable to revision not as formerly at any time, but only at intervals of five years—and besides the limitations resulting from the right of veto vested in the colleague and the right of cancelling vested in the successor, there was added a farther check which operated very powerfully; a usage equivalent to law made it the duty of the censor, on erasing from the list any senator or knight, to specify in writing the grounds for his decision, and thus ordinarily to adopt what was tantamount to a judicial procedure.

In this political position—mainly based on the senate, the equites, and the censorship—the nobility not only usurped in substance the government, but also remodelled the constitution according to their own views. It was part of their policy, with a view to keep up the importance of the public magistracies, to add to the number of these as little as possible, and to keep it far below what was required by the extension of territory and the increase of business. The most urgent exigencies were barely met by the division of the judicial functions hitherto discharged by a single praetor between two judges—one of whom tried the lawsuits between Roman burgesses, and the other those that arose between non-burgesses or between burgess and non-burgess—in $\frac{511}{243}$, and by the nomination of four auxiliary consuls for the four transmarine provinces of Sicily ($\frac{527}{227}$), Sardinia including Corsica ($\frac{527}{227}$), and Hither and Further Spain ($\frac{557}{197}$). The far too summary mode of instituting processes in

Rome, as well as the increasing influence of the official staff, are probably traceable in great measure to the practically inadequate numbers of the Roman magistracy.

Among the innovations originated by the government—which were none the less innovations, that in general they changed not the letter, but merely the practice of the existing constitution—the most prominent were the measures by which the appointment of officers as well as of civil magistrates was made to depend not, as the letter of the constitution allowed and its spirit required, simply on merit and ability, but on birth and seniority. As regards the nomination of staff-officers this was done not in form, but in substance. It had already, during the previous period, been in great part transferred from the general to the burgesses (i. 307); during this period the whole staff-officers of the regular yearly levy—the twenty-four military tribunes of the four ordinary legions—came to be nominated in the *comitia tributa*. Thus a line of demarcation more and more insurmountable was drawn between the subalterns, who gained their promotion from the general by punctual and brave service, and the staff, which obtained its privileged position by canvassing the burgesses (i. 434). With a view to check simply the worst abuses in this respect and to prevent young men quite untried from holding these important posts, it became necessary to require, as a preliminary to the bestowal of staff appointments, evidence of a certain number of years of service. Nevertheless, when once the military tribunate, the true pillar of the Roman military system, was prescribed as the first stepping-stone in the political career of the young aristocrats, the obligation of service inevitably came to be frequently eluded, and the election of officers became liable to all the evils of democratic canvassing and of aristocratic exclusiveness. It was a bitter commentary on the new institution, that in serious wars (as in $\frac{583}{171}$) it was found necessary to suspend the democratic mode of electing officers, and to recommit to the general the appointment of his staff.

In the case of civil officers, the first and chief object was to limit re-election to the supreme magistracies. This was certainly necessary, if the presidency of annual kings was not to be an empty name; and even in the preceding period re-election to the consulship was not permitted till after the lapse of ten years, while in the case of the censorship it was altogether forbidden (i. 310). No farther law was passed in the period before us; but an increased stringency in its application is obvious from the fact that, while the law as to the ten years' interval was suspended in $\frac{537}{217}$ during the continuance of the war in Italy, there was no farther dispensation from it afterwards, and indeed towards the close of this period re-election seldom occurred at all. Moreover, towards the end of this epoch ($\frac{574}{180}$) a decree of the people was issued, binding the candidates for public magistracies to apply for them in a fixed order of succession, and to observe certain intervals between the offices and certain limits of age. Custom, indeed, had long prescribed both of these; but it was a sensibly felt restriction of the freedom of election, when the customary qualification was raised into a legal requirement, and the liberty of disregarding such requirements in extraordinary cases was withdrawn from the electors. In general, admission to the senate was thrown open to persons belonging to the ruling families without distinction as to ability, while not only were the poorer and humbler ranks of the population utterly precluded from access to the offices of government, but all Roman burgesses not belonging to the hereditary aristocracy were practically excluded not indeed exactly from the senate, but from the two highest magistracies, the consulship and the censorship. After the case of Manius Curius (i. 304), no instance can be pointed out of a consul who did not belong to the social aristocracy, and probably no instance of the kind occurred at all. But the number of the *gentes* which appear for the first time in the lists of consuls and censors in the half-century from the beginning of the war with Hannibal to the close of that with Perseus is extremely limited; and by far the most of these, such as Flaminii, Terentii, Porcii, Acilii, and Laelii, may be referred to elections by the opposition, or are traceable to special aristocratic connections. The election of Gaius Laelius in $\frac{564}{190}$, for instance, was evidently due to the Scipios. The exclusion of the poorer classes from the government was, no doubt, required by the altered circumstances of the case. Now that Rome had ceased to be a purely Italian state and had adopted Hellenic culture, it was no longer possible to take a small farmer from the plough and to set him at the head of the community. But it was neither necessary nor beneficial that the elections should almost without exception be confined to the narrow circle of the curule houses, and that a " new man " should only be able to make his way into that circle by a sort of usurpation.[1] No doubt a certain hereditary character was

[1] The stability of the Roman aristocracy may be clearly traced, more especially in the case of the patrician *gentes*, by means of the consular and

inherent not merely in the institution of the senate, in so far as it rested from the first on a representation of the clans (i. 76), but in the nature of the aristocracy generally, in so far as statesmanly wisdom and statesmanly experience are bequeathed from the able father to the able son, and the inspiring spirit of an illustrious ancestry fans every noble spark within the human breast into a speedier and more brilliant flame. In this sense the Roman aristocracy had been at all times hereditary; in fact, it had displayed its hereditary character with great naïveté in the old custom of the senator taking his sons with him to the

aedilician Fasti. As is well known, the consulate was held by one patrician and one plebeian in each year from $\frac{388}{366}$ to $\frac{581}{173}$ (with the exception of the years $\frac{399}{355}$, $\frac{400}{354}$, $\frac{401}{353}$, $\frac{403}{351}$, $\frac{405}{349}$, $\frac{409}{345}$, $\frac{411}{343}$, in which both consuls were patricians). Moreover, the colleges of curule aediles were composed exclusively of patricians in the odd years of the Varronian reckoning, at least down to the close of the sixth century, and they are known for sixteen years, viz., $\frac{541}{213}$, $\frac{545}{209}$, $\frac{547}{207}$, $\frac{549}{205}$, $\frac{551}{203}$, $\frac{553}{201}$, $\frac{555}{199}$, $\frac{557}{197}$, $\frac{561}{193}$, $\frac{565}{189}$, $\frac{567}{187}$, $\frac{575}{179}$, $\frac{585}{169}$, $\frac{589}{165}$, $\frac{591}{163}$, $\frac{593}{161}$. These patrician consuls and aediles are, as respects their *gentes*, distributed as follows:—

	Consuls 388—500 366—254	Consuls 501—581 253—173	Curule aediles of those 16 patrician colleges
Cornelii	15	15	14
Valerii	10	8	4
Claudii	4	8	2
Aemilii	9	6	2
Fabii	6	6	1
Manlii	4	6	1
Postumii . . .	2	6	2
Servilii	3	4	—
Quinctii . . .	2	3	1
Furii	2	3	—
Sulpicii . . .	6	2	2
Veturii	—	2	—
Papirii	3	1	—
Nautii	2	—	—
Julii	1	—	1
Foslii	1	—	—
	70	70	32

Thus the fifteen or sixteen houses of the high nobility, that were powerful in the state at the time of the Licinian laws, maintained their ground without material change in their relative numbers—which no doubt were partly kept up by adoption—for the next two centuries, or, in fact, down to the end of the republic. To the circle of the plebeian nobility new *gentes* doubtless were from time to time added; but in the plebeian Fasti also the old houses, such as the Licinii, Fulvii, Atilii, Domitii, Marcii, Junii, predominate very decidedly throughout three centuries.

senate, and of the public magistrate decorating his sons, as it were by anticipation, with the insignia of the highest official honour—the purple border of the consular, and the golden amulet case of the triumphator.   But, while in the earlier period the hereditary character of the outward dignity had been to a certain extent borne out by the inheritance of intrinsic worth, and the senatorial aristocracy had guided the state not primarily by virtue of hereditary right, but by virtue of the highest of all rights of representation—the right of the superior, as contrasted with the mere ordinary, man—it sank in this epoch (and with specially great rapidity after the end of the Hannibalic war) from its original high position, as the aggregate of those in the community who were most experienced in counsel and action, into an order of lords filling up its ranks by hereditary succession, and exercising collegiate misrule.

Indeed, matters had already at this period reached such a height, that out of the evil of oligarchy there emerged the still worse evil of usurpation of power by particular families.   We have already spoken (p. 265) of the offensive family-policy of the conqueror of Zama, and of his unhappily successful efforts to cover with his own laurels the incapacity and pitifulness of his brother; and the nepotism of the Flaminini was, if possible, still more shameless and offensive than that of the Scipios. Absolute freedom of election in fact turned to the advantage of such coteries far more than of the electors.   The election of Marcus Valerius Corvus to the consulship at twenty-three had doubtless been for the benefit of the state; but now, when Scipio obtained the aedileship at twenty-three and the consulate at thirty, and Flamininus, while not yet thirty years of age, rose from the quaestorship to the consulship, such proceedings involved serious danger to the republic.   Things had already reached such a pass, that the only effective barrier against family rule and its consequences had to be sought in a government strictly oligarchical; and this was the reason why even the party otherwise opposed to the oligarchy agreed to the restriction imposed on absolute freedom of election.

The government bore the stamp of this gradual change in the spirit of the governing class.   It is true that the administration of external affairs was still pervaded at this epoch by the consistency and energy which had established the dominion of the Roman community over Italy.   During the severe disciplinary period of the Sicilian war the Roman aristocracy had gradually raised itself to the height of its new position; and if it uncon-

stitutionally usurped for the senate powers which by right fell
to be shared between the magistrates and the *comitia* alone, it
vindicated the step by its certainly far from brilliant, but sure
and steady, pilotage of the vessel of the state during the Hannibalic storm and the complications thence arising, and showed to
the world that the Roman senate was alone able, and in many
respects alone deserved, to rule the wide circle of the Italo-
Hellenic states. But admitting the noble attitude of the ruling
Roman senate in opposition to the external foe—an attitude
crowned with the noblest results—we may not overlook the fact,
that in the less conspicuous, but far more important and far
more difficult, administration of the internal affairs of the state
both the treatment of the existing arrangements and the new
institutions betray an almost opposite spirit, or, to speak more
correctly, indicate that the opposite tendency has already
acquired the predominance in this field.

In relation, first of all, to the individual burgess the government was no longer what it had been. The term " magistrate "
meant a man who was more than other men; and, if he was the
servant of the community, he was for that very reason the
master of every burgess. But the tightness of the rein was now
visibly relaxed. Where coteries and canvassing flourish as they
did in the Rome of that age, men are chary of forfeiting the good
services of their fellows or the favour of the multitude by stern
words and straightforward action. If now and then magistrates
appeared who displayed the gravity and the sternness of the
olden time, they were ordinarily, like Cotta ($\frac{502}{252}$) and Cato, new
men who had not sprung from the bosom of the ruling class. It
was even deemed something singular, when Paullus, who had
been named commander-in-chief against Perseus, instead of
tendering his thanks in the usual manner to the burgesses,
declared to them that he presumed they had chosen him as
general because they accounted him the most capable of command, and requested them accordingly not to help him to
command, but to be silent and obey.

The supremacy and hegemony of Rome in the territories of
the Mediterranean rested not least on the strictness of her
military discipline and administration of justice. Undoubtedly
she was still, on the whole, at that time infinitely superior in
these respects to the Hellenic, Phoenician, and Oriental states,
which were without exception thoroughly disorganised; nevertheless grave abuses were already occurring in Rome. We have
previously (p. 277 *et seq.*) pointed out how the wretched character

of the commanders-in-chief—and that not merely in the case
of demagogues chosen perhaps by the opposition, like Gaius
Flaminius and Gaius Varro, but of men who were good aristocrats—had already in the third Macedonian war imperilled the
interests of the state. And the mode in which justice was occasionally administered is shown by the scene in the camp of the
consul Lucius Quinctius Flamininus at Placentia ($\frac{562}{192}$). To
compensate a favourite youth for the gladiatorial games of the
capital, which through his attendance on the consul he had
missed the opportunity of seeing, that great lord had ordered a
Boian of rank who had taken refuge in the Roman camp to be
summoned, and had killed him at a banquet with his own hand.
Still worse than the occurrence itself, to which many parallels
might be adduced, was the fact that the perpetrator was not
brought to trial; and not only so, but when the censor Cato on
account of it erased his name from the roll of the senate, his
fellow-senators invited the expelled to resume his senatorial
stall in the theatre. He was, no doubt, a brother of the liberator
of the Greeks, and one of the most powerful coterie-leaders in
the senate.

The financial system of the Roman community also retro-
graded rather than advanced during this epoch. The amount
of their revenues, indeed, was visibly on the increase. The indirect taxes—there were no direct taxes in Rome—increased in
consequence of the enlargement of the Roman territory, which
rendered it necessary, for example, to institute new customs-
offices along the Campanian and Bruttian coasts at Puteoli,
Castra (Squillace), and elsewhere, in $\frac{555}{199}$ and $\frac{575}{179}$. The same
reason led to the new salt-tariff of $\frac{550}{204}$ fixing the scale of prices
at which salt was to be sold in the different districts of Italy, as
it was no longer possible to furnish salt at one and the same price
to the Roman burgesses now scattered throughout the land;
but, as the Roman government probably supplied the burgesses
with salt at cost price, if not below it, this financial measure
yielded no gain to the state. Still more considerable was the
increase in the product of the domains. The land-tax indeed,
which of right was payable to the treasury from the Italian
domain-lands granted for occupation, was in the great majority
of cases neither demanded nor paid. On the other hand the
scriptura was retained; and not only so, but the domains recently
acquired in the second Punic war, particularly the greater
portion of the territory of Capua and that of Leontini (pp. 138,
177), instead of being given up to occupation, were parcelled

out and let to petty temporary lessees, and the attempts at occupation made in these cases were opposed with more than usual energy by the government; by which means the state acquired a considerable and secure source of income. The mines of the state also, particularly the important Spanish mines, were turned to profit on lease. Lastly, the revenue was augmented by the tribute of the transmarine subjects. From extraordinary sources very considerable sums accrued during this epoch to the state treasury, particularly the produce of the spoil in the war with Antiochus, 200 millions of sesterces (£2,000,000), and that of the war with Perseus, 210 millions of sesterces (£2,100,000)—the latter, the largest sum in cash which ever came at one time into the Roman treasury.

But this increase of revenue was for the most part counterbalanced by the increasing expenditure. The provinces, Sicily perhaps excepted, probably cost nearly as much as they yielded; the expenditure on highways and other structures rose in proportion to the extension of territory; the repayment also of the advances (*tributa*) received from the freeholder burgesses during times of severe war formed a burden for many a year on the Roman treasury. To these fell to be added very considerable losses occasioned to the revenue by the mismanagement, negligence, or connivance of the supreme magistrates. Of the conduct of the officials in the provinces, of their luxurious living at the expense of the public purse, of their embezzlement more especially of the spoil, of the incipient system of bribery and extortion, we shall speak in the sequel. How the state fared generally as regarded the farming of its revenues and the contracts for supplies and buildings, may be inferred from the circumstance, that the senate resolved in $\frac{587}{167}$ to desist from the working of the Macedonian mines that had fallen to Rome, because the lessees of the minerals would either plunder the subject or cheat the exchequer—truly a naïve confession of impotence, in which the controlling board pronounced its own censure. Not only was the land-tax of the occupied domain-land allowed tacitly to fall into abeyance, as has been already mentioned, but private buildings in the capital and elsewhere were suffered to encroach on the public property, and the water from the public aqueducts was diverted to private purposes: great dissatisfaction was created on one occasion when the censor took serious steps against such trespassers, and compelled them either to desist from this exclusive use of the public property, or to pay the legal rate for the ground and water.

The conscience of the Romans, otherwise in economic matters so scrupulous, showed, so far as the state was concerned, a remarkable laxity. " He who steals from a burgess," said Cato, " ends his days in chains and fetters; but he who steals from the community ends them in gold and purple." If, notwithstanding the fact that the public property of the Roman community was fearlessly and with impunity plundered by officials and speculators, Polybius still lays stress on the rarity of embezzlement in Rome, while Greece could hardly produce a single official who had not touched the public money, and on the honesty with which a Roman commissioner or magistrate would upon his simple word of honour administer enormous sums, while in the case of the paltriest sum in Greece ten letters were sealed and twenty witnesses were required and yet everybody cheated, this merely implies that social and economic demoralisation had advanced much further in Greece than in Rome, and, in particular, that direct and palpable peculation was not as yet so flourishing in the one case as in the other. The general financial result is most clearly exhibited to us by the state of the public buildings, and by the amount of cash in the treasury. We find in times of peace a fifth, in times of war a tenth, of the revenues expended on public buildings; which, in the circumstances, does not seem to have been a very large outlay. With these sums, as well as with fines which were not directly payable into the treasury, much was doubtless done for the repair of the highways in and near the capital, for the formation of the chief Italian roads,[1] and for the construction of public buildings. Perhaps the most important of the building operations in the capital, known to belong to this period, was the great repair and extension of the network of sewers throughout the city, contracted for probably in $\frac{670}{184}$, for which 24,000,000 sesterces (£240,000) were set apart at once, and to which it may be presumed that the portions of the *cloacae* still extant, at least in the main, belong. To all appearance however, even apart from the severe pressure of war, this period was inferior to the last section of the preceding epoch in respect of public buildings; between $\frac{482}{272}$ and $\frac{607}{147}$ no new aqueduct was constructed at Rome. The treasure of the state, no doubt, increased; the last reserve in $\frac{545}{209}$, when they found themselves under the necessity of

---

[1] The expenses of these were, however, thrown mainly in all probability on the adjoining inhabitants. The old system of making requisitions of task-work was not abolished: it must not unfrequently have happened that the slaves of the landholders were called away to be employed in the construction of roads. (Cato, *de R. R.* 2.)

laying hands on it, amounted only to 4000 pounds of gold (£164,000; p. 162), whereas a short time after the close of this period ($\frac{597}{187}$) close on £860,000 in precious metals were stored in the treasury. But, when we take into account the enormous extraordinary revenues which in the generation after the close of the Hannibalic war came into the Roman treasury, the latter sum surprises us rather by its smallness than by its magnitude. So far as with the extremely meagre statements before us it may be allowable to speak of results, the finances of the Roman state exhibit doubtless an excess of income over expenditure, but are far from presenting a brilliant sum total.

The change in the spirit of the government was most distinctly apparent in the treatment of the Italian and extra-Italian subjects of the Roman community. Formerly there existed in Italy four distinct classes; the ordinary, and the Latin, allied communities, the Roman burgesses *sine suffragio*, and the burgesses with the full franchise. The third of these four classes disappeared during the course of this period, for the communities of passive burgesses either—as was the case with Capua especially—lost their Roman citizenship in consequence of the Hannibalic war, or one after another acquired the full franchise; so that at the close of this period there were no passive burgesses of Rome, except isolated individuals who were for special reasons excluded from the right of voting.

On the other hand there emerged a new class in a position of peculiar inferiority, deprived of municipal freedom and of the right to carry arms and to some extent treated almost like public slaves (*peregrini dediticii*); to which, in particular, the members of the former Campanian, southern Picentine, and Bruttian communities, that had been in alliance with Hannibal (p. 177), belonged. To these were added the Celtic tribes tolerated on the south side of the Alps, whose position in relation to the Italian confederacy is indeed only known imperfectly, but is sufficiently characterised as inferior by the clause embodied in their treaties of alliance with Rome, that no member of these communities should ever be allowed to acquire Roman citizenship (p. 182).

The position of the non-Latin allies had, as we have mentioned before (p. 178), undergone a change greatly to their disadvantage in consequence of the Hannibalic war. Only a few communities in this category, such as Neapolis, Nola, and Heraclea, had during all the vicissitudes of that war remained steadfastly on the Roman side, and therefore retained their former rights as allies unaltered; by far the greater portion were obliged in consequence of having changed sides to acquiesce in a revision of the existing treaties to their disadvantage. The reduced position of the non-Latin allies is attested by the emigration that set in from these towards the Latin communities: when in $\frac{677}{177}$ the Samnites and Paelignians applied to the senate for a reduction of their contingents, their request was based on the ground that of late years 4000 Samnite and Paelignian families had migrated to the Latin colony of Fregellae.

That the Latins—which term now denoted the few towns in old Latium that were not included in the Roman burgess-union, such as Tibur and Praeneste, the allied cities placed in law on the same footing with them, such as several of the Hernican towns, and the Latin colonies dispersed throughout Italy—were still at this time in a better position, is implied in their very name; but they too suffered, in proportion, not much less injuriously. The burdens imposed on them were unjustly increased, and the pressure of military service was more and more transferred from the burgesses to the Latin and other Italian allies. For instance, in 536, nearly twice as many of the allies were called out as of the burgesses: after the end of the Hannibalic war all the burgesses received their discharge, but not all the allies; the latter were chiefly employed for garrison duty and for the odious service in Spain. In the triumphal largess of $\frac{677}{177}$ the allies received not as formerly an equal share with the burgesses, but only the half, so that amidst the unrestrained rejoicing of that soldiers' carnival the divisions thus treated as inferior followed the chariot of victory in sullen silence: in the assignations of land in northern Italy the burgesses received ten *iugera* of arable land each, the non-burgesses three *iugera* each. That liberty of migration was no longer granted to the Latin communities founded after $\frac{486}{268}$, has been already observed (i. 417). It was retained in law by the older Latin cities; but the crowding of their burgesses to Rome, and the complaints of their magistrates as to the increasing depopulation of the cities and the impossibility under such circumstances of furnishing the due contingent, led the Roman government to allow those Latins only to exercise their right of migration when the emigrant left behind children of his own in his native city; and, in conformity with this principle, police-ejections from the capital were carried out to a great extent $\left(\frac{567}{187}, \frac{577}{177}\right)$. The measure might be unavoidable, but it was none the less felt as a material restriction of the right of free migration accorded by treaty to the allied cities. Moreover, the towns founded by Rome in the interior of Italy began towards the close of this period to receive instead of Latin rights the full franchise, which previously had only been given to the maritime colonies; and the enlargement of the Latin body by the accession of new communities, which hitherto had gone on so regularly, thus came to an end. Aquileia, the establishment of which began in $\frac{571}{183}$, was the latest of the Italian colonies of Rome that received Latin rights; the full franchise was given to the colonies, sent forth nearly at the same time, of Potentia, Pisaurum, Parma, Mutina, and Luna ($\frac{570-577}{184-177}$). The reason for this evidently lay in the decline of the Latin as compared with the Roman franchise. The colonists conducted to the new settlements were always, and now more than ever, chosen in preponderating number from the Roman burgesses; and among the very poorer class of these there was no longer found any one willing, even for the acquisition of considerable material advantages, to exchange his rights as a burgess for those of a Latin.

Lastly, in the case of non-burgesses—communities as well as individuals—admission to the Roman franchise was almost completely foreclosed. The earlier course of incorporating the subject communities in that of Rome had been dropped about $\frac{400}{350}$, that the Roman burgess-body might not be too much decentralised by its undue extension; and therefore communities of half-burgesses were instituted (i. 418). Now the centralisation of the community was abandoned, partly through the admission of the half-burgess communities to the full franchise, partly through the accession of numerous more remote burgess-colonies to its ranks; but the older system of incorporation was not resumed. It cannot be shown that after the complete subjugation of Italy even a single Italian community exchanged its position as an ally for the Roman franchise; probably none after that date in reality acquired it. But even the transition of individual Italians to the Roman franchise was at this epoch rendered considerably more difficult, especially by the limitation of the liberty of migration which was in law associated with the passive franchise; and it was confined almost wholly to the case of magistrates of the Latin communities (i. 417) and of non-burgesses admitted, by special favour towards themselves individually, on the founding of burgess-colonies.[1]

---

[1] Thus, as is well known, Ennius of Rudiae received burgess-rights from one of the triumvirs, Q. Fulvius Nobilior, on occasion of the founding of the burgess-colonies of Potentia and Pisaurum (Cic. *Brut.* 20, 79); where-

It cannot be denied that these changes *de facto* and *de jure* in the relations of the Italian subjects exhibit at least an intimate connection and consistency. The situation of the subject classes was throughout deteriorated in proportion to the gradations previously subsisting, and, while the government had formerly endeavoured to soften the distinctions and to provide means of transition from one to another, now the intermediate links were everywhere set aside and the connecting bridges were broken down. As within the Roman burgess-body the ruling class separated itself from the people, uniformly evaded public burdens, and uniformly appropriated honours and advantages, so the burgesses in their turn asserted their distinction from the Italian confederacy, and excluded it more and more from the joint enjoyment of power, while transferring to it a double or triple share in the common burdens. As the nobility, in relation to the plebeians, returned to the close exclusiveness of the declining patriciate, so did the burgesses in relation to the non-burgesses; the plebeiate, which had become great through the liberality of its institutions, now wrapped itself up in the rigid maxims of patricianism. The abolition of the passive burgesses cannot in itself be censured, and, so far as concerned the motive which led to it, belonged in all probability to another category to be mentioned afterwards; but through its abolition an intermediate connecting link was lost. Far more fraught with peril, however, was the disappearance of the distinction between the Latin and the other Italian communities. The privileged position of the Latin nation in Italy was the foundation of the Roman power; that foundation gave way, when the Latin towns began to feel that they were no longer privileged partakers in the dominion of the powerful cognate community, but substantially subjects of Rome like the rest, and when all the Italians began to find their position equally intolerable. It is true, that there were still distinctions: the Bruttians and their companions in misery were treated exactly like slaves and conducted themselves accordingly, deserting, for instance, from the fleet in which they served as galley-slaves, whenever they

upon, according to the well-known custom, he adopted the *praenomen* of the latter. The non-burgesses who were sent to take part in the foundation of a burgess-colony, did not, at least in this epoch, through that circumstance acquire *de jure* Roman citizenship, although they frequently laid claim to it (Liv. xxxiv. 42); but the magistrates charged with the founding of a colony were empowered, by a clause in the decree of the people relative to each case, to confer burgess-rights on a certain number of persons (Cic. *pro Balb.* 21, 48).

could, and gladly taking service against Rome; and the Celtic, and above all the transmarine, subjects formed a class still more oppressed than the Italians were—a class intentionally abandoned by the government to contempt and maltreatment at the hands of the Italians. But such distinctions, while implying a gradation of classes among the subjects, could not in reason afford a compensation for the earlier contrast between the cognate, and the alien, Italian subjects. A profound dissatisfaction prevailed through the whole Italian confederacy, and fear alone prevented it from finding expression. The proposal made in the senate after the battle at Cannae, to give the Roman franchise and a seat in the senate to two men from each Latin community, was made at an unseasonable time, and was rightly rejected; but it shows the apprehension with which men in the ruling community even then viewed the relations between Latium and Rome. Had a second Hannibal now carried the war into Italy, it may be doubted whether he would have again been thwarted by the steadfast resistance of the Latin name to a foreign domination.

But by far the most important institution which this epoch introduced into the Roman commonwealth, and that at the same time which involved the most decided and fatal deviation from the course hitherto pursued, was the new provincial magistracies. The earlier state-law of Rome knew nothing of tributary subjects: the conquered communities were either sold into slavery, or merged in the Roman commonwealth, or admitted to an alliance which secured to them at least communal independence and freedom from taxation. But the Carthaginian possessions in Sicily, Sardinia, and Spain, as well as the kingdom of Hiero, had paid tithe and tribute to their former masters: if Rome was desirous of retaining these possessions at all, it was in the judgment of the short-sighted the most judicious, and undoubtedly the most convenient, course to manage the new territories entirely in accordance with the rules heretofore observed. Accordingly the Romans simply retained the Carthagino-Hieronic provincial constitution, and organised in accordance with it those provinces also, such as Hither Spain, which they wrested from the barbarians. It was the shirt of Nessus which they inherited from the enemy. Beyond doubt at first the Roman government intended, in imposing taxes on their subjects, not strictly to enrich themselves, but only to cover the cost of administration and defence; but they deviated from this course, when they made Macedonia and Illyria tributary without undertaking the government or the guardianship of the frontier there. The fact, however, that they still maintained moderation in the imposition of burdens was of little consequence as compared with the conversion of their sovereignty into a profitable privilege at all; the fall was the same, whether a single apple was taken or the tree was plundered.

Punishment followed in the steps of wrong. The new provincial system necessitated the appointment of governors, whose position was absolutely incompatible not only with the welfare of the provinces, but with the Roman constitution. As the Roman community in the provinces took the place of the former rulers of the land, so the governor appeared there in the position of a king; the Sicilian praetor, for example, resided in the palace of Hiero at Syracuse. It is true, that the governor was nevertheless bound by law to administer his office with republican honesty and frugality. Cato, when governor of Sardinia, appeared in the towns subject to him on foot and attended by a single servant who carried his coat and sacrificial ladle; and, when he returned from his Spanish governorship, he sold his war horse beforehand, because he did not hold himself entitled to charge the state with the expenses of its transport. There is no question that the Roman governors—although certainly but few of them pushed their conscientiousness, like Cato, to the verge of being niggardly and ridiculous—made in many cases a powerful impression on the subjects, more especially on the frivolous and unstable Greeks, by their ancestral piety, by the reverential quietness prevailing at their assemblies, by their comparatively upright administration of office and of justice, especially by their proper severity towards the worst oppressors of the provincials—the Roman revenue-farmers and bankers—and in general by the gravity and dignity of their deportment. The provincials found their government comparatively tolerable. They had not been pampered by their former Carthaginian governors and Syracusan masters, and they were soon to find occasion for recalling with gratitude the present rods as compared with the coming scorpions: it is easy to understand how, in later times, the sixth century of the city appeared as the golden era of provincial rule. But it was not practicable for any length of time to be at once republican and king. Playing the part of governors demoralised the Roman ruling class with fearful rapidity. Haughtiness and arrogance towards the provincials were so natural in the circumstances, as scarcely to form matter of reproach against the individual magistrate. But already it was a rare thing—and the rarer, because the government adhered rigidly to the old principle of not paying public officials—that a governor returned with quite clean hands from his province; it was already remarked upon as something singular that Paullus, the conqueror of Pydna, did not take money. The bad custom of delivering to the governor "honorary wine" and other "voluntary" gifts seems as old as the provincial constitution itself, and may perhaps have been a legacy from the Carthaginians; even Cato in his administration of Sardinia in $\frac{556}{198}$ had to content himself with regulating and moderating such dues. The right of the magistrates, and of those travelling on the business of the state generally, to free quarters and free conveyance was already employed as a pretext for exactions. The more important right of the magistrate to make requisitions of grain from his province—partly for the maintenance of himself and his retinue (*in cellam*), partly for the provisioning of the army in case of war or on other special occasions—at a fair valuation was already so scandalously abused, that on the complaint of the Spaniards the senate in $\frac{583}{171}$ found it necessary to withdraw from the governors the right of fixing the price of the supplies for either purpose (p. 198). Requisitions had begun to be made on the subjects even for the popular festivals in Rome; the unmeasured vexatious demands made on the Italian as well as extra-Italian communities by the aedile Tiberius Sempronius Gracchus, for the festival which he had to provide, induced the senate officially to interfere ($\frac{572}{182}$). The liberties which Roman magistrates at the close of this period allowed themselves to take not only with the unhappy subjects, but even with the dependent free-states and kingdoms, are illustrated by the raids of Gaius Volso in Asia Minor (p. 255), and especially by the scandalous proceedings in Greece during the war with Perseus (p. 277 *et seq.*).

The government had no right to be surprised at such things, for it provided no serious check on the excesses of this capricious military administration. Judicial control, it is true, was not entirely wanting. Although, according to the universal but more than questionable rule of allowing no complaint to be brought against a commander-in-chief during his term of office (i. 251), the Roman governor could ordinarily be called to account only after the mischief had been done, yet he was amenable both to a criminal and to a civil prosecution. In order to the institution of the former, some Roman magistrate who possessed criminal jurisdiction had to undertake the case and bring it before the bar of the people; the civil action was remitted by the senator who administered the corresponding praetorship to a jury appointed, according to the constitution of the tribunal in those times, from the ranks of the senate.   In both cases, therefore, the control lay in the hands of the ruling class, and, although the latter was still sufficiently upright and honourable not absolutely to set aside well-founded complaints, and the senate even in several instances, at the call of those aggrieved, condescended itself to order the institution of a civil process, yet the complaints of poor men and foreigners against powerful members of the ruling aristocracy—submitted to judges and jurymen far remote from the scene and, if not involved in the like guilt, at least belonging to the same order as the accused—could from the first only reckon on success in the event of the wrong being clear and crying; and to complain in vain was almost certain destruction.   The aggrieved no doubt found a sort of support in the hereditary relations of clientship, which the subject cities and provinces were wont to enter into with their conquerors and other Romans who had been brought into contact with them.   The Spanish governors felt that no one could with impunity maltreat the clients of Cato; and the circumstance that the representatives of the three nations conquered by Paullus—the Spaniards, Ligurians, and Macedonians—would not forego the privilege of carrying his bier to the funeral pile, was the noblest dirge in honour of that noble man. But not only did this special protection give the Greeks opportunity to display in Rome all their talent for abasing themselves in presence of their masters, and to demoralise even those masters by their ready servility—the decrees of the Syracusans in honour of Marcellus, after he had destroyed and plundered their city and they had complained of his conduct to the senate in vain, form one of the most scandalous pages in the far from honourable annals of Syracuse—but, in connection with the dangers of a family policy, this patronage on the part of great houses had also its politically perilous side.   In this way the result was that the Roman magistrates in some degree feared the gods and the senate, and for the most part were moderate in their plundering; but still they plundered, and did so with impunity provided they observed such moderation.   The mischievous rule became established, that in the case of minor exactions and moderate violence the Roman magistrate acted in some measure within his sphere and was in law exempt from punishment, so that those who were aggrieved had to keep silence; and from this rule succeeding ages did not fail to draw the fatal consequences.

Nevertheless, even though the tribunals had been as strict as they were lax, the liability to a judicial reckoning could only check the worst evils. The true security for a good administration lay in a strict and uniform supervision by the supreme administrative authority: and this the senate utterly failed to provide. It was in this respect that the laxity and helplessness of the collegiate government became earliest apparent. By right the governors ought to have been subjected to an oversight far more strict and more special than had sufficed for the Italian municipal administration; and now, when the empire embraced great transmarine territories, the arrangements, through which the government preserved to itself the supervision of the whole, ought to have undergone a corresponding expansion. In both respects the reverse was the case. The governors ruled virtually as sovereign; and the most important of the institutions serving for the latter purpose, the census of the empire, was extended to Sicily alone, not to any of the provinces subsequently acquired. This emancipation of the supreme administrative officials from the central authority was more than hazardous. The Roman governor, placed at the head of the armies of the state, and in possession of considerable financial resources; subject to but a lax judicial control, and practically independent of the supreme administration; and impelled by a sort of necessity to separate the interests of himself and of the people whom he governed from those of the Roman community and to treat them as conflicting, far more resembled a Persian satrap than one of the commissioners of the Roman senate at the time of the Samnite wars. The man, moreover, who had just conducted a legalised military tyranny abroad, could with difficulty find his way back to the common civic level, which distinguished between those who commanded and those who obeyed, but not between masters and slaves. Even the government felt that their two fundamental principles—equality within the aristocracy, and the subordination of the power of the magistrates to the senatorial college—began in this instance to give way in their hands. The aversion of the government to the acquisition of new provinces and to the whole provincial system; the institution of the provincial quaestorships, which were intended to take at least the financial power out of the hands of the governors; and the abolition of the arrangement —in itself so judicious—for lengthening the tenure of such offices (p. 198), very clearly evince the anxiety felt by the more far-seeing of the Roman statesmen as to the fruits of the seed thus sown. But diagnosis is not cure. The internal government of the nobility continued to follow the direction once given to it; and the decay of the administration and of the financial system—the precursor of future revolutions and usurpations—steadily pursued its course, if not unnoticed, yet unchecked.

If the new nobility was less strictly defined than the old aristocracy of the clans, and if, while the one encroached on the rest of the burgesses as respected the joint enjoyment of political rights *de jure*, the other only did so *de facto*, the second form of inferiority was for these very reasons worse to bear and worse to throw off than the first. Attempts were, as a matter of course, made to throw it off. The opposition rested on the support of the public assembly, as the nobility did on the senate: in order to understand the opposition, we must first describe the spirit of the burgesses during this period and their position in the commonwealth.

Whatever could be demanded of an assembly of burgesses like the Roman, which was not the motive power, but the firm foundation, of the whole machinery—a sure perception of the common good, a sagacious deference towards the right leader, a steadfast spirit in presperous and evil days, and, above all, the capacity of sacrificing the individual for the general welfare and the comfort of the present for the advantage of the future—all these qualities the Roman community exhibited in so high a degree that, when we look to its conduct as a whole, all censure is lost in reverent admiration. Even now good sense and discretion still thoroughly predominated. The whole conduct of the burgesses with reference to the government as well as to the opposition shows very clearly that the same mighty patriotism before which even the genius of Hannibal had to quit the field prevailed also in the Roman comitia. No doubt they often erred; but their errors originated not in the mischievous impulses of a rabble, but in the narrow-minded views of burgesses and farmers. The machinery, however, by means of which the burgesses influenced the course of public affairs became certainly more and more unwieldy, and the circumstances in which they were placed through their own great deeds far outgrew their power to deal with them. We have already stated, that in the course of this epoch most of the former communities of passive burgesses, as well as a considerable number of newly established colonies, received the full Roman franchise (pp. 311, 313). At the

close of this period the Roman burgess-body, in a tolerably
compact mass, occupied Latium in its widest sense, Sabina, and
a part of Campania, so that it reached on the west coast northward to Caere and southward to Cumae; within this district
there were only a few cities not included in it, such as Tibur,
Praeneste, Signia, Norba, and Ferentinum. To this fell to be
added the maritime colonies on the coasts of Italy which uniformly possessed the full Roman franchise, the Picenian and
Trans-Apennine colonies of most recent foundation to which the
franchise had to be conceded (p. 313), and a very considerable
number of Roman burgesses, who, without forming separate
communities in a strict sense, were dispersed throughout Italy
in market-villages and hamlets (*fora et conciliabula*). To some
extent the unwieldiness of a civic community so constituted was
remedied, as regarded purposes of justice [1] and of administration, by the deputy judges previously mentioned (i. 418); and
already perhaps the maritime (i. 430) and the new Picenian and
Trans-Apennine colonies exhibited at least the first lineaments
of the system under which afterwards smaller urban communities were organised within the great city-commonwealth
of Rome. But in all political questions the general assembly
in the Roman Forum was alone entitled to act. It is obvious
at a glance, that this assembly was no longer, in its composition
or in its collective action, what it had been when all the persons
entitled to vote could exercise their privilege as citizens by
leaving their farms in the morning and returning home the same
evening. Moreover the government—whether from want of
judgment, from negligence, or from any evil design, we cannot
tell—no longer enrolled the communities admitted to the
franchise after $\frac{513}{241}$ in newly instituted tribes, but entered them
in the old; so that gradually each tribe came to be composed of
different townships scattered over the whole Roman territory.
Tribes such as these, containing on an average 8000—the urban
naturally having more, the rural fewer—persons entitled to vote,
without local connection or inward unity, no longer admitted of
any definite leading or of any satisfactory previous deliberation;

[1] In Cato's treatise on husbandry, which, as is well known, primarily
relates to an estate in the district of Venafrum, the judicial discussion of
such processes as might arise is referred to Rome only as respects one
definite case; namely, that in which the landlord leases the winter pasture
to the owner of a flock of sheep, and thus has to deal with a lessee who, as
a rule, is not domiciled in the district (c. 149). It may be inferred from
this, that in ordinary cases, where the contract was with a person domiciled
in the district, such processes as might arise were even in Cato's time
decided not at Rome, but before the local judges.

disadvantages which must have been the more felt, that the voting itself was not preceded by any free debate. Moreover, while the burgesses had quite sufficient capacity to discern their municipal interests, it was foolish and utterly ridiculous to leave the decision of the highest and most difficult questions which the power that ruled the world had to solve to a well-disposed but fortuitous concourse of Italian farmers, and to allow the nomination of generals and the conclusion of treaties of state to be finally judged of by people who understood neither the grounds nor the consequences of their decrees. In all matters transcending mere municipal affairs the Roman popular assemblies accordingly played a childish and even silly part. As a rule, the people stood and assented to all proposals; and, when in exceptional instances they of their own impulse refused their sanction, as on occasion of the declaration of war against Macedonia in $\frac{554}{200}$ (p. 218), the policy of the market-place certainly made a pitiful opposition—and with a pitiful issue— to the policy of the state.

At length the rabble of clients assumed a position, formally of equality and often even, practically, of superiority, alongside of the class of independent burgesses. The institutions in which it originated were of great antiquity. From time immemorial the Roman of quality exercised a sort of government over his freedmen and dependents, and was consulted by them in all their more important affairs; a client, for instance, was careful not to give his children in marriage without having obtained the consent of his patron, and very often the latter directly arranged the match. But as the aristocracy became converted into a special ruling class concentrating in its hands not only power but wealth, the clients became parasites and beggars; and these new partisans of the rich undermined outwardly and inwardly the burgess class. The aristocracy not only tolerated this sort of clientship, but worked it financially and politically for their own advantage. Thus, for instance, the old penny collections, which hitherto had taken place chiefly for religious purposes or in connection with the burial of men of merit, were now employed by lords of high standing—for the first time by Lucius Scipio, in $\frac{568}{186}$, on pretext of a popular festival which he had in contemplation—for the purpose of levying on extraordinary occasions a contribution from the public. Presents were specially placed under legal restriction (in $\frac{550}{204}$), because the senators began under that name to take regular tribute from their clients. But the retinue of clients was above all serviceable to the ruling class as a means of commanding the comitia; and the issue of the elections shows clearly how powerfully the dependent rabble already at this epoch counteracted the influence of the independent middle class.

The very rapid increase of the rabble in the capital particularly, which these facts serve to indicate, is also demonstrable otherwise. The increasing number and importance of the freedmen are shown by the very serious discussions that arose in the previous century (i. 306), and were continued during the present, as to their right to vote in the public assemblies, and by the remarkable resolution, adopted by the senate during the Hannibalic war, to admit honourable freedwomen to a participation in the public collections, and to grant to the legitimate children of manumitted fathers the insignia hitherto belonging only to the children of the free-born (p. 296). The majority of the Hellenes and Orientals who settled in Rome were probably little better than the freedmen, for national servility clung as indelibly to the former as legal servility to the latter.

But not only did these natural causes operate to produce a metropolitan rabble: neither the nobility nor the demagogues, moreover, can be acquitted from the reproach of having systematically nursed its growth, and of having undermined, so far as in them lay, the old public spirit by flattery of the people and things still worse. The electors as a body were still too respectable to admit of direct electoral corruption showing itself on a great scale; but the favour of those entitled to vote was indirectly courted by methods far from commendable. The old obligation of the magistrates, particularly of the aediles, to see that corn could be procured at a moderate price and to superintend the games, began to degenerate into the state of things which at length gave rise to the horrible cry of the city populace under the empire, " Bread for nothing and games for ever! " Large supplies of grain, either placed by the provincial governors at the disposal of the Roman market officials, or delivered at Rome free of cost by the provinces themselves for the purpose of procuring favour with particular Roman magistrates, enabled the aediles, from the middle of the sixth century, to furnish grain to the population of the capital at very low prices. " It was no wonder," Cato considered, " that the burgesses no longer listened to good advice—the belly had no ears."

Popular amusements increased to an alarming extent. For five hundred years the community had been content with one festival in the year, and with one circus. The first Roman demagogue by profession, Gaius Flaminius, added a second festival and a second circus ($\frac{534}{220}$);[1] and by these institutions—the tendency of which is sufficiently indicated by the very name of the new festival, " the plebeian games "—he probably purchased the permission to give battle at the Trasimene lake. When the path was once opened, the evil made rapid progress. The festival in honour of Ceres, the goddess who protected the plebeian order (i. 273), must have been but little, if at all, later than the plebeian games. On the suggestion of the Sibylline and Marcian prophecies, moreover, a fourth festival was added in $\frac{542}{212}$ in honour of Apollo, and a fifth in $\frac{550}{204}$ in honour of the " Great Mother " recently transplanted from Phrygia to Rome. These were the severe years of the Hannibalic war—on the first celebration of the Apollinarian games the burgesses were summoned from the circus itself to arms; the superstitious fear peculiar to Italy was feverishly excited, and persons were not wanting who took advantage of the opportunity to circulate Sibylline and prophetic oracles and to recommend themselves to the people through the medium of their contents and advocacy: we can scarcely blame the government, which was obliged to call for so enormous sacrifices from the burgesses, for yielding in such matters. But what was once conceded had to be continued; indeed, even in more peaceful times ($\frac{581}{173}$) there was added another festival, although of minor importance—the games in honour of Flora. The cost of these new festal amusements was defrayed by the magistrates entrusted with the exhibition of the respective festivals from their own means: thus the curule aediles had, over and above the old national festival, those of the Mother of the Gods and of Flora; the plebeian aediles had the plebeian festival and that of Ceres, and the urban praetor the Apollinarian games. Those who sanctioned the new festivals perhaps excused themselves in their own eyes by the reflection that they were not at any rate a burden on the public purse; but it would have been in reality far less injurious to burden the public budget with a number of useless expenses, than to allow the furnishing of an amusement for the people to become practically a qualification for holding the highest office in the state. The future candidates for the con-

[1] The building of the circus is attested. Respecting the origin of the plebeian games there is no ancient tradition (for what is said by the Pseudo-Asconius, p. 143, *Orell.* is not such); but seeing that they were celebrated in the Flaminian circus (Val. Max. i. 7, 4), and first certainly occur in $\frac{538}{216}$, four years after it was built (Liv. xxiii. 30), what we have stated above is sufficiently proved.

sulship soon entered into a mutual rivalry in their expenditure on these games, which incredibly increased their cost; and of course it was no injury to the interests of the consul expectant, if he gave, over and above this as it were legal contribution, a voluntary " performance " (*munus*), a gladiatorial show at his own expense for the public benefit.   The splendour of the games became gradually the standard by which the electors measured the fitness of the candidates for the consulship.   The nobility had, in truth, to pay dear for their honours—a gladiatorial show on a respectable scale cost 720,000 sesterces (£7200)—but they paid willingly, since by this means they absolutely precluded men who were not wealthy from a political career.

Corruption, however, was not restricted to the Forum; it was transferred even to the camp.   The old burgess militia had reckoned themselves fortunate when they brought home a compensation for their labour in war, and, in the event of success, a trifling gift as a memorial of victory.   The new generals, with Scipio Africanus at their head, lavishly scattered amongst their troops the money of Rome as well as the proceeds of the spoil: it was on this point that Cato quarrelled with Scipio during the last campaigns against Hannibal in Africa. The veterans of the second Macedonian and the Asiatic war already returned home throughout as wealthy men: even the better class began to commend a general, who did not appropriate the gifts of the provincials and the gains of war entirely to himself and his immediate followers, and from whose camp not a few men returned with gold, and many with silver, in their pockets: men began to forget that the movable spoil was the property of the state.   When Lucius Paullus again dealt with it in the old mode, his own soldiers, especially the volunteers who had been allured in numbers by the prospect of rich plunder, were on the point of refusing to decree to the victor of Pydna the honour of a triumph—an honour which they threw away on every one who had subjugated three Ligurian villages.

How much the military discipline and the martial spirit of the burgesses suffered from this conversion of war into a traffic in plunder, may be traced in the campaigns against Perseus; and the spread of cowardice was manifested in a way almost scandalous during the insignificant Istrian war (in $\frac{576}{178}$).   On occasion of a trifling skirmish magnified by rumour to gigantic dimensions, the land army and the naval force of the Romans, and even the Italians at home, took to flight, and Cato found it necessary to address a special reproof to his countrymen for their cowardice. In this too the youth of quality took precedence. Already during the Hannibalic war ($\frac{545}{209}$) the censors found occasion to visit with severe penalties the indolence of those who were bound to serve in the equestrian ranks. Towards the close of this period ($\frac{574}{180}$?) a decree of the people prescribed evidence of ten years' service as a qualification for holding any public magistracy, with a view to compel the sons of the nobility to enter the army.

But perhaps nothing so clearly evinces the decline of genuine pride and genuine honour in high and low alike as the hunting after insignia and titles, which appeared under different forms of expression, but with substantial identity of character, among all ranks and classes. So urgent was the demand for the honour of a triumph that there was difficulty in upholding the old rule, which accorded a triumph only to the ordinary supreme magistrate who augmented the power of the state in open battle, and thus, it is true, not unfrequently excluded from that honour the very authors of the most important successes. There was a necessity for acquiescence, while those generals, who had in vain solicited, or had no prospect of attaining, a triumph from the senate or the burgesses, marched in triumph on their own account at least to the Alban Mount (first in $\frac{523}{231}$). No combat with a Ligurian or Corsican horde was too insignificant to be made a pretext for demanding a triumph. In order to put an end to the trade of peaceful triumphators, such as were the consuls of $\frac{577}{181}$, the granting of a triumph was made to depend on the producing proof of a pitched battle which had cost the lives of at least 5000 of the enemy; but this proof was frequently evaded by false bulletins—already in houses of quality many an enemy's armour might be seen to glitter, which had by no means come thither from the field of battle. While formerly the commander-in-chief of the one year had been proud in that which followed to enter the staff of his successor, the fact that the consular Cato took service as a military tribune under Tiberius Sempronius Longus ($\frac{560}{194}$) and Manius Glabrio ($\frac{563}{191}$; p. 246), was now regarded as a demonstration against the new-fashioned arrogance. Formerly the thanks of the community once for all had sufficed for service rendered to the state: now every meritorious act seemed to demand a permanent distinction. Already Gaius Duilius, the victor of Mylae ($\frac{494}{260}$), had gained an exceptional permission that, when he walked in the evening through the streets of the capital, he should be preceded by a torch-bearer and a piper. Statues and monuments, very often erected at the expense of the person whom they purported to honour, became so common, that it was ironically pronounced a distinction to have none. But such merely personal honours did not long suffice. A custom came into vogue, by which the victor and his descendants derived a permanent surname from the victories they had won—a custom mainly established by the victor of Zama who got himself designated as the hero of Africa, his brother as the hero of Asia, and his cousin as the hero of Spain.[1] The example set by the higher was followed by the humbler classes. When the ruling order did not disdain to settle the funeral arrangements for different ranks and to decree to the man who had been censor a purple winding-sheet, it could not complain of the freedmen for desiring that their sons at any rate might be decorated with the much envied purple border. The robe, the ring, and the amulet-case distinguished not only the burgess and the burgess's wife from the foreigner and the slave, but also the person who was free-born from one who had been a slave, the son of free-born, from the son of manumitted, parents, the son of the knight and the senator from the common burgess, the descendant of a curule house from the common senator (p. 296)—and this in a community where all that was great and good was the work of civil equality!

The dissension in the community was reflected in the ranks of the opposition. Resting on the support of the farmers, the patriots raised a loud cry for reform; resting on the support of the mob in the capital, demagogism began its work. Although the two tendencies do not admit of being wholly separated but in various respects go hand in hand, it will be necessary to consider them apart.

The party of reform emerges, as it were, personified in Marcus Porcius Cato ($\frac{520-605}{234-149}$). Cato, the last statesman of note belonging to that earlier system which restricted its ideas to Italy and was averse to schemes of universal empire, was for that reason accounted in after times the model of a genuine Roman of the antique stamp; he may with greater justice be regarded as the representative of the opposition of the Roman middle class to the new Hellenico-cosmopolite nobility. Brought up at the plough, he was induced to enter on a political career

[1] P. 265. The first certain instance of such a surname is that of Manius Valerius Maximus, consul in $\frac{491}{263}$, who, as conqueror of Messana, assumed the name Messalla (p. 329): that the consul of $\frac{419}{335}$ was, in a similar manner, called Calenus, is an error. The surname of Maximus in the Valerian *gens* (i. 270) is not precisely analogous with the same surname in the Fabian (i. 306).

by a neighbouring proprietor, one of the few nobles who kept aloof from the tendencies of the age, Lucius Valerius Flaccus. That upright patrician deemed the rough Sabine farmer the proper man to stem the current of the times; and he was not deceived in his estimate. Beneath the aegis of Flaccus, and after the good old fashion serving his fellow-citizens and the commonwealth in counsel and action, Cato fought his way up to the consulate and a triumph, and even to the censorship. Having in his seventeenth year entered the burgess-army, he had passed through the whole Hannibalic war from the battle on the Trasimene lake to that of Zama; had served under Marcellus and Fabius, under Nero and Scipio; and at Tarentum and Sena, in Africa, Sardinia, Spain, and Macedonia, had shown equal ability as a soldier, a staff-officer, and a general. He was the same in the Forum, as in the battle-field. His prompt and intrepid address, his rough but pungent rustic wit, his knowledge of Roman law and Roman affairs, his incredible activity and his iron frame, first brought him into notice in the neighbouring towns; and, when at length he made his appearance on the greater arena of the Forum and the senate-house in the capital, constituted him the most influential pleader and political orator of his time. He took up the key-note first struck by Manius Curius, his ideal among Roman statesmen (i. 303): throughout his long life he made it his task honestly, to the best of his judgment, to assail on all hands the prevailing declension; and even in his eighty-fifth year he battled in the Forum with the new spirit of the times. He was anything but comely—he had green eyes, his enemies alleged, and red hair—and he was not a great man, still less a far-seeing statesman. Thoroughly narrow in his political and moral views, and having the ideal of the good old times always before his eyes and on his lips, he cherished an obstinate contempt for everything new. Deeming himself entitled by virtue of his own austere life to manifest an unrelenting severity and harshness towards everything and everybody; upright and honourable, but without a glimpse of any duty beyond the sphere of police discipline and of mercantile integrity; an enemy to all villainy and vulgarity as well as to all genius and refinement, and above all things a foe to those who were his foes; he never made an attempt to stop evils at their source, but waged war throughout life against mere symptoms, and especially against persons. The ruling lords, no doubt, looked down with a lofty disdain on the ignoble barker, and believed, not without reason, that they were far superior; but fashionable corruption in and out of the senate secretly trembled in the presence of the old censor of morals with his proud republican bearing, of the scar-covered veteran of the Hannibalic war, and of the highly influential senator who was the protector of the Roman farmers. He publicly laid before his noble colleagues, one after another, his list of their sins; certainly without being remarkably particular as to the proofs, and certainly also with a peculiar relish in the case of those who had personally crossed or provoked him. With equal fearlessness he reproved and publicly scolded the burgesses for every new injustice and every fresh disorder. His angry attacks provoked numerous enemies, and he lived in declared and irreconcilable hostility with the most powerful aristocratic coteries of the time, particularly the Scipios and Flaminini; he was publicly accused forty-four times. But the farmers—and it is a significant indication how powerful still in the Roman middle class was the spirit which had enabled them to survive the day of Cannae—never allowed the unsparing champion of reform to lack the support of their votes. Indeed when in $\frac{570}{184}$ Cato and his like-minded patrician colleague, Lucius Flaccus, solicited the censorship, and announced beforehand that it was their intention when in that office to undertake a thorough purification of all ranks and classes, the two men so greatly dreaded were elected by the burgesses notwithstanding all the exertions of the nobility; and the latter were obliged to submit, while the great purgation actually took place and erased among others the brother of Africanus from the roll of the equites, and the brother of the deliverer of the Greeks from the roll of the senate.

This warfare directed against individuals, and the various attempts to repress the spirit of the age by means of justice and of police, however deserving of respect might be the sentiments in which they originated, could only at most stem the current of corruption for a short time; and, while it is remarkable that Cato was enabled in spite of that current or rather by means of it to play his political part, it is equally significant that he was as little successful in getting rid of the leaders of the opposite party as they were in getting rid of him. The processes of count and reckoning instituted by him and by those who shared his views before the burgesses uniformly remained, at least in the cases that were of political importance, quite as ineffectual as the counter-accusations directed against him. Nor was much more effect produced by the police-laws, which were issued at this period in unusual numbers, especially with a view to the restriction of luxury and the introduction of a frugal and orderly housekeeping, and some of which have still to be noticed in our view of the national economics.

Far more practical and more useful were the attempts made to counteract the spread of decay by indirect means; among which, beyond doubt, the assignations of new farms out of the domain land occupy the first place. These assignations were made in great numbers and of considerable extent in the period between the first and second war with Carthage, and again from the close of the latter till towards the end of this epoch. The most important of them were the distribution of the Picenian possessions by Gaius Flaminius in $\frac{522}{232}$ (p. 76); the foundation of eight new maritime colonies in $\frac{560}{194}$ (p. 177); and above all the comprehensive colonisation of the district between the Apennines and the Po by the establishment of the Latin colonies of Placentia, Cremona (p. 77), Bononia (p. 184), and Aquileia (p. 183), and of the burgess-colonies, Potentia, Pisaurum, Mutina, Parma, and Luna (p. 210) in the years $\frac{536}{218}$ and $\frac{565-577}{189-177}$. By far the greater part of these valuable foundations may be ascribed to the reforming party. Cato and those who shared his opinions demanded such measures, pointing, on the one hand, to the devastation of Italy by the Hannibalic war and the alarming decrease of the farms and of the free Italian population generally, and, on the other, to the widely extended possessions of the nobles—occupied along with, and similarly to, property of their own—in Cisalpine Gaul, in Samnium, and in the Apulian and Bruttian districts; and although the rulers of Rome did not probably comply with his demands to the extent to which they might and should have complied with them, yet they did not remain deaf to the warning voice of so judicious a man.

Of a kindred character was the proposal, which Cato made in the senate, to remedy the decline of the burgess cavalry by the institution of four hundred new equestrian stalls (p. 299). The exchequer cannot have wanted means for the purpose; but the proposal appears to have been defeated by the exclusive spirit of the nobility and their endeavour to expel from the burgess cavalry those who were troopers merely and not knights. On the other hand, the serious emergencies of the war, which soon induced the Roman government to make an attempt—fortunately unsuccessful—to recruit their armies after the Oriental fashion from the slave-market (p. 128, 155), compelled them to modify the qualifications hitherto required for service in the burgess army, viz., a minimum census of 11,000 *asses* (£43), and free birth. Apart from the fact that they took up for service in the fleet the persons of free birth rated between 4000 *asses* (£17) and 1500 *asses* (£6) and all the freedmen, the minimum census for the legionary was reduced to 4000 *asses* (£17); and, in case of need, both those who were bound to serve in the fleet and the free-born rated between 1500 *asses* (£6) and 375 *asses* (£1 10s.) were enrolled in the burgess infantry. These innovations, which belong probably to the end of the preceding or beginning of the present epoch, doubtless did not originate in party efforts any more than did the Servian military reform; but they gave a material impulse to the democratic party, in so far as those who bore civic burdens necessarily claimed and eventually obtained equalisation of civic rights. The poor and the freedmen began to be of some importance in the commonwealth from the time when they served it; and chiefly from this cause arose one of the most important constitutional changes of this epoch—the remodelling of the *comitia centuriata*, which most probably took place in the same year in which the war concerning Sicily terminated ($\frac{513}{241}$).

According to the order of voting hitherto followed in the centuriate comitia, the wealthy had the preponderance, although the freeholders were no longer—as down to the reform of Appius Claudius (i. 305) they had been—the sole voters. The equites, or in other words the patricio-plebeian nobility, voted first, then those of the highest rating, or in other words those who had exhibited to the censor an estate of at least 100,000 *asses* (£420); [1]

---

[1] As to the original rates of the Roman census it is difficult to lay down anything definite. Afterwards, as is well known, 100,000 *asses* was regarded as the minimum census of the first class; to which the census of the other four classes stood in the (at least approximate) ratio of $\frac{3}{4}, \frac{1}{2}, \frac{1}{4}, \frac{1}{9}$. But these rates are understood already by Polybius, as by all later authors, to refer to the light *as* ($\frac{1}{10}$ of the *denarius*), and apparently this view must be adhered to, although in reference to the Voconian law the same sums are reckoned as heavy *asses* ($\frac{1}{4}$ of the *denarius : Geschichte des Röm. Münzwesens*, p. 302). But Appius Claudius, who first in $\frac{442}{312}$ expressed the census-rates in money instead of in land (i. 305), cannot in this have made use of the light *as*, which only came into existence in $\frac{485}{269}$ (i. 445). Either therefore he expressed the same amounts in heavy *asses*, and these were at the reduction of the coinage converted into light; or he proposed the later figures, and these remained the same notwithstanding the reduction of the coinage, which in this case would have involved a lowering of the class-rates by more than the half. Grave doubts may be raised in opposition to either hypothesis; but the former appears the more credible, for so exorbitant an advance in democratic development is neither probable at the end of the fifth century nor as an incidental consequence of a mere administrative measure, and besides it would hardly have disappeared

and these two divisions, when they concurred, had decided every vote. The suffrage of those assessed under the four following classes had been of doubtful weight; that of those whose valuation remained below the standard of the lowest class, 11,000 *asses* (£43), had been virtually illusory, and the freedmen had with few exceptions been totally destitute of the suffrage. According to the new arrangement the right of priority in voting was withdrawn from the equites, although they retained their separate divisions, and it was transferred to a voting division chosen from the first class by lot; the freedman was placed on an equal footing with the freeborn; and lastly the same number of votes was conceded to each of the five classes,[1] so that, even if the burgesses were at one, it was only by the voting of the third class that the majority was decided. This reform of the centuries was the first important constitutional change which the new opposition won from the nobility, the first victory of democracy proper. It thereby obtained on the one hand the abolition of the priority of voting vested in the nobility, and on the other hand equality of rights in the matter of election. The importance of that aristocratic right of prior voting cannot be estimated too highly, especially at an epoch in which practically the influence of the nobility on the burgesses at large was constantly on the increase. Even the patrician order proper were still at this epoch powerful enough to fill the second consulship and the second censorship, which stood open in law alike to patricians and plebeians, solely with men of their own body, the former up to the close of this period (till $\frac{582}{172}$), the latter even for a generation longer (till $\frac{623}{131}$); and in fact, at the most perilous

wholly from tradition. 100,000 light *asses*, or 40,000 sesterces, may, moreover, be reasonably regarded as the equivalent of the original Roman full hide of perhaps 20 *iugera* (i. 97); so that according to this view the rates of the census as a whole have changed merely in expression, and not in value.

[1] The adjustment of the five class-rates at 100,000, 75,000, 50,000, 25,000, 11,000 *asses* (£420, £315, £210, £105, £43), in combination with the hypothesis that each class gave an equal number of votes, suggests the possibility that the whole number of those rated in a higher class, especially the first, exceeded the number of those entitled to vote in the next following class. But this suspicion, in itself not without ground, carries no great weight, inasmuch as the censors, in fixing the limits of the voting divisions, acted with an arbitrariness which appears to our views astonishing; it may be conjectured that, when this case occurred, they added those of lowest valuation in the higher class to the roll of the following, till the number of persons was at least equal, and probably this is the reason why the census of the first class is stated sometimes at 100,000, sometimes at 110,000 and 125,000 *asses*. The tendency of the measure doubtless was to grant to those entitled to vote at all, more especially the first three classes, a suffrage equal in kind.

moment which the Roman republic ever experienced—in the crisis after the battle of Cannae—they cancelled the duly and legally conducted election of the officer who was in all respects the ablest—the plebeian Marcellus—to the consulship vacated by the death of the patrician Paullus, solely on account of his plebeian origin. At the same time it is a significant token of the nature even of this reform that the right of precedence in voting was withdrawn from the nobility alone, not from those of the highest rating; the right withdrawn from the equestrian centuries passed not to a division chosen incidentally by lot from the whole burgesses, but exclusively to the first class. Still more trenchant in theory at least was the equalisation of the suffrage for the rich and for the poor, for the freeborn and the freedmen, who were assessable, so that, instead of the half, only about a fifth of the whole number of votes remained in the hands of those of the highest rating. But one of the most important, perhaps practically the most important, of these innovations—the equalising of the freedmen with the free-born—was set aside again twenty years later ($\frac{534}{220}$) by one of the most notable men of the reform party itself, the censor Gaius Flaminius, and the freedmen were removed from the centuries—a measure which the censor Tiberius Sempronius Gracchus, the father of the two authors of the Roman revolution, fifty years afterwards ($\frac{585}{169}$) renewed and enforced against the freedmen who were always intruding afresh. The abiding fruit therefore of the reform of the centuries, apart from the enactment directed against the prerogative of the equestrian order, was the political abolition of the distinction as to estate among the burgesses whose valuation exceeded the lowest rating—equality in point of suffrage for the burgesses entitled to vote at all. Substantially in this way all freeholder burgesses of free birth had long enjoyed equality of suffrage in the *comitia tributa*, while the votes of the non-freeholders and freedmen had there been rendered almost practically worthless by being crowded into four of the thirty-five tribes. The general result accordingly was the remodelling of the *comitia centuriata* according to the principle already recognised in the *comitia tributa*; a change which recommended itself by the circumstance, that elections, proposals of laws, criminal charges, and generally all affairs requiring the co-operation of the burgesses, came to be uniformly brought before the *comitia tributa*, and the more unwieldy centuries were seldom convoked except when it was constitutionally necessary to do so for electing the censors, consuls, and praetors, or for decreeing an aggressive war. It thus appears that this reform did not introduce a new principle into the constitution, but only brought into general application the principle that had long regulated the working of the practically more frequent and more important form of the burgess-assemblies. Its democratic, but by no means demagogic, tendency is clearly apparent in the circumstance that the proper supports of every really revolutionary party—the proletariate and the freedmen—still continued as before to hold an inferior position in the centuries as well as in the tribes. For that reason the practical significance of this alteration in the order of voting regulating the popular assemblies must not be estimated too highly. The new law of election doubtless completed in theory civil equality, but did not prevent, and perhaps did not even materially impede, the contemporary formation of a new politically privileged order. It is certainly not owing to the mere imperfection of tradition, defective as it undoubtedly is, that we are nowhere able to point to a practical influence exercised by this much-discussed reform on the course of political affairs. An intimate connection, we may add, subsisted between this reform which equalised the suffrages of the burgesses entitled to vote at all, and the already-mentioned abolition of the Roman burgess-communities *sine suffragio* which were gradually merged in the community of full burgesses. The levelling spirit of the party of progress suggested the abolition of distinctions within the burgess-body, while the chasm between burgesses and non-burgesses was at the same time deepened and widened.

Reviewing what the reform party of this age aimed at and obtained, we find that it undoubtedly exerted itself with patriotism and energy to check, and to a certain extent succeeded in checking, the spread of decay—more especially the falling off of the farmer class and the relaxation of the old strict and frugal habits—as well as the preponderating political influence of the new nobility. But we fail to discover any higher political aim. The discontent of the multitude and the moral indignation of the better classes found doubtless in this opposition their appropriate and powerful expression; but we do not find either a clear insight into the sources of the evil, or any definite and comprehensive plan of remedying it. A certain want of purpose pervaded all these efforts otherwise so deserving of respect, and the purely defensive attitude of the defenders foreboded little good in the issue. Whether the disease could be remedied at all by human skill, remains fairly open to question; the Roman reformers of this period seem to have been good citizens rather than good statesmen, and to have conducted the great struggle between the old civism and the new cosmopolitanism on their part in a somewhat inadequate and narrow spirit.

But, as this period witnessed the rise of a rabble by the side of the burgesses, so it witnessed also the emergence of a demagogism that flattered the populace alongside of the respectable and useful party of opposition. Cato was already acquainted with men who made a trade of demagogism; who had a morbid propensity for speechifying, as others had for drinking or for sleeping; who hired listeners, if they could find no willing audience otherwise; and whom people heard as they heard the market-crier, without attending to their words or, when needing help, entrusting themselves to their care. In his caustic fashion the old man describes these fops formed after the model of the Greek talkers of the *agora*, dealing in jests and witticisms, singing and dancing, ready for anything; such an one was, in his opinion, good for nothing but to exhibit himself as harlequin in a procession and to bandy talk with the public—he would sell his talk or his silence for a bit of bread. In truth these demagogues were the worst enemies of reform. While the reformers insisted above all things and in every direction on moral amendment, demagogism preferred to insist on the limitation of the powers of the government and the extension of those of the burgesses.

Under the former head the most important innovation was the practical abolition of the dictatorship. The crisis occasioned by Quintus Fabius and his popular opponents in $\frac{537}{217}$ (p. 117) gave the death-blow to this all-along unpopular institution. Although the government once afterwards, in $\frac{538}{216}$, under the immediate impression produced by the battle of Cannae, nominated a dictator invested with active command, it could not again venture to do so in more peaceful times. On several occasions subsequently (the last in $\frac{552}{202}$), sometimes after a previous indication by the burgesses of the person to be nominated, a dictator was appointed for urban business; but the office, without being formally abolished, fell practically into desuetude. Through its abeyance the Roman constitutional system, so artificially constructed, lost a corrective which was very desirable with reference to its peculiar feature of collegiate magistrates (i. 253); and the government, which was vested with the sole power of creating a dictatorship or in other words of suspending

the consuls, and ordinarily designated also the person who was
to be nominated as dictator, lost one of its most important
instruments. Its place was but very imperfectly supplied by
the power—which the senate thenceforward claimed—of conferring in extraordinary emergencies, particularly on the sudden
outbreak of revolt or war, a quasi-dictatorial power on the
supreme magistrates for the time being, by instructing them
" to take measures for the safety of the commonwealth at their
discretion," and thus creating a state of things similar to the
modern martial law.

Along with this change the formal powers of the people in
the nomination of magistrates as well as in questions of government, administration, and finance, received a hazardous extension. The priesthoods—particularly those politically most
important, the colleges of men of lore—according to ancient
custom filled up the vacancies in their ranks, and nominated
also their own presidents, where these corporations had presidents
at all; and in fact, for such institutions destined to transmit
the knowledge of divine things from generation to generation,
the only form of election in keeping with their spirit was cooptation. It was therefore—although not of great political importance—an indication of the incipient disorganisation of the
republican arrangements, that at this time (before $\frac{542}{212}$), while
election into the colleges themselves was left on its former
footing, the designation of the presidents—the *curiones* and
pontifices—from the ranks of those corporations was transferred
from the colleges to the community. In this case, however,
with a pious regard for forms that is genuinely Roman, in order
to avoid any error, only a minority of the tribes, and therefore
not the " people," completed the act of election.

Of greater importance was the growing interference of the
burgesses in questions as to persons and things belonging to the
sphere of military administration and external policy. To this
head belong the transference of the nomination of the ordinary
staff-officers from the general to the burgesses, which has been
already mentioned (p. 303); the elections of the leaders of the
opposition as commanders-in-chief against Hannibal (pp. 112,
119); the unconstitutional and irrational decree of the people
in $\frac{537}{217}$, which divided the supreme command between the unpopular generalissimo and his popular lieutenant who opposed
him in the camp as well as at home (p. 118); the tribunician
complaint laid before the burgesses, charging an officer like
Marcellus with injudicious and dishonest management of the

war ($\frac{545}{209}$), which even compelled him to come from the camp and to demonstrate his military capacity before the public of the capital; the still more scandalous attempts to refuse to the victor of Pydna his triumph by a decree of the burgesses (p. 325); the investiture—suggested, it is true, by the senate—of a private man with extraordinary consular authority ($\frac{544}{210}$; p. 147); the dangerous threat of Scipio that, if the senate should refuse him the chief command in Africa, he would seek the sanction of the burgesses ($\frac{349}{205}$; p. 168); the attempt of a man half crazy with ambition to extort from the burgesses, against the will of the government, a declaration of war in every respect unwarranted against the Rhodians ($\frac{587}{167}$; p. 287); and the new constitutional axiom, that every state treaty acquired validity only through the ratification of the people.

This joint action of the burgesses in governing and in commanding was fraught in a high degree with peril. But still more dangerous was their interference with the finances of the state; not only because any attack on the oldest and most important right of the government—the exclusive administration of the public property—struck at the root of the power of the senate, but because the placing of the most important business of this nature—the distribution of the public domains—in the hands of the public assemblies of the burgesses necessarily dug the grave of the republic. To allow the public assembly to decree the transference of public property without limit to its own pocket was not only wrong, but was the beginning of the end; it demoralised the best-disposed citizens, and gave to the proposer a power incompatible with a free commonwealth. Salutary as was the distribution of the public land, and doubly blameable as was the senate accordingly for omitting to cut off this most dangerous of all weapons of agitation by voluntarily distributing the occupied lands, yet Gaius Flaminius, when he came to the burgesses in $\frac{522}{232}$ with the proposal to distribute the domains of Picenum, undoubtedly injured the commonwealth more by the means than he benefited it by the end. Cassius had doubtless two hundred and fifty years earlier proposed the same thing (i. 278); but the two measures, closely as they coincided in the letter, were yet wholly different, inasmuch as Cassius submitted a matter affecting the community to that community while still in its vigour and conducting its own government, whereas Flaminius submitted a public question to the popular assembly of a great state.

Not the party of the government only, but the party of reform also, very properly regarded the military, executive, and financial government as the legitimate domain of the senate, and carefully abstained from making full use of, to say nothing of augmenting, the formal power vested in popular assemblies that were inwardly doomed to inevitable dissolution. Never even in the most limited monarchy was a part so completely null assigned to the monarch as was allotted to the sovereign Roman people: this was no doubt in more than one respect to be regretted, but it was, owing to the existing state of the comitial machinery, even in the view of the friends of reform a matter of necessity. For this reason Cato and those who shared his views never submitted to the burgesses a question, which interfered with the government strictly so called; and never, directly or indirectly, by decree of the people extorted from the senate the political or financial measures which they wished, such as the declaration of war against Carthage and the assignations of land. The government of the senate might be bad; the popular assemblies could not govern at all. Not that an evil-disposed majority predominated in them; on the contrary the counsel of a man of standing, the loud call of honour, and the louder call of necessity were still, as a rule, listened to in the comitia, and averted the most injurious and disgraceful results. The burgesses, before whom Marcellus pleaded his cause, ignominiously dismissed his accuser, and elected the accused as consul for the following year: they suffered themselves also to be persuaded of the necessity of the war against Philip, terminated the war against Perseus by the election of Paullus, and accorded to the latter his well-deserved triumph. But in order to such elections and such decrees there was needed some special stimulus; in general the mass having no will of its own followed the first impulse, and folly or accident dictated the decision.

In the state, as in every organism, an organ which no longer discharges its functions is injurious. The nullity of the sovereign assembly of the people involved no small danger. Any minority in the senate might constitutionally appeal against the majority to the comitia. To every individual who possessed the easy art of addressing untutored ears or of merely throwing away money, a path was opened up for his acquiring a position or procuring a decree in his favour, to which the magistrates and the government were formally bound to do homage. Hence sprang those citizen-generals, accustomed to sketch plans of battle on the tables of taverns and to look down on the regular service with compassion by virtue of their inborn genius for strategy; hence those staff-officers, who owed their command to the canvassing intrigues of the capital and, whenever matters looked serious, had at once to get leave of absence *en masse ;* and hence the battles of the Trasimene lake and of Cannae, and the disgraceful management of the war with Perseus. At every step the government was thwarted and led astray by those unaccountable decrees of the burgesses, and as was to be expected, most of all in the very cases where it was most in the right.

But the weakening of the government and the weakening of the community itself were among the lesser dangers that sprang from this demagogism. Still more directly the factious violence of individual ambition pushed itself forward under the aegis of the constitutional rights of the burgesses. That which formally issued forth as the will of the supreme authority in the state was in reality very often the mere personal pleasure of the mover; and what was to be the fate of a commonwealth in which war and peace, the nomination and deposition of the general and his officers, the public chest and the public property, were dependent on the caprices of the multitude and its accidental leaders? The thunder-storm had not yet burst; but the clouds were gathering in denser masses, and occasional peals of thunder were already rolling through the sultry air. It was a circumstance, moreover, fraught with double danger, that the tendencies which were apparently most opposite met together at their extremes both as regarded ends and as regarded means. Family policy and demagogism carried on a similar and equally dangerous rivalry in patronising and worshipping the rabble. Gaius Flaminius was regarded by the statesmen of the following generation as the initiator of that course from which proceeded the reforms of the Gracchi and—we may add—the democratico-monarchical revolution that ensued. But Publius Scipio also, although setting the fashion to the nobility in arrogance, title-hunting, and client-making, sought support for his personal and almost dynastic policy of opposition to the senate in the multitude, which he not only charmed by the dazzling effect of his personal qualities, but also bribed by his largesses of grain; in the legions, whose favour he courted by all means whether right or wrong; and above all in the body of clients, high and low, that personally adhered to him. Only the dreamy mysticism, on which the charm as well as the weakness of that remarkable man so largely depended, never suffered him to awake at all or allowed him to awake but imperfectly out of the belief that he was nothing, and that he desired to be nothing, but the first burgess of Rome.

To assert the possibility of a reform would be as rash as to deny it: this much is certain, that a thorough amendment of the state in all its departments was urgently required, and that in no quarter was any serious attempt made to accomplish it. Various alterations in details, no doubt, were made on the part of the senate as well as on the part of the popular opposition. The majorities in each were still well disposed, and still frequently, notwithstanding the chasm that separated the parties, united in a common endeavour to effect the removal of the worst evils. But, while they did not stop the evil at its source, it was to little purpose that the better disposed listened with anxiety to the dull murmur of the swelling flood and worked at dikes and dams. Contenting themselves with palliatives, and failing to apply even these—especially such as were the most important, the improvement of justice, for instance, and the distribution of the domains—in proper season and due measure, they helped to prepare evil days for their posterity. By neglecting to break up the field at the proper time, they propagated weeds even when they had no desire to do so. To the later generations who survived the storms of revolution the period after the Hannibalic war appeared the golden age of Rome, and Cato seemed the model of the Roman statesman. It was in reality the calm before the storm and the epoch of political mediocrities, an age like that of the government of Walpole in England; and no Chatham was found in Rome to infuse fresh energy into the stagnant life of the nation. Wherever we cast our eyes, chinks and rents are yawning in the old building; we see workmen busy sometimes in filling them up, sometimes in enlarging them; but we nowhere perceive any trace of preparations for thoroughly rebuilding or renewing it, and the question is no longer whether, but simply when, the structure will fall. During no epoch did the Roman constitution remain formally so stable as in the period from the Sicilian to the third Macedonian war and for a generation beyond it; but the stability of the constitution was here, as everywhere, not a sign of the health of the state, but a token of incipient sickness and the harbinger of revolution.

CHAPTER XII

THE MANAGEMENT OF LAND AND OF CAPITAL

It is in the sixth century of the city that we first find materials for a history of the times exhibiting in some measure the mutual connection of events; and it is in that century also that the economic condition of Rome emerges into view more clearly and distinctly. It was at this epoch that the wholesale system, as regards both the cultivation of land and the management of capital, became first established under the form, and on the scale, which afterwards prevailed; although we cannot exactly discriminate how much of that system is traceable to earlier precedent, how much to an imitation of the methods of husbandry and of speculation among peoples that were earlier civilised, especially the Phoenicians, and how much to the growth of capital and the growth of intelligence in the nation. A summary outline of these economic relations will conduce to a more accurate understanding of the internal history of Rome.

Roman husbandry[1] applied itself either to the farming of

---

[1] In order to gain a true idea of ancient Italy, it is necessary for us to bear in mind the great changes which have been produced there by modern cultivation. Of the *cerealia*, rye was not cultivated in antiquity; and the Romans of the empire were astonished to find that oats, with which they were well acquainted as a weed, was used by the Germans for making porridge. Rice was first cultivated in Italy at the end of the fifteenth, and maize at the beginning of the seventeenth, century. Potatoes and tomatoes were brought from America; artichokes seem to be nothing but a cultivated variety of the cardoon which was known to the Romans, although the peculiar character superinduced by cultivation appears of more recent origin. The almond, again, or " Greek nut," the peach, or " Persian nut," and also the " soft nut " (*nux mollusca*), although originally foreign to Italy, are met with there at least 150 years before Christ. The date-palm, introduced into Italy from Greece as into Greece from the East, and forming a living attestation of the primitive commercial-religious intercourse between the West and the East, was already cultivated in Italy 300 years before Christ (Liv. x. 47; Pallad. v. 5, 2; xi. 12, 1) not for its fruit (Plin. *H. N.* xiii. 4, 26), but, just as in the present day, as a hand-some plant, and for the sake of the leaves which were used at public festivals. The cherry, or fruit of Cerasus on the Black Sea, was later in being introduced, and only began to be planted in Italy in the time of Cicero, although the wild cherry is indigenous there; still later, perhaps, came the apricot, or " Armenian plum." The citron-tree was not cultivated in Italy till the later ages of the empire; the orange was only introduced by the Moors in the twelfth or thirteenth, and the aloe (*Agave*

341

estates, to the occupation of pasture lands, or to the tillage of petty holdings. A very distinct view of the first of these is presented to us in the description given by Cato.

The Roman estates were, considered as larger holdings, uniformly of limited extent. That described by Cato had an area of 240 *iugera;* a very common measure was the so-called *centuria* of 200 *iugera.* Where the laborious culture of the vine was pursued, the unit of husbandry was made still less; Cato assumes in that case an area of 100 *iugera.* Any one who wished to invest more capital in farming did not enlarge his estate, but acquired several estates; accordingly the quantity of 500 *iugera,* fixed as the maximum which it was allowable to occupy, has been conceived to represent the contents of two or three estates.

Heritable leases were not recognised in law, and leases for life occurred as a substitute only in the case of communal land. Leases for shorter periods, granted either for a fixed sum of money or on condition that the lessee should bear all the costs of tillage and should receive in return a share, ordinarily one half, of the produce,[1] were not unknown, but they were exceptional and a makeshift; so that no distinct class of tenant-farmers grew up in Italy.[2] Ordinarily therefore the proprietor

---

Americana) from America only in the sixteenth, century. Cotton was first cultivated in Europe by the Arabs. The buffalo also and the silk-worm belong only to modern, not to ancient Italy.

It is obvious that the products which Italy had not originally are for the most part those very products which seem to us truly "Italian;" and if modern Germany, as compared with the Germany visited by Caesar, may be called a southern land, Italy has since in no less degree acquired a more "southern" aspect.

[1] According to Cato, *de R. R.* 137 (comp. 16), in the case of a lease with division of the produce the gross produce of the estate, after deduction of the fodder necessary for the oxen that drew the plough, was divided between lessor and lessee (*colonus partiarius*) in the proportions agreed upon between them. That the shares were ordinarily equal may be con-jectured from the analogy of the French *bail à cheptel* and the similar Italian system of half-and-half leases, as well as from the absence of all trace of any other scheme of partition. It is erroneous to refer to the case of the *politor,* who got the fifth of the grain or, if the division took place before thrashing, from the sixth to the ninth sheaf (Cato, 136, comp. 5); he was not a lessee sharing the produce, but a labourer assumed in the harvest season, who received his daily wages according to that contract of partnership (p. 346).

[2] There existed no appropriate form for such a lease even in law; for that the contract of *locatio* first applied to the letting of houses, and was only transferred to the leasing of land, is shown very clearly by the rule—applicable to the letting of a house, but not to the leasing of land—that the payment of the tenant must necessarily consist in money; in consequence of which the produce-lease among the Romans comes under the category of contingencies occurring in practical life but not falling within the theory

himself superintended the cultivation of his estates; he did not, however, manage them strictly in person, but only appeared from time to time on the property in order to settle the plan of operations, to look after its execution, and to audit the accounts of his servants. He was thus enabled on the one hand to work a number of estates at the same time, and on the other hand to devote himself, as circumstances might require, to public affairs.

The grain cultivated consisted especially of spelt and wheat, with some barley and millet; turnips, radishes, garlic, poppies, were also grown, and—particularly as fodder for the cattle—lupines, beans, pease, vetches, and other leguminous plants. The seed was sown ordinarily in autumn, only in exceptional cases in spring. Much activity was displayed in irrigation and draining; and drainage by means of covered ditches was early in use. Meadows also for supplying hay were not wanting, and even in the time of Cato they were frequently irrigated artificially. Of equal, if not of greater, economic importance than grain and vegetables were the olive and the vine, of which the former was planted among the crops, the latter in vineyards appropriated to itself.[1] Figs, apples, pears, and other fruit trees were cultivated; and likewise elms, poplars, and other leafy trees and shrubs, partly for the felling of the wood, partly for the sake of the leaves which were useful as litter and as fodder for cattle. The rearing of cattle, on the other hand, held a far less important place in the economy of the Italians than it holds in modern times, for vegetables formed the general fare, and animal food made its appearance at table only exceptionally; where it did appear, it consisted almost solely of the flesh of swine or lambs. Although the ancients did not fail to perceive the economic connection between agriculture and the rearing of cattle, and in particular the importance of producing manure, the modern combination of the growth of corn with the rearing of cattle was a thing foreign to antiquity. The larger cattle were kept only so far as was requisite for the tillage of the fields, and

of jurisprudence. The lease first assumed real importance when the Roman capitalists began to acquire transmarine possessions on a great scale; then indeed they knew how to value it, when a temporary lease was continued through several generations (Colum. i. 7, 3).

[1] That the space between the vines was occupied not by grain, but only at the most by such fodder plants as easily grew in the shade, is evident from Cato (33, comp. 137), and accordingly Columella (iii. 3) calculates on no other accessory gain in the case of a vineyard except the produce of the young shoots sold. On the other hand, the orchard (*arbustum*) was sown like any corn field (Colum. ii. 9, 6). It was only where the vine was trained on living trees that corn was cultivated in the intervals between them.

they were fed not on pasture set apart for the purpose, but, wholly during summer and mostly during winter also, in the stall. Sheep, again, were driven out on the stubble pasture; Cato allows 100 head to 240 *iugera*. Frequently, however, the proprietor preferred to let his winter pasture to a large sheep-owner, or to hand over his flock of sheep to a lessee who was to share the produce, stipulating for the delivery of a certain number of lambs and of a certain quantity of cheese and milk. Swine—Cato assigns to a large estate ten sties—poultry, and pigeons were kept in the farmyard, and fed as there was need; and, where opportunity offered, a small hare-preserve and a fish-pond were constructed—the modest commencement of that nursing and rearing of game and fish which was afterwards prosecuted to so enormous an extent.

The labours of the field were performed by means of oxen which were employed for ploughing, and of asses, which were used specially for the carriage of manure and for driving the mill; perhaps a horse also was kept, apparently for the use of the master. These animals were not reared on the estate, but were purchased; the oxen and horses at any rate were generally castrated. Cato assigns to an estate of 100 *iugera* one, to one of 240 *iugera* three, yoke of oxen; a later writer on agriculture, Saserna, assigns two yoke to the 200 *iugera*. Three asses were, according to Cato's estimate, required for the smaller, and four for the larger, estate.

The human labour on the farm was regularly performed by slaves. At the head of the body of slaves on the estate (*familia rustica*) stood the steward (*vilicus*, from *villa*), who received and expended, bought and sold, went to obtain the instructions of the landlord, and in his absence issued orders and administered punishment. Under him were placed the stewardess (*vilica*), who took charge of the house, kitchen and larder, poultry-yard and dovecot; a number of ploughmen (*bubulci*) and common serfs, an ass-driver, a swineherd, and, where a flock of sheep was kept, a shepherd. The number, of course, varied according to the method of husbandry pursued. An arable estate of 200 *iugera* without orchards was estimated to require two ploughmen and six serfs; a similar estate with orchards two ploughmen and nine serfs, an estate of 240 *iugera* with olive plantations and sheep, three ploughmen, five serfs, and three herdsmen. A vineyard naturally required a larger expenditure of labour: an estate of 100 *iugera* with vine-plantations was supplied with one ploughman, eleven ordinary slaves, and two herdsmen. The steward of course occupied a freer position than the other slaves: the treatise of Mago advised that he should be allowed to marry, to rear children, and to have funds of his own, and Cato advises that he should be married to the stewardess; he alone had some prospect, in the event of good behaviour, of obtaining liberty from his master. In other respects all formed a common household. The slaves were, like the larger cattle, not bred on the estate, but purchased at an age capable of labour in the slave-market; and, when through age or infirmity they had become incapable of working, they were again sent with other refuse to the market.[1] The farm-buildings (*villa rustica*) supplied at once stabling for the cattle, storehouses for the produce, and a dwelling for the steward and the slaves; while a separate country house (*villa urbana*) for the master was frequently erected on the estate. Every slave, even the steward himself, had all the necessaries of life delivered to him on the master's behalf at certain times and according to fixed rates; and upon these he had to subsist. He received in this way clothes and shoes, which were purchased in the market, and which the recipients had merely to keep in repair; a quantity of wheat monthly, which each had to grind for himself; as also salt, olives or salted fish to form a relish to their food, wine, and oil. The quantity was regulated by the labour; on which account the steward, who had easier work than the common slaves, got scantier measure than these. The stewardess attended to all the baking and cooking; and all partook of the same fare. It was not the ordinary practice to place chains on the slaves; but when any one had incurred punishment or was thought likely to attempt an escape, he was set to work in chains and was shut up during the night in the slaves' prison.[2]

[1] Mago, or his translator (in Varro, *R. R.* i. 17, 3), advises that slaves should not be bred, but should be purchased not under 22 years of age; and Cato must have had a similar course in view, as the personal staff of his model farm clearly shows, although he does not exactly say so. Cato (2) expressly counsels the sale of old and diseased slaves. The slave-breeding described by Columella (i. 8), under which female slaves who had three sons were exempted from labour, and the mothers of four sons were even manumitted, was doubtless an independent speculation rather than a part of the regular management of the estate—similar to the trade pursued by Cato himself of purchasing slaves to be trained and sold again (Plutarch, *Cat. Mai.* 21). The characteristic taxation mentioned in this same passage probably has reference to the body of servants properly so called (*familia urbana*).

[2] In this restricted sense the chaining of slaves, and even of the sons of the family (Dionys. ii. 26), was very old; and accordingly chained field-labourers are mentioned by Cato as exceptions, to whom, as they could not themselves grind, bread had to be supplied instead of grain (56). Even in the times of the empire the chaining of slaves uniformly presents itself as a punishment inflicted definitively by the master, provisionally by the

Ordinarily these slaves belonging to the estate were sufficient; in case of need neighbours, as a matter of course, helped each other with their slaves for day's wages. Otherwise labourers from without were not usually employed, except in peculiarly unhealthy districts, where it was found advantageous to limit the amount of slaves and to employ hired persons in their room, and for the ingathering of the harvest, for which the regular supply of labour on the farm did not suffice. At the corn and hay harvests they took in hired reapers, who often instead of wages received from the sixth to the ninth sheaf of the produce reaped, or, if they also thrashed, the fifth of the grain: Umbrian labourers, for instance, went annually in great numbers to the vale of Rieti, to help to gather in the harvest there. The grape and olive harvest was ordinarily let to a contractor, who by means of his men—hired free labourers, or slaves of his own or of others—conducted the gleaning and pressing under the inspection of persons appointed by the landlord for the purpose, and delivered the produce to the master; [1] very frequently the landlord sold the harvest on the tree or branch, and left the purchaser to look after the ingathering.

The whole system was pervaded by the utter unscrupulousness characteristic of the power of capital. Slaves and cattle were placed on the same level; a good watchdog, it is said in a Roman writer on agriculture, must not be on too friendly terms with his "fellow-slaves." The slave and the ox were fed properly so long as they could work, because it would not have been good economy to let them starve; and they were sold like

steward (Colum. i. 8; Gai. i. 13; Ulp. i. 11). If, notwithstanding, the tillage of the fields by means of chained slaves appeared in subsequent times as a distinct system, and the labourers' prison (*ergastulum*)—an underground cellar with window-apertures numerous but narrow and not to be reached from the ground by the hand (Colum. i. 6)—became a necessary part of the farm-buildings, this state of matters was occasioned by the fact that the position of the rural serfs was harder than that of other slaves, and therefore those slaves were chiefly placed in it who had, or seemed to have, committed some offence. That cruel masters, moreover, applied the chains without any occasion to do so, we do not mean to deny, and it is clearly indicated by the circumstance that the law-books do not decree the penalties applicable to slave transgressors against those in chains, but prescribe the punishment of the half-chained. It was precisely the same with branding; it was meant to be, strictly, a punishment, but the whole flock was probably marked (Diodor. xxxv. 5; Bernays, *Phokylides*, p. xxxi).

[1] Cato does not expressly say this as to the vintage, but Varro does so (i. 17), and it is implied in the nature of the case. It would have been economically an error to fix the number of the slaves on a property by the standard of the labours of harvest, and least of all, had such been the case, would the grapes have been sold on the tree, which yet was frequently done (Cato, 147).

a worn-out ploughshare when they became unable to work,
because in like manner it would not have been good economy
to retain them longer. In earlier times religious considerations
had exercised an alleviating influence, and had released the
slave and the plough-ox from labour on the days enjoined for
festivals and for rest.[1] Nothing is more characteristic of the
spirit of Cato and those who shared his sentiments than the way
in which they inculcated the observance of the holiday in the
letter, and evaded it in reality, by advising that, while the plough
should certainly be allowed to rest on these days, the slaves
should even then be incessantly occupied with other labours not
expressly prohibited. On principle no freedom of movement
whatever was allowed to them—a slave, so runs one of Cato's
maxims, must either work or sleep—and no attempt was ever
made to attach the slaves to the estate or to their master by any
bond of human sympathy. The letter of the law in all its naked
hideousness regulated the relation, and the Romans indulged no
illusions as to the consequences. " So many slaves, so many
foes," said a Roman proverb. It was an economic maxim, that
dissensions among the slaves ought rather to be fostered than
suppressed. In the same spirit Plato and Aristotle, and no less
strongly the oracle of the landlords, the Carthaginian Mago,
caution masters against bringing together slaves of the same
nationality, lest they should originate combinations and perhaps
conspiracies of their fellow-countrymen. The landlord, as we
have already said, governed his slaves exactly in the same way
as the Roman community governed its subjects in the " country
estates of the Roman people," the provinces; and the world
learned by experience, that the ruling state had modelled its
new system of government on that of the slave-holder. If,
moreover, we have risen to that little-to-be envied elevation of
thought which values no feature of an economy save the capital
invested in it, we cannot deny to the management of the Roman
estates the praise of consistency, energy, punctuality, frugality,
and solidity. The sound practical husbandman is reflected in
Cato's description of the steward, as he ought to be. He is the

[1] Columella (ii. 12, 9) reckons to the year on an average forty-five rainy
days and holidays; with which accords the statement of Tertullian (De
Idolol. 14), that the number of the heathen festival days did not come up
to the fifty days of the Christian festal season from Easter to Whitsunday.
To these fell to be added the time of rest in the middle of winter after the
completion of the autumnal sowing, which Columella estimates at thirty
days. Within this time, doubtless, the movable " festival of seed-sowing "
(feriae sementivae ; comp. i. 210 and Ovid, Fast. i. 661) uniformly occurred.
This month of rest must not be confounded with the holidays for holding
courts in the season of the harvest (Plin. Ep. viii. 21 2, et al.) and vintage.

first on the farm to rise and the last to go to bed; he is strict in dealing with himself as well as with those under him, and he knows more especially how to keep the stewardess in order, but is also careful of his labourers and his cattle, and in particular of the ox that draws the plough; he puts his hand frequently to work and to every kind of it, but never works himself weary like a slave; he is always at home, never borrows nor lends, gives no entertainments, troubles himself about no other worship than that of the gods of the hearth and the field, and like a true slave leaves all dealings with the gods as well as with men to his master; lastly and above all, he modestly meets that master and faithfully and simply, without carelessness and without excess of care, conforms to the instructions which that master has given. He is a bad husbandman, it is elsewhere said, who buys what he can raise on his own land; a bad father of a household, who takes in hand during the day what can be done by candle-light, unless the weather be bad; a still worse, who does on a working-day what might be done on a holiday; but worst of all is he, who in good weather allows work to go on within doors instead of in the open air. The characteristic enthusiasm too of high farming is not wanting; and the golden rules are laid down, that the soil was given to the husbandman not to be scoured and swept but to be sown and reaped, and that the farmer therefore ought first to plant vines and olives and only thereafter, and that not too early in life, to build himself a villa. A certain boorishness marks the system, and, instead of the rational investigation of causes and effects, the well-known rules of rustic experience are uniformly brought forward; yet there is an evident endeavour to appropriate the experience of others and the products of foreign lands: in Cato's list of the sorts of fruit trees, for instance, Greek, African, and Spanish species appear.

The husbandry of the petty farmer differed from that of the estate-holder only or chiefly in its being on a smaller scale. The owner himself and his children in this case laboured along with the slaves or in their room. The quantity of cattle was reduced, and, where an estate no longer covered the expenses of the plough and of the yoke that drew it, the hoe formed the substitute. The culture of the olive and the vine was less prominent, or was entirely wanting.

In the vicinity of Rome and of other large seats of consumption there existed also carefully irrigated gardens for flowers and vegetables, somewhat similar to those which one now sees around Naples; and these yielded a very abundant return.

Pastoral husbandry was practised on a far greater scale than agriculture. An estate in pasture land (*saltus*) had of necessity in every case an area considerably greater than an arable estate —the least allowance was 800 *iugera*—and it might with advantage to the business be almost indefinitely extended. Italy is so situated in respect of climate that the summer pasture in the mountains and the winter pasture in the plains supplement each other: already at that period, just as at the present day, and for the most part probably along the same paths, the flocks and herds were driven in spring from Apulia to Samnium, and in autumn back again from Samnium to Apulia. The winter pasturage, however, as has been already observed, did not consist entirely of ground kept for the purpose, but was partly the grazing of the stubbles. Horses, oxen, asses, and mules were reared, chiefly to supply the animals required by the landowners, carriers, soldiers, and so forth; herds of swine and of goats also were not neglected. But the almost universal habit of wearing woollen stuffs gave a far greater independence and far higher development to the breeding of sheep. The management was in the hands of slaves, and was on the whole similar to the management of the arable estate, the cattle-master (*magister pecoris*) coming in room of the steward. Throughout the summer the shepherd-slaves lived for the most part not under a roof, but, often miles remote from human habitations, under sheds and sheepfolds; it was necessary therefore that the strongest men should be selected for this employment, that they should be provided with horses and arms, and that they should be allowed far greater freedom of movement than was granted to the slaves on arable estates.

In order to form some estimate of the economic results of this system of husbandry, we must consider the state of prices, and particularly the prices of grain at this period. On an average these were alarmingly low; and that in great measure through the fault of the Roman government, which in this important question was led into the most fearful blunders not so much by its short-sightedness, as by an unpardonable disposition to favour the proletariate of the capital at the expense of the farmers of Italy. The main question here was that of the competition between transmarine and Italian corn. The grain which was delivered by the provincials to the Roman government, sometimes gratuitously, sometimes for a moderate compensation, was in part applied by the government to the maintenance of the Roman official staff and of the Roman armies on the spot, partly given up to the lessees of the *decumae* on condition of their either paying a sum of money for it or of their undertaking to deliver certain quantities of grain at Rome or wherever else it should be required. From the time of the second Macedonian war the Roman armies were uniformly supported by transmarine corn, and, though this tended to the benefit of the Roman exchequer, it cut off the Italian farmer from an important field of consumption for his produce. This however was the least part of the mischief. The government had long, as was reasonable, kept a watchful eye on the price of grain, and, when there was a threatening of dearth, had interfered by well-timed purchases abroad; and now, when the corn-deliveries of its subjects brought into its hands every year large quantities of grain—larger probably than were needed in times of peace—and when, moreover, opportunities were presented to it of acquiring foreign grain in almost unlimited quantity at moderate prices, there was a natural temptation to glut the markets of the capital with such grain, and to dispose of it at rates which either in themselves or as compared with the Italian rates were ruinously low. Already in the years $\frac{551-554}{203-200}$, and in the first instance apparently at the suggestion of Scipio, 6 *modii* ($1\frac{1}{2}$ bush.) of Spanish and African wheat were sold on public account to the citizens of Rome at 24 and even at 12 *asses* (1s. 8d. or 10d.). Some years afterwards ($\frac{558}{196}$), more than 240,000 bushels of Sicilian grain were distributed at the latter illusory price in the capital. In vain Cato inveighed against this short-sighted policy; the rise of demagogism had a part in it, and these extraordinary, but probably very frequent, distributions of grain under the market price by the government or individual magistrates became the germs of the subsequent corn-laws. But, even where the transmarine corn did not reach the consumers in this extraordinary mode, it injuriously affected Italian agriculture. Not only were the masses of grain which the state sold off to the lessees of the tenths beyond doubt acquired under ordinary circumstances by these so cheaply that, when re-sold, it could be disposed of under the price of production; but it is probable that in the provinces, particularly in Sicily—in consequence partly of the favourable nature of the soil, partly of the extent to which wholesale farming and slave-holding were pursued on the Carthaginian system (p. 9.)—the price of production was in general considerably lower than in Italy, while the transport of Sicilian and Sardinian corn to Latium was at least as cheap as, if not cheaper than, its transport thither from Etruria, Campania, or even northern Italy. In the natural course of things therefore transmarine corn could not but flow to the peninsula, and lower the price of the grain produced there. Under the unnatural disturbance of relations occasioned by the lamentable system of slave-labour, it would perhaps have been justifiable to impose a duty on transmarine corn for the protection of the Italian farmer; but the very opposite course seems to have been pursued, and with a view to favour the import of transmarine corn to Italy, a prohibitive system seems to have been applied in the provinces—for though the Rhodians were allowed to export a quantity of corn from Sicily by way of special favour, the exportation of grain from the provinces must probably, as a rule, have been free only as regarded Italy, and the transmarine corn must thus have been monopolised for the benefit of the mother-country.

The effects of this system are clearly evident. A year of extraordinary fertility like $\frac{504}{280}$—when the people of the capital paid for 6 Roman *modii* (1½ bush.) of spelt not more than $\frac{2}{6}$ of a *denarius* (about 5*d.*), and at the same price there were sold 180 Roman pounds (a pound = 11 oz.) of dried figs, 60 pounds of oil, 72 pounds of meat, and 6 *congii* (= 4½ gallons) of wine— is scarcely by reason of its very singularity to be taken into account; but other facts speak more distinctly. Even in Cato's time Sicily was called the granary of Rome. In productive years Sicilian and Sardinian corn was disposed of in the Italian ports for the freight. In the richest corn districts of the peninsula— the modern Romagna and Lombardy—during the time of Polybius victuals and lodgings in an inn cost on an average half an *as* (⅓*d.*) per day; a bushel and a half of wheat was there worth half a *denarius* (4*d.*). The latter average price, about the twelfth part of the normal price elsewhere,[1] shows undeniably that the producers of grain in Italy were wholly destitute of a market for their produce, and in consequence corn and corn-land there were almost valueless.

[1] The medium price of grain in the capital may be assumed at least for the seventh and eighth centuries of Rome at one *denarius* for the Roman *modius*, or 2s. 8d. per bushel of wheat, for which there is now paid (according to the average of the prices in the provinces of Brandenburg and Pomerania from 1816 to 1841) about 3s. 5d. Whether this not very considerable difference between the Roman and the modern prices depends on a rise in the value of corn or on a fall in the value of silver, can hardly be decided.

It is very doubtful, perhaps, whether in the Rome of this and of later times the prices of corn really fluctuated more than is the case in modern times. If we compare prices like those quoted above, of 4d. and 5d. for

In a great industrial state, whose agriculture cannot feed its population, such a result might perhaps be regarded as useful or at any rate as not absolutely injurious; but a country like Italy, where manufactures were inconsiderable and agriculture was altogether the mainstay of the state, was in this way systematically ruined, and the welfare of the nation as a whole was sacrificed in the most shameful fashion to the interests of the essentially unproductive population of the capital, to which in fact bread could never become too cheap. Nothing perhaps evinces so clearly as this, how wretched was the constitution and how incapable was the administration of this so-called golden age of the republic. Any representative system, however meagre, would have led at least to serious complaints and to a perception of the seat of the evil but in those collective assemblages of the burgesses anything was listened to sooner than the warning voice of a foreboding patriot. Any government that deserved the name would of itself have interfered; but the mass of the Roman senate probably with well-meaning credulity regarded the low prices of grain as a real blessing for the people, and the Scipios and Flamininuses had, forsooth, more important things to do—to emancipate the Greeks, and to exercise the functions of republican kings. So the ship drove on unhindered towards the breakers.

When the small holdings ceased to yield any substantial clear return, the farmers were irretrievably ruined, and the more so that they gradually, although more slowly than the other classes, lost the moral tone and frugal habits of the earlier ages of the republic. It is merely a question of time, how rapidly the hides of the Italian farmers would, by purchase or by resignation, become merged in the larger estates. The landlord was better able to maintain himself than the former. The former produced at a cheaper rate than the latter, when, instead of letting his land according to the older system to petty temporary lessees, he caused it according to the newer system to be cultivated by his slaves. Accordingly, where this course had not been adopted even at an earlier period (i. 437), the competition of Sicilian slave-corn compelled the Italian landlord to adopt it,

the bushel and a half, with those of the worst times of war-dearth and famine—such as in the second Punic war when the same quantity rose to 9s. 7d. (1 *medimnus*=15 *drachmae*; Polyb. ix. 44), in the civil war to 19s. 2d. (1 *modius*=5 *denarii*; Cic. *Verr.* iii. 92, 214), in the great dearth under Augustus, even to 21s. 3d. (5 *modii*=27½ *denarii*; Euseb. *Chron. p. Chr.* 7, *Scal.*)—the difference is indeed immense; but such extreme cases are but little instructive, and might in either direction be found recurring under the like conditions at the present day.

and to have the work performed by slaves without wife or child
instead of families of free labourers. The landlord, moreover,
could hold his ground better against competitors by means of
improvements or changes in cultivation, and he could content
himself with a smaller return from the soil than the farmer,
who wanted capital and intelligence and who merely had what
was requisite for his subsistence. Hence the Roman landholder
comparatively neglected the culture of grain—which in many
cases seems to have been restricted to the raising of the quantity
required for the staff of labourers [1]—and gave increased attention
to the production of oil and wine as well as to the breeding of
cattle. These, under the favourable climate of Italy, had no
need to fear foreign competition; Italian wine, Italian oil,
Italian wool not only commanded the home markets, but were
soon sent abroad; the valley of the Po, which could find no
consumption for its corn, provided the half of Italy with swine
and bacon. With this the statements that have reached us
as to the economic results of Roman husbandry very well agree.
There is some ground for assuming that capital invested in land
was reckoned to yield a good return at 6 per cent.; this appears
to accord with the average rate of interest at this period, which
was about twice as much. The rearing of cattle yielded on the
whole better results than arable husbandry: in the latter the
vineyard gave the best return, next came the vegetable garden
and the olive orchard, while meadows and corn-fields yielded
least.[2] It is of course presumed that each species of husbandry

---

[1] Accordingly Cato calls the two estates, which he describes, summarily
"olive plantation" (*olivetum*) and "vineyard" (*vinea*), although not wine
and oil merely, but grain also and other products were cultivated there.
If indeed the 800 *culei*, for which the possessors of the vineyard are directed
to provide themselves with casks (11), formed the maximum of a year's
vintage, the whole of the 100 *iugera* must have been planted with vines,
because a produce of 8 *culei* per *iugerum* was almost unprecedented (Colum.
iii. 3); but Varro (i. 22) understood, and evidently with reason, the estimate
to apply to the case of the possessor of a vineyard who found it necessary
to make the new vintage before he had sold the old.

[2] That the Roman landlord made on an average 6 per cent. on his
capital, we infer from Colum. iii. 3, 9. We have a precise estimate of the
expense and produce only in the case of the vineyard, for which Columella
gives the following calculation of the cost per *iugerum* :—

Price of the ground	1000	sesterces.
Price of the slaves who work it (proportion to		
iugerum)	1143	,,
Vines and stakes	2000	,,
Loss of interest during the first two years . .	497	,,

Total 4640 sesterces=£47.

He calculates the produce as, at any rate, 60 *amphorae*, worth at least was prosecuted under the conditions that suited it, and on the soil which was adapted to its nature. These circumstances were already in themselves sufficient to supersede the husbandry of the petty farmer gradually by the system of farming on a great scale; and it was difficult by means of legislation to counteract them. But an injurious effect was produced by the Claudian law to be mentioned afterwards (shortly before $\frac{536}{218}$), which excluded the senatorial houses from mercantile speculation, and thereby artificially compelled them to invest their enormous capitals mainly in land or, in other words, to replace the old homesteads of the farmers by estates under the management of land-stewards and by pastures for cattle. Moreover special circumstances tended to favour the growth of pastoral husbandry as contrasted with agriculture, although the former was far more injurious to the state. First of all, this form of extracting profit

900 sesterces (£9), which would thus represent a return of 17 per cent. But this is somewhat illusory, as, apart from bad harvests, the cost of gathering in the produce (p. 346), and the expenses of the maintenance of the vines, stakes, and slaves, are omitted from the estimate.

The gross produce of meadow, pasture, and forest is estimated by the same agricultural writer as, at most, 100 sesterces per *iugerum*, and that of corn land as less rather than more: in fact, the average return of 25 *modii* of wheat per *iugerum*, gives, according to the average price in the capital of 1 *denarius* per *modius*, not more than 100 sesterces for the gross proceeds, and at the seat of production the price must have been still lower. Varro (iii. 2) reckons as a good ordinary gross return for a larger estate 150 sesterces per *iugerum*. Estimates of the corresponding expense have not reached us: as a matter of course, the management in this instance cost much less than in that of a vineyard.

All these statements, moreover, date from a century or more after Cato's death. From him we have only the general statement that the breeding of cattle yielded a better return than agriculture (*ap.* Cicero, *De Off.* ii. 25, 89; Colum. vi. *præf.* 4, comp. ii. 16, 2; Plin. *H. N.* xviii. 5, 30; Plutarch, *Cato*, 21); which of course is not meant to imply that it was everywhere advisable to convert arable land into pasture, but is to be understood relatively as signifying that the capital invested in the rearing of flocks and herds on mountain pastures and other suitable grounds yielded, as compared with capital invested in cultivating suitable corn land, a higher interest. Perhaps the circumstance has been also taken into account in the calculation, that the want of energy and intelligence in the landlord operates far less injuriously in the case of pasture land than in the highly developed culture of the vine and olive. On an arable estate, according to Cato, the returns of the soil stood as follows in a descending series:— 1, vineyard; 2, vegetable garden; 3, osier copse, which yielded a large return in consequence of the culture of the vine; 4, olive plantation; 5, meadow yielding hay; 6, corn fields; 7, copse; 8, wood for felling; 9, oak forest for forage to the cattle; all of which nine elements enter into the scheme of husbandry for Cato's model estates.

The higher net return of the culture of the vine as compared with that of corn is attested also by the fact, that under the award pronounced in the arbitration between the city of Genua and the villages tributary to it in $\frac{637}{117}$ the city received a sixth of wine, and a twentieth of grain, as quitrent.

from the soil—the only one which in reality demanded and rewarded operations on a great scale—alone corresponded to the vast capital and to the enterprising spirit of the capitalists of this age. An estate under cultivation, although not demanding the presence of the master constantly, required his frequent appearance on the spot, while the circumstances did not well admit of his enlarging such an estate or of his multiplying his possessions except within narrow limits; whereas an estate under pasture admitted of unlimited enlargement, and claimed little of the owner's attention. For this reason men already began to convert good arable land into pasture even at an economic loss—a practice which was prohibited by legislation (we know not when, perhaps about this period) but hardly with success. The growth of pastoral husbandry was favoured also by the occupation of the domain land. As the portions so occupied were ordinarily large, the system gave rise almost exclusively to great estates; and not only so, but the occupiers of these possessions, which might be resumed by the state at pleasure and were in law always insecure, were afraid to invest any considerable amount in their cultivation—by planting vines for instance, or olives. The consequence was, that these lands were mainly turned to account as pasture.

We are prevented from giving a similar comprehensive view of the moneyed economy of Rome, partly by the want of special treatises descending from Roman antiquity on the subject, partly by its very nature which was far more complex and varied than that of the Roman husbandry. So far as can be ascertained, its principles were, still less perhaps than those of husbandry, the peculiar property of the Romans; on the contrary, they were the common heritage of all ancient civilisation, under which, as under that of modern times, the operations on a great scale naturally were everywhere much alike. The system of mercantile and moneyed speculation appears to have been established in the first instance by the Greeks, and to have been simply adopted by the Romans. Yet the precision with which it was carried out and the magnitude of the scale on which its operations were conducted were so peculiarly Roman, that the spirit of the Roman economy and its grandeur whether for good or evil are pre-eminently conspicuous in its monetary transactions.

The starting-point of the Roman moneyed economy was of course money-lending; and no branch of commercial industry was more zealously prosecuted by the Romans than the trade of the professional money-lender (*fenerator*) and of the money·

dealer or banker (*argentarius*). The transference of the charge
of the larger monetary transactions from the individual capitalists to the mediating banker, who receives and makes payments
for his customers, invests and borrows money, and conducts
their money dealings at home and abroad—which is the mark
of a developed system of capital—was already completely carried
out in the time of Cato. The bankers, however, were not only
the cashiers of the rich in Rome, but everywhere insinuated
themselves into minor branches of business and settled in ever-
increasing numbers in the provinces and dependent states.
Already throughout the whole range of the empire the business
of making advances to those who wanted money began to be,
so to speak, monopolised by the Romans.

Closely connected with this was the immeasurable field of
speculative enterprise. The system of transacting business
through the medium of contract pervaded the whole dealings
of Rome. The state took the lead by letting all its more complicated revenues and all contracts for furnishing supplies and
executing buildings to capitalists, or associations of capitalists,
for a fixed sum to be given or received. But private persons
also uniformly contracted for whatever admitted of being done
by contract—for buildings, for the ingathering of the harvest
(p. 346), and even for the partition of an inheritance among the
heirs or the winding up of a bankrupt estate; in which case the
contractor—usually a banker—received the whole assets, and
engaged on the other hand to settle the liabilities in full or up
to a certain percentage and to pay the balance as the circumstances required.

The prominence of transmarine commerce at an early period
in the Roman national economy has already been adverted to
in its proper place. The further stimulus, which it received
during the present period, is attested by the increased importance
of the Italian customs-duties in the Roman financial system
(p. 308). In addition to the causes of this increase in the
importance of transmarine commerce which need no further
explanation, it was artificially promoted by the privileged position which the ruling Italian nation assumed in the provinces,
and by the exemption from customs-dues which was probably
even now in many of the dependent states conceded by treaty
to the Romans and Latins.

On the other hand, industrial art remained comparatively
undeveloped. Trades were no doubt indispensable, and there
appear indications that to a certain extent they were concentrated

in Rome; Cato, for instance, advises the Campanian landowner
to purchase the slaves' clothing and shoes, the ploughs, vats,
and locks, which he may require, in Rome. From the great
consumption of woollen stuffs the manufacture of cloth must
have been extensive and lucrative.[1] But no endeavours were
apparently made to transplant to Italy any such professional
industry as existed in Egypt and Syria, or even to carry it on
abroad with Italian capital. Flax indeed was cultivated in
Italy and purple dye was prepared there, but the latter branch
of industry at least belonged mainly to the Greek Tarentum,
and probably the importation of Egyptian linen and Milesian
or Tyrian purple even now preponderated everywhere over the
native manufacture.

Under this category, however, falls to some extent the leasing
or purchase by Roman capitalists of landed estates beyond Italy,
with a view to carry on the cultivation of grain and the rearing
of cattle on a great scale. This species of speculation, which
afterwards developed itself to proportions so enormous, probably
began within the period now before us; particularly in Sicily,
where the commercial restrictions imposed on the Siceliots
(p. 63), if not introduced for the very purpose, must have at
least tended to give to the Roman speculators who were exempt
from such restrictions a sort of monopoly of the profits deriv-
able from land.

Business in all these different branches was uniformly carried
on by means of slaves. The money-lenders and bankers
instituted, throughout the range of their business, additional
counting-houses and branch banks under the direction of their
slaves and freedmen. The company which had leased the
customs-duties from the state appointed chiefly their slaves and
freedmen to levy them at each custom-house. Every one who
took contracts for buildings bought architect-slaves; every one
who undertook to provide spectacles or gladiatorial games on
behalf of those to whom that duty pertained purchased or
trained a company of slaves skilled in acting, or a band of serfs
expert in the trade of fighting. The merchant imported his
wares in vessels of his own under the charge of slaves or freedmen, and disposed of them by the same means in wholesale or
retail. We need hardly add that the working of mines and
manufactories was conducted entirely by slaves. The situation

[1] The industrial importance of the Roman cloth-making is evident from
the remarkable part which is played by the fullers in Roman comedy.
The profitable nature of the fullers' pits is attested by Cato (*ap.* Plutarch,
Cat. 21).

of these slaves was, no doubt, far from enviable, and was through-out less favourable than that of slaves in Greece; but, if we leave out of account the classes last mentioned, the industrial slaves found their position on the whole more tolerable than the rural serfs. They had more frequently a family and a practically inde-pendent household, with no remote prospect of obtaining their freedom and property of their own. Hence such positions formed the true training school of those upstarts from the servile class, who by menial virtues and often by menial vices rose to the rank of Roman citizens and not unfrequently attained great prosperity, and who morally, economically, and politically contributed at least as much as the slaves themselves to the ruin of the Roman commonwealth.

The Roman mercantile transactions of this period fully kept pace with the contemporary development of political power, and were no less grand of their kind. In order to gain a clear idea of the activity of the traffic with other lands, we have only to look into the literature, more especially into the comedies of this period, in which the Phoenician merchant is brought on the stage speaking Phoenician, and the dialogue swarms with Greek and half Greek words and phrases. But the extent and energy of the Roman traffic may be traced most distinctly by means of coins and monetary relations. The Roman *denarius* kept pace with the Roman legions. We have already mentioned (p. 62) that the Sicilian mints—last of all that of Syracuse in $\frac{542}{212}$—were closed or at any rate restricted to small money in consequence of the Roman conquest, and that in Sicily and Sardinia the *denarius* obtained legal circulation at least side by side with the older silver currency and probably very soon became the exclusive legal tender. With equal if not greater rapidity the Roman silver coinage penetrated into Spain, where the great silver-mines existed and there was virtually no earlier national coinage; at a very early period the Spanish towns even began to coin after the Roman standard (p. 199). On the whole, as Carthage coined only to a very limited extent (p. 19), there existed not a single important mint in addition to that of Rome in the region of the western Mediterranean, with the exception of the mint of Massilia and perhaps also those of the Illyrian Greeks at Apollonia and Dyrrhachium. Accordingly, when the Romans began to establish themselves in the region of the Po, these mints were about $\frac{525}{229}$, subjected to the Roman standard in such a way, that, while they retained the right of coining silver, they uniformly—and the Massiliots in particular

—were led to adjust their *drachma* to the weight of the Roman three-quarter *denarius*, which the Roman government on its part began to coin, primarily for the use of Upper Italy, under the name of the "coin of victory" (*victoriatus*). This new system, based on the Roman, prevailed throughout the Massiliot, Upper Italian, and Illyrian territories; and these coins even penetrated into the barbarian lands on the north, those of Massilia, for instance, into the Alpine districts along the whole basin of the Rhone, and those of Illyria as far as the modern Transylvania. The eastern half of the Mediterranean was not yet reached by the Roman money, as it had not yet fallen under the direct sovereignty of Rome; but its place was filled by gold, the true and natural medium for international and transmarine commerce. It is true that the Roman government, in conformity with its strictly conservative character, adhered—with the exception of a temporary coinage of gold occasioned by the financial embarrassment during the Hannibalic war (p. 161)—steadfastly to the rule of coining silver only in addition to the national-Italian copper; but commerce had already assumed such dimensions, that it was able in the absence of money to conduct its transactions with gold by weight. Of the sum in cash, which lay in the Roman treasury in $\frac{597}{187}$, scarcely a sixth was coined or uncoined silver, five-sixths consisted of gold in bars,[1] and beyond doubt the precious metals were found in all the chests of the larger Roman capitalists in substantially similar proportions. Already therefore gold held the first place in great transactions; and, as may be inferred from this fact, the preponderance of traffic was maintained with foreign lands, and particularly with the East, which since the times of Philip and Alexander the Great had adopted a gold currency.

The whole gain from these immense transactions of the Roman capitalists flowed in the long run to Rome; for, much as they went abroad, they were not easily induced to settle permanently there, but sooner or later returned to Rome, either realising their gains and investing them in Italy, or continuing to carry on business from Rome as a centre by means of the capital and connections which they had acquired. The moneyed superiority of Rome as compared with the rest of the civilised world was, accordingly, quite as decided as its political and military ascendancy. Rome in this respect stood towards

[1] There were in the treasury 17,410 Roman pounds of gold, 22,070 pounds of uncoined, and 18,230 pounds of coined, silver. The legal ratio of gold to silver was: 1 pound of gold=4000 sesterces, or 1 : 11.91.

other countries somewhat as the England of the present day
stands towards the Continent—a Greek, for instance, observes
of the younger Scipio Africanus, that he was not rich " for a
Roman." We may form some idea of what was considered as
riches in the Rome of those days from the fact, that Lucius
Paullus with an estate of 60 talents (£14,000) was not reckoned
a wealthy senator, and that a dowry—such as each of the
daughters of the elder Scipio Africanus received—of 50 talents
(£12,000) was regarded as a suitable portion for a maiden of
quality, while the estate of the wealthiest Greek of this century
was not more than 300 talents (£72,000).

It was no wonder, accordingly, that the mercantile spirit took
possession of the nation, or rather—for that was no new thing
in Rome—that the spirit of the capitalist now penetrated and
pervaded all aspects and stations of life, and agriculture as well
as the government of the state began to become enterprises of
capitalists. The preservation and increase of wealth positively
formed a part of public and private morality. " A widow's
estate may diminish; " Cato wrote in the practical instructions
which he composed for his son, " a man must augment his substance, and he is deserving of praise and full of a divine spirit,
whose account-books at his death show that he has gained more
than he has inherited." Wherever, therefore, there was giving
and counter-giving, every transaction although concluded without any sort of formality was held as valid, and in case of necessity the right of action was accorded to the party aggrieved if
not by the law, at any rate by mercantile custom and judicial
usage; [1] but the promise of a gift without due form was null alike
in legal theory and in practice. In Rome, Polybius tells us,
nobody gives to any one unless he must do so, and no one pays
a penny before it falls due, even among near relatives. The very
legislation yielded to this mercantile morality, which regarded
all giving away without recompense as squandering; the giving
of presents and bequests and the undertaking of sureties were
subjected to restriction at this period by decree of the people,
and heritages which did not fall to the nearest relatives were
at any rate taxed. In the closest connection with such views
mercantile punctuality, honour, and respectability pervaded
the whole of Roman life. Every ordinary man was morally
bound to keep an account-book of his income and expenditure

---

[1] On this was based the actionable character of contracts of buying,
hiring, and partnership, and, in general, the whole system of non-formal
actionable contracts.

—in every well-arranged house, accordingly, there was a separate record-chamber (*tablinum*)—and every one took care he should not leave the world without having made his will: it was one of the three matters in his life which Cato declares that he regretted, that he had been a single day without a testament. Those household books were universally by Roman usage admitted as valid evidence in a court of justice, nearly in the same way as we admit the evidence of a merchant's ledger. The word of a man of unstained repute was admissible not merely against himself, but in his own favour; nothing was more common than to settle differences between persons of integrity by means of an oath demanded by the one party and given by the other—a mode of settlement which was reckoned valid even in law; and a traditional rule enjoined the jury, in the absence of evidence, to give their verdict in favour of the man of unstained character when opposed to one who was less reputable, and only in the event of both parties being of equal repute to give it in favour of the defendant.[1] The conventional respectability of the Romans was especially apparent in the more and more strict enforcement of the rule, that no respectable man should allow himself to be paid for the performance of personal services. Accordingly magistrates, officers, jurymen, guardians, and generally all respectable men entrusted with public functions, received no recompense for the services which they rendered except, at most, a compensation for their bare outlay; and not only so, but the services which intimate acquaintances (*amici*) rendered to each other—such as giving security, representation in law-suits, custody (*depositum*), lending of objects not intended to be let on hire (*commodatum*), the managing and attending to business in general (*procuratio*)— were treated according to the same principle, so that it was improper to receive any compensation for them and an action was not allowable even where a compensation had been promised. How entirely the man was merged in the merchant, appears most distinctly perhaps in the substitution of a money-payment and an action at law for the duel—even for the political duel—in the Roman life of this period. The usual form of settling questions

---

[1] The chief passage as to this point is the fragment of Cato in Gellius, xiv. 2. In the case of the *obligatio litteris* also, *i.e.*, a claim based solely on the entry of a debt in the account-book of the creditor, this legal recognition of the personal credibility of the party, even where his testimony in his own cause is concerned, affords the key of explanation; and hence it happened that in later times, when this mercantile honour had vanished from Roman life, the *obligatio litteris*, while not exactly abolished, fell of itself into desuetude.

of personal honour was this: a wager was laid between the offender and the party offended as to the truth or falsehood of the offensive assertion, and under the shape of an action for the stake the question of fact was submitted with all the forms of law to a jury; the acceptance of such a wager when offered by the offended or offending party was, just like the acceptance of a challenge to a duel at the present day, left open in law, but in point of honour it could seldom be refused.

One of the most important consequences of this mercantile spirit, which displayed itself with an intensity hardly conceivable by those not engaged in business, was the extraordinary impulse given to the formation of associations. In Rome this was especially fostered by the system already often mentioned as adopted by the government in the transaction of its business —the system of middlemen: for from the extent of the transactions it was natural, and it was probably often required by the state for the sake of greater security, that capitalists should undertake such leases and contracts not individually, but in partnership. All great transactions were organised on the model of these state-contracts. Indications are even found of the occurrence among the Romans of that feature so characteristic of the system of association—a coalition of rival companies in order jointly to establish monopolist prices.[1] In transmarine transactions more especially and such as were otherwise attended with considerable risk, the system of partnership was so extensively adopted, that it practically took the place of insurances, which were unknown to antiquity. Nothing was more common than the nautical loan, as it was called—the modern " bottomry "—by which the risk and gain of transmarine traffic were proportionally distributed among the owners of the vessel and cargo and all the capitalists who had advanced money for the voyage. It was, however, a general rule of Roman economy that one should rather take small shares in many speculations than speculate independently; Cato advised the capitalist not

[1] In the remarkable model contract given by Cato (141) for the letting of the olive-harvest, there is the following paragraph:—
" None [of the persons desirous to contract on the occasion of letting] shall withdraw, for the sake of causing the gathering and pressing of the olives to be let at a dearer rate; except when [the joint bidder] immediately names [the other bidder] as his partner. If this rule shall appear to have been infringed, all the partners [of the company with which the contract has been concluded] shall, if desired by the landlord or the overseer appointed by him, take an oath [that they have not conspired in this way to prevent competition]. If they do not take the oath, the stipulated price is not to be paid." It is tacitly assumed that the contract is taken by a company, not by an individual capitalist.

to fit out a single ship with his money, but to enter into concert with forty-nine other capitalists so as to send out fifty ships and to take an interest in each, to the extent of a fiftieth share. The greater complication thus introduced into business was overcome by the Roman merchant through his punctual laboriousness and his system of management by slaves and freedmen, which, regarded from the point of view of the pure capitalist, was far preferable to our counting-house system. Thus these mercantile companies, with their hundred ramifications, largely influenced the economy of every Roman of note. There was, according to the testimony of Polybius, hardly a man of means in Rome who had not been concerned as an avowed or silent partner in leasing the public revenues; and much more must each have invested on an average a considerable portion of his capital in mercantile associations generally.

All this laid the foundation for that endurance of Roman wealth, which was perhaps still more remarkable than its magnitude. The phenomenon, unique perhaps of its kind, to which we have already called attention (p. 304)—that the condition of the great houses remained almost the same for several centuries—finds its explanation in the somewhat narrow but solid principles on which they managed their mercantile property.

In consequence of the one-sided prominence assigned to capital in the Roman economy, the evils inseparable from a pure capitalist system could not fail to appear.

Civil equality, which had already received a fatal wound through the rise of the ruling order of lords, suffered an equally severe blow in consequence of the line of social demarcation becoming more and more distinctly drawn between the rich and the poor. Nothing more effectually promoted this separation in a downward direction than the already-mentioned rule— apparently a matter of indifference, but in reality involving the deepest arrogance and insolence on the part of the capitalists— that it was disgraceful to take money for work; a wall of partition was thus raised not merely between the common day-labourer or artisan and the respectable landlord or manufacturer, but also between the soldier or subaltern and the military tribune, and between the clerk or messenger and the magistrate. In an upward direction a similar barrier was raised by the Claudian law suggested by Gaius Flaminius (shortly before $\frac{536}{218}$), which prohibited senators and senators' sons from possessing sea-going vessels except for the transport of the produce of their estates, and probably also from participating in public contracts—forbidding them generally from carrying on whatever the Romans included under the head of " speculation " (*quaestus*).[1] It is true that this enactment was not called for by the senators; it was on the contrary a work of the democratic opposition, which perhaps desired in the first instance merely to prevent the evil of members of the governing class personally entering into dealings with the government. It may be, moreover, that the capitalists in this instance, as so often afterwards, made common cause with the democratic party, and seized the opportunity of diminishing competition by the exclusion of the senators. The former object was, of course, only very imperfectly attained, for the system of partnership opened up to the senators ample facilities for continuing to speculate in secret; but this decree of the people drew a regal line of demarcation between those men of quality who did not speculate at all or at any rate not openly and those who did, and it placed alongside of the aristocracy which was primarily political an aristocracy which was purely moneyed—the equestrian order, as it was afterwards called, whose rivalries with the senatorial order fill the history of the following century.

A further consequence of the one-sided power of capital was the disproportionate prominence of those branches of business which were the most sterile and the least productive to the national economy as a whole. Industrial art, which ought to have held the highest place, in fact occupied the lowest. Commerce flourished; but it was universally non-reciprocal. Even on the northern frontier the Romans do not seem to have been able to give merchandise in exchange for the slaves who were brought in numbers from the Celtic and probably even from the Germanic territories to Ariminum and the other markets of northern Italy; at least as early as $\frac{523}{231}$ the export of silver money to the Celtic territory was prohibited by the Roman government. In the intercourse with Greece, Syria, Egypt, Cyrene, and Carthage, the balance of trade was necessarily unfavourable to Italy. Rome began to become the capital of the Mediterranean states, and Italy to become the suburbs of Rome; the Romans had no wish to be anything more, and in their opulent indifference were satisfied with a non-reciprocal

---

[1] Livy (xxi. 63; comp. Cic. *Verr.* v. 18, 45) mentions only the enactment as to the sea-going vessels; but Asconius (*in Or. de Toga Cand.* p. 94. Orell.) and Dio (lv. 10, 5) state that the senator was also forbidden by law to undertake state-contracts (*redemptiones*); and, as according to Livy " all speculation was considered indecorous in a senator," the Claudian law probably went further than he states.

commerce, such as every city which is nothing more than a capital necessarily carries on—they possessed, forsooth, money enough to pay for everything which they needed or did not need. On the other hand the most unproductive of all sorts of business, the traffic in money and the farming of the revenue, formed the true mainstay and stronghold of the Roman economy. And, lastly, whatever elements that economy had contained for the production of a prosperous middle class and of a lower one provided with sufficient subsistence were extinguished by the unhappy system of employing slaves, or, at the best, contributed to the multiplication of the troublesome order of freedmen.

But above all the deep-rooted immorality, which is inherent in an economy of pure capital, ate into the heart of society and of the commonwealth, and substituted an absolute selfishness for humanity and patriotism. The better portion of the nation were very clearly aware of the seeds of corruption which lurked in that pursuit of speculation; and the instinctive hatred of the great multitude, as well as the displeasure of the well-disposed statesman, was especially directed against the trade of the professional money-lender, which for long had been subjected to penal laws and still continued under the letter of the law amenable to punishment. In a comedy of this period the money-lender is told that the class to which he belongs is on a parallel with the *lenones*—

> Eodem hercle vos pono et paro ; parissumi estis ibus.
> Hi saltem in occultis locis prostant : vos in foro ipso :
> Vos fenore, hi male suadendo et lustris lacerant homines.
> Rogitationes plurimas propter vos populus scivit,
> Quas vos rogatas rumpitis : aliquam reperitis rimam.
> Quasi aquam ferventem frigidam esse, ita vos putatis leges.

Cato the leader of the reform party expresses himself still more emphatically than the comedian. " Lending money at interest," he says in the preface to his treatise on agriculture, " has various advantages; but it is not honourable. Our forefathers accordingly ordained, and inscribed it among their laws, that the thief should be bound to pay two-fold, but the man who takes interest four-fold, compensation; whence we may infer how much worse a citizen they deemed the usurer than the thief." There is no great difference, he elsewhere considers, between a money-lender and a murderer; and it must be allowed that his acts did not fall short of his words—when governor of Sardinia, by his rigorous administration of the law he drove the Roman bankers to their wits' end. The great majority of the ruling senatorial order regarded the system of the speculators with dislike, and not only conducted themselves in the provinces on the whole with more integrity and honour than these moneyed men, but frequently acted as a check on them. The frequent changes of the supreme magistrates, however, and the inevitable inequality in their mode of handling the laws, necessarily rendered the effort to check such proceedings in great measure ineffectual.

The Romans perceived moreover—as it was not difficult to perceive—that it was of far more consequence to give a different direction to the whole national economy than to exercise a police control over speculation; it was such views mainly that men like Cato enforced by precept and example on the Roman agriculturist. " When our forefathers," continues Cato in the preface just quoted, " pronounced the eulogy of a worthy man, they praised him as a worthy farmer and a worthy landlord; one who was thus commended was thought to have received the highest praise. The merchant I deem energetic and diligent in the pursuit of gain; but his calling is too much exposed to perils and mischances. On the other hand farmers furnish the bravest men and the ablest soldiers; no calling is so honourable, safe, and inoffensive as theirs, and those who occupy themselves with it are least liable to evil thoughts." He was wont to say of himself, that his property was derived solely from two sources —agriculture and frugality; and, though this was neither very logically expressed nor strictly conformable to the truth,[1] yet Cato was not unjustly regarded by his contemporaries and by posterity as the model of a Roman landlord. Unhappily it is a truth as remarkable as it is painful, that this husbandry, commended so much and certainly with so entire good faith as a remedy, was itself pervaded by the poison of the capitalist system. In the case of pastoral husbandry this was obvious; for that reason it was most in favour with the public and least in favour with the party desirous of moral reform. But how stood the case with agriculture itself? The warfare, which from the third to the fifth century U.C. capital had waged against labour, by withdrawing under the form of interest on debt the

---

[1] Cato, like every other Roman, invested a part of his means in the breeding of cattle, and in commercial and other undertakings. But it was not his habit directly to violate the laws; he neither speculated in state-leases—which as a senator he was not allowed to do—nor practised usury. It is an injustice to charge him with a practice in the latter respect at variance with his theory; the *fenus nauticum*, in which he certainly engaged, was not a branch of usury prohibited by the law; it really formed an essential part of the business of chartering and freighting vessels.

revenues of the soil from the working farmers and bringing them into the hands of the idly consuming fund-holder, had been settled chiefly by the extension of the Roman economy and the transference of the capital which existed in Latium to the field of mercantile activity opened up throughout the range of the Mediterranean. Now even the extended field of business was no longer able to contain the increased mass of capital; and an insane legislation laboured simultaneously to compel the investment of senatorial capital by artificial means in Italian estates, and systematically to depreciate the arable land of Italy by interference with the prices of grain. Thus there began a second campaign of capital against free labour or—what was substantially the same thing in antiquity—against the small farmer system; and, if the first had been bad, it yet seemed mild and humane as compared with the second. The capitalists no longer lent to the farmer at interest—a course which in itself was not now practicable because the petty landholder no longer produced any surplus of consequence, and was moreover not sufficiently simple and radical—but they bought up the farms and converted them, at the best, into estates managed by stewards and wrought by slaves. This also was called agriculture; it was in reality the application of the capitalist system to the produce of the soil. The description of the husbandmen, which Cato gives, is excellent and quite just; but how does it correspond to the system itself which he portrays and recommends? If a Roman senator, as must not unfrequently have been the case, possessed four such estates as that described by Cato, the same space, which in the olden time when small holdings prevailed had supported from 100 to 150 farmers' families, was now occupied by one family of free persons and about 50, for the most part unmarried, slaves. If this was the remedy by which the decaying national economy was to be restored to vigour, it bore, unhappily, an aspect of extreme resemblance to the disease.

The general result of this system is only too clearly obvious in the changed proportions of the population. It is true that the condition of the various districts of Italy was very unequal, and some were even prosperous. The farms, instituted in great numbers in the region between the Apennines and the Po at the time of its colonisation, did not so speedily disappear. Polybius, who visited that quarter not long after the close of the present period, commends its numerous, handsome, and vigorous population: with a just legislation as to corn it would doubtless have been possible to make the basin of the Po, and not Sicily, the granary of the capital. In like manner Picenum and the so-called *ager Gallicus* acquired a numerous body of farmers through the distributions of domain-land consequent on the Flaminian law of $\frac{522}{232}$—a body, however, which was sadly reduced in the Hannibalic war. In Etruria, and perhaps also in Umbria, the internal condition of the subject communities was unfavourable to the flourishing of a class of free farmers. Matters were better in Latium—which could not be entirely deprived of the advantages of the market of the capital, and which had on the whole been spared by the Hannibalic war—as well as in the secluded mountain-valleys of the Marsians and Sabellians. On the other hand the Hannibalic war had fearfully devastated southern Italy and had ruined, in addition to a number of smaller places, its two largest cities, Capua and Tarentum, both once able to send into the field armies of 30,000 men. Samnium had recovered from the severe wars of the fifth century: according to the census of $\frac{529}{225}$ it was in a position to furnish as many men capable of arms as all the Latin towns, and it was probably at that time, next to the *ager Romanus*, the most flourishing region of the peninsula. But the Hannibalic war had desolated the land afresh, and the assignations of land in that quarter to the soldiers of Scipio's army, although considerable, probably did not cover the loss. Campania and Apulia, both hitherto well-peopled regions, were still worse treated in the same war by friend and foe. In Apulia, no doubt, assignations of land were made afterwards, but the colonies instituted there were not successful. The beautiful plain of Campania remained better peopled; but the territory of Capua and of the other communities broken up in the Hannibalic war became public property, and the occupants of it were uniformly not proprietors, but petty temporary lessees. Lastly, in the wide Lucanian and Bruttian territories the population, which was already very thin before the Hannibalic war, was visited by the whole severity of the war itself and of the penal executions that followed in its train; nor was much done on the part of Rome to revive the agriculture there—with the exception perhaps of Valentia (Vibo, now Monteleone), none of the colonies established there attained any real prosperity.

With every allowance for the inequality in the political and economic circumstances of the different districts and for the comparatively flourishing condition of several of them, the retro-gression is yet on the whole unmistakable, and it is confirmed by the most indisputable testimonies as to the general condition of Italy. Cato and Polybius agree in stating that Italy was at the end of the sixth century far weaker in population than at the end of the fifth, and was no longer able to furnish armies so large as in the first Punic war. The increasing difficulty of the levy, the necessity of lowering the qualification for service in the legions, and the complaints of the allies as to the magnitude of the contingents to be furnished by them, confirm these statements; and, in the case of the Roman burgesses, the numbers tell the same tale. In $\frac{502}{252}$, shortly after the expedition of Regulus to Africa, they amounted to 298,000 men capable of bearing arms; thirty years later, shortly before the commencement of the Hannibalic war ($\frac{534}{220}$), they had fallen off to 270,000, or by a tenth, and again twenty years after that, shortly before the end of the same war ($\frac{550}{204}$), to 214,000, or by a fourth; and a generation afterwards—during which no extraordinary losses occurred, but the institution of the great burgess-colonies in the plain of northern Italy in particular occasioned a perceptible and exceptional increase—the numbers of the burgesses had hardly again reached the point at which they stood at the commencement of this period. If we had similar statements regarding the Italian population generally, they would beyond all doubt exhibit a deficit relatively still more considerable. The decline of the national vigour less admits of proof; but it is stated by the writers on agriculture that flesh and milk disappeared more and more from the diet of the common people. At the same time the slave population increased, as the free population declined. In Apulia, Lucania, and the Bruttian land, pastoral husbandry must even in the time of Cato have preponderated over agriculture; the half-savage slave-herdsmen had in reality the command of the country. Apulia was rendered so insecure by them that a strong force had to be stationed there; in $\frac{569}{185}$ a slave-conspiracy planned on the largest scale, and mixed up with the proceedings of the Bacchanalia, was discovered there, and nearly 7000 men were judicially condemned. In Etruria also Roman troops were obliged to take the field against a band of slaves ($\frac{558}{196}$), and even in Latium there were instances in which towns like Setia and Praeneste were in danger of being surprised by a band of runaway serfs ($\frac{556}{198}$). The nation was visibly diminishing, and the community of free burgesses was resolving itself into a body composed of masters and slaves; and, although it was in the first instance the two long wars with Carthage which decimated and ruined both the burgesses and the allies, the Roman capitalists beyond doubt contributed quite as much as Hamilcar and Hannibal to the decline in the vigour and the numbers of the Italian people. No one can say whether the government could have rendered help; but it was an alarming and discreditable fact, that the circles of the Roman aristocracy, well-meaning and energetic as for the most part they were, never once showed any insight into the real gravity of the situation or any foreboding of the full magnitude of the danger. When a Roman lady belonging to the high nobility, the sister of one of the numerous citizen-admirals who in the first Punic war had ruined the fleets of the state, one day got among a crowd in the Roman Forum, she said aloud in the hearing of those around, that it was high time to place her brother once more at the head of the fleet and to relieve the pressure in the market-place by bleeding the citizens afresh ($\frac{508}{246}$). Those who thus thought and spoke were, no doubt, a small minority; nevertheless this outrageous speech was simply a forcible expression of the criminal indifference with which the whole noble and rich world looked down on the common citizens and farmers. They did not exactly desire their destruction, but they allowed it to run its course; and so desolation advanced with gigantic steps over the flourishing land of Italy, where countless numbers of free men had lately rejoiced in moderate and merited prosperity.

CHAPTER XIII

FAITH AND MANNERS

LIFE in the case of the Roman was spent under conditions of austere restraint, and, the nobler he was, the less he was a free man. All-powerful custom restricted him to a narrow range of thought and action; and to have led a serious and strict or, to use the characteristic Latin expressions, a grave and severe life, was his glory. Nothing more or less was expected of him than that he should keep his household in good order and unflinchingly bear his part of counsel and action in public affairs. But, while the individual had neither the wish nor the power to be aught else than a member of the community, the glory and the might of that community were felt by every individual burgess as a personal possession to be transmitted along with his name and his homestead to his posterity; and thus, as one generation after another was laid in the tomb and each in succession added its fresh contribution to the stock of ancient honours, the collective sense of dignity in the noble families of Rome swelled into that mighty pride of Roman citizenship, to which the earth has never perhaps witnessed a parallel, and the traces of which, as strange as they are grand, seem to us whenever we meet them to belong as it were to another world. It was one of the characteristic peculiarities of this powerful pride of citizenship, that, while not suppressed, it was yet compelled by the rigid simplicity and equality that prevailed among the citizens to remain locked up within the breast during life, and was only allowed to find expression after death; but it was displayed in the funeral of the man of distinction so conspicuously and intensely, that this ceremonial is better fitted than any other phenomenon of Roman life to give to us who live in other times a glimpse of that wonderful spirit of the Romans.

It was a singular procession, at which the citizens were invited to be present by the summons of the public crier: " Yonder warrior is dead; whoever can, let him come to escort Lucius Aemilius; he is borne forth from his house." It was opened by bands of wailing women, musicians, and dancers; one of the latter was dressed out and furnished with a mask in imitation of the deceased, and by gesture doubtless and action recalled once more to the multitude the appearance of the well-known man. Then followed the most magnificent and peculiar part of the solemnity—the procession of ancestors—before which all the rest of the pageant so faded in comparison, that men of rank of the true Roman type enjoined their heirs to restrict the funeral pomp to that procession alone. We have already mentioned that the face-masks of those ancestors who had filled the curule aedileship or any higher ordinary magistracy, wrought in wax and painted—modelled as far as possible after life, but not wanting even for the earlier ages up to and beyond the time of the kings—were wont to be placed in wooden niches along the walls of the family hall, and were regarded as the chief ornament of the house. When a death occurred in the family, suitable persons, chiefly actors, were dressed up with these face-masks and the corresponding official costume to take part in the funeral ceremony, so that the ancestors—each in the principal dress worn by him in his lifetime, the triumphator in his gold-embroidered, the censor in his purple, and the consul in his purple-bordered, robe, with their lictors and the other insignia of office —all in chariots gave the final escort to the dead. On the bier overspread with massive purple and gold-embroidered coverlets and fine linen cloths lay the deceased himself, likewise in the full costume of the highest office which he had filled, and surrounded by the armour of the enemies whom he had slain and by the chaplets which in jest or earnest he had won. Behind the bier came the mourners, all dressed in black and without ornament, the sons of the deceased with their heads veiled, the daughters without veil, the relatives and clansmen, the friends, the clients and freedmen. Thus the procession passed on to the Forum. There the corpse was placed in an erect position; the ancestors descended from their chariots and seated themselves in the curule chairs; and the son or nearest gentile kinsman of the deceased ascended the rostra, in order to announce to the assembled multitude in simple recital the names and deeds of each of the men sitting in a circle around him and, last of all, those of him who had recently died.

This may be called a barbarous custom, and a nation of artistic feelings would certainly not have tolerated the continuance of this odd resurrection of the dead down to an epoch of fully developed civilisation; but even Greeks who were very dispassionate and but little disposed to reverence, such as

Polybius, acknowledged the imposing effect produced by the naïve pomp of this funeral ceremony. It was a conception essentially in keeping with the grave solemnity, the uniform movement, and the proud dignity of Roman life, that departed generations should continue to walk, as it were, corporeally among the living, and that, when a burgess weary of labours and of honours was gathered to his fathers, these fathers themselves should appear in the Forum to receive him among their number.

But the Romans had now reached a crisis of transition. Now that the power of Rome was no longer confined to Italy but had spread far and wide to the west and to the east, the days of the old home life of Italy were over, and a Hellenising civilisation came in its room. It is true that Italy had been subject to the influence of Greece, ever since it had a history at all. We have formerly shown how the youthful Greece and the youthful Italy —both of them with some measure of simplicity and originality —gave and received intellectual impulses; and how at a later period Rome endeavoured after a more external manner to appropriate to practical use the language and inventions of the Greeks. But the Hellenism of the Romans of the present period was, in its causes as well as its consequences, something essentially new. The Romans began to feel the lack of a richer intellectual life, and to be startled as it were at their own utter want of mental culture; and, if even nations of artistic gifts, such as the English and Germans, have not disdained in the pauses of their own productiveness to avail themselves of the miserable French culture for filling up the gap, it need excite no surprise that the Italian nation now flung itself with eager zeal on the glorious treasures as well as on the dissolute filth of the intellectual development of Hellas. But it was an impulse still more profound and deep-rooted, which carried the Romans irresistibly into the Hellenic vortex. Hellenic civilisation still doubtless assumed that name, but it was Hellenic no longer; it was, in fact, humanistic and cosmopolitan. It had solved the problem of moulding a mass of different nations into one whole completely in the field of intellect, and to a certain extent also in that of politics; and, now when the same task on a wider scale devolved on Rome, she entered on the possession of Hellenism along with the rest of the inheritance of Alexander the Great. Hellenism therefore was no longer a mere stimulus or accessory influence; it penetrated the Italian nation to the very core. Of course, the vigorous home life of Italy strove against the foreign element. It was only after a most vehement struggle that the Italian farmer abandoned the field to the cosmopolite of the capital; and, as in Germany the French coat called forth the national Germanic frock, so the reaction against Hellenism aroused in Rome a tendency which opposed the influence of Greece on principle, in a fashion altogether foreign to the earlier centuries, and in doing so fell pretty frequently into downright follies and absurdities.

No department of human action or thought remained un-affected by this struggle between the old fashion and the new. Even political relations were largely influenced by it. The whimsical project of emancipating the Hellenes, the well-deserved failure of which has already been described, the kindred, likewise Hellenic, idea of a combination of republics in opposition to kings, and the desire of propagating Hellenic polity at the expense of eastern despotism—which were the two principles that regulated, for instance, the treatment of Mace-donia—were fixed ideas of the new school, just as dread of the Carthaginians was the fixed idea of the old; and, if Cato pushed the latter to a ridiculous excess, Philhellenism now and then indulged in extravagance at least as foolish. For example, the conqueror of king Antiochus not only had a statue of himself in Greek costume erected on the Capitol, but also, instead of calling himself in good Latin *Asiaticus*, assumed the unmeaning and anomalous, but yet magnificent and almost Greek, surname of *Asiagenus*.[1] A more important consequence of this attitude of the ruling nation towards Hellenism was, that the process of Latinising gained ground everywhere in Italy except where it encountered the Hellenes. The cities of the Greeks in Italy, so far as the war had not destroyed them, remained Greek. Apulia, about which, it is true, the Romans gave themselves little concern, appears at this very epoch to have been thoroughly pervaded by Hellenism, and the local civilisation there seems to have attained the level of the decaying Hellenic culture by its side. Tradition is silent on the matter; but the numerous coins of cities, uniformly furnished with Greek inscriptions, and the manufacture of painted vases after the Greek style, which was

[1] That *Asiagenus* was the original title of the hero of Magnesia and of his descendants, is established by coins and inscriptions; the fact that the Capitoline Fasti call him *Asiaticus* is one of several traces indicating that these have undergone a non-contemporaneous revision. The former surname can only be a corruption of Ἀσιαγένης—the form which later authors substituted for it—which signifies not a conqueror of Asia, but an Asiatic by birth.

carried on alone in that part of Italy with more ambition and gaudiness than taste, show that Apulia had completely adopted Greek habits and Greek art.

But the real struggle between Hellenism and its national antagonists during the present period was carried on in the field of faith, of manners, and of art and literature; and we must not omit to attempt some delineation of this great strife of principles, however difficult it may be to present a summary view of the myriad forms and aspects which the conflict assumed.

The extent to which the old simple faith still retained a living hold on the Italians is shown very clearly by the admiration or astonishment which this problem of Italian piety excited among the contemporary Greeks. On occasion of the quarrel with the Aetolians it was reported of the Roman commander-in-chief that during battle he was solely occupied in praying and sacrificing like a priest; whereas Polybius with his somewhat stale moralising calls the attention of his countrymen to the political usefulness of this piety, and admonishes them that a state cannot consist of wise men alone, and that such ceremonies are very convenient for the sake of the multitude.

But if Italy still possessed—what had long been a mere antiquarian curiosity in Hellas—a national religion, it was already visibly beginning to be ossified into theology. The torpor creeping over faith is nowhere perhaps so distinctly apparent as in the alterations in the economy of divine service and of the priesthood. The public service of the gods became not only more tedious, but above all more and more costly. In $\frac{558}{196}$ there was added to the three old colleges of the augurs, pontifices, and keepers of oracles, a fourth consisting of three " banquet-masters " (*tres viri epulones*), solely for the important purpose of superintending the banquets of the gods. The priests, as well as the gods, were in fairness entitled to feast; new institutions, however, were not needed with that view, as every college applied itself with zeal and devotion to its convivial affairs. The clerical banquets were accompanied by the claim of clerical immunities. The priests even in times of grave embarrassment claimed the right of exemption from public burdens, and only after very troublesome controversy submitted to make payment of the taxes in arrear ($\frac{558}{196}$). To the individual, as well as to the community, piety became a more and more costly article. The custom of instituting endowments, and generally of undertaking permanent pecuniary obligations, for religious objects prevailed among the Romans in a manner similar to its prevalence in

Roman Catholic countries at the present day. These endowments—particularly after they came to be regarded by the supreme spiritual and at the same time the supreme juristic authority in the state, the pontifices, as a real burden devolving *de jure* on every heir or other person acquiring the estate—began to form an extremely oppressive charge on property; "inheritance without sacrificial obligation" was a proverbial saying among the Romans somewhat similar to our "rose without a thorn." The dedication of a tenth of their substance became so common, that twice every month a public entertainment was given from the proceeds in the Forum Boarium at Rome. With the Oriental worship of the Mother of the Gods there was imported to Rome among other pious nuisances the practice, annually recurring on certain fixed days, of demanding penny-collections from house to house (*stipem cogere*). Lastly, the subordinate class of priests and soothsayers, as was reasonable, rendered no service without being paid for it; and beyond doubt the Roman dramatist sketched from life, when in the curtain-conversation between husband and wife he represents the account for pious services as ranking with the accounts for the cook, the nurse, and other customary presents:—

> *Da mihi, vir, ———— quod dem Quinquatribus*
> *Praecantrici, conjectrici, hariolae atque haruspicae;*
> *Tum piatricem clementer non potest quin munerem.*
> *Flagitium est, si nil mittetur, quo supercilio spicit.*

The Romans did not create a god of Gold, as they had formerly created one of Silver (i. 432); nevertheless he reigned in reality alike over the highest and lowest spheres of religious life. The old pride of the Latin national religion—the moderation of its economic demands—was irrevocably gone.

At the same time its ancient simplicity also departed. Theology, the spurious offspring of reason and faith, was already occupied in introducing its own tedious prolixity and solemn inanity into the old homely national faith, and thereby expelling the true spirit of that faith. The catalogue of the duties and privileges of the priest of Jupiter, for instance, might well have a place in the Talmud. They pushed the natural rule —that no religious service can be acceptable to the gods unless it is free from flaw—to such an extent in practice, that a single sacrifice had to be repeated thirty times in succession on account of mistakes again and again committed, and that the games, which also formed a part of divine service, were regarded as undone if the presiding magistrate had committed any slip in

word or deed or if the music even had paused at a wrong time,
and so had to be begun afresh, frequently for several, even as
many as seven, times in succession.

This exaggeration of conscientiousness was already a symptom
of its incipient torpor; and the reaction against it—indifference
and unbelief—appeared without delay. Even in the first Punic
war ($\frac{505}{249}$) an instance occurred in which the consul himself made
an open jest of consulting the auspices before battle—a consul,
it is true, belonging to the peculiar clan of the Claudii, which
alike in good and evil was ahead of its age. Towards the end of
this epoch complaints were loudly made that the lore of the
augurs was neglected, and that, to use the language of Cato,
a number of ancient auguries and auspices were falling into
oblivion through the indolence of the college. An augur like
Lucius Paullus, who regarded the priesthood as a science and not
as a mere title, was already a rare exception, and could not but
be so, when the government more and more openly and un-
hesitatingly employed the auspices for the accomplishment of its
political designs, or, in other words, treated the national religion
in accordance with the view of Polybius as a superstition useful
for imposing on the public at large. Where the way was thus
paved, the Hellenistic irreligious spirit found free course. In
connection with the incipient taste for art the sacred images of
the gods began as early as the time of Cato to be employed, like
other furniture, in adorning the apartments of the rich. More
dangerous wounds were inflicted on religion by the rising literature. It could not indeed venture on open attacks, and such
direct additions as were made by its means to religious ideas
—e.g. the Pater Caelus formed by Ennius from the Roman
Saturnus in imitation of the Greek Uranos—were, while Hellenistic, of no great importance. But the diffusion of the doctrines
of Epicharmus and Euhemerus in Rome was fraught with
momentous consequences. The poetical philosophy, which the
later Pythagoreans had extracted from the writings of the old
Sicilian comedian Epicharmus of Megara (about $\frac{280}{470}$), or rather
had, at least for the most part, circulated under cover of his
name, regarded the Greek gods as natural substances, Zeus as
the atmosphere, the soul as a particle of sun-dust, and so forth.
This philosophy of nature, like the Stoic doctrine in later times,
had in its most general outlines a certain affinity with the Roman
religion, and was, in so far, calculated to undermine the national
religion by resolving it into allegory. An historical analysis
of religion was given in the *Sacred Memoirs* of Euhemerus of

Messene (about $\frac{459}{300}$), which, under the form of a narrative of the travels of the author among the marvels of foreign lands, subjected to a thorough and searching investigation the accounts current as to the so-called gods, and resulted in the conclusion that there neither were nor are gods at all. To indicate the character of the book, it may suffice to mention the one fact, that the story of Kronos devouring his children is explained as arising out of the existence of cannibalism in the earliest times and its abolition by king Zeus. Notwithstanding, or even by virtue of, its insipidity and destructive tendency the production had an undeserved success in Greece, and helped, in concert with the current philosophies there, to bury the dead religion. It is a remarkable indication of the expressed and conscious antagonism between religion and the new philosophy that Ennius already translated into Latin those notoriously destructive writings of Epicharmus and Euhemerus. The translators may have justified themselves at the bar of Roman police by pleading that the attacks were directed only against the Greek, and not against the Latin, gods; but the evasion was tolerably transparent. Cato was, from his own point of view, quite right in assailing these tendencies indiscriminately, wherever they met him, with his own peculiar bitterness, and in calling even Socrates a corrupter of morals and offender against religion.

Thus the old national religion was visibly on the decline; and, as the great trees of the primeval forest were uprooted, the soil became covered with a rank growth of thorns and briars and with weeds that had never been seen before. Native superstitions and foreign impostures of the most various hues mingled, competed, and conflicted with each other. No Italian stock remained exempt from this transmuting of old faith into new superstition. As the lore of entrails and of lightning was cultivated among the Etruscans, so the liberal art of observing birds and conjuring serpents flourished luxuriantly among the Sabellians and more particularly the Marsians. Even among the Latin nation, and in fact in Rome itself, we meet with similar phenomena, although they are, comparatively speaking, less conspicuous. Such for instance were the lots of Praeneste, and the remarkable discovery at Rome in $\frac{573}{181}$ of the tomb and posthumous writings of king Numa. These were alleged to prescribe religious rites altogether strange and unheard of; but the credulous were to their regret not permitted to learn more than this, coupled with the fact that the books looked very new; for the senate laid hands on the treasure and ordered the rolls to be summarily thrown into the fire. The home manufacture was quite sufficient to meet such demands of folly as might reasonably be expected; but the Romans were far from being content with it. The Hellenism of that epoch, already de-nationalised and pervaded by Oriental mysticism, introduced not only unbelief but also superstition in its most offensive and dangerous forms to Italy; and these vagaries moreover had a special charm, precisely because they were foreign.

Chaldaean astrologers and casters of nativities were already in the sixth century spread throughout Italy; but a still more important event—one making in fact an epoch in history—was the reception of the Phrygian Mother of the Gods among the publicly recognised divinities of the Roman state, to which the government had been obliged to give their consent during the last weary years of the Hannibalic war ($\frac{550}{204}$). A special embassy was sent for the purpose to Pessinus, a city in the territory of the Celts of Asia Minor; and the rough field-stone, which the priests of the place liberally presented to the foreigners as the real Mother Cybele, was received by the community with un-paralleled pomp. Indeed, by way of perpetually commemorat-ing the joyful event, clubs in which the members entertained each other in rotation were instituted among the higher classes, and seem to have materially stimulated the rising tendency to the formation of cliques. With the permission thus granted for the *cultus* of Cybele the worship of the Orientals gained a footing officially in Rome; and, though the government strictly insisted that the emasculate priests of the new gods should remain Celts (*Galli*) as they were called, and that no Roman burgess should devote himself to this pious eunuchism, yet the barbaric pomp of the " Great Mother "—her priests clad in Oriental costume with the chief eunuch at their head, marching in procession through the streets to the foreign music of fifes and kettledrums, and begging from house to house—and the whole character of the system, half sensuous, half monastic, must have exercised a most material influence over the sentiments and views of the people.

The effect was only too rapidly and fearfully apparent. A few years later ($\frac{568}{186}$) rites of the most abominable character came to the knowledge of the Roman authorities: a secret nocturnal festival in honour of the god Bacchus had been first introduced into Etruria through a Greek priest, and, spreading like a cancer, had rapidly reached Rome and propagated itself over all Italy, everywhere corrupting families and giving rise

to the most heinous crimes, unparalleled unchastity, falsifying
of testaments, and murdering by poison. More than 7000 men
were sentenced to punishment, most of them to death, on this
account, and rigorous enactments were issued as to the future;
yet they did not succeed in repressing the system, and six years
later ($\frac{6}{1}\frac{7}{8}\frac{4}{0}$) the magistrate to whom the matter fell complained
that 3000 men more had been condemned and still there appeared
no end of the evil.

Of course all rational men were agreed in the condemnation
of these spurious forms of religion—as absurd as they were
injurious to the commonwealth: the pious adherents of the
older faith and the partisans of Hellenic enlightenment concurred
in their ridicule of, and indignation at, this superstition. Cato
made it an instruction to his steward, " that he was not to present
any offering, or to allow any offering to be presented on his
behalf, without the knowledge and orders of his master, except
at the domestic hearth and on the wayside-altar at the Com-
pitalia, and that he should consult no *haruspex, hariolus*, or
Chaldaeus." The well-known question as to how a priest could
contrive to suppress laughter when he met his colleague
originated with Cato, and was primarily applied to the Etruscan
haruspex. Much in the same spirit Ennius censures in true
Euripidean style the mendicant soothsayers and their adherents:

> *Sed superstitiosi vates impudentesque arioli,*
> *Aut inertes aut insani aut quibus egestas imperat,*
> *Qui sibi semitam non sapiunt, alteri monstrant viam,*
> *Quibus divitias pollicentur, ab eis drachumam ipsi petunt.*

But in such times reason from the first plays a losing game
against unreason. The government, no doubt, interfered; the
pious impostors were punished and expelled by the police; every
foreign worship not specially sanctioned was forbidden; even
the consulting of the comparatively innocent lot-oracle of Prae-
neste was officially prohibited in $\frac{5}{2}\frac{1}{4}\frac{2}{2}$; and, as we have already
said, those who took part in the Bacchanalia were rigorously
prosecuted. But, when once men's heads are thoroughly
turned, no command of the higher authorities avails to set
them right again. How much the government was obliged to
concede, or at any rate did concede, is obvious from what
has been stated. The Roman custom under which the state
consulted Etruscan sages in certain emergencies and the government accordingly took steps to secure the traditional trans-
mission of Etruscan lore in the noble families of Etruria, as well
as the permission of the secret worship of Demeter which was not

immoral and was restricted to women, may probably be ranked with the earlier innocent and comparatively indifferent adoption of foreign rites. But the admission of the worship of the *Magna Dea* was a bad sign of the weakness which the government felt in presence of the new superstition, perhaps even of the extent to which it was itself pervaded by it; and it showed in like manner either an unpardonable negligence or something still worse, that the authorities only took steps against such proceedings as the Bacchanalia at so late a stage, and even then on an accidental information.

The picture, which has been handed down to us of the life of Cato the Elder, enables us in substance to perceive how, according to the ideas of the respectable Roman citizens of that period, the private life of the Roman should be spent. Active as Cato was as a statesman, pleader, author, and mercantile speculator, family life always formed with him the central object of existence; it was better, he thought, to be a good husband than a great senator. His domestic discipline was strict. The servants were not allowed to leave the house without orders, nor to talk of what occurred in the household to strangers. The more severe punishments were not inflicted capriciously, but sentence was pronounced and executed after a quasi-judicial procedure: the strictness with which offences were punished may be inferred from the fact, that one of his slaves who had concluded a purchase without orders from his master hanged himself on the matter coming to Cato's ears. For slight offences, such as mistakes committed in waiting at table, the consular was wont after dinner to administer to the culprit the proper number of lashes with a thong wielded by his own hand. He kept his wife and children in order no less strictly, but by other means; for he declared it sinful to lay hands on a wife or grown-up children in the same way as on slaves. In the choice of a wife he disapproved marrying for money, and recommended men to look to good descent; but he himself married in old age the daughter of one of his poor clients. Moreover he adopted views in regard to continence on the part of the husband similar to those which everywhere prevail in slave countries; a wife was throughout regarded by him as simply a necessary evil. His writings abound in invectives against the chattering, finery-loving, ungovernable fair sex; it was the opinion of the old lord that " all women are plaguy and proud," and that, " were men quit of women, their life would probably be less godless." On the other hand the rearing of his children born in wedlock was a

matter which touched his heart and his honour, and the wife in
his eyes existed strictly and solely for the children's sake. She
nursed them ordinarily herself, or, if she allowed her children to
be suckled by female slaves, she also allowed their children in
return to draw nourishment from her own breast; one of the
few traits, which indicate an endeavour to mitigate the institution of slavery by ties of human sympathy—the common
impulses of maternity and the bond of foster-brotherhood.
The old general was present in person, whenever it was possible,
at the washing and swaddling of his children. He watched with
reverential care over their childlike innocence; he assures us that
he was as careful lest he should utter an unbecoming word in
presence of his children as if he had been in presence of the Vestal
Virgins, and that he never before the eyes of his daughters embraced their mother, except when she had become alarmed
during a thunder-storm. The education of his son was perhaps
the noblest portion of his varied and variously honourable
activity. True to his maxim, that a ruddy-cheeked boy was
worth more than a pale one, the old soldier in person initiated
his son into all bodily exercises, and taught him to wrestle, to
ride, to swim, to box, and to endure heat and cold. But he
felt very justly, that the time had gone by when it sufficed for a
Roman to be a good farmer and soldier; and he felt also that it
could not but have an injurious influence on the mind of his boy,
if he should subsequently learn that the teacher, who had
rebuked and punished him and had won his reverence, was a
mere slave. Therefore he in person taught the boy what a
Roman was wont to learn, to read and write and know the law
of the land; and even in his later years he worked his way so
far into the general culture of the Hellenes, that he was able to
deliver to his son in his native tongue whatever in that culture he
deemed to be of use to a Roman. All his writings were primarily
intended for his son, and he wrote his historical work for that
son's use with large distinct letters in his own hand. He lived
in a homely and frugal style. His strict parsimony tolerated no
expenditure on luxuries. He allowed no slave to cost him more
than 1500 *denarii* (£65) and no dress more than 100 *denarii*
(£4 6s.); no carpet was to be seen in his house, and for a long
time there was no whitewash on the walls of the rooms.
Ordinarily he partook of the same fare with his servants, and
did not suffer his outlay in cash for the meal to exceed 30 *asses*
(2s.); in time of war even wine was uniformly banished from his
table, and he drank water or, according to circumstances, water

mixed with vinegar. On the other hand, he was no enemy to hospitality; he was fond of associating both with his club in town and with the neighbouring landlords in the country; he sat long at table, and, as his varied experience and his shrewd and ready wit made him a pleasant companion, he disdained neither the dice nor the wine-flask: among other receipts in his book on husbandry he even gives a tried recipe for the case of a too hearty meal and too deep potations. His life up to extreme old age was one of ceaseless activity. Every moment was apportioned and occupied; and every evening he was in the habit of turning over in his mind what he had heard, said, or done during the day. Thus he found time for his own affairs as well as for those of his friends and of the state, and time also for conversation and pleasure; everything was done quickly and without many words, and his genuine spirit of activity hated nothing so much as bustle or a great ado about trifles.

So lived the man who was regarded by his contemporaries and by posterity as the true model of a Roman burgess, and who appeared as it were the living embodiment of the—certainly somewhat coarse-grained—energy and honesty of Rome as opposed to Greek indolence and Greek immorality; as a later Roman poet says:

> *Sperne mores transmarinos, mille habent offucias.*
> *Cive Romano per orbem nemo vivit rectius.*
> *Quippe malim unum Catonem, quam trecentos Socratas.*

Such judgments will not be absolutely adopted by history; but every one who carefully considers the revolution which the degenerate Hellenism of this age accomplished in the modes of life and thought among the Romans, will be inclined to deepen rather than to modify that condemnation of the foreign manners.

The ties of family life became relaxed with fearful rapidity. The evil of grisettes and boy-favourites spread like a pestilence, and, as matters stood, it was not possible to take any material steps in the way of legislation against it. The high tax, which Cato as censor ($\frac{570}{184}$) laid on this most abominable species of slaves kept for luxury, would not be of much moment, and besides fell practically into disuse a year or two afterwards along with the property-tax generally. Celibacy—as to which grave complaints were made as early as $\frac{520}{234}$—and divorces naturally increased in proportion. Horrible crimes were perpetrated in the bosom of families of the highest rank; for instance, the consul Gaius Calpurnius Piso was poisoned by his wife and his stepson, in order to occasion a supplementary election to the consulship and so to procure the supreme magistracy for the latter—a plot which was successful ($\frac{574}{180}$). Moreover the emancipation of women began. According to old custom the married woman was subject in law to the marital power which was parallel with the paternal, and the unmarried woman to the guardianship of her nearest male *agnati* which fell little short of the paternal power; the wife had no property of her own, the virgin and widow had at any rate no right of management. But now women began to aspire to independence in respect to property, and, getting quit of the guardianship of their *agnati* by evasive lawyers' expedients — particularly through mock marriages—they took the management of their property into their own hands, or, in the event of being married, sought by means not much better to withdraw themselves from the marital power, which under the strict letter of the law was necessary. The mass of capital which was collected in the hands of women appeared to the statesmen of the time so dangerous, that they resorted to the extravagant expedient of prohibiting by law the testamentary nomination of women as heirs ($\frac{585}{169}$), and even sought by a highly arbitrary practice to deprive women for the most part of those collateral inheritances which fell to them without testament. In like manner the family jurisdiction over women, which was connected with that marital and tutorial power, became practically more and more antiquated. Even in public matters women already began to have a will of their own and occasionally, as Cato thought, " to rule the rulers of the world;" their influence might be traced in the comitia, and already statues were erected in the provinces to Roman ladies.

Luxury prevailed more and more in dress, ornaments, and furniture, in buildings and at table. Especially after the expedition to Asia Minor in $\frac{564}{190}$ Asiatico-Hellenic luxury, such as prevailed at Ephesus and Alexandria, transferred its empty refinement and its petty trifling, destructive alike of money, time, and pleasure, to Rome. Here too women took the lead: in spite of the zealous invective of Cato they managed to procure the abolition, after the peace with Carthage ($\frac{559}{195}$), of the decree of the people passed soon after the battle of Cannae ($\frac{539}{215}$), which forbade them to use gold ornaments, variegated dresses, or chariots; no course was left to their zealous antagonist but to impose a high tax on those articles ($\frac{570}{184}$). A multitude of new and for the most part frivolous articles—silver plate elegantly figured, table-couches with bronze mounting, Attalic dresses as they were called, and carpets of rich gold brocade—now found their way to Rome. Above all, this new luxury appeared in the appliances of the table. Hitherto without exception the Romans had only partaken of hot dishes once a day; now hot dishes were not unfrequently produced at the second meal (*prandium*), and for the principal meal the two courses formerly in use no longer sufficed. Hitherto the women of the household had themselves attended to the baking of bread and cooking; and it was only on occasion of entertainments that a professional cook was specially hired, who in that case superintended alike the cooking and the baking. Now, on the other hand, a scientific cookery began to prevail. In the better houses a special cook was kept. A division of labour became necessary, and the trade of baking bread and cakes branched off from that of cooking— the first bakers' shops in Rome appeared about $\frac{583}{171}$. Poems on the art of good eating, with long lists of the most palatable fishes and other marine products, found their readers: and the theory was reduced to practice. Foreign delicacies—anchovies from Pontus, wine from Greece—began to be esteemed in Rome, and Cato's receipt for giving to the ordinary wine of the country the flavour of Coan by means of brine would hardly inflict any considerable injury on the Roman wine-merchants. The old decorous singing and reciting of the guests and their boys were supplanted by Asiatic *sambucistriae*. Hitherto the Romans had perhaps drunk pretty deeply at supper, but drinking-banquets in the strict sense were unknown; now formal revels came into vogue, on which occasions the wine was little or not at all diluted and was drunk out of large cups, and the drinking of healths, in which each was bound to follow his neighbour in regular succession, formed the leading feature—" drinking after the Greek style " (*Graeco more bibere*) or " playing the Greek " (*pergraecari, congraecare*) as the Romans called it. In consequence of this debauchery, dice-playing, which had long been in use among the Romans, reached such a height that it was necessary for legislation to interfere. The aversion to labour and the habit of idle lounging were visibly on the increase.[1] Cato pro-

---

[1] A sort of *parabasis* in the Curculio of Plautus describes what went on in the leading thoroughfares of the capital, with little humour perhaps, but with life-like distinctness.

> Commonstrabo, quo in quemque hominem facile inveniatis loco,
> Ne nimio opere sumat operam, si quem conventum velit,
> Vel vitiosum vel sine vitio, vel probum vel improbum.
> Qui perjurum convenire volt hominem, mitto in comitium ;
> Qui mendacem et gloriosum, apud Cloacinae sacrum.

posed to have the market paved with pointed stones, in order to put a stop to the habit of idling; the Romans laughed at the jest and went on to enjoy the pleasure of loitering and gazing around them.

We have already noticed the alarming increase of the popular amusements during this epoch. At the beginning of it, apart from some unimportant foot and chariot races which should rather be ranked with religious ceremonies, only a single general festival was held in the month of September, lasting four days and having a definitely fixed maximum of cost (i. 452). At the close of the epoch, this popular festival had a duration of at least six days; and besides this there were celebrated at the beginning of April the festival of the Mother of the Gods or the so-called Megalensia, towards the end of April that of Ceres and that of Flora, in June that of Apollo, in November the Plebeian games—all of them probably occupying already more days than one. To these fell to be added the numerous cases where the games were celebrated afresh—in which pious scruples probably often served as a mere pretext—and the incessant extraordinary festivals. Among these the already-mentioned banquets furnished from the dedicated tenths (p. 375), the feast of the gods, the triumphal and funeral festivities, were conspicuous; and above all the festal games which were celebrated—for the first time in $\frac{505}{249}$—at the close of one of those longer periods which were marked off in the Etrusco-Roman religion, the *saecula*, as they were called. At the same time domestic festivals were multiplied. During the second Punic war there were introduced

[*Ditis damnosos maritos sub Basilica quaerito.*
Ibidem erunt scorta exoleta, quique stipulari solent.]
Symbolarum collatores apud forum piscarium.
In foro infimo boni homines atque dites ambulant.
In medio propter Canalem, ibi ostentatores meri.
Confidentes garrulique et malevoli supra Lacum,
Qui alteri de nihilo audacter dicunt contumeliam.
Et qui ipsi sat habent quod ipsis vere possit dicier.
Sub Veteribus, ibi sunt, qui dant quique accipiunt foenori.
Pone aedem Castoris, ibi sunt, subito quibus credas male.
In Tusco vico, ibi sunt homines, qui ipsi sese venditant.
In Velabro vel pistorem, vel lanium, vel haruspicem,
Vel qui ipsi vorsant, vel, qui aliis subvorsentur, praebeant.
Ditis damnosos maritos apud Leucadiam Oppiam.

The verses in brackets are a subsequent addition, inserted after the building of the first Roman bazaar ($\frac{570}{184}$). The business of the baker (*pistor*, literally miller) embraced at this time the sale of delicacies and the providing accommodation for revellers (Festus, *Ep. v. alicariae*, p. 7, *Müll.*; Plautus, *Capt.* 160; *Poen.* i. 2, 54; *Trin.* 407). The same was the case with the butchers. Leucadia Oppia probably kept a house of bad fame.

among people of quality, the already-mentioned banquetings on the anniversary of the entrance of the Mother of the Gods (after $\frac{550}{204}$), and, among the lower orders, the similar Saturnalia (after $\frac{537}{217}$), both under the influence of the powers henceforth closely allied—the foreign priest and the foreign cook. A very near approach was made to that ideal condition in which every idler should know where he might kill the time every day; and this in a commonwealth where formerly action had been with all and sundry the very object of existence, and idle enjoyment had been proscribed by custom as well as by law! The bad and demoralising elements in these festal observances, moreover, daily acquired greater ascendancy. It is true that still as formerly the chariot races formed the brilliant finale of the national festivals; and a poet of this period describes very vividly the straining expectancy with which the eyes of the multitude were fastened on the consul, when he was on the point of giving the signal for the chariots to start. But the former amusements no longer sufficed; there was a craving for new and more varied spectacles. Greek athletes now made their appearance (for the first time in $\frac{568}{186}$) alongside of the native wrestlers and boxers. Of the dramatic exhibitions we shall speak hereafter: the introduction of Greek comedy and tragedy to Rome was a gain perhaps of doubtful value; but it formed at any rate the best of their acquisitions at this time. The Romans had probably long indulged in the sport of coursing hares and hunting foxes in presence of the public; now these innocent hunts were converted into formal baitings of wild animals, and the wild beasts of Africa—lions and panthers—were (first so far as can be proved in $\frac{568}{186}$) transported at great cost to Rome, in order that by killing or being killed they might serve to glut the eyes of the gazers of the capital. The still more revolting gladiatorial games, which prevailed in Campania and Etruria, now gained admission to Rome; human blood was first shed for sport in the Roman Forum in $\frac{490}{264}$. Of course these demoralising amusements encountered severe censure: the consul of $\frac{486}{268}$, Publius Sempronius Sophus, sent a divorce to his wife, because she had attended funeral games; the government managed to procure a decree of the people prohibiting the importation of wild beasts to Rome, and strictly insisted that no gladiators should appear at the public festivals. But here too it wanted either the proper power or proper energy: it succeeded, apparently, in checking the practice of baiting animals, but the appearance of sets of gladiators at private festivals, particularly at funeral celebrations, was not suppressed. Still less could the public be prevented from preferring the gladiator to the rope-dancer, the rope-dancer to the comedian, the comedian to the tragedian; or the stage be prevented from revelling by choice amidst the pollution of Hellenic life. Whatever elements of culture were contained in the scenic and artistic entertainments were from the first thrown aside; it was by no means the object of the Roman festivals to elevate—though it should be but temporarily—the whole body of spectators through the power of poetry to the level of feeling of the best, as the Greek stage did in the period of its prime, or to prepare an artistic treat for a select circle, as our theatres endeavour to do. The character of the managers and spectators in Rome is illustrated by a scene at the triumphal games in $\frac{587}{167}$, where the first Greek flute-players, on their melodies failing to please, were instructed by the director to box with one another instead of playing, upon which the delight knew no bounds.

Nor was the evil confined to the corruption of Roman manners by Hellenic contagion; conversely the scholars began to demoralise their instructors. Gladiatorial games, which were unknown in Greece, were first introduced by king Antiochus Epiphanes ($\frac{575-590}{179-184}$), a professed imitator of the Romans, at the Syrian court, and, although they excited at first greater horror than pleasure in the Greek public, which was more humane and had more of a taste for art than the Romans, they yet held their ground and gradually came more and more into vogue.

As a matter of course, this revolution in life and manners brought an economic revolution in its train. Residence in the capital became more and more coveted as well as more costly. Rents rose to an unexampled height. Extravagant prices were paid for the new articles of luxury; a barrel of anchovies from the Black Sea cost 1600 sesterces (£16)—more than the price of a rural slave; a beautiful boy cost 24,000 sesterces (£240)—more than many a farmer's homestead. Money therefore, and nothing but money, became the watchword with high and low. In Greece it had long been the case that nobody did anything without being paid for it, as the Greeks themselves with discreditable candour allowed: after the second Macedonian war the Romans began in this respect also to imitate the Greeks. Respectability had to provide itself with legal buttresses; pleaders, for instance, had to be prohibited by decree of the people from taking money for their services; the jurisconsults alone formed a noble exception, and needed no decree of the people to compel their adherence to the honourable custom of giving their good advice gratuitously. Men did not, if possible, steal outright; but all shifts seemed allowable in order to attain rapidly to riches—plundering and begging, cheating on the part of contractors and swindling on the part of speculators, usurious trading in money and in grain, even the turning of purely moral relations such as friendship and marriage to economic account. Marriage especially became on both sides a matter of mercantile speculation; marriages for money were common, and it appeared necessary to refuse legal validity to the presents which the spouses made to each other. That, under such a state of things, plans for setting fire on all sides to the capital came to the knowledge of the authorities, need excite no surprise. When man no longer finds enjoyment in work, and works merely in order to attain as quickly as possible to enjoyment, it is a mere accident that he does not become a criminal. Destiny lavished all the glories of power and riches with liberal hand on the Romans; but, in truth, the Pandora's box was a gift of doubtful value.

CHAPTER XIV

LITERATURE AND ART

THE influences which stimulated the growth of Roman literature were of a character altogether peculiar and hardly paralleled in any other nation. To estimate them correctly, it is necessary in the first place that we should glance at the national education and national recreations of this period.

Language lies at the root of all mental culture; and this was especially the case in Rome. In a community where so much importance was attached to speeches and documents, and where the citizen, at an age which is still according to modern ideas regarded as boyhood, was already entrusted with the uncontrolled management of his property and might find himself under the necessity of formally addressing the public assembly, not only was great value set all along on the fluent and polished use of the mother-tongue, but efforts were early made to acquire a command of it in the years of boyhood. The Greek language also was already generally diffused in Italy in the time of Hannibal. In the higher circles a knowledge of that language, which was the general medium of intercourse for ancient civilisation, had long been a far from uncommon accomplishment; and now, when the change in the position of Rome had so enormously increased the intercourse with foreigners and the foreign traffic, such a knowledge was, if not necessary, yet in all probability of very material importance to the merchant as well as the statesman. By means of the Italian slaves and freedmen, a very large portion of whom were Greek or half-Greek by birth, the Greek language and Greek knowledge to a certain extent reached even the lower ranks of the population, especially in the capital. The comedies of this period indicate that even the humbler classes of the capital were familiar with a sort of Latin, which could no more be properly understood without a knowledge of Greek than the English of Sterne or the German of Wieland without a knowledge of French.[1] Men of senatorial families,

[1] A distinct set of Greek expressions, such as *stratioticus, machaera, nauclerus, trapezita, danista, drapeta, oenopolium, bolus, malacus, morus,*

however, not only addressed a Greek audience in Greek, but even published their speeches—Tiberius Gracchus (consul in $\frac{577}{177}$ and $\frac{591}{163}$) so published a speech which he had given at Rhodes—and in the time of Hannibal wrote their chronicles in Greek, as we shall have occasion to mention more particularly in the sequel. Individuals went still farther.   The Greeks honoured Flamininus by complimentary demonstrations in the Roman language (p. 231), and he returned the compliment; the " great general of the Aeneiades " dedicated his votive gifts to the Greek gods after the Greek fashion in Greek distichs.[1] Cato reproached another senator with the fact, that he had the effrontery to deliver Greek recitations with the due modulation at Greek revels.

Under the influence of such circumstances Roman education developed itself.   It is a mistaken opinion, that antiquity was materially inferior to our own times in the general diffusion of elementary attainments.   Even among the lower classes and slaves there was considerable knowledge of reading, writing, and counting: in the case of a slave steward, for instance, Cato, following the example of Mago, takes for granted the ability to read and write.   Elementary instruction, as well as instruction in Greek, must have been long before this period imparted to a very considerable extent in Rome.   But the epoch now before us initiated an education, the aim of which was to communicate not merely an outward expertness, but a real mental culture. Hitherto a knowledge of Greek had conferred on its possessor as

graphicus, logus, apologus, techna, schema, forms quite a special feature in the language of Plautus.   Translations are seldom attached, and that only in the case of words not included in the circle of ideas to which those which we have cited belong; for instance, in the Truculentus—in a verse, however, that is perhaps a later addition (i. 1, 60)—we find the explanation: φρόνησις est sapientia.   Fragments of Greek also are common, as in the Casina (iii. 6, 9):

Πράγματά μοι παρέχεις—Dabo μέγα κακὸν, ut opinor.

Greek puns likewise occur, as in the Bacchides (240):

opus est chryso Chrysalo.

Ennius in the same way takes for granted that the etymological meaning of Alexandros and Andromache is known to the spectators (Varro, de L.L. vii. 82).   Most characteristic of all are the half-Greek formations, such as ferritribax, plagipatida, pugilice, or in the Miles Gloriosus (213):

Euge ! euscheme hercle astitit sic dulice et commoedice !

[1] One of these epigrams composed in the name of Flamininus runs thus:

Ζηνὸς ἰὼ κραιπναῖσι γεγαθότες ἱπποσύναισι
Κοῦροι, ἰὼ Σπάρτας Τυνδαρίδαι βασιλεῖς,
Αἰνεάδας Τίτος ὕμμιν ὑπέρτατον ὤπασε δῶρον
Ἑλλήνων τεύξας παισὶν ἐλευθερίαν.

little superiority in civil or social life, as a knowledge of French perhaps confers at the present day in a hamlet of German Switzerland; and the earliest writers of Greek chronicles probably held a position among the senators similar to that of the farmer in the fens of Holstein who has been a student and in the evening, when he comes home from the plough, takes down his Virgil from the shelf. A man who assumed airs of greater importance by reason of his Greek, was reckoned a bad patriot and a fool; and certainly even in Cato's time one who spoke Greek ill or not at all might still be a leading man and become senator and consul. But a change was already taking place. The internal decomposition of Italian nationality had already, particularly in the aristocracy, advanced so far as to render the substitution of a broader human culture for that nationality inevitable: and the craving after a more advanced civilisation was already powerfully stirring the minds of men. Instruction in the Greek language as it were spontaneously met this craving. The classical literature of Greece, the *Iliad* and still more the *Odyssey*, had all along formed the basis of that instruction; the overflowing treasures of Hellenic art and science were already by this means spread before the eyes of the Italians. Without any outward revolution, strictly speaking, in the character of the instruction the natural result was, that the empirical study of the language became converted into a higher study of the literature; that the general culture connected with such literary studies was communicated in increased measure to the scholars; and that these availed themselves of the knowledge thus acquired to dive into that Greek literature which most powerfully influenced the spirit of the age—the tragedies of Euripides and the comedies of Menander.

In a similar way greater importance came to be attached to the study of Latin. The higher society of Rome began to feel the need, if not of exchanging their mother-tongue for Greek, at least of refining it and adapting it to the changed state of culture; and for this purpose too they found themselves in every respect dependent on the Greeks. The economic arrangements of the Romans placed the work of elementary instruction in the mother-tongue—like every other work held in little estimation and performed for hire—chiefly in the hands of slaves, freedmen, or foreigners, or in other words chiefly in the hands of Greeks or half-Greeks;[1] which was attended with the less

---

[1] Such, *e.g.*, was Chilo, the slave of Cato the Elder, who earned money on his master's behalf as a teacher of children (Plutarch, *Cato Mai.* 20).

difficulty, because the Latin alphabet was almost identical with the Greek and the two languages possessed a close and striking affinity. But this was the least part of the matter; the importance of the study of Greek in a formal point of view exercised a far deeper influence over the study of Latin. Any one who knows how singularly difficult it is to find suitable matter and suitable forms for the higher intellectual culture of youth, and how much more difficult it is to set aside the matter and forms once found, will understand how it was that the Romans knew no mode of supplying the want of a more advanced Latin instruction except that of simply transferring the solution of this problem, which the study of the Greek language and literature furnished, to the study of Latin. In the present day a process entirely analogous goes on under our own eyes in the transference of the methods of instruction from the dead to the living languages.

But unfortunately the chief requisite for such a transference was wanting. The Romans could, no doubt, learn to read and write Latin by means of the Twelve Tables; but a Latin culture presupposed a literature, and no such literature existed in Rome.

To this want there was added another. We have already described the multiplication of the amusements of the Roman people. The stage had long played an important part in these recreations; the chariot-races formed strictly the principal amusement in all of them, but these races uniformly took place only on one, viz., the concluding, day, while the earlier days were substantially devoted to stage-entertainments. But for long these stage-representations consisted chiefly of dances and jugglers' feats; the improvised chants, which were produced on these occasions, had neither dialogue nor plot (i. 452). It was only now that the Romans looked around them for a real drama. The Roman popular festivals were throughout under the influence of the Greeks, whose talent for amusing and for killing time naturally rendered them the purveyors of pleasure to the Romans. Now no national amusement was a greater favourite in Greece, and none was more varied, than the theatre; it could not but speedily attract the attention of those who provided the Roman festivals and their staff of assistants. The earlier Roman stage-chant contained within it a dramatic germ capable perhaps of development; but to develop the drama from that germ required on the part of the poet and the public a genial power of imparting and receiving, such as was not to be found among the Romans at all, and least of all at this period; and, had it been possible to find it, the impatience of those entrusted with the amusement of the multitude would hardly have allowed to the noble fruit peace and leisure to ripen. In this case too there was an outward want, which the nation was unable to satisfy; the Romans desired a theatre, but the pieces were wanting.

On these elements Roman literature was based; and its defective character was from the first and necessarily the result of such an origin. All real art has its root in individual freedom and a cheerful enjoyment of life, and the germs of such an art were not wanting in Italy; but, when Roman life substituted for freedom and joyousness the sense of public obligation and the consciousness of duty, art was arrested and, instead of growing, necessarily pined away. The culminating point of Roman development was the period which had no literature. It was not till Roman nationality began to give way and Hellenico-cosmopolite tendencies began to prevail, that literature made its appearance at Rome in their train. Accordingly from the beginning, and by stringent internal necessity, it took its stand on Greek ground and in broad antagonism to the distinctively Roman national spirit. Roman poetry in particular had its immediate origin not in the inward impulse of the poet, but in the outward demands of the school, which needed Latin manuals, and of the stage, which needed Latin dramas. Now both institutions—the school and the stage—were thoroughly anti-Roman and revolutionary. The gaping and staring idleness of the theatre was utterly offensive to the sober earnestness and the spirit of activity which animated the Romans of the olden type; and—inasmuch as it was the deepest and noblest conception lying at the root of the Roman commonwealth, that within the circle of Roman burgesses there should be neither master nor slave, neither *millionnaire* nor beggar, but that above all a like faith and a like culture should signalise all Romans—the school and the necessarily exclusive school-culture were far more dangerous still, and were in fact utterly destructive of the sense of equality. The school and the theatre became the most effective levers in the hands of the new spirit of the age, and all the more so that they used the Latin tongue. Men might perhaps speak and write Greek and yet not cease to be Romans; but in this case they were in the habit of speaking in the Roman language, while the whole inward being and life were Greek. It is not one of the most pleasing, but it is one of the most remarkable and in a historical point of view most instructive, facts in this brilliant era of Roman conservatism, that during its course Hellenism struck root in the whole field of intellect not immediately political, and that the schoolmaster and the *maître de plaisir* of the great public in close alliance created a Roman literature.

In the very earliest Roman author the later development appears, as it were, in embryo. The Greek Andronikos (born before $\frac{482}{272}$, and lived till after $\frac{547}{207}$), afterwards as a Roman burgess called Lucius [1] Livius Andronicus, came to Rome at an early age in $\frac{482}{272}$ among the other captives taken at Tarentum (i. 407) and passed into the possession of the conqueror of Sena (p. 165) Marcus Livius Salinator (consul $\frac{535}{219}$, $\frac{547}{207}$). He was employed as a slave, partly in acting and copying texts, partly in giving instruction in the Latin and Greek languages, which he taught both to the children of his master and to other boys of wealthy parents in and out of the house. He distinguished himself so much in this way that his master gave him freedom, and even the authorities, who not unfrequently availed themselves of his services—commissioning him, for instance, to prepare a thanksgiving-chant after the fortunate turn taken by the Hannibalic war in $\frac{547}{207}$—out of regard for him conceded to the guild of poets and actors a place for their common worship in the temple of Minerva on the Aventine. His authorship arose out of his double occupation. As schoolmaster he translated the *Odyssey* into Latin, in order that the Latin text might form the basis of his Latin, as the Greek text was the basis of his Greek, instruction; and this earliest of Roman school-books maintained its place in education for centuries. As an actor, he not only like every other wrote the texts themselves for his own use, but he also published them as books, that is, he read them in public and diffused them by copies. What was still more important, he substituted the Greek drama for the old essentially lyrical stage poetry. It was in $\frac{514}{240}$, a year after the close of the first Punic war, that the first play was exhibited on the Roman stage. This creation of an epos, a tragedy, and a comedy in the Roman language, and that by a man who was more Roman than Greek, was historically a remarkable event; but we cannot speak of his labours as having any artistic value. They make no sort of claim to originality; viewed as translations, they are characterised by a barbarism which is all the more conspicuous, that his poetry does not naïvely display its own native simplicity, but pedantically labours to imitate the

---

[1] The later rule, by which the freedman necessarily bore the *praenomen* of his patron, was not yet applied in republican Rome.

high artistic culture of the neighbouring people. The wide deviations from the original are due not to the freedom, but to the rudeness of the imitation; the treatment is sometimes insipid, sometimes turgid, the language harsh and quaint.[1] We have no difficulty in believing the statement of the old critics of art, that, apart from the compulsory perusal in school, none of the poems of Livius were taken up a second time. Yet these labours were in various respects models for succeeding times. They formed the commencement of the Roman translation-literature, and naturalised the Greek metres in Latium. The reason why these were adopted only in the dramas, while the *Odyssey* of Livius was written in the national Saturnian measure, evidently was that the iambuses and trochees of tragedy and comedy far more easily admitted of imitation in Latin than the epic dactyls.

But this preliminary stage of literary development was soon passed. The epics and dramas of Livius were regarded by posterity, and undoubtedly with perfect justice, as resembling the rigid statues of Daedalus destitute of emotion or expression—curiosities rather than works of art. But in the following generation, now that the foundations were once laid, there arose a lyric, epic, and dramatic art; and it is of great importance, even in a historical point of view, to trace this poetical growth.

Both as respects extent of production and influence over the public, the drama stood at the head of the poetry thus developed in Rome. In antiquity there was no permanent theatre with

---

[1] One of the tragedies of Livius presented the line—

Quem ego néfrendem alui lácteam immulgéns opem.

The verses of Homer (*Odyssey*, xii. 16):

οὐδ' ἄρα Κίρκην
ἐξ Αἴδεω ἐλθόντες ἐλήθομεν, ἀλλὰ μάλ' ὦκα
ἦλθ' ἐντυναμένη· ἅμα δ' ἀμφίπολοι φέρον αὐτῇ
σῖτον καὶ κρέα πολλὰ καὶ αἴθοπα οἶνον ἐρυθρόν.

are thus interpreted:

Tópper cíti ad aédis—vénimús Círcae
Simúl dúona córam (?)—pórtant ad návis,
Milia ália in ísdem—inserinúntur.

The most remarkable feature is not so much the barbarism as the thoughtlessness of the translator, who, instead of sending Circe to Ulysses, sends Ulysses to Circe. Another still more ridiculous mistake is the translation of αἰδοίοισιν ἔδωκα (Odyss. xv. 373) by *lusi* (Festus, *Ep. v. affatim*, p. 11, *Müller*). Such traits are not in a historical point of view matters of indifference; we recognise in them the level of intellectual culture which marked these earliest Roman verse-making schoolmasters, and we at the same time perceive that, although Andronicus was born in Tarentum, Greek cannot have been properly his mother-tongue.

fixed charges for admission; in Greece as in Rome dramas made their appearance only as an element in the annually recurring or extraordinary amusements of the citizens. Among the measures by which the government counteracted or imagined that they counteracted that extension of the popular festivals which they justly regarded with anxiety, they refused to permit the erection of a stone building for a theatre.[1] Instead of this there was erected for each festival a scaffolding of boards with a stage for the actors (*proscaenium, pulpitum*) and a decorated background (*scaena*) ; and in a semicircle in front of it was staked off the space for the spectators (*cavea*), which was merely sloped without steps or seats, so that, if the spectators had not chairs brought along with them, they squatted, reclined, or stood.[2] The women were probably separated at an early period, and were restricted to the upper and worst places; otherwise there was no distinction of places in law till $\frac{560}{194}$, after which, as already mentioned (p. 301), the lowest and best positions were reserved for the senators.

The audience was anything but genteel. The better classes, it is true, did not keep aloof from the general recreations of the people; the fathers of the city seem even to have been bound for decorum's sake to appear on these occasions. But the very nature of a burgess festival implied that, while slaves and probably foreigners also were excluded, admittance free of charge was given to every burgess with his wife and children;[3] and accordingly the body of spectators cannot have differed much from what one sees in the present day at public fireworks and *gratis* exhibitions. Naturally, therefore, the proceedings were not of the most orderly character; children cried, women talked and shrieked, now and then a wench prepared to make

---

[1] Such a building was, no doubt, constructed for the Apollinarian games in the Flaminian circus in $\frac{575}{179}$ (Liv. xl. 51; Becker, *Top.* p. 605); but it was probably soon afterwards pulled down again (Tertull. *de Spect.* 10).

[2] In $\frac{599}{155}$ there were still no seats in the theatre (Ritschl, *Parerg.* i. p. xviii. xx. 214; comp. Ribbeck, *Trag.* p. 285); but, as not only the authors of the Plautine prologues, but Plautus himself on various occasions, make allusions to a sitting audience (*Mil. Glor.* 82, 83; *Aulul.* iv. 9, 6; *Trucul. ap. fin.* ; *Epid. ap. fin.*), most of the spectators must have brought stools with them or have seated themselves on the ground.

[3] Women and children appear to have been at all times admitted to the Roman theatre (Val. Max. vi. 3, 12; Plutarch, *Quaest. Rom.* 14; Cicero, *de Har. Resp.* 12, 24; Vitruv. v. 3, 1; Suetonius, *Aug.* 44, etc.); but slaves were *de jure* excluded (Cicero, *de Har. Resp.* 12, 26; Ritschl, *Parerg.* i. p. xix. 223), and the same must doubtless have been the case with foreigners, excepting of course the guests of the community, who took their places among or by the side of the senators (Varro, v. 155; Justin. xliii. 5, 10; Sueton. *Aug.* 44).

her way to the stage; the attendants whose duty it was to keep
order had on these festivals anything but a holiday, and found
frequent occasion to confiscate a mantle or to ply the rod.

The introduction of the Greek drama increased the demands
on the dramatic staff, and there seems to have been no redun-
dance in the supply of capable actors: on one occasion for want
of actors a piece of Naevius had to be performed by amateurs.
But this produced no change in the position of the artist; the
poet or, as he was at this time called, the " writer," the actor,
and the composer not only belonged still, as formerly, to the
despised class of labourers for hire (p. 361), but were still, as
formerly, placed in the most marked way under the ban of public
opinion, and subjected to police maltreatment (i. 453). Of
course all reputable persons kept aloof from such an occupation.
The manager of the company (*dominus gregis, factionis*, also
choragus), who was ordinarily also the chief actor, was generally
a freedman, and its members were ordinarily his slaves; the
composers, whose names have reached us, were all of them non-
free. The remuneration was not merely small—a *honorarium*
of 8000 sesterces (£80) given to a dramatist is described shortly
after the close of this period as unusually high—but was, moreover, only paid by the magistrates providing the festival, if the
piece was not a failure. With the payment the matter ended;
dramatic competitions and honorary prizes, such as took place
in Attica, were not yet heard of in Rome—the Romans at this
time appear to have simply applauded or hissed as we now do,
and to have brought forward only a single piece for exhibition
each day.[1] Under such circumstances, where art went for days'
wages and the artist instead of receiving due honour was subjected to disgrace, the new national theatre of the Romans could

---

[1] It is not necessary to infer from the prologues of Plautus (*Cas.* 17;
Amph. 65) that there was a distribution of prizes (Ritschl, *Parerg.* i. 229);
even the passage *Trin.* 706, may very well belong to the Greek original,
not to the translator; and the total silence of the *didascaliae* and prologues,
as well as of all tradition, on the point of prize adjudications and prizes is
decisive.

That only one piece was produced each day we infer from the fact, that
the spectators come from home at the beginning of the piece (*Poen.* 10)
and return home after its close (*Epid. Pseud. Rud. Stich. Truc. ap. fin.*).
They went, as these passages show, to the theatre after the second break-
fast, and were at home again for the midday meal; the performance thus
lasted, according to our reckoning, from about noon till half-past two
o'clock, and a piece of Plautus, with music in the intervals between the
acts, would probably occupy nearly that length of time (comp. Horat.
Ep. ii. 1, 189). The passage in which Tacitus (*Ann.* xiv. 20) makes the
spectators spend " whole days " in the theatre refers to the state of matters
at a later period.

exhibit no original or at all artistic development; and, while the noble rivalry of the noblest Athenians had called into life the Attic drama, the Roman drama taken as a whole could be nothing but a spoiled copy of its predecessor, in which the only wonder is that it has been able to display so much grace and wit in the details.

In the dramatic world comedy greatly preponderated over tragedy: the spectators knit their brows, when instead of the expected comedy a tragedy began. Thus it happened that, while this period exhibits poets who devoted themselves specially to comedy, such as Plautus and Caecilius, it presents none who cultivated tragedy alone; and among the dramas of this epoch known to us by name there occur three comedies for one tragedy. Of course the Roman comic poets, or rather translators, laid hands in the first instance on the pieces which had possession of the Hellenic stage at the time; and thus they found themselves exclusively [1] confined to the range of the newer Attic comedy, and chiefly to its best-known poets, Philemon of Soli in Cilicia ($\frac{394}{360}$? $-\frac{492}{262}$) and Menander of Athens ($\frac{412}{342}-\frac{462}{292}$). This comedy came to be of so great importance as regards the development not only of Roman literature, but even of the nation at large, that history has reason to pause and consider it.

The pieces are of tiresome monotony. Almost without exception the plot turns on helping a young man, at the expense either of his father or of some *leno*, to obtain possession of a sweetheart of undoubted charms and of very doubtful morals. The path to success in love regularly lies through some sort of pecuniary fraud; and the crafty servant, who provides the needful sum and performs the requisite swindling while the lover is mourning over his amatory and pecuniary distresses, is the real mainspring of the piece. There is no want of befitting reflections on the joys and sorrows of love, of tearful parting-scenes, of lovers who in the anguish of their hearts threaten to do themselves a mischief; love or rather amorous intrigue was, as the old critics of art say, the very life-breath of the Menandrian poetry. Marriage forms, at least with Menander, the inevitable finale;

---

[1] The scanty use made of what is called the middle Attic comedy does not require notice in a historical point of view, since it was nothing but the Menandrian comedy in a less developed form. There is no trace of any employment of the older comedy. The Roman tragi-comedy—after the type of the *Amphitruo* of Plautus—was no doubt styled by the Roman literary historians *fabula Rhinthonica ;* but the newer Attic comedians also composed such parodies, and it is difficult to see why the Romans should have resorted for their translations to Rhinthon and the older writers rather than to those who were nearer to their own times.

on which occasion, for the greater edification and satisfaction of the spectators, the virtue of the heroine usually comes forth almost if not wholly untarnished, and the heroine herself proves to be the lost daughter of some rich man and so in every respect an eligible match. Along with these love-pieces we find others of a pathetic kind. Among the comedies of Plautus, for instance, the *Rudens* turns on a shipwreck and the right of asylum; while the *Trinummus* and the *Captivi* contain no amatory intrigue, but depict the generous devotedness of the friend to his friend and of the slave to his master. Persons and situations recur down to the very details like patterns on a carpet; we never get rid of the asides of unseen listeners, of knocking at the house-doors, and of slaves scouring the streets on some errand or other. The standing masks, of which there was a certain fixed number —*e.g.* eight masks for old men, and seven for servants—from which alone in ordinary cases at least the poet had to make his choice, further favoured a stock-model treatment. Such a comedy almost of necessity rejected the lyrical element in the older comedy—the chorus—and confined itself from the first to conversation, or at most recitation; it was devoid not of the political element only, but of all true passion and of all poetical elevation. The pieces judiciously made no pretension to any grand or really poetical effect; their charm resided primarily in furnishing occupation for the intellect, not only through their subject-matter—in which respect the newer comedy was distinguished from the old as much by the greater intrinsic emptiness as by the greater outward complication of the plot —but more especially through their execution in detail, in which the point and polish of the dialogue more particularly formed the triumph of the poet and the delight of the audience. Complications and confusions of one person with another, which very readily allowed scope for extravagant, often licentious, practical jokes—as in the *Casina*, which winds up with the retiring of the two bridegrooms and of the soldier dressed up as bride in genuine Falstaffian style—jests, drolleries, and riddles, which in fact for want of real conversation furnished the staple materials of entertainment at the Attic table of the period, fill up a large portion of these comedies. The authors of them wrote not like Eupolis and Aristophanes for a great nation, but rather for a cultivated society which, like other circles whose ingenuity finds no more fitting field for its exercise, spent its time in guessing riddles and playing at charades. They give us, therefore, no picture of their times; of the great historical and intellectual movements of the age no trace appears in these comedies, and we need to recall, in order to realise, the fact that Philemon and Menander were really contemporaries of Alexander and Aristotle. But they give us a picture, equally elegant and faithful, of that refined Attic society beyond the circles of which comedy never travels. Even in the dim Latin copy, through which we chiefly know it, the grace of the original is not wholly obliterated; and more especially in the pieces which are imitated from Menander, the most talented of these poets, the life which the poet beheld and shared is delicately reflected not so much in its aberrations and distortions as in its amiable every-day course. The friendly domestic relations between father and daughter, husband and wife, master and servant, with their love-affairs and other little interesting incidents, are portrayed with so broad a truthfulness, that even now they do not miss their effect: the servants' feast, for instance, with which the *Stichus* concludes is, in the circumscribed character of its relations and the harmony of the two lovers and the one sweetheart, of unsurpassed gracefulness in its kind. The elegant grisettes, who make their appearance perfumed and adorned, with their hair fashionably dressed and in variegated, gold-embroidered, sweeping robes, or even perform their toilet on the stage, are very effective. In their train come the procuresses, sometimes of the most vulgar sort, such as one who appears in the *Curculio*, sometimes duennas like Goethe's old Barbara, such as Scapha in the *Mostellaria;* and there is no lack of brothers and comrades ready with their help. There is great abundance and variety of parts representing the old: there appear in turn the austere and avaricious, the fond and tender-hearted, and the indulgent accommodating, papas, the amorous old man, the easy old bachelor, the jealous aged matron with her old maid-servant who takes part with her mistress against her master; whereas the young men's parts are less prominent, and neither the first lover, nor the virtuous model son who here and there occurs, claims any great significance. The servant-world—the crafty valet, the stern house-steward, the old vigilant tutor, the rural slave redolent of garlic, the impertinent page—forms a transition to the very numerous professional characters. A standing figure among these is the jester (*parasitus*) who, in return for permission to feast at the table of the rich, has to entertain the guests with drolleries and charades, or, according to circumstances, to submit to have the potsherds flung at his head. This was at that time a formal trade in Athens; and it is certainly no mere poetical fiction which represents such a parasite as expressly preparing himself for his work by means of his books of witticisms and anecdotes. Favourite characters, moreover, are those of the cook, who understands not only how to bully in an unrivalled style, but also how to pilfer like a professional thief; the shameless *leno*, complacently confessing to the practice of every vice, of whom Ballio in the *Pseudolus* is a model specimen; the military bragga-docio, in whom we trace a very distinct embodiment of the free-lance habits that prevailed under Alexander's successors; the professional sharper or sycophant, the stingy money-changer, the solemnly silly physician, the priest, mariner, fisherman, and the like. To these fall to be added, lastly, the parts delineative of character in the strict sense, such as the superstitious man of Menander and the miser in the *Aulularia* of Plautus. The national-Hellenic poetry has preserved, even in this its last creation, its indestructible plastic vigour; but the delineation of character is here copied from without rather than reproduced from inward experience, and the more so, the more the task approaches to the really poetical. It is a significant circum-stance that, in the parts illustrative of character to which we have just referred, the psychological truth is for the most part represented by its logical embodiment; the miser here collects the parings of his nails and laments the tears which he sheds as a waste of water. But the blame of this want of depth in the portraying of character, and generally of the whole poetical and moral hollowness of this newer comedy, lay less with the comic writers than with the nation as a whole. Everything distinctively Greek was expiring: fatherland, national faith, domestic life, all nobleness of action and sentiment were gone; poetry, history, and philosophy were inwardly exhausted; and nothing remained to the Athenian save the school, the fish-market, and the brothel. It is no matter of wonder and hardly a matter of blame, that poetry, which is destined to shed a glory over human existence, could make nothing more of such a life than the Menandrian comedy presents to us. It is at the same time very remarkable that the poetry of this period, wherever it was able to turn away in some degree from the corrupt Attic life without falling into schoolboy imitation, immediately gathers strength and freshness from the ideal. In the only remnant of the mock-heroic comedy of this period—the *Amphi-truo* of Plautus—there breathes throughout a purer and more poetical air than in all the other remains of the contemporary stage. The good-natured gods treated with gentle irony, the

noble forms from the heroic world, and the ludicrously cowardly
slaves present the most wonderful mutual contrasts; and, after
the comical course of the plot, the birth of the son of the gods
amidst thunder and lightning forms an almost grand concluding
effect. But this task of turning the myths into irony was
innocent and poetical, as compared with that of the ordinary
comedy depicting the Attic life of the period. No special
accusation may be brought from a historico-moral point of view
against poets in general, nor ought it to be made matter of
individual reproach to the particular poet that he occupies the
level of his epoch: comedy was not the cause, but the effect
of the corruption that prevailed in the national life. But it is
necessary, more especially with a view to estimate correctly
the influence of these comedies on the life of the Roman
people, to point out the abyss which yawned beneath all that
polish and elegance. The coarsenesses and obscenities, which
Menander indeed in some measure avoided, but of which there
is no lack in the other poets, are the least part of the evil.
Features far worse are, the dreadful aspect of life as a desert
in which the only oases are lovemaking and intoxication; the
fearfully prosaic monotony, in which anything resembling
enthusiasm is to be found only among the sharpers whose heads
have been turned by their own swindling, and who prosecute
the trade of cheating with some sort of zeal; and above all that
immoral morality, with which the pieces of Menander in particular are garnished. Vice is chastised, virtue is rewarded, and any
peccadilloes are covered by conversion at or after marriage.
There are pieces, such as the *Trinummus* of Plautus and several
of Terence, in which all the characters down to the slaves possess
some admixture of virtue; all swarm with honest men who
allow deception on their behalf, with maidenly virtue wherever
possible, with lovers equally favoured and making love in company; moral commonplaces and well-turned ethical maxims
abound. A finale of reconciliation such as that of the *Bacchides*,
where the swindling sons and the swindled fathers by way of a
good conclusion all go to carouse together in the brothel, presents a corruption of morals thoroughly worthy of Kotzebue.

Such were the foundations, and such the elements which
shaped the growth, of Roman comedy. Originality was in
its case excluded not merely by want of aesthetic freedom,
but still more directly, it is probable, by virtue of its liability
to police control. Among the considerable number of Latin
comedies of this sort which are known to us, there is not one

that did not announce itself as an imitation of a definite Greek model; the title was only complete when the names of the Greek piece and of its author were also given, and if, as occasionally happened, the " novelty " of a piece was disputed, the point in dispute was merely whether it had been previously translated. Comedy laid the scene of its plot abroad not only frequently, but regularly and under the pressure of necessity; and the special name of that form of art (*fabula palliata*) was derived from the fact, that the scene was laid out of Rome, usually in Athens, and that the *dramatis personae* were Greeks or at any rate not Romans. The foreign costume is strictly carried out even in detail, especially in those things in which the uncultivated Roman was distinctly sensible of the contrast. Thus the names of Rome and the Romans are avoided, and, where they are referred to, they are called in good Greek " foreigners " (*barbari*); in like manner among the appellations of moneys and coins that so frequently occur there does not once appear a Roman coin. We form a strange idea of men of so great and so versatile talent as Naevius and Plautus, if we refer such caprices to their free choice: this strange and clumsy outlandish aspect of the Roman comedy was undoubtedly occasioned by causes very different from aesthetic considerations. The transference of such a state of social matters as is uniformly delineated in the new Attic comedy to the Rome of the Hannibalic period would have been a direct outrage on its civil order and morality. But, as the dramatic spectacles at this period were regularly given by the aediles and praetors who were entirely dependent on the senate, and even extraordinary festivals, funeral games for instance, could not take place without permission of the government; and as the Roman police, moreover, was not in the habit of standing on ceremony in any case, and least of all in dealing with comedies; the reason is self-evident why this comedy, even after it was admitted as one of the Roman national amusements, still was not allowed to bring forward a Roman on the stage, and remained as it were relegated to foreign lands.

The compilers were still more decidedly prohibited from naming any living person in terms of praise or censure, as well as from any captious allusion to the circumstances of the times. In the whole range of the Plautine and post-Plautine comedy, there is not, so far as we know, matter for a single action of damages. In like manner—if we leave out of view some wholly harmless jests—we meet hardly any trace of invectives levelled at communities (invectives which, owing to the lively municipal spirit of the Italians, would have been specially dangerous), except the significant scoff at the unfortunate Capuans and Atellans (p. 178) and, what is remarkable, various sarcasms on the arrogance and the bad Latin of the Praenestines.[1] In general no references to the events or circumstances of the present occur in the pieces of Plautus. The only exceptions are, good wishes for the progress of the war[2] or for peaceful times; general sallies directed against usurious dealings in grain or money, against extravagance, against bribery by candidates, against the frequency of triumphs, against those who made a trade of collecting forfeited fines, against farmers of the revenue distraining for payment, against the dear prices of the oil-dealers; and once—in the *Curculio*—a more lengthened diatribe as to the doings in the Roman market, resembling the *parabases* of the older Attic comedy, and but little likely to cause offence (p. 385). But even in the midst of such patriotic endeavours, which from a police point of view were entirely in order, the poet interrupts himself;

> *Sed sumne ego stultus, qui rem curo publicam*
> *Ubi sunt magistratus, quos curare oporteat ?*

and taken as a whole, we can hardly imagine a comedy politically tamer than the comedy of Rome in the sixth century.[3] The oldest Roman comic writer of note, Gnaeus Naevius, alone forms

---

[1] *Bacch.* 24; *Trin.* 609; *Truc.* iii. 2, 23. Naevius also, who in fact was generally less scrupulous, ridicules the Praenestines and Lanuvini (*Com.* 21, *Ribb.*). There are indications more than once of a certain variance between the Praenestines and Romans (Liv. xxiii. 20, xlii. 1); and the executions in the time of Pyrrhus (i. 434) as well as the catastrophe in that of Sulla, were certainly connected with this variance.—Innocent jokes, such as *Capt.* 160, 881, of course passed uncensured.—The compliment paid to Massilia in *Cas.* v. 4, 1, deserves notice.

[2] Thus the prologue of the *Cistellaria* concludes with the following words, which may have a place here as the only contemporary mention of the Hannibalic war in the literature that has come down to us:—

> *Haec res sic gesta est.   Bene valete, et vincite*
> *Virtute vera, quod fecistis antidhac ;*
> *Servate vostros socios, veteres et novos ;*
> *Augete auxilia vostris justis legibus ;*
> *Perdite perduelles : parite laudem et lauream*
> *Ut vobis victi Poeni poenas sufferant.*

[3] For this reason we can hardly be too cautious in assuming allusions on the part of Plautus to the events of the times. Recent investigation has set aside many instances of mistaken acuteness of this sort; but might not the reference to the Bacchanalia, which is found in *Cas.* v. 4, 11 (Ritschl, *Parerg.* i. 192), have been expected to incur censure? We may perhaps reverse the case and infer from the notices of the festival of Bacchus in the *Casina* and some other pieces (*Amph.* 703; *Aul.* iii. 1, 3; *Bacch.* 53, 371; *Mil. Glor.* 1016; and especially *Men.* 836), that these were written at a time when it was not yet dangerous to speak of the Bacchanalia.

a remarkable exception. Although he did not write exactly original Roman comedies, the few fragments of his, which we possess, are full of references to circumstances and persons in Rome. Among other liberties he not only ridiculed one Theodotus a painter by name, but even directed against the victor of Zama the following verses, of which Aristophanes need not have been ashamed:

> *Etiam qui res magnas manu saepe gessit gloriose,*
> *Cujus facta viva nunc vigent, qui apud gentes solus praestat,*
> *Eum suus pater cum pallio uno ab amica abduxit.*

As he himself says,

> *Libera lingua loquemur ludis Liberalibus,*

he probably often wrote offensively and put dangerous questions, such as:

> *Cedo qui vestram rem publicam tantam amisistis tam cito?*

which he answered by an enumeration of political sins, such as:

> *Proveniebant oratores novi, stulti adulescentuli.*

But the Roman police was not disposed like the Attic to hold stage-invectives and political diatribes as privileged, or even to tolerate them at all. Naevius was put in prison for these and similar sallies, and was obliged to remain there, till he had publicly made amends and recantation in other comedies. These quarrels, apparently, drove him from his native land; but his successors took warning from his example—one of them indicates very plainly, that he has no desire whatever to incur an involuntary gagging like his colleague Naevius. Thus the result was accomplished—not much less unique of its kind than the conquest of Hannibal—that, during an epoch of the most feverish national excitement, there arose a national stage utterly destitute of political tinge.

But the restrictions thus stringently and laboriously imposed by custom and police on Roman poetry stifled its very breath. Not without reason might Naevius declare the position of the poet under the sceptre of the Lagidae and Seleucidae enviable as compared with his position in free Rome.[1] The degree of success in individual instances was of course determined by the quality of the original which was followed, and by the talent

---

[1] The remarkable passage in the *Tarentilla* can have no other meaning:—

> *Quae ego in theatro hic meis probavi plausibus,*
> *Ea non audere quemquam regem rumpere:*
> *Quanto libertatem hanc hic superat servitus!*

of the individual editor; but amidst all their individual variety
the whole range of translations must have agreed in certain
leading features, inasmuch as all the comedies were adapted
to similar conditions of exhibition and a similar audience. The
treatment of the whole as well as of the details was uniformly
in the highest degree free; and it was necessary that it should
be so. While the original pieces were performed in presence
of that society which they copied, and in this very fact lay their
principal charm, the Roman audience of this period was so
different from the Attic, that it was not even able properly
to understand that foreign world. The Roman comprehended
neither the grace and courtesy, nor the sentimentalism and the
whitened emptiness of the domestic life of the Hellenes. The
slave-world was utterly different; the Roman slave was a piece
of household furniture, the Attic slave was a servant. Where
marriages of slaves occur or a master carries on a kindly conversation with his slave, the Roman translators ask their audience
not to take offence at such things which are usual in Athens;[1]
and, when at a later period comedies began to be written in
Roman costume, the part of the crafty servant had to be rejected
because the Roman public did not tolerate slaves of this sort
overlooking and controlling their masters. The professional
figures and those illustrative of character which were sketched
more broadly and farcically, bore the process of transference
better than the polished figures of every-day life; but even of
those delineations the Roman editor had to lay aside several—
and these probably the very finest and most original, such as
the Thais, the match-maker, the moon-conjuress, and the
mendicant priest of Menander—and to keep chiefly to those
foreign trades, with which the Greek luxury of the table, already
very generally diffused in Rome, had made his audience familiar.
The delineation of the professional cook and the parasite in
the comedy of Plautus with so striking a vividness and relish
finds its explanation in the fact, that Greek cooks at that time
daily offered their services in the Roman market, and that Cato
found it necessary to give orders even to his steward not to keep
a parasite. In like manner the translator could make no use
of a very large portion of the elegant Attic conversation in his

[1] The ideas of the modern Hellas on the point of slavery are illustrated
by the passage in Euripides (*Ion*. 854; comp. *Helena*, 728):—

> Ἐν γάρ τι τοῖς δούλοισιν αἰσχύνην φέρει,
> Τοὔνομα· τὰ δ' ἄλλα πάντα τῶν ἐλευθέρων.
> Οὐδεὶς κακίων δοῦλος, ὅστις ἐσθλὸς ᾖ.

originals. The Roman citizen or farmer stood in much the same relation to the refined revelry and debauchery of Athens, as the German of a provincial town to the mysteries of the Palais Royal. A science of cookery, in the strict sense, never entered into his thoughts; the dinner-parties no doubt continued to be very numerous in the Roman imitation, but everywhere the plain Roman roast pork predominated over the variety of baked meats and the refined sauces and dishes of fish. Of the riddles and drinking songs, of the Greek rhetoric and philosophy, which played so great a part in the originals, we meet only a stray trace now and then in the Roman adaptation.

The havoc, which the Roman editors were compelled in deference to their audience to make in the originals, drove them inevitably into methods of cancelling and amalgamating incompatible with artistic construction. It was usual not only to throw out whole parts occurring in the original, but also to insert others taken from other comedies of the same or of another poet; a treatment indeed which, owing to the outwardly methodical construction of the originals and the recurrence of standing figures and incidents, was not quite so bad as it might seem. Moreover the poets, at least in the earlier period, allowed themselves the most singular liberties in the construction of the plot. The plot of the *Stichus* (performed in $\frac{554}{200}$) otherwise so excellent turns upon the circumstance, that two sisters, whom their father urges to abandon their absent husbands, play the part of Penelopes, till the husbands return home with rich mercantile gains and with a beautiful damsel as a present for their father-in-law. In the *Casina*, which was received with altogether peculiar favour by the public, the bride, from whom the piece is named and around whom the plot revolves, does not make her appearance at all, and the *dénouement* is quite naïvely described by the epilogue as " about to be enacted within." Very often the plot as it thickens suddenly breaks off, the connecting thread is allowed to drop, and other similar signs of an unfinished art appear. The reason of this lay probably far less in the unskilfulness of the Roman editors, than in the indifference of the Roman public to aesthetic laws. Taste, however, gradually formed itself. In the later pieces Plautus has evidently bestowed more care on their construction, and the *Captivi* for instance, the *Pseudolus*, and the *Bacchides* are executed in a masterly manner after their kind. His successor Caecilius, none of whose pieces are extant, is said to have especially distinguished himself by the more artistic treatment of the subject.

In the treatment of details the endeavour of the poet to bring matters as far as possible home to his Roman hearers, and the rule of police which required that the pieces should retain a foreign character, produced the most singular contrasts. The Roman gods, the ritual, military, and legal terms of the Romans, present a strange appearance amid the Greek world; Roman *aediles* and *tresviri* are grotesquely mingled with *agoranomi* and *demarchi;* pieces whose scene is laid in Aetolia or Epidamnus send the spectator without scruple to the Velabrum and the Capitol. Such a patchwork of Roman local tints distributed over the Greek ground is barbarous enough; but interpolations of this nature, which are often in their naïve way very ludicrous, are far more tolerable than that thorough alteration of the pieces into a ruder shape, which the editors deemed necessary to suit the far from Attic culture of their audience. It is true that several even of the new Attic poets probably needed no accession to their coarseness; pieces like the *Asinaria* of Plautus cannot owe their unsurpassed dullness and vulgarity solely to the translator. Nevertheless coarse incidents so prevail in the Roman comedy, that the translators must either have interpolated them or at least have made a very one-sided selection. In the endless abundance of cudgelling and in the lash ever suspended over the back of the slaves we recognise very clearly the household-government inculcated by Cato, just as we recognise the Catonian opposition to women in the never-ending disparagement of wives. Among the jokes of their own invention with which the Roman editors deemed it proper to season the elegant Attic dialogue, several are almost incredibly unmeaning and barbarous.[1]

So far as concerns metrical treatment on the other hand, the flexible and sounding verse on the whole does all honour

---

[1] For instance, in the otherwise very graceful examination which in the *Stichus* of Plautus, the father and his daughters institute into the qualities of a good wife, the irrelevant question—whether it is better to marry a virgin or a widow—is inserted, merely in order that it may be answered by a no less irrelevant and, in the mouth of the interlocutrix, altogether absurd commonplace against women. But that is a trifle compared with the following specimen. In Menander's *Plocium* a husband bewails his troubles to his friend:—

Ἔχω δ' ἐπίκληρον Λάμιαν· οὐκ εἴρηκά σοι
Τοῦτ'; εἶτ' ἄρ' οὐχί; κυρίαν τῆς οἰκίας
Καὶ τῶν ἀγρῶν καὶ πάντων ἀντ' ἐκείνης
Ἔχομεν, Ἄπολλον, ὡς χαλεπῶν χαλεπώτατον.
Ἅπασι δ' ἀργαλέα 'στίν, οὐκ ἐμοὶ μόνῳ,

to the composers. The fact that the iambic trimeters, which predominated in the originals and were alone suitable to their moderate conversational tone, were very frequently replaced in the Latin edition by iambic or trochaic tetrameters, is to be attributed not so much to any want of skill on the part of the editors who knew well how to handle the trimeter, as to the uncultivated taste of the Roman public which was pleased with the sonorous magnificence of the long verse even where it was not appropriate.

Lastly, the arrangements for the exhibition of the pieces bore the like stamp of indifference to aesthetic requirements on the part of the managers and the public. The stage of the ancients —which on account of the extent of the theatre and from the performances taking place by day made no pretension to acting properly so called, employed men to represent female characters, and absolutely required an artificial strengthening of the voice of the actor—was entirely dependent, in a scenic as well as acoustic point of view, on the use of facial and resonant masks. These were well known in Rome; in amateur performances the players appeared without exception masked. But the actors who were to perform the Greek comedies were not supplied with the masks—beyond doubt much more artificial—that were necessary for them; a circumstance which, in connection with the defective acoustic arrangements of the stage,[1] not only compelled the actor to exert his voice unduly, but drove Livius to the highly inartistic but inevitable expedient of having the portions which were to be sung performed by a singer not belonging to the staff of actors, and accompanied by the mere dumb show of the actor within whose part they fell. As little were the givers of the Roman festivals disposed to put themselves to any material expense for decorations and machinery. The Attic stage regularly presented a street with houses in the back-

> Τίῳ, πολὺ μᾶλλονθυγατρί.—πραγμ᾽ ἄμαχον λέγεις·
> Εὖ οἶδα.

In the Latin edition of Caecilius, this conversation, so elegant in its simplicity, is converted into the following uncouth dialogue:—

> Sed tua morosane uxor quaeso est ?—Quam rogas ?—
> Qui tandem ?—Taedet mentionis, quae mihi
> Ubi domum adveni adsedi, extemplo savium
> Dat jejuna anima.—Nil peccat de savio :
> Ut devomas volt, quod foris potaveris.

[1] Even when the Romans built stone theatres, these had not the sounding apparatus by which the Greek architects supported the efforts of the actors (Vitruv. v. 5, 8).

ground, and had no shifting decorations; but, besides various other apparatus, it possessed more especially a contrivance for pushing forward on the chief stage a smaller one representing the interior of a house. The Roman theatre, however, was not provided with this; and we can hardly therefore throw the blame on the poet, if everything, even childbirth, was represented on the street.

Such was the nature of the Roman comedy of the sixth century. The process by which the Greek dramas were transferred to Rome furnishes us with a picture, historically invaluable, of the diversity in the culture of the two nations; but in an aesthetic and a moral point of view the original did not stand high, and the imitation stood still lower. The world of beggarly rabble, to whatever extent the Roman editors might take possession of it under the benefit of the inventory, presented in Rome a forlorn and strange aspect, shorn as it were of its delicate characteristics: comedy no longer rested on the basis of reality, but persons and incidents seemed capriciously or carelessly mingled as in a game of cards; in the original a picture from life, it became in the reproduction a caricature. Under a management which could announce a Greek *agon* with flute playing, choirs of dancers, tragedians, and athletes, and eventually convert it into a boxing-match (p. 388); and in presence of a public which, as later poets complain, ran away *en masse* from the play, if there were pugilists, or rope-dancers, or even gladiators to be seen; poets such as the Roman composers were— workers for hire and of inferior social position—were obliged even perhaps against their own better judgment and their own better taste to accommodate themselves more or less to the prevailing frivolity and rudeness. It was quite possible, nevertheless, that there might arise among them individuals of lively and vigorous talents, who were able at least to repress the foreign and factitious element in poetry, and, when they had found their fitting sphere, to produce pleasing and even important creations.

At the head of these stood Gnaeus Naevius, the first Roman who deserves to be called a poet, and, so far as the accounts preserved regarding him and the few fragments of his works allow us to form an opinion, to all appearance one of the most remarkable and most important names in the whole range of Roman literature. He was a younger contemporary of Andronicus—his poetical activity began considerably before, and probably did not end till after, the Hannibalic war—and felt in a general sense his influence; he was, as is usually the case in artificial literatures, a worker in all the forms of art produced by his predecessor, in epos, tragedy, and comedy, and closely adhered to him in the matter of metres. Nevertheless, an immense chasm separates the poets and their poems. Naevius was neither freedman, schoolmaster, nor actor, but a citizen of unstained character although not of noble descent, belonging probably to one of the Latin communities of Campania, and a soldier in the first Punic war.[1] In thorough contrast to the language of Livius, that of Naevius is easy and clear, free from stiffness and affectation, and seems even in tragedy to avoid pathos as it were on purpose; his verses, in spite of the not unfrequent *hiatus* and several other licences afterwards disallowed, have a smooth and graceful flow.[2] While the quasi-poetry of Livius proceeded, somewhat like that of Gottsched in Germany, from purely external impulses and moved wholly in the leading-strings of the Greeks, his successor emancipated Roman poetry, and with the true divining-rod of the poet struck those springs out of which alone in Italy a native poetry could well up—national history and comedy. Epic poetry no longer merely furnished the schoolmaster with a lesson-book, but

---

[1] The personal notices of Naevius are sadly confused. Seeing that he fought in the first Punic war, he cannot have been born later than $\frac{495}{259}$. Dramas, probably the first, were exhibited by him in $\frac{519}{235}$ (Gell. xii. 21, 45). That he died in $\frac{550}{204}$, as is usually stated, was doubted by Varro (*ap.* Cic. *Brut.* 15, 60), and certainly with reason; if it were so, he must have made his escape during the Hannibalic war to the soil of the enemy. The sarcastic verses on Scipio (p. 406) cannot have been written before the battle of Zama. We may place his life between $\frac{490}{264}$ and $\frac{560}{194}$, so that he was contemporary of the two Scipios who fell in $\frac{543}{211}$ (Cic. *de Rep.* iv. 10), ten years younger than Andronicus, and perhaps ten years older than Plautus. His Campanian origin is indicated by Gellius, and his Latin nationality, if proof of it were needed, by himself in his epitaph. The hypothesis that he was not a Roman citizen, but possibly a burgess of Cales or of some other Latin town in Campania, renders the fact that the Roman police treated him so unscrupulously the more easy of explanation. At any rate he was not an actor, for he served in the army.

[2] Compare, *e.g.* with the verse of Livius the fragment from Naevius' tragedy of *Lycurgus* :—

> *Vos qui regalis corporis custodias*
> *Agitatis, ite actutum in frundiferos locos,*
> *Ingenio arbusta ubi nata sunt, non obsita ;*

or the famous words, which in the *Hector Profisciscens* Hector addresses to Priam:—

> *Laetus sum, laudari me abs te, pater, a laudato viro ;*

and the charming verse from the *Tarentilla* :—

> *Alii adnutat, alii adnictat ; alium amat, alium tenet.*

appealed on its own merits to the hearing and reading public. Composing for the stage had been hitherto, like the preparation of the stage costume, a subsidiary employment of the actor or a mechanical service performed for him; with Naevius the relation was inverted, and the actor now became the servant of the composer. His poetical activity is marked throughout by a national stamp. This stamp is most distinctly impressed on his grave national drama and on his national epos, of which we shall have to speak hereafter; but it also appears in his comedies, which of all his poetic performances seem to have been the best adapted to his talents and the most successful. It was probably, as we have already said (p. 404), external considerations alone that induced the poet to adhere in comedy so much as he did to the Greek originals; and this did not prevent him from far outstripping his successors and probably even the insipid originals in the freshness of his mirth and in the fulness of his living interest in the present; indeed in a certain sense he reverted to the paths of the Aristophanic comedy. He felt full well, and in his epitaph expressed, what he had been to his nation:

> *Mortales immortales flere si foret fas,*
> *Flerent Divae Camenae Naevium poetam ;*
> *Itaque, postquam est Orcino traditus thesauro,*
> *Obliti sunt Romae loquier Latina lingua.*

Such proud language on the part of the man and the poet well befitted one who had witnessed and had personally taken part in the struggles with Hamilcar and with Hannibal, and who had discovered for the thoughts and feelings of that age—so full of deep excitement and so elevated by mighty joy—a poetical expression which, if not exactly the highest, was sound, adroit, and national. We have already mentioned (p. 406) the troubles into which his licence brought him with the authorities, and how, driven in all probability by these troubles from Rome, he ended his life at Utica. In his instance likewise the individual life was sacrificed for the common weal, and the beautiful for the useful.

His younger contemporary, Titus Maccius Plautus ($\frac{500}{254}$? $\frac{570}{184}$), appears to have been far inferior to him both in outward position and in the conception of his poetical calling. A native of the little town of Sassina, which was originally Umbrian but was perhaps by this time Latinised, he earned his livelihood in Rome at first as an actor, and then—after he had lost in mercantile speculations what he had gained by his acting—as a theatrical composer reproducing Greek comedies, without occupying himself with any other department of literature and probably without making any pretension to authorship properly so called. There seems to have been at that time a considerable number of persons who made a trade of thus editing comedies in Rome; but their names, especially as they did not perhaps in general publish their works,[1] were virtually forgotten, and the pieces belonging to this stock of plays, which were preserved, passed in after times under the name of the most popular of them, Plautus. The *litteratores* of the following century reckoned up as many as 130 such "Plautine pieces;" but of these a large portion at any rate were merely revised by Plautus or had no connection with him at all; the best of them are still extant. To form a proper judgment, however, regarding the poetical character of the editor is very difficult, if not impossible, where the originals have not been preserved. That the editors reproduced good and bad pieces without selection; that they were subject and subordinate both to the police and to the public; that they were as indifferent to aesthetical requirements as their audience, and to please the latter, lowered the originals to a farcical and vulgar tone—are objections which apply rather to the whole manufacture of translations than to the individual remodeller. On the other hand we may regard as characteristic of Plautus, the masterly handling of the language and of the varied rhythms, a rare skill in adjusting and working the situation for dramatic effect, the almost always clever and often excellent dialogue, and, above all, a broad and fresh humour, which produces an irresistible comic effect with its happy jokes, its rich vocabulary of nicknames, its whimsical coinage of words, its pungent, often mimic, descriptions and situations—excellences, in which we seem to recognise the former actor. Undoubtedly the editor even in these respects retained what was successful in the originals rather than furnished contributions of his own. Those portions of the pieces which can with certainty be traced to the translator are, to say the least, mediocre; but they enable us to understand why Plautus came to be and continued the true popular poet of Rome and the true mainstay of the Roman stage, and why even after the passing away of the Roman world the theatre has repeatedly reverted to his plays.

[1] This hypothesis appears necessary, because otherwise the ancients could not have hesitated in the way they did as to the genuineness or spuriousness of the pieces of Plautus: in the case of no author, properly so-called, of Roman antiquity, do we find anything like a similar uncertainty as to his literary property. In this respect, as in so many other external points, there exists a most remarkable analogy between Plautus and Shakespeare.

Still less are we able to form a special opinion as to the third and last—for though Ennius wrote comedies, he did so altogether unsuccessfully—comedian of note in this epoch, Statius Caecilius. He resembled Plautus in his position in life and his profession. Born in Cisalpine Gaul in the district of Mediolanum, he was brought among the Insubrian prisoners of war (pp. 75, 182) to Rome, and earned a livelihood, first as a slave, afterwards as a freedman, by remodelling Greek comedies for the theatre down to his probably early death ($\frac{586}{168}$). His language was not pure, as was to be expected from his origin; on the other hand, he directed his efforts, as we have already said (p. 408), to a more artistic construction of the plot. His pieces experienced but a dull reception from his contemporaries, and the public of later times laid aside Caecilius for Plautus and Terence. The critics of the true literary age of Rome—the Varronian and Augustan epoch—assigned to Caecilius the first place among the Roman editors of Greek comedies; but this verdict appears due to the fact, that the mediocrity of the connoisseur gladly prefers a kindred spirit of mediocrity to any special features of excellence in the poet. These art-critics probably took Caecilius under their wing, simply because he was more regular than Plautus and more vigorous than Terence; notwithstanding which he may very well have been far inferior to both.

If therefore the literary historian, while fully acknowledging the very respectable talents of the Roman comedians, cannot recognise in their mere stock of translations a product either artistically important or artistically pure, the judgment of history respecting its moral aspects must necessarily be far more severe. The Greek comedy which formed its basis was morally of little consequence, inasmuch as it was simply on the same level of corruption with its audience; but the Roman drama was, at this epoch when men were wavering between the old austerity and the new corruption, the great school at once of Hellenism and of vice. This Attico-Roman comedy, with its prostitution of body and soul usurping the name of love—equally immoral in shamelessness and in sentimentality—with its offensive and unnatural magnanimity, with its uniform glorification of a life of debauchery, with its mixture of rustic coarseness and foreign refinement, was one continuous lesson of Romano-Hellenic demoralisation, and was felt as such. A proof of this is preserved in the epilogue of the *Captivi* of Plautus:—

Spectatores, ad pudicos mores facta haec fabula est :
Neque in hac subagitationes sunt neque ulla amatio,

Nec pueri suppositio neque argenti circumductio ;
Neque ubi amans adulescens scortum liberet clam suom patrem.
Hujusmodi paucas poetae reperiunt comoedias,
Ubi boni meliores fiant.   Nunc vos, si vobis placet,
Et si placuimus neque odio fuimus, signum hoc mittite.
Qui pudicitiae esse voltis praemium, plausum date !

We see here the opinion entertained regarding the Greek
comedy by the party of moral reform; and it may be added,
that even in the rare instances of moral comedies the morality
was of a character only adapted to ridicule innocence more
surely. Who can doubt that these dramas gave a practical
impulse to corruption? When Alexander the Great derived no
pleasure from a comedy of this sort which its author read before
him, the poet excused himself by saying that the fault lay not
with him, but with the king; that, in order to relish such a piece,
a man must be in the habit of holding revels and of giving and
receiving blows in an intrigue. The man knew his trade: if,
therefore, the Roman burgesses gradually acquired a taste for
these Greek comedies, we see at what a price it was bought. The
Roman government was to blame not for doing so little in behalf
of this poetry, but even for tolerating it at all. Vice no doubt
is powerful without a pulpit; but that is no excuse for the
erection of a pulpit to proclaim it. To debar the Hellenic
comedy from immediate contact with the persons and institutions of Rome, was a subterfuge rather than a serious means of
defence. In fact, comedy would probably have been much less
injurious morally, had they allowed it to have free course, so
that the calling of the poet might have been ennobled and a
Roman poetry in some measure independent might have been
developed; for poetry is a moral power, and, if it inflicts deep
wounds, it is largely able also to heal them. As it was, in this
field also the government erred both in omission and commission;
the political neutrality and moral hypocrisy of its stage-police
contributed their part to the fearfully rapid breaking up of the
Roman nation.

But, while the government did not allow the Roman comedian
to depict the state of things in his native city or to bring his
fellow-citizens on the stage, a national Latin comedy was not
absolutely precluded from springing up; for the Roman burgesses
at this period were not yet identified with the Latin nation, and
the poet was at liberty to lay the plot of his pieces in the Italian
towns of Latin rights just as in Athens or Massilia. In this
way, in fact, the original Latin comedy arose (*fabula togata*)[1] :

[1] *Togatus* denotes, in juristic and generally in technical language, the

the earliest known composer of such pieces, Titinius, flourished probably about the close of this period.[1]

This comedy was also based on the new Attic intrigue-piece; it was not translation, however, but imitation; the scene of the piece lay in Italy, and the actors appeared in the national dress (i. 423), the *toga*. Here the Latin life and habits were brought out with peculiar freshness. The pieces delineate the civil life of the middling towns of Latium; the very titles, such as *Psaltria* or *Ferentinatis, Tibicina, Iurisperita, Fullones*, indicate this; and many particular incidents, such as that of the townsman who has his shoes made after the model of the sandals of the Alban kings, tend to confirm it. The female characters preponderate in a remarkable manner over the male.[2] With

Italian in contradistinction not merely to the foreigner, but also to the Roman burgess. Thus especially *formula togatorum* (*Corp. Inscr. Lat.*, I. n. 200, v. 21, 50) is the list of those Italians bound to render military service, who do not serve in the legions. The designation also of Cisalpine Gaul as *Gallia togata*, which first occurs in Hirtius and not long after disappears again from the ordinary *usus loquendi*, describes this region in all probability according to its legal position, in so far as in the epoch from $\frac{665}{49}$ to $\frac{705}{49}$ the great majority of its communities possessed Latin rights. Virgil appears likewise in the *gens togata*, which he mentions along with the Romans (*Aen.* i. 282), to have thought of the Latin nation.

According to this view we shall have to recognise in the *fabula togata* the comedy which laid its plot in Latium, as the *fabula palliata* had its plot in Greece; the transference of the scene of action to a foreign land is common to both, and the comic writer is wholly forbidden to bring on the stage the city or the burgesses of Rome. That in reality the *togata* could only have its plot laid in the towns of Latin rights, is shown by the fact that all the towns in which, to our knowledge, pieces of Titinius and Afranius had their scene—Setia, Ferentinum, Velitrae, Brundisium—demonstrably had Latin rights down to the Social war. By the extension of the franchise to all Italy the writers of comedy lost this Latin localisation for their pieces, for Cisalpine Gaul, which *de jure* took the place of the Latin communities, lay too far off for the dramatists of the capital, and so the *fabula togata* also seems in fact to have disappeared. But the *de jure* suppressed communities of Italy, such as Capua and Atella, stepped into the gap (pp. 178, 405), and thus the *fabula Atellana* was in some measure the continuation of the *togata*.

[1] Respecting Titinius there is an utter want of literary information; except that, to judge from a fragment of Varro, he seems to have been older than Terence ($\frac{558}{196}$—$\frac{595}{159}$ Ritschl, *Parerg.* i. 194), for in all probability no more can be inferred from that passage, and though, of the two groups there compared, the second (Trabea, Atilius, Caecilius) is on the whole older than the first (Titinius, Terentius, Atta), it does not exactly follow that the oldest of the junior group is to be deemed younger than the youngest of the elder.

[2] Of the fifteen comedies of Titinius, with which we are acquainted, six are named after male characters (*baratus? coecus, fullones, Hortensius, Quintus, varus*), and nine after female (*Gemina, iurisperita, prilia? privigna, psaltria* or *Ferentinatis, Setina, tibicina, Veliterna, Ulubrana?*), two of which, the *iurisperita* and the *tibicina*, are evidently parodies of men's occupations. The feminine world preponderates also in the fragments.

genuine national pride the poet recalls the great times of the
Pyrrhic war, and looks down on his new Latin neighbours,—

Qui Obsce et Volsce fabulantur ; nam Latine nesciunt.

This comedy belongs to the stage of the capital quite as much
as did the Greek; but it was probably pervaded by something
of that rustic antagonism to the ways and the evils of a great
town, which appeared contemporaneously in Cato and afterwards in Varro. As in the German comedy, which proceeded
from the French in much the same way as the Roman comedy
from the Attic, the French Lisette was very soon superseded by
the *Frauenzimmerchen* Franziska, so the Latin national comedy
sprang up, if not with equal poetical power, at any rate with
the same tendency and perhaps with similar success, by the side
of the Hellenising comedy of the capital.

Greek tragedy as well as Greek comedy came in the course of
this epoch to Rome. It was a more valuable, and in some
respects also an easier, acquisition than comedy. The Greek
and particularly the Homeric epos, which was the basis of
tragedy, was not unfamiliar to the Romans, and was already
interwoven with their own national legends; and the susceptible
foreigner found himself far more at home in the ideal world of
the heroic myths than in the fish-market of Athens. Nevertheless tragedy also promoted, only with less abruptness and less
vulgarity, the anti-national and Hellenising spirit; and in this
point of view it was a circumstance of the most decisive importance, that the Greek tragic stage of this period was chiefly
under the sway of Euripides ($\frac{274-348}{480-406}$). This is not the place
for a thorough delineation of that remarkable man and of
his still more remarkable influence on his contemporaries and
posterity; but the intellectual movements of the later Greek
and the Graeco-Roman epoch were to so great an extent affected
by him, that it is indispensable to sketch at least the leading
outlines of his character. Euripides was one of those poets
who raise poetry to a higher level, but in doing so manifest far
more the true sense of what ought to be than the power of
poetically realising it. The profound saying which morally as
well as poetically sums up all tragic art—that action is passion
—holds true no doubt as to ancient tragedy; it exhibits man in
action, but it makes no real attempt to individualise him. The
unsurpassed grandeur with which the struggle between man and
destiny fulfils its course in Aeschylus depends substantially on
the circumstance, that each of the contending powers is only

conceived broadly and generally; the essential humanity in
Prometheus and Agamemnon is but slightly tinged by poetical
individualising. Sophocles seizes human nature in its broader
types, the king, the old man, the sister; but not one of his
figures displays the microcosm of man in all his aspects—the
features of individual character. A high stage was thereby
reached, but not the highest; the delineation of man in his
entireness and the entwining of the individual—in themselves
finished—figures into a higher poetical whole form a greater
achievement, and therefore, as compared with Shakespeare,
Aeschylus and Sophocles represent imperfect stages of development. But, when Euripides undertook to present man as he
is, the advance was logical and in a certain sense historical
rather than poetical. He was able to destroy the ancient
tragedy, but not to create the modern. Everywhere he halted
half way. Masks, through which the expression of the life of
the soul is, as it were, translated from the particular into the
general, were as necessary for the typical tragedy of antiquity
as they are incompatible with the tragedy of character; but
Euripides retained them. With remarkably delicate tact the
older tragedy never presented the dramatic element, to which
it was unable to allow free scope, unmixed, but constantly
fettered it in some measure by the epic subjects from the superhuman world of gods and heroes and by the lyrical choruses.
One feels that Euripides was impatient under these fetters: in
his subjects he descended at least to semi-historic times, and his
choral chants were of so subordinate importance, that they were
frequently omitted from the performance in after times and
hardly perhaps to the injury of the pieces; but yet he has neither
placed his figures wholly on the basis of reality, nor entirely
thrown aside the chorus. Throughout and on all sides he is the
full exponent of an age in which, on the one hand, the grandest
historical and philosophical movement was going forward, but in
which, on the other hand, the primitive fountain of all poetry—
a pure and homely national life—had become turbid. While the
reverential piety of the older tragedians sheds over their pieces
as it were a reflected radiance of heaven; while the limitation of
the narrow horizon of the older Hellenes exercises its satisfying
power over the hearer; the world of Euripides appears in the
pale glimmer of speculation as much denuded of the gods as it
is pervaded by the element of reflection, and gloomy passions
shoot like lightnings athwart the grey clouds. The old deeply-
rooted faith in destiny has disappeared; fate governs as an

outwardly despotic power, and the slaves gnashing their teeth
wear its fetters. The unbelief, which is the despair of faith,
speaks in this poet with superhuman power. Of necessity therefore the poet never attains a plastic conception overpowering
himself, and never reaches a truly poetic effect on the whole;
for which reason he was in some measure careless as to the
construction of his tragedies, and indeed not unfrequently
altogether spoiled them in this respect by providing no central
interest either of plot or person—the slovenly fashion of weaving
the plot in the prologue, and of unravelling it by a *Deus ex
machinâ* or some other platitude, was in reality brought into
vogue by Euripides. All the effect in his case lies in the details;
and with great art certainly every effort has in this respect
been made to conceal the irreparable want of poetic completeness. Euripides is a master in what are called effects; these,
as a rule, have a sensuous sentimental colouring, and often
moreover stimulate the sensuous impression by a special high
seasoning, such as the interweaving of murder or incest with
subjects relating to love. The delineations of Polyxena willing
to die and of Phaedra pining away under the grief of secret love,
above all the splendid picture of the mystic ecstasies of the
Bacchae, are of the greatest beauty in their kind; but they are
neither artistically nor morally pure, and the reproach of Aristophanes, that the poet was unable to paint a Penelope, was
thoroughly well founded. Of a kindred character is the introduction of common compassion into the tragedy of Euripides.
While his stunted heroes or heroines, such as Menelaus in the
Helena, Andromache, Electra as a poor peasant's wife, the sick
and ruined merchant Telephus, are repulsive or ridiculous and
ordinarily both, the pieces, on the other hand, which confine
themselves more to the atmosphere of common reality and
exchange the character of tragedy for that of the touching
family picture or that almost of sentimental comedy, such as
the *Iphigenia in Aulis*, the *Ion*, the *Alcestis*, produce perhaps the
most pleasing effect of all his numerous works. With equal
frequency, but with less success, the poet attempts to bring into
play an intellectual interest. Hence springs the complicated
plot, which is calculated not like the older tragedy to move the
feelings, but rather to keep curiosity on the rack; hence the
dialectically pointed dialogue, to us non-Athenians often
absolutely intolerable; hence the apophthegms, which are
scattered throughout the pieces of Euripides like flowers in a
pleasure-garden; hence above all the psychology of Euripides,

which by no means rests on direct human experience, but on logical reflection. His Medea is certainly in so far painted from life, that she is before departure properly provided with money for her voyage; but of the struggle in the soul between maternal love and jealousy the unbiassed reader will not find much in Euripides. But, above all, poetic effect is replaced in the tragedies of Euripides by moral or political aim. Without strictly or directly entering on the questions of the day, and having in view throughout social rather than political questions, Euripides in the legitimate issues of his principles coincided with the contemporary political and philosophical radicalism, and was the first and chief apostle of that new cosmopolitan humanity which broke up the old Attic national life. This was the ground at once of that opposition which the ungodly and un-Attic poet encountered among his contemporaries, and of that marvellous enthusiasm, with which the younger generation and foreigners devoted themselves to the poet of emotion and of love, of apophthegm and of tendency, of philosophy and of humanity. Greek tragedy in the hands of Euripides stepped beyond its proper sphere and consequently broke down; but the success of the cosmopolitan poet was only promoted by this, since at the same time the nation also stepped beyond its sphere and broke down likewise. The criticism of Aristophanes probably hit the truth exactly both in a moral and in a poetical point of view; but poetry influences the course of history not in proportion to its absolute value, but in proportion as it is able to anticipate the spirit of the age, and in this respect Euripides was unsurpassed. And thus it happened, that Alexander read him diligently; that Aristotle developed the idea of the tragic poet with special reference to him; that the latest poetic and plastic art in Attica as it were originated from him (for the new Attic comedy did nothing but transfer Euripides into a comic form, and the school of painters which we meet with in the designs of the later vases derived their subjects no longer from the old epics, but from the Euripidean tragedy); and lastly that, the more the old Hellas gave place to the new Hellenism, the more the fame and influence of the poet increased, and Greek life abroad, in Egypt as well as in Rome, was directly or indirectly moulded in the main by Euripides.

The Hellenism of Euripides flowed to Rome through very various channels, and probably produced a speedier and deeper effect there by indirect means than in the form of direct translation. The tragic drama in Rome was not exactly later in its

rise than comedy (p. 395); but the far greater expense of bringing a tragedy on the stage—which was undoubtedly felt as a
consideration of moment, at least during the Hannibalic war—
as well as the nature of the audience (p. 397) retarded the
development of tragedy. In the comedies of Plautus the
allusions to tragedies are not very frequent, and most references
of this kind may have been taken from the originals. The first
and only influential tragedian of this epoch was the younger
contemporary of Naevius and Plautus, Quintus Ennius ($\frac{515}{239}$—
$\frac{585}{169}$), whose pieces were already travestied by contemporary
comic writers, and were exhibited and declaimed by posterity
down to the days of the empire.

The tragic drama of the Romans is far less known to us than
the comic: on the whole the same features, which have been
noticed in the case of comedy, are presented by tragedy also.
The dramatic stock, in like manner, was mainly formed by
translations of Greek pieces. The preference was given to
subjects derived from the siege of Troy and the legends immediately connected with it, evidently because this cycle of myths
alone was rendered familiar to the Roman public by their
instruction at school. Incidents of striking horror predominate,
such as matricide or infanticide in the *Eumenides*, the *Alcmaeon*,
the *Cresphontes*, the *Melanippe*, the *Medea*, and the immolation
of virgins in the *Polyxena*, the *Erechthides*, the *Andromeda*, the
Iphigenia—we cannot avoid recalling the fact, that the public
for which these tragedies were prepared was in the habit of
witnessing gladiatorial games. The female characters and
ghosts appear to have made the deepest impression. In addition
to the rejection of masks, the most remarkable deviation of the
Roman edition from the original related to the chorus. The
Roman theatre, fitted up doubtless in the first instance for
comic plays without chorus, had not the special dancing-stage
(*orchestra*) with the altar in the middle, on which the Greek
chorus performed its part, or, to speak more correctly, the space
thus appropriated among the Greeks served with the Romans
as a sort of pit; accordingly the choral dance at least, with its
artistic alternations and intermixture of music and declamation,
must have been omitted in Rome, and, even if the chorus was
retained, it had but little importance. Of course there were
various alterations of detail, changes in the metres, curtail-
ments, and mutilations; in the Latin edition of the *Iphigenia* of
Euripides, for instance, the chorus of women was—either after
the model of another tragedy, or by the editor's own devices—

converted into a chorus of soldiers. The Latin tragedies of the sixth century cannot be pronounced good translations in our sense of the word;[1] yet it is probable that a tragedy of Ennius gave a far less imperfect image of the original of Euripides than a comedy of Plautus gave of the original of Menander.

The historical position and influence of Greek tragedy in Rome were entirely analogous to those of Greek comedy; and while, as the difference in the two kinds of composition necessarily implied, the Hellenistic tendency appeared in tragedy under a purer and more spiritual form, the tragic drama of this period and its principal representative Ennius displayed far more decidedly an anti-national and consciously propagandist aim. Ennius, hardly the most important but certainly the most influential poet of the sixth century, was not a Latin by birth, but on the contrary by virtue of his origin half a Greek. Of Messapian descent and Hellenic culture, he settled in his thirty-fifth year at Rome, and lived there—at first as a resident alien, but after $\frac{570}{184}$ as a burgess (p. 313)—in straitened circumstances, supported partly by giving instruction in Latin and Greek, partly by the proceeds of his pieces, partly by the donations of those Roman grandees, who, like Publius Scipio, Titus Flami-

---

[1] We subjoin, for comparison, the opening lines of the *Medea* in the original of Euripides and in the version of Ennius:—

Εἴθ' ὤφελ' Ἀργοῦς μὴ διαπτάσθαι σκάφος
Κόλχων ἐς αἶαν κυανέας Συμπληγά-δας,
Μηδ' ἐν νάπαισι Πηλίου πεσεῖν ποτε
Τμηθεῖσα πεύκη, μηδ' ἐρετμῶσαι χέρας

Utinam ne in nemore Pelio securibus
Caesa accidisset abiegna ad terram trabes,
Neve inde navis inchoandae exordium
Coepisset, quae nunc nominatur nomine

Ἀνδρῶν ἀρίστων, οἳ τὸ πάγχρυσον δέρος

Argo, quia Argivi in ea dilecti viri
Vecti petebant pellem inauratam arietis

Πελίᾳ μετῆλθον· οὐ γὰρ ἂν δέσποιν' ἐμὴ
Μήδεια πύργους γῆς ἔπλευσ' Ἰωλκίας
Ἔρωτι θυμὸν ἐκπλαγεῖσ' Ἰάσονος.

Colchis, imperio regis Peliae, per dolum.
Nam nunquam era errans mea domo efferret pedem
Medea, animo aegra, amore saevo saucia.

The variations of the translation from the original are instructive—not only its tautologies and periphrases, but also the omission or explanation of the less familiar mythological names, *e.g.* the Symplegades, the Iolcian land, the Argo. But the instances in which Ennius has really misunderstood the original are rare.

ninus, and Marcus Fulvius Nobilior, were inclined to promote the modern Hellenism and to reward the poet who sang their own and their ancestors' praises and even accompanied some of them to the field in the character, as it were, of a poet laureate nominated beforehand to celebrate the great deeds which they were to perform. He has himself elegantly described the client-like qualities requisite for such a calling.[1] From the outset and by virtue of the whole tenor of his life a cosmopolite, he had the skill to appropriate the distinctive features of the nations among which he lived—Greek, Latin, and even Oscan— without devoting himself absolutely to any one of them; and while the Hellenism of the earlier Roman poets was the result rather than the conscious aim of their poetic activity, and accordingly they at least attempted more or less to take their stand on national ground, Ennius on the contrary is very distinctly conscious of his revolutionary tendency, and evidently labours with zeal to bring into vogue neological Hellenic ideas among the Italians. His most serviceable instrument was tragedy. The remains of his tragedies show that he was well acquainted with the whole range of the Greek tragic drama and with Aeschylus and Sophocles in particular; it is the less therefore the result of accident, that he has moulded the great majority of his pieces, and all those that attained celebrity, after the model of Euripides. In the selection and treatment he was doubtless influenced partly by external considerations. But these alone cannot account for his bringing forward so decidedly

[1] Beyond doubt the ancients were right in recognising a sketch of the poet's own character in the passage in the seventh book of the Annals, where the consul calls to his side the confidant,

> quocum bene saepe libenter
> *Mensam sermonesque suos rerumque suarum*
> *Congeriem partit, magnam cum lassus diei*
> *Partem fuisset de summis rebus regundis*
> *Consilio indu foro lato sanctoque senatu :*
> *Cui res audacter magnas parvasque jocumque*
> *Eloqueretur, cuncta simul malaque et bona dictu*
> *Evomeret, si qui vellet, tutoque locaret.*
> *Quocum multa volup ac gaudia clamque palamque.*
> *Ingenium cui nulla malum sententia suadet*
> *Ut faceret facinus lenis aut malus, doctus fidelis*
> *Suavis homo facundus suo contentus beatus*
> *Scitus secunda loquens in tempore commodus verbum*
> *Paucum, multa tenens antiqua sepulta, vetustas*
> *Quem fecit mores veteresque novosque tenentem,*
> *Multorum veterum leges divumque hominumque,*
> *Prudenter qui dicta loquive tacereve possit.*

In the line before the last we should probably read *multarum rerum leges divumque hominumque.*

the Euripidean element in Euripides; for his neglecting the choruses still more than did his original; for his laying still stronger emphasis on sensuous effect than the Greek; nor for his taking up pieces like the *Thyestes* and the *Telephus* so well known from the immortal ridicule of Aristophanes, with their princes' woes and woful princes, and even such a piece as *Menalippa the Female Philosopher*, in which the whole plot turns on the absurdity of the national religion, and the tendency to make war on it from the physicist point of view is at once apparent. The sharpest arrows are everywhere—and that partly in passages which can be proved to have been inserted [1] —directed against faith in the miraculous, and we almost wonder that the censorship of the Roman stage allowed such tirades to pass as the following:—

> *Ego deum genus esse semper dixi et dicam coelitum,*
> *Sed eos non curare opinor, quid agat humanum genus ;*
> *Nam si curent, bene bonis sit, male malis, quod nunc abest.*

We have already remarked (p. 378) that Ennius scientifically inculcated the same religion in a didactic poem; and it is evident that he was in earnest with this freethinking. With this trait other features are in harmony—his political opposition tinged with radicalism, that here and there appears; [2] his singing the praises of the Greek pleasures of the table (p. 385); above all his setting aside the last national element in Latin poetry, the Saturnian measure, and substituting for it the Greek hexameter. That the "multiform" poet executed all these tasks with equal neatness, that he elaborated hexameters out of a language of by no means dactylic structure, and that without checking the natural flow of his style he moved with confidence and freedom amidst unwonted measures and forms—are so many evidences of his extraordinary plastic talent, which was in fact more

---

[1] Comp. p. 380. Euripides (*Iph. in Aul.* 956) defines the soothsayer as a man,

> Ὅς ὀλίγ᾽ ἀληθῆ, πολλὰ δὲ ψευδῆ λέγει
> Τυχών, ὅταν δὲ μὴ τύχῃ, διοίχεται.

This is turned by the Latin translator into the following diatribe against the casters of horoscopes:—

> *Astrologorum signa in coelo quaesit, observat, Jovis*
> *Cum capra aut nepa aut exoritur lumen aliquod beluae.*
> *Quod est ante pedes, nemo spectat : coeli scrutantur plagas.*

[2] In the *Telephus* we find him saying—

> *Palam mutire plebeis piaculum est.*

Greek than Roman; [1] where he offends us, the offence is owing
much more frequently to Greek alliteration [2] than to Roman
ruggedness. He was not a great poet, but a man of graceful
and sprightly talent, throughout possessing the vivid sensibilities
of a poetic nature, but needing the tragic buskin to feel himself
a poet and wholly destitute of the comic vein. We can understand the pride with which the Hellenising poet looked down
on those rude strains

> ——quos olim Faunei vatesque canebant,

and the enthusiasm with which he celebrates his own artistic
poetry:

> Enni poeta salve, qui mortalibus
> Versus propinas flammeos medullitus.

The genius of Ennius instinctively assured him that he had
spread his sails to a prosperous breeze; Greek tragedy became,
and thenceforth remained, a possession of the Latin nation.

Through less frequented paths, and with a less favourable
wind, a bolder mariner pursued a higher aim. Naevius not only
like Ennius—although with far less success—adapted Greek
tragedies for the Roman stage, but also attempted to create,
independently of the Greeks, a grave national drama (*fabula
praetextata*). No outward obstacles here stood in the way; he
brought forward subjects both from Roman legend and from
the contemporary history of the country on the stage of his

---

[1] The following verses, excellent in matter and form, belong to the
adaptation of the *Phoenix* of Euripides:—

> Sed virum virtute vera vivere animatum addecet,
> Fortiterque innoxium (?) vocare adversum adversarios.
> Ea libertas est, qui pectus purum et firmum gestitat:
> Aliae res obnoxiosae nocte in obscura latent.

In the *Scipio*, which was probably incorporated in the collection of
miscellaneous poems the graphic lines occurred:—

> —— mundus coeli vastus constitit silentio,
> Et Neptunus saevus undis asperis pausam dedit.
> Sol equis iter repressit ungulis volantibus;
> Constitere amnes perennes, arbores vento vacant.

This last passage affords us a glimpse of the way in which the poet
worked up his original poems. It is simply an expansion of the words
which occur in the tragedy *Hectoris Lustra* (the original of which was
probably by Sophocles) as spoken by a spectator of the combat between
Hephaestus and the Scamander:—

> Constitit credo Scamander, arbores vento vacant.

and the incident is derived from the *Iliad* (xxi. 381).

[2] Thus in the *Phoenix* we find the line:—

> —— stultust, qui cupita cupiens cupienter cupit.

and this is not the most absurd specimen of such recurring assonances.
He also indulged in acrostic verses (Cic. *de Div.* ii. 54, 111).

native land. Such were his *Nursing of Romulus and Remus* or the *Wolf*, in which Amulius king of Alba appeared, and his *Clastidium*, which celebrated the victory of Marcellus over the Celts in $\frac{532}{222}$ (p. 75). After his example, Ennius in his *Ambracia* described from personal observation the siege of that city by his patron Nobilior in $\frac{565}{189}$ (p. 259). But the number of these national dramas remained small, and that species of composition soon disappeared from the stage; the scanty legend and the colourless history of Rome were unable permanently to compete with the Hellenic mythology. Respecting the poetic value of the pieces we have no longer the means of judging; but, if we may take account of the general poetical intention, there were in Roman literature few such strokes of genius as the creation of a Roman national drama. Only the Greek tragedians of that earliest period which still felt its nearness to the gods—only poets like Phrynichus and Aeschylus—had the courage to bring the great deeds which they had witnessed, and in which they had borne a part, on the stage by the side of those of legendary times; and here, if anywhere, we are enabled vividly to realise what the Punic wars were and how powerful was their effect, when we find a poet who, like Aeschylus, had himself fought in the battles which he sang, introducing the kings and consuls of Rome upon that stage on which men had hitherto been accustomed to see none but gods and heroes.

Recitative poetry also took its rise during this epoch at Rome. Livius naturalised the custom which among the ancients held the place of our modern publication—the public reading of new works by the author—in Rome, at least to the extent of reciting them in his school. As poetry was not in this instance practised with a view to a livelihood, or at any rate not directly so, this branch of it was not regarded by public opinion with such disfavour as writing for the stage: towards the end of this epoch one or two noble Romans had publicly come foward in this manner as poets.[1] Recitative poetry however was chiefly cultivated by those poets who occupied themselves with writing for the stage, and the former held a subordinate place as compared with the latter; in fact, a public to which read poetry might address itself can have existed only to a very limited extent at this period in Rome.

---

[1] Besides Cato, we find the names of two " consulars and poets " belonging to this period (Sueton. *Vita Terent.* 4)—Quintus Labeo, consul in $\frac{571}{183}$, and Marcus Popillius, consul in $\frac{581}{173}$. But it remains uncertain whether they published their poems. Even in the case of Cato this may be doubted.

Lyrical, didactic, and epigrammatic poetry in particular were feebly represented. The religious festival chants—of which the annals of this period certainly have already thought it worth while to mention the author—as well as the monumental inscriptions on temples and tombs, for which the Saturnian remained the regular measure, hardly belong to literature in its proper sense. So far as the minor poetry makes its appearance at all, it is classed ordinarily, and that as early as the time of Naevius, under the name of *satura*. This term was originally applied to the old stage-poem without action which from the time of Livius was driven off the stage by the Greek drama; but in its application to recitative poetry it corresponds in some measure to our "miscellaneous poems," and like the latter denotes not any positive species or style of art, but simply poems not of an epic or dramatic kind, treating of any matters (mostly subjective), and written in any form, at the pleasure of the author. In addition to Cato's "poem on Morals" to be noticed afterwards, which was probably written in Saturnian verses after the precedent of the earlier attempts at a national didactic poetry (i. 454), there came under this category the minor poems of Ennius, which that writer, who was very fertile in this department, published partly in his collection of *saturae*, partly separately. Among these were brief narrative poems relating to the legendary or contemporary history of his country; editions of the religious romance of Euhemerus (p. 377), of the physical poems circulated in the name of Epicharmus (p. 377), and of the gastronomics of Archestratus of Gela, a poet who treated of the higher cookery; as also a dialogue between Life and Death, fables of Aesop, a collection of moral maxims, parodies and epigrammatic trifles—small matters, but indicative of the versatile powers as well as the neological didactic tendencies of the poet, who evidently allowed himself the freest range in this field, which the censorship did not reach.

The attempts at a metrical treatment of the national annals lay claim to greater poetical and historical importance. Here too it was Naevius who gave poetic form to so much of the legendary as well as of the contemporary history as admitted of connected narrative; and who, more especially, recorded in the half-prosaic Saturnian national metre the story of the first Punic war simply and distinctly, with a straightforward adherence to fact, without disdaining anything as unpoetical, and without at all, especially in the description of historical times, going in pursuit of poetical flights or embellishments—maintaining throughout his narrative the present tense.[1] What we have already said of the national drama of the same poet, applies substantially to the work of which we are now speaking. The epic poetry of the Greeks, like their tragedy, had wholly reference to the heroic period; it was an altogether new and, at least in design, an enviably grand idea—to light up the present with the brilliance of poetry. Although in point of execution the chronicle of Naevius was probably not much better than the rhyming chronicles of the middle ages, which are in various respects of kindred character, yet the poet was certainly justified in regarding this work of his with an altogether peculiar complacency. It was no small achievement, in an age when there was absolutely no historical literature except official records, to have composed for his countrymen a connected account of the deeds of their own times and of earlier ages, and in addition to have placed before their eyes the noblest incidents of their history in a dramatic form.

Ennius proposed to himself the very same task as Naevius; but the similarity of the subject only brings out into stronger relief the political and poetical contrast between the national and the anti-national poet. Naevius sought out for the new subject a new form; Ennius fitted or forced it into the forms of the Hellenic epos. The hexameter replaced the Saturnian verse; the ornate style of the Homeridae, striving after plastic vividness of delineation, replaced the homely historic narrative. Wherever the circumstances admit, Homer is directly translated; *e.g.* the burial of those that fell at Heraclea is described after the model of the burial of Patroclus, and under the helmet of Marcus Livius

---

[1] The following fragments will give some idea of its tone. Of Dido he says:

> Blande et docte percontat—Aeneas quo pacto
> Troiam urbem liquerit.

Again of Amulius:

> Manusque susum ad coelum—sustulit suas rex
> Amulius ; gratulatur—divis.

Part of a speech where the indirect construction is remarkable:

> Sin illos deserant for—tissumos virorum
> Magnum stuprum populo—fieri per gentis.

With reference to the landing at Malta in $\frac{498}{256}$:

> Transit Melitam Romanus—insulam in tegram omnem
> Urit populatur vastat—rem hostium concinnat.

Lastly, as to the peace which terminated the war concerning Sicily :

> Id quoque paciscunt moenia—sint Lutatium quae
> Reconcilient ; captivos—plurimos idem
> Sicilienses paciseit—obsides ut reddant.

Stolo, the military tribune who fights with the Istrians, lurks
none other than the Homeric Ajax; the reader is not even spared
the Homeric invocation of the Muse. The epic machinery is
fully set agoing; after the battle of Cannae, for instance, Juno
in a full council of the gods pardons the Romans, and Jupiter
after obtaining the consent of his wife promises them a final
victory over the Carthaginians. Nor do the Annals fail to
betray the neological and Hellenistic tendencies of the author.
The very employment of the gods for the mere purpose of
decoration bears this stamp. The remarkable vision, with which
the poem opens, tells in good Pythagorean style how the soul
now inhabiting Quintus Ennius had previously been domiciled
in Homer and still earlier in a peacock, and then in good physicist
style explains the nature of things and the relation of the body
to the mind. Even the choice of the subject serves the same
purpose—at any rate the Hellenic literati of all ages have found
an especially suitable handle for their Graeco-cosmopolite
tendencies in this very rehabilitation of Roman history. Ennius
lays stress on the circumstance that the Romans were reckoned
Greeks:

> *Contendunt Graecos, Graios memorare solent sos.*

The poetical value of the greatly celebrated Annals may easily
be estimated after the remarks which we have already made
regarding the excellences and defects of the poet in general. A
poet of lively sympathies, he naturally felt himself elevated by
the enthusiastic impulse which the great age of the Punic wars
gave to the national sensibilities of Italy, and he not only often
succeeds in imitating Homeric simplicity, but also and still more
frequently makes his lines strikingly echo the solemnity and
decorum of the Roman character. But the construction of his
epic was defective; indeed it must have been very lax and indifferent, when it was possible for the poet to insert a special
book by way of supplement to please an otherwise forgotten
hero and patron. On the whole the Annals were beyond question the work in which Ennius fell farthest short of his aim. The
plan of making an Iliad pronounces its own condemnation. It
was Ennius, who in this poem for the first time introduced into
literature that changeling compound of epos and of history,
which from that time up to the present day has haunted it like
a ghost, unable either to live or to die. But the poem certainly
had its success. Ennius claimed to be the Roman Homer with
still greater ingenuousness than Klopstock claimed to be the
German, and was received as such by his contemporaries and

still more so by posterity. The veneration for the father of Roman poetry was transmitted from generation to generation; even the polished Quintilian says, " Let us revere Ennius as we revere an ancient sacred grove, whose mighty oaks of a thousand years are more venerable than beautiful; " and, if any one is disposed to wonder at this, he may recall analogous phenomena in the successes of the Aeneid, the Henriad, and the Messiad. A mighty poetical development of the nation would indeed have set aside that almost comic official parallel between the Homeric Iliad and the Ennian Annals as easily as we have set aside the parallels of Sappho and Karschin and of Pindar and Willamov; but no such development took place in Rome. Owing to the interest of the subject especially for aristocratic circles, and the great plastic talent of the poet, the Annals remained the oldest Roman original poem which appeared to the culture of later generations readable or worth reading; and thus, singularly enough, posterity came to honour this thoroughly anti-national epos of a half-Greek *littérateur* as the true model poem of Rome.

A prose literature arose in Rome not much later than Roman poetry, but in a very different way. It experienced neither the artificial stimulus, by which the school and the stage prematurely forced the growth of Roman poetry, nor the artificial restraint, to which Roman comedy in particular was subjected by the strict and narrow-minded censorship of the stage. Nor was this form of literary activity placed from the first under the ban of good society by the stigma which attached to the " ballad-singer." Accordingly the prose literature, while far less extensive and less active than the contemporary poetical authorship, had a far more natural growth. While poetry was almost wholly in the hands of men of humble rank and not a single Roman of quality appears among the celebrated poets of this age, there is, on the contrary, among the prose writers of this period hardly a name that is not senatorial; and it is from the circles of the highest aristocracy, from men who had been consuls and censors —the Fabii, the Gracchi, the Scipios—that this literature throughout proceeds. The conservative and national tendency, in the nature of the case, accorded better with this prose authorship than with poetry; but here too—and particularly in the most important branch of this literature, historical composition—the Hellenistic tendency had a powerful, in fact a preponderant, influence both on matter and form.

Down to the period of the Hannibalic war there was no historical composition in Rome; for the entries in the book of

Annals were of the nature of records and not of literature, and never made any attempt to develop the connection of events. It is a significant illustration of the peculiarity of Roman character, that notwithstanding the extension of Roman power far beyond the bounds of Italy, and notwithstanding the constant contact of the noble society of Rome with the Greeks who were so full of literary activity, it was not till the middle of the sixth century that there sprang up any desire to impart a knowledge of the deeds and fortunes of the Roman people, by means of authorship, to the contemporary world and to posterity. When at length this desire was felt, there were neither literary forms ready at hand for the use of Roman history, nor was there a public prepared to read it, and great talent and considerable time were required to create both. In the first instance, accordingly, these difficulties were in some measure evaded by writing the national history either in the mother tongue and in that case in verse, or in prose and in that case in Greek. We have already spoken of the metrical Annals of Naevius (written about $\frac{550}{204}$?) and of Ennius (written about $\frac{581}{173}$); both belong to the earliest historical literature of the Romans, and those of Naevius may be regarded as the oldest of all Roman historical works. At nearly the same period were composed the Greek Histories of Quintus Fabius Pictor[1] (after $\frac{553}{201}$), a man of noble family who took an active part in state affairs during the Hannibalic war, and of Publius Scipio, the son of Scipio Africanus (who died about $\frac{590}{164}$). In the former case they availed themselves of the poetical art which was already to a certain extent developed, and addressed themselves to a public with a taste for poetry, which was not altogether wanting; in the latter case they found the Greek forms ready to their hand, and addressed themselves

---

[1] That this oldest prose work on the history of Rome was composed in Greek, is established beyond a doubt by Dionys. i. 6, and Cicero, de Div. i. 21, 43. The Latin Annals quoted under the same name by Quintilian and later grammarians remain involved in mystery, and the difficulty is increased by the circumstance, that there is also quoted under the same name a very complete exposition of the pontifical law in the Latin language. But the latter treatise will not be attributed by any one, who has traced the development of Roman literature in its connection, to an author of the age of the Hannibalic war; and Latin annals from that age appear problematical, although it must remain a moot question whether there has been a confusion of the earlier with a later annalist, Quintus Fabius Maximus Servilianus (consul in $\frac{612}{142}$), or whether there existed an old Latin edition of the Greek Annals of Fabius as well as of those of Acilius and Albinus, or whether there were two annalists of the name of Fabius Pictor.

The historical work likewise written in Greek, ascribed to Lucius Cincius Alimentus, a contemporary of Fabius, seems spurious and a compilation of the Augustan age.

—as the interest of their subject stretching far beyond the bounds of Latium naturally suggested—primarily to the cultivated foreigner. The former plan was adopted by the plebeian authors, the latter by those of quality; just as in the time of Frederick the Great an aristocratic literature in the French language subsisted side by side with the native German authorship of pastors and professors, and, while men like Gleim and Ramler wrote war-songs in German, kings and generals wrote military histories in French. Neither the metrical chronicles nor the Greek annals by Roman authors constituted Latin historical composition in the proper sense of the term; this only began with Cato, whose *Origines*, not published before the close of this epoch, formed at once the oldest historical work written in Latin and the first important prose work in Roman literature.[1]

All these works, while not coming up to the Greek conception of history,[2] were, as contrasted with the mere detached notices of the book of Annals, systematic histories with a connected narrative and a more or less regular structure. They all, so far as we can see, embraced the national history from the building of Rome down to the time of the writer, although in point of title the work of Naevius related only to the first war with Carthage, and that of Cato only to the early history. They were thus naturally divided into the three sections of the legendary period, of earlier, and of contemporary, history.

In the legendary period the history of the origin of the city was set forth with great minuteness; and in its case the peculiar difficulty had to be surmounted, that there were, as we have already shown (i. 457), two wholly irreconcilable versions of it in circulation: the national version, which, in its leading outlines at least, was probably already embodied in the book of Annals, and the Greek version of Timaeus, which cannot have remained unknown to these Roman chroniclers. The object of the former was to connect Rome with Alba, that of the latter to connect Rome with Troy; in the former, accordingly, the city was built by Romulus son of the Alban king, in the latter by the Trojan prince Aeneas. To the present epoch, probably either

---

[1] Cato's whole literary activity belonged to the period of his old age (Cicero, *Cat.* 11, 38; Nepos, *Cato*, 3); the composition even of the earlier books of the *Origines* falls not before, and yet probably not long subsequent to, $\frac{586}{168}$ (Plin. *H. N.*, iii. 14, 114).

[2] It is evidently by way of contrast with Fabius that Polybius (xl. 6, 4) calls attention to the fact, that Albinus, the passionate admirer of everything Greek, endeavoured to write a systematic history [πραγματικὴν ἱστορίαν].

to Naevius or to Pictor, belongs the amalgamation of the two stories. The Alban prince Romulus remains the founder of Rome, but becomes at the same time the grandson of Aeneas; Aeneas does not found Rome, but is represented as bringing the Roman Penates to Italy and building Lavinium as their shrine, while his son Ascanius founds Alba Longa, the mother-city of Rome and the ancient metropolis of Latium. All this was a sorry and unskilful patchwork. The view that the original Penates of Rome were preserved not, as had hitherto been believed, in their temple in the Roman Forum, but in the shrine at Lavinium, could not but be offensive to the Romans; and the Greek fiction was a still worse expedient, inasmuch as under it the gods only bestowed on the grandson what they had adjudged to the grandsire. But the amalgamation served its object: without exactly denying the national origin of Rome, it yet deferred to the Hellenising tendency, and legalised in some degree that desire to claim kindred with Aeneas which was already at this epoch greatly in vogue (p. 391); and thus it became the stereotyped, and was soon accepted as the official, account of the origin of the mighty community.

With the exception of the story of the origin of the city, the Greek historiographers had given themselves little or no concern as to the Roman commonwealth; so that the recital of the further course of the national history must have been chiefly derived from native sources. But the scanty information that has been transmitted to us does not enable us to discern distinctly what sort of traditions, in addition to the book of Annals, were at the command of the earliest chroniclers, and what they may possibly have added of their own. The tales inserted from Herodotus [1] were probably still foreign to these earliest annalists; and a direct borrowing of Greek materials for this section cannot be proved. The more remarkable, therefore, is the tendency, which is everywhere, even in the case of Cato the enemy of Hellenism, very distinctly apparent, not only to connect Rome with Hellas, but to represent the Italian and Greek nations as having been originally identical. To this tendency we owe the primitive Italians or aborigines who were immigrants from Greece, and the primitive Greeks or Pelasgians whose wanderings brought them to Italy.

---

[1] For instance the history of the siege of Gabii is compiled from the anecdotes as to Zopyrus and the tyrant Thrasybulus in Herodotus, and one version of the story of the exposure of Romulus is framed on the model of the history of the youth of Cyrus as Herodotus relates it.

The current story presented some sort of connection, though the connecting thread was but weak and loose, throughout the regal period down to the institution of the republic; but at that point the stream of legend dried up, and it was not merely difficult but altogether impossible to form a narrative, in any degree connected and readable, out of the lists of magistrates and the scanty notices appended to them. The poets were the most sensible of the blank. Naevius appears for that reason to have passed at once from the regal period to the war regarding Sicily: Ennius, who in the third of his eighteen books was still occupied with the regal period and in the sixth had already reached the war with Pyrrhus, must have treated the first two centuries of the republic merely in the most general outline. How the annalists who wrote in Greek managed the matter, we do not know. Cato adopted a peculiar course. He felt no pleasure, as he himself says, " in relating what was set forth on the tablet in the house of the Pontifex Maximus, how often wheat had been dear, and when the sun or moon had been eclipsed; " and so he devoted the second and third books of his historical work to accounts of the origin of the other Italian communities and of their admission to the Roman confederacy. He thus got rid of the fetters of chronicle, which reports events year by year under the heading of the magistrates for the time being; the statement, that Cato's historical work narrated events " sectionally," must refer to this feature of his method. This attention bestowed on the other Italian communities, which surprises us in a Roman work, had a bearing on the political position of the author, who leaned throughout on the support of the municipal Italy in his opposition to the proceedings of the capital; while it furnished a sort of substitute for the missing history of Rome from the expulsion of king Tarquinius down to the Pyrrhic war, by presenting in its own way the main result of that history—the union of Italy under the hegemony of Rome.

Contemporary history, again, was treated in a connected and detailed manner. Naevius described the first, and Fabius the second, war with Carthage from their own knowledge; Ennius devoted at least thirteen out of the eighteen books of his Annals to the epoch from Pyrrhus down to the Istrian war (p. 183); Cato narrated in the fourth and fifth books of his historical work the wars from the first Punic war down to that with Perseus, and in the two last books, which probably were on a different and more copious plan, he related the events of the last twenty years of his life. For the Pyrrhic war Ennius may have employed Timaeus or other Greek authorities; but on the whole the accounts given were based, partly on personal observation or communications of eye-witnesses, partly on each other.

Contemporaneously with historical literature, and in some sense as an appendage to it, arose the literature of speeches and letters. This in like manner was commenced by Cato; for the Romans possessed nothing of an earlier age except some funeral orations, most of which probably were only brought to light at a later period from family archives, such as that which the veteran Quintus Fabius, the opponent of Hannibal, delivered when an old man over his son who had died in his prime. Cato on the other hand committed to writing in his old age such of the numerous orations which he had delivered during his long and active public career as were historically important, as a sort of political memoirs, and published them partly in his historical work, partly, it would seem, as independent supplements to it. There also existed a collection of his letters.

With non-Roman history the Romans concerned themselves so far, that a certain knowledge of it was deemed indispensable for the cultivated Roman; even old Fabius is said to have been familiar not merely with the Roman, but also with foreign, wars, and it is distinctly testified that Cato diligently read Thucydides and the Greek historians in general. But, if we leave out of view the collection of anecdotes and maxims which Cato compiled for himself as the fruits of this reading, no trace is discernible of any literary activity in this field.

These first essays in historical literature were all of them, as a matter of course, pervaded by an easy, uncritical spirit; neither authors nor readers readily took offence at inward or outward inconsistencies. King Tarquinius the Second, although he was already grown up at the time of his father's death and did not begin to reign till thirty-nine years afterwards, is nevertheless still a young man when he ascends the throne. Pythagoras, who came to Italy about a generation before the expulsion of the kings, is nevertheless set down by the Roman historians as a friend of the wise Numa. The state-envoys sent to Syracuse in the year $\frac{262}{492}$ transact business with Dionysius the elder, who ascended the throne eighty-six years afterwards ($\frac{348}{406}$). This naïve uncritical spirit is especially apparent in the treatment of Roman chronology. Since according to the Roman reckoning —the outlines of which were probably fixed in the previous epoch—the foundation of Rome took place 240 years before the consecration of the Capitoline temple (i. 459) and 360 years before the burning of the city by the Gauls (i. 454), and the latter event, which is mentioned in Greek historical works, fell according to these in the year of the Athenian archon Pyrgion 388 B.C. Ol. 98, 1, the building of Rome accordingly fell on Ol. 8, 1. This was, according to the chronology of Eratosthenes which was already recognised as canonical, the year 436 after the fall of Troy; nevertheless the common story retained as the founder of Rome the grandson of the Trojan Aeneas. Cato, who like a good financier checked the calculation, no doubt drew attention in this instance to the incongruity; but he does not appear to have proposed any mode of getting over the difficulty—the list of the Alban kings, which was afterwards inserted with this view, certainly did not proceed from him.

The same uncritical spirit, which prevailed in the early history, prevailed also to a certain extent in the representation of historical times. The accounts certainly without exception bore that strong party colouring, for which the Fabian narrative of the origin of the second war with Carthage is censured by Polybius with the calm severity so peculiar to him. Mistrust, however, is more appropriate in such circumstances than reproach. It would be somewhat ridiculous to expect from the Roman contemporaries of Hannibal a just judgment of their antagonist; but no intentional misrepresentation of the facts, except such as a simple-minded patriotism of itself involves, has been proved against the fathers of Roman history.

The beginnings of scientific culture, and even of authorship relating to it, also fall within this epoch. The instruction hitherto given had been substantially confined to reading and writing and a knowledge of the law of the land.[1] But a closer contact with the Greeks gradually suggested to the Romans the idea of a more general culture; and stimulated the endeavour, if not directly to transplant this Greek culture to Rome, at any rate to modify the Roman culture to some extent after its model.

First of all, the knowledge of the mother-tongue began to shape itself into Latin grammar; Greek philology transferred its methods to the kindred idiom of Italy. The active study of grammar began nearly at the same time with Roman authorship. About $\frac{520}{234}$ Spurius Carvilius, a teacher of writing, appears to have regulated the Latin alphabet, and to have given to the letter g, which was not previously included in it (i. 465), the place of the z which could be dispensed with—the place which it still

<hr>

[1] Plautus (*Mostell.* 126) says of parents, that they teach their children *litteras, iura, leges;* and Plutarch (*Cato Mai.* 20) testifies to the same effect.

holds in the modern alphabets of the West. The Roman school-masters must have been constantly working at the adjustment of orthography; the Latin Muses too never disowned their scholastic Hippocrene, and at all times applied themselves to orthography side by side with poetry. Ennius especially—resembling Klopstock in this respect also—not only practised an etymological play on assonance quite after the Alexandrian style; [1] but also introduced, in place of the simple signs for the double consonants that had hitherto been usual, the more accurate Greek double writing. Of Naevius and Plautus, it is true, nothing of the kind is known; the popular poets in Rome must have treated orthography and etymology with the careless-ness which poets usually manifest in such matters.

The Romans of this epoch still remained strangers to rhetoric and philosophy. Public speaking in their case was too decidedly the mainspring of public life to be accessible to the handling of the foreign schoolmaster; the genuine orator Cato poured forth all the vials of his indignant ridicule over the Isocratean folly of ever learning and yet never being able to speak. The Greek philosophy, although it acquired a certain influence over the Romans through the medium of didactic and especially of tragic poetry, was nevertherless viewed with an apprehension com-pounded of boorish ignorance and of instinctive misgiving. Cato bluntly called Socrates a talker and a revolutionist, who was justly put to death as an offender against the faith and the laws of his country; and the opinion, which even Romans addicted to philosophy entertained regarding it, probably finds expression in the words of Ennius:

Philosophari est mihi necesse, at paucis, nam omnino haut placet.
Degustandum ex ea, non in eam ingurgitandum censeo.

Nevertheless the poem on Morals and the instructions in Oratory, which were found among the writings of Cato, may be regarded as the Roman quintessence or, if the expression be preferred, the Roman *caput mortuum* of Greek philosophy and rhetoric. The immediate sources whence Cato drew were, in the case of the poem on Morals, probably the Pythagorean writings on morals (coupled of course with due commendation of the simple an-cestral manners), and, in the case of the book on Oratory, the speeches in Thucydides and more especially the orations of Demosthenes, all of which Cato zealously studied. Of the spirit of these manuals we may form some idea from the golden

[1] Thus in his Epicharmian poems the name of Jupiter is derived from the circumstance *quod iuvat ;* that of Ceres from the fact *quod gerit fruges.*

oratorical rule, oftener quoted than followed by posterity, " to think of the matter and leave the words to follow of themselves."[1]

Similar manuals of a general elementary character were composed by Cato on the Art of Healing, the Science of War, Agriculture, and Jurisprudence—all of which studies were likewise more or less under Greek influence. Physics and mathematics were not much studied in Rome; but the applied sciences connected with them received a certain measure of attention. This was most of all true of medicine. In $\frac{535}{219}$ the first Greek physician, the Peloponnesian Archagathus, settled in Rome and there acquired such repute by his surgical operations, that a residence was assigned to him on the part of the state and he received the freedom of the city; and thereafter his colleagues flocked in crowds to Italy. Cato no doubt not only reviled the foreign medical practitioners with a zeal worthy of a better cause, but attempted, by means of his medical manual compiled from his own experience and probably in part also from the medical literature of the Greeks, to revive the good old fashion under which the father of the family was at the same time the family physician. The physicians and the public gave themselves, as was reasonable, but little concern about his obstinate invectives: at any rate the profession, one of the most lucrative which existed in Rome, continued a monopoly in the hands of the foreigners, and for centuries there were none but Greek physicians in Rome.

Hitherto the measurement of time had been treated in Rome with barbarous indifference, but matters were now at least in some degree improved. With the erection of the first sundial in the Roman Forum in $\frac{491}{263}$ the Greek hour ($\H{\omega}\rho\alpha$, *hora*) began to come into use at Rome: it happened, however, that the Romans erected a sundial which had been prepared for Catana situated four degrees farther to the south, and were guided by this for a whole century. Towards the end of this epoch we find persons of distinction taking an interest in mathematical studies. Manius Acilius Glabrio (consul in $\frac{563}{191}$) attempted to check the confusion of the calendar by a law, which allowed the pontifical college to insert or omit intercalary months at discretion: if the measure failed in its object and in fact aggravated the evil, the failure was probably owing more to the unscrupulousness than to the want of intelligence of the Roman theologians. Marcus Fulvius Nobilior (consul in $\frac{565}{189}$), a man of Greek culture, endeavoured at least to make the Roman calendar more generally known. Gaius Sulpicius Gallus (consul in $\frac{588}{166}$), who not only

---

[1] *Rem tene, verba sequentur.*

predicted the eclipse of the moon in $\frac{586}{168}$ but also calculated the distance of the moon from the earth, and who appears to have come forward even as an astronomical writer, was regarded on this account by his contemporaries as a prodigy of diligence and acuteness.

Agriculture and the art of war were, of course, primarily regulated by the standard of traditional and personal experience, as is very distinctly apparent in that one of the two treatises of Cato on Agriculture which has reached our time. But the results of Graeco-Latin, and even of Phoenician, culture were brought to bear on these subordinate fields just as on the higher provinces of intellectual activity, and for that reason the foreign literature relating to them cannot but have attracted some measure of attention.

Jurisprudence, on the other hand, was only in a subordinate degree affected by foreign elements. The activity of the jurists of this period was still mainly devoted to the answering of parties consulting them and to the instruction of younger listeners; but this oral instruction contributed to form a traditional ground-work of rules, and literary activity was not wholly wanting. A work of greater importance for jurisprudence than the short sketch of Cato was the treatise promulgated by Sextus Aelius Paetus, surnamed the "subtle" (*catus*), who was the first practical jurist of his time, and, in consequence of his exertions for the public benefit in this respect, rose to the consulship ($\frac{556}{198}$) and to the censorship ($\frac{560}{194}$). His treatise—the "*Tripartita*" as it was called—was a work on the Twelve Tables, which appended to each sentence of the text an explanation—chiefly, it is probable, of the antiquated and unintelligible expressions—and the corresponding formula of action. While this process of annotation undeniably indicated the influence of Greek grammatical studies, the portion treating of the formulae of action, on the contrary, was based on the older collection of Appius (i. 463) and on the general system of procedure as developed by national usage and precedent.

The state of science generally at this epoch is very distinctly exhibited in the collection of manuals composed by Cato for his son which, as a sort of encyclopaedia, were designed to set forth in short maxims what a "proper man" (*vir bonus*) ought to be as orator, physician, husbandman, warrior, and jurist. No distinction was yet drawn between an elementary and a special study of the sciences; but so much of science generally as seemed necessary or useful was required of every true Roman.

The work did not include Latin grammar, which consequently cannot as yet have attained that formal development which is implied in a properly scientific instruction in language; and it excluded music and the whole cycle of the mathematical and physical sciences. Throughout it was the directly practical element in science which alone was to be handled, and that with as much brevity and simplicity as possible. The Greek literature was doubtless made use of, but only to furnish some serviceable maxims of experience culled from the mass of chaff and rubbish: it was a favourite saying of Cato, that "Greek literature must be looked into, but not thoroughly studied." Thus arose those household manuals of necessary information, which, while rejecting Greek subtlety and obscurity, banished also Greek acuteness and depth, but through that very peculiarity moulded the position of the Romans towards Greek science for all ages.

Thus poetry and literature came to Rome along with the sovereignty of the world, or, to use the language of a poet of the age of Cicero:

> *Poenico bello secundo Musa pennato gradu*
> *Intulit se bellicosam Romuli in gentem feram.*

In the districts using the Sabellian and Etruscan dialects also there must have been at the same period no want of intellectual movement. Tragedies in the Etruscan language are mentioned, and vases with Oscan inscriptions show that the makers of them were acquainted with Greek comedy. The question accordingly presents itself, whether, contemporarily with Naevius and Cato, a Hellenising literature like the Roman may not have been in course of formation on the Arnus and Volturnus. But all information on the point is lost, and history can in such circumstances only indicate the blank.

The Roman literature is the only one as to which we can still form an opinion; and, however problematical its absolute worth may appear to the aesthetic judge, for those who wish to apprehend the history of Rome it remains of unique value as the reflection of the inner mental life of Italy in that sixth century—so full of the din of arms and so pregnant with the destinies of the future—during which the distinctive development of Italian life closed, and the land began to enter into the broader career of ancient civilisation. In it too there prevailed that antagonism, which everywhere during this epoch pervaded the life of the nation and characterised the age of transition. No one of unprejudiced mind, and who is not misled by the venerable rust of two thousand years, can be deceived as to the defectiveness of the Hellenistico-Roman literature. Roman literature by the side of that of Greece resembles a German orangery by the side of a grove of Sicilian orange-trees; both may give us pleasure, but it is impossible even to conceive them as parallel. This holds true of the literature in the mother-tongue of the Latins still more decidedly, if possible, than of the Roman literature in a foreign tongue; to a very great extent the former was not the work of Romans at all, but of foreigners, of half-Greeks, Celts, and ere long even Africans, whose knowledge of Latin was only acquired by study. Among those who in this age came before the public as poets, none, as we have already said, can be shown to have been persons of rank; and not only so, but none can be shown to have been natives of Latium proper. The very name given to the poet was foreign; even Ennius emphatically calls himself a *poeta*.[1] But not only was this poetry foreign; it was also liable to all those defects which are found to occur where schoolmasters become authors and the great multitude forms the public. We have shown how comedy was artistically debased out of regard to the multitude, and in fact sank into vulgar coarseness; we have further shown that two of the most influential Roman authors were schoolmasters in the first instance and only became poets in the sequel, and that, while the Greek philology which only sprang up after the decline of the national literature experimented merely on the dead body, in Latium grammar and literature had their foundations laid simultaneously and went hand in hand, almost as in the case of modern missions to the heathen. In fact, if we view with an unprejudiced eye this Hellenistic literature of the sixth century—that mechanical poetry destitute of all productive power of its own, that uniform imitation of the very shallowest forms of foreign art, that stock of translations, that changeling of an epos—we are tempted to reckon it simply one of the diseased symptoms of the epoch before us.

But such a judgment, if not unjust, would yet be just only in a very partial sense. We must first of all consider that this artificial literature sprang up in a nation which not only did

---

[1] See the lines already quoted at p. 426.
The formation of the name *poeta* from the vulgar Greek ποιητής instead of ποιητής—as ἐπόησεν was in use among the Attic potters—is characteristic. We may add that *poeta* technically denotes only the author of epic or recitative poems, not the composer for the stage, who at this time was styled *scriba* (p. 398. Festus, *s.v.*, p. 333 *M.*).

not possess any national poetic art, but could never attain any such art. In antiquity, which knew nothing of the modern poetry of individual life, creative poetical activity fell mainly within the mysterious period when a nation was experiencing the fears and pleasures of growth: without prejudice to the greatness of the Greek epic and tragic poets we may assert that their poetry mainly consisted in reproducing the primitive stories of human gods and divine men. This basis of ancient poetry was totally wanting in Latium: where the world of gods remained shapeless and legend remained barren, the golden apples of poetry could not voluntarily ripen. To this falls to be added a second and more important consideration. The inward mental development and the outward political evolution of Italy had equally reached a point at which it was no longer possible to retain the Roman nationality based on the exclusion of all higher and individual mental culture, and to repel the encroachments of Hellenism. The propagation of Hellenism in Italy had certainly a revolutionary and a denationalising tendency, but it was indispensable for the necessary intellectual equalisation of the nations; and this primarily constitutes the historical and even the poetical justification of the Romano-Hellenistic literature. Not a single new and genuine work of art issued from its workshop, but it brought Italy within the intellectual horizon of Hellas. Viewed even in its mere outward aspect, Greek poetry presumes in the hearer a certain amount of positive knowledge. That self-contained completeness, which is one of the most essential peculiarities of the dramas of Shakespeare for instance, was foreign to ancient poetry; a person unacquainted with the cycle of Greek legend would fail to discover the background and often even the ordinary meaning of every rhapsody and every tragedy. If the Roman public of this period was in some degree familiar, as the comedies of Plautus show, with the Homeric poems and the legends of Herakles, and was acquainted with at least the more generally current of the other myths,[1] this knowledge must have found its way to the public primarily through the stage and the school, and thus have formed at least a first step towards the understanding of the Hellenic poetry. But still deeper was the effect

---

[1] Even subordinate figures from the legends of Troy and of Herakles make their appearance, *e.g.* Talthybius (*Stich.* 305), Autolycus (*Bacch.* 275), Parthaon (*Men.* 745). Moreover the most general outlines must have been known in the case of the Theban and the Argonautic legends, and of the stories of Bellerophon (*Bacch.* 810), Pentheus (*Merc.* 467), Procne and Philomela (*Rud.* 604), Sappho and Phaon (*Mil.* 1247).

—on which the most ingenious literary critics of antiquity justly
laid emphasis—produced by the naturalisation of the Greek
poetic language and the Greek metres in Latium. If " conquered
Greece vanquished her rude conqueror by art," the victory was
primarily accomplished by elaborating from the unpliant Latin
idiom a cultivated and elevated poetical language, so that
instead of the monotonous and hackneyed Saturnian the senarius
flowed and the hexameter rushed, and the mighty tetrameters,
the jubilant anapaests, and the artfully intermingled lyrical
rhythms fell on the Latin ear in the mother-tongue. Poetical
language is the key to the ideal world of poetry, poetic measure
the key to poetical feeling; for the man, to whom the eloquent
epithet is dumb and the living image is dead, and in whom the
times of dactyls and iambuses awaken no inward echo, Homer
and Sophocles have composed in vain. Let it not be said that
poetical and rhythmical feeling comes spontaneously. The
ideal feelings are no doubt implanted by nature in the human
breast, but they need favourable sunshine in order to germinate;
and especially in the Latin nation, which was but little susceptible of poetic impulses, they needed external nurture. Nor
let it be said that, by virtue of the widely diffused acquaintance
with the Greek language, its literature might have sufficed for
the susceptible Roman public. The mysterious charm which
language exercises over man, and which poetical language and
rhythm only exercise in a higher degree, attaches not to any
tongue learnt accidentally, but only to the mother-tongue.
From this point of view, we shall form a juster judgment of
the Hellenistic literature, and particularly of the poetry, of the
Romans of this period. If it was the tendency of that literature
to transplant the radicalism of Euripides to Rome, to resolve
the gods either into deceased men or into mental conceptions,
to place a denationalised Latium by the side of a denationalised
Hellas, and to merge all purely and distinctly developed national
peculiarities into the questionable idea of general civilisation,
every one is at liberty to approve or disapprove this tendency,
but none can doubt its historical necessity. From this point
of view the very defectiveness of the Roman poetry, which
cannot be denied, may be explained and so may in some degree
be justified. It is no doubt pervaded by a disproportion
between the trivial and often mutilated contents and the comparatively finished form; but the real significance of this poetry
lay precisely in its formal features, especially those of language
and metre. It was not seemly that poetry in Rome was princi-

CHAP. XIV. **Literature and Art** 445

pally in the hands of schoolmasters and foreigners and was chiefly translation or imitation; but, if the primary object of poetry was simply to form a bridge from Latium to Hellas, Livius and Ennius had certainly a vocation to the poetical pontificate in Rome, and a translated literature was the simplest means to the end. It was still less seemly that Roman poetry preferred to lay its hands on the most prolix and trivial originals; but in this view it was appropriate. No one will desire to place the poetry of Euripides on a level with that of Homer; but, historically viewed, Euripides and Menander were quite as much the oracles of cosmopolitan Hellenism as the *Iliad* and *Odyssey* were the oracles of national Hellenism, and in so far the representatives of the new school had good reason for introducing their audience especially to this cycle of literature. The instinctive consciousness also of their limited poetical powers may partly have induced the Roman composers to keep mainly by Euripides and Menander and to leave Sophocles and even Aristophanes untouched; for, while poetry is essentially national and difficult to transplant, intellect and wit, on which the poetry of Euripides as well as of Menander is based, are in their nature cosmopolitan. Moreover the fact always deserves to be honourably acknowledged, that the Roman poets of the sixth century did not attach themselves to the Hellenic literature of the day of what is called Alexandrinism, but sought their models solely in the older classical literature, although not exactly in its richest or purest fields. On the whole, however innumerable may be the false accommodations and sins against the rules of art which we can point out in them, these were just the offences which were by stringent necessity attendant on the far from scrupulous efforts of the missionaries of Hellenism; and they are, in a historical and even aesthetical point of view, outweighed in some measure by the zeal of faith equally inseparable from propagandism. We may form a different opinion from Ennius as to the value of his new gospel; but, if in the case of faith it does not matter so much what, as how, men believe, we cannot refuse recognition and admiration to the Roman poets of the sixth century. A fresh and strong sense of the power of the Hellenic world-literature, a sacred longing to transplant the marvellous tree to the foreign land, pervaded the whole poetry of the sixth century, and coincided in a peculiar manner with the thoroughly elevated spirit of that great age. The later refined Hellenism looked down on the poetical performances of this period with some degree of contempt; it should rather perhaps have looked up to the poets, who with all their imperfections yet stood in an intimate relation to Greek poetry, and approached nearer to genuine poetical art than their more cultivated successors. In the bold emulation, in the sounding rhythms, even in the mighty professional pride of the poets of this age there is, more than in any other epoch of Roman literature, an imposing grandeur; and even those who are under no illusion as to the weak points of this poetry may apply to it the proud language in which Ennius celebrates its praise:

> *Enni poeta, salve, qui mortalibus*
> *Versus propinas flammeos medullitus.*

As the Hellenico-Roman literature of this period was essentially marked by a dominant tendency, so was also its antithesis, the contemporary national authorship. While the former aimed at neither more nor less than the annihilation of Latin nationality by the creation of a poetry Latin in language but Hellenic in form and spirit, the best and purest part of the Latin nation was driven to reject and place under the ban of outlawry the literature of Hellenism along with Hellenism itself. The Romans in the time of Cato stood opposed to Greek literature, very much as in the time of the Caesars they stood opposed to Christianity; freedmen and foreigners formed the main body of the poetical, as they afterwards formed the main body of the Christian, community; the nobility of the nation and above all the government saw in poetry as in Christianity an absolutely hostile power; Plautus and Ennius were ranked with the rabble by the Roman aristocracy for reasons nearly the same as those for which the apostles and bishops were put to death by the Roman government. In this field too it was Cato, of course, who took the lead as the vigorous champion of his native country against the foreigners. The Greek literati and physicians were in his view the most dangerous scum of the radically corrupt Greek people,[1] and the Roman " ballad-singers " are treated by

---

[1] " As to these Greeks," he says to his son Marcus, " I shall tell at the proper place, what I came to learn regarding them at Athens; and shall show that it is useful to look into their writings, but not to study them thoroughly. They are an utterly corrupt and ungovernable race—believe me, this is true as an oracle; if that people bring hither its culture, it will ruin everything, and most especially if it send hither its physicians. They have conspired to despatch all barbarians by their physicking, nevertheless they get themselves paid for it, that people may trust them and that they may the more easily bring us to ruin. They call us also barbarians, and

him with ineffable contempt (i. 453). He and those who shared his sentiments have been often and harshly censured on this account, and certainly the expressions of his displeasure are not unfrequently characterised by the bluntness and narrowness peculiar to him; but on a closer consideration we must not only confess him to have been in individual points substantially right, but we must also acknowledge that the national opposition in this field, more than anywhere else, abandoned the manifestly inadequate line of mere negative defence. When his younger contemporary, Aulus Postumius Albinus, who was an object of ridicule to the Hellenes themselves by his offensive Hellenising, and who even manufactured Greek verses—when this Albinus in the preface to his historical treatise pleaded in excuse for his defective Greek that he was by birth a Roman—was not the question quite in place, whether he had been condemned by legal authority to meddle with things which he did not understand? Were the trades of the professional translator of comedies and of the poet celebrating heroes for bread and protection more honourable, perhaps, two thousand years ago than they are now? Had Cato not reason to make it a reproach against Nobilior, that he took Ennius—who, we may add, glorified in his verses the Roman potentates without respect of persons, and overloaded Cato himself with praise—along with him to Ambracia as the celebrator of his future achievements? Had he not reason to revile the Greeks, with whom he had become acquainted in Rome and Athens, as an incorrigibly wretched pack? This opposition to the culture of the age and the Hellenism of the day was well warranted; but Cato was by no means chargeable with an opposition to culture and to Hellenism in general. On the contrary it is the highest merit of the national party, that they comprehended very clearly the necessity of creating a Latin literature and of bringing the stimulating influences of Hellenism to bear on it; only their intention was, that Latin literature should not be a mere copy taken from the Greek and intruded on the national feelings of Rome, but should, while quickened by Greek influences, be developed in a manner conformable to Italian nationality. With a genial instinct, which attests not so much the sagacity of

indeed revile us by the still more vulgar name of Opicans. I interdict thee, therefore, from all dealings with the practitioners of the healing art."

Cato in his zeal was not aware that the name of Opicans, which had in Latin an objectionable sense, was in Greek quite free from this, and that the Greeks had in the most innocent way come to designate the Italians by that term (i. 132).

individuals as the general elevation of the epoch, they perceived
that in the case of Rome, owing to the total want of earlier
poetical productiveness, history furnished the only materials
for the development of a distinctive intellectual life. Rome was,
what Greece was not, a state; and the mighty consciousness of
this truth lay at the root both of the bold attempt which Naevius
made to form by means of history a Roman epos and a Roman
drama, and of the creation of Latin prose by Cato. It is true
that the endeavour to replace the gods and heroes of legend by
the kings and consuls of Rome resembles the attempt of the
giants to storm heaven by means of mountains piled one above
another: without a mythologic world there is no ancient epos
and no ancient drama, and poetry knows no substitutes. With
greater moderation and good sense Cato left poetry proper, as
a thing irremediably lost, to the party opposed to him; although
his attempt to create a didactic poetry in national measure after
the model of the earlier Roman productions—the Appian poem
on Morals and the poem on Agriculture—remains significant
and deserving of respect, if not in point of success, yet in point
of intention. Prose afforded him a more favourable field, and
accordingly he applied the whole varied power and energy
peculiar to him to the creation of a prose literature in his native
tongue. This effort was all the more Roman and all the more
deserving of respect, that the public which he primarily addressed
was the family circle, and that in such an effort he stood almost
alone in his time. Thus arose his *Origines*, his remarkable
state-speeches, his treatises on special branches of science. They
are certainly pervaded by a national spirit, and turn on national
subjects; but they are far from anti-Hellenic: in fact they
originated essentially under Greek influence, although in a
different sense from that in which the writings of the opposite
party so originated. The idea and even the title of his chief
work were borrowed from the Greek " foundation-histories "
(κτίσεις). The same is true of his oratorical authorship; he
ridiculed Isocrates, but he tried to learn from Thucydides
and Demosthenes. His encyclopaedia is substantially the result
of his study of Greek literature. Of all the undertakings of
that active and patriotic man none was more fruitful of results
and none more useful to his country than his literary activity,
little esteemed in comparison as it probably was by himself.
He found numerous and worthy successors in oratorical and
scientific authorship; and though his original historical treatise,
which of its kind may be compared with the Greek logography,

was followed by no Herodotus or Thucydides, yet he was the means of establishing the principle that literary occupation in connection with the useful sciences as well as with history was not merely becoming but honourable in a Roman.

Let us glance, in conclusion, at the state of the arts of architecture, sculpture, and painting. So far as concerns the former, the traces of growing luxury were less observable in public than in private buildings. It was not till towards the close of this period, and especially from the time of the censorship of Cato ($\frac{570}{184}$), that the Romans began in the case of the former to have respect to public convenience as well as to public exigency; to line with stone the basins (*lacus*) supplied from the aqueducts ($\frac{570}{184}$); to erect colonnades ($\frac{575}{179}$, $\frac{580}{174}$); and above all to transfer to Rome the Attic halls for courts and business—the *basilicae* as they were called. The first of these buildings, somewhat corresponding to our modern bazaars—the Porcian or silversmiths' hall—was erected by Cato in $\frac{570}{184}$ alongside of the senate-house; others were soon associated with it, till gradually along the sides of the Forum the private shops were replaced by these splendid columnar halls. Every-day life, however, was more deeply influenced by the revolution in domestic architecture which must, at latest, be placed in this period. The dwelling-room (*atrium*), court (*cavum aedium*), garden and garden colonnade (*peristylium*), the record-chamber (*tablinum*), chapel, kitchen, and bedrooms were by degrees severally provided for; and, as to the internal fittings, the column began to be applied both in the court and in the dwelling-room for the support of the open roof and also for the garden colonnades: throughout these arrangements it is probable that Greek models were copied or at any rate made use of. Yet the materials used in building remained simple; "our ancestors," says Varro, "dwelt in houses of brick, and laid merely a moderate foundation of stone to keep away damp."

Of Roman plastic art we scarcely encounter any other trace than, perhaps, the embossing in wax of the images of ancestors. Painters and painting are mentioned somewhat more frequently. Manius Valerius caused the victory which he obtained over the Carthaginians and Hiero in $\frac{491}{263}$ off Messana (p. 33) to be depicted on the side wall of the senate-house—the first historical frescoes in Rome, which were followed by many of similar character, and which were in the domain of the arts of design what the national epos and the national drama became not much later

in the domain of poetry. We find named as painters, one
Theodotus who, as Naevius scoffingly said—

> *Sedens in cella circumtectus tegetibus*
> *Lares ludentis peni pinxit bubulo ;*

Marcus Pacuvius of Brundisium, who painted in the temple of
Hercules in the Forum Boarium—the same who, when more
advanced in life, made himself a name as an editor of Greek
tragedies; and Marcus Plautius Lyco, a native of Asia Minor,
whose beautiful paintings in the temple of Juno at Ardea
procured for him the freedom of that city.[1] But these very
facts clearly indicate, not only that the exercise of art in Rome
was altogether of subordinate importance and more of a manual
occupation than an art, but also that it fell, probably still more
exclusively than poetry, into the hands of Greeks and half
Greeks.

On the other hand there appeared in genteel circles the first
traces of the tastes subsequently displayed by the dilettante
and the collector. They admired the magnificence of the
Corinthian and Athenian temples, and regarded with contempt
the old-fashioned terra-cotta figures on the roofs of those of
Rome: even a man like Lucius Paullus, who shared the feelings
of Cato rather than of Scipio, viewed and judged the Zeus of
Phidias with the eye of a connoisseur. The custom of carrying
off the treasures of art from the conquered Greek cities was first
introduced on a large scale by Marcus Marcellus after the capture
of Syracuse ($\frac{542}{212}$). The practice met with severe reprobation
from men of the old school of training, and the stern veteran
Quintus Fabius, for instance, on the capture of Tarentum ($\frac{545}{209}$)
gave orders that the statues in the temples should not be
touched, but that the Tarentines should be allowed to retain
their indignant gods. Yet the plundering of temples in this way
became of more and more frequent occurrence. Titus Flami-
ninus in particular ($\frac{560}{194}$) and Marcus Fulvius Nobilior ($\frac{567}{187}$), two
leading champions of Roman Hellenism, and Lucius Paullus
($\frac{587}{167}$) were the means of filling the public buildings of Rome with
the master-pieces of the Greek chisel. In taking such steps the
Romans had a dawning consciousness of the truth that an

---

[1] Plautius belongs to this or to the beginning of the following period, for
the inscription on his pictures (Plin. *H.N.* xxxv. 10, 115) being hexa-
metrical, cannot well be older than Ennius, and the bestowal on the
citizenship of Ardea must have taken place before the Social War through
which Ardea lost its independence.

interest in art as well as an interest in poetry formed an essential part of Hellenic culture or, in other words, of modern civilisation; but, while the appropriation of Greek poetry was impossible without some sort of poetical activity, in the case of art the mere beholding and procuring of its productions seemed to suffice, and therefore, while a native literature was formed in an artificial way in Rome, no attempt even was made to develop a native art.

MADE AT THE TEMPLE PRESS LETCHWORTH IN GREAT BRITAIN

EVERYMAN'S LIBRARY

By ERNEST RHYS

VICTOR HUGO said a Library was "an act of faith,"
and some unknown essayist spoke of one so beautiful,
so perfect, so harmonious in all its parts, that he who
made it was smitten with a passion. In that faith the promoters
of Everyman's Library planned it out originally on a large
scale; and their idea in so doing was to make it conform as
far as possible to a perfect scheme. However, perfection is a
thing to be aimed at and not to be achieved in this difficult world;
and since the first volumes appeared, now several years ago,
there have been many interruptions. A great war has come and
gone; and even the City of Books has felt something like a
world commotion. Only in recent years is the series getting
back into its old stride and looking forward to complete its
original scheme of a Thousand Volumes. One of the practical
expedients in that original plan was to divide the volumes into
sections, as Biography, Fiction, History, Belles Lettres, Poetry,
Romance, and so forth; with a compartment for young people,
and last, and not least, one of Reference Books. Beside the
dictionaries and encyclopædias to be expected in that section,
there was a special set of literary and historical atlases. One of
these atlases dealing with Europe, we may recall, was directly
affected by the disturbance of frontiers during the war; and the
maps had to be completely revised in consequence, so as to chart

the New Europe which we hope will now preserve its peace under the auspices of the League of Nations set up at Geneva.

That is only one small item, however, in a library list which runs already to the final centuries of the Thousand. The largest slice of this huge provision is, as a matter of course, given to the tyrannous demands of fiction. But in carrying out the scheme, publishers and editors contrived to keep in mind that books, like men and women, have their elective affinities. The present volume, for instance, will be found to have its companion books, both in the same section and even more significantly in other sections. With that idea too, novels like Walter Scott's *Ivanhoe* and *Fortunes of Nigel*, Lytton's *Harold* and Dickens's *Tale of Two Cities*, have been used as pioneers of history and treated as a sort of holiday history books. For in our day history is tending to grow more documentary and less literary; and "the historian who is a stylist," as one of our contributors, the late Thomas Seccombe, said, "will soon be regarded as a kind of Phœnix." But in this special department of Everyman's Library we have been eclectic enough to choose our history men from every school in turn. We have Grote, Gibbon, Finlay, Macaulay, Motley, Prescott. We have among earlier books the Venerable Bede and the Anglo-Saxon Chronicle, have completed a Livy in an admirable new translation by Canon Roberts, while Cæsar, Tacitus, Thucydides and Herodotus are not forgotten.

"You only, O Books," said Richard de Bury, "are liberal and independent; you give to all who ask." The delightful variety, the wisdom and the wit which are at the disposal of Everyman in his own library may well, at times, seem to him a little embarrassing. He may turn to Dick Steele in *The Spectator* and learn how Cleomira dances, when the elegance of her motion is unimaginable and "her eyes are chastised with the simplicity and innocence of her thoughts." He may turn to Plato's Phædrus and read how every soul is divided into three parts (like Cæsar's Gaul). He may turn to the finest critic of Victorian times, Matthew Arnold, and find in his essay on Maurice de Guerin the perfect key to what is there called the "magical power of poetry." It is Shakespeare, with his

> "daffodils
> That come before the swallow dares, and take
> The winds of March with beauty;"

it is Wordsworth, with his

> "voice . . . heard
> In spring-time from the cuckoo-bird,
> Breaking the silence of the seas
> Among the farthest Hebrides;"

or Keats, with his

> ". . . . moving waters at their priest-like task
> Of cold ablution round Earth's human shores."

William Hazlitt's "Table Talk," among the volumes of Essays, may help to show the relationship of one author to another, which is another form of the Friendship of Books. His incomparable essay in that volume, "On Going a Journey," forms a capital prelude to Coleridge's "Biographia Literaria" and to his and Wordsworth's poems. In the same way one may turn to the review of Moore's Life of Byron in Macaulay's *Essays* as a prelude to the three volumes of Byron's own poems, remembering that the poet whom Europe loved more than England did was as Macaulay said: "the beginning, the middle and the end of all his own poetry." This brings us to the provoking reflection that it is the obvious authors and the books most easy to reprint which have been the signal successes out of the many hundreds in the series, for Everyman is distinctly proverbial in his tastes. He likes best of all an old author who has worn well or a comparatively new author who has gained something like news-paper notoriety. In attempting to lead him on from the good books that are known to those that are less known, the publishers may have at times been too adventurous. The late *Chief* himself was much more than an ordinary book-producer in this critical enterprise. He threw himself into it with the zeal of a book-lover and indeed of one who, like Milton, thought that books might be as alive and productive as dragons' teeth, which, being "sown up and down the land, might chance to spring up armed men."

Mr. Pepys in his *Diary* writes about some of his books, "which are come home gilt on the backs, very handsome to the eye." The pleasure he took in them is that which Everyman may take in the gilt backs of his favourite books in his own Library, which after all he has helped to make good and lasting.

EVERYMAN'S LIBRARY
A CLASSIFIED LIST OF THE 953 VOLUMES

In each of the thirteen classifications in this list (except BIOGRAPHY) the volumes are arranged alphabetically under the *authors' names*, but Anthologies and works by various hands are listed under titles. Where authors appear in more than one section, a cross-reference is given, viz.: (*See also* FICTION). The number at the end of each item is the number of the volume in the series.

All the volumes are obtainable in the standard Cloth binding, and in the special Library binding; selected volumes obtainable in Leather are marked L.

BIOGRAPHY

BIOGRAPHY—continued

CLASSICAL

ESSAYS AND BELLES-LETTRES

ESSAYS AND BELLES-LETTRES—*continued*

Landor's Imaginary Conversations and Poems: A selection. Edited with Introduction by Havelock Ellis. 890

Lowell's (James Russell) Among My Books. 607

Macaulay's Essays. 2 vols. Introduction by A. J. Grieve, M.A. 225–6
,, Miscellaneous Essays and The Lays of Ancient Rome. 439
(*See also* HISTORY *and* ORATORY)

Machiavelli's Prince. Special Trans. and Intro. by W. K. Marriott. 280
(*See also* HISTORY)

Martinengo-Cesaresco (Countess): Essays in the Study of Folk-Songs. 673

Mazzini's Duties of Man, etc. Introduction by Thomas Jones, M.A. 224

Milton's Areopagitica, etc. Introduction by Professor C. E. Vaughan. 795
(*See also* POETRY)

L Mitford's Our Village. Edited, with Intro., by Sir John Squire. 927

Montagu's (Lady) Letters. Introduction by R. Brimley Johnson. 69

Newman's On the Scope and Nature of University Education, and a paper on Christianity and Scientific Investigation. Introduction by Wilfred Ward. 723
(*See also* PHILOSOPHY)

Osborne's (Dorothy) Letters to Sir William Temple. Edited and connotated by Judge Parry. 674

Penn's The Peace of Europe. Some Fruits of Solitude, etc. 724

Prelude to Poetry, The. Edited by Ernest Rhys. 789

Reynold's Discourses. Introduction by L. March Phillipps. 118

Rhys's New Book of Sense and Nonsense. 813

Rousseau's Emile. Translated by Barbara Foxley. 518
(*See also* PHILOSOPHY AND THEOLOGY)

Ruskin's Crown of Wild Olive and Cestus of Aglaia. 323
,, Elements of Drawing and Perspective. 217
,, Ethics of the Dust. Introduction by Grace Rhys. 282
,, Modern Painters. 5 vols. Introduction by Lionel Cust. 208–12
,, Pre-Raphaelitism. Lectures on Architecture and Painting, Academy Notes, 1855–9, and Notes on the Turner Gallery. Introduction by Laurence Binyon. 218
L ,, Sesame and Lilies, The Two Paths, and The King of the Golden River. Introduction by Sir Oliver Lodge. 219
,, Seven Lamps of Architecture. Intro. by Selwyn Image. 207
,, Stones of Venice. 3 vols. Intro. by L. March Phillipps. 213–15
,, Time and Tide with other Essays. 450
,, Unto This Last. The Political Economy of Art. 216
(*See also* FOR YOUNG PEOPLE)

Spectator, The. 4 vols. Introduction by G. Gregory Smith. 164–7

Spencer's (Herbert) Essays on Education. Intro. by C. W. Eliot. 504

Sterne's Sentimental Journey and Journal and Letters to Eliza. Intro. by George Saintsbury. 796
(*See also* FICTION)

Stevenson's In the South Seas and Island Nights' Entertainments. 769
L ,, Virginibus Puerisque and Familiar Studies of Men and Books. 765
(*See also* FICTION, POETRY, *and* TRAVEL)

Swift's Tale of a Tub, The Battle of the Books, etc. 347
(*See also* BIOGRAPHY *and* FOR YOUNG PEOPLE)

Swinnerton's (Frank) The Georgian Literary Scene. 943

Table Talk. Edited by J. C. Thornton. 906

Taylor's (Isaac) Words and Places, or Etymological Illustrations of History, Ethnology, and Geography. Intro. by Edward Thomas. 517

Thackeray's (W. M.) The English Humorists and The Four Georges. Introduction by Walter Jerrold. 610
(*See also* FICTION)

Thoreau's Walden. Introduction by Walter Raymond. 281

Trench's On the Study of Words and English Past and Present. Introduction by George Sampson. 788

Tytler's Essay on the Principles of Translation. 168

Walton's Compleat Angler. Introduction by Andrew Lang. 70

FICTION

FICTION—*continued*

FICTION—*continued*

FICTION—*continued*

Melville's (Herman) Omoo. Introduction by Ernest Rhys. 297
L   „   „   Typee. Introduction by Ernest Rhys. 180
L Meredith's (George) The Ordeal of Richard Feverel. 916
    Mérimée's Carmen, with Prévost's Manon Lescaut. Intro. by Philip
        Henderson. 834
    Mickiewicz's (Adam) Pan Tadeusz. 842
L Moore's (George) Esther Waters. 933
    Mulock's John Halifax, Gentleman. Introduction by J. Shaylor. 123
    Neale's (J. M.) The Fall of Constantinople. 655
    Paltock's (Robert) Peter Wilkins; or, The Flying Indians. Introduction
        by A. H. Bullen. 676
    Pater's Marius the Epicurean. Introduction by Osbert Burdett. 903
    Peacock's Headlong Hall and Nightmare Abbey. 327
L. Poe's Tales of Mystery and Imagination. Intro. by Padraic Colum. 336
        (*See also* POETRY)
    Prévost's Manon Lescaut, with Mérimée's Carmen. Introduction by
        Philip Henderson. 834
L Priestley's Angel Pavement. 938
    Pushkin's (Alexander) The Captain's Daughter and Other Tales. Trans.
        by Natalie Duddington. 898
    Quiller-Couch's (Sir Arthur) Hetty Wesley. 864   [2 vols. 865–6
    Radcliffe's (Ann) Mysteries of Udolpho. Intro. by R. Austin Freeman.
L Reade's (C.) The Cloister and the Hearth. Intro. by A. C. Swinburne. 29
    „   Peg Woffington and Christie Johnstone. 299
    Richardson's (Samuel) Pamela. Intro. by G. Saintsbury. 2 vols. 683–4
    „   „   Clarissa. Intro. by Prof. W. L. Phelps. 4 vols.
        882–5
    Russian Authors, Short Stories from. Trans. by R. S. Townsend. 758
    Sand's (George) The Devil's Pool and François the Waif. 534
    Scheffel's Ekkehard: a Tale of the Tenth Century. 529
    Scott's (Michael) Tom Cringle's Log. 710

SIR WALTER SCOTT'S WORKS:

Abbot, The. 124	L Ivanhoe. Intro. Ernest Rhys. 16
Anne of Geierstein. 125	L Kenilworth. 135
Antiquary, The. 126	Monastery, The. 136
Black Dwarf and Legend of	Old Mortality. 137
Montrose. 128	Peveril of the Peak. 138
Bride of Lammermoor. 129	Pirate, The. 139
Castle Dangerous and the Sur-	Quentin Durward. 140
geon's Daughter. 130	Redgauntlet. 141
Count Robert of Paris. 131	Rob Roy. 142
Fair Maid of Perth. 132	St. Ronan's Well. 143
Fortunes of Nigel. 71	Talisman, The. 144
Guy Mannering. 133	Waverley. 75
Heart of Midlothian, The. 134	Woodstock. Intro. by Edward
Highland Widow and Betrothed. 127	Garnett. 72

        (*See also* BIOGRAPHY *and* POETRY)

    Shchedrin's The Golovlyov Family. Translated by Natalie Duddington.
        Introduction by Edward Garnett. 908
    Shelley's (Mary Wollstonecraft) Frankenstein. 616
    Sheppard's Charles Auchester. Intro. by Jessie M. Middleton. 505
    Shorter Novels, Vol. I. Elizabethan and Jacobean. Edited by Philip
        Henderson. 824
    „   „   Vol. II. Jacobean and Restoration. Edited by Philip
        Henderson. 841
    „   „   Vol. III. Eighteenth Century (Beckford's Vathek,
        Walpole's Castle of Otranto, and Dr. Johnson's
        Rasselas). 856
    Sienkiewicz (Henryk). Tales from. Edited by Monica M. Gardner. 871
    Smollett's Peregrine Pickle. 2 vols. 838–9
    „   Roderick Random. Introduction by H. W. Hodges. 790
    Stendhal's Scarlet and Black. Translated by C. K. Scott Moncrieff.
        2 vols. 945–6

FICTION—*continued*

HISTORY

HISTORY—*continued*

Green's Short History of the English People. Edited and Revised by L. Cecil Jane, with an Appendix by R. P. Farley, B.A. 2 vols. 727–8
Grote's History of Greece. Intro. by A. D. Lindsay. 12 vols. 186–97
Hallam's (Henry) Constitutional History of England. 3 vols. 621–3
Holinshed's Chronicle as used in Shakespeare's Plays. Introduction by Professor Allardyce Nicoll. 800
Irving's (Washington) Conquest of Granada. 478
    (*See also* ESSAYS *and* BIOGRAPHY)
Josephus' Wars of the Jews. Introduction by Dr Jacob Hart. 712
Macaulay's History of England. 3 vols. 34–6
    (*See also* ESSAYS *and* ORATORY)
Maine's (Sir Henry) Ancient Law. 734
Merivale's History of Rome. (An Introductory vol. to Gibbon.) 433
Mignet's (F. A. M.) The French Revolution. 713
Milman's History of the Jews. 2 vols. 377–8
Mommsen's History of Rome. Translated by W. P. Dickson, LL.D. With a review of the work by E. A. Freeman. 4 vols. 542–5
Motley's Dutch Republic. 3 vols. 86–8
Parkman's Conspiracy of Pontiac. 2 vols. 302–3
Paston Letters, The. Based on edition of Knight. Introduction by Mrs Archer-Hind, M.A. 2 vols. 752–3
Pilgrim Fathers, The. Introduction by John Masefield. 480
L Pinnow's History of Germany. Translated by M. R. Brailsford. 929
Political Liberty, The Growth of. A Source-Book of English History. Arranged by Ernest Rhys. 745   [M.A. 2 vols. 397–8
Prescott's Conquest of Mexico. With Introduction by Thomas Seccombe.
    ,,   Conquest of Peru. Intro. by Thomas Seccombe, M.A. 301
Sismondi's Italian Republics. 250
Stanley's Lectures on the Eastern Church. Intro. by A. J. Grieve. 251
Tacitus. Vol. I. Annals. Introduction by E. H. Blakeney. 273
    ,,   Vol. II. Agricola and Germania. Intro. E. H. Blakeney. 274
Thierry's Norman Conquest. Intro. by J. A. Price, B.A. 2 vols. 198–9
Villehardouin and De Joinville's Chronicles of the Crusades. Translated, with Introduction, by Sir F. Marzials, C.B. 333
Voltaire's Age of Louis XIV. Translated by Martyn P. Pollack. 780

ORATORY

Anthology of British Historical Speeches and Orations. Compiled by Ernest Rhys. 714
Bright's (John) Speeches. Selected with Intro. by Joseph Sturge. 252
Burke's American Speeches and Letters. 340.   (*See also* ESSAYS)
Demosthenes: Select Orations. 546
Fox (Charles James): Speeches (French Revolutionary War Period). Edited with Introduction by Irene Cooper Willis, M.A. 759
Lincoln's Speeches, etc. Intro. by the Rt Hon. James Bryce. 206
    (*See also* BIOGRAPHY)
Macaulay's Speeches on Politics and Literature. 399
    (*See also* ESSAYS *and* HISTORY)
Pitt's Orations on the War with France. 145

PHILOSOPHY AND THEOLOGY

L A Kempis' Imitation of Christ. 484
Ancient Hebrew Literature. Being the Old Testament and Apocrypha. Arranged by the Rev. R. B. Taylor. 4 vols. 253–6
Aristotle, The Nicomachean Ethics of. Translated by D. P. Chase. Introduction by Professor J. A. Smith. 547
    (*See also* CLASSICAL)
Bacon's The Advancement of Learning. 719   (*See also* ESSAYS)
Berkeley's (Bishop) Principles of Human Knowledge, New Theory of Vision. With Introduction by A. D. Lindsay. 483

PHILOSOPHY AND THEOLOGY—*continued*

Boehme's (Jacob) The Signature of All Things, with Other Writings. Introduction by Clifford Bax. 569

Browne's Religio Medici, etc. Intro. by Professor C. H. Herford. 92

Bunyan's Grace Abounding and Mr Badman. Introduction by G. B. Harrison. 815 *(See also* ROMANCE)

Burton's (Robert) Anatomy of Melancholy. Introduction by Holbrook Jackson. 3 vols. 886–8

Butler's Analogy of Religion. Introduction by Rev. Ronald Bayne. 90

Descartes' (René) A Discourse on Method. Translated by Professor John Veitch. Introduction by A. D. Lindsay. 570

L Ellis' (Havelock) Selected Essays. Introduction by J. S. Collis. 930

L Gore's (Charles) The Philosophy of the Good Life. 924

Hindu Scriptures. Edited by Dr Nicol Macnicol. Introduction by Rabindranath Tagore. 944

Hobbes' Leviathan. Edited, with Intro. by A. D. Lindsay, M.A. 691

Hooker's Ecclesiastical Polity. Intro. by Rev. H. Bayne. 2 vols. 201–2

Hume's Treatise of Human Nature, and other Philosophical Works. Introduction by A. D. Lindsay, M.A. 2 vols. 548–9

James (William): Selected Papers on Philosophy. 739

Kant's Critique of Pure Reason. Translated by J. M. D. Meiklejohn. Introduction by A. D. Lindsay, M.A. 909

Keble's The Christian Year. Introduction by J. C. Shairp. 690

King Edward VI. First and Second Prayer Books. Introduction by the Right Rev. Bishop of Gloucester. 448

L Koran, The. Rodwell's Translation. 380

Latimer's Sermons. Introduction by Canon Beeching. 40

Law's Serious Call to a Devout and Holy Life. 91

Leibniz's Philosophical Writings. Selected and trans. by Mary Morris. Introduction by C. R. Morris, M.A. 905

Locke's Two Treatises of Civil Government. Introduction by Professor William S. Carpenter. 751

Malthus on the Principles of Population. 2 vols. 692–3

Mill's (John Stuart) Utilitarianism, Liberty, Representative Government. With Introduction by A. D. Lindsay, M.A. 482

„ Subjection of Women. *(See* Wollstonecraft, Mary, *under* SCIENCE)

More's Utopia. Introduction by Judge O'Hagan. 461

New Testament. Arranged in the order in which the books came to the Christians of the First Century. 93

Newman's Apologia pro Vita Sua. Intro. by Dr Charles Sarolea. 636 *(See also* ESSAYS)

Nietzsche's Thus Spake Zarathustra. Trans. by A. Tille and M. M. Bozman.

Paine's Rights of Man. Introduction by G. J. Holyoake. 718 [718

Pascal's Pensées. Translated by W. F. Trotter. Introduction by T. S. Eliot. 874 [C.I.E. 403

Ramayana and the Mahabharata, The. Translated by Romesh Dutt.

Renan's Life of Jesus. Introduction by Right Rev. Chas. Baron, D.D. 805

Robertson's (F. W.) Sermons on Christian Doctrine, and Bible Subjects. Each Volume with Introduction by Canon Burnett. 3 vols. 37–9 *(Note: No. 37 is out of print.)*

Robinson's (Wade) The Philosophy of Atonement and Other Sermons. Introduction by Rev. F. B. Meyer. 637

Rousseau's (J. J.) The Social Contract, etc. 660. *(See also* ESSAYS)

St Augustine's Confessions. Dr Pusey's Translation. 200

L St Francis: The Little Flowers, and The Life of St. Francis. 485

Seeley's Ecce Homo. Introduction by Sir Oliver Lodge. 305

Selection from St Thomas Aquinas. Edited by The Rev. Father M. C. D'Arcy. 953 *(Ready Summer 1939)*

Spinoza's Ethics, etc. Translated by Andrew J. Boyle. With Introduction by Professor Santayana. 481

Swedenborg's (Emmanuel) Heaven and Hell. 379

    „   „   The Divine Love and Wisdom. 635

    „   „   The Divine Providence. 658

L   „   „   The True Christian Religion. 893

POETRY AND DRAMA

POETRY AND DRAMA—*continued*

REFERENCE

ROMANCE

Aucassin and Nicolette, with other Medieval Romances. 497
Boccaccio's Decameron. (Unabridged.) Translated by J. M. Rigg. Introduction by Edward Hutton. 2 vols. 845–6
L Bunyan's Pilgrim's Progress. Introduction by Rev. H. E. Lewis. 204
Burnt Njal, The Story of. Translated by Sir George Dasent. 558
Cervantes' Don Quixote. Motteux's Translation. Lockhart's Introduction. 2 vols. 385–6
Chrétien de Troyes: Eric and Enid. Translated, with Introduction and Notes, by William Wistar Comfort. 698
French Medieval Romances. Translated by Eugene Mason. 557
Geoffrey of Monmouth's Histories of the Kings of Britain. 577
Grettir Saga, The. Newly Translated by G. Ainslie Hight. 699
Gudrun. Done into English by Margaret Armour. 880
Guest's (Lady) Mabinogion. Introduction by Rev. R. Williams. 97
Heimskringla: The Olaf Sagas. Translated by Samuel Laing. Introduction and Notes by John Beveridge. 717
    „   Sagas of the Norse Kings. Translated by Samuel Laing. Introduction and Notes by John Beveridge. 847
Holy Graal, The High History of the, 445
Kalevala. Introduction by W. F. Kirby, F.L.S., F.E.S. 2 vols. 259–60
Le Sage's The Adventures of Gil Blas. Intro. by Anatole Le Bras. 2 vols.
MacDonald's (George) Phantastes: A Faerie Romance. 732   [437–8
    (See also FICTION)
Malory's Le Morte d'Arthur. Intro. by Professor Rhys. 2 vols. 45–6
L Morris (William): Early Romances. Introduction by Alfred Noyes. 261
    „   „   The Life and Death of Jason. 575
Morte d'Arthur Romances, Two. Introduction by Lucy A. Paton. 634
Nibelungs, The Fall of the. Translated by Margaret Armour. 312
Rabelais' The Heroic Deeds of Gargantua and Pantagruel. Introduction by D. B. Wyndham Lewis. 2 vols. 826–7
Wace's Arthurian Romance. Translated by Eugene Mason. Layamon's Brut. Introduction by Lucy A. Paton. 578

SCIENCE

Boyle's The Sceptical Chymist. 559
Darwin's The Origin of Species. Introduction by Sir Arthur Keith. 811
    (See also TRAVEL)   [E. F. Bozman. 922
L Eddington's (Sir Arthur) The Nature of the Physical World. Intro. by
Euclid: the Elements of. Todhunter's Edition. Introduction by Sir Thomas Heath, K.C.B. 891
Faraday's (Michael) Experimental Researches in Electricity. 576
Galton's Inquiries into Human Faculty. Revised by Author. 263
George's (Henry) Progress and Poverty. 560
Hahnemann's (Samuel) The Organon of the Rational Art of Healing. Introduction by C. E. Wheeler. 663
Harvey's Circulation of the Blood. Introduction by Ernest Parkyn. 262
Howard's State of the Prisons. Introduction by Kenneth Ruck. 835
Huxley's Essays. Introduction by Sir Oliver Lodge. 47
    „   Select Lectures and Lay Sermons. Intro. Sir Oliver Lodge. 498
Lyell's Antiquity of Man. With an introduction by R. H. Rastall. 700
Marx's (Karl) Capital. Translated by Eden and Cedar Paul. Introduction by G. D. H. Cole. 2 vols. 848–9
Miller's Old Red Sandstone. 103
Owen's (Robert) A New View of Society, etc. Intro. by G. D. H. Cole. 799
L Pearson's (Karl) The Grammar of Science. 939
Ricardo's Principles of Political Economy and Taxation. 590
Smith's (Adam) The Wealth of Nations. 2 vols. 412–13
Tyndall's Glaciers of the Alps and Mountaineering in 1861. 98
White's Selborne. Introduction by Principal Windle. 48
Wollstonecraft (Mary), The Rights of Woman, with John Stuart Mill's The Subjection of Women. 825